Textual Sources 1

A330   Myth in the Greek and Roman worlds

This publication forms part of the Open University module A330 *Myth in the Greek and Roman worlds*. Details of this and other Open University modules can be obtained from the Student Registration and Enquiry Service, The Open University, PO Box 197, Milton Keynes MK7 6BJ, United Kingdom (tel. +44 (0)845 300 60 90; email general-enquiries@open.ac.uk).

Alternatively, you may visit the Open University website at www.open.ac.uk where you can learn more about the wide range of modules offered at all levels by The Open University.

To purchase a selection of Open University materials visit www.ouw.co.uk, or contact Open University Worldwide, Walton Hall, Milton Keynes MK7 6AA, United Kingdom for a brochure (tel. +44 (0)1908 858793; fax +44 (0)1908 858787; email ouw-customer-services@open.ac.uk).

The Open University
Walton Hall, Milton Keynes
MK7 6AA

First published 2010

Edited and designed by The Open University.

Typeset in India by Alden Prepress Services, Chennai.

Printed in the United Kingdom by Charlesworth Press, Wakefield.

ISBN 978 1 8487 3194 3

1.1

Contents

Primary Sources   5
Introduction   6
Block 1   The myth of Hippolytus and Phaedra   10
Block 2   Myth in Rome: power, life and afterlife   17

Secondary Sources   69
Introduction   70
Block 1   The myth of Hippolytus and Phaedra   72
Block 2   Myth in Rome: power, life and afterlife   138

Acknowledgements   306

Primary Sources

Introduction 6
Primary Source I   Ovid, *The Art of Love*, Book 2   6
Primary Source II   Ovid, *The Art of Love*, Book 1   8

Block 1   The myth of Hippolytus and Phaedra   10
Primary Source 1.1   Ovid, 'Phaedra to Hippolytus'   10
Primary Source 1.2   Euripides, *Hippolytus*   14
Primary Source 1.3   Virgil, *The Aeneid* 7.761–84   15
Primary Source 1.4   Servius, *Ad Aeneid* 6.136   16

Block 2   Myth in Rome: power, life and afterlife   17
Primary Source 2.1   Livy, extract from *The Early History of Rome*   17
Primary Source 2.2   Virgil, 'Evander takes Aeneas on a tour of Rome'
(*The Aeneid* 8.305–69)   29
Primary Source 2.3   Virgil, 'The shield of Aeneas'
(*The Aeneid* 8.609–732)   30
Primary Source 2.4   Ovid, 'The rape of the Sabine women'   33
Primary Source 2.5   Suetonius, Nero's entertainments   34
Primary Source 2.6   Tacitus, extracts from *Annals*
(Books 15 and 16)   39
Primary Source 2.7   Cassius Dio, 'Nero's spectacles'   41
Primary Source 2.8   Lucan, extract from *The Civil War* (*Pharsalia*)   46
Primary Source 2.9   Seneca the Younger, *Apocolocyntosis* 4   47
Primary Source 2.10   Cassius Dio, 'The Golden Day'   48
Primary Source 2.11   Suetonius, 'Nero's Golden House'   49
Primary Source 2.12   Tacitus, 'Innocent victims'   50
Primary Source 2.13   Martial, *On The Spectacles* 2   50
Primary Source 2.14   Pliny the Elder, 'Nero's Golden House'   51
Primary Source 2.15   Seneca the Younger, *Letter* 115   52
Primary Source 2.16   Epitaphs from gladiatorial tombstones   55
Primary Source 2.17   Martial, *On the Spectacles* 6, 10 and 24,
Epigrams 5.24   56
Primary Source 2.18   Apuleius, *Metamorphoses* 10.29–32   56
Primary Source 2.19   Petronius, extracts from *The Satyricon*   58
Primary Source 2.20   Polybius, *The Rise of the Roman Empire* 6.56   60
Primary Source 2.21   Lucretius, *On Nature* 3.830–69   61
Primary Source 2.22   Cicero, *Tusculan Disputations* I.v.9–I.vi.13   61
Primary Source 2.23   Cicero, *In Defence of Cluentis* 171   63
Primary Source 2.24   Cicero, *Philippics* 14.12.32   63
Primary Source 2.25   Cicero, *On the Republic* 6.13   63
Primary Source 2.26   Lucian, *Menippus* 17–21   63
Primary Source 2.27   Lucian, *On Funerals* 1–9   65
Primary Source 2.28   Seneca, *Consolation to Marcia* 19.4–5   67
Primary Source 2.29   Pliny the Elder, *Natural History*
7.55.188–189   67
Primary Source 2.30   Juvenal, *Satire* 2.149–52   67
Primary Source 2.31   Four epitaphs   67

Introduction

Primary Source I   Ovid, *The Art of Love*, Book 2

(Source: Melville, A.D. (trans.) (1990) *Ovid: The Love Poems*, Oxford, Oxford University Press, pp. 108–10)

iambic pentameter

Oh Venus, Love, and Erato, who are	15
Love's namesake[1] now, if ever, take my part;	
Great is my task, to tell what arts can stay	
The flight of Love, that world-wide runaway,	
An airy creature with a pair of wings;	
It's hard to put restraint upon such things.	20

With every exit barred by Minos' hand,	
A bold escape on wings his prisoner planned.	
When Daedalus had pent the monster[2] in,	
Half bull, half man,[3] fruit of a mother's sin,	
'Just monarch, let my exile end', he prayed,	25
'In my own country let my bones be laid.	
Since in my home a cruel destiny[4]	
Forbade me live, there grant me leave to die.	
Release my child, if age can earn no ruth,	
Or pity age, if you'll not pity youth'.	30
These words he spoke, but all, and more beside,	
Were said in vain: release was still denied.	
Whereat quoth he: 'Now, Daedalus, ah now	
Your cleverness you have a chance to show!	
O'er earth and ocean[5] Minos wields his might,	35
Nor land nor sea is open to my flight.	
The skyey path remains, we'll tempt the skies:	
Great Jove, look kindly on my enterprise.	

[1]   *Love's namesake:* the etymological connection (real or false is immaterial) between Erato and *eros* is as old as Plato (*Phaedrus* 259b). Ovid expects his readers to remember that she is invoked by Apollonius at the beginning of his account of the love of Jason and Medea (*Argonautica* iii. I). There may also possibly be an arch 'correction' of Virgil, whose commentators, from Servius onwards ('Erato for Calliope or for any Muse') have been hard put to it to explain why he chose to introduce the second, 'Iliadic', half of the Aeneid by invoking Erato (vii. 37). Ovid makes it clear that she has every right to figure in *his* poem and lends it status by the invocation.

[2]   *pent the monster in*: in the Labyrinth; i. 527–64 n.

[3]   *Half bull, half man*: *Amores* ii. II. 10 n.

[4]   *a cruel destiny*: he had had to flee Athens after murdering his nephew Perdix in jealousy of his inventive powers (*Metamorphoses* viii. 235–59).

[5]   *and ocean*: 'Minos was the first ruler to build a fleet and to take command of the sea' (Thucydides i. 4).

I'll not aspire to reach your starred abode,[6]
   To flee a tyrant I've no other road.   40
I'd swim the Styx, if that way lay escape;
   In me shall nature all her laws reshape.'
Woes sharpen wits; who'er would think it true
   That man could cleave a pathway through the blue?
The oary plumes of birds he sets in line   45
   And binds the fragile texture fast with twine,
Makes firm the ends with wax dissolved in heat,
   And now the craftsman's novel work's complete.
With wax and plumes his laughing youngster played
   Nor guessed such engines for himself were made.   50
'These craft shall bear us home,' his father said,
   'By aid of these from Minos we'll be sped.
All else he bars, to bar the skies he fails,
   The skies are free, the skies my genius scales.
But not by armed Orion steer your way,   55
   Bootes' comrade,[7] nor Callisto's ray.[8]
I'll pilot you; behind me wing your flight;
   Thy task's to follow; I shall guide you right.
For if through heaven's ether towards the sun
   We mount, beneath his rays the wax will run,   60
And if too near the sea our pinions scud,
   The airy plumes will sodden in the flood.
Fly midway, child; of breezes too beware,
   And trim your sails to catch the favouring air.'
He fits the gear thus warning, and explains   65
   Its working, as a bird her fledglings trains.
Then his own pinions binding on his back
   With trembling limbs he tests the novel track.
A parting kiss he gives his son so dear,
   Nor could a father's cheeks resist a tear.   70
A low-browed hill that rose above the plain
   Upon their venture launched the luckless twain.
Still Daedalus maintains his steadfast poise,
   Sways his own wings and turns to watch the boy's.
Now feels the lad his novel journey's thrill,   75
   He casts off fear and flies with daring skill.

---

[6] *aspire to reach your starred abode*: like the Giants (*Amores* ii. 1. 11–12, 13 nn.). Icarus in his youthful heedlessness does just this and incurs destruction. The story is abruptly introduced, and its moral—the difficulty of Ovid's undertaking (97–8)—seems to be at odds with the confident manifesto that ushered in the poem. In Horace Daedalus figures as a warning of the originally sacrilegious character of seafaring (*Odes* i. 3. 33 ff.; cf. *Amores* ii. 11.1 n.), and Icarus as a type of the daring that courts destruction (iv. 2. 1–4; cf. ii. 20. 13–16), as he does in Ovid's later comments on his own fate (*Tristia* i. 2. 89–90, iii. 4. 21–4). Rather than taking all this as a serious reflection on 'the limits of *ars*' (Myerowitz) it seems preferable to see it as a mock-solemn warning to the lover to 'follow reason and avoid extremes' (Green). Resort to magic (the next precept) is a case in point: that, like Icarus' attempt to scale the heavens, is impious (*nefas*, 107).

[7] *Bootes*: the Wagoner.

[8] *Callisto*: the Great Bear; the story of her double metamorphosis is told by Ovid at *Metamorphoses* ii. 401–535.

These one who fished with quivering rod espied;
   Straight from his fingers dropped the task he plied.
Left Samos lay, with Naxos in the rear,
   And Paros and the isle to Phoebus[9] dear;   80
To right Astypalaea's fishy deeps,
   Lebynthos and Calymne's wooded steeps,
When all with boyhood's recklessness afire
   The youngster soars aloft and leaves his sire.
He nears the sun, the waxen bonds dissolve,   85
   Nor buoyant on the breeze his arms revolve.
Aghast he scans the deep from heaven's height,
   And darkness surges o'er his stricken sight.
The wax gives out, the naked limbs contort,
   He flutters, clutching vainly for support,   90
He drops, and dropping, 'Father, Father,' shrieks,
   'I'm lost'; the green flood chokes him as he speaks.
'Icarus,' wails his sire, a sire no more,
   'Where's Icarus? Oh whither do you soar?
Ah Icarus!' He sees the wave-tossed plumes.   95
   Earth has his bones: the sea his name assumes.[10]

A mortal's wings not Minos could restrain,
   A winged god I purpose to enchain.

Primary Source II   Ovid, *The Art of Love*, Book 1

(Source: Melville, A.D. (trans.) (1990) *Ovid: The Love Poems*, Oxford,
Oxford University Press, pp. 94–5)

First tell yourself all women can be won:
   Just spread your nets; the thing's as good as done.   270
Spring birds and summer crickets shall be mute
   And greyhounds flee before the hare's pursuit,
Ere woman spurns a wooer's blandishments;
   Even she you'd swear would ne'er consent, consents.
To stolen joys both man and woman thrill;   275
   She hides her yearnings, he dissembles ill.
Could men agree to ask no woman first,
   The asker's role perforce would be reversed.
Cow lows to bull across the balmy mead,
   The mare still whinnies to the horn-shod steed.   280
More calm and sober burn the lusts of men,
   In lawful bounds our ardours do we pen.
Take Byblis, who with halter unafraid
   The price of her incestuous passion paid;
Myrrha, who loved, but in no filial wise,   285
   Her father, prisoned in a tree-trunk lies,
That fragrant tree that from her tears of shame

---

[9]   *the isle to Phoebus dear*: Delos, his birthplace. Here and in the later retelling of the story at *Metamorphoses* viii. 220–2 scholars have puzzled over Daedalus' route, which is not altogether easy to square with the geographical facts. Ovid was more concerned with the evocative qualities of the Greek names of these islands than with their precise locations.

[10]   *the sea his name assumes*: the Icarian Sea, between the Cyclades and south-west Asia Minor.

Distils the perfume that preserves her name.
In Ida's shady valleys once was reared
   A snow-white bull, the glory of the herd.   290
Betwixt his horns one streak of umber thin
   Was the sole blemish on his milky skin.
Cnossos' and Cydon's heifers all aflame
   To bear the burden of his courtship came.
Pasiphae, longing for a bestial mate,   295
   Eyed the fair cows with jealousy and hate.
Known truth I sing: not even that land of lies,
   Crete of the hundred towns, my tale denies.
Herself, it's said, fresh leaves and softest sward
   With hands unskilled she gathered for her lord.   300
She joins the herds nor recks her husband's case,
   And Minos to a bull yields pride of place.
Pasiphae, why don that raiment fine?
   No gauds can move that paramour of thine.
What use that mirror 'mid the mountain flocks?   305
   What use, fond fool, to smooth your ordered locks?
Yet trust your glass that shows you you're no cow:
   How welcome would be horns upon that brow!
Oh! love your spouse and for no stranger lust,
   Or sin with your own kind, if sin you must.   310
She quits her palace and through glades and groves
   Like a hag-ridden bacchanal she roves.
How oft she eyed a heifer in despite,
   Exclaiming 'Why should *she* my lord delight?
See on the turf she gambols at his feet;   315
   The fool thinks doubtless that she looks so sweet.'
She had her harmless victim, as she spoke,
   Torn from the herd and set to bear the yoke,
Or, a sham offering, at the altar felled,
   And gloated as her rival's heart she held.   320
Oft to the Gods her rivals did she vow,
   And took their hearts and said 'Go, charm him now!'
And for Europa's lot or Io's prayed,
   One the bull's rider, one the heifer-maid;
Till cozened by a wooden cow his seed   325
   He gave her, and the child betrayed its breed.

Block 1   The myth of Hippolytus and Phaedra

Primary Source 1.1   Ovid, 'Phaedra to Hippolytus'

(Source: Isbell, H. (trans.) (1990) *Ovid: Heroides*, Harmondsworth, Penguin,
pp. 30–5, 37–8)

A girl from Crete sends her greeting to a man
   who is the son of an Amazon.
This maiden wishes for him the good fortune
   she lacks unless he gives it to her.
Whatever words are here, read on to the end.   5
   How could reading this letter hurt you?
Indeed, my words might even give you pleasure.
   These letters carry my secret thoughts
over land and sea; even enemies read
   letters another enemy sends.   10
Three times have I tried to speak with you, three times
   my tongue has stuck in my mouth, three times
the sound of my voice has been stopped at my lips.
   If Love is joined with modesty then
love should never be deprived of modesty.   15
   Modesty is shy but Love is bold;
it is Love that commands me to write to you
   because modesty made me silent.
Whatever Love commands must not be ignored.
   The gods, the lords of all, are themselves   20
subject to Love's command. Could I disobey?
   When I was so confused Love said, 'Write.
Though made of iron, he will surely give his hand.'
   Love will aid me: while warming my bones
with fire may he turn your heart to heed my prayers.   25
   You may inquire, but I tell you now:
I will not basely forsake my marriage vows;
   my name is free from all infamy.
Because it has come late, love has come deeper.
   I am on fire with love within me;   30
my breast is burned by an invisible wound.
   As a young steer is chafed by the yoke
and a colt barely endures the first bridle,
   so has my heart rebelled against love.
This heavy load does not rest well on my soul.   35
   When the art is learned in youth, a first
love is simple; but love that comes after youth
   always burns with a harsher passion.
I offer you a purity long preserved;
   let us both be equal in our guilt.   40
Fruit picked from a heavy branch is good, the first
   rose pinched by a slender nail is best.
But even if the innocent purity
   in which I have always lived my life
were to be stained by this unaccustomed sin,   45
   I would regard this fortune that burns
me with such flames a kindly fortune. Base love

is worse than love merely forbidden.
If Juno gave me her brother and husband,
    Jove, I would prefer Hippolytus.[1]   50
Now, incredibly, I turn to strange pastimes:
    I want to be among the wild beasts.
Delia, who is known to all for her bow,
    is mine; like you, I have chosen her.[2]
I take my pleasure in the forest driving   55
    deer to the net and urging my hounds
over the hills. I hurl the quivering spear
    and I rest my body in the grass.
I drive a chariot around the dusty track
    and twist the bit in the horse's mouth.   60
At other times I am swept up like the mad
    screaming disciples of Bacchus who
are driven by their god's frenzy or like those
    who worship on the ridge of Ida
rattling drums and snares or like those possessed and   65
    given up to the sacred madness
brought by half-divine dryads and fauns with horns.[3]
    When the madness leaves me I return
and others tell me what I was; in my heart
    I know I have been possessed by love.   70
Perhaps I am paying a debt to Venus
    for the favours my family enjoyed:
Jove founded our line by loving Europa –
    he came to her disguised as a bull;
Pasiphae, my mother, was raped by a bull   75
    by whom she bore her burden of shame.
Aegeus' lying son used the helpful thread
    my sister gave and escaped the maze.
I too, a child of Minos, must be subject
    to the same law that rules my family.   80
It is our common fate that one house took us –
    your great beauty has conquered my heart,
your father captured the heart of my sister.
    Theseus and his son together
have been the destruction of we two sisters;   85
    you could erect a double trophy.
Once when I went to Ceres' Eleusis[4] –
    the soil of Crete should have held me back –
you pleased me most though you had pleased me
    before.
    Dressed in white with flowers in your hair,   90
your sun-tanned cheeks were coloured by modesty.

---

[1]   Jove or Jupiter (the Greek Zeus) was the king of the gods. Juno (the Greek Hera) was his sister and his wife and thus queen of the gods.

[2]   The name Delia is sometimes given to Diana in a poetic context. The term is derived from the place of her birth, the island of Delos.

[3]   This is a reference to the maenads, female followers of Dionysus (the Roman Bacchus or Liber). Wherever the god went, in heaven or on earth, he was followed by satyrs and maenads.

[4]   Eleusis was an Attic city not far from the Isthmus of Corinth. In ancient times it became sacred to Ceres (the Greek Demeter). According to the myth, in the time of Theseus Eleusis was governed jointly with Athens.

It was then that love pierced my body.
Some would have called you stern; I saw only strength.
  Get rid of these men who look like girls;
men who are truly men are more than handsome.   95
  That frown, the hair that falls where it must,
the light dust on your splendid face, suit you well.
  I admire you when you rein in the
stubborn necks of your high-spirited horses,
  forcing a turn in a slight circle.[5]   100
I admire your arm whether it hurls a lance
  or grasps the iron-headed hunting spear.
There is no more for me to say except that
  whatever you do delights my eyes.
Exhaust your harshness there in the wilderness;   105
  do not wage a campaign against me.
You live the chastity of Diana while
  you pilfer what is owed to Venus.
Something which never takes rest will not endure.
  Rest repairs the limbs and renews strength.   110
If the bow is never relaxed it will lose
  the tension that makes it a bow; you
would do well to imitate the weapons of
  Diana while you follow her lead.
Indeed, Cephalus was a mighty hunter,   115
  and many beasts fell beneath his spear
to the ground, yet he did no harm in yielding
  himself to enjoy Aurora's love.
Many times that goddess shrewdly went to him
  leaving behind her aged husband;   120
and Venus, too, often reclined with the son
  of Cinyras by a holly oak.
Moreover, Oeneus' son blazed with love
  for Atalanta of Maenalus –
he gave her the wild beast's pelt to be a pledge   125
  of his love for her. We too can be
counted as lovers like these. If one removes
  love, your forest in only rustic.
I will come to you, I fear neither the cliffs
  nor the slashing tusks of the wild boar.   130
There is a slender isthmus which hears throughout
  its length and breadth the roar of two seas.
In that place, land of Troezen, Pittheus'
  kingdom, a place dearer now to me
than my native land, we together can dwell.   135
  Neptune's heroic son is absent
now, detained by his dearest friend, Pirithous.
  Theseus, we must conclude, loves him
more than he loves Phaedra; loves him more than he
  loves you, his son.[6] But that is not all.   140
We have both been deeply hurt by Theseus.
  With his club he crushed my brother's bones

---

[5]   Hippolytus, as his name suggests, was renowned for his skill in breeding and training horses. This would be in keeping with this devotion to Diana.

[6]   Neptune was the god of the sea whom the Romans associated with the Greek god, Poseidon.

and scattered them over the soil; then he left
  my sister helpless with the wild beasts.
Your mother was a most courageous warrior   145
  and worthy to bear such a strong son.
Where is she? She is dead, speared by Theseus.
  Even such a promising baby
as you were was not enough to save her life.
  I ask you, why did they not marry?   150
Why, unless perhaps he feared you as rival.
  He sired brothers but took them from me,
raising them in his own way to be his heirs.
  I wish my breast which has injured you
so greatly, fairest man, had been torn open.   155
  Go now, pay your respects to the bed
which your father denies by his wicked deeds.
  If I seem a stepmother who would
lie with her husband's son, ignore such silly
  words. Such virtue was out of date in   160
Saturn's reign and it died in the next age when
  Jove decreed that virtue was pleasure.
Because Jove made his sister his wife the gods
  have come to see that nothing is wrong.[7]
The only enduring contract is that which   165
  is preserved by the chains of Venus.
Do not worry that our love must be concealed,
  only ask the help of Venus and
she will hide us in the mantle of kinship;
  we will be praised for our embraces   170
and I will seem to be a good stepmother.
  The same roof will always shelter us
no austere husband's gate will need unbolting
  in the dark of night, no guard must be
evaded, all doors will always be open.   175
  No one will question your presence here.
You have kissed me in public, this will not change;
  even on my couch you will be safe:
indeed, your fault will earn you the highest praise.
  Hurry, do not delay, tie our bond   180
together now, I shall pray that love will spare
  you all the bitterness I must feel.
Though I am proud, I can bend my knee in prayer.
  But where now is pride, my high-flown words?
All are fallen. I was determined – if love   185
  can determine anything – to fight
long rather than be conquered, but I confess
  I am overcome. I beseech you,
I extend to you a queen's regal arms, let
  me only clasp your knees. Love does not   190

---

[7] Cronos, the King of the Titans whom the Romans identified with Saturn, took Rhea, his sister, to be his wife. Cronos was warned that one of his children would overthrow him. To prevent this, as Rhea bore each of their offspring Cronos ate the infant. However, the youngest, Zeus, was hidden away by Rhea and her mother Ge. In time, Zeus grew to manhood and rescued his siblings from the body of their father. The young gods then defeated Cronos. Zeus also took Hera, his sister, as his wife.

care for what is proper, modesty has fled
    the field of battle and its standards.
If this letter offends you, give me pardon;
    let your hard heart grow softer for me.
My father is Minos who governs the seas,   195
    my ancestor hurls the lightning and
my grandfather drives his gleaming chariot through
    the day wearing a crown of sunlight.[8]
Nobility lies underneath love. Pity
    my family, if you cannot spare me.   200
Jove's island, Crete, is a part of my dowry;
    each one in my court can be your slave.
Cruel man, change your mind: my mother made a bull
    desire her; are you fiercer than that?
By Venus, who is closest to me, spare me.   205
    May your love never be rejected,
may the nimble goddess guard you in the glades,
    may the forests give you beasts to kill,
may your friends be satyrs and the mountain gods,
    may your flying spear pierce the wild boar,   210
may the nymphs – though I hear you despise women –
    relieve your thirst with flowing water.
I mingle my prayer with weeping: you are reading
my words; I beg you, try to imagine my tears.

Primary Source 1.2   Euripides, *Hippolytus*

(Source: Halleran, M.R. (trans. and ed.) (1995) *Euripides: Hippolytus*, Oxford, Aris & Phillips, pp. 29–33)

Hippolytus 1 Fragments

F 443 (=A Barrett)

O bright air and holy light of day,
how sweet it is to gaze on you for those who fare well
and for those who are unfortunate; to this group I belong.
Phaedra speaking; very likely the play's opening lines.

Plu., *Moralia* 27f–28a (p. 491 Nauck) (= B Barrett)

And [Euripides] represented Phaedra also as accusing Theseus that she fell in love with Hippolytus on account of his [Theseus'] transgressions.
Probably early in the play.

F 430 (= C Barrett)

But I have as an instructor of boldness and daring
Eros, most resourceful in impossible circumstances,
and the hardest god of all to fight against.
Phaedra speaking, perhaps in an early dialogue with the Nurse.

[...]

---

[8]   The sun-god was Helios, the father of Pasiphaë and thus Phaedra's grandfather.

F 440 (= K Barrett)

Theseus, I advise you for the best, if you have sense:
Don't believe a woman even when you hear the truth.
No clear speaker; it comes most likely after Phaedra's charge against
Hippolytus.

[...]

F 439 (= N Barrett)

Alas, alas, that the facts have no voice
for humans, so that those who are clever at speaking would be nothing.
But as things are, they conceal with glib tongues
what is truest, so that what ought to appear to be so does not.
Either Theseus (complaining about Hippolytus) or Hippolytus
(complaining about Phaedra or Theseus).

F 446 (= U Barrett)

O blessed hero Hippolytus,
what honors you have obtained for your virtue.
Never for mortals
is another power greater than excellence.
For either sooner or later comes
the good reward for piety.
The Chorus; perhaps the concluding lines of the play.

Primary Source 1.3   Virgil, *The Aeneid* 7.761–84

(Source: West, D. (trans.) (2003) *Virgil: The Aeneid*, London, Penguin, pp. 162–3)

There too, sent by his mother Aricia, glorious Virbius came
to the war, the lovely son of Hippolytus. He had grown to
manhood in the grove of Egeria around the dank lake-shores by
the altar where rich sacrifices win the favour of Diana. For after
Hippolytus had been brought to his death by the wiles of his
stepmother Phaedra, torn to pieces by bolting horses and paying
with his blood the penalty imposed by his father, men say he
came back under the stars of the sky and the winds of heaven,
restored by healing herbs and the love of Diana. Then the   770
All-powerful Father was enraged that any mortal should rise
from the shades below into the light of life and with his own
hand he took the inventor of those healing arts, Asclepius, son
of Apollo, and hurled him with his thunderbolt down into the
wave of the river Styx. But Diana Trivia, in her loving care,
found a secret refuge for Hippolytus and consigned him to the
nymph Egeria and her grove, where, alone and unknown, his
name changed to Virbius, he might live out his days. Thus it is
that horn-hooved horses are not admitted to the sacred grove of
the temple of Trivia because in their terror at the monsters of the   780
deep the horses of Hippolytus had overturned his chariot and
thrown him on the shore. But none the less his son was driving
fiery horses across the level plain as he rushed to the wars in a chariot.

Primary Source 1.4   Servius, *Ad Aeneid* 6.136

(Source: Green, C.M.C. (2007) *Roman Religion and The Cult of Diana at Aricia*, Cambridge and New York, Cambridge University Press, pp. 297–9)

Frazer has been attacked (e.g., by J.Z. Smith 1978, West 1990) for his interpretation of the rex nemorensis on the grounds that he mistranslated Servius' Latin. Smith has directed particular criticism toward Frazer's understanding of AD Aen. 6.136, and presented a new version of the passage, a translation which itself had flaws [...] I offer here my own version [...]

LATET ARBORE OPACA AUREUS licet de hoc ramo hi qui de sacris Proserpinae scripsisse dicuntur, quiddam esse mysticum adfirment, publica tamen opinio hoc habet. Orestes post occisum regem Thoantem in regione Taurica cum sorore Iphigenia, ut supra (2.116) diximus, fugit et Dianae simulacrum inde sublatum haud longe ab Aricia collocavit. in huius templo post mutatum ritum sacrificiorum fuit arbor quaedam, de qua infringi ramum non licebat. dabatur autem fugitivis potestas, ut si quis exinde ramum potuisset auferre, monomachia cum fugitivo templi sacerdote dimicaret: nam fugitivus illic erat sacerdos AD priscae imaginem fugae. dimicandi autem dabatur facultas quasi AD pristini sacrificii reparationem. nunc ergo istum inde sumpsit colerem [...]

A golden [bough] lies hidden in a shady tree. Although, in the matter of this branch, those who are said to have written about the rites of Proserpine assert that it is something used in the mysteries, nevertheless the general view is as follows: Orestes, after the killing of King Thoas in the Tauric land, fled with his sister (as we stated above [2.116]), and the image of Diana that he brought from there he set up not far from Aricia. In her precinct, after the sacrificial ritual was changed, there was a certain tree, from which it was not permitted to break off a branch. Moreover, the right was given to any fugitive who contrived to remove a branch thence to contend in single combat with the fugitive priest of the temple, for the priest there was [also] a fugitive, to symbolize the original flight. And indeed, this opportunity of fighting was given as though in renewal of the original sacrifice: it follows that, at this point in his narrative, he [i.e. Vergil] has taken his rhetorical effects from here [...]

Block 2   Myth in Rome: power, life and afterlife

Primary Source 2.1   Livy, extract from *The Early History of Rome*

(Source: de Sélincourt, A. (trans.) (1960) *Livy: The Early History of Rome*, Harmondsworth, Penguin, pp. 33–51)

The task of writing a history of our nation from Rome's earliest days fills me, I confess, with some misgiving, and even were I confident in the value of my work, I should hesitate to say so. I am aware that for historians to make extravagant claims is, and always has been, all too common: every writer on history tends to look down his nose at his less cultivated predecessors, happily persuaded that he will better them in point of style, or bring new facts to light. But however that may be, I shall find satisfaction in contributing – not, I hope, ignobly – to the labour of putting on record the story of the greatest nation in the world. Countless others have written on this theme and it may be that I shall pass unnoticed amongst them; if so, I must comfort myself with the greatness and splendour of my rivals, whose work will rob my own of recognition.

My task, moreover, is an immensely laborious one. I shall have to go back more than seven hundred years, and trace my story from its small beginnings up to these recent times when its ramifications are so vast that any adequate treatment is hardly possible. I am aware, too, that most readers will take less pleasure in my account of how Rome began and in her early history; they will wish to hurry on to more modern times and to read of the period, already a long one, in which the might of an imperial people is beginning to work its own ruin. My own feeling is different; I shall find antiquity a rewarding study, if only because, while I am absorbed in it, I shall be able to turn my eyes from the troubles which for so long have tormented the modern world, and to write without any of that over-anxious consideration which may well plague a writer on contemporary life, even if it does not lead him to conceal the truth.

Events before Rome was born or thought of have come to us in old tales with more of the charm of poetry than of a sound historical record, and such traditions I propose neither to affirm nor refute. There is no reason, I feel, to object when antiquity draws no hard line between the human and the supernatural: it adds dignity to the past, and, if any nation deserves the privilege of claiming a divine ancestry, that nation is our own; and so great is the glory won by the Roman people in their wars that, when they declare that Mars himself was their first parent and father of the man who founded their city, all the nations of the world might well allow the claim as readily as they accept Rome's imperial dominion.

These, however, are comparatively trivial matters and I set little store by them. I invite the reader's attention to the much more serious consideration of the kind of lives our ancestors lived, of who were the men, and what the means both in politics and war by which Rome's power was first acquired and subsequently expanded; I would then have him trace the process of our moral decline, to watch first, the sinking of the foundations of morality as the old teaching was allowed to lapse, then the rapidly increasing disintegration, then the final collapse of the whole edifice, and the dark dawning of our modern day when we can neither endure our vices nor face the remedies needed to cure them. The study of history is the best medicine for a sick mind; for in history you have a record of the infinite variety of human experience plainly set out for all to see; and in that record you can find for yourself and your country both examples and warnings; fine things to take as models, base things, rotten through and through, to avoid.

I hope my passion for Rome's past has not impaired my judgement; for I do honestly believe that no country has ever been greater or purer than ours or richer in good citizens and noble deeds; none has been free for so many generations from the vices of avarice and luxury; nowhere have thrift and plain living been for so long held in such esteem. Indeed, poverty, with us, went hand in hand with contentment. Of late years wealth has made us greedy, and self-indulgence has brought us, through every form of sensual excess, to be, if I may so put it, in love with death both individual and collective.

But bitter comments of this sort are not likely to find favour, even when they have to be made. Let us have no more of them, at least at the beginning of our great story. On the contrary, I should prefer to borrow from the poets and begin with good omens and with prayers to all the host of heaven to grant a successful issue to the work which lies before me.

It is generally accepted that after the fall of Troy the Greeks kept up hostilities against all the Trojans except Aeneas and Antenor. These two men had worked consistently for peace and the restoration of Helen, and for that reason, added to certain personal connections of long standing, they were allowed to go unmolested. Each had various adventures: Antenor joined forces with the Eneti, who had been driven out of Paphlagonia and, having lost their king, Pylaemenes, at Troy, wanted someone to lead them as well as somewhere to settle. He penetrated to the head of the Adriatic and expelled the Euganei, a tribe living between the Alps and the sea, and occupied that territory with a mixed population of Trojans and Eneti. The spot where they landed is called Troy and the neighbouring country the Trojan district. The combined peoples came to be known as Venetians.

Aeneas was forced into exile by similar troubles; he, however, was destined to lay the foundations of a greater future. He went first to Macedonia, then in his search for a new home sailed to Sicily, and from Sicily to the territory of Laurentum. This part of Italy too, like the spot where Antenor landed, is known as Troy. Aeneas's men in the course of their almost interminable wanderings had lost all they possessed except their ships and their swords; once on shore, they set about scouring the countryside for what they could find, and while thus engaged they were met by a force of armed natives who, under their king Latinus, came hurrying up from the town and the surrounding country to protect themselves from the invaders. There are two versions of what happened next: according to one, there was a fight in which Latinus was beaten; he then came to terms with Aeneas and cemented the alliance by giving him his daughter in marriage. According to the other, the battle was about to begin when Latinus, before the trumpets could sound the charge, came forward with his captains and invited the foreign leaders to a parley. He then asked Aeneas who his men were and where they had come from, why they had left their homes and what was their object in landing on Laurentian territory. He was told in reply that the men were Trojans, their leader Aeneas, the son of Anchises and Venus; that their native town had been burnt to the ground and now they were fugitives in search of some place where they could build a new town to settle in. Latinus, hearing their story, was so deeply impressed by the noble bearing of the strangers and by their leader's high courage either for peace or war, that he gave Aeneas his hand in pledge of friendship from that moment onward. A treaty was made; the two armies exchanged signs of mutual respect; Aeneas accepted the hospitality of Latinus, who gave him his daughter in marriage, thus further confirming the treaty of alliance by a private and domestic bond solemnly entered into in the presence of the Gods of his hearth.

The Trojans could no longer doubt that at last their travels were over and that they had found a permanent home. They began to build a settlement, which Aeneas named Lavinium after his wife Lavinia. A child was soon born of the marriage: a boy, who was given the name Ascanius.

The Trojans and the Latins were soon jointly involved in war. Turnus, prince of the Rutuli, to whom Latinus's daughter Lavinia had been pledged before Aeneas's arrival, angered by the insult of having to step down in favour of a stranger, attacked the combined forces of Aeneas and Latinus. Both sides suffered in the subsequent struggle: the Rutuli were defeated, but the victors lost their leader Latinus. Turnus and his people, in their anxiety for the future, then looked for help to Mezentius, king of the rich and powerful Etruscans, whose seat of government was at Caere, at that time a wealthy town. Mezentius, needed little persuasion to join the Rutuli, as from the outset he had been far from pleased by the rise of the new settlement, and now felt that the Trojan power was growing much more rapidly than was safe for its neighbours. In this dangerous situation Aeneas conferred the native name of Latins upon his own people; the sharing of a common name as well as a common polity could, he felt, strengthen the bond between the two peoples. As a result of this step the original settlers were no less loyal to their king Aeneas than were the Trojans themselves. Trojans and Latins were rapidly becoming one people, and this gave Aeneas confidence to make an active move against the Etruscans, in spite of their great strength. Etruria, indeed, had at this time both by sea and land filled the whole length of Italy from the Alps to the Sicilian strait with the noise of her name; none the less Aeneas refused to act on the defensive and marched out to meet the enemy. The Latins were victorious, and for Aeneas the battle was the last of his labours in this world. He lies buried on the river Numicus. Was he man or god? However it be, men call him Jupiter Indiges – the local Jove.

Aeneas's son Ascanius was still too young for a position of authority; Lavinia, however, was a woman of great character, and acted as regent until Ascanius came of age and was able to assume power as the successor of his father and grandfather. There is some doubt – and no one can pretend to certainty on something so deeply buried in the mists of time – about who precisely this Ascanius was. Was it the one I have been discussing, or was it an elder brother, the son of Creusa, who was born before the sack of Troy and was with Aeneas in his escape from the burning city – the Iulus, in fact, whom the Julian family claim as their eponym? It is at any rate certain that Aeneas was his father, and – whatever the answer to the other question may be – it can be taken as a fact that he left Lavinium to found a new settlement. Lavinium was by then a populous and, for those days, a rich and flourishing town, and Ascanius left it in charge of his mother (or stepmother, if you will) and went off to found his new settlement on the Alban hills. This town, strung out as it was along a ridge, was named Alba Longa. Its foundation took place about thirty years after that of Lavinium; but the Latins had already grown so strong, especially since the defeat of the Etruscans, that neither Mezentius, the Etruscan king, nor any other neighbouring people dared to attack them, even when Aeneas died and the control of things passed temporarily into the hands of a woman, and Ascanius was still a child learning the elements of kingship. By the terms of the treaty between the Latins and Etruscans the river Albula (now the Tiber) became the boundary between the two territories.

Ascanius was succeeded by his son Silvius – 'born in the woods' – and he by his son Aeneas Silvius, whose heir was Latinus Silvius. By him several new settlements were made, and given the name of Old Latins. All the kings of Alba subsequently kept the cognomen Silvius. Next in succession to Latinius was

Alba; then Atys, then Capys, then Capetus, then Tiberinus – who was drowned crossing the Albula and gave that river the name of which succeeding generations have always known it. Tiberinus was succeeded by Agrippa, Agrippa by his son Romulus Silvius, who was struck by lightning and bequeathed his power to Aventinus. Aventinus was buried on the hill, now a part of the city of Rome, and still bearing his name. Proca, the next king, had two sons, Numitor and Amulius, to the elder of whom, Numitor, he left the hereditary realm of the Silvian family; that, at least, was his intention, but respect for seniority was flouted, the father's will ignored and Amulius drove out his brother and seized the throne. One act of violence led to another; he proceeded to murder his brother's male children, and made his niece, Rhea Silvia, a Vestal, ostensibly to do her honour, but actually by condemning her to perpetual virginity to preclude the possibility of issue.

But (I must believe) it was already written in the book of fate that this great city of ours should rise, and the first steps be taken to the founding of the mightiest empire the world has known – next to God's. The Vestal Virgin was raped and gave birth to twin boys. Mars, she declared, was their father – perhaps she believed it, perhaps she was merely hoping by the pretence to palliate her guilt. Whatever the truth of the matter, neither gods nor men could save her or her babes from the savage hands of the king. The mother was bound and flung into prison; the boys, by the king's order, were condemned to be drowned in the river. Destiny, however, intervened; the Tiber had overflowed its banks; because of the flooded ground it was impossible to get to the actual river, and the men entrusted to do the deed thought that the flood-water, sluggish though it was, would serve their purpose. Accordingly they made shift to carry out the king's orders by leaving the infants on the edge of the first flood-water they came to, at the spot where now stands the Ruminal fig-tree – said to have once been known as the fig-tree of Romulus. In those days the country thereabouts was all wild and uncultivated, and the story goes that when the basket in which the infants had been exposed was left high and dry by the receding water, a she-wolf, coming down from the neighbouring hills to quench her thirst, heard the children crying and made her way to where they were. She offered them her teats to suck and treated them with such gentleness that Faustulus, the king's herdsman, found her licking them with her tongue. Faustulus, took them to his hut and gave them to his wife Larentia to nurse. Some think that the origin of this fable was the fact that Larentia was a common whore and was called Wolf by the shepherds.

Such, then, was the birth and upbringing of the twins. By the time they were grown boys, they employed themselves actively on the farm and with the flocks and began to go hunting in the woods; their strength grew with their resolution, until not content only with the chase they took to attacking robbers and sharing their stolen goods with their friends the shepherds. Other young fellows joined them, and they and the shepherds would fleet the time together, now in serious talk, now in jollity.

Even in that remote age the Palatine hill (which got its name from the Arcadian settlement Pallanteum) is supposed to have been the scene of the gay festival of the Lupercalia. The Arcadian Evander, who many years before held that region, is said to have instituted there the old Arcadian practice of holding an annual festival in honour of Lycean Pan (afterwards called Inuus by the Romans), in which young men ran about naked and disported themselves in various pranks and fooleries. The day of the festival was common knowledge, and on one occasion when it was in full swing brigands, incensed at the loss of their ill-gotten gains, laid a trap for Romulus and Remus.

Romulus successfully defended himself, but Remus was caught and handed over to Amulius. The brigands laid a complaint against their prisoner, the main charge being that he and his brother were in the habit of raiding Numitor's land with an organized gang of ruffians and stealing the cattle. Thereupon Remus was handed over for punishment to Numitor.

Now Faustulus had suspected all along that the boys he was bringing up were of royal blood. He knew that two infants had been exposed by the king's orders, and the rescue of his own two fitted perfectly in point of time. Hitherto, however, he had been unwilling to declare what he knew, until either a suitable opportunity occurred or circumstances compelled him. Now the truth could no longer be concealed, so in his alarm he told Romulus the whole story; Numitor, too, when he had Remus in custody and was told that the brothers were twins, was set thinking about his grandsons; the young men's age and character, so different from the lowly born, confirmed his suspicions; and further inquiries led him to the same conclusion, until he was on the point of acknowledging Remus. The net was closing in, and Romulus acted. He was not strong enough for open hostilities, so he instructed a number of the herdsmen to meet at the king's house by different routes at a pre-ordained time; this was done, and with the help of Remus, at the head of another body of men, the king was surprised and killed. Before the first blow was struck, Numitor gave it out that an enemy had broken into the town and attacked the palace; he then drew off all the men of military age to garrison the inner fortress, and, as soon as he saw Romulus and Remus, their purpose accomplished, coming to congratulate him, he summoned a meeting of the people and laid the facts before it: Amulius's crime against himself, the birth of his grandsons, and the circumstances attending it, how they were brought up and ultimately recognized, and, finally, the murder of the king for which he himself assumed responsibility. The two brothers marched through the crowd at the head of their men and saluted their grandfather as king, and by a shout of unanimous consent his royal title was confirmed.

Romulus and Remus, after the control of Alba had passed to Numitor in the way I have described, were suddenly seized by an urge to found a new settlement on the spot where they had been left to drown as infants and had been subsequently brought up. There was, in point of fact, already an excess of population in Alba, what with the Albans themselves, the Latins, and the addition of the herdsmen: enough, indeed, to justify the hope that Alba and Lavinium would one day be small places compared with the proposed new settlement. Unhappily the brothers' plans for the future were marred by the same source which had divided their grandfather and Amulius – jealous and ambition. A disgraceful quarrel arose from a matter in itself trivial. As the brothers were twins and all questions of seniority was thereby precluded, they determined to ask the tutelary gods of the countryside to declare by augury which of them should govern the new town once it was founded, and give his name to it. For this purpose Romulus took the Palatine hill and Remus the Aventine as their respective stations from which to observe the auspices. Remus, the story goes, was the first to receive a sign – six vultures; and no sooner was this made known to the people than double the number of birds appeared to Romulus. The followers of each promptly saluted their master as king, one side basing its claim upon priority, the other upon number. Angry words ensued, followed all too soon by blows, and in the course of the affray Remus was killed. There is another story, a commoner one, according to which Remus, by way of jeering at his brother, jumped over the half-built walls of the new settlement, whereupon Romulus killed him in a fit of rage, adding the threat, 'So perish whoever else shall overleap my battlements.'

This, then, was how Romulus obtained the sole power. The newly built city was called by its founder's name.

Romulus's first act was to fortify the Palatine, the scene of his own upbringing. He offered sacrifice to the gods, using the Alban forms except in the case of Hercules, where he followed the Greek ritual as instituted by Evander. According to the old tale, Hercules after killing Greyon came into these parts driving his oxen. The oxen were exceedingly beautiful, and close to the Tiber, at the spot where he had swum across with them, he came upon a grassy meadow; here, weary with walking, he lay down to rest and allowed the beasts to refresh themselves with the rich pasture. Being drowsy with food and drink he fell asleep, and, while he slept, a shepherd of that region, a fierce giant named Cacus, saw the oxen and was instantly taken by their beauty. Purposing to steal them, he was aware that, if he drove them in the ordinary way to his cave, their tracks could not fail to guide their master thither as soon as he began his search; so choosing the finest from the herd he dragged them backwards by their tails and hid them in his cavern. Hercules awoke at dawn, and casting his eye over the herd noticed that some of the animals were missing. He went at once to the nearest cave on the chance that there were tracks leading into it, but found that they all led outwards, apparently to nowhere. It was very odd; so full of vague misgivings he started driving the remainder of his herd away from this eerie spot. Some of the beasts, naturally enough, missed their companions and began to low, and there came an answering low from the cave. Hercules turned. He walked towards the cave, and Cacus, when he saw him coming, tried to keep him off. But all in vain; Hercules struck him with this club, and the robber, vainly calling upon his friends for help, fell dead.

In those days Evander held sway over that part of the country. He was an exile from the Peloponnese and his position depended less upon sovereign power than upon personal influence; he was revered for his invention of letters – a strange and wonderful thing to the rude uncultivated men amongst whom he dwelt – and, still more, on account of his mother Carmenta, who was supposed to be divine and before the coming of the Sibyl into Italy had been revered by the people of those parts as a prophetess.

On the occasion of which I am writing Evander could not but observe the shepherds who were excitedly mobbing the unknown killer. He joined them, and upon being informed of their crime and its cause, directed his gaze upon the stranger. Seeing him to be of more than human stature and of a preternatural dignity of bearing, he asked him who he was, and, hearing his name and parentage and country, cried: 'Hercules, son of Jupiter, I bid you welcome. You are the subject of my mother's prophecy; for she, a true prophet, declared that you would increase the number of the Gods, and that here an altar would be dedicated to you, and the nation destined to be the mightiest in the world would one day name it Greatest of Altars and serve it with your own proper rites.'

Hercules gave him his hand and replied that he accepted the inspired words and would himself assist the course of destiny by building and consecrating an altar. A splendid beast was chosen from the herd, and on the new altar sacrifice, for the first time, was offered to Hercules; the rite itself, and the subsequent feast, being administered by members of the two most distinguished local families, the Potitii and Pinarii.

It so happened that the Pinarii were late for the feast. The Potitii were there in time, and were served in consequence with the entrails of the victim; the Pinarii came in only for the remainder. From this circumstance the custom became established that no member of the Pinarian family, throughout its history, was ever served with his portion of entrails at a sacrifice to Hercules. The Potitii were taught by Evander, and furnished the priests of this cult for many generations, until the solemn duty they had so long performed was delegated to public slaves and the family became extinct. This was the only foreign religious rite adopted by Romulus; by so doing he showed, even then, his respect for that immortality which is the prize of valour. His own destiny was already leading him to the same reward.

Having performed with proper ceremony his religious duties, he summoned his subjects and gave them laws, without which the creation of a unified body politic would not have been possible. In his view the rabble over whom he ruled could be induced to respect the law only if he himself adopted certain visible signs of power; he proceeded, therefore, to increase the dignity and impressiveness of his position by various devices, of which the most important was the creation of the twelve lictors to attend his person. Some have fancied that he made the lictors twelve in number because the vultures, in the augury, had been twelve; personally, however, I incline to follow the opinion which finds for this an Etruscan origin. We know that the State Chair – the 'curule' chair – and the purple-bordered toga came to us from Etruria; and it is probable that the idea of attendants, as well as, in this case, of their number, came across the border from Etruria too. The number twelve was due to the fact that the twelve Etruscan communities united to elect a king, and each contributed one lictor.

Meanwhile Rome was growing. More and more ground was coming within the circuit of its walls. Indeed, the rapid expansion of the enclosed area was out of proportion to the actual population, and evidently indicated an eye to the future. In antiquity the founder of a new settlement, in order to increase its population, would as a matter of course shark up a lot of homeless and destitute folk and pretend that they were 'born of earth' to be his progeny; Romulus now followed a similar course: to help fill his big new town, he threw open, in the ground – now enclosed – between the two copses as you go up the Capitoline hill, a place of asylum for fugitives. Hither fled for refuge all the rag-tag-and-bobtail from the neighbouring peoples: some free, some slaves, and all of them wanting nothing but a fresh start. That mob was the first real addition to the City's strength, the first step to her future greatness.

Having now adequate numbers, Romulus proceeded to temper strength with policy and turned his attention to social organization. He created a hundred senators – fixing that number either because it was enough for his purpose, or because there were no more than a hundred who were in a position to be made 'Fathers', as they were called, or Heads of Clans. The title of 'fathers' (*patres*) undoubtedly was derived from their rank, and their descendants were called 'patricians'.

Rome was now strong enough to challenge any of her neighbours; but, great though she was, her greatness seemed likely to last only for a single generation. There were not enough women, and that, added to the fact that there was no intermarriage with neighbouring communities, ruled out any hope of maintaining the level of population. Romulus accordingly, on the advice of his senators, sent representatives to the various peoples across his borders to negotiate alliances and the right of intermarriage for the newly established state. The envoys were instructed to point out that cities, like everything else, have to begin small; in course of time, helped by their own worth and the favour of heaven, some, at least, grow rich and famous, and of these Rome would assuredly be one: Gods had blessed her birth, and the valour of her people would not fail in the days to come. The Romans were men, as they were; why, then, be reluctant to intermarry with them?

Romulus's overtures were nowhere favourably received; it was clear that everyone despised the new community, and at the same time feared, both for themselves and for posterity, the growth of this new power in their midst. More often than not his envoys were dismissed with the question of whether Rome had thrown open her doors to female, as well as to male, runaways and vagabonds, as that would evidently be the most suitable way for Romans to get wives. The young Romans naturally resented this jibe, and a clash seemed inevitable. Romulus, seeing it must come, set the scene for it with elaborate care. Deliberately hiding his resentment, he prepared to celebrate the Consualia, a solemn festival in honour of Neptune, patron of the horse, and sent notice of his intention all over the neighbouring countryside. The better to advertise it, his people lavished upon their preparations for the spectacle all the resources – such as they were in those days – at their command. On the appointed day crowds flocked to Rome, partly, no doubt out of sheer curiosity to see the new town. The majority were from the neighbouring settlements of Caenina, Crustumium, and Antemnae, but all the Sabines were there too, with their wives and children. Many houses offered hospitable entertainment to the visitors; they were invited to inspect the fortifications, layout, and numerous buildings of the town, and expressed their surprise at the rapidity of its growth. Then the great moment came; the show began, and nobody had eyes or thoughts for anything else. This was the Romans' opportunity: at a given signal all the able-bodied men burst through the crowd and seized the young women. Most of the girls were the prize of whoever got hold of them first, but a few conspicuously handsome ones had been previously marked down for leading senators, and these were brought to their houses by special gangs. There was one young woman of much greater beauty than the rest; and the story goes that she was seized by a party of men belonging to the household of someone called Thalassius, and in reply to the many questions about whose house they were taking her to, they, to prevent anyone else laying hands upon her, kept shouting 'Thalassius, Thalassius!' This was the origin of the use of this word at weddings.

By this act of violence the fun of the festival broke up in panic. The girls' unfortunate parents made good their escape, not without bitter comments on the treachery of their hosts and heartfelt prayers to the God to whose festival they had come in all good faith in the solemnity of the occasion, only to be grossly deceived. The young women were no less indignant and as full of foreboding for the future.

Romulus, however, reassured them. Going from one to another he declared that their own parents were really to blame, in that they had been too proud to allow intermarriage with their neighbours; nevertheless, they need not fear; as married women they would share all the fortunes of Rome, all the privileges of the community, and they would be bound to their husbands by the dearest bond of all, their children. He urged them to forget their wrath and give their hearts to those to whom chance had given their bodies. Often, he said, a sense of injury yields in the end to affection, and their husbands would treat them all the more kindly in that they would try, each one of them, not only to fulfil their own part of the bargain but also to make up to their wives for the homes and parents they had lost. The men, too, played their part: they spoke honeyed words and vowed that it was passionate love which had prompted their offence. No plea can better touch a woman's heart.

The women in course of time lost their resentment; but no sooner had they learned to accept their lot than their parents began to stir up trouble in earnest. To excite sympathy they went about dressed in mourning and pouring out their grief in tears and lamentations. Not content with confining these demonstrations within the walls of their own towns, they marched in mass to the house of Titus Tatius the Sabine king, the greatest name in that part of the country. Official embassies, too, from various settlements, waited upon him.

It seemed to the people of Caenina, Crustumium, and Antemnae, who had been involved in the trouble, that Tatius and the Sabines were unduly dilatory, so the three communities resolved to take action on their own. Of the three, however, Crustumium and Antemnae proved too slow to satisfy the impatient wrath of their partner, with the result that the men of Caenina invaded Roman territory without any support. Scattered groups of them were doing what damage they could, when Romulus, at the head of his troops, appeared upon the scene. A few blows were enough and defeat soon taught them that angry men must also be strong, if they would achieve their purpose. The Romans pursued the routed enemy; Romulus himself cut down their prince and stripped him of his arms, then, their leader dead, took the town at the first assault. The victorious army returned, and Romulus proceeded to dispose of the spoils. Magnificent in action, he was no less eager for popular recognition and applause; he took the armour which he had stripped from the body of the enemy commander, fixed it on a frame made for the purpose, and carried it in his own hands up to the Capitol, where, by an oak which the shepherds regarded as a sacred tree, he laid it down as an offering to Jupiter. At the same time he determined on the size of a plot of ground to be consecrated to the God, and uttered this prayer: 'Jupiter Feretrius (such was the new title he bestowed), to you I bring these spoils of victory, a king's armour taken by a king; and within the bounds already clear to my mind's eye I dedicate to you a holy precinct where, in days to come, following my example, other men shall lay the "spoils of honour", stripped from the bodies of commanders or kings killed by their own hands.' Such was the origin of the first temple consecrated in Rome. The gods ordained that Romulus, when he declared that others should bring their spoils thither, should not speak in vain; it was their pleasure, too, that the glory of that offering should not be cheapened by too frequent occurrence. The distinction of winning the 'spoils of honour' has been rare indeed: in the countless battles of succeeding years it has been won on two occasions only.

These proceedings on the Capitol had temporarily drawn the Romans from their farms, and a force from Antemnae took the opportunity of making a raid. Once again Roman troops pounced. The scattered groups of raiders were taken by surprise; a single charge sufficed to put them to flight, their town was taken, and Romulus had a double victory to his credit. His wife Hersilia had long been pestered by the young women who had been carried off at the festival, so she took this opportunity, when he was congratulating himself on his success, to ask him to pardon the girls' parents and allow them to come and live in Rome. It would, she urged, form a strong and valuable bond of union. The request was readily granted.

Romulus's next move was against the men of Crustumium, who were on the march against him: but the defeat of their neighbours had already undermined their confidence, and they were even more easily broken up. Settlers were sent out both to Antemnae and Crustumium, the fertility of the soil in the latter attracting the greater number of volunteers. On the other hand a number of people, chiefly parents or relatives of the captured women, moved from Crustumium to Rome.

The last to attack Rome were the Sabines, and the ensuing struggle was far more serious than the previous ones. The enemy gave no notice of their intentions and acted upon no hasty impulse of revenge or cupidity. Their plans were carefully laid, and backed by treachery. Spurius Tarpeius, the commander of the Roman citadel, had a daughter, a young girl, who, when she had gone outside the walls to fetch water for a sacrifice, was bribed by Tatius, the king of the Sabines, to admit a party of his soldiers into the fortress. Once inside, the men crushed her to death under their shields, to make it look as if they had taken the place by storm – or, it may be, to show by harsh example that there must be no trusting a traitor. There is also a story that this girl had demanded as the price of her services 'What they had on their shield-arms'. Now the Sabines in those days used to wear on their left arms heavy gold bracelets and fine jewelled rings – so they kept their bargain: paying, however, not, as the girl hoped, with golden bracelets, but with their shields. Some say that after bargaining for what they 'had on their left arms' she did actually demand their shields, and, being proved a traitor, was killed, as it were, by the very coin that paid her.

The Sabines were now in possession of the citadel. Next day the Roman troops occupied all the ground between the Palatine and Capitoline hills and there waited till they could tolerate the situation no longer. Fiercely determined to recover the citadel, they pressed forward to the attack. This was the signal for the enemy to move down to meet them. The first blows were struck by the rival champions Mettius Curtius, the Sabine, and Hostius Hostilius of Rome. The Romans were in the worse position, but they were kept going for a time by the great gallantry of Hostius; when he fell, their resistance at once collapsed and they retreated in disorder to the Palatine Old Gate. Romulus himself was swept along by the fugitive rabble, but, as he rode, he waved his sword above his head and shouted, 'Hear me, O Jupiter! At the bidding of your eagles I laid the foundations of Rome here on the Palatine. Our fortress is in Sabine hands, basely betrayed – thence are they coming sword in hand across the valley against us. Father of Gods and men, suffer them not to set foot on the spot where now we stand. Banish fear from Roman hearts and stop their shameful retreat. I vow a temple here – to you, O Jupiter, Stayer of Flight – that men may remember hereafter that Rome in her trouble was saved by your help.' It was almost as if he felt that his prayer was granted: a moment later, 'Turn on them, Romans,' he cried, 'and fight once more. Jupiter himself commands it.'
The Romans obeyed what they believed to be the voice from heaven. They rallied, and Romulus thrust his way forward to the van.

Mettius Curtius had led the Sabine advance down the slope from the citadel. He had driven the Roman troops back in disorder over the ground today occupied by the Forum, and nearly reached the gate of the Palatine. 'Comrades,' he cried, 'we have beaten our treacherous hosts – our feeble foes. They know now that catching girls is a different matter from fighting against men!'
The boast had hardly left his lips when Romulus, with a handful of his best and most courageous troops, was on him. The fact that Mettius was mounted proved a disadvantage to him; he turned and galloped off, the Romans in pursuit, and this bold stroke on the part of their leader inspired the Roman troops elsewhere on the field to make a fresh effort and to rout their opponents.

The yells of the pursuers so scared Mettius's horse that he took the bit between his teeth and plunged with his rider into the swamps. The Sabines were aghast; the imminent threat to their champion for the moment diverted them from the work in hand, and they tried to help him by shouting advice and signalling, until at last by a supreme effort he struggled out to safety. The battle was then renewed in the valley between the two hills, and this time the Romans had the best of it.

This was the moment when the Sabine women, the original cause of the quarrel, played their decisive part. The dreadful situation in which they found themselves banished their natural timidity and gave them courage to intervene. With loosened hair and rent garments they braved the flying spears and thrust their way in a body between the embattled armies. They parted the angry combatants; they besought their fathers on the one side, their husbands on the other, to spare themselves the curse of shedding kindred blood. 'We are mothers now,' they cried; 'our children are your sons – your grandsons: do not put on them the stain of parricide. If our marriage – if the relationship between you – is hateful to you, turn your anger against *us*. *We* are the cause of strife; on our account our husbands and fathers lie wounded or dead, and we would rather die ourselves than live on either widowed or orphaned.' The effect of the appeal was immediate and profound. Silence fell and not a man moved. A moment later the rival captains stepped forward to conclude a peace. Indeed, they went further: the two states were united under a single government, with Rome as the seat of power. Thus the population of Rome was doubled, and the Romans, as a gesture to the Sabines, called themselves the Quirites, after the Sabine town of Cures. In memory of the battle the stretch of shallow water where Curtius and his horse first struggled from the deep swamps into safety, was named Curtius's Lake.

This happy and unlooked-for end to a bitter war strengthened the bond between the Sabine women and their parents and husbands. Romulus moreover marked his own special awareness of this deepened feeling by giving the women's names to the thirty wards into which he then divided the population. No doubt there were more than thirty of the women; but it is not known on what principle they were selected to give their names – whether it was by lot, or age, or their own or their husbands' rank. At the same time three centuries of knights were created, the Ramnenses named after Romulus, the Titienses after Tatius, and the Luceres, the origin of whose name is uncertain. As a result of these measures the joint rule of the two kings was brought into harmony.

Some years later the kinsmen of Tatius offered violence to some Laurentian envoys. The Laurentian people claimed redress under what passed in those days for international law, and Tatius allowed the ties of blood to influence his decision. The result of this was that he drew their revenge upon himself: he was murdered in a riot at Lavinium, whither he had gone to celebrate the annual sacrifice. Romulus is said to have felt less distress at his death than was strictly proper: possibly the joint reign was not, in fact, entirely harmonious; possibly he felt that Tatius deserved what he got. But whatever the reason, he refused to go to war, and, to wipe out the double stain of Tatius's murder and the insult to the envoys, renewed the pact between Rome and Lavinium.

Thus there was peace with Lavinium, as welcome as it was unexpected; all the same, Rome was at once involved in hostilities with an enemy almost at the city gates. This time it was the men of Fidenae, who, in alarm at the rapid growth of a rival on their very doorstep, decided to take the offensive and to nip its power in the bud. They dispatched a force to devastate the country between the two towns; then, turning left (the other way was barred by the river), carried on their work amongst the farms. The men working on the farms fled in sudden alarm and confusion to the protection of the town, and the arrival of this mob brought the first news of the raid. Romulus acted promptly. With the enemy so close delay was dangerous. He marched out at the head of his troops and took up a position about a mile from Fidenae, where he left a small holding force. Of his main body he ordered a part to lie in ambush where dense undergrowth afforded cover, while with the rest, the greater number, and all his mounted troops he challenged the enemy with a feint attack, riding with his cavalry right up to the gates of Fidenae. The ruse succeeded; the enemy were drawn, and the cavalry skirmish lent an air of genuineness to the subsequent Roman withdrawal of their mounted troops, which deliberately broke discipline as if undecided whether to fight or run. Then, when the Roman foot also began to give way, the deluded enemy came pouring *en masse* from behind their defences, flung themselves with blind fury upon their retreating enemy, and were led straight into the ambush. Their flanks were promptly attacked by the Roman troops there concealed. At the same moment the standards of the holding force left behind by Romulus were seen to be advancing, and these combined threats proved too much for the Fidenates, who began a hurried retreat before Romulus and his mounted men even had time to wheel to the attack. A moment before, the Fidenates had been following up a feigned withdrawal; now, in good earnest and far greater disorder, they were themselves on the run for the protection of their own walls. But they were not destined to escape; the Romans in hot pursuit burst into the town close on their heels, before the gates could be shut against them.

The war fever soon spread to Veii, which, like Fidenae, was an Etruscan town. It was also a close neighbour of Rome, and the danger of such propinquity in the event of Rome proving hostile to all her neighbouring communities was a further exacerbation. Accordingly she sent a raiding force into Roman territory. It was not an organized movement; the raiders took up no regular position, but simply picked up what they could from the countryside and returned without waiting for countermeasures from Rome. The Romans, however, on finding them still in their territory, crossed the Tiber fully prepared for a decisive struggle, and assumed a position with a view to an assault upon the town. At the news of their approach the Veientes took the field, to fight it out in the open rather than be shut up within their walls and forced to stand a siege. In the fight which ensued Romulus used no strategy; the sheer power of his veteran troops sufficed for victory, and he pursued the retreating enemy to the walls of Veii. The town itself was strongly fortified and well sited for defence; Romulus, accordingly, made no attempt to take it, but contented himself on the return march with wasting the cultivated land, more by way of revenge than for what he could take from it. The loss the Veientes suffered from the devastation did as much as their defeat in the field to secure their submission and they sent envoys to Rome to treat for peace. They were mulcted of a part of their territory and granted a truce for a hundred years.

Such is the story of Rome's military and political achievements during the reign of Romulus. All of them chime well enough with the belief in his divine birth and the divinity ascribed to him after his death. One need but recall the vigour he displayed in recovering his ancestral throne; his wisdom in founding Rome and bringing her to strength by the arts of both war and peace. It was to him and no one else that she owed the power which enabled her to enjoy untroubled tranquillity for the next forty years.

Great though Romulus was, he was better loved by the commons than by the senate, and best of all by the army. He maintained, in peace as well as in war, a personal armed guard of three hundred men, whom he called Celeres – 'the Swift'.

Such, then, were the deeds of Romulus, and they will never grow old. One day while he was reviewing his troops on the Campus Martius near the marsh of Capra, a storm burst, with violent thunder. A cloud enveloped him, so thick that it hid him from the eyes of everyone present; and from that moment he was never seen again upon earth.

The troops, who had been alarmed by the sudden storm, soon recovered when it passed over and the sun came out again. Then they saw that the throne was empty, and, ready though they were to believe the senators, who had been standing at the king's side and now declared that he had been carried up on high by a whirlwind, they none the less felt like children bereft of a father and for a long time stood in sorrowful silence. Then a few voices began to proclaim Romulus's divinity; the cry was taken up, and at last every man present hailed him as a god and son of a god, and prayed to him to be for ever gracious and to protect his children. However, even on this great occasion there were, I believe, a few dissentients who secretly maintained that the king had been torn to pieces by the senators. At all events the story got about, though in veiled terms; but it was not important, as awe, and admiration for Romulus's greatness, set the seal upon the other version of his end, which was, moreover, given further credit by the timely action of a certain Julius Proculus, a man, we are told, honoured for his wise counsel on weighty matters. The loss of the king had left the people in an uneasy mood and suspicious of the senators, and Proculus, aware of the prevalent temper, conceived the shrewd idea of addressing the Assembly. 'Romulus,' he declared, 'the father of our City, descended from heaven at dawn this morning and appeared to me. In awe and reverence I stood before him, praying for permission to look upon his face without sin. "Go," he said, "and tell the Romans that by heaven's will my Rome shall be capital of the world. Let them learn to be soldiers. Let them know, and teach their children, that no power on earth can stand against Roman arms." Having spoken these words, he was taken up again into the sky.'

Proculus's story had a most remarkable effect; the army and commons, cruelly distressed at the loss of their king, were much comforted once they were assured of his immortality.

Primary Source 2.2 Virgil, 'Evander takes Aeneas on a tour of Rome' (*The Aeneid* 8.305–69)

(Source: West, D. (trans.) (1991) *Virgil: The Aeneid, A New Prose Translation*, Harmondsworth, Penguin, pp. 199–201)

As soon as the sacred rites were completed, they all returned to the city. The king, weighed down with age, kept Aeneas and his son Pallas by his side as he walked, and made the way seem shorter by all the things he told them. Aeneas was lost in admiration and his eyes were never still as he looked about him enthralled by the places he saw, asking questions about them and joyfully listening to Evander's explanations of all the relics of the men of old. This is what was said that day by Evander, the founder of the citadel of Rome: 'These woods used to be the haunt of native fauns and nymphs and a race of men born from the hard wood of oak-tree trunks. They had no rules of conduct and no civilization. They did not know how to yoke oxen for ploughing, how to gather wealth or husband what they had, but they lived off the fruit of the tree and the harsh diet of huntsmen. In those early days, in flight from the weapons of Jupiter, came Saturn from heavenly Olympus, an exile who had lost his kingdom. He brought together this wild and scattered mountain people, gave them laws and resolved that the name of the land should be changed to Latium, since he had *lain* hidden within its borders. His reign was what men call the Golden Age, such was the peace and serenity of the people under his rule. But gradually a worse age of baser metal took its place and with it came the madness of war and the lust for possessions. Then bands of Ausonians arrived and Sicanian peoples, and the land of Saturn lost its name many times.

Next there were kings, among them the cruel and monstrous Thybris, after whom we Italians have in later years called the river Thybris, and the old river Albula has lost its true name. I had been driven from my native land and was setting course for the most distant oceans when Fortune, that no man can resist, and Fate, that no man can escape, set me here in this place, driven by fearsome words of warning from my mother, the nymph Carmentis, and by the authority of the god Apollo.'

He had just finished saying this and moved on a little, when he pointed out the Altar of Carmentis and the Carmental Gate, as the Romans have called it from earliest times in honour of the nymph Carmentis. She had the gift of prophecy and was the first to foretell the future greatness of the sons of Aeneas and the future fame of Pallanteum. From here he pointed out the great grove which warlike Romulus set up as a sanctuary – he was to call it the Asylum – and also the Lupercal there under its cool rock, then called by Arcadian tradition they had brought from Parrhasia, the cave of Pan Lycaeus, the wolf god. He also pointed out the grove of the Argiletum, and, calling upon that consecrated spot to be his witness, he told the story of the killing of his guest Argus.

From here he led the way to the house of Tarpeia and the Capitol, now all gold, but in those distant days bristling with rough scrub. Even then a powerful sense of a divine presence in the place caused great fear among the country people, even then they went in awe of the wood and the rock. 'This grove,' said Evander, 'this leafy-topped hill, is the home of some god, we know not which. My Arcadians believe they have often seen Jupiter himself shaking the darkening aegis in his right hand to drive along the storm clouds. And then here are the ruined walls of these two towns. What you are looking at are relics of the men of old. These are their monuments. One of these citadels was founded by Father Janus; the other by Saturn. This one used to be called the Janiculum; the other, Saturnia.'

Talking in this way they were coming up to Evander's humble home, and there were cattle everywhere, lowing in the Roman Forum and the now luxurious district of the Carinae. When they arrived at his house, Evander said: 'The victorious Hercules of the line of Alceus stooped to enter this door. This was a palace large enough for him. You are my guest, and you too must have the courage to despise wealth. You must mould yourself to be worthy of the god. Come into my poor home and do not judge it too harshly.' With these words he led the mighty Aeneas under the roof-tree of his narrow house and set him down on a bed of leaves covered with the hide of a Libyan bear. Night fell and its dark wings enfolded the earth.

Primary Source 2.3   Virgil, 'The shield of Aeneas' (*The Aeneid* 8.609–732)

(Source: West, D. (trans.) (1991) *Virgil: The Aeneid, A New Prose Translation*, Harmondsworth, Penguin, pp. 209–13)

But the goddess Venus, bringing her gifts, was at hand, shining among the clouds of heaven. When she saw her son at some distance from the others, alone in a secluded valley across the icy river, she spoke to him, coming unasked before his eyes: 'Here now are the gifts I promised you, perfected by my husband's skill. When the time comes you need not hesitate, my son, to face the proud Laurentines or challenge fierce Turnus to battle.' With these words the goddess of Cythera came to her son's embrace and laid the armour in all its shining splendour before him under an oak tree.

Aeneas rejoiced at these gifts from the goddess and at the honour she was paying him and could not have his fill of gazing at them. He turned them over in his hands, in his arms, admiring the terrible, crested, fire-spurting helmet, the death-dealing sword, the huge, unyielding breastplate of blood-red bronze like a dark cloud fired by the rays of the sun and glowing far across the sky, then the polished greaves of richly refined electrum and gold, the spear and the fabric of the shield beyond all words to describe. There the God of Fire, with his knowledge of the prophets and of time that was to be, had laid out the story of Italy and the triumphs of the Romans, and there in order were all the generations that would spring from Ascanius and all the wars they would fight.

He had made, too, a mother wolf stretched out in the green cave of Mars with twin boys playing round her udders, hanging there unafraid and sucking at her as she bent her supple neck back to lick each of them in turn and mould their bodies into shape with her tongue.

Near this he had put Rome and the violent rape of the Sabines at the great games in the bowl of the crowded Circus, and a new war suddenly breaking out between the people of Romulus and the stern Sabines from Cures led by their aged king Tatius. Then, after these same kings had put an end to their conflict, they stood in their armour before the altar of Jupiter with sacred vessels in their hands, sacrificing a sow to ratify the treaty.

Close by, four-horse chariots had been driven hard in opposite directions and had torn Mettus in two – the man of Alba should have stood by his promises – and Tullus was dragging the deceiver's body through a wood while a dew of blood dripped from the brambles.

There too was Porsenna ordering the Romans to take Tarquin back after they had expelled him, and mounting a great siege against the city while the descendants of Aeneas were running upon the drawn swords of the enemy in the name of liberty. There you could see him as though raging and blustering because Horatius Cocles was daring to tear the bridge down and Cloelia had broken her chains and was swimming the river.

At the top of the shield Manlius, the keeper of the citadel on the Tarpeian rock, stood in front of the temple and kept guard on the heights of the Capitol. The new thatch stood out rough on the roof of Romulus's palace, and here was a silver goose fluttering through the golden portico, honking to announce that the Gauls were at the gates. There were the Gauls close by, among the thorn bushes, climbing into the citadel under the cover of darkness on that pitch-black night. Their hair was gold, their clothing was gold, their striped cloaks gleamed and their milk-white necks were encircled by golden torques. In each right hand there glinted two heavy Alpine spears and long shields protected their bodies. Here too Vulcan had hammered out the leaping Salii, the priests of Mars, and the naked Luperci, the priests' conical hats tufted with wool, the figure-of-eight shields which had fallen from heaven and chaste matrons leading sacred processions through the city in cushioned carriages.

At some distance from these scenes he added the habitations of the dead in Tartarus, the tall gateway of Dis and the punishments of the damned, with Catiline hanging from his beetling crag and shivering at the faces of the Furies. There too were the righteous, in a place apart, and Cato administering justice.

Between all these there ran a representation of a broad expanse of swelling sea, golden, but dark blue beneath the white foam on the crests of the waves, and all round it in a circle swam dolphins picked out in silver, cleaving the sea and feathering its surface with their tails.

In the middle were the bronze-armoured fleets at the battle of Actium. There before your eyes the battle was drawn up with the whole of the headland of Leucas seething and all the waves gleaming in gold. On one side was Augustus Caesar, leading the men of Italy into battle alongside the Senate and the People of Rome, its gods of home and its great gods. High he stood on the poop of his ship while from his radiant forehead there streamed a double flame and his father's star shone above his head. On the other wing, towering above the battle as he led his ships in line ahead, sailed Agrippa with favouring winds and favouring gods, and the beaks of captured vessels flashed from the proud honour on his forehead, the Naval Crown. On the other side, with the wealth of the barbarian world and warriors in all kinds of different armour, came Antony in triumph from the shores of the Red Sea and the peoples of the Dawn. With him sailed Egypt and the power of the East from as far as distant Bactria, and there bringing up the rear was the greatest outrage of all, his Egyptian wife! On they came at speed, all together, and the whole surface of the sea was churned to foam by the pull of their oars and the bow-waves from their triple beaks. They steered for the high sea and you would have thought that the Cycladic Islands had been torn loose again and were floating on the ocean, or that mountains were colliding with mountains, to see men in action on those ships with their massive, turreted sterns, showering blazing torches of tow and flying steel as the fresh blood began to redden the furrows of Neptune's fields. In the middle of all this the queen summoned her warships by rattling her Egyptian timbrels – she was not yet seeing the two snakes there at her back – while Anubis barked and all manner of monstrous gods levelled their weapons at Neptune and Venus and Minerva. There in the eye of battle raged Mars, engraved in iron, the grim Furies swooped from the sky and jubilant Discord strode along in her torn cloak with Bellona at her heels cracking her bloody whip. But high on the headland of Actium, Apollo saw it all and was drawing his bow. In terror at the sight of the whole of Egypt and of India, all the Arabians and all the Shebans were turning tail and the queen herself could be seen calling for winds and setting her sails by them. She had untied the sail-ropes and was even now paying them out. There in all the slaughter the God of Fire had set her, pale with the pallor or approaching death, driven over the waves by the Iapygian winds blowing off Calabria. Opposite her he had fashioned the Nile with grief in every line of his great body, opening his robes and with every fold of drapery beckoning his defeated people into his blue-grey breast and the secret waters of his river.

But Caesar was riding into Rome in triple triumph, paying undying vows to the gods of Italy and consecrating three hundred great shrines throughout the city. The streets resounded with joy and festivities and applause. There was a chorus of matrons at every temple, at every temple there were altars and the ground before the altars was strewn with the bodies of slaughtered bullocks. He himself was seated at the white marble threshold of gleaming white Apollo, inspecting the gifts brought before him by the peoples of the earth and hanging them high on the posts of the doors of the temple, while the defeated nations walked in long procession in all their different costumes and in all their different armour, speaking all the tongues of the earth. Here Mulciber, the God of Fire, had moulded the Nomads and the Africans with their streaming robes; here, too, the Lelegeians and Carians of Asia and the Gelonians from Scythia with their arrows. The Euphrates was now moving with a chastened current, and here were the Gaulish Morini from the ends of the earth, the two-horned Rhine, the undefeated Dahae from beyond the Caspian and the river Araxes chafing at his bridge.

Such were the scenes spread over the shield that Vulcan made and Venus gave to her son. Marvelling at it, and rejoicing at the things pictured on it without knowing what they were, Aeneas lifted on to his shoulder the fame and the fate of his descendants.

Primary Source 2.4   Ovid, 'The rape of the Sabine women'

(Source: Green, P. (trans.) (1982) *Ovid: The Erotic Poems*, London, Penguin, pp. 168–70)

But the theatre's curving tiers should form your favourite
    Hunting-ground: here you are sure to find   90
The richest returns, be your wish for lover or playmate,
    A one-night stand or a permanent affair.
As ants hurry to and fro in column, mandibles
    Clutching grains of wheat
(Their regular diet), as bees haunt fragrant pastures   95
    And meadows, hovering over the thyme,
Flitting from flower to flower, so our fashionable ladies
    Swarm to the games in such crowds, I often can't
Decide which I like. As spectators they come, come to be
       inspected:
    Chaste modesty doesn't stand a chance.   100
Such incidents at the games go back to Romulus –
    Men without women, Sabine rape.
No marble theatre then, no awnings, no perfumed saffron
    To spray the stage red:
The Palatine woods supplied a leafy backdrop (nature's   105
    Scenery, untouched by art),
While the tiers of seats were plain turf, and spectators shaded
    Their shaggy heads with leaves.
Urgently brooding in silence, the men kept glancing
    About them, each marking his choice   110
Among the girls. To the skirl of Etruscan flutes' rough triple
    Rhythm, the dancers stamped
And turned. Amid cheers (applause then lacked discrimination)
    The king gave the sign for which
They'd so eagerly watched. Project Rape was on. Up they
       sprang then   115
    With a lusty roar, laid hot hands on the girls.
As timorous doves flee eagles, as a lambkin
    Runs when it sees the hated wolf,
So this wild charge of men left the girls all panic-stricken,
    Not one had the same colour in her cheeks as before –   120
The same nightmare for all, though terror's features varied:
    Some tore their hair, some just froze
Where they sat; some, dismayed, kept silence, others vainly
    Yelled for Mamma; some wailed; some gaped;
Some fled, some just stood there. So they were carried off as   125
    Marriage-bed plunder; even so, many contrived
To make panic look fetching. Any girl who resisted her pursuer
    Too vigorously would find herself picked up

And borne off regardless. 'Why spoil those pretty eyes with
    weeping?'
She'd hear, 'I'll be all to you   130
That your Dad ever was to your Mum.' (You alone found
    the proper
    Bounty for soldiers, Romulus: give me that,
And I'll join up myself!) Ever since that day, by hallowed
    custom.
    Our theatres have always held dangers for pretty girls.

Primary Source 2.5   Suetonius, Nero's entertainments

(Source: Graves, R. (trans.) (1979 [1957]) *Gaius Suetonius Tranquillus: The Twelve Caesars*, revised with an intro. by M. Grant, Harmondsworth, Penguin, pp. 218–20, 222–7, 246–7)

10.   As a further guarantee of his virtuous intentions, he promised to model his rule on the principles laid down by Augustus, and never missed an opportunity of being generous or merciful, or of showing how affable he was. He lowered, if he could not abolish, some of the heavier taxes; and reduced by three-quarters the fee for denouncing evasions of the Papian Law. Moreover, he presented the commons with forty gold pieces each; settled annual salaries on distinguished but impoverished senators – to the amount of 5,000 gold pieces in some case – and granted the Guards cohorts a free monthly issue of grain. If asked to sign the usual execution order for a felon, he would sigh: 'Ah, how I wish that I had never learned to write!' He seldom forgot a face, and would greet men of whatever rank by name without a moment's hesitation. Once, when the Senate passed a vote of thanks to him, he answered: 'Wait until I deserve them!' He allowed even the commons to watch him taking exercise on the Campus Martius, and often gave public declamations. Also, he recited his own poems, both at home and in the Theatre: a performance which so delighted everyone that a Thanksgiving was voted him, as though he had won a great victory, and the passages he had chosen were printed in letters of gold on plaques dedicated to Capitoline Jupiter.

11.   He gave an immense variety of entertainments – coming-of-age parties, chariot races in the Circus, stage plays, a gladiatorial show – persuading even old men of consular rank, and old ladies, too, to attend the coming-of-age parties. He reserved seats for the knights at the Circus, as he had done in the Theatre; and actually raced four-camel chariots! At the Great Festival, as he called the series of plays devoted to the eternity of the Empire, parts were taken by men and women of both Orders; and one well-known knight rode an elephant down a sloping tight-rope. When he staged 'The Fire', a Roman play by Afranius, the actors were allowed to keep the valuable furnishings they rescued from the burning house. Throughout the Festival all kinds of gifts were scattered to the people – 1,000 assorted birds daily, and quantities of food parcels; besides vouchers for grain, clothes, gold, silver, precious stones, pearls, paintings, slaves, transport animals, and even trained wild beasts – and finally for ships, blocks of city apartments, and farms.

12.   Nero watched from the top of the proscenium. The gladiatorial show took place in a wooden theatre, near the Campus Martius, which had been built in less than a year; but no one was allowed to be killed during these combats, not even criminals. He did, however, make 400 senators and 600 knights, some of them rich and respectable, do battle in the arena; and some had to fight wild

beasts and perform various duties about the ring. He staged a naval engagement on an artificial lake of salt water which had sea-monsters swimming in it; also Pyrrhic performances by certain young Greeks, to whom he presented certificates of Roman citizenship when their show ended. At one stage of the *Minotaur* ballet an actor, disguised as a bull, actually mounted another who played Pasiphaë and occupied the hind-quarters of a hollow wooden heifer – or that, at least, was the audience's impression. In the *Daedalus and Icarus* ballet, the actor who played Icarus, while attempting his first flight, fell beside Nero's couch and spattered him with blood.

Nero rarely presided at shows of this sort, but would recline in the closed imperial box and watch through a small window; later, however, he opened the box. He inaugurated the Neronia, a festival of competitions in music, gymnastics, and horsemanship, modelled on the Greek ones and held every five years; and simultaneously opened his Baths and gymnasium, and provided free oil for knights and senators. Ex-consuls, drawn by lot, presided over the Neronia, and occupied the praetors' seats. Then Nero descended to the orchestra where the senators sat, to accept the wreath for Latin oratory and verse, which had been reserved for him by the unanimous vote of all the distinguished competitors. The judges also awarded him the wreath for a lyre solo, but he bowed reverently to them, and said: 'Pray lay it on the ground before Augustus' statue!' At an athletic competition held in the Enclosure, oxen were sacrificed on a lavish scale; that was when he shaved his chin for the first time, put the hair in a gold box studded with valuable pearls and dedicated it to Capitoline Jupiter. He had invited the Vestal Virgins to watch the athletics, explaining that the priestesses of Ceres at Olympia were accorded the same privilege.

13.   The welcome given Tiridates when he visited Rome deserves inclusion in the list of Nero's spectacles. Tiridates was the Armenian king whom he had lured to Rome with wonderful promises. Cloudy weather prevented Tiridates from being displayed to the people on the day fixed by imperial edict; however, Nero brought him out as soon as possible afterwards. The Guards cohorts were drawn up in full armour around the temples of the Forum, while Nero occupied his curule chair on the Rostrum, wearing triumphal dress and surrounded by military insignia and standards. Tiridates had to walk up a ramp and then prostrate himself in supplication; whereupon Nero stretched out his hand, drew him to his feet, kissed him, and took the turban from his head, replacing it with a diadem. When Tiridates' supplication had been translated into Latin and publicly recited by an interpreter of praetorian rank he was taken to the Theatre (where he made a further supplication) and offered a seat on Nero's right. The people then hailed Nero as Imperator and, after dedicating a laurel-wreath in the Capitol, he closed the double doors of the Temple of Janus, as a sign that all war was at an end.

[...]

19.   Nero planned only two foreign tours: one to Alexandria, the other to Greece. A warning portent made him cancel the Alexandrian voyage, on the very day when his ship should have sailed: during his farewell round of the Temples he had sat down in the shrine of Vesta, but when he rose to leave, the hem of his robe got caught and then a temporary blindness overcame him. While in Greece he tried to have a canal cut through the Isthmus, and addressed a gathering of Praetorian Guards, urging them to undertake the task. Nero took a mattock himself and, at a trumpet blast, broke the ground and carried off the first basket of earth on his back. He had also planned an expedition to the

Caspian Gates, enrolling a new legion of Italian-born recruits, all six feet tall, whom he called 'The Phalanx of Alexander the Great'.

I have separated this catalogue of Nero's less atrocious acts – some deserving no criticism, some even praiseworthy – from the others; but I must begin to list his follies and crimes.

20.   Music formed part of his childhood curriculum, and he early developed a taste for it. Soon after his accession, he summoned Terpnus, the greatest lyre-player of the day, to sing to him when dinner had ended, for several nights in succession; until very late. Then, little by little, he began to study and practise himself and conscientiously undertook all the usual exercises for strengthening and developing the voice. He would lie on his back with a slab of lead on his chest, use enemas and emetics to keep down his weight, and refrain from eating apples and every other food considered deleterious to the vocal cords. Ultimately, though his voice was feeble and husky, he was pleased enough with his progress to begin to nurse theatrical ambitions, and would quote to his friends the Greek proverb: 'Unheard melodies are never sweet.' His first stage appearance was at Neapolis where, disregarding an earthquake which shook the theatre, he sang his piece through to the end. He often sang at Neapolis, for several consecutive days, too; and even while giving his voice a brief rest could not stay out of sight, but after bathing went to dine in the orchestra where he promised the crowd in Greek that, when he had downed a drink or two, he would give them something to make their ears ring. So captivated was he by the rhythmic applause of a crowd of Alexandrians from a fleet which had just put in, that he sent to Alexandria for more. He also chose some young knights, and more than 5,000 sturdy ordinary youths, whom he divided into groups to learn the Alexandrian method of applause – they were known, respectively, as 'Bees', 'Roof-tiles', and 'Bricks' – and provide it liberally whenever he sang. It was easy to recognize them by their bushy hair, splendid dress, and the absence of rings on their left hands. The knights who led them earned four hundred gold pieces a performance.

21.   Appearances at Rome as well meant so much to Nero that he held the Neronia again before the required five years elapsed. When the crowd clamoured to hear his heavenly voice, he answered that he would perform in the Palace gardens later if anyone wanted to hear him; but when the Guards on duty seconded the appeal, he delightedly agreed to oblige them. He wasted no time in getting his name entered on the list of competing lyre-players, and dropped his ticket into the urn with the others. The Guards prefects carried his lyre as he went up to play in his turn and a group of colonels and close friends accompanied him. After taking his place and finishing his preliminary oration, he made Cluvius Rufus, the ex-Consul, announce the title of the song. It was *Niobe*; and he sang on until two hours before dusk. Then he postponed the rest of the contest to the following year, which would give him an opportunity to sing oftener. But since a year was a long time to wait, he continued to make frequent appearances. He toyed with the idea of playing opposite professional actors in public shows staged by magistrates; because one of the praetors had offered him 10,000 gold pieces if he would consent. And he did actually sing in tragedies, taking the parts of heroes and gods, sometimes even of heroines and goddesses, wearing masks either modelled on his own face, or on the face of whatever woman he happened to be in love with at the time. Among his performances were *Canace in Childbirth*, *Orestes the Matricide*, *Oedipus Blinded*, and *Distraught Hercules*. There is a story that a young recruit on guard recognized him in the rags and fetters demanded by the part of Hercules, and dashed forward to his assistance.

22.   Horses had been Nero's main interest since childhood; despite all efforts to the contrary, his chatter about the chariot races at the Circus could not be stopped. When scolded by one of his tutors for telling his fellow-pupils about a Green charioteer who got dragged by his team, Nero untruthfully explained that he had been discussing Hector's fate in the *Iliad*. At the beginning of his reign he used every day to play with model ivory chariots on a board, and came up from the country to attend all the races, even minor ones, at first in secret and then without the least embarrassment; so that there was never any doubt that he would be at Rome on that particular day. He frankly admitted that he wished the number of prizes increased, which meant that more contests were included and that they lasted until a late hour, and the faction-managers no longer thought it worth while to bring out their teams except for a full day's racing.

Very soon Nero set his heart on driving a chariot himself, and to display himself more frequently, and after a preliminary trial in the Palace gardens before an audience of slaves and loungers, made a public appearance at the Circus; on this occasion one of his freedmen replaced the magistrate who dropped the napkin as the starting signal.

However, these incursions into the arts at Rome did not satisfy him, and he headed for Greece, as I mentioned above. His main reason was that the cities which regularly sponsored musical contests had adopted the practice of sending him every available prize for lyre-playing; he always accepted these with great pleasure, giving the delegates the earliest audience of the day and invitations to private dinners. Some of them would beg Nero to sing when the meal was over, and applaud his performance to the echo, which made him announce: 'The Greeks alone are worthy of my efforts, they really listen to music.' So he sailed off hastily and, as soon as he arrived at Cassiope, gave his first song recital before the altar of Jupiter Cassius; after which he went the round of the contests.

23.   For this purpose, he ordered those contests which normally took place only at intervals to be held during his visit, even if it meant repeating them; and broke tradition at Olympia by introducing a musical competition into the athletic games. When Helius, his freedman, reminded him that he was urgently needed at Rome, he would not be distracted by official business, but answered: 'Yes, you have made yourself quite plain. I am aware that you want me to go home; you will do far better, however, if you encourage me to stay until I proved myself worthy of Nero.'

No one was allowed to leave the theatre during his recitals, however pressing the reason. We read of women in the audience giving birth, and of men being so bored with listening and applauding that they furtively dropped down from the wall at the rear, since the gates were kept barred, or shammed dead and were carried away for burial. Nero's stage fright and general nervousness when he took part in the competitions, his jealousy of rivals, and his awe of the judges, can scarcely be believed. Though usually gracious and charming to other competitors, whom he treated as equals, he abused them behind their backs, and sometimes insulted them to their faces; and if any were particularly good singers, he would bribe them not to do themselves justice. Before every performance he would address the judges with the utmost deference: saying that he had done what he could, and that the issue was now in Fortune's hands; but that since they were men of judgement and experience, they would know how to eliminate the factor of chance. When they told him not to worry he felt a little better, but still anxious; and mistook the silence and embarrassment of some for alienation and disfavour, admitting that he suspected every one of them.

24.   During the competitions he strictly observed the rules, never daring to clear his throat and even using his arm to wipe the sweat from his brow. Once, while acting in a tragedy, he dropped his sceptre and quickly recovered it, but was terrified of disqualification. The accompanist, however – who played a flute and made the necessary dumbshow to illustrate the words – swore that the slip had passed unnoticed, because the audience were listening with such rapt attention; so he took heart again. Nero insisted on announcing his own victories; which emboldened him to enter the competition for heralds. To destroy every trace of previous winners in these contests he ordered all their statues and busts to be taken down, dragged away with hooks, and hurled into public lavatories. On several occasions he took part in the chariot racing, and at Olympia drove a ten-horse team, a novelty for which he had censured King Mithridates in one of his own poems. He fell from the chariot and had to be helped in again; but, though he failed to stay the course and retired before the finish, the judges nevertheless awarded him the prize. On the eve of his departure, he presented the whole province with its freedom and conferred Roman citizenship as well as large cash rewards on the judges. It was during the Isthmian Games at Corinth that he stood in the middle of the stadium and personally announced these benefits.

25.   Returning to Italy, Nero disembarked at Neapolis, where he had made his debut as a singer, and ordered part of the city wall to be razed – which is the Greek custom whenever the victor in any of the Sacred Games comes home. He repeated the same performance at Antium, at Albanum, and finally at Rome. For his processional entry into Rome he chose the chariot which Augustus had used in his triumph in a former age; and wore a Greek mantle spangled with gold stars over a purple robe. The Olympic wreath was on his head, the Pythian wreath in his right hand, the others were carried before him, with placards explaining where and against whom he had won them, what songs he had sung, and in what plays he had acted. Nero's chariot was followed by his claque, who behaved like a triumphal escort and shouted that they were the Augustus men celebrating his triumph. The procession passed through the Circus (he had the entrance arch pulled down to allow more room), then by way of the Velabrum and the Forum to the Palatine Hill and the Temple of Apollo. Victims were sacrificed in his honour all along the route, which was sprinkled from time to time with perfume, and the populace showered him with birds, ribbons, and sweetmeats. He hung the wreaths above the couches in his sleeping quarters, and set up several statues of himself playing the lyre. He also had a coin struck with the same device. After this, it never occurred to him that he ought to refrain from singing, or even sing a little less; but he saved his voice by addressing the troops only in written orders, or in speeches delivered by someone else; and would attend no entertainment or official business unless he had a voice-trainer standing by, telling him when to spare his vocal cords, and when to protect his mouth with a handkerchief. Whether he offered people his friendship or plainly indicated his dislike for them, often depended on how generously or how feebly they had applauded.

[...]

52.   As a boy Nero read most of the usual humanities subjects except philosophy which, Agrippina warned him, was no proper study for a future ruler. His tutor Seneca hid the works of the early rhetoricians from him, intending to be admired himself as long as possible. So Nero turned his hand to poetry, and would dash off verses enthusiastically, without any effort. It is often claimed that he published other people's work as his own; but notebooks and papers have come into my possession which contain some of Nero's best-known poems in his own handwriting. Many erasures and cancellations, as well

as words substituted above the lines prove that he was neither copying nor dictating, and are written just as people write when they are thinking and composing. Nero also took more than an amateur's interest in painting and sculpture.

53.   His dominant characteristics were his thirst for popularity and his jealousy of men who caught the public eye by any means whatsoever. Because he had won so many stage victories, most people expected him to take part in athletic contests at the next Olympiad. For he practised wrestling all the time, and everywhere in Greece had watched the gymnastic competitions like the judges, squatting on the ground in the stadium, and if any pair of competitors worked away from the centre of the ring, would push them back himself. Because of his singing he had been compared to Phoebus Apollo and because of his chariot-riding to the Sun-God; now, apparently, he planned to become a Hercules, for according to one story he had a lion so carefully trained that he could safely face it naked before the entire amphitheatre; and then either kill it with his club or strangle it.

54.   Just before the end Nero took a public oath that if he managed to keep his throne he would celebrate the victory with a festival, performing successively on water-organ, flute, bagpipes; and when the last day came would dance the role of Turnus in Virgil's *Aeneid*. He was supposed to have killed the actor Paris because he considered him a serious professional rival.

Primary Source 2.6   Tacitus, extracts from *Annals* (Books 15 and 16)

(Source: Grant M. (trans.) (1956) *Tacitus: The Annals of Imperial Rome*, London, Penguin, pp. 320–1 and 360)

NERO had long desired to drive in four-horse chariot races. Another equally deplorable ambition was to sing to the lyre, like a professional. 'Chariot-racing', he said, 'was an accomplishment of ancient kings and leaders – honoured by poets, associated with divine worship. Singing, too, is sacred to Apollo: that glorious and provident god is represented in a musician's dress in Greek cities, and also in Roman temples.'

There was no stopping him. But Seneca and Burrus tried to prevent him from gaining both his wishes by conceding one of them. In the Vatican valley, therefore, an enclosure was constructed, where he could drive his horses, remote from the public eye. But soon the public were admitted – and even invited; and they approved vociferously. For such is a crowd: avid for entertainment, and delighted if the emperor shares their tastes. However, this scandalous publicity did not satiate Nero, as his advisers had expected. Indeed, it led him on. But if he shared his degradation, he thought it would be less; so he brought on to the stage members of the ancient nobility whose poverty made them corruptible. They are dead, and I feel I owe it to their ancestors not to name them. For though they behaved dishonourably, so did the man who paid them to offend (instead of not to do so). Well-known knights, too, he induced by huge presents to offer their services in the arena. But gifts from the man who can command carry with them an obligation.

However, Nero was not yet ready to disgrace himself on a public stage. Instead he instituted 'Youth Games'.[1] There were many volunteers. Birth, age, official career did not prevent people from acting – in Greek or Latin style – or from

---

[1]   Instituted by Nero to celebrate the first shaving of his beard.

accompanying their performances with effeminate gestures and songs. Eminent women, too, rehearsed indecent parts. In the wood which Augustus had planted round his Naval Lake, places of assignation and taverns were built, and every stimulus to vice was displayed for sale. Moreover, there were distributions of money. Respectable people were compelled to spend it; disreputable people did so gladly. Promiscuity and degradation throve. Roman morals had long become impure, but never was there so favourable an environment for debauchery as among this filthy crowd. Even in good surroundings people find it hard to behave well. Here every form of immorality competed for attention, and no chastity, modesty, or vestige of decency could survive.

The climax was the emperor's stage debut. Meticulously tuning his lyre, he struck practice notes to the trainers beside him. A battalion attended with its officers. So did Burrus, grieving – but applauding. Now, too, was formed the corps of Roman knights known as the Augustiani. These powerful young men, impudent by nature or ambition, maintained a din of applause day and night, showering divine epithets on Nero's beauty and voice. They were grand and respected as if they had done great things.

But the emperor did not obtain publicity by his theatrical talents only. He also aspired to poetic taste. He gathered round himself at dinner men who possessed some versifying ability but were not yet known. As they sat on, they strung together verses they had brought with them, or extemporized – and filled out Nero's own suggestions, such as they were. This method is apparent from Nero's poems themselves, which lack vigour, inspiration, and homogeneity. To philosophers, too, he devoted some of his time after dinner, enjoying their quarrelsome assertions of contradictory views. There were enough of such people willing to display their glum features and expressions for the amusement of the court.

[...]

The same year witnessed gladiatorial displays on a no less magnificent scale than before, but exceeding all precedent in the number of distinguished women and senators disgracing themselves in the arena. When the new year began, with Gaius Laecanius Bassus and Marcus Licinius Crassus Frugi (II) as consuls, Nero showed daily-increasing impatience to appear regularly on the public stage. Hitherto, he had sung at home, or at the Youth Games held in his Gardens. But he began to disdain such occasions as insufficiently attended and too restricted for a voice like his. Not venturing, however, to make his début at Rome, he selected Neapolis, as being a Greek city. Starting there, he planned to cross to Greece, win the glorious and long-revered wreaths of its Games, and thus increase his fame and popularity at home.

The Neapolitan theatre was filled. Besides the local population, it contained visitors from all around attracted by the notable occasion. Present, too, were those who attend the emperor out of respect or to perform various services – and even units of troops. The theatre now provided what seemed to most people an evil omen, but to Nero a sign of divine providence and favour. For when it was empty (the crowd having left), it collapsed. But there were no casualties; and Nero composed a poem thanking the gods for the happy outcome of the incident.

[...]

The five-yearly Games were now close. The senate tried to avert scandal by offering the emperor, in advance, the first prize for song, and also conferred on him a crown 'for eloquence' to gloss over the degradation attaching to the stage. But Nero declared that there was no need for favouritism or the senate's authority; he would compete on equal terms and rely on the conscience of the judges to award him the prize he deserved. First he recited a poem on the stage. Then, when the crowd shouted that he should 'display all his accomplishments' (those were their actual words), he made a second *entrée* as a musician.

Nero scrupulously observed harpists' etiquette. When tired, he remained standing. To wipe away perspiration, he used nothing but the robe he was wearing. He allowed no moisture from his mouth or nose to be visible. At the conclusion, he awaited the verdict of the judges in assumed trepidation, on bended knee, and with a gesture of deference to the public. And the public at least, used to applauding the poses even of professional actors, cheered in measured, rhythmical cadences. They sounded delighted. Indeed, since the national disgrace meant nothing to them, perhaps they were.

But people from remote country towns of austere, old-fashioned Italy, or visitors from distant provinces on official or private business, had no experience of outrageous behaviour; they found the spectacle intolerable. Their unpractised hands tired easily and proved unequal to the degrading task, thereby disorganizing the expert applauders and earning many cuffs from the Guardsmen who, to prevent any momentary disharmony or silence, were stationed along the benches. Numerous knights, it is recorded, were crushed to death forcing their way up through the narrow exits against the crowd. Others, as they sat day and night, collapsed and died. For absence was even more dangerous than attendance, since there were many spies unconcealedly (and more still secretly) noting who was there – and noting whether their expressions were pleased or dissatisfied. Humble offenders received instant punishment. Against important people the grudge was momentarily postponed, but paid later. Vespasian, the story went, nodded somnolently; he was reprimanded by an ex-slave called Phoebus, and only rescued by enlightened intercession. Nor was this the last time he was in peril. But his imperial destiny saved him.

Primary Source 2.7   Cassius Dio, 'Nero's spectacles'

(Source: Cary, E. (trans.) (1925) *Dio Cassius: Roman History, Books LXI–LXX*, The Loeb Classical Library, Cambridge MA and London, Harvard University Press, pp. 45–7, 53–5, 73–81, 109, 137–9, 151–3, 169–71.

Book 61.6

[...]

Such was Nero's general character. I shall now proceed to details. He had such enthusiasm for the horse-races that he actually decorated the famous race-horses that had passed their prime with the regular street costume for men and honoured them with gifts of money for their feed. Thereupon the horsebreeders and charioteers, encouraged by this enthusiasm on his part, proceeded to treat both the praetors and the consuls with great insolence; and Aulus Fabricius, when praetor, finding them unwilling to take part in the contests on reasonable terms, dispensed with their services, and training dogs to draw chariots, introduced them in place of horses. At this, the wearers of the White and of the Red immediately entered their chariots for the races; but as the Greens and the Blues would not participate even then, Nero himself furnished the prizes for the horses and the horse-race took place.

Book 61.9

[…]

At one spectacle men on horseback overcame bulls while riding along beside them, and the knights who served as Nero's bodyguard brought down with their javelins four hundred bears and three hundred lions. On the same occasion thirty members of the equestrian order fought as gladiators. Such were the proceedings which the emperor sanctioned openly; secretly, however, he carried on nocturnal revels throughout the entire city, insulting women, practising lewdness on boys, stripping the people whom he encountered, beating, wounding and murdering. He had an idea that his identity was not known, for he used various costumes and different wigs at different times; but he would be recognized both by his retinue and by his deeds, since no one else would have dared commit so many and so serious outrages in such a reckless manner. Indeed, it was becoming unsafe even for a person to remain at home, since Nero would break into shops and houses. Now a certain Julius Montanus, a senator, enraged on his wife's account, fell upon him and inflicted many blows upon him, so that he had to remain in concealment several days by reason of the black eyes he had received. And yet Montanus would have suffered no harm for this, since Nero thought the violence had been all an accident and so was not disposed to be angry at the occurrence, had not the other sent him a note begging his pardon. Nero on reading the letter remarked: "So he knew that he was striking Nero." Thereupon Montanus committed suicide.

In the course of producing a spectacle at one of the theatres he suddenly filled the place with sea water so that fishes and sea monsters swam about in it, and he exhibited a naval battle between men representing Persians and Athenians. After this he immediately drew off the water, dried the ground, and once more exhibited contests between land forces, who fought not only in single combat but also in large groups equally matched.

[…]

Book 61.17–21

In honour of his mother he celebrated a most magnificent and costly festival, the events taking place for several days in five or six theatres at once. It was on this occasion that an elephant was led up to the highest gallery of the theatre and walked down from that point on ropes, carrying a rider. There was another exhibition that was at once most disgraceful and most shocking, when men and women not only of the equestrian but even of the senatorial order appeared as performers in the orchestra, in the Circus, and in the hunting-theatre, like those who are held in lowest esteem. Some of them played the flute and danced in pantomimes or acted in tragedies and comedies or sang to the lyre; they drove horses, killed wild beasts and fought as gladiators, some willingly and some sore against their will. So the men of that day beheld the great families—the Furii, the Horatii, the Fabii, the Poreii, the Valerii, and all the rest whose trophies and whose temples were to be seen—standing down there below them and doing things some of which they formerly would not even watch when performed by others. So they would point them out to one another and make their comments, Macedonians saying: "There is the descendant of Paulus"; Greeks, "There is Mummius' descendant"; Sicilians, "Look at Claudius"; Epirots, "Look at Appius"; Asiatics naming Lucius, Iberians Publius, Carthaginians Africanus, and Romans naming them all. For such, apparently, were the introductory rites by which Nero desired to usher in his own career of disgrace.

All who had any sense lamented likewise the huge outlays of money. For all the costliest viands that men eat and everything else of the highest value—horses, slaves, teams, gold, silver, and raiment of divers hues—was given away by means of tokens, as follows. Nero would throw among the crowd tiny balls, each one appropriately inscribed, and the articles called for by the balls would be presented to those who had seized them. Sensible people, I say, were grieved, reflecting that when he was spending so much in order that he might disgrace himself, he would not be likely to abstain from any of the most terrible crimes, in order that he might gain money. When some portents took place at this time, the seers declared that they meant destruction for him and they advised him to divert the evil upon others. He would accordingly have put numerous persons out of the way immediately, had not Seneca said to him: "No matter how many you may slay, you cannot kill your successor."

It was at this time that he celebrated so many sacrifices for his preservation, as he expressed it, and dedicated the provision market called the Macellum. Later he instituted a new kind of festival called Juvenalia, or Games of Youth. It was celebrated in honour of his beard, which he now shaved for the first time; the hairs he placed in a small golden globe and offered to Jupiter Capitolinus. For this festival members of the noblest families as well as all others were bound to give exhibitions of some sort. For example, Aeilia Catella, a woman not only prominent by reason of her family and her wealth but also advanced in years (she was an octogenarian), danced in a pantomime. Others, who on account of old age or illness could not do anything by themselves, sang in choruses. All devoted themselves to practising any talent that they possessed as best they could, and all the most distinguished people, men and women, girls and lads, old women and old men, attended schools designated for the purpose. And in case anyone was unable to furnish entertainment in any other fashion, he would be assigned to the choruses. And when some of them out of shame put on masks, to avoid being recognized, Nero caused the masks to be taken off, pretending that this was demanded by the populace, and exhibited the performers to a rabble whose magistrates they had been but a short time before. Now, more than ever, not only these performers but the rest as well regarded the dead as fortunate. For many of the foremost men had perished in the course of that year; some of them, in fact, charged with conspiring against Nero, had been surrounded by the soldiers and stoned to death.

As a fitting climax to these performances, Nero himself made his appearance in the theatre, being announced under his own name by Gallio. So there stood this Caesar on the stage wearing the garb of a lyre player. This emperor uttered the words: "My lords, of your kindness give me ear," and this Augustus sang to the lyre some piece called "Attis" or "The Bacchantes,"[1] while many soldiers stood by and all the people that the seats would hold sat watching. Yet he had, according to report, but a slight and indistinct voice, so that he moved his whole audience to laughter and tears at once. Beside him stood Burrus and Seneca, like teachers, prompting him; and they would wave their arms and togas at every utterance of his and lead others to do the same. Indeed, Nero had got ready a special corps of about five thousand soldiers, called Augustans; these would lead the applause, and all the rest, however loath, were obliged to shout with them. Thrasea was the single exception, since he would never help Nero in these matters; but all the rest and especially the prominent men, assembled with alacrity, grieved though they were, and joined in all the shouts of the Augustans, as if they were delighted. And one might have heard them exclaiming: "Glorious Caesar! Our Apollo, our Augustus, another Pythian! By thyself we

---

[1]   These are actual titles of poems by Nero.

swear, O Caesar, none surpasses thee." After this performance he entertained the people at a feast on boats on the site of the naval battle given by Augustus; thence at midnight he sailed through a canal into the Tiber.

These things, then, he did to celebrate the shaving of his beard; and in behalf of his preservation and the continuance of his power, as his proclamation put it, he instituted some quadrennial games, which he called Neronia. In honour of this event he also erected the gymnasium,[2] and at its dedication made a free distribution of olive oil to the senators and knights. The crown for lyre-playing he took without a contest; for all others were debarred, on the assumption that they were unworthy of being victors. And immediately, wearing the garb of this guild, he entered the gymnasium itself to be enrolled as victor. Thereafter all other crowns awarded as prizes for lyre-playing in all the contests were sent to him as the only artist worthy of victory.

Book 62.15

[...]

To such lengths did Nero's licence go that he actually drove chariots in public. And on one occasion after exhibiting a wild-beast hunt he immediately piped water into the theatre and produced a sea-fight; then he let the water out again and arranged a gladiatorial combat. Last of all, he flooded the place once more and gave a costly public banquet. Tigellinus had been appointed director of the banquet and everything had been provided on a lavish scale. The arrangements made were as follows. In the centre of the lake there had first been lowered the great wooden casks used for holding wine, and on top of these, planks had been fastened, while round about this platform taverns and booths had been erected. Thus Nero and Tigellinus and their fellow-banqueters occupied the centre, where they held their feast on purple rugs and soft cushions, while all the rest made merry in the taverns.

[...]

Book 62.29

[...]

Nero continued to do many ridiculous things. Thus, on the occasion of a certain popular festival, he descended to the orchestra of the theatre, where he read some Trojan lays of his own; and in honour of these, numerous sacrifices were offered, as was the case with everything else that he did. He was now making preparations to write an epic narrating all the achievements of the Romans; and even before composing a line of it he began to consider the proper number of books, consulting among others Annaeus Cornutus, who at this time was famed for his learning. This man he came very near putting to death and did deport to an island, because, while some were urging him to write four hundred books, Cornutus said that this was too many and nobody would read them. And when someone objected, "Yet Chrysippus, whom you praise and imitate, composed many more," the other retorted: "But they are a help to the conduct of men's lives." So Cornutus incurred banishment for this. Lucan, on the other hand, was debarred from writing poetry because he was receiving high praise for his work.

[...]

---

[2]   Gymnasium here means a school of music.

Book 63.9

[...]

Had he merely done this, he would have been the subject of ridicule. Yet how could one endure even to hear about, let alone behold, a Roman, a senator, a patrician, a high priest, a Caesar, an emperor, an Augustus, named on the programme among the contestants, training his voice, practising various songs, wearing long hair on his head the while his chin was smooth-shaven, throwing his toga over his shoulder in the races, walking about with one or two attendants, looking askance at his opponents, and constantly uttering taunting remarks to them, standing in dread of the directors of the games and the wielders of the whip and lavishing money on them all secretly to avoid being brought to book and scourged? And all this he did, though by winning the contests of the lyre-players and tragedians and heralds he would make certain his defeat in the contest of the Caesars. What harsher proscription could there ever be than this, in which it was not Sulla that posted the names of others, but Nero that posted his own name? What stranger victory than one for which he received the crown of wild olive, bay, parsley or pine and lost the political crown? Yet why should one lament these acts of his alone, seeing that he also elevated himself on the high-soled buskins only to fall from the throne, and in putting on the mask threw off the dignity of his sovereignty to beg in the guise of a runaway slave, to be lead about as a blind man, to be heavy with child, to be in labour, to be a madman, or to wander an outcast, his favourite roles being those of Oedipus, Thyestes, Heracles, Alcmeon and Orestes?[3] The masks that he wore were sometimes made to resemble the characters he was portraying and sometimes bore his own likeness; but the women's masks were all fashioned after the features of Sabina, in order that, though dead, she might still take part in the spectacle. All the situations that ordinary actors simulate in their acting he, too, would portray in speech or action or in submitting to the action of others—save only that golden chains were used to bind him; for apparently it was not thought proper for a Roman emperor to be bound in iron shackles.

Book 63.20–21

[...]

When he entered Rome, a portion of the wall was torn down and a section of the gates broken in, because some asserted that each of these ceremonies was customary upon the return of crowned victors from the games. First entered men bearing the crowns which he had won, and after them others with wooden panels borne aloft on spears, upon which were inscribed the name of the games, the kind of contest, and a statement that Nero Caesar first of all the Romans from the beginning of the world had won it. Next came the victor himself on a triumphal car, the one in which Augustus had once celebrated his many victories; he was clad in a vestment of purple covered with spangles of gold, was crowned with a garland of wild olive, and held in his hand the Pythian laurel. By his side in the vehicle rode Diodorus the lyre-player. After passing in this manner through the Circus and through the Forum in company with the soldiers and the knights and the senate he ascended the Capitol and proceeded thence to the palace. The city was all decked with garlands, was ablaze with lights and reeking with incense, and the whole population, the senators

---

[3] With the addition of Canace (from the *Aeolus*) from ch. 10, the characters here named may possibly suffice for all the situations just described. For Thyestes as a beggar see Aristophanes *Ach.* 433; yet little is known of this play, and it is more natural to think of the famous Telephus. Alcmeon and Orestes could each serve for both the madman and the outcast. It is to be noted that all the plays, except the *Oedipus Coloneus*, are by Euripides.

Pythian Games at Delphi (590 BCE)

themselves most of all, kept shouting in chorus; "Hail, Olympian Victor! Hail, Pythian Victor! Augustus! Augustus! Hail to Nero our Hercules! Hail to Nero, our Apollo! The only Victor of the Grand Tour, the only one from the beginning of time! Augustus! Augustus! O, Divine Voice! Blessed are they that hear thee." I might, to be sure, have used circumlocutions, but why not declare their very words? The expressions that they used do not disgrace any history; rather, the fact that I have not concealed any of them lends it distinction.

When he had finished these ceremonies, he announced a series of horse-races, and carrying into the Circus these crowns as well as all the others that he had secured by his victories in chariot-racing, he placed them round the Egyptian obelisk. The number of them was one thousand eight hundred and eight. And after doing this he appeared as a charioteer. Now a certain Larcius, a Lydian, approached him with an offer of a million sesterces if he would play the lyre for them. Nero, however, would not take the money, disdaining to do anything for pay (albeit Tigellinus collected it, as the price of not putting Larcius to death), but he did appear in the theatre, nevertheless, and not only played the lyre but also acted in a tragedy. (As for the equestrian contests, he never failed to take part in them.) Sometimes he would voluntarily let himself be defeated, in order to make it more credible that he really won on most occasions.

[...]

Primary Source 2.8   Lucan, extract from *The Civil War* (*Pharsalia*)

(Source: Duff, J.D. (trans.) (1928) *Lucan: The Civil War (Pharsalia)*, The Loeb Classical Library, Cambridge MA and London, Harvard University Press and William Heinemann, Book 1, lines 33–66, pp. 5–7, footnotes added)

[...]

Still, if Fate could find no other way for the advent of Nero; if an everlasting kingdom costs the gods dear and heaven could not be ruled by its sovran, the Thunderer, before the battle with the fierce Giants,—then we complain no more against the gods: even such crimes and such guilt are not too high a price too pay. Let Pharsalia heap her awful plains with dead; let the shade of the Carthaginian[1] be glutted with carnage;[2] let the last battle be joined at fatal Munda;[3] and though to these be added the famine of Perusia[4] and the horrors of Mutina,[5] the ships overwhelmed near stormy Leucas[6] and the war against slaves hard by the flames of Etna,[7] yet Rome owes so much to civil war, because what was done was done for you, Caesar. When your watch on earth is over and you seek the stars at last, the celestial palace you prefer will welcome you, and the sky will be glad. Whether you choose to wield Jove's sceptre, or to mount the fiery chariot of Phoebus and circle earth with your moving flame—earth

[1]   Hannibal.

[2]   At Thapsus.

[3]   Munda in Spain, the site of a battle in 45 BCE at which the sons of Pompey were defeated with the loss of 30,000 men.

[4]   Augustus besieged Perusia (in Etruria, Italy) for several months in 41 BCE before it was compelled by famine to surrender.

[5]   Mutina (Modena, Italy) was besieged in 44 and 43 BCE by Marc Antony.

[6]   A reference to the battle of Actium (31 BCE). Actium was near the Isle of Leucas or Leucadia.

[7]   A reference to the defeat of Pompey's son in 36 BCE in the Sicilian seas, where a large number of slaves had joined his forces.

unterrified by the transference of the sun; every god will give place to you, and Nature will leave it to you to determine what deity you wish to be, and where to establish your universal throne. But choose not your seat either in the Northern region or where the sultry sky of the opposing South sinks down: from these quarters your light would look aslant at your city of Rome. If you lean on any one part of boundless space, the axle of the sphere will be weighed down[8]; maintain therefore the equipoise of heaven by remaining at the centre of the system. May that region of the sky be bright and clear, and may no clouds obstruct our view of Caesar! In that day let mankind lay down their arms and seek their own welfare, and let all nations love one another; let Peace fly over the earth and shut fast the iron gates of warlike Janus.[9] But to me you are divine already; and if my breast receives you to inspire my verse, I would not care to trouble the god who rules mysterious Delphi, or to summon Bacchus from Nysa:[10] you alone are sufficient to give strength to a Roman bard.

[...]

Primary Source 2.9   Seneca the Younger, *Apocolocyntosis* 4

(Source: Eden, P.T. (trans.) (1984) *Seneca: Apocolocyntosis*, Cambridge, Cambridge University Press, pp. 30–1)

4.   So she spoke, and, twirling the thread on an ugly spool, she snapped off the duration of that right royal lumpish life. But Lachesis, with tresses tied and locks adorned, garlanding her hair and brow with Pierian laurel, plucked shining white yarn from a snowy fleece to fashion it with a lucky touch; yet when teased out it suddenly took on a wonderful colour. The Sisters marvelled at their stints: the common wool changed to precious metal; a Golden Age spun down on the beautiful thread. And there was no end to it: the fleeces they teased out were lucky; and they delighted to fill their hands: their stints were charming. The work sped of its own accord and with no toil the soft threads spun down on the twisting spool. They surpassed the years of Tithonus and of Nestor. Phoebus was at hand, and helped with his singing, and delighted in the years to come, and now joyfully plied his quill, now joyfully handed them their stints. He kept them intent on his singing and beguiled their toil; and while they praised their brother's lyre and songs extravagantly, their hands had spun more than usual, and the commended work exceeded human destinies. 'Take nothing away, Fates,' Phoebus said, 'let the duration of human life be surpassed by him who is my like in looks and grace, and my equal in voice and song. He will guarantee an era of prosperity to the weary and break the silence of the laws. Like the Morning Star, as he rises scattering the stars in flight, or like the Evening Star, as he rises when the stars return (at dusk), like the gleaming Sun, as soon as rosy Dawn has dispelled the shadows and led in the day, as he gazes on the world and begins to whip up his chariot from the starting-barrier: such a Caesar is at hand, such a Nero shall Rome now gaze upon. His radiant face blazes with gentle brilliance and his shapely neck with flowing hair.'

So Apollo. Then Lachesis, because she too fancied such a very shapely fellow, behaved open-handedly and gave Nero many years from her own supply. But as for Claudius, they ordered everybody

to carry him out from the house with rejoicing and fair-speaking.

---

[8]   Weight is a regular attribute of divinity in ancient mythology.

[9]   The doors of the temple of Janus were closed during peacetime.

[10]   Nysa was the name of several cities sacred to Bacchus.

And he did indeed gurgle his life out, and from then on ceased to have even the appearance of existence. However, he breathed his last while he was listening to some comic actors, so you know I have good reason to be afraid of them. This was the last utterance of his to be heard in this world, after he had let out a louder sound from that part by which he found it easier to communicate: 'Oh dear, I think I've shit myself.' I rather suspect he did. He certainly shat up everything else.

Primary Source 2.10   Cassius Dio, 'The Golden Day'

(Source: Cary, E. (trans.) (1925) *Dio Cassius: Roman History, Books LXI–LXX*, The Loeb Classical Library, Cambridge MA and London, Harvard University Press, pp. 139–45)

Book 63.1–6

In this consulship of Gaius Telesinus and Suetonius Paulinus one event of great glory and another of deep disgrace took place. For one thing, Nero contended among the lyre-players, and after Menecrates, the teacher of this art, had celebrated a triumph for him in the Circus, he appeared as a charioteer. On the other hand, Tiridates presented himself in Rome, bringing with him not only his own sons but also those of Vologaesus, of Pacorus, and of Monobazus. Their progress all the way from the Euphrates was like a triumphal procession. Tiridates himself was at the height of his reputation by reason of his age, beauty, family and intelligence; and his whole retinue of servants together with all his royal paraphernalia accompanied him. Three thousand Parthian horsemen and numerous Romans besides followed in his train. They were received by gaily decorated cities and by peoples who shouted many compliments. Provisions were furnished them free of cost, a daily expenditure of 800,000 sesterces for their support being thus charged to the public treasury. This went on without change for the nine months occupied in their journey. The prince covered the whole distance to the confines of Italy on horseback, and beside him rode his wife, wearing a golden helmet in place of a veil, so as not to defy the traditions of her country by letting her face be seen. In Italy he was conveyed in a two-horse carriage sent by Nero, and met the emperor at Neapolis, which he reached by way of Picenum. He refused, however, to obey the order to lay aside his dagger when he approached the emperor, but fastened it to the scabbard with nails. Yet he knelt upon the ground, and with arms crossed called him master and did obeisance. Nero admired him for this action and entertained him in many ways, especially by giving a gladiatorial exhibition at Puteoli. It was under the direction of Patrobius, one of his freedmen, who managed to make it a most brilliant and costly affair, as may be seen from the fact that on one of the days not a person but Ethiopians—men, women, and children—appeared in the theatre. By way of showing Patrobius some fitting honour Tiridates shot at wild beasts from his elevated seat, and—if one can believe it—transfixed and killed two bulls with a single arrow.

After this event Nero took him up to Rome and set the diadem upon his head. The entire city had been decorated with lights and garlands, and great crowds of people were to be seen everywhere, the Forum, however, being especially full. The centre was occupied by the civilians, arranged according to rank, clad in white and carrying laurel branches; everywhere else were the soldiers, arrayed in shining armour, their weapons and standards flashing like the lightning. The very roof-tiles of all the buildings in the vicinity were completely hidden from view by the spectators who had climbed to the roofs. Everything had been thus got ready during the night; and at daybreak Nero, wearing the triumphal garb and accompanied by the senate and the Praetorians, entered the Forum.

He ascended the rostra and seated himself upon a chair of state. Next Tiridates and his suite passed between lines of heavy-armed troops drawn up on either side, took their stand close to the rostra, and did obeisance to the emperor as they had done before. At this a great roar went up, which so alarmed Tiridates that for some moments he stood speechless, in terror of his life. Then, silence having been proclaimed, he recovered courage and quelling his pride made himself subservient to the occasion and to his need, caring little how humbly he spoke, in view of the prize he hoped to obtain. These were his words: "Master, I am the descendant of Arsaces, brother of the kings Vologaesus and Pacorus, and thy slave. And I have come to thee, my god, to worship thee as I do Mithras. The destiny thou spinnest for me shall be mine; for thou art my Fortune and my Fate." Nero replied to him as follows: "Well hast thou done to come hither in person, that meeting me face to face thou mightest enjoy my grace. For what neither thy father left thee nor thy brothers gave and preserved for thee, this do I grant thee. King of Armenia I now declare thee, that both thou and they may understand that I have power to take away kingdoms and to bestow them." At the close of these words he bade him ascend by the approach which had been built in front of the rostra expressly for this occasion, and when Tiridates had been made to sit beneath his feet, he placed the diadem upon his head. At this, too, there were many shouts of all sorts. By special decree there was also a celebration in the theatre. Not merely the stage but the whole interior of the theatre round about had been gilded, and all the properties that were brought in had been adorned with gold, so that people gave to the day itself the epithet of "golden." The curtains stretched overhead to keep off the sun were of purple and in the centre of them was an embroidered figure of Nero driving a chariot, with golden stars gleaming all about him.   'Apollo'

Such, then, was this occasion; and of course they had a costly banquet. Afterwards Nero publicly sang to the lyre, and also drove a chariot, clad in the costume of the Greens and wearing a charioteer's helmet. This made Tiridates disgusted with him; but he praised Corbulo, in whom he found only this one fault, that he would put up with such a master. [...]

Primary Source 2.11   Suetonius, 'Nero's Golden House'

(Source: Graves, R. (trans.) (1957) *Gaius Suetonius Tranquillus: The Twelve Caesars*, revised with an intro. by M. Grant, Harmondsworth, Penguin, pp. 229–30, 236–7)

31.   His wastefulness showed most of all in the architectural projects. He built a palace, stretching from the Palatine to the Esquiline, which he called 'The Passageway'; and when it burned down soon afterwards, rebuilt it under the new name of 'The Golden House'. The following details will give some notion of its size and magnificence. The entrance-hall was large enough to contain a huge   *megalomania?* statue of himself, 120 feet high; and the pillared arcade ran for a whole mile. An enormous pool, like a sea, was surrounded by buildings made to resemble cities, and by a landscape garden consisting of ploughed fields, vineyards, pastures, and woodlands – where every variety of domestic and wild animals roamed about. Parts of the house were overlaid with gold and studded with precious stones and mother-of-pearl. All the dining-rooms had ceilings of fretted ivory, the panels of which could slide back and let a rain of flowers, or of perfume from hidden sprinklers, shower upon his guests. The main dining-room was circular, and its roof revolved, day and night, in time with the sky. Sea water, or sulphur water, was always on tap in the baths. When the palace had been decorated throughout in this lavish style, Nero dedicated it, and condescended to remark: 'Good, now I can at last begin to live like a human being!'

[...]

38.   Nero showed no greater mercy to the common folk, or to the very walls of Rome. Once, in the course of a general conversation, someone quoted the line:

> When I am dead, may fire consume the earth,

but Nero said that the first part of the line should read: 'While I yet live,' and soon converted this fancy into fact. Pretending to be disgusted by the drab old buildings and narrow, winding streets of Rome, he brazenly set fire to the city; and though a group of ex-consuls caught his attendants, armed with tow and blazing torches, trespassing on their property, they dared not interfere. He also coveted the sites of several granaries, solidly built in stone, near the Golden House; having knocked down their walls with siege-engines, he set the interiors ablaze. This terror lasted for six days and seven nights, causing many people to take shelter in monuments and tombs. Nero's men destroyed not only a vast number of apartment blocks, but mansions which had belonged to famous generals and were still decorated with their triumphal trophies; temples, too, vowed and dedicated by the kings, and others during the Punic and Gallic wars – in fact, every ancient monument of historical interest that had hitherto survived. Nero watched the conflagration from the Tower of Maecenas, enraptured by what he called 'the beauty of the flames'; then put on his tragedian's costume and sang *The Sack of Ilium* from beginning to end.
He offered to remove corpses and rubble free of charge, but allowed nobody to search among the ruins even of his own mansion; he wanted to collect as much loot and spoils as possible himself. Then he opened a Fire Relief Fund and insisted on contributions, which bled the provincials white and practically beggared all private citizens.

[...]

Primary Source 2.12   Tacitus, 'Innocent victims'

(Source: Grant, M. (trans.) (1956) *Tacitus: The Annals of Imperial Rome*, London, Penguin, pp. 383–4)

But Nero profited by his country's ruin to build a new palace. Its wonders were not so much customary and commonplace luxuries like gold and jewels, but lawns and lakes and faked rusticity – woods here, open spaces and view there. With their cunning, impudent artificialities, Nero's architects and engineers, Severus and Celer, did not balk at effects which Nature herself had ruled out as impossible.

Primary Source 2.13   Martial, *On The Spectacles* 2

(Source: Shackleton Bailey, D.R. (ed. and trans.) (1993) *Martial: Epigrams*, Loeb Classical Library, Cambridge MA and London, Harvard University Press, vol. 1, pp. 13–15)

Where the starry colossus[1] sees the constellations at close range and lofty scaffolding[2] rises in the middle of the road, once gleamed the odious halls of a cruel monarch, and in all Rome there stood a single house.[3] Where rises before our eyes the august pile of the Amphitheater, was once Nero's lake. Where

---

[1]   A colossal statue of Nero, transferred from its place in his Golden House to the Via Sacra by Vespasian, who replaced the head to make it into a statue of the Sun, complete with rays (1.70.7).

[2]   The purpose of this is in doubt; see A. Boethius' discussion in *Eranos* 50 (1952) 129–137.

[3]   The Golden House of Nero, built in 64 after the great fire of Rome.

we admire the warm baths,[4] a speedy gift, a haughty tract of land had robbed the poor of their dwellings. Where the Claudian colonnade unfolds its wide-spread shade, was the outermost part of the palace's[5] end. Rome has been restored to herself, and under your rule, Caesar, the pleasances that belonged to a master now belong to the people.

Primary Source 2.14   Pliny the Elder, 'Nero's Golden House'

(Sources: Rackham, H. (trans.) (1952) *Pliny: Natural History, Books 33–35*, The Loeb Classical Library, Cambridge MA and London, Harvard University Press, pp. 45 and 161 for extracts (a) and (b); Eichholz, D.E. (trans.) (1962) *Pliny: Natural History Books 36–37*, The Loeb Classical Library, Cambridge MA and London, Harvard University Press and William Heinemann, pp. 129–131 for extracts (c) and (d))

(a) Pliny, *Natural History* 33.16.54

[...]

His immediate successor Nero covered the theatre of Pompey with gold for one day's purpose, when he was to display it to Tiridates King of Armenia. Yet how small was the theatre in comparison with Nero's Golden Palace which goes all round the city!

(b) Pliny, *Natural History* 34.18.45

[...]

But all the gigantic statues of this class have been beaten in our period by Zenodorus with the Hermes or Mercury which he made in the community of the Arverni in Gaul; it took him ten years and the sum paid for its making was 40,000,000 sesterees. Having given sufficient proof of his artistic skills in Gaul he was summoned to Rome by Nero, and there made the colossal statue, 106½ ft. high, intended to represent that emperor but now, dedicated to the sun after the condemnation of that emperor's crimes, it is an object of awe. In his studio we used not only to admire the remarkable likeness of the clay model but also to marvel at the frame of quite small timbers[1] which constituted the first stage of the work put in hand. This statue has shown that skill in bronze-founding has perished, since Nero was quite ready to provide gold and silver, and also Zenodorus was counted inferior to none of the artists of old in his knowledge of modelling and chasing.

(c) Pliny, *Natural History* 36.46.163

[...]

During Nero's principate there was discovered in Cappadocia a stone as hard as marble, white and, even where deep-yellow veins occurred, translucent. In token of its appearance it was called 'phengites' or the 'Luminary Stone.'[2]

---

[4]   Of Titus, one of Rome's three great public baths, along with those of Agrippa and Nero. M. regularly refers to these as *thermae* ("warm baths") as distinct from privately built and owned establishments (*balnea*).

[5]   The Golden House.

[1]   A skeleton for the model; or, according to Eugénie Sellers, slender wax tubes covering a wax model, which was then cased in loam before bronze was poured in.

[2]   Perhaps a variety of onyx marble.

Of this stone Nero rebuilt the temple of Fortune, known as the shrine of Sejanus,[3] but originally consecrated by King Servius Tullius and incorporated by Nero in his Golden House. Thanks to this stone, in the daytime it was as light as day in the temple, even when the doors were shut; but the effect was not that of windows of specular stone, since the light was, so to speak, trapped within rather than allowed to penetrate from without.

[...]

Primary Source 2.15   Seneca the Younger, *Letter* 115

(Source: Gummere, R.M. (trans.) (1925) *Seneca: Ad Lucilium Epistulae Morales, Volume III*, The Loeb Classical Library, Cambridge MA and London, Harvard University Press and William Heinemann, pp. 319–31)

[...]

CXV. On the superficial blessings

I wish, my dear Lucilius, that you would not be too particular with regard to words and their arrangement; I have greater matters than these to commend to your care. You should seek what to write, rather than how to write it—and even that not for the purpose of writing but of feeling it, that you may thus make what you have felt more your own and, as it were, set a seal on it. Whenever you notice a style that is too careful and too polished, you may be sure that the mind also is no less absorbed in petty things. The really great man speaks informally and easily; whatever he says, he speaks with assurance rather than with pains.

You are familiar with the young dandies, natty as to their beards and locks, fresh from the bandbox; you can never expect from them any strength or any soundness. Style is the garb of thought: if it be trimmed, or dyed, or treated, it shows that there are defects and a certain amount of flaws in the mind. Elaborate elegance is not a manly garb. If we had the privilege of looking into a good man's soul, oh what a fair, holy, magnificent, gracious, and shining face should we behold—radiant on the one side with justice and temperance, on another with bravery and wisdom! And, besides these, thriftiness, moderation, endurance, refinement, affability, and—though hard to believe—love of one's fellow-men, that Good which is so rare in man, all these would be shedding their own glory over that soul. There, too, forethought combined with elegance and, resulting from these, a most excellent greatness of soul (the noblest of all these virtues)—indeed what charm, O ye heavens, what authority and dignity would they contribute! What a wonderful combination of sweetness and power! No one could call such a face lovable without also calling it worshipful. If one might behold such a face, more exalted and more radiant than the mortal eye is wont to behold, would not one pause as if struck dumb by a visitation from above, and utter a silent prayer, saying: "May it be lawful to have looked upon it!"? And then, led on by the encouraging kindliness of his expression, should we not bow down and worship? Should we not, after much contemplation of a far superior countenance, surpassing those which we are wont to look upon,

---

[3]   Sejanus, prefect of the praetorian guard under Tiberius, was executed in A.D. 31. He no doubt restored the temple. According to Juvenal (X. 74), he was a devotee of Nortia, the Etruscan goddess of luck.

mild-eyed and yet flashing with life-giving fire—should we not then, I say, in reverence and awe, give utterance to those famous lines of our poet Vergil:

> O maiden, words are weak! Thy face is more
> Than mortal, and thy voice rings sweeter far
> Than mortal man's;
> Blest be thou; and, whoe'er thou art, relieve
> Our heavy burdens.[1]

And such a vision will indeed be a present help and relief to us, if we are willing to worship it. But this worship does not consist in slaughtering fattened bulls, or in hanging up offerings of gold or silver, or in pouring coins into a temple treasury; rather does it consist in a will that is reverent and upright.

There is none of us, I declare to you, who would not burn with love for this vision of virtue, if only he had the privilege of beholding it; for now there are many things that cut off our vision, piercing it with too strong a light, or clogging it with too much darkness. If, however, as certain drugs are wont to be used for sharpening and clearing the eyesight, we are likewise willing to free our mind's eye from hindrances, we shall then be able to perceive virtue, though it be buried in the body—even though poverty stand in the way, and even though lowliness and disgrace block the path. We shall then, I say, behold that true beauty, no matter if it be smothered by unloveliness. Conversely, we shall get a view of evil and the deadening influences of a sorrow-laden soul—in spite of the hindrance that results from the widespread gleam of riches that flash round about, and in spite of the false light—of official position on the one side or great power on the other—which beats pitilessly upon the beholder.

Then it will be in our power to understand how contemptible are the things we admire—like children who regard every toy as a thing of value, who cherish necklaces bought at the price of a mere penny as more dear than their parents or than their brothers. And what, then, as Ariso says,[2] is the difference between ourselves and these children, except that we elders go crazy over paintings and sculpture, and that our folly costs us dearer? Children are pleased by the smooth and variegated pebbles which they pick up on the beach, while we take delight in tall columns of veined marble brought either from Egyptian sands or from African deserts to hold up a colonnade or a dining-hall large enough to contain a city crowd; we admire walls veneered with a thin layer of marble, although we know the while what defects the marble conceals. We cheat our own eyesight, and when we have overlaid our ceilings with gold, what else is it but a lie in which we take such delight? For we know that beneath all this gilding there lurks some ugly wood.

Nor is such superficial decoration spread merely over walls and ceilings; nay, all the famous men whom you see strutting about with head in air, have nothing but a gold-leaf prosperity. Look beneath, and you will know how much evil lies under that thin coating of titles. Note that very commodity which holds the attention of so many magistrates and so many judges, and which creates both magistrates and judges—that money, I say, which ever since it began to be regarded with respect, has caused the ruin of the true honour of things; we become alternately merchants and merchandise, and we ask, not what a thing truly is, but what it costs; we fulfil duties if it pays, or neglect them if it pays, and we follow an honourable course as long as it encourages our expectations, ready to veer across to the opposite course if crooked conduct shall promise

---

[1]   *Aen.* i. 327 ff.

[2]   Frag. 372 von Arnim.

more. Our parents have instilled into us a respect for gold and silver; in our early years the craving has been implanted, settling deep within us and growing with our growth. Then too the whole nation, though at odds on every other subject, agrees upon this; this is what they regard, this is what they ask for their children, this is what they dedicate to the gods when they wish to show their gratitude—as if it were the greatest of all man's possessions! And finally, public opinion has come to such a pass that poverty is a hissing and a reproach, despised by the rich and loathed by the poor.

Verses of poets also are added to the account—verses which lend fuel to our passions, verses in which wealth is praised as if it were the only credit and glory of mortal man. People seem to think that the immortal gods cannot give any better gift than wealth—or even possess anything better:

> The Sun-god's palace, set with pillars tall,
> And flashing bright with gold.[3]

Or they describe the chariot of the Sun:[4]

> Gold was the axle, golden eke the pole,
> And gold the tires that bound the circling wheels,
> And silver all the spokes within the wheels.

And finally, when they would praise an epoch as the best, they call it the "Golden Age." Even among the Greek tragic poets there are some who regard pelf as better than purity, soundness, or good report:

> Call me a scoundrel, only call me rich!
> All ask how great my riches are, but none
> Whether my soul is good.
>
> None asks the means or source of your estate,
> But merely how it totals.
>
> All men are worth as much as what they own
>
> What is most shameful for us to possess?
> Nothing!
>
> If riches bless me, I should love to live;
> Yet I would rather die, if poor.
>
> A man dies nobly in pursuit of wealth.[5]
>
> Money, that blessing to the rise of man,
> Cannot be matched by mother's love, or lisp
> Of children, or the honour due one's sire.
> And if the sweetness of the lover's glance
> Be half so charming, Love will rightly stir
> The hearts of gods and men to adoration.[6]

When these last-quoted lines were spoken at a performance of one of the tragedies of Euripides, the whole audience rose with one accord to hiss the actor

[3]   Ovid, *Metam.* ii 1f.

[4]   *Id.ib.* ii. 107 ff.

[5]   *cf.* Nauck, *Trag. Gr. fragg. adesp.* 181. 1 and 461.

[6]   *cf. id., Eurip. Danaë, Frag.* 324, and Hense's note (ed. of 1914, p. 559)

and the play off the stage. But Euripides jumped to his feet, claimed a hearing, and asked them to wait for the conclusion and see the destiny that was in store for this man who gaped after gold. Bellerophon, in that particular drama, was to pay the penalty which is exacted of all men in the drama of life. For one must pay the penalty for all greedy acts; although the greed is enough of a penalty in itself. What tears and toil does money wring from us! Greed is wretched in that which it craves and wretched in that which it wins! Think besides of the daily worry which afflicts every possessor in proportion to the measure of his gain! The possession of riches means even greater agony of spirit than the acquisition of riches. And how we sorrow over our losses—losses which fall heavily upon us, and yet seem still more heavy! And finally, though Fortune may leave our property intact, whatever we cannot gain in addition, is sheer loss!

"But," you will say to me, "people call yonder man happy and rich; they pray that some day they may equal him in possessions." Very true. What, then? Do you think that there is any more pitiable lot in life than to possess misery and hatred also? Would that those who are bound to crave wealth could compare notes with the rich man! Would that those who are bound to seek political office could confer with ambitious men who have reached the most sought-after honours! They would then surely alter their prayers, seeing that these grandees are always gaping after new gain, condemning what is already behind them. For there is no one in the world who is contented with his prosperity, even if it comes to him on the run. Men complain about their plans and the outcome of their plans; they always prefer what they have failed to win.

So philosophy can settle this problem for you, and afford you, to my mind, the greatest boon that exists—absence of regret for your own conduct. This is a sure happiness; no storm can ruffle it; but you cannot be steered safely through by any subtly woven words, or any gently flowing language. Let words proceed as they please, provided only your soul keeps its own sure order,[7] provided your soul is great and holds unruffled to its ideals, pleased with itself on account of the very things which displease others, a soul that makes life the test of its progress, and believes that its knowledge is in exact proportion to its freedom from desire and its freedom from fear. Farewell.

Primary Source 2.16   Epitaphs from gladiatorial tombstones

(Sources: (a) = Robert, L. (1940), *Les gladiateurs dans l'Orient grec*, n. 109 in Futrell, A. (ed.) (2006) *The Roman Games: A Sourcebook*, Malden MA, Oxford and Victoria, Blackwell Publishing, p. 149; (b) = Di Cinzia, V. and Caldelli, M.L. (2000) *Epigrafia Anfiteatrale Dell'Occidente Romano*, vol. 5, Rome, Edizioni Quasar di Severino Tognon, p. 109)

(a) Hermes

For Hermes. Paitraeites with his cell-mates set this up in memory.

[From a now lost tombstone which was decorated with a figure holding a net and trident, the weapons of a retiarius.]

(b) Hector

Hector, vic(toriarum) III. [Hector of 3 victories.]

[The tombstone was decorated with two gladiators in combat. It was found at Moirans (France), but is now lost. First century CE.]

---

[7]   A play on the *compositio* of rhetoric.

Primary Source 2.17   Martial, *On the Spectacles* 6, 10 and 24, *Epigrams* 5.24

(Source: Shackleton Bailey, D.R. (ed. and trans.) (1993) *Martial: Epigrams*, The Loeb Classical Library, Cambridge MA and London, Harvard University Press, vol. 1 (pp. 17, 19, 29, 377)

On the Spectacles 6

Believe that Pasiphae was mated to the Dictaean bull; we have seen it, the old legend has won credence. And let not hoary antiquity plume itself, Caesar: whatever Fame sings of, the arena affords you.

On the Spectacles 10

Daedalus, when you are being thus torn by a Lucanian bear, how you wish you now had your wings![1]

On the Spectacles 24

Whatever Rhodope is said to have watched on Orpheus' stage, the arena, Caesar, displayed to you. Rocks crept and a wondrous forest ran, such as the grove of the Hesperides is believed to have been. Every kind of wild beast was present, mingling with the tame, and many a bird hovered above the bard. But himself lay torn by an ungrateful bear. This thing alone was done contrary to the legend.

Epigram 5.24

Hermes, favorite fighter of the age; Hermes skilled in all weaponry; Hermes, gladiator and trainer both; Hermes, tempest and tremor[2] of his school; Hermes, who (but none other) makes Helius afraid; Hermes, before whom (but none other) Advolans falls; Hermes, taught to win without wounding;[3] Hermes, himself his own substitute;[4] Hermes, gold mine of seat-mongers; Hermes, darling and distress of gladiators' women;[5] Hermes, proud with battling spear; Hermes, menacing with marine trident;[6] Hermes, formidable in drooping[7] helmet; Hermes, glory of Mars universal; Hermes, all things in one and thrice unique.

Primary Source 2.18   Apuleius, *Metamorphoses* 10.29–32

(Source: Kenney, E.J. (ed.) (1998) *Apuleius: The Golden Ass: A New Translation*, London, Penguin, pp. 190–93)

[...]

This then was the woman with whom I was to be publicly joined in holy matrimony. It was with feelings of deep distress and painful anticipation that I looked forward to the day of the games. More than once I was minded to do away with myself rather than be defiled by contact with this wicked woman and be put to shame and disgraced by being made a public spectacle. However, lacking as I did hands and fingers, I could find no way with my stubby rounded hooves of drawing a sword. My one consolation and ray of hope – slender

---

[1]   Daedalus will have been a criminal or beast-fighter.

[2]   i.e. earthquake.

[3]   He disarmed his opponents.

[4]   Never vanquished, and so never replaced by another gladiator.

[5]   They adored him or feared he would kill their men.

[6]   As a *retiarius* armed with net and trident.

[7]   The meaning of the epithet *languida* is doubtful; some have thought it corrupt.

enough – in my desperate plight was that spring had come once more. Everywhere there was colour: flowers were in bud, the meadows were putting on their bright summer garments, and roses were just beginning to break out of their thorny coverings and diffuse their fragrant scent – the roses which could make me once again the Lucius I had been.

Now the day of the games had arrived, and I was led to the theatre in ceremonial procession, escorted by crowds of people. While the show was being formally inaugurated by a troupe of professional dancers, I was left for a while outside the gate, where I had the pleasure of cropping the lush grass which was growing in the entrance. At the same time, as the gates were left open, I was able to feast my eyes on the very pretty sight inside.

First I saw boys and girls in the very flower of their youth, handsome and beautifully dressed, expressive in their movements, who were grouping themselves to perform a pyrrhic dance in Greek style. In the graceful mazes of their ballet they now danced in a circle, now joined hands in a straight line, now formed a hollow square, now divided into semi-choruses. Then a trumpet-call signalled an end to their complicated manoeuvres and symmetrical interweavings, the curtain was raised and the screens folded back to reveal the stage.

There was a hill of wood in the shape of that famous mount Ida sung by the poet Homer. It was a lofty structure, planted with shrubs and living trees, and on its summit the architect had contrived a spring from which a stream flowed down. Some goats were browsing on the grass; and a young man got up as the Phrygian shepherd Paris in a handsome tunic, draped in a mantle of oriental style, with a golden tiara on his head, was playing herdsman. To him there entered an extremely pretty boy, naked except for a cloak such as teenage boys wear over his left shoulder. From his blond hair, a striking sight, there projected a matching pair of little golden wings; the wand he carried identified him as Mercury. He danced forward and extended to the actor who represented Paris an apple plated with gold which he was carrying in his right hand, while with a nod he conveyed Jupiter's orders; then he gracefully retired and left the stage. Next there appeared a handsome girl representing Juno, with a shining diadem on her head and carrying a sceptre. She was followed by another girl, who could only be Minerva; she wore on her head a gleaming helmet with a wreath of olive round it and held aloft a shield and brandished a spear, just as she appears in battle.

After them there entered a third girl, the loveliest of the three, proclaimed as Venus by her ravishing ambrosial complexion, Venus as she was when still a virgin. She was completely naked, showing off her beauty in all its perfection, except for a wisp of thin silk that covered her pretty secrets. This little bit of material, however, the prurient wind in its amorous play now wafted aside to reveal the blossom of her youth and now skittishly flattened against her to cling closely and outline every detail of her voluptuous figure. The white colour of the goddess's skin, symbolizing her descent from heaven, contrasted with the blue of her dress, recalling her connection with the sea.

Each of the girls enacting the goddesses had a supporting escort. Juno was attended by actors impersonating Castor and Pollux, wearing egg-shaped helmets with a star for crest. This actress with restrained and natural gestures performed a dignified piece of miming, moving to an accompaniment of airs on the Ionian pipe, in which she promised to confer on the shepherd, if he adjudged the prize of beauty to her, dominion over Asia. The girl whose warlike get-up had made a Minerva of her was flanked by two boys, the armed attendants of the goddess of battles, Terror and Fear, leaping about with naked swords. Behind them a Dorian piper sounded a martial strain, alternating bass notes with strident trumpet-like tones to stimulate their brisk and vigorous dancing. This goddess, tossing her head and glaring threateningly, with rapid and complicated gestures indicated vividly to Paris that if he awarded her the victory in the beauty contest, he would with her aid be a great warrior with a glorious roll of battle-honours.

But now Venus, to immense applause from the audience, took centre stage. Surrounded by a throng of happy little boys, she stood sweetly smiling, an enchanting sight. These chubby children with their milk-white skin were for all the world like real Cupids just flown in from the sky or the ocean. Their little wings and their little bows and arrows and the rest of their costume made the resemblance perfect; and as if their mistress was on her way to a wedding-breakfast they lighted her footsteps with flaming torches. Next there entered a crowd of pretty unmarried girls, on this side the gracefullest of Graces, on that the loveliest of Hours, strewing garlands and flowers in honour of their goddess and in the intricacies of their artful dance essaying to delight the queen of heaven with all the rich bounty of the spring. Now the pipes breathed sweet Lydian harmonies; and while these were seducing the hearts of the spectators, Venus, even more seductive, began to dance. Advancing with slow and deliberate steps, her supple figure gently swaying and her head moving slightly in time to the music, she responded to the languishing melody of the pipes with elegant gestures. Now her eyes fluttered provocatively, now they flashed sharp menaces, and at times she danced only with them. As soon as she appeared before the judge it was plain from the movement of her hands that she was promising that, if she were preferred to the other goddesses, she would give Paris a wife of pre-eminent loveliness matching her own. At this the Phrygian youth readily handed the girl the golden apple he was holding as the token of her victory.

Primary Source 2.19   Petronius, extracts from *The Satyricon*

(Source: Sullivan, J. (trans.) (1965) *Petronius: The Satyricon and The Fragments*, Harmondsworth, Penguin, pp. 46–7, 50–1, 64, 71; notes omitted)

Dinner with Trimalchio

29.   As I was gaping at all this, I almost fell over backwards and broke a leg. There on the left as one entered, not far from the porter's cubbyhole, was a huge dog with a chain round its neck. It was painted on the wall and over it, in big capitals, was written:

BEWARE OF THE DOG

My colleagues laughed at me, but when I got my breath back I went on to examine the whole wall. There was a mural of a slave market, price tags and all. Then Trimalchio himself, holding a wand of Mercury and being led into Rome by Minerva. After this a picture of how he learned accounting and, finally, how he became a steward. The painstaking artist had drawn it all in great detail with descriptions underneath. Just where the colonnade ended Mercury hauled him up by the chin and rushed him to a high platform. Fortune with her flowing cornucopia and the three Fates spinning their golden threads were there in attendance.

[...]

35.   After our applause the next course was brought in. Actually it was not as grand as we expected, but it was so novel that everyone stared. It was a deep circular tray with the twelve signs of the Zodiac arranged round the edge. Over each of them the chef had placed some appropriate dainty suggested by the subjects. Over Aries the Ram, butter beans; over Taurus the Bull, a beef-steak; over the Heavenly Twins, testicles and kidneys; over Cancer the Crab, a garland; over Leo the Lion, an African fig; over Virgo the Virgin, a young sow's udder; over Libra the Scales, a balance with a tart in one pan and a cake in the other; over Scorpio, a lobster; over Sagittarius the Archer, a bull's eye; over Capricorn, a horned fish; over Aquarius the Water-carrier, a goose; over Pisces the Fishes, two mullets. In the centre was a piece of grassy turf bearing a honeycomb. A young Egyptian slave carried bread around in a silver oven ... and in a sickening voice he mangled a song from the show *The Asafoetida Man*.

36.   As we started rather reluctantly on this inferior fare, Trimalchio said: 'Let's eat, if you don't mind. This is the sauce of all order.' As he spoke, four dancers hurtled forward in time to the music and removed the upper part of the great dish, revealing underneath plump fowls, sows' udders, and a hare with wings fixed to his middle to look like Pegasus. We also noticed four little figures of Marsyas, which let a peppery fish-sauce go running over some fish which seemed to be swimming in a little channel. We all joined in the servants' applause and amid some laughter we helped ourselves to these quite exquisite things.

Trimalchio was every bit as delighted as we were with this piece of ingenuity: 'Carve 'er!' he cried. Up came the man with the carving knife and with his hands moving in time to the orchestra, he sliced up the victuals like a charioteer battling to the sound of organ music. And still Trimalchio went on saying insistently: 'Carve 'er! Carve 'er!'

I suspected this repetition was connected with some joke, and I went so far as to ask the man on my left what it meant. He had watched this sort of game quite often and said:

'You see the fellow doing the carving – he's called Carver. So whenever he says "Carver!", he's calling out his name and his orders.'

[...]

52.   'Now I'm very keen on silver. I have some three-gallon bumpers ... showing how Cassandra killed her sons, and the boys are lying there dead– very lifelike. I have a bowl my patron left – with Daedalus shutting Niobe in the Trojan Horse. What's more, I have the fights of Hermeros and Petraites on some cups – all good and heavy. No, I wouldn't sell my know-how at any price.'

— mockery.

[...]

59.   Ascyltus began to answer this abuse but Trimalchio, highly amused by his friend's fluency, said:

'No slanging matches! Let's all have a nice time. And you, Hermeros, leave the young fellow alone. His blood's a bit hot – you should know better.
In things like this, the one who gives in always comes off best. Besides, when you were just a chicken, you shouted cock-a-doodle too, and you had no more brains yourself. So let's start enjoying ourselves again, that'll be much better. Let's watch the recitations from Homer.'

In came the troupe immediately and banged their shields with their spears. Trimalchio sat up on his cushion and while the reciters spouted their Greek lines at one another in their usual impudent way, he read aloud in Latin in a sing-song voice. After a while, he got silence and asked:

'Do you know which scene they were acting? Diomede and Ganymede were the two brothers. Their sister was Helen. Agamemnon carried her off and offered a hind to Diana in her place. So now Homer is describing how the Trojans and Tarentines fought each other. Agamemnon, of course, won and married off his daughter Iphigenia to Achilles. This drove Ajax insane, and in a moment or two he'll explain how it ended.'

As Trimalchio said this, the reciters gave a loud shout, the servants made a lane, and a calf was brought in on a two-hundred pound plate: it was boiled whole and wearing a helmet. Following it came Ajax, slashing at the calf with a drawn sword like a madman. Up and down went his arm – then he collected the pieces on the point of his sword and shared them among the surprised guests.

[...]

Primary Source 2.20   Polybius, *The Rise of the Roman Empire* 6.56

(Source: Scott-Kilvert, I. (trans.) (1979) *Polybius: The Rise of the Roman Empire*, Harmondsworth, Penguin, p. 349)

[...]

However, the sphere in which the Roman commonwealth seems to me to show its superiority most decisively is in that of religious belief. Here we find that the very phenomenon which among other peoples[1] is regarded as a subject for reproach, namely superstition, is actually the element which holds the Roman state together. These matters are treated with such solemnity and introduced so frequently both into public and into private life that nothing could exceed them in importance. Many people may find this astonishing, but my own view is that the Romans have adopted these practices for the sake of the common people. This approach might not have been necessary had it ever been possible to form a state composed entirely of wise men. But as the masses are always fickle, filled with lawless desires, unreasoning anger and violent passions, they can only be restrained by mysterious terrors or other dramatizations of the subject. For this reason I believe that the ancients were by no means acting foolishly or haphazardly when they introduced to the people various notions concerning the gods and belief in the punishments of Hades, but rather that the moderns are foolish and take great risks in rejecting them. At any rate the result is that among the Greeks, apart from anything else, men who hold public office cannot be trusted with the safe-keeping of so much as a single talent, even if they have ten accountants and as many seals and twice as many witnesses, whereas among the Romans their magistrates handle large sums of money and scrupulously perform their duty because they have given their word on oath. Among other nations it is a rare phenomenon to find a man who keeps his hands off public funds and whose record is clean in this respect, while among the Romans it is quite the exception to find a man who has been detected in such conduct.

[...]

[1]   In particular among the Greeks.

Primary Source 2.21   Lucretius, *On Nature* 3.830–69

(Source: Geer, R.M. (trans.) (1965) *Lucretius: On Nature*, The Library of Liberal Arts, New York, Bobbs-Merrill Company, pp. 105–106, notes omitted)

Death is not to be feared

[...]

elite commentators

Death is nothing to us and does not concern us at all, inasmuch   830
as the soul is mortal. Just as we felt nothing painful in
the time now past when the Carthaginians were pressing to the
attack on all sides, when everything beneath the high shores of
heaven, struck by the confused tumult of war, trembled and
shuddered, and it was a question to which of the two the rule of
all mankind on land and sea would fall; so when we shall not
be, when soul and body by those uniting we exist will have   840
been sundered from each other, surely then nothing can happen
to us, who shall not exist, or stir our senses, not even if the earth
be mingled with the sea and the sea with the heaven. And if our
mind and soul do feel after they have been torn from the body,
yet this is nothing to us who exist as individuals formed by the
union and association of body and soul. If, after our death,
time should again gather together once more the atoms of which
we were formed, and should restore them to the positions that
they now occupy, and if the light of life should again be
granted—even if this should happen, it would not pertain at   850
all to us once the chain of consciousness had been broken. Even
now no concern troubles us about the selves we formerly were,
no pain touches us about them. For when you consider the
whole past expanse of unmeasured time and how manifold are
the motions of the atoms, you could easily believe that these
same atoms from which we are now formed have often been
arranged in the same order in which they now are. Yet we are
not able to grasp this in our memory, since an interruption of   860
life has been thrown between, and all the motions have wandered
far from sense. For if perchance pain and wretchedness
are to occur, a man to whom they can occur must also exist at
the same time. Since death removes this possibility and prevents
the existence of the dead man to whom the discomfort of death
would be assigned, we may be sure that there is nothing in death
to be feared by us, that he who does not exist cannot be made
miserable, and that a man is as if he had never been when once
immortal death has taken away his mortal life.

[...]

Primary Source 2.22   Cicero, *Tusculan Disputations* I.v.9–I. vi.13

(Source: King, J.E. (trans.) (1960) *Cicero: Tusculan Disputations*, The Loeb Classical Library, Cambridge MA and London, Harvard University Press and William Heinemann, pp. 13–17)

V. [...] M. There is no one then who is not wretched. A. Absolutely no one.
M. And in fact, if you wish to be consistent, everyone who has been born or will
be born is not only wretched but always wretched as well. For if your meaning

were that only those who had to die were wretched, you would make an exception of no living person—for all have to die—still there would have been an end of wretchedness in death; seeing however that the dead too were wretched we are born to eternal wretchedness. For it must follow that those who died a hundred thousand years ago are wretched, or rather everyone who has been born. A. That is precisely my opinion. M. Tell me, pray! You are not terrified, are you, by the stories of three-headed Cerberus in the lower world, the roar of Cocytus, the passage of Acheron, and "chin the water touching, Tantalus worn out with thirst"?[1] Again, are you frightened at the tale that Sisyphus

> Rolleth the stone as he sweateth in toil yet never advanceth?

Or it may be also at the pitiless judges Minos and Rhadamanths? At whose bar L. Crassus will not defend you nor M. Antonius,[2] nor—since the case will be tried before Greek judges—will you be able to engage Demosthenes:[3] you will have to plead your cause in person before a vast audience. From such prospects it may be you shrink and therefore consider death an unending evil.

VI. A. Do you suppose me so crazy as to believe such tales? M. You don't believe them true? A. Certainly not. M. My word! that's a sad story. A. Why so? M. Because I could have been so eloquent in speaking against such tales. A. Who could not on such a theme? Or what trouble is there in proving the falsity of these hobgoblins of poets and painters? M. And yet there are portly volumes in which philosophers argue against these self-same fables. A. They must have little to do; for who is so stupid as to be influenced by such things? M. If then the wretched are not in the lower world, there cannot be any beings in the lower world at all. A. I am precisely of that opinion. M. Where then are those whom you describe as wretched, or what is their place of habitation? For if they exist they must be somewhere. A. Well! I suppose they are not anywhere. M. Therefore you suppose they have no existence either. A. Exactly as you say; still I suppose them to be wretched for the simple reason that they do not exist at all. M. I must say now I should have preferred you to quail at Cerberus rather than find you making such rash statements. A. How so, pray? M. You are affirming the existence of the being whose existence you deny. Where have your wits gone? Once say a being who does not exist *is* miserable and you affirm his existence.[4] A. I am not so dull as to say such a thing. M. What do you say then? A. I say that M. Crassus[5] for example, because he lost a noble fortune by death, is wretched, that Cn. Pompeius[6] is wretched because he was robbed of a splendid reputation, in a word that all are wretched who quit the light of day. M. You come back to the same position, for they must exist if they *are* wretched: but just now you said that the dead did not exist. Now if they do not exist they cannot be anything. Therefore they cannot be wretched either. A. I do not perhaps express my meaning. I think that the mere fact of not existing, when one has existed, is utter wretchedness. M. What? more wretched than never to have existed at all? It follows that those who are not yet born are wretched now, because they do not exist, and that we, if we are to be wretched after death, have been wretched before we were born. My recollections previous to my birth do

---

[1]   Cf. § 98, and for the terrors of the lower world, Lucret. III. 978 ff., Virg. *Aen*. VI. 548 ff.

[2]   The chief orators of the generation preceding Cicero.

[3]   Cf. V. § 103.

[4]   A. should have said that the copula "*is*" is simply a connecting particle and implies no notion of existence, as is clear in such a proposition as "He is a nonentity."

[5]   M. Licinius Crassus the Triumvir, killed at Carrhae fighting with the Parthians in 53 B.C.

[6]   Killed in Egypt after his defeat at Pharsalus in 48 B.C. cf. § 86.

not report me wretched: if you have a better memory I should like to know what your recollections of your state are. [...]

Primary Source 2.23   Cicero, *In Defence of Cluentis* 171

(Source: Grose Hodge, H. (trans.) (1966) *Cicero: The Speeches*, Cambridge MA and London, Harvard University Press and William Heinemann, pp. 407–409)

[...]

For what harm at all has death done him, now that he is actually dead? Unless perhaps we are led by silly stories to suppose that he is enduring the torments of the damned in the nether world, and that he has there encountered more of his enemies than he left on earth; that the avenging spirits of his mother-in-law, his wives, his brother, and his children have driven him headlong into the abiding-place of the wicked. But if these stories are false, as every one knows they are, what is it that death has taken from him except the power to feel pain?

[...]

Primary Source 2.24   Cicero, *Philippics* 14.12.32

(Source: Ker, W.C.A. (trans.) (1926) *Cicero: Philippics*, The Loeb Classical Library, Cambridge MA and London, Harvard University Press and William Heinemann, p. 637)

[...] O fortunate death, the debt to nature, best paid on behalf of country! you I verily regard as born for your country; your very name is from Mars, so that it seems the same God begot this city for the world, and you for this city. In flight death is disgraceful; in victory glorious; for Mars himself is wont to claim out of the battle-line the bravest as his own.[1] Those impious wretches then whom you have slain will even among the shades below pay the penalty of their treason; but you who have poured out your last breath in victory have won the seats and abodes of the pious. Brief is the life given us by nature; but the memory of life nobly resigned is everlasting. [...]

Primary Source 2.25   Cicero, *On the Republic* 6.13

(Source: Hope, V.M. (ed.) (2007) *Death in Ancient Rome: A Sourcebook*, Abingdon, Routledge, p. 221)

Be certain of this so that you will be even more eager to defend the Republic: all those who have saved, helped or extended their country have a special place fixed for them in the heavens, where they will enjoy a life of eternal happiness.

Primary Source 2.26   Lucian, *Menippus* 17–21

(Source: Harmon, A.M. (trans.) (1925) *Lucian: In Eight Volumes, Vol. IV*, Cambridge MA and London, Harvard University Press and William Heinemann, pp. 101–109)

FRIEND

But tell me, Menippus; those who have such expensive, high monuments on earth, and tombstones and statues and inscriptions—are they no more highly honoured there than the common dead?

---

[1]   A reminiscence of Soph. *Phil.* 437: πόλεμος οὐδέν' ἄνδρ' ἑκὼν αἱρεῖ πονηρόν, ἀλλὰ τοὺς χρηστοὺς ἀεί. A similar sentiment is found in Aesch. *Fr.* 52 and Eur. *Fr.* 649 and 721.

MENIPPUS

Nonsense, man! If you had seen Mausolus himself—I mean the Carian, so famous for his monument—I know right well that you would never have stopped laughing, so humbly did he lie where he was flung, in a cubby-hole, inconspicuous among the rest of the plebeian dead, deriving, in my opinion, only this much satisfaction from his monument, that he was heavy laden with such a great weight resting upon him. When Aeacus measures off the space for each, my friend—and he gives at most not over a foot—one must be content to lie in it, huddled together to fit its compass. But you would have laughed much more heartily, I think, if you had seen our kings and satraps reduced to poverty there, and either selling salt fish on account of their neediness or teaching the alphabet, and getting abused and hit over the head by all comers, like the meanest of slaves. In fact, when I saw Philip of Macedon, I could not control my laughter. He was pointed out to me in a corner, cobbling worn-out sandals for pay! Many others, too, could be seen begging at the cross-roads—your Xerxeses, I mean, and Dariuses and Polycrateses.

FRIEND

What you say about the kings is extraordinary and almost incredible. But what was Socrates doing, and Diogenes, and the rest of the wise men?

MENIPPUS

As to Socrates, there too he goes about cross-questioning everyone. His associates are Palamedes, Odysseus, Nestor, and other talkative corpses. His legs, I may say, were still puffed up and swollen from his draught of poison. And good old Diogenes lives with Sardanapalus the Assyrian, Midas the Phrygian, and several other wealthy men. As he hears them lamenting and reviewing their former good-fortune, he laughs and rejoices; and often he lies on his back and sings in a very harsh and unpleasant voice, drowning out their lamentations, so that the gentlemen are annoyed and think of changing their lodgings because they cannot stand Diogenes.

FRIEND

Well, enough of this, but what was the motion that in the beginning you said had been passed against the rich?

MENIPPUS

Thanks for reminding me. Somehow or other, in spite of my intention to speak about that, I went very much astray in my talk.

During my stay there, the city fathers called a public meeting to discuss matters of general interest; so when I saw many people running in the same direction, I mingled with the dead and speedily became one of the electors myself. Well, various business was transacted, and at last that about the rich. After many dreadful charges of violence and mendacity and superciliousness and injustice had been brought against them, at length one of the demagogues rose and read the following motion.

(MOTION)

"Whereas many lawless deeds are done in life by the rich, who plunder and oppress and in every way humiliate the poor,

"Be it resolved by the senate and people, that when they die their bodies be punished like those of the other malefactors, but their souls be sent back up into life and enter into donkeys until they shall have passed two hundred and fifty thousand years in the said condition, transmigrating from donkey to donkey, bearing burdens, and being driven by the poor; and that thereafter it be permitted them to die.

"On motion of Scully Fitzbones of Corpsebury, Cadavershire."

After this motion had been read, the officials put it to the vote, the majority indicated assent by the usual sign, Brimo brayed and Cerberus howled. That is the way in which their motions are enacted and ratified.

Well, there you have what took place at the meeting. For my part, I did what I came to do. Going to Teiresias, I told him the whole story and besought him to tell me what sort of life he considered the best. He laughed (he is a blind little old gentleman, pale, with a piping voice) and said: "My son, I know the reason for your perplexity; it came from the wise men, who are not consistent with themselves. But it is not permissible to tell you, for Rhadamanthus has forbidden it." "Don't say that, gaffer," said I. "Tell me, and don't allow me to go about in life blinder than you are." So he took me aside, and after he had led me a good way apart from the others, he bent his head slightly toward my ear and said: "The life of the common sort is best, and you will act more wisely if you stop speculating about heavenly bodies and discussing final causes and first causes, spit your scorn at those clever syllogisms, and counting all that sort of thing nonsense, make it always your sole object to put the present to good use and to hasten on your way, laughing a great deal and taking nothing seriously."

[...]

Primary Source 2.27   Lucian, *On Funerals* 1–9

(Source: Harmon, A.M. (trans.) (1925) *Lucian: In Eight Volumes, Vol. IV*, Cambridge MA and London, Harvard University Press and William Heinemann, pp. 113–19)

Truly, it is well worth while to observe what most people do and say at funerals, and on the other hand what their would-be comforters say; to observe also how unbearable the mourners consider what is happening, not only for themselves but for those whom they mourn. Yet, I swear by Pluto and Persephone, they have not one whit of definite knowledge as to whether this experience is unpleasant and worth grieving about, or on the contrary delightful and better for those who undergo it. No, they simply commit their grief into the charge of custom and habit. When someone dies, then, this is what they do—but stay! First I wish to tell you what beliefs they hold about death itself, for then it will become clear why they engage in these superfluous practices.

The general herd, whom philosophers call the laity, trust Homer and Hesiod and the other myth-makers in these matters, and take their poetry for a law unto themselves. So they suppose that there is a place deep under the earth called Hades, which is large and roomy and murky and sunless; I don't know how they imagine it to be lighted up so that everything in it can be seen. The king of the abyss is a brother of Zeus named Pluto, who has been honoured with that appellative, so I was told by one well versed in such matters, because of his wealth of corpses.[1] This Pluto, they say, has organized his state and the world below as follows. He himself has been allotted the sovereignty of the dead, whom he receives, takes in charge, and retains in close custody, permitting nobody whatsoever to go back up above, except, in all time, a very few for most important reasons. His country is surrounded by great rivers, fearful even in name; for they are called "Wailing," "Burning Fire," and the like. But the principal feature is Lake Acheron, which lies in front and first receives visitors; it cannot be crossed or passed without the ferryman, for it is too deep to ford afoot and too broad to swim across—indeed, even dead birds cannot fly across it![2] Hard by the descent and the portal, which is of adamant, stands the king's nephew, Aeacus, who is commander of the guard; and beside him is a three-headed dog, very long-fanged, who gives a friendly, peaceable glance to those who come in, but howls at those who try to run away and frightens them with his great mouth. After passing the lake on going in, one comes next to a great meadow overgrown with asphodel, and to a spring that is inimical to memory; in fact, they call it "Oblivion" for that reason. All this, by the way, was told to the ancients by people who came back from there, Alcestis and Protesilaus of Thessaly, Theseus, son of Aegeus, and Homer's Odysseus, highly respectable and trustworthy witnesses, who, I suppose, did not drink of the spring, or else they would not have remembered it all.

Well, Pluto and Persephone, as these people said, are the rulers and have the general over-lordship, with a great throng of understrappers and assistants in administration—Furies, Tormentors, Terrors, and also Hermes, who, however, is not always with them.[3] As prefects, moreover, and satraps and judges, there are two that hold court, Minos and Rhadamanthus of Crete, who are sons of Zeus. These receive the good, just men who have lived virtuously, and when many have been collected, send them off, as if to a colony, to the Elysian fields to take part in the best life. But if they come upon any rascals, turning them over to the Furies, they send them to the Place of the Wicked, to be punished in proportion to their wickedness. There—ah! what punishment do they not undergo? They are racked, burned, devoured by vultures, turned upon a wheel; they roll stones uphill; and as for Tantalus, he stands on the very brink of the lake with a parched throat, like to die, poor fellow, for thirst! But those of the middle way in life, and they are many, wander about in the meadow without their bodies, in the form of shadows that vanish like smoke in your fingers. They get their nourishment, naturally, from the libations that are poured in our world and the burnt-offerings at the tomb; so that if anyone has not left a friend or kinsman behind him on earth, he goes about his business there as an unfed corpse, in a state of famine.

So thoroughly are people taken in by all this that when one of the family dies, immediately they bring an obol and put it into his mouth, to pay the ferryman for setting him over. They do not stop to consider what sort of coinage is customary and current in the lower world, and whether it is the Athenian or the

---

[1]   The Greeks derived the name Ploutōn (Pluto) from ploutein (to be rich), and generally held that it was given to Hades because he owned and dispensed the riches that are in the earth. So Lucian in the *Timon* (21). Here, however, we have in substance the view of Cornutus (5): "He was called Pluto because, of all that is perishable, there is nothing which does not at last go down to him and become his property."

[2]   Many places on earth, men thought, exhaled vapours so deadly that birds, attempting to cross them, fell dead; the most famous of these "Plutonia" was the lake near Cumae, called Ἄορνος par excellence, whence Avernus. If live birds could not fly across Avernus, surely the ghost of a bird could not fly across Acheron.

[3]   Hermes had to serve two masters, Zeus and Pluto. See *Downward Journey*, 1–2 (ii, 5).

Macedonian or the Aeginetan obol that is legal tender there; nor, indeed, that it would be far better not to be able to pay the fare, since in that case the ferryman would not take them and they would be escorted back to life again.

[...]

Primary Source 2.28   Seneca, *Consolation to Marcia* 19.4–5

(Source: Hope, V.M. (ed.) (2007) *Death in Ancient Rome: A Sourcebook*, Abingdon, Routledge, p. 227)

[...]

Know that there are no ills to be suffered after death, that the reports that make the underworld terrible to us are only tales, that no darkness awaits the dead, no prison, no blazing streams of fire, no river of oblivion, that no judgement seats are there, nor culprits, nor in that lax freedom are there any tyrants. All these things are the fancies of the poets, who have worried us with false terrors. Death is a release from all our suffering, a boundary beyond which our ills cannot cross; it restores us to that peaceful condition in which we were before birth.

Primary Source 2.29   Pliny the Elder, *Natural History* 7.55.188–189

(Source: Hope, V.M. (ed.) (2007) *Death in Ancient Rome: A Sourcebook*, Abingdon, Routledge, p. 230)

All men are in the same condition from their final day as they were before their first day. Neither body nor mind has any sensation after death, any more than it did before birth. It is vanity that extends itself into the future and creates for itself a life lasting beyond death, sometimes giving the soul immortality, sometimes transfiguration, sometimes giving senses to those below, and worshipping ghosts and making a god of one who has already ceased to be even a man. It is as if man's method of breathing were different from that of other animals and no one predicts a similar immortality for other animals that live as long. But in itself what is the substance of the soul? What is its material? Where is its thought? How does it see, hear and touch? What use does it get from these senses, or what good can it have without them? Next, where is the home and how great is the crowd of all the souls and shades of the ages? These are childish delusions and the inventions of mortality greedy for unceasing life.

Primary Source 2.30   Juvenal, *Satire* 2.149–52

(Source: Hope, V.M. (ed.) (2007) *Death in Ancient Rome: A Sourcebook*, Abingdon, Routledge, p. 228)

These days not even children, except those small enough to get a free bath, believe in such things as spirits, or underground kingdoms and rivers, or the waters of Styx black with frogs, or thousands of dead men crossing in a single boat.

Primary Source 2.31   Four epitaphs

(Sources: Courtney, E. (ed.) (1995) *Musa Lapidaria: A Selection of Latin Verse Inscriptions*, Atlanta, Scholars Press, p. 87 for extract (a) and Hope, V.M. (ed.) (2007) *Death in Ancient Rome: A Sourcebook*, Abingdon, Routledge, pp. 228 and 231 for extracts (b), (c) and (d))

(a) To the soul of Petronius Antigenes (CIL II 6435)[1]

You, traveller, who make your way along the path with your foot laced up, halt, I ask you, and, I beseech you, do not spurn my epitaph. Delicately nurtured and loved I lived on earth for ten years, two months, two days. I traversed the doctrines of Pythagoras and the views of the philosophers, I read the lyric poets and the holy epics of Homer, I knew what Euclid had laid down on his abacus. At the same time I enjoyed diversions and impudent amusements. All this my father Hilarus had bestowed on me, and he himself (would have been) my patron had not I, with my unhappy lot, encountered the hostility of destiny. Now in the underworld by the waters of infernal Acheron I dwell under murky stars. I have escaped tempestuous life. Farewell, hope and fortune; I have nothing to do with you, cheat others, please. This is my eternal home, here I lie, here shall I be for ever.

(b) CIL I 6298

To the spirits of the departed, Cerellia Fortunata, a very dear wife, with whom I lived 11 years without quarrel. Marcus Antonius Encolpus made this for himself and Antonius Athenaeus, his very dear freed slave, and for his freedmen and freedwomen and their descendants, except Marcus Antonius Athenionus.

Traveller, do not pass by my epitaph, but stop and listen, and then, when you have learned the truth, carry on. There is no boat in Hades, no ferryman Charon, no Aeacus holder of the keys, nor any dog called Cerberus. All of us who have died and gone below are bones and ashes: there is nothing else. What I have told you is true. Now leave, traveller, so that you will not think that, although dead, I talk too much.

(c) CIL XIII 530

To the spirits of the departed. I was not, I was, I am not, I don't care. Donnia Italia aged 20, rests here. Caius Munatius and Donnia Calliste for a devoted freed slave.

(d) CIL VI 26003

Lucius Scaterius Celer. We are and we were nothing. See, reader, how quickly we return from nothing to nothing. Lucius Scaterius Amethystus made this according to the will.

Secondary Sources

Introduction   70
Secondary Source I   W.H. Auden, 'Musée des Beaux Arts'   70
Secondary Source II   W.H. Auden, from 'Twelve Songs' ('Stop All the Clocks')   70

Block 1   The myth of Hippolytus and Phaedra   72
Secondary Source 1.1   Richard Buxton, 'Tragedy and Greek myth'   72
Secondary Source 1.2   Oliver Taplin, 'Escaping the "philodramatist" versus "iconocentric" polarity'   89
Secondary Source 1.3   Alan Cameron, 'Mythology and culture'   93
Secondary Source 1.4   Sir James George Frazer, *The Golden Bough*, chapters 1 and 24   96
Secondary Source 1.5   Eric Csapo, 'Frazer's *Golden Bough*'   118
Secondary Source 1.6   Eric Csapo, 'Comparative Approaches'   124
Secondary Source 1.7   Eric Csapo, 'Frazer's comparative method'   135

Block 2   Myth in Rome: power, life and afterlife   138
Secondary Source 2.1   'Fact or Legend? Debate over the origins of Rome'   138
Secondary Source 2.2   Edward Champlin, 'Nero'   143
Secondary Source 2.3   Miriam T. Griffin, 'The tyranny of art'   173
Secondary Source 2.4   J. Elsner, 'Constructing decadence: the representation of Nero as Imperial Builder'   179
Secondary Source 2.5   Alan Cameron, 'Myth and society'   193
Secondary Source 2.6   Paul Zanker, 'A miniature villa in the town'   202
Secondary Source 2.7   John R. Clarke, 'The villa as model for middle-class houses'   212
Secondary Source 2.8   Verity Platt, 'Viewing, desiring, believing: confronting the divine in a Pompeian house'   213
Secondary Source 2.9   Lauren Hackworth Petersen, 'Disney World in Pompeii: the House of Octavius Quartio'   234
Secondary Source 2.10   Alan E. Bernstein 'Useful death'   241
Secondary Source 2.11   Michael Koortbojian, 'Adonis's tale'   257
Secondary Source 2.12   Susan Wood, 'Mortals, empresses and earth goddesses'   280

Introduction

Secondary Source I   W.H. Auden, 'Musée des Beaux Arts'

(Source: W.H. Auden (1966) *Collected Shorter Poems 1927–1957*, London, Faber and Faber)

About suffering they were never wrong,   1
The Old Masters: how well they understood
Its human position; how it takes place
While someone else is eating or opening a window or just walking
    dully along;
How, when the aged are reverently, passionately waiting   5
For the miraculous birth, there always must be
Children who did not specially want it to happen, skating
On a pond at the edge of the wood:
They never forgot
That even the dreadful martyrdom must run its course   10
Anyhow in a corner, some untidy spot
Where the dogs go on with their doggy life and the torturer's horse
Scratches its innocent behind on a tree.

In Brueghel's *Icarus*, for instance: how everything turns away
Quite leisurely from the disaster: the ploughman may   15
Have heard the splash, the forsaken cry,
But for him it was not an important failure; the sun shone
As it had to on the white legs disappearing into the green
Water; and the expensive delicate ship that must have seen
Something amazing, a boy falling out of the sky,   20
Had somewhere to get to and sailed calmly on.

[Handwritten margin note: "Hunters in the Snow" (1565) in Vienna]

Secondary Source II   W.H. Auden, from 'Twelve Songs' ('Stop All the Clocks')

(Source: W.H. Auden (1966) *Collected Shorter Poems 1927–1957*, London, Faber and Faber)

IX

Stop all the clocks, cut off the telephone,   1
Prevent the dog from barking with a juicy bone,
Silence the pianos and with muffled drum
Bring out the coffin, let the mourners come.

Let aeroplanes circle moaning overhead   5
Scribbling on the sky the message He Is Dead,
Put crêpe bows round the white necks of the public doves,
Let the traffic policemen wear black cotton gloves.

He was my North, my South, my East and West,
My working week and my Sunday rest,   10
My noon, my midnight, my talk, my song;
I thought that love would last for ever: I was wrong.

The stars are not wanted now: put out every one;
Pack up the moon and dismantle the sun;
Pour away the ocean and sweep up the wood;   15
For nothing now can ever come to any good.

Block 1   The myth of Hippolytus and Phaedra

Secondary Source 1.1   Richard Buxton, 'Tragedy and Greek myth'

(Source: Woodward, R.D. (ed.) (2007) *The Cambridge Companion to Greek Mythology,* Cambridge and New York, Cambridge University Press, Chapter 4, pp. 166–89 and selected references)

The theatre of Dionysus in fifth-century-BC Athens provided a unique context for myth-telling.[1] At the annual festival of the City Dionysia, myths were reembodied in performances by members of the citizen group. In these reembodiments, as heroes and divinities walked the stage, myths were not just narrated as past events: they were actualised as present happenings. Then and there, but also now and here; remote enough to allow room for pity, but close enough to inspire awe.[2]

In the present attempt to characterise tragic myths, I begin with a discussion (Section 1) of an apparently simple question: What happens in Greek tragedies? In order to suggest an answer, I contrast tragedy with the nontragic mythological tradition, examining in particular the kinds of actions and sufferings ascribed to heroes and heroines. In Section 2 I ask another seemingly straightforward question: Where are Greek tragedies imagined as taking place? My answer involves politics and psychology as well as topography and geography. Finally, in Section 3, I discuss ways in which tragedy represents the gods. Throughout the chapter, my aim is to ask how far it is possible to isolate features which are distinctively tragic.[3]

What happens in Greek tragedies?

Across a wide range of Greek mythological narratives, in both texts and visual representations, the mighty heroes Heracles, Theseus, Agamemnon, and Oedipus are credited with formidable and triumphantly successful exploits. Heracles is the monster-slayer *par excellence*; Theseus, champion of idealised Athenian values, rids the world of unpleasant villains and puts an end to the Minotaur; Agamemnon leads the expedition which captures Troy, so justly avenging Paris' abduction of Helen; Oedipus destroys the oppressive power of the Sphinx. These same heroes appear, more specifically, in tragedies, including four which survive to the present day: Euripides' *The Madness of Heracles* and *Hippolytus*; Aeschylus' *Agamemnon*; Sophocles' *Oedipus Tyrannus*. What is noticeable about the way in which these heroes are represented in tragedy is the kind of *selection* of mythical material which tragedy practises. When in Euripides' play the peerless Heracles returns home after his culminating Labour (the seizing of the hell-hound Cerberus), he is struck by a frenzy sent upon him by Hera; while out of his senses he slaughters his wife and children and is only prevented from killing his father Amphitryon when Athena hurls a rock at him. In *Hippolytus*, Theseus witnesses the utter destruction of his family: when his son Hippolytus slights Aphrodite, the goddess's punishment leads to the suicide

---

[1]   See Pickard-Cambridge (1968); Csapo and Slater (1994).

[2]   However exaggerated one may consider the reverence paid to Aristotle's *Poetics* over the centuries, the composite Aristotelian concept of pity-and-fear remains a pointer towards reconstructing the experience of Greek tragedy; cf. Buxton (2002). On the whole question of the role of the *Poetics* in the history of the interpretation of tragedy, see now Lurje (2004).

[3]   There are many ways of asking and answering this question: two examples, complementary both to my own approach and to each other, are the general account of Burian (1997) and the more specific one by Calame (2000a).

of Theseus' wife Phaedra and to the death of Hippolytus, intemperately cursed by his father in the false belief that the young man had raped Phaedra.

In *Agamemnon*, Troy's conqueror is humiliatingly stabbed to death in his bath by his vengeful and unfaithful wife Clytemnestra. In *Oedipus Tyrannus*, the saviour of Thebes becomes an abhorred outcast, revealed as the killer of his father and as the husband to whom his own mother bore four children.

This pattern is typical. Greek tragedies do not narrate heroic exploits: instead, they explore the disruptions and dilemmas generated by such heroism, disruptions and dilemmas which almost invariably involve the catastrophic destruction of a household. Now of course tragedy is not the only genre to highlight the problematic aspects of heroism. We need only think of the *Iliad*, where heroic values are put under enormous strain by the conflict between Agamemnon and Achilles; where Achilles' clear-eyed awareness of the brevity of his glory contrasts with the all-too-human, indeed 'tragically' limited vision which characterizes Hector;[4] and where one of the poem's greatest affective climaxes, in which Priam ransoms from Achilles the body of his dead son Hector, precisely exemplifies the kind of emotional intensity later exploited in Attic tragedy.[5] Or we may think of the *Odyssey*, in which Odysseus' slaying of the suitors is by no means morally unambiguous (this is especially clear in Book 24, where the suitors' grieving families step forward to exact vengeance for their murdered brothers and sons). Nevertheless, it is above all in tragedy that the underside of heroism becomes pervasive, not simply as a 'theme,' but as the predominant perspective from which mythical events are selected and depicted. It will be useful to illustrate this in more detail, by examining one myth, that of Jason and Medea, in three different versions.

In *Pythian 4*, the praise-poet Pindar honours Arcesilas of Cyrene, victor in the chariot-race at Delphi in 462 BC. The poem includes what is, for Pindar, an unusually extended account of a myth, namely Jason's quest for the Golden Fleece. In spite of its length, this account is not a detailed narration, but rather a spotlighting of significant moments. Given that Pindar is celebrating the return of a victorious athlete after a competitive triumph, the choice of the myth of the Argonauts makes perfect sense as a paradigm of success in the world of heroic adventure: Jason left home in search of glory, and returned home having won it.[6] The Pindaric Jason is formidable, handsome, and gentle of speech, even when he confronts Pelias, who has forcibly usurped sovereignty from Jason's 'rightfully ruling parents' (110). Thanks to his trust in the god (232) and to Medea's passionate assistance, Jason wins the Fleece, and is wreathed by his comrades like a victor in the Games (240). What of Medea? It is true that Aphrodite teaches Jason how to induce Medea to lose her shame for her parents and to desire a country – Hellas – which is not her own, so that she shall be burned and whirled by the lash of Persuasion (216–19). It is true, too, that her chaotic and disruptive emotions have been taken to exemplify her 'disturbing ambiguity.'[7] Nor can it be denied that at one point Medea is described as 'the murder(ess) of Pelias' (250), presumably an allusion to the later brutal episode

---

[4]   See Redfield (1975).

[5]   Plato (*Republic* 602b9–10) significantly takes 'tragic poetry' to be a quality of *both* epic *and* drama. Plato identifies a 'tragic' viewpoint which stresses humanity's subjection to indifferent or hostile divine forces – the opposite of his own metaphysical and ethical position, which locates happiness exclusively in the individual soul's capacity to choose between good and evil. On this, see the excellent discussion in Halliwell (2002).

[6]   For an insightful account of the motif of the return home in Pindaric poetry, see Crotty (1982), esp. 104–38.

[7]   O'Higgins (1997) 121.

in which she deceived Pelias' daughters into butchering and boiling him, in an attempt to effect his rejuvenation. Nevertheless, although this allusion has been cited as evidence of Medea's 'infamous duplicity,'[8] there is surely no implication that to be a murder(ess)-of-Pelias is necessarily a negative quality, since earlier in the poem Pelias has been portrayed as unlawfully and violently insolent (*athemin, biaios, hubrin* ... 109–12). Moreover, about any possible future dissension between the Colchian princess and her Greek lover, Pindar is silent: Jason took her away secretly but *sun autai ...*, 'with her acquiescence' (250). To put the matter in broad and direct terms: in *Pythian* 4 the central function of the myth of the *Argo* is to shed lustre on the human victor Arcesilas by praising the mythical hero who stands as his exemplar.[9]

Argonautica, the great Hellenistic epic poem by Apollonius of Rhodes, narrates the tale of Jason and Medea in far richer detail than anything we find in Pindar; and in Apollonius it does indeed become imperative to recognise ambiguity. The portrayal of the two principals is subtle and complex: for the bright light of Pindaric heroism Apollonius substitutes something far more troubling. Jason can only achieve his goal by relying on others: even though, before yoking the fire-breathing Colchian bulls, he exults in the strength of his limbs like a proud warhorse (3.1259–62), he has by that stage already been sprinkled by Medea with potions which confer invulnerability. Not only is he far from self-reliant, but he also enters deeply worrying moral territory: his treacherous and religiously polluting murder of Medea's brother Apsyrtus overshadows the latter part of the epic, and partly determines the return course taken by the *Argo*, as Jason and Medea visit first Circe, and then Alcinous on Phaeacia, in a quest for purification.[10]

The difference between the Pindaric and the Apollonian Medeas are even greater than those between their Jasons. Compared to the near-evanescence of Medea in *Pythian 4*, the Medea of Apollonius is a strong and disturbing presence from the moment that she appears. When she abandons her home, she is torn apart by grief (4.34–40); she threatens Jason with the terrible consequences of his breaking of his oath to her, when it seems that he will negotiate with the pursuing Colchians (4.383–93). There is even a subtext which hints at the future rupture between Jason and Medea, since the myth of Ariadne, mentioned several times (3.997–1004, 1096–1108; 4.430–34), cannot but recall Theseus' abandoning of *his* foreign princess. Nevertheless, in spite of these darker characteristics of Jason and Medea, as the *Argo* sails into its home port of Pagasae at the end of the poem there is no mention of impending trouble. Indeed, about Medea's future career, we have learned explicitly only two things. First, according to Hera's plan, Medea will arrive in Iolcus as a *kakon* (κακόν), 'bane,' to Pelias (3.1134–6). Second – so Hera assures Thetis – Medea will ultimately marry Achilles in the Elysian Fields (4.810–16).[11] Whatever has

---

[8]   O'Higgins (1997) 103.

[9]   On the whole I am sceptical of attempts, for example, by Segal (1986: 15–29), to emphasise at every turn the craftiness and duplicity of the Pindaric Jason-with-Medea; I prefer Burton's more straightforward reading (1962: 150–73). To find ambiguity *everywhere* is to risk bleaching out its impact when it does occur.

[10]   For a fascinating treatment of the Apsyrtus story, see Bremmer (1997).

[11]   According to the scholiast on this passage in Apollonius (Schol. Ap. Rhod. 4.814–15, p. 293 W), this intriguing detail was apparently also found in Ibycus and Simonides (*PMG* 291 Ibycus = *PMG* 558 Simonides); cf. Gantz (1993) 133.

gone before, the ending of the epic is serene, concluding as it does at the moment when the *Argo* itself bows out of the story:

> You sailed untroubled past the coast of Cecrops' land, past
> Aulis inside Euboea, past the towns of the Opuntian Locrians,
> and joyfully you stepped ashore at Pagasae.

(4.1778–81)

Chronologically intermediate between the Pindaric and the Apollonian narratives is Euripides' tragedy. As might be expected from a story incorporating so many episodes of violent conflict, the myth of Medea was a favourite with the Greek tragedians;[12] but the only play on this theme to survive to the present day is the Euripidean masterpiece. Within the world of this play, the expedition of the *Argo* is just a memory; equally remote is the recollected love between Jason and Medea. From the perspective of the tragedy's Corinthian setting, Colchis and Iolcus lie in the past; Athens, Medea's eventual refuge, lies in the future. Concentrated into the transitional Corinthian present is an episode of horrifying cruelty, which encompasses the destruction of two families.

Jason has decided to put Medea aside in favour of a new bride, the daughter of the Corinthian king Creon. When Medea cunningly obtains from a nervous and reluctant Creon the permission to remain for just one more day before leaving Corinth, she seizes the opportunity to inflict a ghastly vengeance on her former lover and his prospective second family. As wedding presents to Jason's new bride, Medea sends a lovely gown and coronet, conveyed by her own little sons to make the gifts more persuasively welcome. But the gifts turn out to contain a fiery, flesh-eating poison, which causes the excruciating deaths of the girl and her father. A Newsbringer[13] recounts the final stages of the torment:

> Overcome by disaster, she fell to the ground;
> Except to her father, she was indeed hard to recognise;
> The form of her eyes was not clear, and her face was disfigured;
> Blood mingled with flame dripped down from her head; her
>   flesh,
> Eaten away by the invisible jaws of poison, flowed away
> From the bones, like drops of pine resin –
> A terrible sight. Everyone was afraid to touch
> Her corpse. We had learned the lesson from what had happened.

(*Med.* 1195–1203)

Going beyond even these horrors. Medea then kills her own two young sons – acting not as a monstrous psychopath, but as a mother torn apart by conflicting drives. At first she had found the thought of infanticide hideous beyond imagining:

> What am I to do? My courage has gone,
> Women, when I saw the bright eyes of my children,
> I could not do it. Farewell to the plans
> I had before. I'll take my children from this land.
> Why should I cause harm to my children in order to make
> Their father suffer, when I shall suffer twice as much myself?

(1042–7)

---

[12] See Moreau (1994) 174.

[13] Modern critics usually refer to such characters as 'Messengers,' but as often as not there is no message: just news from elsewhere.

But finally, overcome by the urge to punish the partner who has betrayed her, Medea convinces herself that she has no choice:

> Friends, the deed is decided: with all speed
> To kill the children and then leave Corinth;
> Not to delay, giving the children up to another
> More malevolent hand to murder them.
> At all events, they must die; and since they must,
> It is I who shall kill them, I who gave them birth.
> Arm yourself, my heart: why do I hesitate
> To perform wicked deeds that are terrible, yet inevitable?

(1236–43)

With the boys lying dead, it might seem that any possibility for still greater cruelty has been exhausted. Yet as a final refinement Medea conveys her sons' corpses away from Corinth, in order to prevent Jason from embracing them in a last farewell. 'You are not yet mourning,' she chillingly informs Jason (1396): 'Wait until you are old.'

In exploring the catastrophic underside of heroism, Euripides' *Medea* exemplifies the inflection typically given by tragic playwrights to the mythical tradition. Tragedy is a world in which the tensions which ordinarily beset family life are unbearably intensified. In marriages, ancient and modern, husbands and wives quarrel and even fight: in tragedy, Clytemnestra goes further: she slaughters Agamemnon. In families, ancient and modern, children often face conflicts of loyalty towards their father and mother: in tragedy, Orestes goes further: he kills his mother because she killed his father. Tragedy is a crucible, a burning glass, an arena which displays events so terrible that one can hardly bear to contemplate them, yet so compelling that one cannot but watch to the end.

Where do Greek tragedies happen?

We now turn to the *location* of tragic myths. The action of Greek tragedies is, I shall suggest, imagined as unfolding 'in between.' The Euripidean Medea may once more serve as our initial guide.

Medea is in many senses an outsider. Not only is she a stranger to Corinth: this Colchian princess is a stranger to the Greek world altogether. At first she relies on Jason; later – for her escape plan – she relies on Aigeus. But throughout, her status is that of one who is 'citiless' (*apolis* [ἄπολις], 255, cf. 644).[14] This condition of exclusion applies, literally or metaphorically, to a large proportion of the protagonists in Greek tragedy. In Sophocles' *Philoctetes* the eponymous hero, abandoned on the island of Lemnos, lacks all the comforts which would have brought his life closer to that of a civilised human being; only his magically unerring bow raises him above the level of a brute. (The desolation and isolation attributed to Lemnos in this play constitute another example of tragic 'selection': inhabited since prehistoric times, the real Lemnos was by no means devoid of human population.) Another Sophoclean work, *Ajax*, depicts a hero whose position at the very edge of the beached Greek ships (*Aj.* 4) reflects his martial indomitability – the extremity of an army's lines in one of its points of maximum vulnerability – but also symbolises other aspects of his marginality, including his madness and his attainment, albeit briefly, of a sublime linguistic register unparalleled elsewhere in the play;[15] eventually he

---

[14]   Compare also the Nurse's remarkable expression at 34–5, where she observes that Medea has realized what it means *not* to have been uprooted from one's native land.

[15]   I have explored the unique language of Ajax in Buxton (2006).

commits the ultimate act of self-exclusion by falling on his sword. In these and many other tragedies, explorations of the moral and emotional implications of exclusion and marginality illustrate the genre's predilection for 'testing to destruction' the concepts and categories of ordinary Greek life.[16] By dramatising the experiences of individuals driven out of their usual frameworks for living, tragedies depict actions which are simultaneously extreme and representative – just as the chorus of *Oedipus Tyrannus* can characterize the utterly extraordinary events surrounding Oedipus as a 'paradigm' of human existence (*OT* 1193).

There are various ways in which tragic actions may unfold in the gaps between states. Sometimes these states are *city*-states, as in Sophocles' *Oedipus at Colonus*, in which the plot concerns an outcast wandering in the no-man's-land between Thebes and Athens. Will hospitable Athens agree to admit a wanderer with a horrific past? Will Creon and Polynices, with their threats and persuasion, draw Oedipus back to Thebes? At the end Oedipus mysteriously crosses an even more dangerous, because sacred, boundary, that between life and death, eventually to occupy a post mortem position between the two poles – as a dead hero with the power to affect the living.

A similar sense of the precarious balance between states typically underlies works which turn on the acceptance or rejection of a ritual supplication. Central to Aeschylus' *Suppliant Maidens* is the dilemma faced by the Argive ruler Pelasgus, obliged to decide whether to accept a group of refugees in a crisis where such acceptance will entail the dangerous enmity of those angrily pursuing them. The asylum-seekers in question are the daughters of Danaus, desperate to avoid being forced into marriage with their cousins, the sons of Aegyptus. To intensify Pelasgus' dilemma still further, the Danaids threaten to commit suicide upon the city's holy shrines. As Pelasgus expresses it to the chorus of Danaid maidens:

> Yes, I see difficulties everywhere, hard to wrestle with;
> A surge of troubles overwhelms me like a river.
> I have entered upon a sea of ruin, bottomless and dangerous,
> With nowhere a harbour to escape from misfortune.
> If I do not fulfil this duty to help you,
> You threatened us with pollution unsurpassed;
> But if I stand against your cousins, Aegyptus' sons,
> Before our walls and fight the matter out,
> Is the cost not a bitter one, that men
> Should soak the earth in blood for women's sake?
> Yet I must fear the wrath of Zeus, the suppliants' god:
> For mortals that is the supreme fear.

(*Supp.* 468–79)

The boundary between one community and another is a place of tension, and potentially a powerful generator of dramatic meaning.[17]

The gaps between states explored in Euripides' *Trojan Women* are at once political and more than political. The action is suspended between Troy and

---

[16]   See Buxton (2002) 184.

[17]   This kind of 'boundary decision,' while typical of tragedy, is certainly not exclusive to it. A classic case from epic is that from Book 4 of Apollonius' *Argonautica*. The Phaeacian king Alcinous has to find a criterion by which to determine whether to return Medea to the pursuing Colchians, or to allow her to remain with Jason. His Solomon-like judgement is that, if Medea is still a virgin, she must go back to Colchis; but if she has already been united with Jason, she should not be forced to leave him (*Ap. Rhod.* 4.1106–9).

Greece, but also between past and present and, for the Trojan women themselves, between one male and another. The surviving women of Troy find themselves in a city whose past already lies in smouldering ruins, and whose future will consist of a slave existence across the sea in Greece. Cassandra will be transferred from the service of Apollo to the bed of Agamemnon; it is proposed that Hecuba and Andromache shall serve Odysseus and Neoptolemus. The Trojan men, it is true, died good deaths, achieving 'the most beautiful glory' by dying for their country (*Tro.* 386–7). But dead they are: the only living Trojan male to appear in the play is young Astyanax, a silent victim soon to be hurled to his death from the city walls. In so far as a *polis* is defined by the presence of its male citizens, Troy is a *polis* no longer; rather, it is an empty space, abandoned even by Poseidon and Athena, who had ended their prologue by walking away. The minimal scope for the expression of personal preference which had momentarily opened up earlier on ('I would rather go to the famed and blessed land of Theseus' – i.e., Athens – the chorus had observed (207)) has given way by the end to ineluctable trek toward the Greek ships.

Yet another boundary explored in tragedy is the problematic interface between 'Greek' and 'Barbarian.' *Medea* again provides a reference point. In the face of Medea's accusations about broken vows, Jason retorts that moving to Greece has introduced her to a society which respects justice and the rule of law (*Med.* 536–8). Yet, notwithstanding the 'barbaric' cruelty of Medea's revenge, Jason's breaking of his vows to her hardly allows such a dichotomy to stand unchallenged: there is heartlessness on either side of the division between Greek and non-Greek. An equivalent overlap between these two categories pervades Aeschylus' *Agamemnon*, whose subtitle might be 'A Tale of Two Cities.' The play evokes a series of characters who travel, or who once travelled, from Argos to Troy or vice versa, and one of the questions implicitly raised in the play is this: Will the generalisations which applied in Troy (for example: that the gods punish mortals who are impious) apply also in Argos? When Agamemnon is persuaded by Clytemnestra to perform the symbolically tremendous gesture of trampling on rich fabric as he reenters his palace, he admits that this is exactly what Priam would have done (*Ag.* 935–6) – another example of the characteristically tragic collapsing of boundaries.

In several other plays an analogous to-ing and fro-ing takes place; but in these cases the opposed locations are features of the landscape rather than different communities. More often than not, the *skene* (stage building), in front of which tragedies were played out, was designed to represent part of the built environment such as a house or palace, which in turn usually belonged within a *polis*.[18] Yet it often happens that significant action takes place in the off-stage space imagined to lie beyond the *skene* – typically in a mountain region adjacent to and contrasting with the world of human habitation. The reciprocal relationship between mountain and city constitutes yet one more permutation of the interstitial status of tragic action, since the action of many tragedies oscillates between an ostensibly civilised household/city and the sacred wildness of a mountain. The most obvious example is the role of Mount Cithaeron in myths based in the city of Thebes.[19] In both *Oedipus Tyrannus* and

---

[18]   The imagined location of the building need not be Greece: cf. Euripides' *Helen* (set in Egypt) or Aeschylus' *Persians* (set in Persia); and there may be *equivalents* of a house, such as a more-or-less permanent warrior-tent (*Ajax*, set in the Greek camp at Troy). But there are exceptions: the scene of *Prometheus Bound* is the extreme wilderness of the Caucasus; that of Sophocles' *Philoctetes* is before a cave on the sea-shore of Lemnos.

[19]   N.b. also Mt. Oeta in Sophocles' *Women of Trachis*. On tragic mountains see Buxton (1992) 12–14.

Bacchae, this mountain is where human beings come unusually and dangerously close to the sacred. For Oedipus, this proximity is strange and eerie: Cithaeron is where he was left to die and then miraculously saved. For the mortals swept up in the arrival of Dionysus in Greece, Cithaeron has a more sharply defined role: it is where the women go in search of Dionysus, abandoning their proper domestic role in a civilised community. By the end of the play, the mountain has become a place of nightmarish carnage, and yet the religious experiences which take place there are, at least when properly channelled through ritual, an integral part of the world of civilisation.

'Spaces between' are found not only in the physical world, but also in the mind. Several tragedies are shaped by the interplay of sanity and madness, though there are marked variations, from play to play, about what constitutes being out of one's 'right' mind, and what the causes and effects of such a condition might be. For Io in *Prometheus Bound* (attributed to Aeschylus), the distortion of her mind is provoked by the jealousy of Hera, whose agent is a fly which stings unremittingly. Being driven out of her senses is for Io analogous to other disastrous upheavals which she endures, namely metamorphosis from human to cow, and exile from her homeland as she wanders from continent to continent. Throughout all this, Io is a victim: she suffers but does not act. To some extent comparable is the madness of Cassandra in *Agamemnon*: she too has become a victim, having lost credibility as a prophetess after refusing to satisfy Apollo's lust. Io and Cassandra have in common the linguistic turmoil which the playwright lends to each: as they lurch in and out of frenzy, their utterances alternate between reasoned lucidity and tormented, wordless exclamation, whether it be the *otototoi popoi da* (ὀτοτοτοτοῖ πόποι δᾶ) of Cassandra (*Ag.* 1072) or Io's *io moi moi; he he'* (ἰώ μοί μοι ἒ ἔ, *Prom.* 742).

For Heracles in *The Madness of Heracles* and Agave in *Bacchae*, the sufferings produced by madness are even more 'tragic' (if we take that word to signify, this time, a quality of experience, rather than 'that which is represented in a tragedy'). The agent of Heracles' delusion is once more the jealous Hera (acting now through Lyssa, goddess of Madness); the result is Heracles' commission of acts not less terrible for being unwitting. As for Agave, the god she offends is Dionysus, whose divinity she, like her sisters, denies. Her punishment is to be maddened, and in that state to dismember her still-living son Pentheus. Both of these explorations of madness involve the agonising return of the protagonists to their normal condition of mind, a process guided in each case by their father. Heracles' guide is Amphitryon:

AMPH.   There: look at the bodies of these children, lying where they fell.

HER.   Ah! What is this that I see? Ah no!

AMPH.   They were no enemies, these children you fought against, my son.

HER.   Fought? Who killed these children?

AMPH.   You did, my son: your bow – and whichever god is responsible.

(*Her.* 1131–5)

For Agave, it is Cadmus who gently steers her mind onto the path of horrified recognition:

CADM.   Whose house did you go to when you were married?

AGAVE   You gave me to Echion, one of the Sown Men, so they said.

CADM.   What son was born to your husband in your home?

AGAVE   Pentheus, the product of my union with his father.

CADM.   Whose head are you holding in your arms?

AGAVE   A lion's head – at least, so said the woman who hunted it.

CADM.   Look directly at it: it is but a small labour to look upon it.

AGAVE   Ah! What am I looking at? What am I carrying in my hands?

CADM.   Gaze at it; learn the truth more clearly.

AGAVE   I see the greatest pain. I am wretched.

(*Ba.* 1273–82)

That Heracles was out of his 'right' mind when he slew his children is clear enough. But was Agave really deluded, while she was ecstatically worshipping Dionysus? How is 'true wisdom' to be defined? These are some of the many disturbing issues which *Bacchae* confronts.

In summary: tragedy does not occupy a comfortable space within accepted concepts and assumptions. The distinctive location of tragic myths is in the gaps between certainties. Tragedy is a place of edges and margins, an in-between territory where boundaries – literal and metaphorical – are ripe for exploration and contestation.

Divinities and mortals

I turn finally to a question fundamental to any attempt to clarify tragedy's distinctiveness within the mythical tradition: How are the gods portrayed?

The actions of divinities are highlighted in every narrative genre which retells Greek myths. In Homeric epic, and in all subsequent Greek epics down to Nonnus, the gods play a decisive part.[20] Hesiod's *Theogony* evidently centres on divinities, but the same poet's *Works and Days* also accords a crucial role to the gods, for example, through the interrelated fates of Prometheus and Pandora – the gods' gift to humanity. Pindaric praise-poetry – composed for victors in the Games celebrated for Zeus, Apollo, and Poseidon – depends on constant reference to the gods' transcendent power, as a foil and a paradigm for the deeds of mortal heroes and the victors who strive to emulate them. Herodotus' *Histories* may focus on the glorious exploits of mortals in the Greco-Persian War, but the backdrop to these events is a structure of religious assumptions anchored in the mythical past.[21] As for comedy, Aristophanes' plays take the existence of the gods as read, even if the nature of the reading allows for outrageous mockery of the rulers of the universe; half a millennium later, in a quite different comic vein, the dialogues of Lucian still mine the deeds of the gods in order to extract humour. To all this textual evidence must be added countless visual images from every period of classical antiquity, including objects as disparate as temple friezes, statues, coins, vases, and gems, all of which embody or are adorned by representations of divinities involved in mythological episodes.[22] Each of these genres, indeed each individual poet or artist, works from a particular perspective; the same is true of tragedy and tragedians. What, then, can we identify as distinctive about the tragic portrayal of gods and goddesses?

---

[20]   On Homer see, for example, Griffin (1980) 144–204; Kraus (1984); Kullmann (1992); Kearns (2004). On post-Homeric epic, Feeney (1991) is fundamental.

[21]   For an incisive contribution to this much-discussed topic, see Gould (2001) 359–77.

[22]   The first place to turn for information about visual evidence for Greek mythology is the indispensable *Lexicon Iconographicum Mythologiae Classicae*.

First, a crucial preliminary. It must be stressed that the gods only very rarely form the centrepiece of a tragedy.[23] They are, rather, its framework, its backdrop, that which is beyond and behind the action – action which is carried forward by the mortal heroes and heroines, who choose, are deluded, come to grief, struggle courageously, in fear or madness or generosity or hatred. Nevertheless, those human actions always resonate against a more-than-human background, and it is this which we shall now investigate.

No single 'voice' dominates this portrayal. Tragedy was competitive: in the contest at the City Dionysia, each playwright staged his own version of the mythological past, striving to be adjudged superior to his rivals. Just as the music, choreography, and costuming of tragedies varied between play and play, so too did the representation of the gods. This variety is evident even in the tiny proportion of the total tragic output constituted by the surviving plays. To take one example: the dramatic device found in so many Euripidean works, whereby, during the prologue or epilogue, a divinity speaks authoritatively from the stage apparatus known as 'the machine,' is by contrast unusual in extant Sophocles, where we encounter a predominant sense of the *difficulty* of determining the gods' views and intentions.[24] Even within a single work we find changing emphases. In Aeschylus' *Oresteia*, the first play of the trilogy offers a picture of divine action which is at best enigmatic and at worst baffling;[25] only in the third play do the gods stride forth upon the stage, as Apollo, the Furies, and Athena argue their cases and defend their individual, explicitly stated perspectives on the action.

Making every allowance for such variations, however, we may still plausibly suggest a number of generalisations about the gods in tragedy. I shall mention four.

Tragedy explores conflicts among the Gods

Emphasis on conflict between divinities is far from being unique to tragedy. We need only think of the cosmic wars narrated in Hesiod's *Theogony*; of the battles between the gods in the *Iliad*; of the struggle between Athena and Poseidon in the *Odyssey* over the homecoming of Odysseus; of the squabble between Hermes and Apollo in the *Homeric Hymn to Hermes*, concerning the theft of his brother's cattle by the newborn trickster god. Nevertheless, tragedy does show a marked interest in such conflicts – another aspect of tragedy's location in 'the space between.' Sometimes these conflicts are about power and sovereignty; sometimes they are generated by boundary disputes over the various provinces of interest with which the gods are associated. In both kinds of conflict, human beings play the role of victims.

A classic struggle over sovereignty is dramatised in *Prometheus Bound*, in which Zeus, the new and (as depicted by his adversaries) tyrannical ruler of the universe, is pitted against the no less divine Prometheus. For having dared to champion humanity in the face of Zeus' intention to annihilate them, Prometheus is subjected to an interminable and horrible punishment: fixed to a rock in the Caucasus, he will have his endlessly self-regenerating liver torn to shreds daily by an eagle. However, the Titan, whose suffering is compounded

---

[23]   Even in the case of *Prometheus Bound*, it could be argued that the central character is not simply a Titan, but also a kind of honorary hero, in virtue of his steadfast support for humankind.

[24]   The two appearances of divinities in the extant plays are those of Athena at the beginning of *Ajax* and the deified Heracles at the end of *Philoctetes*. For four other instances in the fragmentary plays, cf. the discussion in Parker (1999) 11–12.

[25]   On tragic 'bafflement,' see Buxton (1988).

by his knowledge of the full duration of his future torment (his name means 'Forethought'), refuses to defer to his tormentor, or to his tormentor's lackey:

HERMES   Bring yourself, rash fool, at last
            To think correctly in face of your present anguish.

PROM.   You exhort me in vain, as if you were talking to the waves.
            Never convince yourself that I, in fear
            Of Zeus' intent, will become feminised in my mind,
            Begging my greatly hated enemy, with hands
            Upturned in womanish supplication, to free me from these bonds.
            No, never.

(Prom. 999–1006)

One aspect of the cosmic power-struggle dramatised in *Prometheus Bound* is the clash between two successive generations of gods. The same is true of the *Oresteia*, though here the climactic struggle is fought not over the fate of humanity as a whole, but over the fate of a single individual. Orestes' act of matricide is defended by the 'younger' god Apollo and attacked by the 'older' Furies, the goddesses whose primordial authority to punish kin-murderers long predates the coming to power of the Olympians. When Apollo's side of the argument is confirmed by the casting vote of his fellow Olympian Athena, the Furies' resentment is couched in terms of generational conflict:

> You younger gods, you have ridden down
> The ancient laws, and torn them from my hands.

(Eum. 778–9)

Seniority was not the only reason for a divinity to assert a claim to honour, or to resent the behaviour of a fellow god. Differences in spheres of operation between deities also held ample potential for clashes of interest. In *Hippolytus*, the conflict between Artemis and Aphrodite works itself out through the lives and deaths of the family of Theseus; the goddesses themselves merely frame the action by appearing in the prologue (Aphrodite) and in the finale (Artemis). When the young hunter Hippolytus prefers the chaste pursuits associated with the virginal Artemis to the world of sexuality presided over by Aphrodite, his agonising death at the hands of the goddess of love leads Artemis, at the end of the play, to locate the action firmly within the context of the eternal rivalry between the two goddesses. As she says to the dying Hippolytus:

> Let be. For, even when you are under the dark of earth,
> Aphrodite's zealous anger shall not fall upon you
> Unavenged; your piety and noble spirit deserve requital.
> I, by my own hand, with these unerring arrows
> Shall wreak vengeance on the mortal she holds dearest.

(Hipp. 1417–22)

The time of gods is not the time of mortals. Human lives may come and go, but Artemis and Aphrodite will forever embody antithetical perceptions of sexuality.

In tragedy the gods' use of power can be openly criticised, yet at the same time that power must be acknowledged, because it is omnipresent and unavoidable

One feature of ancient Greek religion which can be particularly difficult to comprehend for a modern observer – especially one from a morally polarised monotheistic background – is its readiness to tolerate overt criticism of the gods' behaviour. In few works of Greek literature is the conduct of a god placed under more intense scrutiny than in Euripides' *Ion*. The plot narrates the consequences of the god's rape of Creusa, an event which she recollects in an aria of extraordinary bitterness:

> You came with hair flashing
> Gold, as I gathered
> Into my cloak flowers ablaze
> With their golden light.
> Clinging to my pale wrists
> As I cried for my mother's help
> You led me to a bed in a cave,
> A god and my lover,
> With no shame,
> Doing a favour to the Cyprian.
> In misery I bore you
> A son, whom in fear of my mother
> I placed in that bed
> Where you cruelly forced me.[26]

(*Ion* 887–901)

This is not, to be sure, the only view of Apollo which the play presents. In the opening scene a servant of the god's Delphic temple, a young man by the name of Ion – who (it will turn out) was born from Creusa's union with Apollo – associates this shrine and its patron deity with the qualities of brightness, healing, and, above all, purity – in a very literal sense (Ion reports that his duties include frightening away birds from the temple, and sweeping the floor of the shrine when it has been fouled). Moreover, after many twists and turns in the plot, mother and son will recognise each other, and Apollo's paternity will be cast in a positive light when Athena pronounces ex machina that 'Apollo then has managed all things well' (1595). However, such a view is expressed only after the goddess has excused Apollo's own attendance at the denouement in highly equivocal terms:

> I have come here in haste, sent by Apollo,
> Who did not think it right to come himself
> Into your sight, in case there should be blame
> For what has happened in the past ...

(1556–8)

When Creusa does at last utter praises of Apollo, it is because he has restored her son to her, not because she feels any differently about the sexual mistreatment which she herself received at the god's hands (1609–10). The weight of the play leaves Apolline morality in at best an ambiguous light.[27]

Though the criticisms of Apollo in *Ion* are especially sustained and strident, in other tragedies too the conduct of various divinities is presented, at least by some of the characters, as worthy of censure. Sophocles' *Women of Trachis* highlights the ritual importance of Zeus, in relation to his oracle at Dodona and his altar at Cenaeum; Zeus is the addressee of numerous invocations, prayers and oaths; Zeus holds sway over Mount Oeta, the location of the funeral pyre to which Heracles will be conveyed. But as an agent within the drama the father of the gods is noticeable by his complete absence, even when his son Heracles

[26] Adapted from translation by R. F. Willetts (*The Complete Greek Tragedies*, Chicago, 1958). (The other translations from tragedy in the present chapter – which make no claim to literary merit – are my own.)

[27] See chapter 3 of Zacharia (2003) for an explanation of the ambiguity of Apollo in this play.

cries out to him in anguish ('O Zeus, where in the world have I come?' – the hero's very first words, 983–4). Furthermore, although Heracles' expression 'Zeus in the stars' (1106) does not necessarily imply a tone of irony or resentment, the concluding reference by Heracles' son Hyllus to 'the great cruelty of the gods displayed in what is being done, gods who beget children and are called fathers but who can look upon such sufferings as these' (1266–9) can only be taken as a bitter accusation of a state of divinely ordered affairs which can tolerate such a waste of human life. And yet the seeds of a perception which counterbalances Hyllus' accusations are already present in the choral coda to the play:

'There is none of these things which is not Zeus.'

(*Trach.* 1278)[28]

important — The gods are *there*, and they are powerful: mortals ignore them at their peril.

Two other Sophoclean plays bring home this realisation with particular force. In *Ajax*, long before the eponymous hero made his attempt on the lives of the Greek commanders, he had (so a Newsbringer reports) made a reckless boast about his lack of need of divine help: 'Father, together with the gods even one who is nothing could win mastery; but I trust that I shall grasp this glory even without them!' (767–9). When seen in the light of Athena's concluding words in the opening scene ('Look, then, at such things, and never yourself speak an arrogant word against the gods ... For one day brings down all mortal things, and one day raises them up; the gods love those who think sensibly and hate the wicked' (127–33)), Ajax's arrogance shows a fatal misunderstanding of the proper relationship between mortals and gods. Equally heedless of the divine framework of human ethical behaviour is Creon in *Antigone*. Though Antigone herself might merely be using self-justifying rhetoric when she invokes 'the unwritten and unfailing laws of the gods' (454) to back her defiant burial of her traitorous brother Polynices, her position receives unequivocal support from the seer Tiresias, who describes how a horrific distortion of sacrificial practice has been precipitated by the exposing of Polynices' corpse (1016–22). Creon rescinds his decree forbidding burial, but too late; his refusal to comprehend how the world works culminates, not only in the death of Antigone, but also in the suicides of his own son and wife.

The omnipresence of divine influence on human action in tragedy does not negate the importance of human choice

Contrary to a common misperception of what Greek tragedy is like, tragic myths do not simply illustrate the inevitability of 'fate.' It is true that spectators and readers are often confronted with the subjecting of human beings to irresistible pressure from the gods: Heracles is sent mad by Hera, and Ajax by Athena; Phaedra does not choose to fall in love with her stepson – her passion is caused by Aphrodite; when Pentheus suddenly expresses a desire to see the maenads on Mount Cithaeron, it is because his mind has been invaded by Dionysus. But such cases must be set against those where the preponderant dramatic meaning is borne by actions which are squarely the consequence of human choice.

Two plays by Sophocles will exemplify this point. *Oedipus Tyrannus* has often been taken to be the paradigm of a work in which a human being is shown to be powerless against fortune. And yet the *plot* of the play – as opposed to the

---

[28]   In spite of the views of some scholars who assign this and the preceding three lines to Hyllus, I believe that the concluding voice of the play should be that of the chorus. For a justification of this view see Buxton (1988) 43–4.

mythical events, and in particular the oracular predictions, which constitute its *antecedents* – concerns a man who, whatever the cost, is bent upon two interrelated courses of action: at first, doing everything necessary to free his city from the pollution which has engulfed it; then, finding out his own identity, from the moment when this has been called into question. These courses of action are, to put it crudely, what the play is about; and they are the product of Oedipus' own choosing. Even when the now blind king cries out to the chorus that 'It was Apollo, friends, Apollo who brought about these cruel, cruel sufferings of mine!' (1329–30), not only is it unclear in what sense Apollo can possible be 'responsible' for what has occurred, but also Oedipus immediately goes on to maintain his own responsibility for the most shocking deed to have taken place within the time-frame of the play – his self-blinding ('And no other hand but mine struck my eyes, miserable that I am!' 1331–2). Whatever Apollo's oracle may have predicted, and whatever the putative relationship between such predictions and the eventual outcome, what is undeniable is that nothing in the play for a moment suggests that the truth was 'fated' to come out *in this way* – and it is the *manner* of the revelation of the truth which bears the weight of the work's dramatic significance.

Ajax offers another example of the overriding importance of human choice. The play begins with a demonstration of the cool, terrifying power of a divinity, Athena, first to drive a great hero mad, and then to mock and toy with him while he is in that condition: mighty Ajax ignominiously drips with the blood of sacrificial sheep, which he believes to be the blood of the Greek commanders whom he has, he thinks, put to death because (in his view) they had slighted him. But this state of helpless delusion, of powerless submission to the gods, soon gives way: initially to a consciousness of profound shame, and then to a decision to commit suicide. This decision is Ajax's alone: a decision taken with deliberation, like the deliberation with which he fixes in the earth the sword upon which he will fall (815–22). This is not the only crucial moment in the play for which the frame of reference is presented as completely within the hands of mortals. The rancorous debate about whether or not to allow burial to Ajax is driven exclusively by human emotions: anger, invective, loyalty, together with the ultimately decisive ingredient of self-interest added by Odysseus ('I too shall come to that need,' 1365). Athena's controlling presence left the stage long ago.

We have mentioned some cases where the gods evidently compel, and others where mortals unambiguously choose. But in still other cases tragic action occupies an intermediate ground between compulsion and choice. When, in *Agamemnon*, the chorus recalls the episode in which the Greek commander sacrificed his daughter Iphigenia in order to appease the anger of Artemis, the words they use are 'When he had put on the yoke-strap of necessity ...' (218). The paradox could not be more stark. Agamemnon *put on* the yoke-strap: it was a freely chosen act. But the yoke-strap which he put on was that of *necessity*: he had no choice. In representing the involvement of the gods in human life, tragic myths dwell on crises in which precisely this kind of paradox comes into focus.

The gods of tragedy are partially comprehensible, but aspects of them remain unfathomable, incommensurable, and unknowable

We have already met several instances in which the role and attitude of the gods is explicitly set out in the tragic action. Usually this is when the gods themselves appear on the scene and speak. Sometimes a divinity will set out the ground rules of the action only to depart for good (e.g., Athena in *Ajax*, Hermes in *Ion*, Athena and Poseidon in *The Trojan Women*); in other cases it will be left to

[margin note, left: *Similar to Phaedra's to die.*]

[margin note, right: *Don't the gods create situations where the humans are compelled to act. Whether they wish to or not.*]

a divinity at the end of a play to reintegrate the action into the audience's experience by referring to ritual (Artemis at the end of *Hippolytus*; Athena at the end of *Iphigenia in Tauris*) or by placing the events of the play in a wider mythical context (Castor in Euripides' *Electra*; Apollo in *Orestes*; Thetis in *Andromache*). Less often, divinities express their own point of view either throughout the action or at its midpoint, rather than at its beginning or end: Dionysus is on stage for much of *Bacchae*; Iris and Lyssa appear midway through *Heracles*; in *Eumenides* Apollo, the Furies, and Athena dominate the action in person.

But there are also cases in which that which receives emphasis is not the gods' visibility but their ultimate unpredictability and unfathomability. Of the three great Athenian tragedians, Euripides is the one who most insistently confronts spectators with what they seemingly could not have anticipated, so much so that a choral coda to this effect becomes a refrain in several of his works:

> Many are the shapes of the divinities;
> The gods bring many matters to surprising ends;
> The things we thought would happen do not happen;
> For the unexpected the god finds a way.
> Such was the conclusion of this story.[29]

Although it is usually impossible to determine precisely how far the spectators' background knowledge of mythology might have shaped their expectations, the manner in which Euripides introduces abrupt changes of dramatic direction suggests that even an audience acquainted with the general outlines of a myth might have reacted with astonishment: one example is the shocking arrival, in *Heracles*, of Lyssa goddess of madness; another – this time narrated as opposed to enacted – is the appearance of the monstrous bull from the sea as reported by the Newsbringer in *Hippolytus*. Such epiphanies sharpen an audience's sense of the gulf between mortal and divinity and dramatize the ultimate incommensurability of human with divine, even in a medium such as tragedy, in which god and mortal visibly tread the stage side by side.[30]

Fundamental though the unexpected may be to Euripidean dramaturgy, some of the most striking illustrations of the gods' unfathomability are to be found in works by the other two great tragedians. Near the beginning of *Agamemnon*, in the course of the chorus's monumental opening ode, the old men of Argos recall an episode from the outset of the Greek expedition against Troy. When the fleet was gathered at Aulis, two eagles were seen devouring a pregnant hare. The beginning of any military campaign was a sensitive and dangerous time, when – given a belief-system in which human and cosmic events were perceived to be mutually interconnected[31] – anything remotely unusual would be interpreted as ominous. The Greek seer Calchas duly read the strange occurrence as a sign: in this case, a sign of the displeasure of Artemis, who 'hates the eagles' feast' (138). But why Artemis should not only 'hate' this natural event, but also, if the Aeschylean text is taken to mean what it says,[32] take it as a justification for her subsequent injunction upon Agamemnon to sacrifice his own daughter – these matters are left opaque. At the origin of

---

[29] This passage occurs at the end of *Alcestis* (1159–63), *Andromache* (1284–8), *Helen* (1688–92), and *Bacchae* (1388–92), and, with a variation in the first line (which now runs: 'Zeus on Olympus is dispenser of many things'), *Medea* (1415–19).

[30] See Gould (2001) 203–34, on the incommensurability of the divine with the human.

[31] A thought-provoking study of 'interconnectedness' is to be found in Oudemans and Lardinois (1987).

[32] Compare Page (1957) xxv.

the action of the *Oresteia* is an enigma wrapped in a riddle; and at the centre of the enigma is the attitude of the gods towards humanity.

But it is neither Aeschylus nor Euripides who presents the purposes of the gods at their most inscrutable. The tragedian who does *this* is Sophocles; above all, in *Oedipus Tyrannus*. 'To the gods,' Oedipus maintains, just as the play is about to end (1519), 'I am most hateful.' If Oedipus *is* hated by the gods – as opposed to simply *feeling* that he is hated – then there must be a reason for it, since it would be out of keeping with everything we know of Greek religion if one or more divinities were to conceive an *unmotivated* hatred for a mortal. And the reason is not far to seek: the sending of the plague upon Thebes, an unambiguous indication of divine displeasure, follows inexorably upon the miasma generated by Oedipus' hideous transgressions. But that is far from being the end of the matter. For why should it have been precisely Oedipus, and not someone else, who has been put into the position, unwittingly, of incurring this displeasure? Did the gods will *that*? Nothing in the play entitles us to give an answer; indeed, nothing in the play raises the question at all. What the gods want for Oedipus remains as enigmatic at the end of the play as it was at the beginning.

Tragic myths offer a spectacle of a world in which mortals try to cope with events at the limits of or beyond their comprehension; even when these events *are* comprehended, they are comprehended too late. But Greek tragedy is not just a record of human inadequacy. The sense of limitation is offset by a whole range of positives: Oedipus' moral strength in his relentless quest for the truth; Neoptolemus' change of heart, when he decides to abandon his deception of Philoctetes and to take him home (even though the decision is eventually countermanded by Heracles); Theseus' generosity of spirit towards Heracles and Oedipus; the linguistic sublimity of Ajax and Cassandra when they gain insight into how the world is.[33] Most of the characteristics which I have described as 'distinctively tragic' can be paralleled in one or more other genres of myth-telling. But the combination of all of them in tragedy is what makes the genre unique. It is nothing less than an exploration, through the medium of traditional tales, of the place of humanity in the world, an exploration both popular and profound. Of all the ancient forms of myth-telling, only the Homeric poems can rival the tragedies in their continuing power to hold, enchant, shock, and unsettle.[34]

Works cited in the text

Bremmer, J.N. (1997) "Why did Medea kill her brother Apsyrtos?" in J.J. Clauss and S.I. Johnston, eds. *Medea: Essays on Medea in Myth, Literature, Philosophy, and Art*, 83–100. Princeton.

Burian, P. (1997) "Myth into *muthos*: the shaping of tragic plot," in P.E. Easterling, ed., *The Cambridge Companion to Greek Tragedy*, 178–208. Cambridge.

Burton, R.W.B. (1962) *Pindar's Pythian Odes: Essays in Interpretation*. Oxford.

Buxton, R. (1988) "Bafflement in Greek Tragedy." *Mètis* 3: 41–51.

Buxton, R. (1992) "Imaginary Greek Mountains." *JHS* 112: 1–15.

Buxton, R. (2002) "Time, Space and Ideology: Tragic Myths and the Athenian Polis," in J.A. López Férez, ed., *Mitos en la literatura griega arcaica y clásica*, 175–89. Madrid.

---

[33]   *Aj.* 669–77 and *Agam.* 1327–30.

[34]   Several friends and colleagues have helped me to think through the issues developed in this chapter. In particular, I must single out Michael Lurje, whose detailed and thoughtful comments enabled me to remove at least some of the shortcomings in my argument.

Buxton, R. (2006) "Weapons and Day's White Horses: The Language of *Ajax*," in I.J.F. de Jong and A. Rijksbaron, eds., *Sophocles and the Greek Language. Aspects of Diction, Syntax, and Pragmatics*, 13–23. Leiden.

Calame, C. (2000a) "Iô, les Danaïdes, l'extérieur et l'inflexion tragique," in C. Calame, *Poétique des mythes dans la Grèce antique,* 117–44. Paris.

Crotty, K. (1982) *Song and Action: The Victory Odes of Pindar.* Baltimore.

Csapo, E. and W.J. Slater (1994) *The Context of Ancient Drama.* Ann Arbor, MI.

Feeney, D.C. (1991) *The Gods in Epic: Poets and Critics of the Classical Tradition.* Oxford.

Gantz, T. (1993) *Early Greek Myth: A Guide to Literary and Artistic Sources.* Baltimore/ London.

Gould, J. (2001) *Myth, Ritual, Memory and Exchange: Essays in Greek Literature and Culture.* Oxford.

Griffin, J. (1980) *Homer on Life and Death.* Oxford.

Halliwell, S. (2002) "Mimesis and the Best Life," in *The Aesthetics of Mimesis: Ancient Texts and Modern Problems*, 98–117. Princeton.

Kearns, E. (2004) "The gods in the Homeric epics," in R. Fowler, ed., *The Cambridge Companion to Homer*, 59–73. Cambridge.

Kraus, W. (1984) "Götter und Menschen bei Homer," in *Aus Allem Eines. Studien zur antiken Geistesgeschichte*, 15–27. Heidelberg. (Reprinted from *Wiener Humanistische Blätter* 18 [1976]: 20–32.)

Kullmann, W. (1992) "Gods and Men in the *Iliad* and *Odyssey*," in *Homerische Motive: Beiträge zur Entstehung, Eigenart und Wirkung von Ilias und Odyssee*, 243–63. Stuttgart. (Reprinted from *Harv. Stud.* 89 [1985]: 1–23.)

Lurje, M. (2004) *Die Suche nach der Schuld: Sophokles' Oedipus Rex, Aristoteles' Poetik und das Tragödienverständnis der Neuzeit.* Munich/Leipzig.

Moreau, A. (1994) *Le Mythe de Jason et Médée: Le va-nu-pied et la sorcière.* Paris.

O'Higgins, D.M. (1997) "Medea as Muse: Pindar's *Pythian* 4," in J.J. Clauss and S.I. Johnston, eds., *Medea: Essays on Medea in Myth, Literature, Philosophy, and Art*, 103–26. Princeton.

Oudemans, T.C.W. and Lardinois, A.P.M.H. (1987) *Tragic Ambiguity: Anthropology, Philosophy and Sophocles'* Antigone. Leiden.

Page, D.L. (1957) *Euripides*: Medea. Oxford.

Parker, R. (1999) "Through a Glass Darkly: Sophocles and the Divine," in J. Griffin, ed., *Sophocles Revisited. Essays Presented to Sir Hugh Lloyd-Jones*, 11–30. Oxford.

Pickard-Cambridge, A. (1968) *The Dramatic Festivals of Athens*, second ed., revised by J. Gould and D.M. Lewis. Oxford.

Redfield, J.M. (1975) *Nature and Culture in the Iliad: The Tragedy of Hector.* Chicago.

Segal, C. (1986) *Pindar's Mythmaking: The Fourth Pythian Ode.* Princeton.

Willetts, R.F. (1958) *The Complete Greek Tragedies.* Chicago.

Zacharia K. (2003) *Converging Truths: Euripides' Ion and the Athenian Quest for Self-Definition.* Leiden.

Secondary Source 1.2   Oliver Taplin, 'Escaping the "philodramatist" versus "iconocentric" polarity'

(Source: Taplin, O. (2007) *Pots and Plays: Interactions between Tragedy and Greek Vase-painting of the Fourth Century BC*, Los Angeles, CA, J. Paul Getty Museum, pp. 22–6 and selected references from pp. 296–301)

This book is the first of its kind to be produced in thirty-five years—in some important ways it is entirely the first of its kind. A central reason for this is that it has become hotly contested what kind of relationship vase-painting and tragedy have to each other. More than that, it is hotly contested whether they have any significant relationship at all. And the approach that rejects any relationship between tragedy and visual art, or at least strongly questions or problematizes any connection, has become the dominant position in the last two decades. So there has not been a lot of recent work drawing the two forms together; what does exist has usually been pulled to pieces by the strategies of demolition deployed by those opposed to making these connections. I am, then, taking a position in this book that goes against the current flow of the tide. But I must emphasize that I am not attempting this by going back to the old "unfashionable" position, nor by advocating some compromise between the two poles: I am coming at the question from a different angle, which accepts neither of the current positions.

The only clear way to bring out what is at issue is to set out the two embattled camps in their extreme forms. The approach that argues for—or, all too often, takes for granted—a close relationship between the paintings and a pre-existent play is usually set up as the "old" view. Guiliani has more neutrally dubbed it the "philodramatic" position.[1] The key assumption of this viewpoint is that the painting is secondary to the work of literature, ancillary to it, and to be interpreted in light of it. The usual language speaks of "inspired by," "derived from", and in its strongest terms—terms that make its opponents see red—the painting is said to "show" or "illustrate" the play. This philodramatic position, which goes back to the nineteenth-century studies of the newly discovered vases,[2] tends to be embraced, understandably enough, by those whose first interest is the plays, and by those who have come to the vases through philology and literature. It is, broadly speaking, espoused by the three big books on the subject: Séchan (1926);[3] Trendall and Webster (1971), who actually use the word "Illustrations" in their title; and Kossatz-Deissmann (1978). It also to a considerable extent underlies the methods and organization of the great project of *LIMC*, although it is not by any means supported by all the relevant articles. In the last twenty-five years, some leading scholars, including Margot Schmidt and Richard Green, have been much more careful and sceptical in relating the vases to the plays, while still proposing that a serious relationship may be valid. And Trendall himself retreated a long way from the overconfidence of the 1971 book. But the tide has been running so strongly the other way that even circumspect collocations of art and literature have often met with polemical and impatient rejection.

Before going further, it will be best to set out the opposing "new" position, the "iconocentric" school.[4] Actually, this too has a long pedigree in the age-old

---

[1]   Giuliani 1996, 72; in Taplin 1993, 21, I called these advocates "philologist-iconographers."

[2]   For some bibliography, see Giuliani 1996, 72 n. 4.

[3]   On the title page, "Études sur la tragédie grecque" is printed in a far larger font than "dans ses rapports avec la céramique."

[4]   Giuliani 1996, 74–75; in Taplin 1993, 21, I called these advocates "autonomous iconologists."

contest between the visual arts and verbal literature (reflected most famously by Gotthold Ephraim Lessing's *Laokoön*, 1766), and their rival claims to superior wisdom and access to truth; the scholarship of this position, with application to Greek drama and vase-painting, also goes back to the nineteenth century.[5] But it has made its mark most clearly in recent times, through Jean-Marc Moret's fine book on the iconography of the Sack of Troy.[6] This view has become the dominant orthodoxy in Francophone scholarship and is now becoming widespread.[7]

Moret shows with a wealth of detail how the vase-painters have their own language for telling stories; how certain poses and tableaux and patterns of composition are employed again and again in putting together a wide variety of mythological narratives. The painting is derived, it is then claimed, not from drama nor from any other literature, but from the repertoire and techniques of the painters themselves. The paintings are, so this school maintains, "self-sufficient." They do not need literature in order to be understood and appreciated: "far from being banal illustrations of tragedy, they reflect their own new conception of myth."[8] Many scholars would also wish to emphasize the place of oral, non-literary tellings of myths. While not every advocate of this view would insist that the paintings have nothing whatsoever to do with tragedy, they do insist, in strong opposition to the philodramatists, that any relationship to any particular play is distanced and dispensable. This, I shall argue, is to throw the baby out with the bathwater: in rejecting all the unacceptable assumptions of the philodramatists, they have thrown out the interesting and important connections that *are* worth exploring—with due caution and perspective.

The philodramatic position in its strong form is quite simply untenable. Not only are there not, with very rare exceptions, any pictures of tragic theatrical performances ..., the vases are not even pictures of scenes from the plays, let alone illustrations. Many of the vases that are the strongest candidates for being "tragedy related" show episodes that were narrated by messengers and not enacted onstage (on this, see further below). Many include extra figures who have no identifiable role in the play, and many combine characters and incidents that belong in separate scenes of the play. Almost all show young men naked, as was the convention in heroic art but was almost certainly not the convention in the theater.

And there are often more detailed discrepancies or mismatches between the painting and the play. Philodramatists tend to play down these "contraindications": but they should be taken seriously as possible warnings that the painting has little or nothing to do with the play that is allegedly being invoked. On the other hand, the discrepancies may be too unimportant to outweigh the positive signs, the "pro-indications." [...]

It is noticeable that in their arguments, iconocentrists tend to seize on any discrepancy, however slight, to refute any claimed connection—they can, on occasion, "out-pedant the pedants." But due consideration should be given to other explanations, which may well be more plausible than a total prohibition

---

[5]   Notably Robert 1881; cf. Metzger 1965.

[6]   Moret 1975, further exemplified by Moret 1984 on the iconography of Oedipus and the Sphinx.

[7]   The "interpretation" sections by Christian Aellen in Aellen-Cambitoglou-Chamay 1986 are particularly important because they reject, or do not even raise, any connection between tragedy and the vases published there, which were collected at that time in Geneva. Several are important for this work, and no fewer than eight of them will be discussed later; these are nos. 4, 16, 39, 68, 88, 93, 99, 108.

[8]   Aellen in Aellen-Cambitoglou-Chamay 1986, 268, slightly paraphrased.

of relationship between art and literature. These include, for example, technical and compositional and iconographic considerations—factors of the kind that are, in fact, emphasized by the iconocentrics themselves when it suits them. Another might be performance traditions: later reperformances were under no obligation to stick exactly to the implied "stage directions" that are built into the texts of the original performances at Athens.[9] The actors do not even seem to have observed any strong obligation to stick to the words of the original text, leading to Lykourgos' attempt to impose an authorized version [...] Evidently it rapidly became the iconographic convention, for example, to represent Erinyes (Furies) with wings, which contradicts the text of Aeschylus' *Oresteia*. It is more than likely that this had become the performance convention also, although whether it was the painters or the performers who first gave the Erinyes wings, we are not able to say. But, even allowing these reservations about iconocentric attacks, it has to be recognized that these paintings are not *pictures of play*; they do not display any sense of obligation to be faithful to the detail of texts (and, a fortiori, they cannot be securely used to reconstruct lost texts).

The popularity of mythological paintings that draw images from messenger speeches is interesting in this connection. At first sight one might not expect such speeches to be taken up in tragedy-related paintings, since the events were not seen onstage. But, in fact, they supply the subject of a significant proportion of the most plausible instances.[10] The visualization of the myth is informed by the vivid tragic messenger, and those who witnessed the tragedy can "see" the scene the messenger described. The vase does not show them what they saw onstage, but the myth as they envisaged it under the spell of the play.

The iconocentric position, on the other hand, even in an extreme form, is not simply disprovable. Strictly speaking, it is tenable. It is true that visual artists of myth build up their own vocabulary for telling stories; furthermore, they can build up their own versions of stories. It is also true that, generally speaking, the paintings can stand on their own feet; they are self-sufficient, they do not need a tragedy or any other verbal version of the story in order to have meaning. But it is my thesis that the viewers of these vases, with their experiences of mythological narratives, have to be brought into the picture. It is not the mentality of the producer/painter that is at issue so much as that of the perceiver. Once that is allowed, it should be registered that the interest for the viewer of some of the paintings in question is severely curtailed without a particular tragic narrative to inform them.

[...]

So we come to my crucial departure from the iconocentric position. The artistic language of the paintings—recurrent postures, etc.—may not need a particular version of the myth in order to engage a viewer, but the works are much informed by the narrative of the myth in question. The specific version makes the painting more powerful. If it is true that the performance of tragedy was one of the main means through which the viewers of these vases knew the myths, [...] then their familiarity with the tragic telling would have, in at least some cases, informed their appreciation of the vase. It would have *enriched* its meaning for them. The vases are not, then, according to my approach, "banal illustrations," nor are they dependent on or derived from the plays. They are

---

[9]   Those "original" stage directions were a central subject of Taplin 1977 and 1978.

[10]   Thus, of those pictures in part 2 that are variously related to surviving plays of Euripides (nos. 31–54), more than a third connect with messenger speeches.

informed by the plays; they mean more, and have more interest and depth, for someone who knows the play in question. That is the core of what I mean by calling a vase "related to tragedy."

I shall try to give more substance to this idea of "enriching" or "informing" by means of a simplified analogy drawn from another period—I offer it for purely heuristic purposes and will not cite any actual manifestations. Suppose that we have a series of paintings that all evidently share the same basic iconography: they show a young man in black, with a white blouse, staring at a skull. Within that basic composition, which (let us suppose) draws on an iconographic tradition of contemplation scenes, there are many variants. In most he stands, but occasionally he sits; in most, but not quite all, the man has a companion standing behind him; in nearly all, but not all, there is an open grave with earth and bones lying around it; and in most, but not all, there is a grave digger, and sometimes two grave diggers, down in the grave. In some of the pictures, there are indications of a church; in a few a boat can be seen on the sea in the distance; and in a few a funeral procession can be seen approaching. Now, at least some of these paintings are (again, let us suppose) fine works of art in their own right; they convey a vivid sense of youth and decay and of the prospect of death in life. They do not *need* the Hamlet story, let alone Shakespeare's text. But even a rudimentary recollection of the Shakespeare, whether from reading or performance, will surely inform and enrich the picture. "Alas, poor Yorick! I knew him, Horatio ..." The grave digger identifies himself; but it is the Shakespeare that identifies the skull, the loyal Horatio, the funeral procession. It is important to register that none of these (imagined) paintings is presented as the play in performance: they include no painted scenery, lights, make-up, actors, and so forth. At the same time, one might note that the white blouse is drawn from a much-loved performance tradition; it is not essential to the scene and is not indicated by the text of the play. (I shall return to this matter of performance in the next section.)

The sine qua non of this iconography is the young man with the skull; the open grave is standard but not essential. If the man is old, then this is not Hamlet (it might be Saint Jerome). If he is looking at a decapitated head, it is not Hamlet (perhaps something to do with John the Baptist?). If he is looking at a leg bone, not a skull, then that is not Hamlet, unless perhaps it is some kind of secondary variant. The same would be true if the scene were set indoors. If the man is in colorful clothes, this is still presumably Hamlet, though it might jar with the picture that many have derived from the performance tradition. If Hamlet has two or more companions, that might also offend purists, but he is still presumably Hamlet; so too if he is holding two skulls, one in either hand. These are the kind of variations and discrepancies that (mutatis mutandis) we shall encounter again and again in part 2 of this book. The pro- and contraindications have to be weighed against each other.

There are all sorts of ways in which this Hamlet analogy does not fully match the situation in the fourth-century B.C. Greek world, but I hope it makes clearer the basic point that paintings can be informed by plays. They mean more to those who recall the story as it is told in a particular play than they do to those who do not. The painting can be enjoyed through knowing some other narrative of the "myth," but it is less enriched. It is by coming at the issue through the *viewers* of the vases that I believe I have eluded the polarization between philodramatists and iconocentrics. Whatever it was that the viewers wanted from the mythological paintings, it was clearly not pictures of plays and not pictures of tragic performances. But, given the presence of tragic theater in their lives, there was no reason for them to keep these two art forms running separately along parallel lines.

Works cited in the text

C. Aellen, A. Cambitoglou, and J. Chamay. *Le peintre de Darius et son milieu: Vases grecs d'Italie méridionale*. Geneva: Association Hellas et Roma, 1986.

Giuliani, L. "Rhesus between Dream and Death: On the Relation of Image to Literature in Apulian Vase-Painting." *BICS* 41 (1996): 71–86.

Kossatz-Deissmann, A. *Dramen des Aischylos auf west-griechischen Vasen*. Mainz: von Zabern, 1978.

Metzger, H. *Recherches sur l'imagerie*. Paris: de Boccard, 1965.

Moret, J.M. *L'Ilioupersis dans la céramique italiote: Les mythes et leur expression figurée au IVe siècle*. Geneva: Institut Suisse de Rome, 1975.

Moret, J.M. *Oedipe, la Sphinx et les Thébains: Essai de mythologie iconographique*. Geneva: Institut Suisse de Rome, 1984.

Robert, C. *Bild und Lied: Archäologische Beiträge zur Geschichte der griechischen Heldensage*. Berlin: Weidmann, 1881.

Séchan, L. *Études sur la tragédie grecque dans ses rapports avec la céramique*. Paris: Champion, 1926.

Taplin, O. *The Stagecraft of Aeschylus*. Oxford: Oxford Univ. Press, 1977.

Taplin, O. *Greek Tragedy in Action*. London: Routledge, 1978.

Trendall, A.D. and T.B.L. Webster. *Illustrations of Greek Drama*. London: Phaidon, 1971.

Secondary Source 1.3   Alan Cameron, 'Mythology and culture'

(Source: Cameron, A. (2004) *Greek Mythography and the Roman World*, New York, Oxford University Press, pp. 220–4)

The role of Greek mythology in the culture that defined and unified the elite of the Greco-Roman world is so immense that it tends to be taken for granted.[1] It would be easy to fill an entire book and still not do justice to the subject. Mythology in Strabo and Pausanias alone (not to mention Diodorus) would fill substantial dissertations. This chapter simply collects a few illustrations from a variety of different fields.

We tend to think of myth as the subject matter par excellence of poetry. The first century was the golden age of Roman poetry but saw a low ebb for Greek poetry. The Greek world was dominated by the so-called Second Sophistic; it was the age rather of epideictic oratory. But sophists no less than poets were expected to adorn their work with clever and appropriate mythological allusions. Modern readers are less struck by all these allusions than perhaps they should be, largely because the only people who are still able to read the imperial sophists are classical scholars, who have effortlessly absorbed the necessary mythological knowledge in the course of their own study of the classics and so take them for granted.

---

[1]   Not directly mentioned, for example, in Simon Swain, *Hellenism and Empire: Language, Classicism and Power in the Greek World, AD 50–250* (Oxford 1996); see (briefly) W. Liebeschuetz, "Pagan Mythology in the Christian Empire," *International Journal of the Classical Tradition* 2 (1995), 193–208.

While strongly recommending mythological allusions for the budding orator, Menander Rhetor warns that he has less license than the poets and should dispatch them as briefly as possible.[2] But this did not mean that either writer or reader needed to know less. Quite the contrary; allusions had to be picked up from a single, preferably paradoxical detail. One handbook suggests the Alcestis story to illustrate the importance of choosing the right wife: that was how Admetus escaped his destined death![3] In four lines the Michigan dictionary gives just what a member of the second-century elite needed to know about the shearwater story: the names and parentage of the unfortunate girls before their transformation, a picturesque detail (the crows), and a classical citation. On this basis he could casually allude to shearwaters hating crows "as Aeschylus says."

Display oratory continued in importance down into Byzantine times, but the third century also saw a major revival of mythological poetry, beginning with Dionysius Periegetes and the prolific father-and-son team of Nestor and Peisandros of Laranda,[4] a movement that culminated in the 48-book *Dionysiaca* of Nonnus in the fifth century. Even epigrams inscribed on the statue bases of local dignitaries and imperial officials are full of mythological references.[5]

Greek mythology was the cultural currency of even the remotest corners of the Roman world. One of the most famous sophists of the mid-fourth century was Prohaeresius, a man of Armenian family born in Cappadocia (incidentally a Christian) who held a chair in Athens. Around 357 the Emperor Constans offered him any reward he wanted for his achievements, and Prohaeresius asked for the gift of a few islands to provide Athens with a corn supply. The gift had to be confirmed by the praetorian prefect of Illyricum, at the time a man called Anatolius, born in Beirut. Prohaeresius gathered a number of his supporters to address the prefect on his behalf, but instead Anatolius called on Prohaeresius to speak extempore himself. So Prohaeresius spoke off the cuff "about the imperial gift, and cited Celeus and Triptolemus and how Demeter sojourned among men that she might bestow on them the gift of corn. With that famous narrative he combined the tale of the generosity of Constans, and very speedily he invested the occurrence with the splendour and dignity of ancient legend."[6]

Anyone with any pretensions to culture knew Greek myths in the same way that medieval Christians knew Bible stories. Yet while Christianity superseded paganism as the religion of the Roman and post-Roman world, educated people continued to know the stories of Greek myth as well as they knew the Bible. For all its deep Christian piety, it would be impossible to make head or tail of much Byzantine literature without extensive knowledge of classical mythology.[7] As we have seen, our knowledge of many details on the oldest myths comes from scholia laboriously copied into Byzantine manuscripts of classical poets. By far the longest subject category in the index to Herbert Hunger's great work on Byzantine secular literature is "Mythologie."[8]

---

[2]   339. 1, p. 17 Russell-Wilson.

[3]   Ps-Dionysius p. 264 Radermacher, translated in Russell-Wilson, *Menander Rhetor* p. 367.

[4]   For a brief account, Ewen Bowie, "Greek Poetry in the Antonine Age," in D. A. Russell (ed.), *Antonine Literature* (Oxford 1990), 53–90.

[5]   L. Robert, *Épigrammes du Bas-Empire* (Paris 1948), passim.

[6]   Eunap. *Vit. Soph.* 492.

[7]   For a single, albeit striking example, K. Demoen, *Pagan and Biblical Exempla in Gregory Nazianzen* (Turnout 1996), 211–31.

[8]   *Die hochsprachliche profane Literatur der Byzantiner* i–ii (Munich 1978).

But it was by no means in and for literature alone that mythology was important. A comprehensive knowledge of Greek myth was essential for anyone who wanted to hold his head up in polite society, throughout the length and breadth of the Roman world. Not just for reading the classics or identifying allusions in contemporary poets and orators but for understanding the conversation of peers, scenes on wall paintings, silver plate, mosaic floors, and (above all) the decoration of the sarcophagi in which loved ones were now interred.[9] The most important comprehensive aid to understanding the role of art in ancient society to appear in recent years is the (happily now complete) *Lexicon Iconographicum Mythologiae Classicae* (1981–97).

Given the sheer number of surviving examples (several thousand), the case of sarcophagus decoration raises the question of the reading of mythological scenes in a particularly acute form. Among the most popular are Dionysus (more than 430 examples), Meleager (200 from Rome alone), the Muses (200), Endymion (120 from Rome alone), the rape of Persephone (90), Amazons (60), Heracles (40) and Hippolytus (40). The meaning of such scenes in this context has been long debated. It is naturally tempting to read them as evoking some aspect of the life of the deceased or the promise of life after death, and many learned and ingenious studies have been devoted to this pursuit. Many of the issues for and against were summarized in Arthur Darby Nock's famous critical review of Franz Cumont's *Recherches sur le symbolisme funéraire des Romains* (Paris 1942).[10] As Nock remarked, while it is easy to see funerary significance in (say) the death of Actaeon or the Niobids or Dionysiac processions, there are many scenes that seem utterly inappropriate. Notably the 16 Medea sarcophagi, all featuring the murder of her children.[11] There are also 40-odd Orestes sarcophagi, divided fairly evenly between two scenes: Orestes killing Aegisthus and Clytemnestra and (evidently based on Euripides's *Iphigeneia among the Taurians*) Orestes and Pylades with Iphigeneia fighting Scythians to board a ship.[12] Neither seems at all appropriate for a sarcophagus.

Paul Zanker has recently argued that preoccupation with the afterlife is a modern perspective. In the second and third centuries sarcophagi were a focus of celebrations by the family of the deceased and so reflected the concerns of the living rather than the expectations of the dead.[13] The deceased is sometimes represented reclining on a couch, cup in hand, with an inscription exhorting his survivors to drink and be merry.[14] This may be the simplest explanation for the overwhelming dominance of Dionysiac themes, with their festive processions. Both here and in a great many Meleager sarcophagi, outdoor picnics are a favorite theme, perhaps reflecting real-life banquets round the sarcophagus. Meleager was popular because so many members of the elite were keen hunters; a woman might be represented as Persephone simply because "she was beautiful and charming like Persephone when Hades seized her." Rather than

---

[9]   For a comprehensive study of sarcophagi reliefs myth by myth, G. Koch and H. Sichtermann, *Römische Sarkophage* (Munich 1982); M. Koorbojian, *Myth, Meaning and Memory on Roman Sarcophagi* (Berkeley 1995); D. Grassinger, *Die mythologischen Sarkophage I: Achill ... Amazonen* (Berlin 1999), and H. Sichtermann, *Die mythologischen Sarkophage II: Apollon ... Grazien* (Berlin 1992), with M. Koortbojian, *JRA* 8 (1995), 421–34.

[10]   Nock, "Sarcophagi and Symbolism," *AJA* 50 (1946), 140–70 = *Essays on Religion and the Ancient World* ii (Oxford 1972), 606–41.

[11]   Koch and Sichtermann 1982, 159–61.

[12]   Koch and Sichtermann 1982, 170–1.

[13]   Zanker, "Die mythologischen Sarkophagenreliefs und ihre Betrachter," *Sitzungsberichte d. Bay. Akad.* 2000, 2 (Munich 2000), 1–47.

[14]   See Zanker 2000, 9–14.

classifying mythological sarcophagi iconographically by myth (Zanker suggests), perhaps we should classify them by the message they were intended to convey. Here just as in the poets and orators or indeed the mosaic floors or domestic wall paintings of the age, the stories of mythology are used "not only because they are familiar but because they are exemplary, because they illustrate and explain something about the order of the world and the relationship of gods and men."[15]

More simply still, according to Nock,[16]

> We are left with classicism and culture as a prime factor when we look at these representations or at a grave-altar with the tale of Pasiphaë. ... Any scene out of the heritage of antiquity, whether it was pathetic or not, whether it was in any sense capable of being regarded as parallel to personal experience or hopes for the future, gave dignity.

This is no less true of the frequent mythological allusions and comparisons in funerary poetry, in some ways (as Nock saw) more obviously so when badly done. One delightful example is the often unmetrical 52-line inscription in which an evidently grief-stricken man mourns for his freedwoman concubine. Among other things he gives a detailed physical description of this incomparable woman: fair complexion, golden hair, small breasts, skin carefully depilated, and what about her legs (*quid crura*?)? "Atalanta's figure would be comic beside hers." She kept her quarrelsome sons together, like Pylades and Orestes. How different what Helen did to Troy! While the execution is grotesque, the intention is clear. The writer must have believed that his mythological comparisons created a patina of classical dignity.

Secondary Source 1.4   Sir James George Frazer, *The Golden Bough*, chapters 1 and 24

(Source: Frazer, Sir J.G. (1949 [1922]) *The Golden Bough: A Study In Magic And Religion* (abridged edn), London, Palgrave Macmillan, pp. 1–9, 264–83)

Chapter 1

The King of the Wood

§ I. *Diana and Virbius.*—Who does not know Turner's picture of the Golden Bough? The scene, suffused with the golden glow of imagination in which the divine mind of Turner steeped and transfigured even the fairest natural landscape, is a dream-like vision of the little woodland lake of Nemi—"Diana's Mirror," as it was called by the ancients. No one who has seen that calm water, lapped in a green hollow of the Alban hills, can ever forget it. The two characteristic Italian villages which slumber on its banks, and the equally Italian palace whose terraced gardens descend steeply to the lake, hardly break the stillness and even the solitariness of the scene. Dian herself might still linger by this lonely shore, still haunt these woodlands wild.

In antiquity this sylvan landscape was the scene of a strange and recurring tragedy. On the northern shore of the lake, right under the precipitous cliffs on which the modern village of Nemi is perched, stood the sacred grove and sanctuary of Diana Nemorensis, or Diana of the Wood. The lake and the grove were sometimes known as the lake and grove of Aricia. But the town of Aricia (the modern La Riccia) was situated about three miles off, at the foot of the

---

[15]   Jasper Griffin, *The Mirror of Myth: Classical Themes and Variations* (London 1986), 17.

[16]   Nock 1946, 166 = 1972, 637.

Alban Mount, and separated by a steep descent from the lake, which lies in a small crater-like hollow on the mountain side. In this sacred grove there grew a certain tree round which at any time of the day, and probably far into the night, a grim figure might be seen to prowl. In his hand he carried a drawn sword, and he kept peering warily about him as if at every instant he expected to be set upon by an enemy. He was a priest and a murderer; and the man for whom he looked was sooner or later to murder him and hold the priesthood in his stead. Such was the rule of the sanctuary. A candidate for the priesthood could only succeed to office by slaying the priest, and having slain him, he retained office till he was himself slain by a stronger or a craftier.

The post which he held by this precarious tenure carried with it the title of king; but surely no crowned head ever lay uneasier, or was visited by more evil dreams, than his. For year in year out, in summer and winter, in fair weather and in foul, he had to keep his lonely watch, and whenever he snatched a troubled slumber it was at the peril of his life. The least relaxation of this vigilance, the smallest abatement of his strength of limb or skill of fence, put him in jeopardy; grey hairs might seal his death-warrant. To gentle and pious pilgrims at the shrine the sight of him might well seem to darken the fair landscape, as when a cloud suddenly blots the sun on a bright day. The dreamy blue of Italian skies, the dappled shade of summer woods, and the sparkle of waves in the sun, can have accorded but ill with that stern and sinister figure. Rather we picture to ourselves the scene as it may have been witnessed by a belated wayfarer on one of those wild autumn nights when the dead leaves are falling thick, and the winds seem to sing the dirge of the dying year. It is a sombre picture, set to melancholy music—the background of forest showing black and jagged against a lowering and stormy sky, the sighing of the wind in the branches, the rustle of the withered leaves under foot, the lapping of the cold water on the shore, and in the foreground, pacing to and fro, now in twilight and now in gloom, a dark figure with a glitter of steel at the shoulder whenever the pale moon, riding clear of the cloud-rack, peers down at him through the matted boughs.

The strange rule of this priesthood has no parallel in classical antiquity, and cannot be explained from it. To find an explanation we must go farther afield. No one will probably deny that such a custom savours of a barbarous age, and, surviving into imperial times, stands out in striking isolation from the polished Italian society of the day, like a primaeval rock rising from a smooth-shaven lawn. It is the very rudeness and barbarity of the custom which allow us a hope of explaining it. For recent researches into the early history of man have revealed the essential similarity with which, under many superficial differences, the human mind has elaborated its first crude philosophy of life. Accordingly, if we can show that a barbarous custom, like that of the priesthood of Nemi, has existed elsewhere; if we can detect the motives which led to its institution; if we can prove that these motives have operated widely, perhaps universally, in human society, producing in varied circumstances a variety of institutions specifically different but generically alike; if we can show, lastly, that these very motives, with some of their derivative institutions, were actually at work in classical antiquity; then we may fairly infer that at a remoter age the same motives gave birth to the priesthood of Nemi. Such an inference, in default of direct evidence as to how the priesthood did actually arise, can never amount to demonstration. But it will be more or less probable according to the degree of completeness with which it fulfils the conditions I have indicated. The object of this book is, by meeting these conditions, to offer a fairly probable explanation of the priesthood of Nemi.

I begin by setting forth the few facts and legends which have come down to us on the subject. According to one story the worship of Diana at Nemi was instituted by Orestes, who, after killing Thoas, king of the Tauric Chersonese (the Crimea), fled with his sister to Italy, bringing with him the image of the Tauric Diana hidden in a faggot of sticks. After his death his bones were transported from Aricia to Rome and buried in front of the temple of Saturn, on the Capitoline slope, beside the temple of Concord. The bloody ritual which legend ascribed to the Tauric Diana is familiar to classical readers; it is said that every stranger who landed on the shore was sacrificed on her altar. But transported to Italy, the rite assumed a milder form. Within the sanctuary at Nemi grew a certain tree of which no branch might be broken. Only a runaway slave was allowed to break off, if he could, one of its boughs. Success in the attempt entitled him to fight the priest in single combat, and if he slew him he reigned in his stead with the title of King of the Wood (*Rex Nemorensis*). According to the public opinion of the ancients the fateful branch was that Golden Bough which, at the Sibyl's bidding, Aeneas plucked before he essayed the perilous journey to the world of the dead. The flight of the slave represented, it was said, the flight of Orestes; his combat with the priest was a reminiscence of the human sacrifices once offered to the Tauric Diana. This rule of succession by the sword was observed down to imperial times; for amongst his other freaks Caligula, thinking that the priest of Nemi had held office too long, hired a more stalwart ruffian to slay him; and a Greek traveller, who visited Italy in the age of the Antonines, remarks that down to his time the priesthood was still the prize of victory in a single combat.

Of the worship of Diana at Nemi some leading features can still be made out. From the votive offerings which have been found on the site, it appears that she was conceived of especially as a huntress, and further as blessing men and women with offspring, and granting expectant mothers an easy delivery. Again, fire seems to have played a foremost part in her ritual. For during her annual festival, held on the thirteenth of August, at the hottest time of the year, her grove shone with a multitude of torches, whose ruddy glare was reflected by the lake; and throughout the length and breadth of Italy the day was kept with holy rites at every domestic hearth. Bronze statuettes found in her precinct represent the goddess herself holding a torch in her raised right hand; and women whose prayers had been heard by her came crowned with wreaths and bearing lighted torches to the sanctuary in fulfilment of their vows. Some one unknown dedicated a perpetually burning lamp in a little shrine at Nemi for the safety of the Emperor Claudius and his family. The terra-cotta lamps which have been discovered in the grove may perhaps have served a like purpose for humbler persons. If so, the analogy of the custom to the Catholic practice of dedicating holy candles in churches would be obvious. Further, the title of Vesta borne by Diana at Nemi points clearly to the maintenance of a perpetual holy fire in her sanctuary. A large circular basement at the north-east corner of the temple, raised on three steps and bearing traces of a mosaic pavement, probably supported a round temple of Diana in her character of Vesta, like the round temple of Vesta in the Roman Forum. Here the sacred fire would seem to have been tended by Vestal Virgins, for the head of a Vestal in terra-cotta was found on the spot, and the worship of a perpetual fire, cared for by holy maidens, appears to have been common in Latium from the earliest to the latest times. Further, at the annual festival of the goddess, hunting dogs were crowned and wild beasts were not molested; young people went through a purificatory ceremony in her honour; wine was brought forth, and the feast consisted of a kid, cakes served piping hot on plates of leaves, and apples still hanging in clusters on the boughs.

But Diana did not reign alone in her grove at Nemi. Two lesser divinities shared her forest sanctuary. One was Egeria, the nymph of the clear water which, bubbling from the basaltic rocks, used to fall in graceful cascades into the lake at the place called Le Mole, because here were established the mills of the modern village of Nemi. The purling of the stream as it ran over the pebbles is mentioned by Ovid, who tells us that he had often drunk of its water. Women with child used to sacrifice to Egeria, because she was believed, like Diana, to be able to grant them an easy delivery. Tradition ran that the nymph had been the wife or mistress of the wise king Numa, that he had consorted with her in the secrecy of the sacred grove, and that the laws which he gave the Romans had been inspired by communion with her divinity. Plutarch compares the legend with other tales of the loves of goddesses for mortal men, such as the love of Cybele and the Moon for the fair youths Attis and Endymion. According to some, the trysting-place of the lovers was not in the woods of Nemi but in a grove outside the dripping Porta Capena at Rome, where another sacred spring of Egeria gushed from a dark cavern. Every day the Roman Vestals fetched water from this spring to wash the temple of Vesta, carrying it in earthenware pitchers on their heads. In Juvenal's time the natural rock had been encased in marble, and the hallowed spot was profaned by gangs of poor Jews, who were suffered to squat, like gypsies, in the grove. We may suppose that the spring which fell into the lake of Nemi was the true original Egeria, and that when the first settlers moved down from the Alban hills to the banks of the Tiber they brought the nymph with them and found a new home for her in a grove outside the gates. The remains of baths which have been discovered within the sacred precinct, together with may terra-cotta models of various parts of the human body, suggest that the waters of Egeria were used to heal the sick, who may have signified their hopes or testified their gratitude by dedicating likenesses of the diseased members to the goddess, in accordance with a custom which is still observed in many parts of Europe. To this day it would seem that the spring retains medicinal virtues.

The other of the minor deities at Nemi was Virbius. Legend had it that Virbius was the young Greek hero Hippolytus, chaste and fair, who learned the art of venery from the centaur Chiron, and spent all his days in the greenwood chasing wild beasts with the virgin huntress Artemis (the Greek counterpart of Diana) for his only comrade. Proud of her divine society, he spurned the love of women, and this proved his bane. For Aphrodite, stung by his scorn, inspired his stepmother Phaedra with love of him; and when he disdained her wicked advances she falsely accused him to his father Theseus. The slander was believed, and Theseus prayed to his sire Poseidon to avenge the imagined wrong. So while Hippolytus drove in a chariot by the shore of the Saronic Gulf, the sea-god sent a fierce bull forth from the waves. The terrified horses bolted, threw Hippolytus from the chariot, and dragged him at their hoofs to death. But Diana, for the love she bore Hippolytus, persuaded the leech Aesculapius to bring her fair young hunter back to life by his simples. Jupiter, indignant that a mortal man should return from the gates of death, thrust down the meddling leech himself to Hades. But Diana hid her favourite from the angry god in a thick cloud, disguised his features by adding years to his life, and then bore him far away to the dells of Nemi, where she entrusted him to the nymph Egeria, to live there, unknown and solitary, under the name of Virbius, in the depth of the Italian forest. There he reigned a king, and there he dedicated a precinct to Diana. He had a comely son, Virbius, who, undaunted by his father's fate, drove a team of fiery steeds to join the Latins in the war against Aeneas and the Trojans. Virbius was worshipped as a god not only at Nemi but elsewhere; for in Campania we hear of a special priest devoted to his service. Horses were excluded from the Arician grove and sanctuary because horses had killed Hippolytus. It was unlawful to touch his image. Some thought that he was the sun. "But the truth is," says Servius, "that he is a deity associated with Diana, as Attis is associated with the Mother of the Gods, and Erichthonius with Minerva, and Adonis with Venus." What the nature of that association was we shall enquire presently. Here it is worth observing that in his long and chequered career this mythical personage has displayed a remarkable tenacity of life. For we can hardly doubt that the Saint Hippolytus of the Roman calendar, who was dragged by horses to death on the thirteenth of August, Diana's own day, is no other than the Greek hero of the same name, who, after dying twice as a heathen sinner, has been happily resuscitated as a Christian saint.

It needs no elaborate demonstration to convince us that the stories told to account for Diana's worship at Nemi are unhistorical. Clearly they belong to that large class of myths which are made up to explain the origin of a religious ritual and have no other foundation than the resemblance, real or imaginary, which may be traced between it and some foreign ritual. The incongruity of these Nemi myths is indeed transparent, since the foundation of the worship is traced now to Orestes and now to Hippolytus, according as this or that feature of the ritual has to be accounted for. The real value of such tales is that they serve to illustrate the nature of the worship by providing a standard with which to compare it; and further, that they bear witness indirectly to its venerable age by showing that the true origin was lost in the mists of a fabulous antiquity. In the latter respect these Nemi legends are probably more to be trusted than the apparently historical tradition, vouched for by Cato the Elder, that the sacred grove was dedicated to Diana by a certain Egerius Baebius or Laevius of Tusculum, a Latin dictator, on behalf of the peoples of Tusculum, Aricia, Lanuvium, Laurentum, Cora, Tibur, Pometia, and Ardea. This tradition indeed speaks for the great age of the sanctuary, since it seems to date its foundation sometime before 495 B.C., the year in which Pometia was sacked by the Romans and disappears from history. But we cannot suppose that so barbarous a rule as that of the Arician priesthood was deliberately instituted by a league of civilised communities, such as the Latin cities undoubtedly were. It must have been handed down from a time beyond the memory of man, when Italy was still in a far ruder state than any known to us in the historical period. The credit of the tradition is rather shaken than confirmed by another story which ascribes the foundation of the sanctuary to a certain Manius Egerius, who gave rise to the saying, "There are many Manii at Aricia." This proverb some explained by alleging that Manius Egerius was the ancestor of a long and distinguished line, whereas others thought it meant that there were many ugly and deformed people at Aricia, and they derived the name Manius from *Mania*, a bogy or bugbear to frighten children. A Roman satirist uses the name Manius as typical of the beggars who lay in wait for pilgrims on the Arician slopes. These differences of opinion, together with the discrepancy between Manius Egerius of Aricia and Egerius Laevius of Tusculum, as well as the resemblance of both names to the mythical Egeria, excite our suspicion. Yet the tradition recorded by Cato seems too circumstantial, and its sponsor too respectable, to allow us to dismiss it as an idle fiction. Rather we may suppose that it refers to some ancient restoration or reconstruction of the sanctuary, which was actually carried out by the confederate states. At any rate it testifies to a belief that the grove had been from early times a common place of worship for many of the oldest cities of the country, if not for the whole Latin confederacy.

§ 2. *Artemis and Hippolytus.*—I have said that the Arician legends of Orestes and Hippolytus, though worthless as history, have a certain value in so far as they may help us to understand the worship of Nemi better by comparing it with the ritual and myths of other sanctuaries. We must ask ourselves, Why did the authors of these legends pitch upon Orestes and Hippolytus in order to explain Virbius and the King of the Wood? In regard to Orestes, the answer is obvious. He and the image of the Tauric Diana, which could only be appeased with human blood, were dragged in to render intelligible the murderous rule of succession to the Arician priesthood. In regard to Hippolytus the case is not so plain. The manner of his death suggests readily enough a reason for the exclusion of horses from the grove; but this by itself seems hardly enough to account for the identification. We must try to probe deeper by examining the worship as well as the legend or myth of Hippolytus.

He had a famous sanctuary at his ancestral home of Troezen, situated on that beautiful, almost landlocked bay, where groves of oranges and lemons, with tall cypresses soaring like dark spires above the garden of the Hesperides, now clothe the strip of fertile shore at the foot of the rugged mountains. Across the blue water of the tranquil bay, which it shelters from the open sea, rises Poseidon's sacred island, its peak veiled in the sombre green of the pines. On this fair coast Hippolytus was worshipped. Within his sanctuary stood a temple with an ancient image. His service was performed by a priest who held office for life: every year a sacrificial festival was held in his honour; and his untimely fate was yearly mourned, with weeping and doleful chants, by unwedded maids. Youths and maidens dedicated locks of their hair in his temple before marriage. His grave existed at Troezen, though the people would not show it. It has been suggested, with great plausibility, that in the handsome Hippolytus, beloved of Artemis, cut off in his youthful prime, and yearly mourned by damsels, we have one of those mortal lovers of a goddess who appear so often in ancient religion, and of whom Adonis is the most familiar type. The rivalry of Artemis and Phaedra for the affection of Hippolytus reproduces, it is said, under different names, the rivalry of Aphrodite and Proserpine for the love of Adonis, for Phaedra is merely a double of Aphrodite. The theory probably does no injustice either to Hippolytus or to Artemis. For Artemis was originally a great goddess of fertility, and, on the principles of early religion, she who fertilises nature must herself be fertile, and to be that she must necessarily have a male consort. On this view, Hippolytus was the consort of Artemis at Troezen, and the short tresses offered to him by the Troezenian youths and maidens before marriage were designed to strengthen his union with the goddess, and so to promote the fruitfulness of the earth, of cattle, and of mankind. It is some confirmation of this view that within the precinct of Hippolytus at Troezen there were worshipped two female powers named Damia and Auxesia, whose connexion with the fertility of the ground is unquestionable. When Epidaurus suffered from a dearth, the people, in obedience to an oracle, carved images of Damia and the Auxesia out of sacred olive-wood, and no sooner had they done so and set them up than the earth bore fruit again. Moreover, at Troezen itself, and apparently within the precinct of Hippolytus, a curious festival of stone-throwing was held in honour of these maidens, as the Troezenians called them; and it is easy to show that similar customs have been practised in many lands for the express purpose of ensuring good crops. In the story of the tragic death of the youthful Hippolytus we may discern an analogy with similar tales of other fair but mortal youths who paid with their lives for the brief rapture of the love of an immortal goddess. These hapless lovers were probably not always mere myths, and the legends which traced their spilt blood in the purple bloom of the violet, the scarlet stain of the anemone, or the crimson flush of the rose were no idle poetic emblems of youth and beauty fleeting as the summer flowers. Such fables contain a deeper philosophy of the relation of the life of man to the life of nature—a sad philosophy which gave birth to a tragic practice. What that philosophy and that practice were, we shall learn later on.

§ 3. *Recapitulation.*—We can now perhaps understand why the ancients identified Hippolytus, the consort of Artemis, with Virbius, who, according to Servius, stood to Diana as Adonis to Venus, or Attis to the Mother of the Gods. For Diana, like Artemis, was a goddess of fertility in general, and of childbirth in particular. As such she, like her Greek counterpart, needed a male partner. That partner, if Servius is right, was Virbius. In his character of the founder of the sacred grove and first king of Nemi, Virbius is clearly the mythical predecessor or archetype of the line of priests who served Diana under the title of Kings in the Wood, and who came, like him, one after the other, to a violent end. It is natural, therefore, to conjecture that they stood to the goddess of the grove in the same relation in which Virbius stood to her; in short, that the mortal King of the Wood had for his queen the woodland Diana herself. If the sacred tree which he guarded with his life was supposed, as seems probable, to be her special embodiment, her priest may not only have worshipped it as his goddess but embraced it as his wife. There is at least nothing absurd in the supposition, since even in the time of Pliny a noble Roman used thus to treat a beautiful beech-tree in another sacred grove of Diana on the Alban hills. He embraced it, he kissed it, he lay under its shadow, he poured wine on its trunk. Apparently he took the tree for the goddess. The custom of physically marrying men and women to trees is still practised in India and other parts of the East. Why should it not have obtained in ancient Latium?

Reviewing the evidence as a whole, we may conclude that the worship of Diana in her sacred grove at Nemi was of great importance and immemorial antiquity; that she was revered as the goddess of woodlands and of wild creatures, probably also of domestic cattle and of the fruits of the earth; that she was believed to bless men and women with offspring and to aid mothers in childbed; that her holy fire, tended by chaste virgins, burned perpetually in a round temple within the precinct; that associated with her was a water-nymph Egeria who discharged one of Diana's own functions by succouring women in travail, and who was popularly supposed to have mated with an old Roman king in the sacred grove; further, that Diana of the Wood herself had a male companion Virbius by name, who was to her what Adonis was to Venus or Attis to Cybele; and lastly, that this mythical Virbius was represented in historical times by a line of priests known as Kings of the Wood, who regularly perished by the swords of their successors, and whose lives were in a manner bound up with a certain tree in the grove, because so long as that tree was uninjured they were safe from attack.

Clearly these conclusions do not of themselves suffice to explain the peculiar rule of succession to the priesthood. But perhaps the survey of a wider field may lead us to think that they contain in germ the solution of the problem. To that wider survey we must now address ourselves. It will be long and laborious, but may possess something of the interest and charm of a voyage of discovery, in which we shall visit many strange foreign lands, with strange foreign peoples, and still stranger customs. The wind is in the shrouds: we shake out our sails to it, and leave the coast of Italy behind us for a time.

Chapter XXIV

The Killing of the Divine King

§ 1. *The Mortality of the Gods.*—Man has created gods in his own likeness and being himself mortal he has naturally supposed his creatures to be in the same sad predicament. Thus the Greenlanders believed that a wind could kill their most powerful god, and that he would certainly die if he touched a dog. When they heard of the Christian God, they kept asking if he never died, and being informed that he did not, they were much surprised, and said that he must be a very great god indeed. In answer to the enquiries of Colonel Dodge, a North American Indian stated that the world was made by the Great Spirit. Being asked which Great Spirit he meant, the good one or the bad one, "Oh, neither of *them*," replied he, "the Great Spirit that made the world is dead long ago. He could not possibly have lived as long as this." A tribe in the Philippine Islands told the Spanish conquerors that the grave of the Creator was upon the top of Mount Cabunian. Heitsi-eibib, a god or divine hero of the Hottentots, died several times and came to life again. His graves are generally to be met with in narrow defiles between mountains. When the Hottentots pass one of them, they throw a stone on it for good luck, sometimes muttering "Give us plenty of cattle." The grave of Zeus, the great god of Greece, was shown to visitors in Crete as late as about the beginning of our era. The body of Dionysus was buried at Delphi beside the golden statue of Apollo, and his tomb bore the inscription, "Here lies Dionysus dead, the son of Semele." According to one account, Apollo himself was buried at Delphi; for Pythagoras is said to have carved an inscription on his tomb, setting forth how the god had been killed by the python and buried under the tripod.

The great gods of Egypt themselves were not exempt from the common lot. They too grew old and died. But when at a later time the discovery of the art of embalming gave a new lease of life to the souls of the dead by preserving their bodies for an indefinite time from corruption, the deities were permitted to share the benefit of an invention which held out to gods as well as to men a reasonable hope of immortality. Every province then had the tomb and mummy of its dead god. The mummy of Osiris was to be seen at Mendes; Thinis boasted of the mummy of Anhouri; and Heliopolis rejoiced in the possession of that of Toumou. The high gods of Babylon also, though they appeared to their worshippers only in dreams and visions, were conceived to be human in their bodily shape, human in their passions, and human in their fate; for like men they were born into the world, and like men they loved and fought and died.

§ 2. *Kings killed when their Strength fails.*—If the high gods, who dwell remote from the fret and fever of this earthly life, are yet believed to die at last, it is not to be expected that a god who lodges in a frail tabernacle of flesh should escape the same fate, though we hear of African kings who have imagined themselves immortal by virtue of their sorceries. Now primitive peoples, as we have seen, sometimes believe that their safety and even that of the world is bound up with the life of one of these god-men or human incarnations of the divinity. Naturally, therefore, they take the utmost care of his life, out of regard for their own. But no amount of care and precaution will prevent the man-god from growing old and feeble and at last dying. His worshippers have to lay their account with this sad necessity and to meet it as best they can. The danger is a formidable one; for if the course of nature is independent on the man-god's life, what catastrophes may not be expected from the gradual enfeeblement of his powers and their final extinction in death? There is only one way of averting these dangers. The man-god must be killed as soon as he shows symptoms that his powers are beginning to fail, and his soul must be transferred to a vigorous successor before it has been seriously impaired by the threatened decay.

The advantages of thus putting the man-god to death instead of allowing him to die of old age and disease are, to the savage, obvious enough. For if the man-god dies what we call a natural death, it means, according to the savage, that his soul has either voluntarily departed from his body and refuses to return, or more commonly that it has been extracted, or at least detained in its wanderings, by a demon or sorcerer. In any of these cases the soul of the man-god is lost to his worshippers, and with it their prosperity is gone and their very existence endangered. Even if they could arrange to catch the soul of the dying god as it left his lips or his nostrils and so transfer it to a successor, this would not effect their purpose; for, dying of disease, his soul would necessarily leave his body in the last stage of weakness and exhaustion, and so enfeebled it would continue to drag out a languid, inert existence in any body to which it might be transferred. Whereas by slaying him his worshippers could, in the first place, make sure of catching his soul as it escaped and transferring it to a suitable successor; and, in the second place, by putting him to death before his natural force was abated, they would secure that the world should not fall into decay with the decay of the man-god. Every purpose, therefore, was answered, and all dangers averted by thus killing the man-god and transferring his soul, while yet at its prime, to a vigorous successor.

The mystic kings of Fire and Water in Cambodia are not allowed to die a natural death. Hence when one of them is seriously ill and the elders think that he cannot recover, they stab him to death. The people of Congo believed, as we have seen, that if their pontiff the Chitomé were to die a natural death, the world would perish, and the earth, which he alone sustained by his power and merit, would immediately be annihilated. Accordingly when he fell ill and seemed likely to die, the man who was destined to be his successor entered the pontiff's house with a rope or a club and strangled or clubbed him to death. The Ethiopian kings of Meroe were worshipped as gods; but whenever the priest chose, they sent a messenger to the king, ordering him to die, and alleging an oracle of the gods as their authority for the command. This command the king always obeyed down to the reign of Ergamenes, a contemporary of Ptolemy II., King of Egypt. Having received a Greek education which emancipated him from the superstitions of his countrymen, Ergamenes ventured to disregard the command of the priests, and, entering the Golden Temple with a body of soldiers, put the priests to the sword.

Customs of the same sort appear to have prevailed in this part of Africa down to modern times. In some tribes of Fazoql the king had to administer justice daily under a certain tree. If from sickness or any other cause he was unable to discharge this duty for three whole days, he was hanged on the tree in a noose, which contained two razors so arranged that when the noose was drawn tight by the weight of the king's body they cut his throat.

A custom of putting their divine kings to death at the first symptoms of infirmity or old age prevailed until lately, if indeed it is even now extinct and not merely dormant, among the Shilluk of the White Nile, and in recent years it has been carefully investigated by Dr. C. G. Seligman. The reverence which the Shilluk pay to their king appears to arise chiefly from the conviction that he is a reincarnation of the spirit of Nyakang, the semi-divine hero who founded the dynasty and settled the tribe in their present territory. It is a fundamental article of the Shilluk creed that the spirit of the divine or semi-divine Nyakang is incarnate in the reigning king, who is accordingly himself invested to some extent with the character of a divinity. But while the Shilluk hold their kings in high, indeed religious reverence and take every precaution against their accidental death, nevertheless they cherish "the conviction that the king must not be allowed to become ill or senile, lest with his diminishing vigour the cattle should sicken and fail to bear their increase, the crops should rot in the fields, and man, stricken with disease, should die in ever-increasing numbers."

To prevent these calamities it used to be the regular custom with the Shilluk to put the king to death whenever he showed signs of ill-health or failing strength. One of the fatal symptoms of decay was taken to be an incapacity to satisfy the sexual passions of his wives, of whom he has very many, distributed in a large number of houses at Fashoda. When this ominous weakness manifested itself, the wives reported it to the chiefs, who are popularly said to have intimated to the king his doom by spreading a white cloth over his face and knees as he lay slumbering in the heat of the sultry afternoon. Execution soon followed the sentence of death. A hut was specially built for the occasion: the king was led into it and lay down with his head resting on the lap of a nubile virgin: the door of the hut was then walled up; and the couple were left without food, water, or fire to die of hunger and suffocation. This was the old custom, but it was abolished some five generations ago on account of the excessive sufferings of one of the kings who perished in this way. It is said that the chiefs announce his fate to the king, and that afterwards he is strangled in a hut which has been specially built for the occasion.

From Dr. Seligman's enquiries it appears that not only was the Shilluk king liable to be killed with due ceremony at the first symptoms of incipient decay, but even while he was yet in the prime of health and strength he might be attacked at any time by a rival and have to defend his crown in a combat to the death. According to the common Shilluk tradition any son of a king had the right thus to fight the king in possession and, if he succeeded in killing him, to reign in his stead. As every king had a large harem and many sons, the number of possible candidates for the throne at any time may well have been not inconsiderable, and the reigning monarch must have carried his life in his hand. But the attack on him could only take place with any prospect of success at night; for during the day the king surrounded himself with his friends and bodyguards, and an aspirant to the throne could hardly hope to cut his way through them and strike home. It was otherwise at night. For then the guards were dismissed and the king was alone in his enclosure with his favourite wives, and there was no man near to defend him except a few herdsmen, whose huts stood a little way off. The hours of darkness were therefore the season of peril for the king. It is said that he used to pass them in constant watchfulness, prowling round his huts fully armed, peering into the blackest shadows, or himself standing silent and alert, like a sentinel on duty, in some dark corner. When at last his rival appeared, the fight would take place in grim silence, broken only by the clash of spears and shields, for it was a point of honour with the king not to call the herdsmen to his assistance.

Like Nyakang himself, their founder, each of the Shilluk kings after death is worshipped at a shrine, which is erected over his grave, and the grave of a king is always in the village where he was born. The tomb-shrine of a king resembles the shrine of Nyakang, consisting of a few huts enclosed by a fence; one of the huts is built over the king's grave, the others are occupied by the guardians of the shrine. Indeed the shrines of Nyakang and the shrines of the kings are scarcely to be distinguished from each other, and the religious rituals observed at all of them are identical in form and vary only in matters of detail, the variations being due apparently to the far greater sanctity attributed to the shrines of Nyakang. The grave-shrines of the kings are tended by certain old men or women, who correspond to the guardians of the shrines of Nyakang. They are usually widows or old men-servants of the deceased king, and when they die they are succeeded in their office by their descendants. Moreover, cattle are dedicated to the grave-shrines of the kings and sacrifices are offered at them just as at the shrines of Nyakang.

In general the principal element in the religion of the Shilluk would seem to be the worship which they pay to their sacred or divine kings, whether dead or alive. These are believed to be animated by a single divine spirit, which has been transmitted from the semi-mythical, but probably in substance historical, founder of the dynasty through all his successors to the present day. Hence, regarding their kings as incarnate divinities on whom the welfare of men, of cattle, and of the corn implicitly depends, the Shilluk naturally pay them the greatest respect and take every care of them; and however strange it may seem to us, their custom of putting the divine king to death as soon as he shows signs of ill-health or failing strength springs directly from their profound veneration for him and from their anxiety to preserve him, or rather the divine spirit by which he is animated, in the most perfect state of efficiency: nay, we may go further and say that their practice of regicide is the best proof they can give of the high regard in which they hold their kings. For they believe, as we have seen, that the king's life or spirit is so sympathetically bound up with the prosperity of the whole country, that if he fell ill or grew senile the cattle would sicken and cease to multiply, the crops would rot in the fields, and men would perish of widespread disease. Hence, in their opinion, the only way of averting these calamities is to put the king to death while he is still hale and hearty, in order that the divine spirit which he has inherited from his predecessors may be transmitted in turn by him to his successor while it is still in full vigour and has not yet been impaired by the weakness of disease and old age. In this connexion the particular symptom which is commonly said to seal the king's death-warrant is highly significant; when he can no longer satisfy the passions of his numerous wives, in other words, when he has ceased, whether partially or wholly, to be able to reproduce his kind, it is time for him to die and to make room for a more vigorous successor. Taken along with the other reasons which are alleged for putting the king to death, this one suggests that the fertility of men, of cattle, and of the crops is believed to depend sympathetically on the generative power of the king, so that the complete failure of that power in him would involve a corresponding failure in men, animals, and plants, and would thereby entail at no distant date the entire extinction of all life, whether human, animal, or vegetable. No wonder, that with such a danger before their eyes the Shilluk should be most careful not to let the king die what we should call a natural death of sickness or old age. It is characteristic of their attitude towards the death of the kings that they refrain from speaking of it as death: they do not say that a king has died but simply that he has "gone away" like his divine ancestors Nyakang and Dag, the two first kings of the dynasty, both of whom are reported not to have died but to have disappeared. The similar legends of the mysterious disappearance of early kings in other lands, for example at Rome and in Uganda, may well point to a similar custom of putting them to death for the purpose of preserving their life.

On the whole the theory and practice of the divine kings of the Shilluk correspond very nearly to the theory and practice of the priests of Nemi, the Kings of the Wood, if my view of the latter is correct. In both we see a series of divine kings on whose life the fertility of men, of cattle, and of vegetation is believed to depend, and who are put to death, whether in single combat or otherwise, in order that their divine spirit may be transmitted to their successors in full vigour, uncontaminated by the weakness and decay of sickness or old age, because any such degeneration on the part of the king would, in the opinion of his worshippers, entail a corresponding degeneration on mankind, on cattle, and on the crops. Some points in this explanation of the custom of putting divine kings to death, particularly the method of transmitting their divine souls to their successors, will be dealt with more fully in the sequel. Meantime we pass to other examples of the general practice.

The Dinka are a congeries of independent tribes in the valley of the White Nile. They are essentially a pastoral people, passionately devoted to the care of their numerous herds of oxen, though they also keep sheep and goats, and the women cultivate small quantities of millet and sesame. For their crops and above all for their pastures they depend on the regularity of the rains: in seasons of prolonged drought they are said to be reduced to great extremities. Hence the rain-maker is a very important personage among them to this day; indeed the men in authority whom travellers dub chiefs or sheikhs are in fact the actual or potential rain-makers of the tribe or community. Each of them is believed to be animated by the spirit of a great rain-maker, which has come down to him through a succession of rain-makers; and in virtue of this inspiration a successful rain-maker enjoys very great power and is consulted on all important matters. Yet in spite, or rather in virtue, of the high honour in which he is held, no Dinka rain-maker is allowed to die a natural death of sickness or old age; for the Dinka believe that if such an untoward event were to happen, the tribe would suffer from disease and famine, and the herds would not yield their increase. So when a rain-maker feels that he is growing old and infirm, he tells his children that he wishes to die. Among the Agar Dinka a large grave is dug and the rain-maker lies down in it, surrounded by his friends and relatives. From time to time he speaks to the people, recalling the past history of the tribe, reminding them how he has ruled and advised them, and instructing them how they are to act in the future. Then, when he has concluded his admonition, he bids them cover him up. So the earth is thrown down on him as he lies in the grave, and he soon dies of suffocation. Such, with minor variations, appears to be the regular end of the honourable career of a rain-maker in all the Dinka tribes. The Khor-Adar Dinka told Dr. Seligman that when they have dug the grave for their rain-maker they strangle him in his house. The father and paternal uncle of one of Dr. Seligman's informants had both been rain-makers and both had been killed in the most regular and orthodox fashion. Even if a rain-maker is quite young he will be put to death should he seem likely to perish of disease. Further, every precaution is taken to prevent a rain-maker from dying an accidental death, for such an end, though not nearly so serious a matter as death from illness or old age, would be sure to entail sickness on the tribe. As soon as a rain-maker is killed, his valuable spirit is supposed to pass to a suitable successor, whether a son or other near blood relation.

In the Central African kingdom of Bunyoro down to recent years custom required that as soon as the king fell seriously ill or began to break up from age, he should die by his own hand; for, according to an old prophecy, the throne would pass away from the dynasty if ever the king were to die a natural death. He killed himself by draining a poisoned cup. If he faltered or were too ill to ask for the cup, it was his wife's duty to administer the poison. When the king of Kibanga, on the Upper Congo, seems near his end, the sorcerers put a rope round his neck, which they draw gradually tighter till he dies. If the king of Gingiro happens to be wounded in war, he is put to death by his comrades, or, if they fail to kill him, by his kinsfolk, however hard he may beg for mercy. They say they do it that he may not die by the hands of his enemies. The Jukos are a heathen tribe of the Benue river, a great tributary of the Niger. In their country "the town of Gatri is ruled by a king who is elected by the big men of the town as follows. When in the opinion of the big men the king has reigned long enough, they give out that 'the king is sick'—a formula understood by all to mean that they are going to kill him, though the intention is never put more plainly. They then decide who is to be the next king. How long he is to reign is settled by the influential men at a meeting; the question is put and answered by each man throwing on the ground a little piece of stick for each year he thinks the new king should rule. The king is then told, and a great feast prepared, at which the king gets drunk on guinea-corn beer. After that he is speared, and the man who was chosen becomes king. Thus each Juko king knows that he cannot have very many more years to live, and that he is certain of his predecessor's fate. This, however, does not seem to frighten candidates. The same custom of king-killing is said to prevail at Quonde and Wukari as well as at Gatri." In the three Hausa kingdoms of Gobir, Katsina, and Daura, in Northern Nigeria, as soon as a king showed signs of failing health or growing infirmity, an official who bore the title of Killer of the Elephant appeared and throttled him.

The Matiamvo is a great king or emperor in the interior of Angola. One of the inferior kings of the country, by name Challa, gave to a Portuguese expedition the following account of the manner in which the Matiamvo comes by his end. "It has been customary," he said, "for our Matiamvos to die either in war or by a violent death, and the present Matiamvo must meet this last fate, as, in consequence of his great exactions, he has lived long enough. When we come to this understanding, and decide that he should be killed, we invite him to make war with our enemies, on which occasion we all accompany him and his family to the war, when we lose some of our people. If he escapes unhurt, we return to the war again and fight for three or four days. We then suddenly abandon him and his family to their fate, leaving him in the enemy's hands. Seeing himself thus deserted, he causes his throne to be erected, and, sitting down, calls his family around him. He then orders his mother to approach; she kneels at his feet; he first cuts off her head, then decapitates his sons in succession, next his wives and relatives, and, last of all, his most beloved wife, called Anacullo. This slaughter being accomplished, the Matiamvo, dressed in all his pomp, awaits his own death, which immediately follows, by an officer sent by the powerful neighbouring chiefs, Caniquinha and Canica. This officer first cuts off his legs and arms at the joints, and lastly he cuts off his head; after which the head of the officer is struck off. All the potentates retire from the encampment, in order not to witness his death. It is my duty to remain and witness his death, and to mark the place where the head and arms have been deposited by the two great chiefs, the enemies of the Matiamvo. They also take possession of all the property belonging to the deceased monarch and his family, which they convey to their own residence. I then provide for the funeral of the mutilated remains of the late Matiamvo, after which I retire to his capital and proclaim the new government. I then return to where the head, legs, and arms have been deposited, and, for forty slaves, I ransom them, together with the merchandise and other property belonging to the deceased, which I give up to the new Matiamvo, who has been proclaimed. This is what has happened to many Matiamvos, and what must happen to the present one."

It appears to have been a Zulu custom to put the king to death as soon as he began to have wrinkles or grey hairs. At least this seems implied in the following passage written by one who resided for some time at the court of

the notorious Zulu tyrant Chaka, in the early part of the nineteenth century: "The extraordinary violence of the king's rage with me was mainly occasioned by that absurd nostrum, the hair oil, with the notion of which Mr. Farewell had impressed him as being a specific for removing all indications of age. From the first moment of his having heard that such a preparation was attainable, he evinced a solicitude to procure it, and on every occasion never forgot to remind us of his anxiety respecting it; more especially on our departure on the mission his injunctions were particularly directed to this object. It will be seen that it is one of the barbarous customs of the Zoolas in their choice or election of their kings that must neither have wrinkles nor grey hairs, as they are both distinguishing marks of disqualification for becoming a monarch of a warlike people. It is also equally indispensable that their king should never exhibit those proofs of having become unfit and incompetent to reign; it is therefore important that they should conceal these indications so long as they possibly can. Chaka had become greatly apprehensive of the approach of grey hairs; which would at once be the signal for him to prepare to make his exit from this sublunary world, it being always followed by the death of the monarch."
The writer to whom we are indebted for this instructive anecdote of the hair oil omits to specify the mode in which a grey-haired and wrinkled Zulu chief used "to make his exit from this sublunary world"; but on analogy we may conjecture that he was killed.

The custom of putting kings to death as soon as they suffered from any personal defect prevailed two centuries ago in the Caffre kingdom of Sofala. We have seen that these kings of Sofala were regarded as gods by their people, being entreated to give rain or sunshine, according as each might be wanted. Nevertheless a slight bodily blemish, such as the loss of a tooth, was considered a sufficient cause for putting one of these god-men to death, as we learn from the following passage of an old Portuguese historian: "It was formerly the custom of the kings of this land to commit suicide by taking poison when any disaster or natural physical defect fell upon them, such as impotence, infectious disease, the loss of their front teeth, by which they were disfigured, or any other deformity or affliction. To put an end to such defects they killed themselves, saying that the king should be free from any blemish, and if not, it was better for his honour that he should die and seek another life where he would be made whole, for there everything was perfect. But the Quiteve (king) who reigned when I was in those parts would not imitate his predecessors in this, being discreet and dreaded as he was; for having lost a front tooth he caused it to be proclaimed throughout the kingdom that all should be aware that he had lost a tooth and should recognise him when they saw him without it, and if his predecessors killed themselves for such things they were very foolish, and he would not do so; on the contrary, he would be very sorry when the time came for him to die a natural death, for his life was very necessary to preserve his kingdom and defend it from his enemies; and he recommended his successors to follow his example."

The king of Sofala who dared to survive the loss of his front tooth was thus a bold reformer like Ergamenes, king of Ethiopia. We may conjecture that the ground for putting the Ethiopian kings to death was, as in the case of the Zulu and Sofala kings, the appearance on their person of any bodily defect or sign of decay; and that the oracle which the priests alleged as the authority for the royal execution was to the effect that great calamities would result from the reign of a king who had any blemish on his body; just as an oracle warned Sparta against a "lame reign," that is, the reign of a lame king. It is some confirmation of this conjecture that the kings of Ethiopia were chosen for their size, strength, and beauty long before the custom of killing them was abolished. To this day the Sultan of Wadai must have no obvious bodily defect, and the king of Angoy cannot be crowned if he has a single blemish, such as a broken or a filed tooth or the scar of an old wound. According to the Book of Acaill and many other authorities no king who was afflicted with a personal blemish might reign over Ireland at Tara. Hence, when the great King Cormac Mac Art lost one eye by an accident, he at once abdicated.

Many days' journey to the north-east of Abomey, the old capital of Dahomey, lies the kingdom of Eyeo. "The Eyeos are governed by a king, no less absolute than the king of Dahomey, yet subject to a regulation of state, at once humiliating and extraordinary. When the people have conceived an opinion of his ill-government, which is sometimes insidiously infused into them by the artifice of his discontented ministers, they send a deputation to him with a present of parrots' eggs, as a mark of its authenticity, to represent to him that the burden of government must have so far fatigued him that they consider it full time for him to repose from his cares and indulge himself with a little sleep. He thanks his subjects for their attention to his ease, retires to his own apartment as if to sleep, and there gives directions to his women to strangle him. This is immediately executed, and his son quietly ascends the throne upon the usual terms of holding the reins of government no longer than whilst he merits the approbation of the people." About the year 1774, a king of Eyeo, whom his ministers attempted to remove in the customary manner, positively refused to accept the proffered parrots' eggs at their hands, telling them that he had no mind to take a nap, but on the contrary was resolved to watch for the benefit of his subjects. The ministers, surprised and indignant at his recalcitrancy, raised a rebellion, but were defeated with great slaughter, and thus by his spirited conduct the king freed himself from the tyranny of his councillors and established a new precedent for the guidance of his successors. However, the old custom seems to have revived, and persisted until late in the nineteenth century, for a Catholic missionary, writing in 1884, speaks of the practice as if it were still in vogue. Another missionary, writing in 1881, thus describes the usage of the Egbas and the Yorubas of West Africa: "Among the customs of the country one of the most curious is unquestionably that of judging and punishing the king. Should he have earned the hatred of his people by exceeding his rights, one of his councillors, on whom the heavy duty is laid, requires of the prince that he shall 'go to sleep,' which means simply 'take poison and die.' If his courage fails him at the supreme moment, a friend renders him this last service, and quietly, without betraying the secret, they prepare the people for the news of the king's death. In Yoruba the thing is managed a little differently. When a son is born to the king of Oyo, they make a model of the infant's right foot in clay and keep it in the house of the elders (*ogboni*). If the king fails to observe the customs of the country, a messenger, without speaking a word, shows him his child's foot. The king knows what that means. He takes poison and goes to sleep." The old Prussians acknowledged as their supreme lord a ruler who governed them in the name of the gods, and was known as "God's Mouth." When he felt himself weak and ill, if he wished to leave a good name behind him, he had a great heap made of thorn-bushes and straw, on which he mounted and delivered a long sermon to the people, exhorting them to serve the gods and promising to go to the gods and speak for the people. Then he took some of the perpetual fire which burned in front of the holy oak-tree, and lighting the pile with it burned himself to death.

§ 3. *Kings killed at the End of a Fixed Term.*—In the cases hitherto described, the divine king or priest is suffered by his people to retain office until some outward defect, some visible symptom of failing health or advancing age, warns them that he is no longer equal to the discharge of his divine duties; but not until such symptoms have made their appearance is he put to death. Some peoples, however, appear to have thought it unsafe to wait for even the slightest symptom of decay and have preferred to kill the king while he was still in the full vigour of life. Accordingly, they have fixed a term beyond which he might not reign, and at the close of which he must die, the term fixed upon being short enough to exclude the probability of his degenerating physically in the interval. In some parts of Southern India the period fixed was twelve years. Thus, according to an old traveller, in the province of Quilacare, "there is a Gentile house of prayer, in which there is an idol which they hold in great account, and every twelve years they celebrate a great feast to it, whither all the Gentiles go as to a jubilee. This temple possesses many lands and much revenue: it is a very great affair. This province has a king over it, who has not more than twelve years to reign from jubilee to jubilee. His manner of living is in this wise, that is to say: when the twelve years are completed, on the day of this feast there assemble together innumerable people, and much money is spent in giving food to Bramans. The king has a wooden scaffolding made, spread over with silken hangings: and on that day he goes to bathe at a tank with great ceremonies and sound of music, after that he comes to the idol and prays to it, and mounts on to the scaffolding, and there before all the people he takes some very sharp knives, and begins to cut off his nose, and then his ears, and his lips, and all his members, and as much flesh off himself as he can; and he throws it away very hurriedly until so much of his blood is spilled that he begins to faint, and then he cuts his throat himself. And he performs this sacrifice to the idol, and whoever desires to reign other twelve years and undertake this martyrdom for love of the idol, has to be present looking on at this: and from that place they raise him up as king."

The king of Calicut, on the Malabar coast, bears the title of Samorin or Samory. He "pretends to be of a higher rank than the Brahmans, and to be inferior only to the invisible gods; a pretention that was acknowledged by his subjects, but which is held as absurd and abominable by the Brahmans, by whom he is only treated as a Sudra." Formerly the Samorin had to cut his throat in public at the end of a twelve years' reign. But towards the end of the seventeenth century the rule had been modified as follows: "Many strange customs were observed in this country in former times, and some very odd ones are still continued. It was an ancient custom for the Samorin to reign but twelve years, and no longer. If he died before his term was expired, it saved him a troublesome ceremony of cutting his own throat, on a publick scaffold erected for the purpose. He first made a feast for all his nobility and gentry, who are very numerous. After the feast he saluted his guests, and went on the scaffold, and very decently cut his own throat in the view of the assembly, and his body was, a little while after, burned with great pomp and ceremony, and the grandees elected a new Samorin. Whether that custom was a religious or a civil ceremony, I know not, but it is now laid aside. And a new custom is followed by the modern Samorins, that jubilee is proclaimed throughout his dominions, at the end of twelve years, and a tent is pitched for him in a spacious plain, and a great feast is celebrated for ten or twelve days, with mirth and jollity, guns firing night and day, so at the end of the feast any four of the guests that have a mind to gain a crown by a desperate action, in fighting their way through 30 or 40,000 of his guards, and kill the Samorin in his tent, he that kills him succeeds him in his empire. In anno 1695, one of those jubilees happened, and the tent pitched near Pennany, a seaport of his, about fifteen leagues to the southward of Calicut. There were but three men that would venture on that desperate action, who fell in, with sword and target, among the guard, and, after they had killed and wounded many, were themselves killed. One of the desperados had a nephew of fifteen or sixteen years of age, that kept close by his uncle in the attack on the guards, and, when he saw him fall, the youth got through the guards into the tent, and made a stroke at his Majesty's head, and had certainly despatched him if a large brass lamp which was burning over his head had not marred the blow; but, before he could make another, he was killed by the guards; and, I believe, the same Samorin reigns yet. I chanced to come that time along the coast and heard the guns for two or three days and nights successively."

The English traveller, whose account I have quoted, did not himself witness the festival he describes, though he heard the sound of the firing in the distance. Fortunately, exact records of these festivals and of the number of men who perished at them have been preserved in the archives of the royal family at Calicut. In the latter part of the nineteenth century they were examined by Mr. W. Logan, with the personal assistance of the reigning king, and from his work it is possible to gain an accurate conception both of the tragedy and of the scene where it was periodically enacted down to 1743, when the ceremony took place for the last time.

The festival at which the king of Calicut staked his crown and his life on the issue of battle was known as the "Great Sacrifice." It fell every twelfth year, when the planet Jupiter was in retrograde motion in the sign of the Crab, and it lasted twenty-eight days, culminating at the time of the eighth lunar asterism in the month of Makaram. As the date of the festival was determined by the position of Jupiter in the sky, and the interval between two festivals was twelve years, which is roughly Jupiter's period of revolution round the sun, we may conjecture that the splendid planet was supposed to be in a special sense the king's star and to rule his destiny, the period of its revolution in heaven corresponding to the period of his reign on earth. However that may be, the ceremony was observed with great pomp at the Tirunavayi temple, on the north bank of the Ponnani River. The spot is close to the present railway line. As the train rushes by, you can just catch a glimpse of the temple almost hidden behind a clump of trees on the river bank. From the western gateway of the temple a perfectly straight road, hardly raised above the level of the surrounding rice-fields and shaded by a fine avenue, runs for half a mile to a high ridge with a precipitous bank, on which the outlines of three or four terraces can still be traced. On the topmost of these terraces the king took his stand on the eventful day. The view which it commands is a fine one. Across the flat expanse of the rice-fields, with the broad placid river winding through them, the eye ranges eastward to high tablelands, their lower slopes embowered in woods, while afar off looms the great chain of the western Ghauts, and in the furthest distance the Neilgherries or Blue Mountains, hardly distinguishable from the azure of the sky above.

But it was not to the distant prospect that the king's eyes naturally turned at this crisis of his fate. His attention was arrested by a spectacle nearer at hand. For all the plain below was alive with troops, their banners waving gaily in the sun, the white tents of their many camps standing sharply out against the green and gold of the rice-fields. Forty thousand fighting men or more were gathered there to defend the king. But if the plain swarmed with soldiers, the road that cuts across it from the temple to the king's stand was clear of them. Not a soul was stirring on it. Each side of the way was barred by palisades, and from the palisades on either hand a long hedge of spears, held by strong arms, projected into the empty road, their blades meeting in the middle and forming a glittering arch of steel. All was now ready. The king waved his sword. At the same moment a great chain of massy gold, enriched with bosses, was placed on an elephant at his side. That was the signal. On the instant a stir might be seen half a mile away at the gate of the temple. A group of swordsmen, decked with flowers and smeared with ashes, has stepped out from the crowd. They have just partaken of their last meal on earth, and they now receive the last blessings and farewells of their friends. A moment more and they are coming down the lane of spears, hewing and stabbing right and left at the spearmen, winding and turning and writhing among the blades as if they had no bones in their bodies. It is all in vain. One after the other they fall, some nearer the king, some farther off, content to die, not for the shadow of a crown, but for the mere sake of approving their dauntless valour and swordsmanship to the world. On the last days of the festival the same magnificent display of gallantry, the same useless sacrifice of life was repeated again and again. Yet perhaps no sacrifice is wholly useless which proves that there are men who prefer honour to life.

"It is a singular custom in Bengal," says an old native historian of India, "that there is little of hereditary descent in the succession to the sovereignty. ... Whoever kills the king, and succeeds in placing himself on that throne, is immediately acknowledged as king; all the *amirs*, *wazirs*, soldiers, and peasants instantly obey and submit to him, and consider him as being as much their sovereign as they did their former prince, and obey his orders implicitly. The people of Bengal say, 'We are faithful to the throne; whoever fills the throne we are obedient and true to it.'" A custom of the same sort formerly prevailed in the little kingdom of Passier, on the northern coast of Sumatra. The old Portuguese historian De Barros, who informs us of it, remarks with surprise that no wise man would wish to be king of Passier, since the monarch was not allowed by his subjects to live long. From time to time a sort of fury seized the people, and they marched through the streets of the city chanting with loud voices the fatal words, "The kings must die!" When the king heard that song of death he knew that his hour had come. The man who struck the fatal blow was of the royal lineage, and as soon as he had done the deed of blood and seated himself on the throne he was regarded as the legitimate king, provided that he contrived to maintain his seat peaceably for a single day. This, however, the regicide did not always succeed in doing. When Fernão Peres d'Andrade, on a voyage to China, put in at Passier for a cargo of spices, two kings were massacred, and that in the most peaceable and orderly manner, without the smallest sign of tumult or sedition in the city, where everything went on its usual course, as if the murder or execution of a king were a matter of everyday occurrence. Indeed, on one occasion three kings were raised to the dangerous elevation and followed each other on the dusty road of death in a single day. The people defended the custom, which they esteemed very laudable and even of divine institution, by saying that God would never allow so high and mighty a being as a king, who reigned as his vicegerent on earth, to perish by violence unless for his sins he thoroughly deserved it. Far away from the tropical island of Sumatra a rule of the same sort appears to have obtained among the old Slavs. When the captives Gunn and Jarmerik contrived to slay the king and queen of the Slavs and made their escape, they were pursued by the barbarians, who shouted after them that if they would only come back they would reign again instead of the murdered monarch, since by a public statute of the ancients the succession to the throne fell to the king's assassin. But the flying regicides turned a deaf ear to promises which they regarded as mere baits to lure them back to destruction; they continued their flight, and the shouts and clamour of the barbarians gradually died away in the distance.

When kings were bound to suffer death, whether at their own hands or at the hands of others, on the expiration of a fixed term of years, it was natural that they should seek to delegate the painful duty, along with some of the privileges of sovereignty, to a substitute who should suffer vicariously in their stead. This expedient appears to have been resorted to by some of the princes of Malabar. Thus we are informed by a native authority on that country that "in some places all power both executive and judicial were delegated for a fixed period to natives by the sovereign. This institution was styled *Thalavettiparothiam* or authority obtained by decapitation. ... It was an office tenable for five years during which its bearer was invested with supreme despotic powers within his jurisdiction. On the expiry of the five years the man's head was cut off and thrown up in the air amongst a large concourse of villagers, each of whom vied with the other in trying to catch it in its course down. He who succeeded was nominated to the post for the next five years."

When once kings, who had hitherto been bound to die a violent death at the end of a term of years, conceived the happy thought of dying by deputy in the persons of others, they would very naturally put it in practice; and accordingly we need not wonder at finding so popular an expedient, or traces of it, in many lands. Scandinavian traditions contain some hints that of old the Swedish kings reigned only for periods of nine years, after which they were put to death or had to find a substitute to die in their stead. Thus Aun or On, king of Sweden, is said to have sacrificed to Odin for length of days and to have been answered by the god that he should live so long as he sacrificed one of his sons every ninth year. He sacrificed nine of them in this manner, and would have sacrificed the tenth and last, but the Swedes would not allow him. So he died and was buried in a mound at Upsala. Another indication of a similar tenure of the crown occurs in a curious legend of the deposition and banishment of Odin. Offended at his misdeeds, the other gods outlawed and exiled him, but set up in his place a substitute, Oller by name, a cunning wizard, to whom they accorded the symbols both of royalty and of godhead. The deputy bore the name of Odin, and reigned for nearly ten years, when he was driven from the throne, while the real Odin came to his own again. His discomfited rival retired to Sweden and was afterwards slain in an attempt to repair his shattered fortunes. As gods are often merely men who loom large through the mists of tradition, we may conjecture that this Norse legend preserves a confused reminiscence of ancient Swedish kings who reigned for nine or ten years together, then abdicated, delegating to others the privilege of dying for their country. The great festival which was held at Upsala every nine years may have been the occasion on which the king or his deputy was put to death. We know that human sacrifices formed part of the rites.

There are some grounds for believing that the reign of many ancient Greek kings was limited to eight years, or at least that at the end of every period of eight years a new consecration, a fresh outpouring of the divine grace, was regarded as necessary in order to enable them to discharge their civil and religious duties. Thus it was a rule of the Spartan constitution that every eighth year the ephors should choose a clear and moonless night and sitting down observe the sky in silence. If during their vigil they saw a meteor or shooting star, they inferred that the king had sinned against the deity, and they suspended him from his functions until the Delphic or Olympic oracle should reinstate him in them. This custom, which has all the air of great antiquity, was not suffered to remain a dead letter even in the last period of the Spartan monarchy; for in the third century before our era a king, who had rendered himself obnoxious to the reforming party, was actually deposed on various trumped-up charges, among which the allegation that the ominous sign had been seen in the sky took a prominent place.

If the tenure of the regal office was formerly limited among the Spartans to eight years, we may naturally ask, why was the precise period selected as the measure of a king's reign? The reason is probably to be found in those astronomical considerations which determined the early Greek calendar. The difficulty of reconciling lunar with solar time is one of the standing puzzles which has taxed the ingenuity of men who are emerging from barbarism. Now an octennial cycle is the shortest period at the end of which sun and moon really mark time together after overlapping, so to say, throughout the whole of the interval. Thus, for example, it is only once in every eight years that the full moon coincides with the longest or shortest day; and as this coincidence can be observed with the aid of a simple dial, the observation is naturally one of the first to furnish a base for a calendar which shall bring lunar and solar times into tolerable, though not exact, harmony. But in early days the proper adjustment of the calendar is a matter of religious concern, since on it depends a knowledge of the right seasons for propitiating the deities whose favour is indispensable to the welfare of the community. No wonder, therefore, that the king, as the chief priest of the state, or as himself a god, should be liable to deposition or death at the end of an astronomical period. When the great luminaries had run their course on high, and were about to renew the heavenly race, it might well be thought that the king should renew his divine energies, or prove them unabated, under pain of making room for a more vigorous successor. In Southern India, as we have seen, the king's reign and life terminated with the revolution of the planet Jupiter round the sun. In Greece, on the other hand, the king's fate seems to have hung in the balance at the end of every eight years, ready to fly up and kick the beam as soon as the opposite scale was loaded with a falling star.

Whatever its origin may have been, the cycle of eight years appears to have coincided with the normal length of the king's reign in other parts of Greece beside Sparta. Thus Minos, king of Cnossus in Crete, whose great palace has been unearthed in recent years, is said to have held office for periods of eight years together. At the end of each period he retired for a season to the oracular cave on Mount Ida, and there communed with his divine father Zeus, giving him an account of his kingship in the years that were past, and receiving from him instructions for his guidance in those which were to come. The tradition plainly implies that at the end of every eight years the king's sacred powers needed to be renewed by intercourse with the godhead, and that without such a renewal he would have forfeited his right to the throne.

Without being unduly rash we may surmise that the tribute of seven youths and seven maidens whom the Athenians were bound to send to Minos every eight years had some connexion with the renewal of the king's power for another octennial cycle. Traditions varied as to the fate which awaited the lads and damsels on their arrival in Crete; but the common view appears to have been that they were shut up in the labyrinth, there to be devoured by the Minotaur, or at least to be imprisoned for life. Perhaps they were sacrificed by being roasted alive in a bronze image of a bull, or of a bull-headed man, in order to renew the strength of the king and of the sun, whom he personated. This at all events is suggested by the legend of Talos, a bronze man who clutched people to his breast and leaped with them into the fire, so that they were roasted alive. He is said to have been given by Zeus to Europa, or by Hephaestus to Minos, to guard the island of Crete, which he patrolled thrice daily. According to one account he was a bull, according to another he was the sun. Probably he was identical with the Minotaur, and stripped of his mythical features was nothing but a bronze image of the sun represented as a man with a bull's head. In order to renew the solar fires, human victims may have been sacrificed to the idol by being roasted in its hollow body or placed on its sloping hands and allowed to roll into a pit of fire. It was in the latter fashion that the Carthaginians sacrificed their offspring to Moloch. The children were laid on the hands of a calf-headed image of bronze, from which they slid into a fiery oven, while the people danced to the music of flutes and timbrels to drown the shrieks of the burning victims. The resemblance which the Cretan traditions bear to the Carthaginian practice suggests that the worship associated with the names of Minos and the Minotaur may have been powerfully influenced by that of a Semitic Baal. In the tradition of Phalaris, tyrant of Agrigentum, and his brazen bull we may have an echo of similar rites in Sicily, where the Carthaginian power struck deep roots.

In the province of Lagos the Ijebu tribe of the Yoruba race is divided into two branches, which are known respectively as the Ijebu Ode and the Ijebu Remon. The Ode branch of the tribe is ruled by a chief who bears the title of Awujale and is surrounded by a great deal of mystery. Down to recent times his face might not be seen even by his own subjects, and if circumstances obliged him to communicate with them he did so through a screen which hid him from view. The other or Remon branch of the Ijebu tribe is governed by a chief, who ranks below the Awujale. Mr. John Parkinson was informed that in former times this subordinate chief used to be killed with ceremony after a rule of three years. As the country is now under British protection the custom of putting the chief to death at the end of a three years' reign has long been abolished, and Mr. Parkinson was unable to ascertain any particulars on the subject.

At Babylon, within historical times, the tenure of the kingly office was in practice lifelong, yet in theory it would seem to have been merely annual. For every year at the festival of Zagmuk the king had to renew his power by seizing the hands of the image of Marduk in his great temple of Esagil at Babylon. Even when Babylon passed under the power of Assyria, the monarchs of that country were expected to legalise their claim to the throne every year by coming to Babylon and performing the ancient ceremony at the New Year festival, and some of them found the obligation so burdensome that rather than discharge it they renounced the title of king altogether and contented themselves with the humbler one of Governor. Further, it would appear that in remote times, though not within the historical period, the kings of Babylon or their barbarous predecessors forfeited not merely their crown but their life at the end of a year's tenure of office. At least this is the conclusion to which the following evidence seems to point. According to the historian Berosus, who as a Babylonian priest spoke with ample knowledge, there was annually celebrated in Babylon a festival called the Sacaea. It began on the sixteenth day of the month Lous, and lasted for five days, during which masters and servants changed places, the servants giving orders and the masters obeying them. A prisoner condemned to death was dressed in the king's robes, seated on the king's throne, allowed to issue whatever commands he pleased, to eat, drink, and enjoy himself, and to lie with the king's concubines. But at the end of the five days he was stripped of his royal robes, scourged, and hanged or impaled. During his brief term of office he bore the title of Zoganes. This custom might perhaps have been explained as merely a grim jest perpetrated in a season of jollity at the expense of an unhappy criminal. But one circumstance—the leave given to the mock king to enjoy the king's concubines—is decisive against this interpretation. Considering the jealous seclusion of an oriental despot's harem we may be quite certain that permission to invade it would never have been granted by the despot, least of all to a condemned criminal, except for the very gravest cause. This cause could hardly be other than that the condemned man was about to die in the king's stead, and that to make the substitution perfect it was necessary he should enjoy the full rights of royalty during his brief reign. There is nothing surprising in this substitution. The rule that the king must be put to death either on the appearance of any symptom of bodily decay or at the end of a fixed period is certainly one which, sooner or later, the kings would seek to abolish or modify. We have seen that in Ethiopia, Sofala, and Eyeo the rule was boldly set aside by enlightened monarchs; and that in Calicut the old custom of killing the king at the end of twelve years was changed into a permission granted to any one at the end of the twelve years' period to attack the king, and, in the event of killing him, to reign in his stead; though, as the king took care at these times to be surrounded by his guards, the permission was little more than a form. Another way of modifying the stern old rule is seen in the Babylonian custom just described. When the time drew near for the king to be put to death (in Babylon this appears to have been at the end of a single year's reign) he abdicated for a few days, during which a temporary king reigned and suffered in his stead. At first the temporary king may have been an innocent person, possibly a member of the king's own family; but with the growth of civilisation the sacrifice of an innocent person would be revolting to the public sentiment, and accordingly a condemned criminal would be invested with the brief and fatal sovereignty. In the sequel we shall find other examples of a dying criminal representing a dying god. For we must not forget that, as the case of the Shilluk kings clearly shows, the king is slain in his character of a god or a demigod, his death and resurrection, as the only means of perpetuating the divine life unimpaired, being deemed necessary for the salvation of his people and the world.

A vestige of a practice of putting the king to death at the end of a year's reign appears to have survived in the festival called Macahity, which used to be celebrated in Hawaii during the last month of the year. About a hundred years ago a Russian voyager described the custom as follows: "The taboo Macahity is not unlike to our festival of Christmas. It continues a whole month, during which the people amuse themselves with dances, plays, and sham-fights of every kind. The king must open this festival wherever he is. On this occasion his majesty dresses himself in his richest cloak and helmet, and is paddled in a canoe along the shore, followed sometimes by many of his subjects.
He embarks early, and must finish his excursion at sunrise. The strongest and most expert of the warriors is chosen to receive him on his landing. This warrior watches the canoe along the beach; and as soon as the king lands, and has thrown off his cloak, he darts his spear at him, from a distance of about thirty paces, and the king must either catch the spear in his hand, or suffer from it: there is no jesting in the business. Having caught it, he carries it under his arm, with the sharp end downwards, into the temple or *heavoo*. On his entrance, the assembled multitude begin their sham-fights, and immediately the air is obscured by clouds of spears, made for the occasion with blunted ends. Hamamea [the king] has been frequently advised to abolish this ridiculous ceremony, in which he risks his life every year; but to no effect. His answer always is, that he is as able to catch a spear as any one of the island is to throw it at him. During the Macahity, all punishments are remitted throughout the country; and no person can leave the place in which he commences these holidays, let the affair be ever so important."

That a king should regularly have been put to death at the close of a year's reign will hardly appear improbable when we learn that to this day there is still a kingdom in which the reign and the life of the sovereign are limited to a single day. In Ngoio, a province of the ancient kingdom of Congo, the rule obtains that the chief who assumes the cap of sovereignty is always killed on the night after his coronation. The right of succession lies with the chief of the Musurongo; but we need not wonder that he does not exercise it, and that the throne stands vacant. "No one likes to lose his life for a few hours' glory on the Ngoio throne."

Secondary Source 1.5   Eric Csapo, 'Frazer's *Golden Bough*'

(Source: Csapo, E. (2005) *Theories of Mythology*, Malden MA and Oxford, Blackwell Publishing, pp. 36–43 and selected references)

Frazer's magnum opus, *The Golden Bough*, is one of the truly great works of modern anthropology, a professional as well as a popular classic. For over a century it has adorned the shelves of more home libraries than any anthropological work written before or since. It was originally published in two volumes in 1890, expanded to three in the second edition of 1900, to twelve in a third edition of 1911–15, and acquired a further supplement volume in 1936. In 1922 a 714-page abridgment of the work was made, largely by Frazer's wife; Frazer himself "was constitutionally incapable of abridging anything" (Frazer in Frazer 1994: xl). Much is said about Frazer's style when we note that the abridgment reduced the bulk of the work by a whopping 84 percent, mainly by eliminating the notes and thousands of superfluous examples. Another abridgment by Gaster (1959) reduces the work by a further 30 percent, only to make up for it in endnotes. The best abridgment is by Robert Fraser (1994), but the 1922 version is better known, and is therefore cited here wherever possible.

Any attempt to summarize this enormous work undercuts its persuasive eloquence and the compelling weight of its widely researched and sometimes detailed examples. Frazer's impulse to expand, rather than contract, was well-founded: when the liopleurodon is stripped to its bare bones, robbed of the intimidating bulk of its scholarship and the narcotic splendor of its poetry, one finds a fairly thin line of argument with sometimes very loose and awkward joins. This in itself makes the exercise worthwhile; though it can only be done at the cost of obscuring typical features of argumentation which make the work rhetorically persuasive despite the tenuous logical links. Conspicuous features of Frazer's style of argument (and that of most of his contemporary comparatists) are: (1) the looseness of the equations; (2) the reliance on suggestive and circumstantial detail; (3) the tendency to persuade by suggesting a large number of alternatives, all tending in the same direction, as if exhausting the possibilities, and cumulatively overdetermining the desired connection; (4) the disparate quality of the sources of evidence; and (5) the tendency to list all positive examples, but either no or few negative ones. Feature 1 arises from the assumptions behind Frazer's use of the comparative method. Convinced that human society everywhere goes through the same stages, then "if some behaviour has been observed in, say, the jungles of the Amazon but, unfortunately , not in the jungles of the Congo ... then it is perfectly in order to use data from the Amazon to make a point about the Congo" (Ackerman 1987: 47). The logical "knight's move" may be observed also in the reliance on circumstantial detail (feature 2). Not all the examples given in Frazer's lists include the details relevant to the point he is making, but are included because they resemble relevant examples in other circumstantial details, and so allow the missing links to be inferred. This feature also appears at more important junctures in the argument of the *Golden Bough*: note, for example, Frazer's argument which connects mistletoe to the fire of the sun. Frazer can find no example of a direct link, but he can make a direct link between fern-seed and the sun; as there are many similarities in the cultivation and treatment of mistletoe and fern-seed (both are collected in midsummer and midwinter and used in divining rods), it only stands to reason that the recorded folktale which makes fern-seed the blood of the sun uncovers a primitive logic which must assert the same of mistletoe. Features 4 and 5 have to some extent been discussed in ... Chapter 1, though in relation to the former it is worth noting that the early part of *The Golden Bough* relies most heavily on ethnographic data from contemporary savages, the central section on Greco-Roman and Near Eastern myth, and the last section on modern European folklore.

The Golden Bough opens with a skilfully drawn landscape with figures. A few miles south of Rome in the Alban hills of Latium there is a small volcanic basin which contains a lake, surrounded, in antiquity, by a dark oak forest. This forest was sacred to Diana, and in it she had a temple. The priest of the temple was selected by a bizarre rite. Only a runaway slave could accede to the priesthood by finding his way into the grove, plucking a branch (called "the golden bough") from a sacred tree, and then killing the former priest in single combat. In his turn, the new priest would spend his days and nights vigilantly guarding the tree, and waiting for the ineluctable appearance of his own assassin and successor. The priest was called the "King of the Wood."

True to his method, Frazer begins immediately by identifying this rite as a "survival": "No one will probably deny that such a custom savours of a barbarous age, and, surviving into imperial times, stands out in striking isolation from the polished Italian society of the day, like a primaeval rock rising from a smooth-shaven lawn" (1922: 2). But an explanation is possible, thanks to the very rudeness of the custom (2):

> For recent researches into the early history of man have revealed the essential similarity with which, under many superficial differences, the human mind has elaborated its first crude philosophy of life. Accordingly, if we can show that a barbarous custom, like that of the priesthood of Nemi, has existed elsewhere; if we can detect the motives which led to its institution; if we can prove that these motives have operated widely, perhaps universally, in human society, producing in varied circumstances a variety of institutions specifically different but generically alike; if we can show, lastly, that these very motives, with some of their derivative institutions were actually at work in classical antiquity; then we may fairly infer that at a remoter age the same motives gave birth to the priesthood of Nemi.

Frazer begins by drawing attention to Diana's character as a goddess of fertility and as a keeper of sacred fire. The cult was initiated when Orestes brought the image of Artemis (= Diana) to the grove, from Taurus, where she notoriously demanded human sacrifice. In myth Diana's young lover Hippolytus was said to have been brought back to life, transported to Nemi, and given as a consort to the nymph Egeria. Frazer finds parallels to the relationship between the goddess and the king in the relationship of other goddesses to short-lived mortal consorts, such as Aphrodite and Adonis or Cybele and Attis. The grove of Nemi is also the place where Numa, the Roman king, consorted with Egeria. The overture ends with many hanging questions: Why is this priest a "King of the Wood?" What is his relation to Diana? What is their relation to Numa and Egeria? Why is he sacrificed? What is the "King's" relation to the sacred fire? What is his relation to the golden bough?

Frazer then elaborates a three-stage scheme for the history of human culture upon which the answers to these questions will depend. An Age of Magic, surviving still among the Australian aborigines, is followed by an Age of Religion, and then by an Age of Science, known so far only in the West. Magic is a straightforward attempt to manipulate nature on the basis of an erroneous theory of natural causality, whereas religion is an attempt to control nature through the propitiation of spirits or gods. Magic is paradoxically more scientific than religion: it is a false science based upon a spurious system of natural law. Of magic, there are two types. The first Frazer calls "imitative" (or "homeopathic") magic, which operates through a law of similarity. This is the belief that by acting on something which resembles another object, you act upon that belief itself, as, for example, when you put pins into a voodoo doll with the intention of harming the person in whose image the doll is made. The second type is "contagious" magic, which operates through a law of contact, so that acting upon a part of something is supposed to affect the whole, as, for example, when a witch strikes a knife in a person's footprint in the hope of laming that person. Religion arises when the belief that nature is governed by "immutable laws acting mechanically" is abandoned for a belief that the course of nature is determined "by the passions or caprice of personal beings"; religion is thus defined as "a propitiation or conciliation of powers superior to man which are believed to direct and control the course of nature and of human life" (50–1). The Age of Magic shades into the Age of Religion through stages as magical powers become increasingly concentrated. At first magic was practiced communally, then concentrated in the hands of a caste of medicine men, and finally in the hands of a single all-powerful "priest king." Later, when greater magical powers are ascribed to a particular individual, somewhere "midway between the age of magic and the age of religion" (162), there are "divine kings." The Age of Religion properly begins when divinity is finally abstracted from the person of the king. In the age of divine kings, though there is a notion of divinity, nature can still be manipulated, through contagious magic, by acting upon the person of the king.

Turning his attention now to the priest of Diana, who was also styled "King of the Wood," Frazer examines the plentiful evidence for belief in tree-spirits. The progress from animism to polytheism is demonstrated by the replacement of the belief that the tree embodies a spirit by the belief that the spirit only occasionally inhabits the tree. Tree-spirits come to be thought of as having human or animal form. Male and female tree-spirits are sometimes represented as bridegroom and bride, sometimes also as king and queen. Frazer infers from European spring festivals (deemed "remnants") that "our rude forefathers personified the powers of vegetation as male and female, and attempted, on the principle of homeopathic or imitative magic, to quicken the growth of trees and plants by representing the marriage of the sylvan deities in the persons of the King and Queen of May" (135). Ancient sacred marriages also served to promote fertility. Thus, Frazer concludes, the King of the Wood and Diana formed a sacred couple for fertility magic. The same divinities appear in the marriage of Numa, the Roman king, with Egeria, another name for the goddess of the grove.
The Roman kings represented themselves as Jupiter at times, and Jupiter must have been the divine embodiment of the early Roman kings. Jupiter was god of the oak and of lightning. The early kings must have represented themselves as oak-spirits with the power to control the lightning and the rain. Early Rome, like many early societies, was matrilineal – the kingship was handed down by marriage with the princess, who was won in a contest, held annually. The King of the Wood was none other than Dianus (or Janus a form of Jupiter), the Aryan god of the thunder and the oak. His consort was Diana (a form of Juno), goddess of the oak (Egeria was a dryad, an oak nymph) and the sacred fire. In Aryan religion the communal, perpetual (Vestal) fire was fed with oak-wood. Nemi was an oak grove. So the fire and the oak were identical.

After demonstrating that the King of the Wood was originally a "divine king," Frazer turns his attention to the manner of his ritual killing. The comparanda show, he argues, that divine kings are normally sacrificed and replaced, at first when their powers begin to wane (so as not to allow a sympathetic withering of the crops), in order to renew nature, ensure fertility, and secure the food supply. The memory of this sacrifice is preserved in the myths of the death and rebirth of the god/mortal lover of the goddess (e.g., Adonis, Attis, Osiris, Dionysus). Later, the dying god is thought of as a vegetation spirit (tree-spirit, corn-spirit). Hence the sacrifice, earlier linked to the life of the king, is synchronized with the agrarian cycle and becomes an annual sacrifice to guarantee the renewal of spring. Sacrifice evolved from the periodic sacrifice of the divine king to the sacrifice of a substitute, then to the sacrifice of a human victim only in times of emergency, and finally to animal sacrifice. Scapegoat rituals are explained in terms of the primitive belief that evil could be transferred to inanimate objects, then to sacrificial victims. Since the king (or his substitute) was being sacrificed anyway, it was convenient to transfer sins to him so that he could take them away.

Having dealt with the sacrificial combat of the divine King of the Wood, Frazer probes further into his relationship to the sacred fire kept in Diana's temple. In Europe, since the Middle Ages, at certain times of year fire ceremonies take place which show traces of human sacrifice: usually an effigy of Winter, Old Age, or Death is burnt or one of the company is selected for mock-immolation (in some cases dressed up in green leaves), while the peasants dance around the fire or leap over it, which they do for fertility and purification (cf. divine king and scapegoat). These customs, he urges, originate in the burning of the vegetation-spirit: in addition to renewal through replacing the old spirit, the fire imitates the light and heat of the sun, necessary to the growth of crops, and so is a form of sympathetic magic. Sacrifice by burning the victim alive has wider cosmological implications than simple blood-sacrifice, since it renews not only the fertility of nature but also the light of the sun. Later, Frazer surmises that the King of the Wood originally met his end in a fire-sacrifice.

The final sections of *The Golden Bough* are taken up in a search for the rationale behind the requirement that the challenger of the King of the Wood pluck a branch from the sacred oak. In the Norse myth of Balder, Balder is invulnerable to everything but the mistletoe, by which he is slain, and thereafter he is consumed by a great fire. Ancient Aryans attributed great powers to the mistletoe which they thought sent from heaven, notably by lightning falling upon oak trees. In Nordic countries mistletoe is collected on Midsummer's Eve at the time of bonfires called "Balder's balefires." "In other words, we may assume with some degree of probability that the myth of Balder's death was not merely a myth, that is, a description of physical phenomena in imagery borrowed from human life, but that it was at that same time the story which people told to explain why they annually burned a human representative of the god and cut the mistletoe with solemn ceremony" (664). In view of the importance of the oak to Aryan mythology and the use of oak in the fire festivals, Frazer concludes Balder was the tree-spirit of the oak. The myth of Balder is to be explained by a belief that the seat of life of the oak was the mistletoe which grows evergreen upon the deciduous tree, and that in order to take the life of the tree-spirit, one had first to remove the mistletoe. The mistletoe was apparently thought to be indestructible and communicated its indestructibility to the oak so long as it was attached.

If the mistletoe had to be removed before killing the tree or the tree-spirit, this does not quite explain why a branch of the oak had to be removed before killing the tree- or vegetation-spirit behind the King of the Wood. To explain the plucking of the golden bough, Frazer has recourse to a large number of modern folktales (Punchkin) in Indo-European languages which show a belief in an "external soul," i.e., an inanimate object, animal, or plant in which a person deposits his soul or life for safekeeping (and for the apparent Aryan belief in the external soul, Frazer can find ample comparanda in the totemistic practices of various non-Aryans). Balder's life, he concludes, was deposited in the mistletoe just as the life of the oak. The same must have been true of the King of the Wood and the golden bough. Conveniently, a passage of Virgil's *Aeneid* compares the golden bough growing in the holm oak to a mistletoe. "The inference is almost inevitable that the Golden Bough was nothing but the mistletoe seen through the haze of poetry or of popular superstition" (703). Hence the life or external soul of the King of the Wood (= oak spirit) was deposited in the golden bough (= mistletoe), and this is why the bough had to be plucked before he could be killed in combat. "And to complete the parallel," Frazer adds (703–4),

> it is only necessary to suppose that the King of the Wood was formerly burned, dead or alive, at the midsummer fire festival which, as we have seen, was annually celebrated in the Arician grove. The perpetual fire which burned in the grove, like the perpetual fire which burned in the temple of Vesta at Rome and under the oak at Romove, was probably fed with the sacred oak-wood; and thus it would be in a great fire of oak that the King of the Wood formerly met his end. At a late time, as I have suggested, his annual tenure of office was lengthened or shortened, as the case might be, by the rule which allowed him to live so long as he could prove his divine right by the strong hand. But he only escaped the fire to fall by the sword. ... The rite was probably an essential feature in the ancient Aryan worship of the oak.

But why is the bough "golden" when mistletoe is in fact white, or at best a yellowish-white? To answer this question Frazer invokes the analogy of the fern-seed, said in a German fairytale to be the blood of the sun, and also collected by peasants throughout Europe at the time of the summer and winter solstice (like mistletoe). Contemporary European peasants used it, like the mistletoe, as a charm against fire (homeopathic magic), and also as a divining rod for finding gold. Mistletoe is therefore conceived as an emanation of the golden fire of the sun. Now the reason for the midsummer bonfires, according to Frazer, is to "feed" the sun at the time of the solstice; hence it was also thought that the sun's fire was an emanation of the mistletoe, as the seed of this fire, or as the soul of the oak which fed the fire. One last flourish: the Aryans connected the oak with lightning because, among trees, it is the most likely to be struck. The Druids thought that the mistletoe descended from heaven, and in Aargau mistletoe is called "thunder-besom." This shows that the old Aryans believed the mistletoe to be celestial fire descended from heaven by lightning on Midsummer's Eve. The oak is struck by lightning more often than other trees and so was thought to be the sacred terrestrial repository of the sky-god's soul. Mistletoe is thought to be golden because the fire from heaven remains smoldering inside.

The priest at Nemi was therefore a degenerate survival of a divine king/ vegetation-spirit, later turned sky-god. The rule of succession through combat is the survival of a time when divine kings were sacrificed (first by fire and then by the sword) and replaced in order to ensure the reinvigoration of the crops. The particular requirement that the golden bough be plucked was a survival of the time when the sky-god/tree-spirit's soul was thought to be deposited in the mistletoe. Various aspects of the sky-god/tree-spirit's cult were transferred to his consort, Diana, originally Queen of Heaven: in particular she remained the guardian of forests and animal life, and the guardian of the sacred flame.

Lurking in the shadows behind the priest of Nemi is another divine king: Jesus Christ is in an important sense the real subject of the book. Frazer's full revised edition has seven parts (some with two volumes), of which the sixth is devoted to discussion of the scapegoat. This section of the work is barely mentioned in my summary because totally irrelevant to the explanation of the priesthood at Nemi. It has, however, a great deal to do with the impact and success of the *Golden Bough*. Implicitly in the first edition, then explicitly in the second, Frazer characterized Jesus Christ as a typical Near Eastern dying-god figure, a fertility spirit, rooted in primeval magic, whose death and resurrection were designed to promote agriculture. But Christ also took away men's sins, and so Frazer's sixth section, the climax of the whole work, ends with an extended comparison of Christ with typically barbaric rites of human sacrifice. Christianity is reduced to just another example of the murky confusion of savage thought. As if in fear the point might be lost to subtlety, Frazer's great peroration in the last paragraph of the twelfth volume describes the traveler/reader returning on the Appian Way in language that insists that Christ and the Christian martyrs descend in a direct lineage from the runaway slave burned in the wood at Nemi: "glimpsing the sky aflame with sunset, its golden glory resting like the aureole of a dying saint over Rome and touching with a crest of fire the dome of St. Peter's," and as he looks back at the unchanging grove of Diana, he hears borne on the wind (at an impossible distance) the church bells of Rome ringing the Angelus. "Sweet and solemn they chime out from the distant city and die lingeringly away across the wide Campagnan marshes. *Le roi est mort, vive le roi! Ave Maria!*" (714). The Golden Bough really does argue "the essential similarity with which, under many superficial differences, the human mind has elaborated its first crude philosophy of life." Christianity was just one of those superficial differences and Christian morality could no longer be reckoned among the features that distinguished the European from the savage. Only science could.

Despite all the delicious scandal aroused by this treatment of Christianity and the notoriety and success it guaranteed for his work, Frazer was cowed by the criticism it provoked. In his third edition the section dealing with the crucifixion of Christ was relegated to an appendix. In Frazer's abridgment it was deleted altogether, along with several other sections implicitly relevant to Christian beliefs (Fraser's 1994 abridgment reinserts it in its proper place). Robert Graves suggested that Frazer muffled his iconoclasm in order to keep his nice office at Trinity College. But this is surely too cynical: by all accounts Frazer was a shy and retiring man, sensitive to criticism, and indeed a regular churchgoer, able, in the name of social respectability, like many of the great Victorian atheists, to separate science and religion in practice as easily as they did in thought.
We have seen the care Frazer took, in *Folklore in the Old Testament*, to characterize his method and scholarship as an *advocatus dei*, however hollow or subtly ironic the claim.

References

Ackerman, R. 1987. *J. G. Frazer: His Life and Work.* Cambridge.

Frazer, J. G. 1994. *The Golden Bough.* Abridged ed. R. Fraser. Cambridge.

Gaster, T. H. 1959. *The New Golden Bough: A New Abridgement of the Classic Work by Sir James George Frazer.* New York.

Secondary Source 1.6   Eric Csapo, 'Comparative Approaches'

(Source: Csapo, E. (2005) *Theories of Mythology*, Malden, MA and Oxford, Blackwell Publishing, chapter 2, pp. 10–21, 30–2 and selected references)

> From one perspective, the British may indeed have seen the peoples of their empire as alien, as other, as beneath them – to be lorded over and condescended to. But from another, they also saw them as similar, as analogous, as equal and sometimes even as better than they were themselves. ... And this view was not just socially conservative, but politically conservative too. ... the whole purpose of the British Empire was "to maintain traditional rulerships as a fortress of societal security in a changing world." And in that enterprise, the colour of a person's skin was less significant than their position in the local social hierarchy: "the really important category was status," and as such it was "fundamental to all other categories."
>
> D. Cannadine, *Ornamentalism*, 123–4

> He is a barbarian, and thinks that the customs of his tribe and island are the laws of nature.
>
> G.B. Shaw, *Caesar and Cleopatra*, act 2

2.1   THE RISE OF THE COMPARATIVE METHOD

Some social conditions behind the birth of comparative mythology

Comparative mythology became a discipline during the age of European imperialism. More than coincidence links the method with its social context. Since the Renaissance, anything that might be regarded as "myth" had been only of interest to students of Greco-Roman literature, and principally because of its transformation into literature. For any other purpose "myths" were objects of revulsion and contempt. But the fortunes of myth rose gradually with the imperial enterprise, when, increasingly, it was myth in its raw, preliterary state which captured the European imagination. This is not to say that myth rose significantly in estimation. Myths were still objects of revulsion and contempt, but interesting objects, mainly for the light they supposedly shed upon the character of the mythmaker. The mythmaker, in his turn, whether non-European or ancient European, was primarily of interest as an object of comparison – a foil – for his European observer. Myth became a tool of European self-discovery.

The story of the invention of the modern science of mythology is inseparable from the story of the invention of anthropology. When Europe began to expand, first by exploration and then by trade, finally by conquest, exploitation, and colonization, Europeans came into contact with a great many races with strange customs, languages, and religions. It was useful to gain some understanding of the ways and manners of these many diverse nations, if only to learn to deal with them more effectively. But neither the ability nor the desire to describe others comes naturally. The earliest travelers' reports are surprisingly uninformative about native peoples, tending toward superficial sketches in the midst of more detailed inventories of the real estate and its mineral, botanical, and zoological riches. Even when the natives managed in some way to make an impression upon the early explorers' consciousness, the descriptions tended to be contradictory, even self-contradictory, and the contradictions tended to extremes. Tzvetan Todorov's *Conquest of America* (1984) shows that Columbus's letters describe the "discovered" populations at times as vicious beasts, and at others as "noble savages" living in a state of Edenic innocence. Indeed, he was able to reach these opposite conclusions while observing the very same traits in different contexts. The Caribbean aboriginals had no concept of private property. When they allowed him to help himself to their goods, Columbus declared them the most upright, generous, and liberal people in the world. A little later they helped themselves to Columbus's goods; he declared them vicious, perverse schemers and cut off their ears and noses. Both explanations missed the point because Columbus could only understand the actions of the Indians within his own cultural framework. Both explanations create an absolute distance between the aboriginals and Europeans. Civilization for the early European explorers meant European culture. With such a definition, the Caribbean Indians could only exist either in a subhuman or in a precivilized state. Columbus was completely unable to perceive that their system of values was simply different from his own. He mistook the difference for an absence of values. "These two elementary figures of the experience of alterity are both grounded in egocentrism, in the identification of our own values with values in general, of our *I* with the universe – in the conviction that the world is one" (39–40).

So long as Europe adhered to its traditional values with unswerving conviction, the perception of similarities and differences, whether of institutions, customs, or myths, would rarely exceed an interpretive framework which was itself explicitly mythical. For example, Diego Durán, a Dominican friar who accompanied Cortez, is one of the most acute observers of the Aztecs. He noted many similarities in their rituals to Christian rituals, but exaggerated them. They were nearly the same or "exactly" alike, and the doctrine was often treated as identical: the Aztecs "revered the Father, the Son and the Holy Ghost, and called them Tota, Topiltzin and Yolometl; these words mean Our Father, Our Son, and the Heart of Both, honouring each one separately and all three as a unity" (1967.1:8). To explain this Durán offered two theories: that St. Thomas had come to Mexico to spread the Gospel, but it degenerated and came to be mixed "with their idolatry, bloody and abominable" (9); or that "the devil our cursed adversary forced the Indians to imitate the ceremonies of the Christian Catholic religion in his own service and cult" (3). Myths and rituals either preserve the true faith or are parodies scripted by the devil.

So long as Europeans remained confidently centered in their traditional ways and beliefs, the "other" could be observed, but the data could only be measured on a single scale, which might show the savage better or worse than the European, but never qualitatively different. European exploration and conquest do not, in themselves, explain the rise of mythology or anthropology: they provided only the experience of foreign cultures, the raw data, but not the mindset which could turn their observations into a meaningful science. This depended on fundamental changes in Europe itself, which undermined the European's confident assumption that his ways were God's. The most intense period of European expansion, from the seventeenth into the twentieth century, was also a period of rapid change, upheaval, and serious division within European society. Economically there was a change from the dominance of agriculture to the dominance of industry. Politically and socially there was a shift from a hierarchic to a more egalitarian configuration of power. These processes sufficed to install a new and very different set of values, but in the context of imperialism, they did much more: they engendered what sociologists call "a crisis in values."

In *Ideology and Utopia* (1936) Karl Mannheim explains how a process of democratization in combination with an imperial enterprise is likely to lead to a crisis in values. Democratization creates a period of high social mobility, in which people of one class change social status and learn to see their society through the eyes of another class. Imperialism brings people into contact with other nations with different ways and different values. Neither imperialism nor democratization by themselves need upset traditional values. But one source of cultural disorientation reinforces the other, and the combined impact of vertical mobility between classes and horizontal mobility between cultures is very likely to shake the belief in the eternal and universal validity of one's traditional way of thinking. Mannheim was describing, in the first instance, the ancient Greek, not the modern European "Enlightenment," though the latter was very much in his mind. With the addition of industrial capitalism this process is only intensified, since the new economic system displaced huge segments of the population from rural to urban areas, greatly increased the mobility between classes, upward and downward, by increasing the volubility of wealth, and also increased the traffic of people and goods to the colonies by integrating them within the economy of the imperial capital as sources of raw materials, sources of labor, and markets for manufactured goods.

The large-scale vertical and horizontal displacements of the modern era enabled Europeans to perceive and then to entertain different systems of values, and eventually to be more tolerant and finally more receptive to other ways of thinking and doing things. The once unified, absolute, and authoritarian code of Christian belief yielded to the pluralistic, relativistic, and (more) egalitarian discourse of today's "global culture" (which despite its name, is thoroughly Western). In four hundred years European civilization and its offshoots passed from a state of absolute assurance that their ways were the ways of God, while the ways of other peoples were curiosities, perversions, errors, or heresies, to a belief in the artificiality and constructedness of all values. The final victim of European imperialism was Europe itself. As Terry Eagleton puts it: "it is hard to remain convinced that your way of doing things is the only possible one when you are busy trying to subjugate another society which conducts its affairs in a radically different but apparently effective way" (1991: 107). It becomes impossible, when, through the inner dynamics of one's own culture, one's values are in doubt even before confronting the other.

Comparative mythology and comparative anthropology would never have been interesting, nor really possible, unless European values were shaken both internally through rapid cultural change and externally through rapid imperial expansion. Comparative social science has no place in a world of cultural absolutism. In such a world there is only one culture and nothing to compare it to but an absence of culture. But comparatism fares little better in a world of complete cultural relativism. In such a world there are no grounds for comparison, and no evident profit in the exercise. The discipline found its ideal habitat somewhere in the middle ground between the cultural absolutism of the seventeenth century and cultural relativism of the twenty-first, when cultures were looked upon as different, and different in their own right, but not so different that they defied common measure, no matter how abstract the scale. The heyday of comparative mythology lasted from about the 1850s to the 1920s when there was still a confident belief in the superiority of European culture, but far less agreement about how precisely one defined its distinctive difference: one could still draw direct comparisons, and, not coincidentally, profit from an air of scandal whether one insisted on the sameness or difference of another culture's ways to one's own.

Mythology was an especially important figure in the discourse of self and other. It was thought to give direct access to mentality and intelligence. When, in its heyday, comparative mythology explicitly compared myths, beliefs, and cultures, it implicitly compared the mental powers of men of different races, in terms of agility, rationality, the capacity to rise above superstition, see truth, give direction, and provide leadership – at stake ultimately was the justification of European hegemony. But if much of the excitement generated by early comparatism had to do implicitly or explicitly with race and imperial relations, it was also connected implicitly or explicitly with the competing value systems within Europe itself. If the image of the savage, with all its contradictions, was essentially a foil for European self-definition, sometimes the poles of its contradictions were set by opposed value systems within European society. Savage societies, and often even highly civilized ones, were reconfigured after the image of European society, in such a way as to offset differentially the chief divisions within European ideology. We will see this double-determination at work in the comparative method, practiced by Müller, Frazer, and other myth-theorists examined in this volume.

William Jones and the discovery of Indo-European

The development of an administrative apparatus for the effective maintenance and commercial exploitation of Europe's overseas empires provided the stimulus for the earliest scientific ethnographic research. In particular, it was the administration of British India, the most complex and sophisticated of all European dominions, which supplied the immediate context for the creation of comparative linguistics and comparative mythology.

Imperial expansion eastward brought a new interest in Oriental languages to English schools. In the mid-eighteenth century the middle-class Welshman William Jones (1746–94) was able to acquire at Harrow and Oxford, in addition to the usual fare of Greek and Latin, a knowledge of Hebrew, Arabic, Persian, Turkish, and Chinese. (Sanskrit the ancient language of India, written from about 1500 BC, first acquired a place in the curriculum of a European institution of higher learning with the foundation of a training school for the East India Company, East India College, in England in 1806.) Despite his interest in Oriental languages, Jones, by his own admission, would never have studied Sanskrit, even when appointed Justice of the High Court of Bengal in Calcutta in 1783, if not for his distrust of the pandits hired by the Court to advise him on indigenous law (which was based on the interpretation of ancient texts). He soon became an enthusiast, however, and when he founded an "Asiatic Society" in Calcutta, he delivered a number of lectures comparing Sanskrit language and mythology with others. In one of these lectures in 1786 Jones declared (1807: 34–5).

> The Sanskrit language, whatever be its antiquity, is of a wonderful structure; more perfect than the Greek, more copious than the Latin, and more exquisitely refined than either, yet bearing to both of them a stronger affinity, both in the roots of verbs and in the forms of grammar, than could possibly have been produced by accident; so strong indeed, that no philologer could examine them all three, without believing them to have sprung from some common source, which, perhaps, no longer exists: there is a similar reason, though not quite so forcible, for supposing that both the Gothick and the Celtick, though blended with a very different idiom, had the same origin with Sanskrit; and the old Persian might be added to the same family.

With these words Jones is credited with the discovery of the language family that later came to be known variously as Indo-Aryan, Indo-Germanic (so called by German scholars after 1823), or Indo-European (coined in 1813). Jones was not in fact the first to notice close similarities in the vocabulary of contemporary and classical European languages, nor the first to posit a common origin for them (nationalistic European scholars had been claiming a privileged connection between their mother tongues and Greek and Latin since Giraldus Cambrensis in the twelfth century; most influentially, Marcus Boxhorn in the seventeenth century, derived European languages from Scythian!). Though Jones's linguistic arguments showed better scientific method (nothing, after all, is known of Scythian), his success had a great deal to do with immediate ideological concerns. He was, as Lincoln says, "the right man in the right time and place: that which he said was – or was taken to be – very much the right thing" (1999: 84).

Once the primordial unity of European languages was scientifically demonstrated this "fact" could be and was invested with mythical values. A common linguistic origin was immediately taken to imply a historical, cultural, and racial unity, and once the Proto-Indo-European or "Aryan" nation became an object of imagination, whether scientific or popular, it began to accumulate characteristics, usually to the detriment of other races and cultures. The accomplishments of the highly idealized cultures of Classical Antiquity, like the art and literature of ancient India, testified to the superior talents of this prodigious race in its earliest recorded history and purest expression. This tendency was equally pronounced among those who, like Jones himself, believed that linguistic comparison vindicated the biblical account of the original unity and dispersal of all mankind (Edenic unity, the Fall, the tower of Babel, the sons of Noah). For though European theorists might posit an original unity for all mankind (not just Europeans), they tended not to treat all the races as equal any more than did the biblical story, but established hierarchies among races by arranging the descendants of Shem, Ham, and Japheth in various orders of priority, and ascribing different ethical qualities to them.

Herder, Grimm, Romanticism, and comparative philology

Paradoxically Jones's "discovery" had its greatest impact on Germany, where internal turmoil and, above all, the fragmentation of the German-speaking population into numerous small and independent principalities with strong political and regional differences had prevented effective participation in the colonial enterprise so successfully pursued by European powers to the West and East. In its stead, however, the aspirations of a largely liberal and middle class for the unification of Germany within a modern nation-state created a deep need for the creation of a common German national identity. In the struggle for the political unification of Germany (which succeeded in 1871), language, literature, and folklore proved indispensable ideological tools.

In Germany the equation of language and *Volk* (common people, folk, nation) was an easy one. According to the highly influential critic and philosopher Johann Gottfried von Herder (1744–1803), language, folksong, and mythology were all the spontaneous (and true) expressions of national character. Great poetry, the highest form of cultural expression, was only possible if a language was itself poetic (and Herder's study of German syntax and phonetics demonstrated the still untapped poetic potential of German). But poetry was healthiest when a people was permitted spontaneous expression of emotion and imagination through its national language, and the best poetry was rooted in traditional folksong and folktale. By contrast, a language, and its literature, were prematurely withered by rationalism, or stunted by foreign influence. Herder argued that the vigorous development of German literature in the Middle Ages had been stunted by Enlightenment rationalism and all the foreign political, cultural, and religious influences that had seeped into Germany since the European Renaissance. Herder's ideas had an incalculable influence upon the nationalistic movements in Germany and throughout Europe. They also directly inspired two successive literary movements: *Sturm und Drang* and Romanticism owed Herder their characteristic antirationalism, medievalism, and patriotism, their cults of spontaneity, emotion, nature, and original genius, and their pursuit of the *Volksgeist* (national spirit) through folklore and myth.

In *Thoughts on the Philosophy of Human History* (1784–91) Herder had in fact anticipated Jones in asserting the historical unity of all mankind (which he also located in Central Asia). Once the various races had dispersed from their ancestral home they developed different physical, spiritual, and moral characteristics through subgroup endogamy (i.e., marriage exclusively between members of the community), the process of adaptation to the climates and geographical features of the countries they inhabited, and, most importantly, through the development of separate languages and mythologies. The theory made the historical study of poetry, language, and folk mythology the key to the reconstruction and recovery of the national psyche in its originary and pure form.

Typical of the intellectual ferment of post-Herderian Germany was the range of activities pursued by the brothers Jakob (1785–1863) and Wilhelm Grimm (1786–1859). Among their numerous publications they produced critical editions, collections, and studies of Old German poetry, minstrelsy, epics, legends, mythology and folktales, even ancient German law. Most important, however, were Jakob Grimm's *History of the German Language* and *German Grammar.* Taking advantage of Jones's discovery of Indo-European, Grimm was able, through comparing the forms of German with other Indo-European languages, to reach much farther back into the linguistic history of the Germanic peoples than written records allowed. In his study of grammar, notably, Jakob Grimm applied a rigorous method for describing consonant shifts in Indo-European, for which many credit him, along with his compatriot Franz Bopp (1791–1867), as founder of the science of historical linguistics.

As a simple illustration of what has come to be known as "Grimm's Law," consider the following list of stop consonants (sounds made by blocking the airflow of the vocal column) and aspirates (constriction but not complete stoppage of vocal column):

	1 *Voiceless stop*	2 *Voiced stop*	3 *Voiceless aspirate*	4 *Voiced aspirate*
Labial	p	b	ph or f	bh
Dental	t	d	th	dh
Palatal	k	g	kh	gh

According to Grimm, the changes from Proto-Indo-European to Germanic languages (including English) could be mapped as a general shift of consonants from column 1 to column 3, from column 2 to column 1, and from column 4 to column 2. This can be demonstrated by comparing words in Germanic languages with words in Indo-European languages thought to be closer to the original form. Thus the first rule (voiceless stop to voiceless aspirate) is illustrated by English "foot" (cf. German *Fuss*) compared to Sanskrit *pat (a)-*, Greek *pod-*, Latin *ped-*. The second rule is demonstrated by English "knee" (cf. German *Knie*) compared to Greek *gonu*, and Latin *genu*. The third rule is illustrated by English "brother" (German *Bruder*) compared to Sanskrit *bhrátar*. The observation of regular patterns such as these facilitated the reconstruction of the original Proto-Indo-European vocabulary, helped to identify linguistic subfamilies (e.g., "Germanic," "Celtic," "Italic," etc.), and also held out the prospect of a historical reconstruction of the relative departure and movements of the various linguistic groups from the common Indo-European homeland (this, however, has proved more problematic). [...]

2.2   MAX MÜLLER AND SOLAR MYTHOLOGY

Max Müller and attitudes toward British India

Friedrich Maximilian Müller (1823–1900), alias Max Müller (the more aristocratic-sounding double surname he adopted), is generally regarded as the founder of comparative mythology. A German by birth, he studied Sanskrit in Leipzig, Berlin (with Bopp), and Paris, and went to England in 1846 to edit and translate the (Sanskrit) *Rig Veda*. Upon receiving a commission for the work from the East India Company, he settled in Oxford and became a British subject. In 1868 Müller was appointed to a chair of Comparative Philology created specially for him, partly in consolation for narrowly missing an appointment as Boden Professor of Sanskrit. It seems his foreign birth and his political and religious views counted against his candidacy for the chair in Sanskrit (endowed expressly for the purpose of spreading Christianity to India by translating the Bible into Sanskrit). The bane of race theorists and assimilationists, throughout his life Müller spread admiration for India's languages, social structure, religion, and culture, emphasizing, wherever possible, not only their essential similarity, but their genetic relationship to their British equivalents. He counted it as one of the great accomplishments of nineteenth-century Orientalist research (as championed by himself) that the people of India had not only "ceased to be [regarded as] mere idolaters and niggers, they have been recognised as our brothers in language and thought" (1892: 34).

This is not to suggest that Müller's theories were generally anti-racist and anti-imperialist. They were so only with regard to India, and indeed only with regard to certain castes and regions of the Subcontinent. Müller adopted a two-race theory of the history of India. In remote antiquity the "Aryan" ("Japhetic" or "Caucasian") conquest brought the benefits of civilization to the "black" "Hamitic" races. The direct descendants of these Aryan warriors/culture heroes were, according to Müller, the upper-caste Brahmans (a priestly and scholarly caste which preserved and studied the Sanskrit texts). They were natural allies of Britain's own "civilizing mission." Indeed, Aryan and Briton played parallel roles at either end of the long history of Indian civilization: "it is curious to see," he declared, "how the descendants of the same race [i.e., the Aryan English], to which the first conquerors and masters of India belonged, returned, after having followed the northern development of the Japhetic race to their primordial soil, to accomplish the glorious work of civilization, which had been left unfinished by their Aryan brethren" (1847: 349). But he showed, through the example of India itself, that the task of civilization succeeded best where the conquerors worked through the medium of the conquered people's own language and culture. What was good for India seems pretty neatly to have coincided with what was good for Sanskrit studies: indeed, Müller knew and cared for only so much of the Indian subcontinent as was exactly coterminous with his academic discipline.

Despite Müller's triumphant claims, there were many even among Orientalists who continued to urge the inferiority of Indians in race and culture. Vigorous and widespread opposition to Müller came from two camps, described by Trautmann as "race science, which theorized the English common-sense view that the Indians, whatever the Sanskritists might say, were a separate, inferior, and *unimprovable* race"; and "a developmentalist, progressivist, liberal, and non-racial-essentialist critique of Hindu civilization in aid of a program for the improvement of India along European lines" (1997: 187–8). The latter urged a slightly less high-handed variety of coercion through assimilation, anxious to extend the benefits of science, technology, and economic progress, in sympathy with the broader spectrum of the British bourgeoisie, who were anxious to reap them. Both attitudes were doubtless common in the administrative culture of the East India Company: its East India College, typically, was founded to prepare British youths for the trials of life among "People every way dissimilar to their own" (Trautmann 1997: 115). The view that British and Indian were polar opposites allowed no hope of cultural coalescence.

Yet in the imperial administration, if not in academic circles, attitudes sympathetic to Müller's eventually prevailed. In 1858, in the wake of the Indian Mutiny, when the East India Company ceded administrative control of India to the Crown, the new imperial administration acquired a much more traditionally aristocratic character, less likely to see racial difference in "every way" than to find an appealing similarity between the hierarchical social stratification of India and Britain. Race became less interesting than pedigree, and indiscriminate claims of ethnic superiority less compelling than graded class distinctions. As David Cannadine's *Ornamentalism* amply demonstrates, British aristocrats came to regard India's culture as an idealized vision of a way of life that they as a class hoped to preserve – traditional, timeless, agrarian, intricately layered, and perfectly integrated: "it was atop this layered, Burkeian, agrarian image of Indian society that the British constructed a system of government that was simultaneously direct and indirect, authoritarian and collaborationist, but that always took for granted the reinforcement and preservation of tradition and hierarchy" (2001: 43). Viceroy, Governor, Maharajah, and Brahman were truly collaborators and brothers in the Aryan reconquest.

[...]

2.3 JAMES FRAZER

The rise of comparative anthropology

Even today James Frazer (1854–1941) is the most widely read exponent of the "comparative method" in the study of myth. Frazer's comparative method could not have been more different from Müller's. The latter was a direct borrowing from comparative linguistics. Müller subordinated anthropological interpretations to linguistic etymologies: his crude equations (e.g., Zeus = Dyaus) were based chiefly on linguistic arguments. Frazer's method was more purely anthropological. Having no interest in linguistics, he compared myths with myths and rites with rites.

Anthropology only gradually came unto its own as a formal discipline in the nineteenth century. Despite some initial impetus from linguistics and comparative philology at the beginning of the century, anthropology's chief sources of inspiration lay elsewhere. The first was the gradual increase (in quantity and quality) of available ethnographic data. Much of this was in the form of government reports or government-sponsored research. The nineteenth century produced the first serious studies of the indigenous cultures of Africa, the South Pacific, and Australia. Significantly, most of these cultures were simple societies based on tribal units.

Further stimulus came from the neighboring disciplines of geology and archaeology. Until about 1860 European scholars generally accepted a short chronology for human (and world) history: most influential was the chronology of Archbishop James Ussher who, in the 1650s, calculated, on the basis of a close reading of the Bible, that Creation began in 4004 BC. Charles Lyell, in *Principles of Geology* (1830–3), demonstrated that the geological features of the earth were to be explained as the result of processes that continue to operate. Moreover, he was able to show the great antiquity of life-forms through fossils contained in geological strata, and even the possibility of dating human remains, through stratigraphic analysis, to a much remoter antiquity than previously imagined. Lyell's lesson in chronology was slow to penetrate scholarly consciousness and only finally struck home a quarter-century later, when an only remotely related archaeological discovery captured the popular imagination. In 1858 quarrymen at Brixham in southwest England discovered a sealed cavern. A select committee of eminent geologists probed the cavern floor and found stone tools in a mix of mammoth, rhinoceros, and cave-bear bones. For the scientifically minded, philologically based theories, like Müller's, now barely a year out of press, lost some of their éclat. The "Aryan family," which, on the traditional chronology, was close to Eden in time and place, lost some of its pristine and originary glamour, when it acquired, almost overnight, a two-million-year prehistory, which threatened to compromise its putative racial purity and, with it, its biological uniqueness.

Archaeology, with the aid of geological chronology, not only gave human prehistory greater depth, but it also suggested a new field in which European science could engage the other. At the same time as the ethnographic material was flooding in with reports of distant races of men, differently shaped, living in the most elementary tribal societies and using stone tools, amateur archaeologists, closer to home, were digging up bones and artifacts which showed that European ancestors once lived in comparable simplicity, with primitive technology and measurably smaller and thicker skulls. The irresistible temptation was to equate the European distant past with the conditions of life in the ethnographic present in Africa, Australia and the South Seas. All that was needed was the formulation of an evolutionary stage theory to justify the use of data drawn from the observation of contemporary savages to be used in the reconstruction of European prehistory. Darwin's *Origin of the Species*, published within a year of the discovery of the Brixham Cave, only acted to confirm the plausibility of the evolutionary model. As human history was now to be measured in what seemed geological ages, rather than a few millennia, it was not difficult to transfer the image of layered stratigraphy from geology and archaeology to history.

John Lubbock, banker, politician, naturalist, archaeologist, was also first president of the Royal Anthropological Institute, "whose founding in 1871 was effectively the beginning of British anthropology as we know it" (Trautman 1997: 166). Inspired by Darwin, Lubbock pioneered just the kind of evolutionary cultural stratigraphy that could bring archaeology and ethnography together within a single science (he notably coined the terms "paleolithic" and "neolithic"). Lubbock's *Pre-Historic Times, as Illustrated by Ancient Remains and the Manners and Customs of Modern Savages*, published in 1865, is one of the first attempts to distill history from a mishmash of archaeological and ethnographical data. He justifies his approach with a direct appeal to Lyell's geology (1865: 416):

> the archaeologist is free to follow the methods which have been so successfully pursued in geology – the rude bone and stone implements of bygone ages being to the one what the remains of extinct animals are to the other. The analogy may be pursued even further than this. Many mammalia which are extinct in Europe have representatives still living in other countries. Our fossil pachyderms, for instance, would be almost unintelligible but for the species which still inhabit some parts of Asia and Africa;the secondary marsupials are illustrated by their existing representatives in Australia and South America; and in the same manner, if we wish clearly to understand the antiquities of Europe, we must compare them with the rude implements and weapons still, or until lately, used by the savage races in other parts of the world. In fact, the Van Diemaner and South American are to the antiquary what the opossum and the sloth are to the geologist.

The image of the fossilized pachyderm evokes *in ovo* a second key concept for anthropological comparatism. Not only do evolutionary stages exist which permit the direct comparison of stone-age Europeans and modern savages, but there is yet a third source of evidence which links later with earlier stages of evolution, a kind of cultural "fossil" or "survival." A cultural "survival" is a custom or belief which arises in one stage of social development but lingers on in further stages of social development despite the loss of much of its original function, meaning, or importance. Thus certain beliefs or practices at home in savage societies were seen to survive in later ages up to the present, like the sloths Lubbock assigned to glacial times, or the ossified and forgotten Indo-European expressions which, Müller supposed, gave rise to myth. The notion of the survival is "an integral part of the comparative method" and "in one form or another it came into use more or less simultaneously in the writings of the great evolutionists" (Harris 1968: 165). But Edward Tylor's *Primitive Culture* (1871) was the first to use the term "survival" and give it explicit definition: "These are processes, customs, opinions, and so forth which have been carried on by force of habit into a new state of society different from that in which they had their original home, and they thus remain as proofs and examples of an older condition of culture out of which a newer has been evolved." Survivals might be such things as magicians' rattles, which are powerful instruments in primitive culture but lived on in Victorian Europe as children's toys. Survivals might also be ritual acts which in later cultures appear as actions in myths or fairytales, long after the ritual is forgotten. As Tylor's words indicate, survivals are not just the corollary of theories of cultural evolution, but the proof.

Among survivals, the most useful for the anthropologist and the most exciting for his readers are those which Tylor identifies as "worn out, worthless, or even bad with downright harmful folly," preserved by "stupidity, unpractical conservatism and dogged superstition" which a more "practical utilitarianism would have remorselessly swept away" (1958: 156). It is these conspicuously irrational traits that stand out, at least in the modern world, as ill-fitting, absurd, or contradictory.

[...]

References

Cannadine, D. 2001. *Ornamentalism: How the British Saw their Empire.* Oxford.

Durán, D. 1967. *Historia de las Indias de Nueva España.* 2 vols. Mexico City.

Eagleton, T. 1991. *Ideology.* London.

Harris, M. 1968. *The Rise of Anthropological Theory.* New York.

Jones, W. 1807. *Works of Sir William Jones.* Vol. 3. London.

Lincoln, B. 1999. *Theorizing Myth: Narrative, Ideology, and Scholarship.* Chicago and London.

Lubbock, J. 1865. *Pre-Historic Times, as Illustrated by Ancient Remains and the Manners and Customs of Modern Savages.* London.

Mannheim, K. 1936. *Ideology and Utopia.* London.

Müller, F. M. 1847. "On the Relation of the Bengali to the Asian and Aboriginal Languages of India," *Report of the British Association for the Advancement of Science*, 1848: 319–50.

Müller, F. M. 1892. *Address Delivered at the Opening of the Ninth International Congress of Orientalists held in London, September 5, 1892.* Oxford.

Todorov, T. 1984. *The Conquest of America.* New York. Trans. R. Howard. [French original 1982.]

Trautmann, T. R. 1997. *Aryans and British India.* Berkeley, CA.

Tylor, E. B. 1958. *Primitive Culture.* New York. [Original 1871.]

Secondary Source 1.7   Eric Csapo, 'Frazer's comparative method'

(Source: Csapo, E. (2005) *Theories of Mythology*, Malden MA and Oxford, Blackwell Publishing, pp. 33–6)

Frazer's comparative method could be described as an easy four-step process. The first step is to find a particular problem: a rite, myth, or institution which seems odd or self-contradictory, or simply one that evades rational comprehension: chances are that the oddity is a survival from a previous stage of cultural development. The second step consists in gathering as many examples of this particular rite, myth, or institution from as many cultures as one can find. The third step is to find a generalizing explanation for the phenomenon. This will often emerge from some of the specific examples collected, since some are likely to be closer to the "origin" of the phenomenon than others. The correct explanation will be the one which has the power to account for all of the collected examples with the least degree of complexity and special pleading. The fourth step is simply to wrap up by reapplying the general explanation to the original problem.

An easy example is Frazer's treatment of the story of Cain and Abel from the Old Testament. The biblical text reads as follows (Genesis 4):

> Now Adam knew Eve his wife, and she conceived and bore Cain, saying, "I have gotten a man with the help of the Lord." And again, she bore his brother Abel. Now Abel was a keeper of sheep, and Cain a tiller of the ground. In the course of time Cain brought to the Lord an offering of the fruit of the ground, and Abel brought of the firstlings of his flock and of their fat portions. And the Lord had regard for Abel and his offering, but for Cain and his offering he had no regard. So Cain was very angry, and his countenance fell. The Lord said to Cain, "Why are you angry, and why has your countenance fallen? If you do well, will you not be accepted? And if you do not do well, sin is crouching at the door; its desire is for you, but you must master it." Cain said to Abel his brother, "Let us go into the field." And when they were in the field, Cain rose up against his brother Abel, and killed him. Then the Lord said to Cain, "Where is Abel your brother?" He said, "I do not know; am I my brother's keeper?" And the Lord said, "What have you done? The voice of your brother's blood is crying to me from the ground. And now you are cursed from the ground, which has opened its mouth to receive your brother's blood from your hand. When you till the ground, it shall no longer yield to you its strength; you shall be a fugitive and a great wanderer on the earth." Cain said to the Lord, "My punishment is greater than I can bear. Behold, thou has driven me this day away from the ground; and from thy face I shall be hidden; and I shall be a fugitive and a wanderer on the earth and whoever finds me will slay me." Then the Lord said to him, "Not so! If anyone slays Cain, vengeance shall be taken on him sevenfold." And the Lord put a mark on Cain, lest any who came upon him should kill him. Then Cain went away from the presence of the Lord, and dwelt in the land of Nod, east of Eden.

In *Folklore in the Old Testament* (1918.1: 78–103) Frazer problematizes this mark that God puts on Cain. On the usual interpretation the mark served to protect Cain from human assailants. But there are as yet no other human assailants (no one yet lives on earth, according to Frazer's reading of the Bible, except the murderer and his parents). Moreover, the biblical passage makes

Abel's blood and the ground itself, which will become barren, the agents of
Cain's exile. Frazer compares this to the widespread belief in blood pollution
causing infection or crop failure. Many cultures, therefore, preserve the custom
of driving murderers into exile or temporary seclusion for fear of famine or
contagion. These parallels suggest that the mark of Cain was a warning to
others to avoid contact with him. But other examples show that revenge was
sought not only by the blood of the murdered man, but by his ghost. Frazer
gives many examples of rituals performed to appease the ghost of a murdered
man. The examples, however, do not become immediately relevant until Frazer
discusses the use of marks and disguises to protect a murderer from the ghost of
his victim. Of the twenty-two selected examples we need to take only three of
the shorter ones – the style is already familiar from Chapter 1 (1918.1: 92–7):

> Among the Ba-Yaka ... "a man who has been killed in battle is
> supposed to send his soul to avenge his death on the person of the
> man who killed him; the latter, however, can escape the vengeance of
> the dead by wearing the red tail-feathers of the parrot in his hair, and
> painting his forehead red." ... Among the Borana Gallas, when a war-
> party has returned to the village, the victors who have slain a foe are
> washed by the woman with a mixture of fat and butter, and their faces
> are painted red and white. Among the Southern Massim ... a warrior
> who has slain a man remains secluded in his house for six days.
> During the first three days he may eat only roasted food and must
> cook it for himself. Then he bathes and blackens his face for the
> remaining three days.

"Thus," Frazer concludes, "the mark of Cain may have been a mode of
disguising a homicide, or of rendering him so repulsive or formidable in
appearance that his victim's ghost would either not know him or at least give
him a wide berth" (1918.1: 98–9).

The essay moves from the discovery of the problem, to the collection of
evidence of similar beliefs and practices, to a generalizing explanation. But the
example also shows that the process may be a little less straightforward than
the four-step description allowed. In practice, step one at least sometimes
presupposes step two: i.e., the "problem" often emerges (or is constructed) only
after the comparative material has already been gathered and sifted. Also, step
two must to some extent presuppose step three: just what constitutes "examples
of this particular rite, myth, or institution" can generally only be determined
once one has decided where the original logic lay. In the present example, it is
only with the help of the anthropological parallels that the "mark" or "sign"
seems problematic: it seems to be an indication that Cain was under God's
special protection and not a disguise of any sort. Nor would anyone begin to
solve this problem, supposing it was noticed in the first place, by collecting
passages relating to the protection of murderers from ghosts. This is not just a
similar example of the practice, since there is no mention of ghosts of any sort
in the biblical passage: both the identification of the initial "problem" and the
selection of relevant comparanda depend on the decision that the mark is a
disguise against ghosts.

Frazer defends his generalizing explanation on the grounds that it has "the advantage of relieving the Biblical narrative from a manifest absurdity" (1918.1: 100–1):

> For on the usual interpretation God affixed the mark of Cain in order to save him from human assailants, apparently forgetting that there was nobody to assail him, since the earth was as yet inhabited only by the murderer himself and his parents. Hence by assuming that the foe of whom the first murderer went in fear was a ghost instead of a living man, we avoid the irreverence of imputing to the deity a grave lapse of memory little in keeping with the divine omniscience. Here again, therefore, the comparative method approves itself a powerful *advocatus Dei*.

But the conclusion, far from protecting God from a lapse of memory, calls attention to a hitherto unnoticed absurdity in the biblical passage (for neither God's nor Cain's "anyone" can really refer to the world's first ghost), and it compounds the absurdity by supposing God to threaten punishment to a ghost. Frazer's dry sense of humor (so arid that many doubt its existence) will not allow us to decide whether he really hopes some fundamentalist Christian reader will accept his interpretation as a defense of the literalness of the Bible, or whether he is just having more fun at the expense of those who insist on the literal truth of this text. (Immediately before this passage he wonders whether God "decorated Cain with red, black, or white paint, or perhaps with a tasteful combination of these colours" or just painted him red like a Fijian, white like a Ngoni, black like an Arunta, or half-red and half-white like the Masai and the Nanadi, "or he may have plastered his head with mud, like the Pimas, or his whole body with cow's dung, like the Kavirondo.") The real moral of the story appears in the essay's final paragraph 1918.1: 103):

> The venerable framework of society rests on many pillars, of which the most solid are nature, reason, and justice; yet at certain stages of its slow and laborious construction it could ill have dispensed with the frail prop of superstition. If the day should ever come when the great edifice has been carried to completion and reposes in simple majesty on adamantine foundations, it will be possible, without risk to its stability, to cut away and destroy the rotten timbers that shored it up in the process of building.

So much for Frazer's defense of scripture.

Reference

Frazer, J. G. 1918. *Folklore in the Old Testament.* 3 vols. London.

Block 2   Myth in Rome: power, life and afterlife

Secondary Source 2.1   'Fact or Legend? Debate over the origins of Rome'

(Source: Slayman, A. (2007) 'Fact or Legend? Debate over the Origins of Rome', *Archaeology*, vol. 60, no. 4, July/August 2007, pp. 23–7)

Archaeologist Andrea Carandini claims he has evidence for a flesh-and-blood Romulus, the legendary founder of Rome. Many of his colleagues dispute his interpretation, believing Romulus to be a mythic figure. Who's right? In this special report, we present both sides of the debate, plus interviews with Carandini and critic Albert Ammerman.

April 21, 753 B.C.—After being raised by a she-wolf along the banks of the Tiber River, the orphan twins Romulus and Remus decide to found a city. They consult the augurs to see which of them will be king, and the answer comes back: "Romulus." So he marks out a sacred boundary on the Palatine Hill and orders his men to dig a ditch and build a wall around it. Remus, in a fit of jealousy and rage, jumps over the wall. For this sacrilegious transgression, Romulus kills his brother and goes on to fulfil the prophecy by becoming the first king of Rome.

For more than 2,000 years, historians have made a living poking holes in this legend, pointing out that there are inconsistent versions of the story and that parts of it are simply impossible. But over the past two decades, Italian archaeologist Andrea Carandini has uncovered startling evidence in the heart of the Roman Forum that seems to confirm parts of the myth. A professor at the University of Rome, Carandini is one of the deans of contemporary Italian archaeology. His discoveries include a wall (possibly the sacred boundary of legend) and a "royal palace" that he has connected to Rome's earliest years. Based on this evidence he argues that Romulus was a real historical figure. His defence of Rome's mythic origins, which has earned him the admiration of the Roman public but the disapproval of many of his colleagues, represents a sharp break with two millennia of scholarship.

How seriously should we take the legendary accounts of Rome's founding? The Roman historian Livy (59 B.C.–A.D. 17) characterized the traditions surrounding the city's earliest years as "old tales with more of the charm of poetry than of sound historical record." Over the years, the doubt expressed by Livy and other ancient authors crystallized into the archskepticism of historian Theodor Mommsen, who wrote in 1854, "The founding of a city in the strict sense, such as the legend assumes, is of course to be reckoned altogether out of the question: Rome was not built in a day." In 1899, however, Italian archaeologist Giacomo Boni discovered a stele in the Forum with an archaic Latin inscription that included the word *rex* (king), possibly a reference to Romulus or one of the six legendary kings said to have succeeded him. Boni identified the site where he found the stele as the legendary tomb of Romulus, and as a result, the Livian tradition concerning royal Rome once again became a subject of serious debate.

Over the years a scholarly consensus emerged that went something like this: In very ancient times, from the sixteenth through the ninth centuries B.C., a few small villages occupied the area that was to become Rome.

Historians generally avoided the period, because the early literature was thought to be based on pure myth, and archaeologists wrote of it only in terms of Bronze Age, Iron Age, and numbered ceramic phases. The so-called Latial II and III cultures flourished during the eighth century B.C., when the literary sources said Rome had been founded, but nothing in the archaeological record could be tied to a man named Romulus. By the seventh and sixth centuries B.C. these villages were beginning to coalesce into a city, and by the fifth century B.C. Boni's inscription announced the presence of a king. But no one even thought of claiming that someone had founded a city on virgin soil, and certainly not someone named Romulus one April day in 753 B.C.

Decades of carefully crafted consensus seemed on the brink of crumbling when, in 1988, Carandini announced the discovery of an ancient wall on the Palatine. There, on the hill's north slope, he found a natural gully shaped into a ditch by human tools. Next to it were the remains of four successive walls, the oldest being of wood and clay and almost five feet wide, dating from the mid-eighth century B.C., bordered on one side by a strip of ground free from construction. "When I excavated the Romulean-age wall I realized that I was looking at the very origins of Rome as a city-state...the first of Romulus's great works," Carandini recently told ARCHAEOLOGY (see interview below).

Carandini continued his excavations, and two years ago made yet another major discovery, this time in the form of a large, elaborate structure that he described as a "royal palace," also dating from the eighth century B.C. To him, this confirmed the idea that Rome, although built atop a preexisting settlement, was really founded in the mid-eighth century, and that a king named Romulus truly existed.

The notion that Rome's famous founding myth might actually be true has enduring appeal to the populace of a city steeped from birth in ancient grandeur—and to fans of A.S. Roma, one the city's major soccer teams, whose logo sports a wolf suckling the twins. And Carandini's discoveries have made him something of a celebrity, at least by archaeological standards. A lecture he gave last fall in Rome attracted a crowd of some 5,000 according to *La Repubblica*, which compared Carandini's popularity favourably with that of Leonardo DiCaprio.

But his argument that Romulus was real has provoked massive scholarly controversy, with an assortment of archaeologists and historians admiring his excavations but reserving judgment on—or even rejecting—many of his conclusions. University of Exeter historian T.P. Wiseman has been one of Caradini's most vocal critics, faulting him for using "the legends of Romulus in the Greek and Latin authors (writing seven centuries or more after the alleged events) as if they were historical evidence that can explain the results of his excavations."

For now, at least, Carandini appears to be in the minority, but there is always the possibility that he might be right. "If he is right—and we might not know this in our lifetimes—he will have made major discoveries of a kind only Boni made 100 years ago," says classical archaeologist Albert Ammerman of Colgate University, who excavated in Rome from 1987 until 2003 [...]. "He will have done something to reverse the skeptical tradition of ancient authors and modern ancient historians totally, but in practical terms this will take decades." Either way, only time will tell—time and more excavations.

Andrea Carandini on the evidence for Romulus

Interviewed by MARCO MEROLA

MM: What was Rome like before Romulus—that is, before the eighth century B.C.?

AC: Before the eighth century B.C., a big settlement existed which had no forum or capitol. Around the mid-ninth century B.C., necropolises built between the hills were moved to the outskirts, and the hills were given over completely to huts. The boundaries of the necropolises, therefore, give us a "negative" photograph of the settlement itself, which probably covered about 500 acres. All the other settlements of the time covered at most 25 acres.

The pre-Romulean settlement consisted of a federation of quarters that had roughly the same importance. There were 27 shrines of the Argei, a ritual in which human effigies made of bulrushes were cast into the Tiber, presumably to appease the gods. As the shrines were located in 27 different areas of Rome, this means that there were 27 sections of the city. What we know about the Argei comes from ancient authors who described the location of the different quarters.

MM: What are the available written sources for Rome's founding?

AC: The Roman historian Quintus Fabius Pictor, who worked in the third and second centuries B.C., wrote the first actual account of Rome's origins. What he reports is much older; it dates back to centuries before. Pictor would have seen Rome's Archaic monuments still standing—the Temple of Capitoline Jupiter, various buildings that had not been destroyed by the Gauls [in 390 B.C.]. Many buildings built in the sixth century B.C. survived [in Pictor's time]. Unfortunately, none of the historian's original works have survived, but a number of later writers—Cicero, for example, in *De Republica*—picked up what he wrote.

There are many other significant written sources for early Rome, such as the Law of the 12 Tables. This law dates back to the mid-fifth century B.C., and it includes customary rules that date back to a much earlier time—even to the eighth century B.C. Think also of the famous Praenestine mirror [a fourth-century B.C. mirror decorated with mythological scenes], which may depict the legend of Romulus. All are important elements that help in reconstructing the origins of Rome.

MM: Romulus and Remus are supposed to have been semidivine brothers, like Castor and Pollux. But did they really exist?

AC: There is archaeological evidence of the existence of Romulus and Remus. When I excavated the Romulean-age wall on the Palatine, I realized that I was looking at the very origins of Rome as a city-state. This wall, which was the first of Romulus's great works, destroyed the [earlier] hut villages and is dated through a number of foundation deposits to about 775–750 B.C. These were not fortifications but should be regarded as sacred walls protecting a sacred place.

Then, in the second half of the eighth century, Romulus commissioned the reclamation of the land beneath the Forum, which had been a swamp, and the construction of a new sacred and political center. There we have uncovered the oldest cobble paving, dating back to the eighth century, which was covered by a newer layer dating from about 650 B.C. The Forum was bounded on one side by the sanctuary of Vesta. The excavations at the Temple of Vesta have given me the ultimate evidence, the actual "marks" of the early city. In the sanctuary of Vesta I actually excavated down to virgin soil. The earth was marked, as if someone had used a tool like a plowshare to demarcate the location of a building.

Opposite the entrance to the Temple of Vesta was the House of the Vestal Virgins. Beneath it I found a hut dating back to between 750 and 725 B.C.; given its location I think it represents the first House of the Vestal Virgins. While the ancients associated the sanctuary of Vesta with Numa Pompilius [the second king of Rome], the archaeological dating corresponds to Romulus. Hence, my theory is that the construction of the sanctuary started before Numa's accession to the throne, but had been ordered by Romulus himself a few years after the Palatine walls were built.

On the side of the sanctuary facing east, where the Arch of Titus is, we found an extraordinarily innovative small palace that I have identified as the Domus Regia [royal palace]. Literary sources tell us that Numa Pompilius and Ancus Marcius [the fourth king of Rome] lived in this place.

Finally, Romulus created an organization composed of tribes, with a king backed by a royal council and an assembly. There was a shift from the community of the *patres* [the early Roman senate] to a monarchy. Romulus also rationalized the system of the 27 sections. There were three tribes with nine *curiae* [assemblies] each, and he added one in order to have a total of 10 curiae [per tribe]. But with Romulus the curiae were no longer independent and equal; instead, they were subjected to a central power.

MM: What do your archaeological discoveries tell us about early Rome?

AC: These excavations prove that it all started around the mid-eighth century B.C. in these central, public places of worship and politics. After 750 B.C. everything was born. There was no gradual expansion of an old core but the sudden evolution of a city that was great and remains great. At last today we are witnessing a notable convergence of the literary tradition and the archaeological evidence.

MM: Did you expect to find any of this when you began work on the northern slope of the Palatine in 1986?

AC: When I decided to excavate the northern slopes of the Palatine Hill I was looking not for the founding of Rome, but for the origin of the buildings. My intention was to study the heart of this city, comprising about 2.5 acres and stretching from the Arch of Titus to the Temple of Vesta. I now have tons of evidence for my theories, but I still need to enrich this picture.

MM: What still needs to be discovered to clarify your ideas about Rome's founding?

AC: I would like to find the worship hut of Jupiter Feretrius, a small temple on the Capitoline in which Romulus is supposed to have worshipped, or try to understand how a curia was made and how the fabric of the city was composed. I would also like to know more about the rural settlements and the *oppida*, the main fortified settlements, and excavate beneath the Basilica Julia in the Forum.

After years of excavation, I think I have a profile of the city, but I am still missing the details. If I were young I would excavate at least another hectare. Doing this would be a heroic enterprise, but I am not a youngster. Archaeology can find anything. Rome is below our feet. But unfortunately in two or three years of excavations we could not find enough. We would need to work uninterrupted for years and years.

Marco Merola *is* ARCHAEOLOGY's *Naples correspondent.*

Albert Ammerman on the origins of Rome

Interviewed by ANDREW SLAYMAN

AS: What do ancient historians have to say about the founding of Rome?

AA: Two main figures have come down to us: Livy [59 B.C.–A.D. 17] and Dionysius of Halicarnassus [who wrote around 25 B.C.]. Livy says that when we're dealing with very remote times he will neither confirm nor deny the historicity of what he's saying; he's just going to repeat what is said.

In the case of Dionysius, who was a Greek historian writing in Greek, he naturally envisioned the founding of Rome by Romulus as if it were a Greek city. The notion of a "foundation" came from the Greek historiographical tradition, in which if you had a major city, like Syracuse or Crotone [Greek colonies in Sicily and southern Italy], you had to have a narrative talking about its founder, the date of its foundation, and so forth. In Rome's case we have the great stories of Romulus and Remus, which have been honed over the centuries to make a wonderful narrative account.

There is also Plutarch on the life of Romulus, together with his parallel life of Theseus, the legendary founder of Athens. Plutarch [about A.D. 46–120] says specifically that these stories sound too good to be true. He tells us all kinds of things about the lives of Theseus and Romulus, but he treats them as elaborations added over time, viewing the story as a whole as tradition that is myth-history. It's like George Washington chopping down the cherry tree. No American historian today accepts or believes the story, but they might retell it because it's part of the tradition.

AS: If ancient historians don't believe their own stories, then what should modern scholars do with them?

AA: The consensus embodied in the traditional version of the story—that Romulus founded Rome in 753 B.C.—obscures endless variations in the ancient texts. The classic example is that Livy has Romulus dying in two different ways. In one, he goes to the Forum and the people tear him apart; in the other, he goes up in apotheosis.

The consensus version also embodies its fair share of impossibilities. Seven kings are said to have reigned between 753 and 510 B.C. but if you look at the average length of a reign that this implies, almost 35 years, it's quite clear that either the dates or the list of kings must be wrong.

When you have so many alternative versions, it indicates that elaborations took place as the stories were passed down over the centuries. That there are so many different versions fuels the skeptics—people who, like [nineteenth-century historian] Theodor Mommsen, would say that it's all a pack of lies. In reality you can use it, but you have to take the whole literary tradition together, with all its problems and inconsistencies and anachronisms.

AS: What do modern historians have to say about the origins of Rome?

AA: Looking back at the ancient historians, if you read Dionysius of Halicarnassus he tries to pack the origins of Rome into a great founding figure: Romulus. But if you follow the lead of Livy, the development of the different functions of the city are distributed over the seven kings. They are not all packed into one figure.

Similarly, most historians working today don't want to "front-load" the origins of the city—that is, to say, that it all happened in the eighth century B.C. Instead they want to have a certain sequence. They tend to acknowledge that things were happening before the eighth century, but to look for the development of the city as a city in the seventh.

AS: What about the archaeology?

AA: It's clear from Carandini's work that there's a lot happening in the eighth century, and that there may be a kernel of truth in the legend. We may even be able to accept Roma Quadrata on the Palatine—that is a small, early town with four sides and a sacred boundary known as the *pomerium*—but I would argue *that* in itself doesn't make Rome. The traditional story of the founding of Rome isn't about urbanism; it's about a sacred entity that can be called an *urbs* [a city]. The real urban takeoff —roofs with tiles, foundation blocks, landscape transformation, inscriptions, art, imports of exotic things from the Greek world—all of those things took place after 650 B.C.

Where I feel Carandini goes too far is in saying that if you can show that some piece of the archaeological record exists, this somehow validates the literary tradition. In other words, if the literary tradition says that Romulus built a wall on the Palatine in 753 B.C., and you find a wall on the Palatine dating to around 750 B.C., then the wall must be Romulus's wall, and Romulus must have been real. Just because you find a wall somewhere in Scotland, that's not enough to call it Hadrian's Wall.

crux of the matter

AS: What new work is needed to understand Rome's origins?

AA: We see the origins of the Forum as a major event. Many people now think it's the creation of the Forum that was key to the development of the urban fabric. Carandini is hoping to push this back as far as possible, but we think it's probably more like 650 or 625 B.C. That said, at present it's not possible to reliably date the fill that contributed to the creation of the Forum. To do so, we would have to date the most recent pieces in the fill, but Boni did not keep all of his finds. So to know when Rome began to develop as a city, we need to reexcavate the Forum. This would require digging 20 feet below the marble pavement of the Forum and four feet below the water table, so it is unlikely to happen anytime soon.

Andrew Slayman *is a former* ARCHAEOLOGY *editor and the director of ArtfulMedia.*

Secondary Source 2.2   Edward Champlin, 'Nero'

(Source: Champlin, E. (2003) *Nero*, Cambridge MA, Harvard University Press, pp. 92–111, 126–32 and 200–209)

The power of myth

NERO'S STRATEGY is best understood in the context of two related phenomena in Roman public life of the late Republic and early Empire. The first may be called the power of myth.

In the middle and late Republic a fashion developed among the Roman upper classes for linking themselves genealogically with the gods and heroes (the latter themselves being children or descendants of the former) of myth, typically by claiming descent from a Greek or Trojan hero who had wandered to Italy, often to found not just a family but a town or city. Thus, Julius Caesar and his adoptive son Augustus could present themselves as representatives of the Trojan prince Aeneas, the founder of Rome and son of Venus (hence the claim of their heir Nero to "spring from the great family of Aeneas"); indeed, almost every contemporary politician could lay claim to a similarly grand origin[1]. This genealogical fashion is itself but one aspect of the massive hellenization of every aspect of Roman and Italian culture—or the domestication of classical and hellenistic Greek culture—over the third, second, and first centuries BC, as Rome established herself, by conquest, by imitation, and by attraction, as the epicentre of a Graeco-Roman world. That such genealogies were not strictly verifiable is irrelevant. They were a single facet of the reconciliation between Greek and Roman cultures, part of a much larger bilateral accommodation to the realities of power. Greek orators and poets could address their new masters in terms of praise already forged for other, Hellenic rulers; while Roman statesmen could present themselves as legitimate participants in a culture that was older than their own. But heroic pedigrees also had a more immediate purpose, as weapons deployed in politics at Rome.

Legendary genealogies form a single strand, the most literal-minded, in the general weaving of myth into contemporary Roman political life. By appropriating the gods and heroes of myth and legendary history, if not as ancestors, then at least as exemplars, politicians could present images laden with meanings which were quickly recognizable to a broad public[2]. Hence everywhere, from the coins in their purses to the decorative programs of their greatest public buildings, citizens could decipher with relative ease the claims of their leaders when they were couched artistically in mythical and legendary terms, messages which the literate could also read in contemporary writings. Thus world conquerors and benefactors like Alexander or Pompey the Great, or a would-be conqueror-benefactor like Mark Antony, would turn naturally to the global exploits of Dionysus or Hercules to represent their own deeds. Antony's rival, the future emperor Augustus, early on in his career adopted the symbols of a persona of Apollo, the god of peace and the arts, the bringer of the new Golden Age. He took, for instance, the sphinx (a symbol of Apollo) for his signet ring, wore Apollo's laurel wreath in public, attributed the final victory at Actium over Antony and Cleopatra to the god's protection (as the poets would proclaim at length), and built the great Temple of Apollo on the Palatine, beside and connected to his own house[3].

The clearest example of the use of myth (and legend), in a city overflowing with similar architectural complexes, is the Forum of Augustus in the center of Rome, an open rectangle about 125 by 90 meters. In the center of the square stood a large statue of the *princeps* Augustus, riding in a triumphal chariot with inscriptions added to its base which described his victories and called him by the title given him at the time of the dedication of the Forum in 2 BC, *Pater Patriae*, father of his country. Running the whole length of both sides of the square were two-story colonnades, with niche after niche holding over-life-size

---

[1]   See the splendid paper of Wiseman, T.P., "Legendary Genealogies in Late-Republican Rome," *G&R* 21 (1974): 153–64 = *Roman Studies Literary and Historical* (Liverpool, 1987).

[2]   For an excellent introduction to the whole question of "myth as example of history," see Hölscher, T., "Mythen als Exempel der Geschichte," in F. Graf, ed., *Mythos in mythenloser Gesellschaft. Das Paradigma Roms* (Colloquium Rauricum 3, Stuttgart, Leipzig, 1993), 67–87.

[3]   See Zanker, *The Power of Images in the Age of Augustus* (Ann Arbor, 1988), especially 33–77, on the rival mythological images of Antony and Octavian (Augustus) expressed visually in coins, freestanding and relief sculpture, gems, earthenware, and monumental architecture.

statues of all the great Romans of the past. On one side, near the top end, stood Romulus, the founder of Rome, larger than all the rest, shown with the spear and military spoils, the *spolia opima*, which were awarded to the rare Roman commander who killed the enemy leader in personal combat. On the other side, facing Romulus, stood father Aeneas, the founder of the Roman race, in the classic pose of piety, carrying his father and leading his son by the hand, away from the flames of Troy. Aeneas was flanked by statues of his descendants, including the family of Julius Caesar, the mythical and historical ancestors of Augustus. Thus the two founders of Rome and all her great men gazed down on Augustus in the center. The top end of the Forum was dominated by the great Temple of Mars Ultor, Mars the Avenger, the avenger of Augustus' father, Julius Caesar, against his assassins, and the avenger of Rome against the Parthians. The god Mars was shown fully armed at the center of the temple's pediment, flanked by his wife Venus on one side, the ancestor of the Julian family, and on the other by the goddess Fortuna, the Fortune pointedly brought back to Rome by Augustus in 19 BC: a nice family affair, then, Mars the father of Romulus, his wife Venus, the mother of Aeneas, both looking down on their descendant Augustus in the middle of the square. A brief and selective description does scant justice to the elements of the complex, but their programmatic nature is clear. Augustus the conqueror was presented as the culmination of Roman history—the new Aeneas, the new Romulus, the third founder of Rome and guardian of its military glory[4].

These were but a few of the images which were displayed in every public corner of the city of Augustus, replicated in private works of art, and elaborated by the poets, orators, and historians of the day. Indeed, there was no need to portray the emperor exclusively in terms of a single god or hero. Augustus, for example, was also linked to portrayals of the Athenian hero Theseus, western conqueror of the Amazons of the East (just as Octavian/Augustus would overcome Antony), or of Diomedes, or of Orestes, each figure of myth bearing with him an often simplified message that would be significant to contemporary observers[5]. The point here is that daily life was permeated by such examples from the past, all dedicated to comment on the present. It was customary to present Rome's leaders wrapped in the deeds and virtues of figures from myth and legend, and the Roman people were thoroughly accustomed to read and appreciate the messages they bore.

We have already seen the second phenomenon to be considered here, *theatralis licentia*, theatrical license. Where the power of myth can be taken to convey the manipulation of a symbolic vocabulary by the leaders of the state, theatrical license suggests the other side of the coin, the vigorous expression of popular sentiment on public issues within a privileged public space. One striking aspect of this license is particularly important: the prominence of the double entendre in plays, if we can stretch the phrase to include both speech and action. Again from the late Republic onward, an abundance of evidence shows that Roman theatrical audiences were extra-ordinarily quick to hear the words spoken and to see the actions presented on stage as offering pointed commentary on contemporary public life[6].

[4] See Zanker 1988, 192–215, based on P. Zanker, *Forum Augustum* (Tübingen, 1968).

[5] Hölscher 1993, 80. On Augustus as Orestes, a figure of interest to his descendant Nero, see also Hölscher, "Augustus and Orestes," *Travaux du centre d'archéologie méditerranéenne de l'Académie Polonaise des Sciences*, Études et Travaux 15 (1991): 164–8.

[6] Examples can be found in Cameron, A., *Circus Factions: Blues and Greens at Rome and Byzantium* (Oxford, 1976), 158–161, 171–172, and Reynolds, R. W., "Criticism of Individuals in Roman Popular Comedy," *CQ* 37 (1943): 37–45.

[margin note: opposite of the power of myth : expression of popular sentiment to undermine credibility of Emperors : used in imperial age.]

How such messages were transmitted varied. The playwright himself might be the source, as when Julius Caesar forced the elderly Laberius to perform in one of his own mimes; Laberius got his own back by appearing as a slave who had just been whipped and crying out the line, "Henceforth citizens we have lost our liberty," at which the whole audience turned to look at Caesar. Such outspokenness might be dangerous under the empire: Caligula had a writer burned alive in the arena for writing a humorous double entendre, *ob ambigui ioci versiculum*. But more often it was the actors themselves who would speak lines, even changing words, so as to produce an appropriate effect, a proclivity that made performers very dangerous indeed. Cicero describes at length (and probably with some exaggeration) how the great actor Aesop wound up his audience to a fever-pitch of sympathy for the orator when he was in exile, emphasizing appropriate lines such as those dealing with a father driven away and his house demolished (as Cicero's had been), encouraging requests for encores of pointed remarks, adding his own lines, and gesturing to different parts of the audience as they seemed relevant. The play, a tragedy, takes on a new life. Under the empire such behavior was riskier: a good emperor like Marcus Aurelius might sit unmoved through an exaggerated pun on the name of his wife's alleged lover, but less philosophical rulers like Nero and Commodus sent foolhardy performers into exile[7].

Not only the author and the actors but the producer of the play himself might also make a statement through the drama he chose or the manner in which it was presented. The best example is that of the general Pompey who, for his great Eastern conquests, celebrated a triumph of unprecedented magnificence in 61 BC, at the same time dedicating a temple to Venus Victrix, victorious Venus, where his military trophies would be on permanent display. Attached to this temple and likewise built from spoils, was to be a theater, and at the dedication of the complex in 55 Pompey presented plays whose production gave new meaning to the word "theatricality": in *Clytemnestra* there appeared 600 mules bearing Agamemnon's plunder from Troy, while *The Trojan Horse* saw hundreds of extras carrying 3,000 bowls heaped with booty. The props were real, the identification of the Greek king Agamemnon, first among equals, on stage with the Roman *triumphator* behind it irresistible[8].

What gives a special flavour to the transmission and reception of these double entendres is their occasional spontaneity. That is, "the audience sometimes saw an allusion where none was intended."[9] Augustus for instance was embarrassed once when a crowd leapt to its feet and applauded the line "O just and good lord." But in 68, when actors in a performance at Rome took up the comic song "Onesimus is coming from his villa" (otherwise unknown), their audience finished the words and repeated them several times, apparently in mockery of the new emperor Galba, then on his way from Spain[10]. This remarkable sensitivity on the part of the audience underscores the heightening of awareness

---

[7]   Laberius: Macrobius *Saturnalia* 2. 7. 4. Caligula: Suetonius *Caligula* 27. Cicero: *Pro Sestio* 120–122. Marcus: *HA Marcus* 29. Nero: above. Commodus: *HA Commodus* 3. Gallienus allegedly burned some impudent actors alive: *HA Gallieni* 7–9. Rawson, E., "Theatrical Life in Republican Rome and Italy," *PBSR* 53 (1985): 97–113 = *Roman Culture and Society: Collected Papers* (Oxford, 1991), 468–87, at 470, points out that the tradition of the political double entendre goes back at least into the 90s BC, citing two examples.

[8]   Cicero *Ad Familiares* 7.1, with Beacham, R. C., *The Roman Theatre and Its Audience* (London, 1991), 156–158. For other examples of plays produced for their contemporary relevance, see Cameron 1976, 171.

[9]   Reynolds 1943, 40.

[10]   Suetonius *Augustus* 53, *Galba* 13.

within a Roman theater: audiences *expected* to find contemporary relevance in the productions; performers *expected* to have their pointed remarks and actions caught, interpreted, and appreciated.

Theatrical license meets and merges with the power of myth in the conveyance of messages between rulers and ruled: almost all tragic drama and some comic drama portrayed the already familiar adventures of Greek gods and heroes. In short, the Roman people were accustomed to seeing their rulers everywhere presented as figures of well-known myths, and they were accustomed to performances on stage that commented directly on their own contemporary concerns. We must remember the expectations of the Roman audience when we read the hostile or dismissive accounts of Nero's performances: every person there would expect that when their emperor himself entered the theater to perform, he would be identifying himself in some way with the character he played: he could not have avoided it, he could not have done it unthinkingly. On occasion, in his most extravagantly theatrical gesture—one that seriously undermines the nature of ancient drama—Nero would wear a mask showing his own features. That could not possibly leave anyone in doubt: Nero *was* Orestes the matricide, Orestes was Nero; Nero *was* Oedipus, the man who had killed his father and married his own mother.

EVEN THOUGH he did not appear on the tragic stage until 66, it was the death of Agrippina in 59 that prompted Nero's interest in acting. Orestes and Oedipus were two of his favorite roles[11].

The tale of Orestes was one of the best known (and most complex) in antiquity. His father, Agamemnon, King of Mycenae, had been commander-in-chief of the Greek army at Troy. Returning home after the Trojan War, Agamemnon had been slaughtered in his bath by his wife, Clytemnestra, and her lover, Aegisthus. His son, Orestes, was spirited away, and when he had grown to manhood he inquired of Apollo's oracle at Delphi whether he should avenge his father by killing his murderers. The god replied that he must. In disguise he went to Mycenae to inform the murderous adulterers that he, Orestes was dead. They were completely taken in, and Orestes slew Aegisthus. Recognizing her son, Clytemnestra tried to appeal to his filial feelings by baring the bosom which had nourished him, but he struck her down as well. That same night the terrible Erinyes, the Furies, appeared with their scourges to harry the matricide, and he fled for protection to Delphi. There the god told him after a year of exile he must make his way to Athens, where Athena would end the curse.
He wandered through many lands, often in a state of madness, and he was ritually purified many times, but with no success: always the Furies pursued him, spurred on by the ghost of Clytemnestra. At last, in a great murder trial at Athens, with Apollo defending and the eldest Fury prosecuting him, Orestes was acquitted by one vote, the vote of Athena[12].

For Nero, the golden key to the story of Orestes was not that he was a matricide, but that he was a *justified* matricide[13]. Indeed, there were two justifications

---

[11]   It should be noted that the myths discussed here are those which Nero *acted*, not those which he sang about [...] That his roles were relevant to his real life is not a new idea, but their nature and purpose have been little explored.

[12]   Details for this and the following stories, with full references to the ancient sources, may be found in L. Preller, *Griechische Mythologie*, 4th ed., rev. C. Robert (Leipzig, 1894–1921), and W.H. Roscher, ed., *Ausführliches Lexikon der griechischen und römischen Mythologie* (Berlin, 1884–1937). The two major ancient collections are Hyginus' *Fabulae* and Apollodorus' *Bibliotheca*.

[13]   Delcourt, M., *Oreste et Alcméon. Étude sur la projection légendaire du matricide en Grèce* (Paris, 1959), 65–67, is central to what follows.

which might palliate the horror of the deed. One was vengeance for the murdered father, vengeance which was not only proper but demanded. Nero at 16 had played no role in the death of Claudius, his father by adoption, but Agrippina, in her passionate resentment of her son's rejection of her, did apparently claim responsibility for murder, portraying herself as the mother who had sacrificed everything so that her son might rule. Yet there seems to be no hint that the image of Nero as avenger of his father Claudius was ever developed, or even that anyone at the time took seriously the notion that Claudius had been murdered. *?? What did Nero know? What did he assume?*

But Nero did offer the other reasonable defense against the charge of matricide. Orestes had killed his mother not just because his father's death and the command of Apollo clamored for vengeance, but because Clytemnestra had stolen his inheritance from him and the people of Mycenae were suffering under the tyranny of a woman. In the words given him by Aeschylus:

> Here numerous desires converge to drive me on:
> the god's urgency and my father's passion, and
> with these the loss of my estates wears hard on me;
> the thought that these my citizens, most high renowned
> of men, who toppled Troy in show of courage, must
> go subject to this brace of women ...[14]

This was the essence of the posthumous campaign against Agrippina, especially as recounted in Seneca's letter to the senate, that she had gone beyond her womanly role to aim at supreme power, undermining loyalties and even planning to murder her son, as indeed Clytemnestra was said to have threatened the infant Orestes: Nero's preservation, as we have seen, was closely tied to the preservation of the empire, *aeternitas imperii*. A skilful performance might even draw a parallel between Agrippina pointing to her womb and Clytemnestra baring the breast which had nourished Orestes: the public good had overcome filial piety[15]. Just as Orestes' heroic act had liberated Mycenae, so Nero's great sacrifice saved Rome.

Of course Nero carried the performance as Orestes beyond the limits of the stage, in his complaint for the rest of his days that he was harried by his mother's ghost and by the Furies with their scourges and their flaming torches. Again his interest first appears seven years after her death, in 66, when he came into contact with the *magi*, Persian wise men. Through them he tried to summon and appease his mother's ghost, but he soon found that they were frauds and gave up magic when the implacable spirit of his mother proved to be uncharacteristically shy[16]. The following year, during his tour of Greece, as Suetonius records, he avoided the mystery rites at Eleusis as one who was impure. Dio, perhaps misreporting this same refusal, adds that he kept away from Athens "because of the story about the Furies," and from Sparta because

---

[14]   *Choephoroi* 299–304, translated by Richmond Lattimore. The brace of women is Clytemnestra and the womanish Aegisthus, who had not gone to war at Troy.

[15]   The parallel is suggested in Krappe, A. H., "La fin d'Agrippine," *REA* 42 (1940): 466–72, at 471–472, but cf. Delcourt 1959, 66–67.

[16]   Suetonius 34; see Pliny *NH* 30. 14–17, for the date and for Nero's disgust.

of the restrictive laws of Lycurgus[17]. But there is a far more plausible explanation for his avoidance of these places: he had no interest in them. He was there for the games[18]. The story about the Furies was a dramatic excuse, possibly by then even a joke, but he was quite willing up to his last days to identify himself with the archetypal matricide.

The identification with Orestes was further emphasized when Nero added to his repertoire another favorite character, Alcmaeon—a virtual double, the other matricide of myth. His tale is far less familiar today[19]. Alcmaeon was the son of the seer Amphiaraus, who was one of the Seven against Thebes, the heroes from Argos who took the part of Polyneices against his brother Eteocles when those two sons of Oedipus fell out over the rule of their father's kingdom. Amphiaraus, who foresaw his own death, refused to march against Thebes, but Polyneices bribed his wife, Eriphyle, with an antique necklace to persuade her husband to go. He went to Thebes and died there, along with most of the Argive heroes, or at least he disappeared forever. His son Alcmaeon was likewise reluctant to march against Thebes, when he was asked to lead an expedition of the sons of the Seven seeking vengeance. Thersander, the son of Polyneices, then bribed Alcmaeon's mother, the same Eriphyle, with an ancient robe to persuade her son to go to war. Under Alcmaeon's leadership Thebes was captured, and it was only then that he learned by chance that his mother's greed had brought death to his father and danger to himself. An ambiguous oracle from Apollo, that Eriphyle deserved to die, led to his murdering his mother. The Furies pursued him and he wandered, sometimes mad, until the river god Achelous purified him and gave him his daughter in marriage; but the necklace and the robe led eventually, through a separate sequence of events in which the Furies played a role, to Alcmaeon's own murder by another father-in-law outraged at his bigamy[20].

The parallels between the tale of Alcmaeon and the tale of Orestes make it clear why the role of Alcmaeon appealed to Nero: the perfidious mother who caused the death of the father and threatened the safety of her son, the ambiguous oracle from Delphi, the matricide, the pursuit by the Furies and the madness. The divergences between the two also suggest why Alcmaeon might be less attractive to Nero, and why less is heard of the role: no kingdom was at stake, reports differed as to whether the father had died or disappeared, the hero himself was responsible for his own death.

The central point is that it was Nero and not his enemies who chose to mythologize the murder of his mother. By presenting Orestes as one of his favorite roles, by underscoring this predilection with Alcmaeon, by dramatizing the torments of conscience in his life offstage, by performing the matricide on stage in a mask that bore his own features, Nero framed the terms of the debate over his own guilt.

[Handwritten margin notes: Apollo / Poetry etc etc / Orestes/ Alcmaeon / realization of what he must do to save himself]

[17] Dio may be confused: Athens should have been a place of refuge for the new Orestes.

[18] Convincingly argued by Kennell N. M., "ΝΕΡΩΝ ΠΕΡΙΟΔΟΝΙΚΗΣ," *AJP* 109 (1988): 239–51 [...]. Dio 63. 14. 3. Athens was something of a backwater at the time, and Nero made no effort even to visit a city far more attractive to him, Alexandria. Nor is it at all clear why the Furies should have kept him from Athens: Athena had after all been the goddess who had saved Orestes from them there, and in her Italian form as Minerva she had saved Nero.

[19] And Alcmaeon is routinely linked with Orestes in standard attacks on Nero: Suetonius 39. 2, Dio, Philostratus *Apollonius*.

[20] Besides Hyginus and Apollodorus, the main sources are Pausanias and two plays by Euripides which survive only in fragments. The story clearly had greater resonance in antiquity than now. The only known representation of Alcmaeon in Roman art (if it is Alcmaeon) appears in a Pompeian fresco contemporary with Nero ("third quarter of the first century"): *LIMC* 1. 1, 549, 552.

Unquestionably, he succeeded. The clue lies in this: his ancient critics were compelled to react by seeking to demonstrate that he was *not* comparable with Orestes. Juvenal objected that Orestes had acted on the authority of the gods, and he never killed his sister or his wife, poisoned his relatives—or sang the part of Orestes on stage, or wrote a *Troica*! Philostratus, in his *Life of Apollonius of Tyana*, noted that Orestes' father had been murdered by his mother, but that Nero owed his adoption and the empire to his mother. The elder Philostratus pointed out that while Orestes had been avenging his father, Nero had no such excuse. The contemporary graffito recorded by Suetonius runs in the same vein: the first part seems to represent the heroic posturing of the official version, "Nero Orestes Alcmaeon, mother-slayer," parodying his official name, Nero Claudius Caesar; but the second half refocuses attention on its simple horror: "Or put it another way: Nero killed his own mother."[21]

The clearest glimpse into the public debate over guilt comes in an obscure anecdote. One day, as Nero was passing by, the Cynic philosopher Isidorus loudly reproached him in public, crying out "that he sang the ills of Nauplius well, but disposed of his goods badly." Around the clever puns on good and evil (*mala bene / bona male*) was built a pointed contrast between Nero's success on stage and his failure as emperor, a criticism that sent Isidorus into exile. The ills of Nauplius, *Naupli mala*, need explanation. Nauplius was the father of the wise Palamedes, a great inventor and one of the leaders of the Greek army at Troy. Odysseus, to settle a personal grudge, and with the connivance or acquiescence of the other kings, accused Palamedes of betraying the Greek army to the Trojans for gold. He was convicted on the strength of fabricated evidence, and stoned to death. In revenge, his father Nauplius later lured the Greek fleet to its destruction by false signals, as it was sailing home from the war. The evils of Nauplius have been taken to refer in some way to the death of his son Palamedes, and it has been assumed that Nero must have written a poem on the theme[22]. But it is simpler to understand *mala* not as the woes suffered by Nauplius, but as the evils he caused. For when he had failed to win any recompense for his son's death from the Greek leaders, Nauplius sailed back from Troy and visited many of their wives in turn, telling each one that she would be replaced by a Trojan concubine. Several of the queens then fell into adultery, chief among them being Clytemnestra, the wife of Agamemnon. Thus, with the *Naupli mala*, Isidorus was alluding to the tragic events which culminated in the story of Orestes, and which were performed in public by Nero—rather well performed, as he had to admit, if only to keep the epigram pointed. On that reading, Isidorus tried to rebuild the barrier between theatrical myth and real life; he tried as well to sever the specious bond between the tale of Orestes and the fortunes of Nero's empire.

[21]   Juvenal 8. 215–221; Philostratus *VA* 4. 38; Pseudo-Lucian [Philostratus the Elder] *Nero* 10; Suetonius 39. 2. I am not sure what to make of the late scholiast's note on Lucan, *Bellum Civile* 5. 113 (cf. 139, 178), which claims that the Delphic oracle replied to Nero, "I do not respond to parricides": that is precisely what it *had* done to Orestes and Alcmaeon. The rhetorical response is not at all Delphic.

[22]   See, e.g., Crum, R. H., "Petronius and the Emperors," *CW* 45 (1951/1952): 161–167, 197–201, building on a point made by R. S. Rogers, *CW* 35 (1945/1946), 53–54: in one version of the myth Palamedes was first lured down a well by a false report of treasure there, then stones were tossed down on him. This is taken by Crum as an allusion, made in a *Nauplius* written by Nero, to the hunt for Dido's treasure (Suetonius 31. 3, et al.). Frazer, R. M., "Nero the Artist-Criminal," *CJ* 62 (1966/1967): 17–20 prefers the version that has Palamedes murdered by drowning while on a fishing expedition. Nero would then be dramatizing his own disposal of his young stepson while the boy was fishing (Suetonius 35.5). *Mala Naupli:* Suetonius 39. 3.

THE STORY of Oedipus must be examined next to that of Orestes. If anything even more familiar, and as a folktale even more widespread, it was a story whose retelling had a similar goal.

Laius, King of Thebes, was warned by the Delphic oracle that a son born to him and his wife Jocasta would kill him. In time a baby was born, exposed by the king on Mount Cithaeron, and by a series of coincidences saved and reared as their own son by the king and queen of Sicyon. Later the youth Oedipus was told by Delphi that he would kill his father and marry his mother. Horrified at the thought, he fled, only to fall in with Laius, his true father, and kill him in a roadside brawl. He then came to Thebes, which he freed from the shadow of the murderous Sphinx by correctly answering her riddle. The thankful Thebans made him their king and he married the now-widowed queen, Jocasta, by whom he had two sons and two daughters. When his city was ravaged by plague, Oedipus consulted Delphi, which ordered him to expel the murderer of Laius. Obediently he cursed the unknown killer and sentenced him to exile. Soon thereafter it was dramatically and irrefutably proven that he, Oedipus, had killed his father, Laius, and married his mother, Jocasta. Jocasta hanged herself and Oedipus stabbed out his eyes with her brooch. He was then driven from the city by her brother Creon and wandered the world, guided by his daughter Antigone and hounded by the Furies until he finally died at Colonus near Athens.

It is clear that Nero portrayed Oedipus as he was after the gods had stricken him with the knowledge of murder and incest. Suetonius writes of Nero's Oedipus Blinded, *Oedipus Excaecatus*, Dio of his being led about as a blind man[23]. He probably played the role in his victory at the Olympic Games in the summer of 67. Suetonius, in his account of Nero's punctilious attention to the rules of competition at Olympia, recalls his fear that he might be disqualified when he dropped his *baculus*, a staff or sceptre, during a performance, a fear that was relieved when the actor appearing with him (his *hypocrita*) assured him that no one had noticed the accident amid the uproar of acclaim. What may be a distorted version of this anecdote appears in the third-century novelistic *Life of Apollonius of Tyana* by Philostratus, when the hero criticizes the emperor's excesses at the Olympics: "What do you think of his being so perfect in the role of Creon and Oedipus that he is worried he may accidentally get his entrance or his costume or his sceptre wrong?"[24] And in Nero's last public performance in Rome the following year, he sang Oedipus the Exile, presumably the same as or a sequel to Oedipus Blinded; with Roman alertness for the double significance, someone noticed that the last line he sang in public was "My father and co-husband drives me to my death."[25]

The unconscious but intentional murder of the father is less important in the story and for Nero than is its central element, the unconscious and unintended

[23]   Dio 63. 9. 4–10; 22. 6; Suetonius 21. 3.

[24]   Philostratus *Apollonius* 5. 7.

[25]   Dio 63. 9. 4; Suetonius 46. 3. The idea that the ghost of Laius pursued his murderous son first appeared in a horrific scene of necromancy in Seneca's near-contemporary play *Oedipus*. Webster, T. B. L, *The Tragedies of Euripides* (London, 1967), 242–243, suggested that "*excaecatum* could hardly refer to self-blinding," hence that Nero was following a tradition much less familiar to us but central to the (lost) *Oedipus* of Euripides, wherein Oedipus was exposed as the murderer of Laius and blinded at the order of Creon *before* it was revealed that he was Laius' son. This alternative Oedipus, more dignified and more passive, was sent into exile with Antigone after the deaths of his fratricidal sons, Polyneices and Eteocles, at the end of Euripides' (surviving) *Phoenissae:* Nero's line would be appropriate for such an ending, although there is nothing like it in Euripides. Whichever the case may be, I presume that Juvenal's association of Nero with the mask of Antigone (8. 299) refers to his *Oedipus Exul*.

incest with the mother, whereby the father is supplanted. Incest between mother and son, though relatively rare in life and legend, had a clear symbolic significance, and stories about it share one characteristic, that the hero was or wished to be the conqueror of a homeland from which he was at the time in some way excluded[26]. Great men could be assured by consulting dreambooks that their mothers symbolized their country, so that when they dreamed of lying with their mothers they would either win power over their land, or at least die and be buried in it. Nero had to look no further than his own family for precedent: the night before Julius Caesar crossed the river Rubicon to begin his domination of the Roman world, he was said to have dreamed that he slept with his mother. To conquer one's mother was to conquer the earth, mother of all[27].

Again, it was Nero and not his enemies who made the comparison with Oedipus. After all, it was he who chose to flaunt a concubine who looked like Agrippina and to say when he was with her that he was having intercourse with his mother, and it was he who chose to play the role of Oedipus before a public which was notoriously quick to pounce upon any contemporary parallel, real or imagined. Oedipus conveyed a lesson which Orestes could not: he was indeed guilty of incest, but it was not his fault—he had acted out of ignorance[28].

The myth of Oedipus intersects with the myth of Orestes (and its doublet, Alcmaeon) in Neronian ideology: both traced the close relationship between royal mother and royal son which led to or was revealed as a crime; both crimes required the death of the mother; both crimes were intimately linked with the seizure of power by the legitimate heir. Sleeping with and killing one's mother are taboo for ordinary men, but both myths might be harnessed to show how the breaking of a private taboo by a prince could be tantamount to, even excused as, the legitimate seizing of public power. A great deal of the process is lost to us. We can never know Nero's state of mind or the opinions of his counselors before and after the murder of his mother; we may never know for certain the truth behind the rumors of incest; we will never know (the worst loss of all) the texts which Nero performed, the words he sang, the gestures he acted out. But we can see the boldness and the skill with which he acted to mitigate the horror of his act. Rome by Nero's day was a city thoroughly accustomed to the widespread, programmatic representation of myth in public life, and to the deep implication of the audience in theatrical performance. As emperor he deliberately invited comparison with the most familiar of Greek heroes, and as a competent performer he acted out the parallels in his life and on the stage. By mythologizing himself and his crime, he both distanced the crime and clothed himself in the aura of a hero. The goal was not to prove his innocence, but to accept guilt and to justify it.

[26]   Again, the following depends on Delcourt, M., *Oedipe ou la légende du conquérant* (Liège, 1944: repr. Paris 1981), especially 190–213.

[27]   According to Plutarch *Caesar* 32. 6. Suetonius *Divus Iulius* 7. 2 places the incident much earlier in Caesar's career, making explicit the interpretation that "mother ... is no other than the earth, which is considered the parent of all." For other instances, see Delcourt 1944, 192–203.

[28]   The death of Jocasta in Seneca's *Oedipus* poses an interesting problem. On the verge of suicide, she debates where to stab herself, in the breast or in the throat, but settles on the place where all the troubles began, her womb (*Oedipus* 1032–1039). As Hind, J. G. F., "The Death of Agrippina and the Finale of the 'Oedipus' of Seneca," *AUMLA* 38 (1972) pointed out, her suicide by striking the womb appears in no extant Greek tragedy, but it does strongly recall Agrippina's *ventrem feri*. Unfortunately the date of Seneca's play is unknown. Hind canvasses three possibilities: it was written before Agrippina's death, and she was playing a role; it was written after her death, and Seneca was perhaps implying that she killed herself; or it was written before her death, and popular rumor embroidered her death with a Senecan reminiscence. All three are quite possible, with a variant of the third being more likely, that is, the literary embroidery shows the hand of Nero, who controlled the story of his mother's death.

A LITTLE over six years after the death of his mother, in the early summer of 65, the 27-year-old Nero inadvertently killed his second wife, Poppaea Sabina, who was then in her early thirties. All the sources agree that he had been madly in love with her since the year 58. In their significance for Nero, the life and death of Poppaea rivaled those of Agrippina.

The real Poppaea is all but lost to history, permanently obscured by the ferocious caricature of her in the fourteenth book of the *Annals* of Tacitus as the implacable mistress who drives Nero into removing her rivals, first his mother Agrippina in 59, then his wife Octavia in 62. Tacitus asserts (without evidence) that behind a veil of modesty she was sexually voracious, and he charges her with using sex as a means to power. But she rarely appeared in public, and it is remarkable how little the historian says about her, introducing her only five times into his narrative: at her original seduction of Nero, at the two dramas of 59 (the Death of Agrippina) and 62 (the Death of Octavia), at the birth of her child in 63, and at her own death. Tacitus offers much about her motives, much about her speeches exhorting Nero to crime, but not a word about her four years as mistress and three years as empress[29]. Dio paints the same picture, but without the nagging. Suetonius does no more than report without any criticism, Nero's infatuation with her, their marriage, and her death. Her only crime may have been to supplant Octavia, who was canonized by some as the rightful empress. Soon after Nero's death the anonymous play *Octavia* would label Poppaea as the proud mistress, *superbam paelicem*, and the word "mistress" seems to have stuck[30].

The woman Nero chose to marry—Octavia was not his choice—would have to be extraordinary. Tacitus, for all that he detested her morality, admitted that Poppaea was indeed that: "Her mother, who had surpassed all the women of her day in beauty, had given her both fame and good looks, and her wealth matched the splendor of her family. She was pleasant to converse with and her nature was by no means dull: she made a show of modesty."[31] She took great pains with her beauty, keeping wrinkles at bay by daily baths in the milk from 500 she-asses, and she prayed that she might die before she began to lose her looks. Her hair was the color of amber, and when Nero praised it in a poem other women copied what had previously been thought an unattractive shade[32]. Yet she was as intelligent as she was beautiful. The poet Leonides of Alexandria gave to Poppaea Augusta a globe of the heavens as a birthday present because, as he says in the accompanying epigram, she enjoyed gifts worthy of her marriage-bed (as the "wife of Zeus") and of her learning (*sophie*). She also took a fashionable interest in Judaism, twice interceding compassionately with her husband on the Jews' behalf, and subsidizing the future historian Josephus[33]. Nero's third wife and widow, Statilia Messalina, was similarly remarkable for

---

[29]   *Annals* 13. 45–46, 14. 1, 14. 60–61, 16. 6–7.

[30]   *Octavia* 125, cf. 186. Compare Tacitus 14. 60, *paelex et adultera*; Dio 62. 13. 1, *pallikida*.

[31]   Tacitus 13. 45. The whole description is meant to recall, sometimes to echo, Sallust's description of another wild and immoral noblewoman, Sempronia, in *Catilina* 25: Syme, R., *Tacitus* (Oxford, 1958), 353.

[32]   Milk baths: Pliny ii. 238, 28. 183 (and favorite mules were shod with gold: Pliny 33. 140); *Scholia AD Juvenalem* 6. 462; Dio 62. 28. I (along with the prayer for early death). Amber-colored hair (*sucini*): Pliny 37. 50. It is usually thought that this comes from an erotic poem by the emperor; it may reflect an amber craze which sprang up in the reign (Pliny 37. 45–46). A face cream, *pinguia Poppaeana*, was named after her: Juvenal 6. 462.

[33]   Astronomy: *Anthologia Palatina* 9. 355 = D. L. Page, *Further Greek Epigrams* (Cambridge, 1981), 535–536, Leonides xxxii. Judaism: Josephus *Jewish Antiquities* 20. 189–195, *Vita* 16. Williams, M. H., "'Θεοσεβὴς γὰρ ἦν' – The Jewish Tendencies of Poppaea Sabina," *JTS* 39 (1988): 97–111 showed conclusively what should never have been doubted—that Josephus was both precise and accurate in calling the empress *theosebes*, pious (that is, in her support for the pious).

her wealth, her beauty, and her character, and was such a devotee of oratory that she even practiced the art of declamation: would he have settled for anything less in her predecessor?[34]

On 21 January 63 Poppaea bore Nero his first child, a daughter, Claudia, at Nero's own birthplace, Antium, an event which Nero greeted "with more than mortal joy." Mother and daughter were both given the imperial title of Augusta, the gods were elaborately thanked, a temple was proposed for the goddess Fecundity, public games were decreed, golden statues of Fortune (the two Fortunes, goddesses of Antium) were added to the throne of Capitoline Jupiter in Rome, and a chariot race was established at Antium in honor of the Claudian and the Domitian families. Within four months the baby died, and Nero's grief was as unrestrained as his former joy: the baby girl became the Goddess Claudia, *diva Claudia*, with a temple and a priest[35].

Within two years, Poppaea was again pregnant with a potential heir. The alleged manner of her death in the summer of 65 was to become as notorious to later ages as that of Agrippina. According to Tacitus, it was after the celebration of the second Neronian games that Nero chanced to kick his pregnant wife, and she died. Some writers, he adds, swayed more by hatred than by love of truth, had suggestion poison, but Tacitus (rightly) refused to believe them, because Nero wanted children and was deeply in love with his wife. Suetonius embellishes the tale somewhat: Poppaea, pregnant and ill, reproached him for returning home late from chariot-racing (nothing about the Neronia), and Nero killed her with a blow of his heel (*ictu calcis*, the same phrase used by Tacitus). Cassius Dio says simply that he kicked her to death, either intentionally or unintentionally[36]. Again, while the stories generally cohere, there is that hint of doubt—was it really an accident, did he mean to poison her?—but the standard version was that Nero had lashed out in blind ferocity. It was a tragically domestic incident: a wife in discomfort nags her husband, perhaps he has had a bad day at the races, a flash of temper, an eternity of sorrow.

Nero's mourning was worthy of Nero. Rather than the normal cremation, Poppaea's body was embalmed with spices in the Egyptian fashion and placed in the mausoleum of Augustus. At a great public funeral, a fortune in perfume was burned and Nero himself delivered her eulogy from the Rostra in the Forum, praising Poppaea's beauty and counting it among her virtues that she had been the mother of a divine child. She was deified as a matter of course, appearing as the goddess Poppaea, *diva Poppaea Augusta*, on coins and inscriptions, and just before his own death three years later Nero completed and dedicated a temple to the goddess Sabina Venus, with an inscription proclaiming that the women of Rome had built it[37]. But the extravagance of his

---

[34]   *Scholia AD Juvenalem* 6. 434. It might be argued that his third marriage was part of his extravagant plan to keep Poppaea alive (see below). As graffiti attest, Poppaea and Nero were both highly popular at Pompeii, which may well have been her native town: Van Buren A. W., "Pompeii – Nero – Poppaea," in G. E. Mylonas and D. Raymond, eds., *Studies Presented to David Moore Robinson*, II (Saint Louis, 1953), 970–974; Della Corte, M., *Case ed abitanti di Pompeii*[3] (Naples,1965), 72–80; Carcopino, J., "Un procurateur méconnu de Néron," *BSNAF* 1960, 150–158, at 153–154; add the laudatory *AE* 1977, 217–218.

[35]   She appears as such, or as *diva Claudia virgo*, on coins and inscriptions: *PIR*[2]C 1061. There seems to be no trace of the temple.

[36]   Tacitus 16. 6; Suetonius 35. 3; Dio 62. 27. 4.

[37]   Funeral: Tacitus 16. 6. Perfume: Pliny 12. 83. Deification: Tacitus 16. 21; Dio 62. 26. 3; RPC (Corinth/Patrae); AFA (ad 66); *ILS* 232, 8902. Temple: see Dio 63. 26. 3, observing that most of the money had been extorted. The temple appears to have escaped notice in *LTUR* and Richardson 1992, and Sabina Venus does not seem to appear on coins or inscriptions. However, note the close connection between Poppaea, Nero, and Venus on the Pompeian graffiti, *AE* 1977, 217–218.

mourning went far beyond anything ever seen at Rome. Embalming the corpse was not enough. Eerily recalling his treatment of Agrippina, Nero sent for a woman who reportedly looked like Poppaea and kept her, presumably as a concubine. But the next year he discovered an ex-slave boy who so resembled his late wife that he castrated him, called him Sabina, married him in a solemn ceremony, and dressed and treated him in all ways as his empress.

And whenever he played a woman's part on stage, he wore a mask with the features of Poppaea[38]. Again, as after the death of Agrippina, Nero chose his parts with care.

His most unusual role was Canace in Childbirth, *Canace Parturiens*, noted by Suetonius as one he undertook after the second Neronia, that is, after the death of his wife. The joke went around, apparently during the Grecian tour in 67, that a soldier who asked, "What is the emperor doing?" received the reply, "He is in labor."[39] Canace was the daughter of Aeolus, the king of the winds and friend of the gods, who lived with his wife and their six sons and six daughters in isolation on the Aeolian Islands in the Tyrrhenian Sea. Versions of the story differ substantially in details, but the essential elements are that Canace bore a child to her brother Macareus and that when their father discovered the affair he sent a sword to Canace, with which she killed herself. Macareus persuaded his father to change his mind, but it was too late and he too killed himself.

This minor tale would be familiar to the educated from the now lost play *Aeolus* by Euripides, but even more from the *Heroides* of Ovid, the collection of letters in verse from heroines of myth to their husbands or lovers, published less than eighty years before Nero's performance. Ovid subscribed to the version that portrayed Canace as her brother's eager lover. Through her he describes in detail the shame and pain of the childbirth. Aeolus hears the cries of the newborn and flies into a rage, threatening his daughter even as she lies on her bed. He orders the baby to be cast out to the wild animals, and almost immediately after he leaves her room, a messenger brings in the sword. After recounting these events, Canace bids her brother farewell, asking him to place her own and their child's remains in one urn and to mourn them both[40].

The version performed by Nero was surely close to this in its pathos. The parallels between life and myth need not be exact—the emotional resonance would be enough—and events succeed each other in Ovid's poem so rapidly that the tale could easily be encompassed within a piece entitled Canace in Childbirth. Out of the whole repertoire Nero deliberately chose a rather obscure myth in which he played on stage a mother giving birth who was soon after killed at the same time as her baby and bitterly mourned by the child's father and grandfather. He did so as he wore the mask of his late wife Poppaea Sabina, struck down in her pregnancy. Bizarre though the whole affair might appear to us, no Roman audience could miss the personal relevance of the tale; some might even be touched.

---

[38]   Dio 62. 28. 2–3, 63. 9. 5, 63. 12. 3 – 13.2 [...].

[39]   Suetonius 21. 3; Dio 63. 9. 4, 10. 2.

[40]   Ovid *Heroides* ii. 121ff. For Euripides' *Aeolus*, see Webster 1967, 157–160. In this version Macareus rapes his sister and she bears his child in secret. He then persuades his father to let the twelve siblings marry each other, which they do by lot, and Canace marries another brother. Aeolus discovers the truth and sends Canace the sword; Macareus confesses and persuades his father to forgive Canace, but it is too late. He finds his sister dying and kills himself with the same sword. But it appears that the child survives (Webster 1967, 159), and neither that nor the rape would be to Nero's purpose.

Another favorite role taken up by the emperor after his wife's death was that of *Hercules Furens*, Hercules Gone Mad, best known from Euripides' play *Heracles* and from Seneca's *Hercules Furens*. Briefly stated, the great hero is driven mad by the goddess Hera and slays his sons and their mother, his wife Megara, the daughter of Creon, King of Thebes. The oracle at Delphi then orders him to serve King Eurystheus, for whom he will perform the Twelve Labors. In Euripides' play the height of pathos is reached when the hero comes to his senses to discover that he is bound to a column, surrounded by the corpses of his family and by his bow and arrows, and learns to his mounting horror that he was the murderer. This scene was certainly replicated by Nero in his performance, for rumor asserted that once a young soldier, who was posted to guard the entrance, rushed to the emperor's assistance when he saw him in his finery and bound with chains, as the role required. The chains were, of course, of gold[41].

The story of Hercules is key—the father who kills his wife and his sons and heirs but who is not responsible for the deed, driven mad as he is by the anger of a god[42]. As with the death of Agrippina, so with that of Poppaea: Nero consciously presented his own versions of myths on stage before an audience eager to discover the slightest nuance of contemporary relevance. The desired response is likewise clear, though not explicit. Like Hercules, whom he wished to imitate in other ways, Nero had destroyed the woman he loved, and the child who was to succeed him, not because he was a murderer, but in a fit of divine madness. In short, the story was true: he had killed Poppaea Sabina as rumor had it, and he had slaughtered their unborn child, but like Hercules (and like Aeolus in his own way), he was innocent.

BUT *WAS* the story true? Probably not. It was certainly not original. Despite the absolute silence of our sources, it looks as if Nero tried to reinvent publicly a significant part of his private life in the image of one specific model: the notorious Periander, tyrant of Corinth in the first half of the sixth century BC[43]. The distinctive reminiscences are stunning.

First, Periander was the only other important figure of Graeco-Roman antiquity who was accused of sleeping with his mother, and, as with Nero, the event was the turning point in his life. The story is best known as presented in Chapter 17 of the *Unhappy Love Stories, Erotika Pathemata*, written by the Greek poet Parthenius in the first century BC. As he grew to be a gentle and handsome youth, Periander's mother fell ever more passionately in love with him. Unable to restrain herself, she finally persuaded her reluctant son to meet secretly with a beautiful married woman who was hopelessly enamored of him. Conditions of modesty were set: they were to meet in a room without a light, and he was not to make the woman speak to him. They met, and Periander was delighted with his unseen mistress. Naturally his curiosity grew without being satisfied as his mother continued to protect the woman's identity. At last, when she came to the

---

[41]   Suetonius 21. 3; cf. Dio 63. 10. 2 (soldier), 63. 9. 5. (golden chains). Dio at 63. 9. 4 mentions Nero playing a madman, and that Hercules was one of his favorite roles. The young soldier's impetuous act was presumably a shrewd tribute to the emperor's acting genius.
Two other roles are attributed to Nero for which it is hard to find any contemporary relevance: Thyestes (Dio 63. 94. 4, 22. 6; Juvenal 8. 227–230) and Melanippe (Juvenal 8. 229).

[42]   There is an echo of the theme of the loss of the heir in the tale of Canace, as her father Aeolus destroys mother and child in his fury but soon repents of the deed—in part at least because, in the Euripidean version, he has earlier expressed "his desire for male grandchildren who will be good fighters and wise counselors": Webster 1967, 158.

[43]   The parallels were first noted by the folklorist A. H. Krappe: Krappe 1940, 470–471; cf. Delcourt 1944, 203. See also Mayer, R., "What caused Poppaea's Death?" *Historia* 31 (1982): 248–249 ("It does not seem to have been noticed …").

room one night he lit a lamp; then, struck with horror to discover that his lover was his own mother, he tried to slay her. The gods intervened to prevent him, his mother killed herself, and Periander, his mind unbalanced, sank into ferocious tyranny. His biographer, Diogenes Laertius, quotes a much-truncated version of this folktale, to the effect that the tyrant committed incest with his mother and when the truth was revealed turned brutal. The mother's name, we are told, was *Crateia*, Power[44].

Next, as Diogenes relates the matter in his brief Life of Periander, "in a fit of anger, he killed his wife by throwing a footstool at her, or by a kick, when she was pregnant."[45] He had been egged on by the lies of his concubines, whom he later burned alive, and in a (fictitious) letter to his father-in-law he protests that he had not meant to do it. In destroying the unborn baby he also ensured that he would leave no child as the heir to his power: one son was feeble-minded, the other was killed later, and Periander was succeeded by his nephew.

Herodotus adds a strange story[46]. Happening to lose an object of value one day, Periander sent an embassy to an oracle of the dead. The ghost of his wife Melissa appeared but would not help: "She was chill," she said, "having no clothes; the garments buried with her were of no manner of use, since they had not been burnt. And this should be her token to Periander, that what she said was true – the oven was cold when he baked his loaves in it." Periander understood the sign at once, for he had made love to her dead body. He therefore summoned the women of Corinth to the temple of Hera. When they arrived in their finery, as for a festival, he stripped them all naked, slave and free alike, and burned their clothes for Melissa. She then told a second inquiry to the oracle where to find the lost valuable. Thus, even though incest with a mother and unintentionally kicking to death a pregnant wife in a fit of fury might be enough to draw the parallel, Nero went further. The embalming of Poppaea, the union with her double, the marriage with Sporus, might all be taken to echo Periander's obsession with his dead wife; certainly the temple dedicated to the divine Sabina Venus by the women of Rome was built with money extorted from them, just as Periander had forced the women of Corinth to dedicate their finest clothes to his dead Melissa[47].

Finally, Periander was the first to think of cutting a canal through the Isthmus of Corinth. Others after him were said to have considered the attempt—Demetrius Poliorcetes, Julius Caesar, Caligula—but only Nero, a lover of grand engineering projects, tried seriously to put the plan into action. The cutting of the Isthmus, although of undoubted benefit to mankind, came to be regarded as an act of hubris, an overbearing trespass into the affairs of the gods, and the mark of a tyrant[48]. The next man after Nero who was said to have weighed the possibility was the wealthy and imperious Athenian orator and sophist Herodes Atticus, a Roman senator and consul in the year 143. Not a tyrant

---

[44]   Diogenes Laertius, *Lives of the Philosophers* 1. 96. His *Life of Periander*, 1. 94–100, is the main ancient source for the tyrant. Cf. Plutarch *Moralia* 146D.

[45]   Diogenes Laertius 1. 94.

[46]   Herodotus 5. 92. Explained as the historicizing of myth by J. Stern. "De-mythologization in Herodotus: 5. 92. ε," *Eranos* 87 (1989): 13–20.

[47]   Nero's extortion: Dio 63. 26. 3–4. Diogenes Laertius offers a doublet of the clothing/enforced dedication story at 1. 96. Periander vowed a golden statue if he won the chariot race at the Olympic Games. He won but, being short of gold, he helped himself to the ornaments which he had seen the women wearing at a festival.

[48]   Gerster 1884; Traina, G., "L'impossibile taglio dell'Istmo (Ps. Lucian, *Nero* 1–5)," *RFIC* 115 (1987): 40–49. Pliny *NH* 4. 10, grumbling about impiety, gives the standard list of names of those who dared (without Periander); each is confirmed by other sources.

himself, he nevertheless had several run-ins with the democratic elements in Athens, and his grandfather had actually been condemned on a charge of aiming at tyranny. More peculiarly, Herodes was charged by his brother-in-law with beating his wife so as to cause her death in the eight month of her pregnancy, in the year 157. We are told, moreover, in addition to his accuser's inability to bring any proof, that Herodes' defense was helped by the fact that he had not intended to kill her, and that his grief for her was uncommonly extravagant[49]. Just the man to dream of a Corinthian canal.

The Periander of legend provided for Nero a veritable mirror for princes. On the surface, as we see it, the image is horrific: the savage sexuality of a man who violated his mother, who violated the mother of his child, who violated Mother Earth; the violent conquest and exertion of unrestrained power; the proverbial cruelty. Periander had learned well from his teacher, the older tyrant Thrasybulus of Miletus. In a celebrated tale which attaches itself to other similar figures, Periander sent to Thrasybulus to ask what was the best way to govern. Thrasybulus replied by taking the messenger for a walk, during which he lopped off all the tallest heads of grain. The messenger was mystified that Thrasybulus said nothing, but Periander understood, and the lesson was not lost on Nero[50].

Yet the mirror reflects simultaneously a quite different image. Periander had made Corinth great. He built up its navy and dominated the seas, he conquered, he colonized widely, he promoted trade from Illyria to Egypt. He legislated against luxury, forced his subjects to work hard, abolished taxes. His court attracted artists and poets, chief among them the singer Arion. He beautified the city with great buildings. He won the chariot race at the Olympic Games. At the heart of it all lay his own tremendous personality, and a practical and gnomic wisdom that gained him a place on lists of the Seven Sages of Greece. Many Greeks had trouble accepting Periander as one of the wise men. Plato omitted him; Aristotle included him; several others in their discomfort concluded that there must have been two Perianders, the despot and the sage[51]. Nero would be quite happy with the paradox of the man whose superior virtues and abilities absolved him from the moral constraints of society.

FOR NERO, it was not a matter of art for art's sake. He used the stage—he could not have avoided using the stage—as a platform for his views, presented in mythological dress. From that assumption several conclusions follow.

First, we can see at least three messages in transmission. One is the image of the matricide, driven by the gods, tormented by the Furies, but ultimately absolved for his crime—in the case of Orestes, seizing power from the female usurper. The second is that of the incestuous son who sleeps unawares with his mother; and the third is that of the man who unintentionally causes the death of wife and child. No myth was, or was expected to be, an exact fit with real life; an allusion was enough for the audience to create its own story[52]. The common thread of the tales enacted by Nero on stage, sometimes in a mask displaying his own features, was one of justification for acts that were essentially unjustifiable. At some deeper level, he was saying, he was innocent.

[49]   Discussed in connection with Nero, Periander, and the standard image of the tyrant by Ameling, W., "Tyrannen und schwangeren Frauen," *Historia* 35 (1986): 507–508. On the death, the trial, and the extravagant mourning, see W. Ameling, *Herodes Atticus* I, *Biographie* (Hildensheim, Zürich, New York, 1983), 100–107.

[50]   Herodotus 5. 92; Diogenes Laertius 1. 100.

[51]   Diogenes Laertius 1. 98–99.

[52]   The point is made by Coleman, K. M., "Fatal Charades: Roman Executions Staged as Mythological Enactments," *JRS* 80 (1990): 44–73, at 62–63, 66.

Moreover, since Nero chose to act out the tales on stage, he himself must either have created or soon appropriated them. This is best seen in the identification with Orestes, which was asserted by him and rejected by his critics, but it casts light on the other notorious stories as well. In folklore, mother-son incest normally occurs between two unwitting parties, or else the mother seduces the son; seldom is the son at fault[53]. Nero brilliantly combined elements of the Oedipus tale with elements of Orestes to double the horror of Agrippina's lust for power. He also succeeded in getting his message across. The serious doubt that incest actually occurred, and the certainty shared by all but his most virulent detractors that, if it did occur, Agrippina must have been the aggressor—not having ones' cake, but eating it anyway—surely both can only have started with Nero. Whatever later generations made of the affair, popular rumor, *fama*, blamed Agrippina.

Similarly with the treatment of the death of Poppaea, Nero got his message across, whatever later generations made of it. Despite grumbling, most agreed that it was an accident. No one really questioned whether Nero had kicked her, or even whether Poppaea was pregnant at all. The claim that he was innocent of the crime by reason of temporary insanity brilliantly diverts attention from the fact of the crime itself. That Nero seems to have studied the life of Periander with extraordinary care strongly suggests that there may have been no crime at all—that Poppaea's fortuitous death was made into something more interesting and the excuse for even more immoderate mourning. Sleeping with his mother and kicking his pregnant wife to death are stories too good to be true.

Finally, behind the masks lies a daring new conception of Roman power. By presenting himself as the heroes and heroines of myth, Nero of course raised himself above the level of ordinary action and responsibility. That fits in well with the model of Periander drawn from legend. There were other models which he could imitate, the most obvious being Augustus and Alexander. Augustus followed by his successors was the civil prince, *civilis princeps*, the first among equals, but poised between Republican nobleman and Hellenistic monarch. Alexander followed by his successors was something different: world-conqueror, patron of arts and letters, close to divinity on earth. But Periander was something quite different again, an older and much more elemental creature, not a god or godlike but a great tyrant, superhuman in his emotions and his wisdom, writer and Olympic victor, conqueror and patron of the arts—in short, a Greek rather than a Hellenistic or Roman monarch, and one much closer to the heroes of myth than of history[54].

---

[53] Thompson, S., *Motif-Index of Folk Literature* (Bloomington, Indianapolis, 1953), motifs K 2111. 5; M 344; N 365. 1; T 412 passim.

[54] Vernant, J. P., "The Lame Tyrant: from Oedipus to Periander," in J. P. Vernant and P. Vidal-Naquet, *Myth and Tragedy in Ancient Greece* (New York, 1988), 207–236 brilliantly compares the legendary kings of Thebes, the Labdacids, the family of Oedipus, with the historical tyrants of Corinth, the Cypselids, the family of Periander. Concluding at 226–227: "in the way that the Greeks imagined the figure of the tyrant, as projected in the fifth and fourth centuries, he took on the features of the hero of legend, an individual at once elect yet accursed," and so on. And quoting Gernet about the tyrant as a "natural" product of the past: "His excesses had their models in legends." Rejecting social norms, he is "relegat[ed] to an isolation comparable both to that of a god, who is too far above men to come down to their level, and to that of a beast, so dominated by its appetites that it can brook no restraint. The tyrant despises the rules that control the ordering of the social fabric and, through its regularly woven mesh, determine the position of each individual in relation to all the rest, in other words—to put it more crudely, as Plato does—he is perfectly prepared to kill his father, sleep with his mother, and devour the flesh of his own children."
Also relevant to Nero's interests in performance and Periander is R. P. Martin, "The Seven Sages as Performers of Wisdom," in C. Dougherty and L. Kurke, eds., *Cultural Poetics in Archaic Greece: Cult, Performance, Politics* (Cambridge, 1993), 108–128.

Shining Apollo

[...]

THE NEW ERA that dawned in 64 was a Golden Age. In 65, Nero was for a time the willing dupe of a deranged North African knight named Caesellius Bassus, who claimed that the hidden treasure of Queen Dido of Carthage had been revealed to him in a dream: a mass of gold bullion lying in a great cave under his estates. Without checking either the source or the story itself, Nero dispatched an army of treasure-seekers. After a long and frenzied search nothing was found, and Bassus killed himself. But during the weeks and months of waiting, gold fever consumed the capital, rumors flew, and the emperor was alleged to have spent vast sums recklessly, in the anticipation that his treasury would soon be replenished[55]. This period of happy suspense coincided with the second celebration of the Neronian Games, and the competing orators seized the occasion to heap praise on the emperor: the earth, they claimed, teemed with new fertility and the gods were bringing forth unexpected wealth—pure gold, not gold alloyed with other metals as before. Gold indeed glitters everywhere in Nero's reign, from the emperor's poems written in letters of gold to the gold casket containing his first beard; from his golden fishing net to the gold chains he wore on stage as Hercules to his golden box of poisons; from Poppaea's gold-shod mules to Nero's golden chamber pot[56]. But there is more here than just imperial luxury. Gold was the symbol of the sun, Apollo was the god with the golden hair and the gilded face, and the Sun was the source of life[57]. From 64 on Nero tried to make the Golden Age of the Sun a reality, in the most flamboyant way.

In late May of 66, Rome witnessed the extraordinary Golden Day[58]. This was the day on which the emperor crowned Tiridates King of Armenia at fabulous expense. It received its name from the people because of a stunning embellishment of the Theater of Pompey, where the stage, the walls, everything portable, were all in some way gilded. Pliny the Elder, who must have seen it, says simply that Nero covered the theater with gold for that one day. It would have been blinding were the crowd not protected from the sun by the awning, at the center of which was Nero driving the chariot of the Sun.

Earlier on the Golden Day the emperor had received the homage of Tiridates in the Forum and crowned him before a vast crowd[59]. The ceremony was timed to begin at sunrise, and Dio's source remarked on the white clothes of the civilians who crowded everywhere, even on the roof-tops, and the shining armor of the soldiers in their ranks, with their weapons flashing like lightning. The theatrical effect when the rising sun first hit the Forum must have been dazzling. It was indeed an effect, one that was deliberately planned: an earlier day for the

---

[55]   Tacitus 16. 1–3 and Suetonius 31. 4–32. 5, both depending on the same source.

[56]   Hemsoll, D., "The Architecture of Nero's Golden House," in M. Henig ed., *Architecture and Architectural Sculpture in the Roman Empire* (Oxford, 1990), 10–38, at 36, n. 87, gives a long list of golden items connected with Nero.

[57]   On gold as the attribute of the Sun, see L'Orange, H. P., *Likeness and Icon: Selected Studies in Classical and Early Mediaeval Art* (Odense 1973), 292–294.

[58]   The prime sources are Dio 63. 1–6 and Suetonius 13; cf. Pliny 33. 54, Tacitus 16. 23–24.

[59]   In a carefully staged ceremony, complete with dialogue, Tiridates proclaimed himself to be Nero's slave who had come to worship him as a god, as he did Mithras. [...]

ceremony had been set by edict, but it had been postponed *because of clouds*. In the Forum as in the gilded theater, where Nero repeated the coronation under his solar awning, the Golden Day was also the Day of the Sun[60].

Pliny remarked that the gilded Theater of Pompey was but a fraction of the size of the *aurea domus*, Nero's famed Golden House, which (he claimed) surrounded the city[61]. The name of the house, it must be understood, was Nero's own, and he coined it after the Great Fire of 64. Construction had been undertaken of a palace which connected the complex on the Palatine Hill with the imperial gardens on the Esquiline, and to which Nero had given the simple name of *Domus Transitoria*, the Connecting House. This had been destroyed by the Fire and was afterwards redesigned and rebuilt at lavish expense. The new palace, which was going up even as the Golden Day dawned, he called simply the Golden House, *Domus Aurea*. He planned to erect a 120-foot statue of Sol in its enormous vestibule: no one could doubt that this was the house of the Sun.

Petronius, in his contemporary novel, the *Satyricon*, would mock Roman youths who wasted their hard-conquered spoils in raising buildings of gold, but Nero's old tutor, Seneca, knew that there was more to the Golden House than the luxury, which he too condemned. Writing in the late summer or autumn of 64—that is, after the Golden House had begun to rise from the ruins of the Domus Transitoria—he offered a clear and precise denunciation of the new solar ideology:

> People seem to think that the immortal gods cannot give any better gift than wealth—or even possess anything better [here he quotes Ovid's *Metamorphoses* 2.1]:
>
> The sun-god's palace, set with pillars tall
> And flashing bright with gold
>
> Or look at the chariot of the Sun:
>
> Gold was the axle, golden too the pole
> And gold the tires that bound the circling wheels
> And silver all the spokes within the wheels
>
> And finally, when they would praise an epoch as the best, they call it the "Golden Age" (*saeculum aureum*)[62].

This passage shows startlingly open contempt for the new Golden Age, as Seneca attacks the very equation of gold with the Sun which underlay Nero's project, drawing on the tale of Phaethon in Ovid for small all-too-apt quotations. The vulgarity, the superficiality of people who define the gods in terms of gold are mercilessly etched in Neronian terms—the *palace* of the Sun, the *chariot* of the Sun—and the concept of a new Golden Age is turned upside down, not sublime but ignoble.

---

[60] Dio 63. 3. 4–6; Suetonius 13, noting the postponement *propter nubilem;* Pliny 33. 54 (and possibly 19. 24, though he writes there of the sky-colored, star-strewn awnings as being over the *amphitheatrum Neronis*). On the wearing of white clothes at public spectacles, see, e.g., Martial 4. 2, 14. 137.

[61] Pliny 33. 54, cf. 36. 111. On the Golden House, see ['One house' below].

[62] Petronius *Satyrica* 120. 87; Seneca *Epistulae Morales* 115. 12–13, cited in Hemsoll 1990, 31. Blaison, M., 'Suétone et *l'ekphrasis* de la *Domus Aurea* (Suét., *Ner.* 31)," *Latomus* 57 (1998): 617–624 argues that Suetonius' description of the Golden House should be taken not literally but literarily, suggesting that it was heavily influenced by Ovid's description of the House of the Sun; but the Ovidian lens was provided by Seneca, who actually knew the Golden House.

Seneca goes on to dissect lines from the Greek tragedians which seemed to praise wealth. In one, from a play by Euripides about Bellerophon, money is deemed superior to love. When, at its first performance, the entire audience rose as one to eject from the theater the actor who had spoken these words, Euripides himself (writes Seneca) jumped up and urged them to wait and see *quem admirator auri exitum faceret*, how one who adored gold would die[63]. Not perhaps the most political anecdote for Seneca to repeat when his gold-obsessed former pupil was raising his Golden House: Nero was overjoyed at his old teacher's enforced suicide the following year[64].

Earlier in the same letter, Seneca dwells on being dazzled by light, in a remarkable discussion of moral chiaroscuro. The philosopher distinguishes between misleading superficial beauty and the true inner radiance of the virtuous soul. The problem is a matter of vision: we cannot see inner beauty because we have been blinded by too much exterior *splendor*, or by too much darkness. It we could but purify our vision we would see internal beauty, however buried it might be beneath outward poverty, or lowliness, or disgrace. "Conversely," he continues, "we shall get a view of evil and the deadening influences of a sorrow-laden soul, in spite of the hindrance that results from the widespread gleam of riches that flash round about, *divitiarum radiantium splendor*, and in spite of the false light, *falsa lux, ...* of great power which beats pitilessly upon the beholder"[65]. The evil, unhappy soul, masked by the splendor of radiant riches, the false light of great power—all this just before Seneca turns to describe the Sun god's palace.

Seneca wrote, in Ovid's words, of the Sun god's palace flashing bright with gold, *regia Solis ... clara micante auro*. Safely after Nero's death, Martial would sing of new works rising where the hateful hall of a savage king once shone, *invidiosa feri radiabant atria regis*. Why did it shine? In his precious account of the Golden House, Suetonius describes in order the vestibule, the lake, its buildings, and the open countryside; then he says, "in other parts everything was covered with gold and studded with gems and pearls"—after which his tour proceeds to the dining-rooms and baths. Presumably the gilt and jewel adornment covered not just the interiors but also the exteriors of the Golden House, just as the Theater of Pompey was gilded throughout for one day. Nero, as we have seen from the Golden Day, was interested in dazzling light effects. Curiously, Pliny tells of a Temple of the Fortune of Sejanus which the emperor set up somewhere in the grounds of the Golden House to house an ancient statue of the goddess Fortuna, rescued from a shrine supposed originally to have been built by King Servius Tullius in sixth century BC and probably damaged or destroyed in the Great Fire. What made Nero's temple memorable was that it was built of a marble-hard stone recently discovered in Cappadocia—*phengites*, the shining stone, white, streaked with yellow veins. Pliny was deeply impressed by its translucence, which made the temple as light as day even when the doors were shut, uncannily striking the viewer as lit from within[66].

Imagine a visitor toiling up the straightened and splendidly redeveloped Via Sacra from the Forum, to approach the doors of the Domus Aurea. There, in the enormous vestibule, dominating the vista, indeed visible throughout much of

---

[63] Seneca *Epistulae Morales* 115. 15.

[64] Tacitus 15. 60: *caedes Annaei Senecae, laetissima principi.*

[65] Seneca *Epistulae Morales* 115. 6–7.

[66] Martial *De Spectaculis* 2. 3; Suetonius 31; Pliny *NH* 36. 163. On the complex history of the Fortune of Sejanus, see Coarelli, F., *Il Foro Boario: dalle origini alla fine della Repubblica* (Rome, 1988), 265–288; cf. *LTUR* II, 278, "Fortuna Seiani, Aedes" (L. Anselmino and M. J. Strazulla).

the city, Nero intended to install the dazzling bronze colossal statue of the Sun which he had commissioned. It would view the stars close-up (in Martial's words), and would mark the transition from the old center of Republican Rome to the new imperial palace[67]. It is standardly and authoritatively asserted, and almost universally accepted, that the notorious Colossus was erected in Nero's lifetime, and that the Sun was depicted with the emperor's own features[68]. However, R.R.R. Smith has argued with great force that neither assumption is warranted: Pliny the Elder, who had watched in awe as the sculptor Zenodorus built his model, erected the scaffolding, and molded the great work out of bronze, does *not* say that it was a remarkable likeness of the emperor, only that it was remarkably lifelike; Suetonius does *not* say that it stood in the vestibule, but rather that the vestibule was one in which the 120-foot Colossus might stand, *staret* (that is, the vestibule was also very large; others have pointed this out, as Smith notes)[69]. Both observations are correct.

Of the two questions—did the statue originally represent Nero? and was it erected during his lifetime?—the second is the easier to answer. As Smith remarks, "When Pliny saw it, it was still in the workshop, and Tacitus, always keen-eyed for any new signs of Nero's *audacia*, does not even mention it." Since, moreover, Suetonius cannot be taken to say that the statue stood in the vestibule in Nero's day, and since Dio tells us straightforwardly that in 75, under Vespasian, the Colossus was erected in the Sacred Way, there is absolutely no reason to believe that Nero saw the statue standing in the Domus Aurea before his death in 68[70].

Less clear is the answer to the first question. That the Colossus which survived into the fourth century represented the sun, there is no doubt: "the mass of the marvelous Colossus, crowned with rays, delights in overcoming the work of Rhodes."[71] The scholarly consensus has been that after his death the emperor's image was reworked into the more standard features of the sun, although no ancient author says so[72]. This view rests mainly on Pliny's assertion that the

[67]   Martial *De Spectaculis* 2. 1. The Colossus remained a byword for its huge size even to those who had never seen it: *CLE* 1552 A, 82–83 (from Cillium, in Tunisia, c. AD 150).

[68]   The large bibliography on the Colossus is collected and superseded by the paper of Lega, C., "Il Colosso di Nerone," *BCAR* 93(1989–1990): 339–378 (cf. her article in *LTUR* I, 295–298, "Colossus: Nero"), and by the book of Bergmann, M., *Die Strahlen der Herrscher. Theomorphes Herrschebild und politische Symbolik im Hellenismus und in der römischen Kaiserzeit* (Mainz, 1998).

[69]   See Smith, R. R. R., "Nero and the Sun-god: Divine Accessories and Political Symbols in Roman Imperial Images," JRA 13 (2000): 532–542 [review of Bergmann 1998], 536–538, on Pliny 34. 45 and Suetonius 31.

[70]   Dio 66. 15. 1. Note also Martial *De Spectaculis* 2, which works a series of contrasts between the contemporary valley of the Colosseum in 80 and its state in 64, when the Golden House occupied the area. Where the Colosseum now stands, was Nero's Lake; where the Baths of Titus now stand, was once a stretch of open country after the houses of the poor were removed; where now the Colonnade of the Temple of the Divine Claudius stands, was the boundary of the House; and (beginning the list of contrasts) where the Colossus itself now stands were the halls of the tyrant; *if* we were to follow Martial to the letter, this *should* mean that the Colossus, like the Colosseum, the Baths, and the Temple, was raised after Nero's death.

[71]   Lega 1989–1990 discusses the evidence. The quote is from Martial (1. 70), writing under Domitian. The Colossus stood in the same location for half a century, until in the later 120s the emperor Hadrian, needing to clear the area for his new Temple of Venus and Rome, moved the statue to a site next to the Colosseum (which was built by the Flavians and took its name from the statue). The statue itself disappeared sometime after the fourth century, but its new base survived until it was demolished as late as 1933.

[72]   The case is summarized in Lega 1989–1990, 349–351, and Bergmann, M., "Der Koloss Neros, die Domus Aurea und der Mentalitätswandel im Rom der frühen Kaiserzeit," *Trierer Winckelmannsprogramme* 13 (1993): 3–37, at 4–6, 14–17.

statue was intended, *destinatum*, to represent Nero, but was dedicated to the sun after the emperor's crimes were condemned; and on Suetonius' observation in passing that Vespasian richly rewarded the restorer, *refector*, of the Venus of Cos and the Colossus (generally taken to signal the reworking of the statue from Nero into Sol, although Smith observes that it can mean merely that the statue was finished under Vespasian). There is no evidence that the statue was reworked into the sun—Pliny certainly does not say so—and Smith argues that Nero's alleged "intention" to portray himself as the sun was the invention of posthumous rhetoric, designed as an index of a "bad" emperor's megalomania. Thus Suetonius' observation that the vestibule was large enough to contain a 120-foot colossus "with his own features" is simply misleading, and it should be noted that, according to Dio's source, some said the statue erected in 75 bore Nero's features, others those of Titus[73]. Smith concludes, "There are many other paper monuments and untestable rhetorical charges attached to these figures [that is, "bad" or failed emperors] ... which are often accepted as unproblematic evidence on a kind of *ad hominem* basis simply because no ground rules have been established for engaging with this genre of literary representation." That Nero intended to erect a huge statue of himself looming over the city certainly fits in with other unfounded posthumous allegations against him, and it does not correspond either with his other, real intentions or with the program of the Golden House.

Whether he lived to see the Colossus in place or not, let us pursue Nero's intentions. Past the overwhelming vestibule his amazed visitor would find not the expected "house," but a bowl of open countryside dotted with woods, pastures, fields, animals, and different buildings, all scattered around an artificial lake: the "Golden House" was not a house at all, but a large suburban villa set down in the heart of the city, *rus in urbe*[74]. Its grounds covered the valley where the lake lay (the site today of the Colosseum) and the slopes of the surrounding hills—the Esquiline to the north, the Caelian to the south, the Palatine to the west.

Looking from the vestibule to the left across the valley, the visitor's eye would be drawn immediately to the tremendous façade of the main residential complex, set carefully on, out from, into, the side of the Oppian Hill, which was part of the Esquiline. Carefully indeed, for terraces were imposed on the landscape, as part of the hill was removed behind and strong substructures were added in front[75]. This must have been intended to facilitate one of the most remarkable features of the building, its alignment, which was imposed on, not by, the topography. The Oppian complex (along with the later, dependent

---

[73] What the post-Neronian Colossus looked like can be deduced from coins or medallions of the third-century emperors Severus Alexander and Gordian III. Those of Alexander are difficult to decipher, but Gordian's clearly show next to the Colosseum a standing nude figure with radiate head, his right hand held forward and resting on the rudder of Fortune, his left arm perhaps bent with the hand holding a globe: *LTUR* I, fig. 17. Moreover, very happily, Bergmann has drawn attention to a carved amethyst, now in Berlin, which seems to present the figure of Helios is precisely the same way as the medallion of Gordian. On the rudder, see J. Gagé, "Le colosse et la Fortune de Rome," *MEFR* 45 (1928): 109–122, arguing cleverly but unconvincingly for a transformation of the statue into the symbol of Rome's fate.

[74] In fact, where one might expect to discover just such a scene painted in a vestibule, one would see a reality—a double *trompe l'oeil*.

[75] The following paragraph depends heavily on Voisin, J.-L., "*Exoriente sole* (Suétone, *Ner.* 6). D'Alexandrie à la *Domus Aurea*," *L'Urbs: Espace urbain et histoire Ier siècle av. J. C.-IIIe ap. J. C.* (Rome, 1987): 509–543, 509–519.

Baths of Titus) is unique among the public buildings of Rome in its strict orientation, lying precisely on an east-west axis. The significance of this is still not known[76], but undoubtedly a building that faced due south would be washed with sunshine throughout the day. The effect of sunlight hitting a gilded and bejeweled façade, over 360 meters long, from dawn till dusk, would be blinding: "the sun-god's palace, set with pillars tall and flashing bright with gold."

This Golden House looked down from the periphery of the area onto a world in miniature[77]. Tacitus curtly dismisses the artificiality of the landscaping imposed on downtown Rome by Nero's engineers, as "fields and lakes and, to give the impression of wilderness, woods here and open spaces and prospects there." But Suetonius is more precise as he moves methodically in his description from the vestibule where the Colossus might stand over to the actual villa itself:

> There was also a lake like the sea, encircled by buildings meant to look like cities. There was moreover countryside of various kinds, fields, vineyards, pastures, and woods, along with a great number of every kind of tame and wild animals[78].

What the visitor standing by the Colossus would realize immediately was that this artificial landscape was a microcosm of the world. More precisely, the "sea" surrounded by "cities," farms and wild countryside, humans and animals, may have represented the Roman Empire in miniature, with the Mediterranean at its center. Overlooking this world from the Oppian Hill was the glittering façade of the Palace of the Sun, while high above its entrance would stand the shining statue of the Sun, its master, holding the world in his hand.

One house

[...]

OF NERO'S many follies, none was more magnificent than his Xanadu, the legendary Domus Aurea, the Golden House. Suetonius, by far our most important source, captures its breathtaking "size and splendor" with fascinated disapproval:

> Its vestibule was high enough to contain a colossal statue of the Emperor a hundred and twenty feet high. So large was the house that it had a triple colonnade a mile long. There was lake in it too, a sea surrounded with buildings to represent cities, besides tracts of country, varied with tilled fields, vineyards, pastures and woods, with great numbers of wild and domestic animals. In the rest of the house all parts were overlaid with gold and adorned with jewels and mother-of-pearl. There were dining-rooms with fretted ceilings of ivory, whose

[76] Voisin 1987 suggests fascinating astrological intentions. There certainly does seem to be a singular prominence accorded to the *oculus*, the large circular opening in the dome of the great central octagonal hall. At noon on the equinoxes, the circle of light cast by the *oculus* precisely touches the four corners of the door leading into the great nymphaeum: the circle is, as it were, squared. Unfortunately, a cupola stood over the dome (Hemsoll, D., "Reconstructing the Octagonal Dining Room of Nero's Golden House," *Architectural History* 32 (1989): 1–17; Hemsholl 1990): unless it were ingeniously opened or removable in some way, the light would have great difficulty penetrating.

[77] It should be noted that the extent of the Golden House has been exaggerated by both ancients and moderns: see Chapter 7 below. The practical effect of properly recognizing its size, which will be relevant to the argument here, is that the so-called Oppian or Esquiline "wing" (as the residence is known) was at the periphery of the area.

[78] Tacitus 15. 42; Suetonius 31. On the surprising form of the lake, revealed by excavation, see [below].

panels could turn and shower down flowers and were fitted with pipes for sprinkling the guests with perfumes. The main banquet hall was circular and constantly revolved day and night, like the heavens. He had baths supplied with sea water and sulphur water. When the edifice was finished in this style and he dedicated it, he deigned to say nothing more in the way of approval than that he was at last beginning to be housed like a human being.

Tacitus is much briefer, to the same effect:

Nero ... erected a mansion in which jewels and gold, long familiar objects, quite vulgarized by our extravagance, were not so marvellous as the fields and lakes and artificial wilderness with woods on one side, open spaces and extensive views on another.

One other important literary source for the Golden House survives, an epigram of Martial published in the year 80 to celebrate spectacles sponsored by the emperor Titus in the newly built Colosseum. Since the new amphitheater stood squarely in the grounds of the Golden House, the poet took the occasion to contrast the state of the area in 64 with its current condition:

Where the starry colossus sees the constellations at close range and lofty scaffolding rises in the middle of the road, once gleamed the odious halls of a cruel monarch [i.e., the vestibule], and in all Rome there stood a single house. Where rises before our eyes the august pile of the Amphitheater [the Colosseum], was once Nero's lake. Where we admire the warm baths [of Titus], a speedy gift, a haughty tract of land had robbed the poor of their dwellings. Where the Claudian colonnade [the portico of the Temple of the Divine Claudius] unfolds it widespread shade, was the outermost part of the palace's end. Rome has been restored to herself, under your rule, Caesar, the pleasances that belonged to a master now belong to the people[79].

Part of the Golden House survives today, vast underground ruins on the Mons Oppius, a spur of the Esquiline Hill. Unfinished at Nero's death, later damaged by fire, it was filled in and built over by the emperor Trajan almost fifty years later to serve as the substructure of his great bath complex. Rediscovered in the Renaissance, its rooms, now "grottoes," served to stimulate generations of artists with their "grotesque" paintings. The shadowy subterranean ruins, and the dazzling literary accounts of what they once were, have fascinated kings, artists, and academics ever since. But the question is rarely asked directly: *why* did Nero build the Golden House? Or, in more romantic terms, what did he mean by saying "housed like a human being"? The answer to that lies in the answer to another question: *where* did he build the Golden House?

Suetonius tells us: "He made a palace extending all the way from the Palatine to the Esquiline, which at first he called the House of Passage, *Domus Transitoria*, but when it was burned shortly after its completion and rebuilt, the Golden House, *Domus Aurea*."[80] Tacitus adds that Nero returned from Antium to Rome when the flames approached the *domus* by which he had connected, *continuaverat*, the Palatine and the *horti Maecenatis*, the Gardens of Maecenas

---

[79] Suetonius 31. 1–2; Tacitus 15. 42. 1 (Church and Brodribb translation, modified); Martial *De Spectaculis* 2.

[80] Suetonius 31. 1: *Non in alia re tamen damnosior quam in aedificando domum a Palatio Esquilias usque fecit, quam primo transitoriam, mox incendio absumptam restitutamque auream nominavit.*

(which lay on the Esquiline)[81]. All this seems perfectly clear. By Nero's day, the formerly residential area of the Palatine Hill was dominated by two large imperial palace complexes: the Palatina Domus, the House of Augustus, in the southwest, overlooking the Circus Maximus; and to the north of it, the Domus Tiberiana, the House of Tiberius, which overlooked the Via Sacra and the eastern end of the Forum. The Esquiline Hill to the east, on the other hand, was particularly associated with "gardens," *horti*, that is, grand country villas of the inner suburb, most notably the large tracts of the Gardens of Maecenas and the Lamian Gardens, both now owned by the emperor. These were the areas that Nero now joined together, the public Palatine and the private Esquiline, through the valley where the Colosseum would later be built.

Despite these fairly precise indications, Nero's ancient critics would leave us in no doubt: the House was everywhere, it was taking over the city. As Tacitus sneered in passing, after the fire Nero rebuilt "so much [of the city] as was left unoccupied by his mansion." After the emperor's death, Martial (who had been in Rome when it was being built) complained that a single house stood in the whole city. The strongly disapproving Elder Piny (who was also there) asserted explicitly, not once but twice, that the Golden House surrounded Rome. Why stop there? In Nero's own day the anonymous lampoon mentioned earlier continued: "Rome is becoming a house: migrate to Veii, Romans, / unless that house takes over Veii as well."[82] The spell of the Golden House seems to invite hyperbole. Did it really take over the whole city, occupy most of it, surround it? For that matter, did the *immensa domus* of Vedius Pollio, "the work of a city," really cover an area larger than many small towns, as Ovid maintained? Was Herodian strictly accurate in claiming that the later palace of the Severi was larger than a whole city?[83]

Modern scholars have been entranced by the supposed vastness of the fabulous Golden House. Elements of its predecessor, the Domus Transitoria, have long been identified in a marvelously elegant fountain-court on the Palatine, the so-called Bagni di Livia, certainly Neronian in date and covered over by the later Domus Flavia of the Flavian emperors; that is, it lay to the east of the House of Augustus. And since the splendid Domus Tiberiana was revealed in the 1980s to be in essence a Neronian palace, it too has been claimed as part of the Golden House—indeed it has been grandly described as the Palatine nucleus of the Domus Aurea complex, a *domus-villa* balancing the celebrated *villa-domus* nucleus on the Oppian[84]. That is, the Golden House took over the Palatine.

---

[81]   Tacitus 15. 39: *Eo in tempore Nero Antii agens non ante urbem regressus est quam domui eius, qua Palatium et Maecenatis hortos continuaverat, ignis propinquaret.*

[82]   Tacitus 43.1; Martial *Spect.* 2. 4; Pliny 33. 54, 36. III; Suetonius 39. 2.

[83]   Ovid *Fasti* 6. 639–642; Herodian 4.1.2.

[84]   For the Bagni di Livia, in fact a nymphaeum, on the Palatine: *LTUR* II (1995), 199–202, *s.v. Domus Transitoria* (M. de Vos). (In fact, all but seven lines of this article are devoted to the nymphaeum.) Domus Tiberiana: Carandini, A., "Il giardino Romano nell'età tardo repubblicana e Guilio-Claudia," in Morganti, G., ed., *Gli Orti Farnesiani sul Palatino* (Rome, 1990), 14–15. Carandini's formulation of domus-villa and villa-domus (that is, I presume, structures that combine elements of townhouse and country villa, with one or the other predominating), for which there is no ancient evidence, has been taken over by others: Krause, C., "Wo residierten die Flavier? Überlegungen zur flavischen Bautätigkeit auf dem Palatin," in F. E. Koenig and S. Rebertz, eds., *Arculiana, receuil d'hommages offerts à Hans Bögli* (Avenches, 1995), 459–468, at 462–463, cf. *LTUR* II (1995), 189–197, *s.v. Domus Tiberiana* (C. Krause). On other structures attributed to the Domus Aurea, see Royo, M., *Domus imperatoriae. Topographie, formation et imaginaire des palais imipriaux (IIe siècle av. J.-C.-Ier siècle ap. J.-C.* (Rome, 1999), 311, and *LTUR* II (1995), 49, *s.v. Domus Aurea* (A. Cassatella). *LTUR*, the standard repertory of Roman topography, unfortunately includes an entry entitled *Domus Aurea: Complesso del Palatino: LTUR* II (1995), 63–64 (A. Cassatella).

At the other extreme, it has been suggested that the Golden House engulfed the Gardens of Maecenas on the Esquiline, to the east[85]. It also included, so we have been told, a large tract on the Esquiline to the north and east of the Oppian ruins, to take in the cisterns of the Baths of Trajan at Sette Sale; it included the huge Temple of the Divine Claudius and a large expanse to the south of it on the Caelian Hill; the Servian Wall must have functioned as a boundary[86]. Unfortunately, there is no evidence for any of this.

The underlying scholarly assumption has been that *any* Neronian remains on or even near the Palatine, the Esquiline or in the valley in between, must be part of the Golden House. As it happens, some of the remains confidently assigned to it have turned out not to be Neronian at all: the edifice beneath the Temple of Venus and Rome is now known to antedate Nero, while the cisterns of Trajan's Baths are now known to be Trajanic[87]. But what of the rich Neronian remains on the Palatine Hill? It is universally assumed by modern scholarship that the Golden House included the imperial residences on the Palatine. Yet there is no support at all for this assumption in the ancient sources, and good reason to doubt it.

By combining Suetonius' account with Martial's poem and with the archaeological evidence (some unearthed very recently), we can be sure that the grounds of the Golden House included the following: a huge vestibule intended for the Colossus on the Velia, its platform closely corresponding to the surviving platform of the Hadrianic Temple of Venus and Rome; a large, rectangular lake, surrounded by elaborate terraces and colonnades, in the floor of the valley of the later Colosseum; a grand nymphaeum, that is, a huge, spectacular, artificially "natural" fountain on the northeast slope of the Caelian Hill; the mansion sprawled along the Oppian; and an indeterminate open area dotted (apparently) with other, smaller buildings such as a Temple of Fortune, not to mention the "cities" and rustic scenes described by Suetonius. That is,

---

[85]   La Rocca, E., "Il lusso come espressione di potere," in M. Cima and E. La Rocca, *Le tranquille dimore degli dei. La residenza imperiale degli horti Lamiani* (Venice, 1986), 3–35, at 32.

[86]   Van Essen, C. C., "La topographie de la Domus Aurea Neronis," *Mededelingen der Koninklijke Nederlandse Akademie van Wetenschappen, Afd. Letterkunde,* n.s. 17, 12 (Amsterdam, 1954), 371–398. Van Essen's deeply flawed study has been tremendously influential. His sketch plan of the Golden House is commonly reproduced, as in Ward-Perkins 1981, 60. Compare the elaborate map in *LTUR* II (1995), 397.
Warden, P. G., "The Domus Aurea Reconsidered," *JSAH* 40 (1981): 271–278 sensibly reduced the area by half, from about 200 to about 100 acres, confining "The Golden House" to the slopes, not the summits, of the hills. Although nobody has paid this view much attention, it has the great advantage of making the area covered by the Oppian house and its grounds much more "transitional," not including but in a sense joining the hills (see below). It is still too large.
W. V. Harris, reviewing *LTUR* II, in *JRA* 10 (1997): 383–388, writes at 385: "I suspect that we may be in danger of exaggerating the amount of land which this admittedly huge complex occupied."

[87]   House under Venus and Rome (e.g., MacDonald, W. L., *The Architecture of the Roman Empire, I: An Introductory Study* (rev. ed., New Haven, 1982), 21–35): *LTUR* II (1993), s.v. *Domus Domitiana*, 92 (E. Papi). Cisterns of the Baths of Trajan: de Fine Licht, K., *Untersuchungen an den Trajansthermen zu Rom 2, Sette Sale* (*Analecta Romana Instituti Danici*, Suppl. 19, Rome, 1990), 27. (Traces of remains beneath the cisterns are too scanty to attribute to the Golden House: ibid., 96–98.) As it also happens, Martial seems to indicate that the portico of the Temple of the Divine Claudius on the Caelian was the boundary of the Golden House—*Claudia diffusas ubi porticus explicit umbras, / ultima pars aulae deficientis erat* (*De Spectaculis* 2. 9–10)—and Nero, who tore down the temple under construction (Vespasian completed the building), covered the hillside with a nymphaeum meant to be viewed from the house itself on the other side of the valley (Colini, A. M., *Storia e topografia del Celio nell'Antichità* (*Atti della Pontificia Accademia Romana d'Archeologia*, ser. 3, *Memorie*, vol. VII, Rome, 1944), 154–156). Despite Van Essen and *LTUR* I (1993), 277–278, s.v. *Claudius, Divus, Templum* (C. Buzzetti), I can see no reason for assigning the area of the temple to the Golden House.

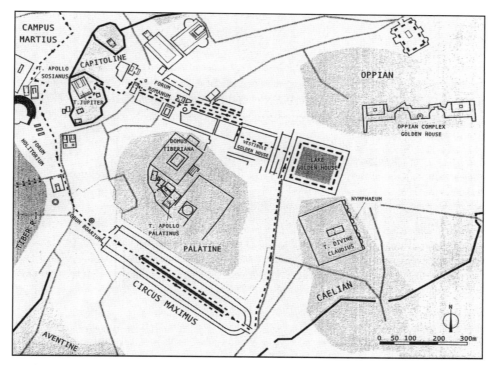

Nero's Rome: Golden House and Triumphal Route. The route of a Roman triumph is shown with dotted lines and arrows.

what our sources describe is the entrance on the Velia, the mansion on the Oppian, and the open country below it. Both Suetonius and Tacitus speak clearly of only *one* house; indeed Suetonius describes just one house, one estate, however extravagant, however surrounded with open spaces, buildings, lakes, porticoes, and so forth. Of complexes of adjacent palaces such as existed on the Palatine, some of them new, some of them reconstructed under Nero, they say nothing. Neronian though such buildings undoubtedly were, there is no hint that Nero or anyone else thought of any palace on the Palatine as being part of the Golden House.

Moreover, as we have seen, Suetonius says, literally, that "he made a house from the Palatine all the way to (*usque ad*) the Esquiline," while Tacitus speaks of "the house by which he had joined (*continuaverat*) the Palatine and the Gardens of Maecenas [on the Esquiline]." Suetonius also clearly conceives of one house that was built, burned, and rebuilt: *domum ... primo transitoriam, mox incendio absumptam restitutamque auream nominavit*. The Domus Transitoria (Nero's own name for it) is eclipsed by its golden namesake. What precisely did Nero mean by the bland "*transitoria*"? It should signify something that connects, a passageway between places. Can we then think of structures *on* the Palatine and the Esquiline hills as "transitional," *transitoria*, when those hills were just what was being connected? The name surely implies rather that the Golden House lay *between* the hills.

A precise analogy in the topography of Rome bears this out: the Forum of Nerva, which was widely known in Late Antiquity as the Forum Transitorium[88]. This narrow, elongated forum was essentially a magnificent passageway between the Subura district and the Forum Romanum, begun by Domitian and dedicated by Nerva. But if we applied to it the same criteria that

---

[88]   Forum Transitorium: see *LTUR* II (1993), *s.v. Forum Nervae*, 307–311 (H. Bauer and C. Morselli), for the references. Note that Aurelius Victor also calls it (at 12. 2) "Forum Pervium," the Forum of Passage, or Thoroughfare.

have been applied to Nero's mansion, it would not just transitorily "lie between," "offer a passageway," "connect," it would also overrun and absorb all that it touched—the Forum of Augustus, the Forum of Julius Caesar, the Temple of Peace, the Forum Romanum, the Subura itself—which is absurd. By this analogy, the Domus Transitoria and consequently the Domus Aurea, must *not* have included the Palatine, or the Esquiline, or any building on them: it lay *between* them; it connected them; it was a passageway between two areas. What Nero meant by this transition remains to be seen.

Behind modern inflation of its size there lies a fundamental assumption about the Golden House, that Nero wished to be private. Here the question of boundaries is central: wherever they may have lain, what *were* the boundaries? How was the Golden House defined? If there were walls over open spaces or gates blocking off streets, no sign of them survives, and this lack of clear boundaries (other than such obvious constructions as the vestibule or the nymphaeum) has allowed free rein to scholarly imagination. Roads, some of them important, certainly crossed the area. Did praetorian guards bar the way, forcing traffic to circumnavigate what was by any measurement a huge swath of downtown Rome? Were the citizens of Rome not to visit the Temple of Fortune, originally constructed under the kings and now reconstructed by Nero on the grounds of his house? The only scholar who has considered the matter of access seriously is Miriam Griffin, in her biography of Nero. She observed that the standard discussions of these matters fifty years ago "worked on two premises: that Nero would follow the terrain as much as possible, and that he would want to be isolated." Both assumptions, she pointed out, are incorrect, disregarding Nero's notorious fondness for rearranging nature on a large scale, and assuming contrary to the evidence that Nero wished for privacy. Griffin's discussions and her conclusion, that "nothing suggests that Nero meant to shut himself up in the Domus Aurea," have been largely ignored by subsequent scholarship on the Golden House[89]. Yet the conclusion is surely correct—that a man who "was carried away," in the words of Suetonius, "by a craze for popularity," and whose popularity did not wane after the fire, would do nothing to exclude his people.

IN 64, just a few months before the Great Fire, Nero offered the most elaborate portrayal yet of himself as the friend of the people, staging through Tigellinus one of his great popular parties that pointedly recalled the aristocratic pleasures of maritime Baiae. It was then too that he offered the novel conceit that all Rome was his house and its citizens were his family. Again, how does the Golden House fit in?

When Nero came to the throne there were two large, permanent, artificial bodies of water in Rome, the Stagnum Agrippae in the Campus Martius and the Naumachia Augusti across the Tiber. Both were fed by aqueducts, both were surrounded by parks, around both Nero erected pavilions, and the area of the Lake of Agrippa (at least) he stocked with exotic birds and animals. Both were

---

[89]   See Griffin, M. T., *Nero: The End of a Dynasty* (London, 1984), 138–141, discussing Van Essen 1954: an excellent summary of the problem, acknowledging discussion with N. Purcell. Largely ignored: but cf. now Darwall-Smith, R. H., *Emperors and Architecture: A Study of Flavian Rome* (Brussels, 1996), 37–38, who correctly concludes that the picture of the Golden House as Nero's private retreat is overdrawn, noting that it stood on arterial roads and contained public shrines, that the Macellum was too close to ensure privacy, and that Nero enjoyed giving large public banquets for which the House was a suitable setting: "Nero might see himself building a house where all the people of Rome could enjoy themselves with him." Similarly but independently: Champlin, E., "God and Man in the Golden House", in M. Cima and E. La Rocca, eds., *Horti Romani* (*BCAR Supplemento* 6, Rome, 1998), 333–344 (from a conference held in 1995). Craze for popularity: Suetonius 53.

the scenes of elaborate nautical banquets and boating parties, reminiscent of Baiae. In 64 the emperor moved to add a third large, permanent, artificial body of water to the city, one surrounded by parkland, animals, and pavilions: the Stagnum Neronis, Nero's Lake, at the heart of the Golden House.

Two observations about the Stagnum Neronis link it and the Golden House to the Campus Martius. The first concerns its relationship with the later Baths of Titus (dedicated by that emperor in 80), which lay immediately to the west of the villa on the Oppian and which are the only other public buildings in Rome to share its precise east-west axis. Filippo Coarelli has suggested that they were originally conceived as the baths of the Golden House. As Inge Nielsen expressed the matter, this would solve two problems. First, it would explain why there is otherwise no trace of baths serving the huge Neronian complex on the Oppian: that is, the Baths of Titus, or their forerunner, were planned as the baths of the Golden House. And second, it would also explain why the Baths of Titus lacked the usual amenities of gardens, pool, porticoes: that is, the lake and gardens of the Golden House provided them. Thus the baths and the house complex would fit together very nicely[90]. If this were true—and it is, admittedly, purely speculative—the Domus Aurea baths would then have been intended as a strong and conscious echo of the very recent bath complex in the Campus Martius, erected by Nero himself. Certainly the Baths of Titus strikingly imitated on a smaller scale the new and innovative Baths of Nero in the Campus, with their great square palaestra; and where the Baths of Nero were integrated with the other facilities around the adjacent Lake of Agrippa in the Campus Martius, the Baths of Titus were or would be connected by a splendid staircase with the Lake of Nero in the Domus Aurea complex[91].

There is more to be said about the Lake, as we have learned something astonishing about it in the last decade. Excavations at the Meta Sudans, the fountain later erected at the western end of the valley of the Colosseum, have revealed that the Stagnum Neronis, far from being an irregularly shaped rustic pond, surrounded by vegetation (as it has been universally conceived), was in fact a huge rectangle, bordered by elaborate porticoed colonnades: that is, it looked very much like the Stagnum Agrippae[92]. In short, the Domus Aurea offered another version of, a pendant to, a central complex of the Campus Martius. On this view, part of the Golden House was a clear image of one of the most public areas of Rome, an area where Nero meant to introduce the maritime pleasures of Baiae to the people of Rome.

Looking down on this rectangle of water fringed by colonnades was the great façade of the mansion on the Oppian, which has been defined as a porticus villa. The complex, as has often been observed, in many ways recalls the Campanian *villae maritimae*, those seaside villas familiar both from wall paintings and from archaeology, with their terraces, gardens, long cool porticoes, and (above all) grand panoramic views of the sea. Let us go further: the Domus Aurea *was* a

---

[90]   See Nielsen, I., *Thermae et Balnea: The Architectual and Cultural History of Roman Public Baths* (Aarhus, 1990), 45–47, with bibliography; cf. briefly F. Coarelli, *Roma*, new edition (Bari, 1995), 211. Not mentioned in *LTUR* V (1999), 66–67, *s.v. Thermae Titi/Titianae* (G. Caruso).

[91]   Baths of Nero in the Campus Martius: Ghini, G., "Terme Neroniano-Alessandrine", in *Roma. Archeologia nel centro* (Rome, 1985), 395–399; Ghini, G., "Le terme Alessandrine nel Campo Marzio," *Monumenti Antichi* ser. Misc. 3 4 (1988): 121–177; cf. *LTUR* V (1999), 60–62, *s.v. Thermae Neronianae/Alexandrinae* (G. Ghini).

[92]   See Panella, C., "La valle del Colosseo nell'Antichità," *Boll.Arch* 1–2 (1990): 34–88, 67–68, and especially her splendid book, Panella, C. ed., *Meta Sudans*, I *Un area sacra in Palatio e la valle del Colosso prima e dopo Nerone* (Rome, 1996), 180–188; cf. *LTUR* II (1995), 51–55, *s.v. Domus Aurea: Area dello Stagnum* (C. Panella).

Campanian seaside villa[93]. Like its counterpart in the Campus Martius, it was intended to recall the pleasures of Baiae in the heart of Rome. Is there any reason to think that it too did not welcome the people of Rome to forget their cares as their city rose from the ashes?

THE STANDARD charge against Nero, formulated during his lifetime and later echoed by Pliny and Martial, was that his house was taking over the city. Accordingly, the Flavians dismantled or built over the components of the Golden House and ostentatiously dedicated them to new public use: the Baths of Titus, the Temple of the Divine Claudius, the paintings removed to the Temple of Peace—and above all the Colosseum, a monument to military virtue at the heart of Nero's pleasure palace[94]. But here a basic principle must be stressed: criticisms of Nero are very often direct distortions of his own words and deeds. The idea of the city as house *originated* with Nero, not with his critics, who turned a popular act into one of tyranny. Yes, he treated the whole city as his house, as we know; yes, he even sought to make the city into his house: but his intention thereby was not to *ex*clude the people, as his critics claimed. It was to *in*clude them. The *princeps* and the *populus Romanus* were *necessitudines*: sharing the delights of Baiae, they would share the Campus Martius *and* the Domus Aurea.

How then do we define the Domus Aurea? In the last few years, the historical evolution of the *horti Romani* has been charted in a variety of modes—political, social, architectural, religious, philosophical, theatrical—and Nero surely understood them at least as well as we do. *Horti* have been defined as a singular unit, an urban villa with a park. They were luxurious, inner suburban dwellings of the Roman aristocracy which imitated in several respects the palace complexes of Hellenistic kings. One of the great markers separating *horti* from *domus*, or great townhouses, was the line between private and public, and the deepest luxury of the *horti* was their sense of privacy and space virtually within the city. Nero, with his Domus Transitoria, connecting the imperial *domus* on the Palatine with the great *horti* on the Esquiline, meant to cross that boundary between public and private and create something new: it was to be, as it were, a fusion of *domus* and *horti*. It must be emphasized: here alone, not everywhere. Public business would still be transacted in the *aulae*, the halls of the real *domus* on the Palatine. True privacy—or at least urban privacy—would still be found in the *horti* of Maecenas or Lamia or Servilius.

The Golden House should be conceived as something new, physically separate from the structures, public or private, which crowned the Palatine, the Caelian, and the Esquiline hills. In essence it was a bowl formed by the valley and the hillsides, and it seems designed for visual effect, calculating what a viewer would observe when looking around from the vestibule on the Velia, or up from the lake to the façade of the palace on the Oppian, or down from the palace to the lake: it is, in short, a theater, or rather an amphitheater. People were meant to look. Privacy was not an issue.

At least two spectacles were being presented simultaneously—the House of the Sun-God, and the Villa of the People—and actor/spectators were essential. Nero's association with Sol/Helios in the Domus Aurea is so much a part of his public solar ideology, and the visual effects of the exteriors (at least) of the

---

[93]   Thus portrayed, independently, by Zevi, F., "Nerone, Baiae e la Domus Aurea", in B. Andreae and C. Precisse, *Ulisse. Il mito e la memoria* (Rome, 1996), 320–331; Champlin 1998.

[94]   In fact, much of Nero's construction after 64 did not tamper with private property, and if Vespasian returned one square foot to any previous owner we do not hear of it: see the excellent paper by Morford, M. P. O., "The Distortion of the Domus Aurea Tradition," *Eranos* 66 (1968): 158–179.

Golden House are so calculated to impress spectators, and there are simply so many rooms in it, that it is hard to imagine the Palace of the Sun-God *not* being a place open to the public. <u>At the same time, the Golden House conforms to Nero's fondness for consciously upsetting the hierarchies of Roman society, sharing pleasure with his people, staging at Rome riotous scenes of public license on sets reminiscent of a Campanian resort that was, until then, the playground of the rich.</u> The godlike *princeps* is, after all, just a human being like the rest of us, and he invites us to share his house. It was indeed a private house, but it was the house of the whole Roman people as well.

Next to the glamorous Domus Aurea, its original name, the bland Domus Transitoria, the Connecting House, never draws a second glance. Yet it too was to be taken both literally and metaphorically. The adjective *transitorius* is extremely rare in Latin, and this is its earliest attestation[95]. It may be that Nero, ever creative, invented the word.

Secondary Source 2.3   Miriam T. Griffin, 'The tyranny of art'

(Source: Griffin, M.T. (1984) *Nero: The End of a Dynasty*, New Haven and London, Yale University Press, pp. 133–42)

Of the area that we know to have been occupied by the Domus Aurea much was already in imperial hands, such as the parts of the Palatine and Esquiline Hills already used for the Domus Transitoria. Nero may have occupied the sites of some of the grand houses on the Palatine that had been damaged by the Fire, though some were still in private possession later on[1]. In the valley of the Colosseum, where he had his famous lake, there might previously have been shops of the kind the Fire destroyed when it started in the adjoining area to the south. The likelihood that this was, at least partially, a commercial area is increased by a plausible identification of the *horrea* or warehouses whose destruction Suetonius dramatises as a work of organised demolition: they could be those found under the nave of the Church of S. Clemente not far to the east of the Colosseum[2]. To the north, the Flavian poet Martial indicates that houses of the poor were sacrificed to Nero's park in the area, covered in his day by Titus' Baths. And here, on the Oppian Hill, next to the extant portions of the palace, have been found the remains of private houses of Republican date with various kinds of mosaic flooring indicating that some of them were quite modest dwellings[3]. To the south, Nero used the site of the temple of Divus Claudius, which he had authorised while his mother was alive, and on which much work had already been done[4].

---

[95]   Other than the Domus Transitoria, the word seems in literature to be applied only to the Forum Transitorium: see references in *LTUR* II (1995), 308, *s.v.* Forum Nervae (H. Bauer and C. Morselli). Later epigraphy produces an otherwise unknown public location at Puteoli (*ILS* 5919, where the editor, H. Dessau, cites *Dig*. 43. 8. 2. 17: a small forum?), and a late fourth century Forum Transitorium at Lambaesis in Numidia (*CIL* VIII. 2722).

[1]   Pliny *NH* 17. 5 notes that trees belonging to the house of Caecina Largus (*cos. ord.* 42) were destroyed in the Fire of 64 and speaks of the house as no longer in existence. For a house in the Palatine later: *Ann*. 15. 69 (Vestinus Atticus); perhaps also the house of Salvidienus Orfitus (Suet. *Nero* 37. 1; Dio 62. 27, 1).

[2]   Suet. *Nero* 38. 1. These particular buildings, however, do not seem to have been taken over by Nero, but reconstructed at an undetermined date: Blake, *Roman Construction*, 28–9; Rickman, *Roman Granaries and Stone Buildings* (1971), 107.

[3]   Martial *Spec*. 2 (cited p.138). Sanguinetti, *Bollettino del centro di studi per la storia dell'architettura* 12 (1958), 45.

[4]   Suet. *Vesp*. 9. 1.

It is clear then that some private owners, rich and poor, saw the great palace and its parks laid out over the places in which they had lived and worked. It was traditional to approve of utilitarian building, but even public buildings whose purposes were not clearly for the public good could be criticised. All the more vulnerable then was Nero's Golden House. It could still be adduced half a century later in distant Bithynia as an example of selfish building to which citizens might reasonably object, in contrast with 'lofty edifices worthy of a great city'[5]. By that time successive Emperors had covered the major areas of the palace with public buildings of undoubted utility: the temple of Divus Claudius rebuilt by Vespasian, his great amphitheatre The Colosseum and perhaps a temple of the Sun for the redesigned Colossus[6]; then came the Baths of Titus, the gladiatorial school (the Ludus Magnus) of Domitian, his imperial residence of the Palatine, and finally Trajan's Baths. Except for Domitian's palace, all of these were meant to advertise the genuine public spirit of these Emperors, in contrast with Nero's selfishness. Vespasian had also made a point of moving the art treasures that had adorned Nero's palace into the temple of Peace.

Nero's selfishness as it damaged the interests of the public at large was the theme particularly developed by the Flavians, who did not wish to restore so much imperial property to its original owners. But selfishness was not all that worried Nero's contemporaries: at least among the upper orders there was a feeling that the Domus Aurea rendered visible a more monarchical conception of the Principate[7]. No one who saw the entrance of the palace could have doubted that self-glorification played a part in its conception. On the summit of the Velia, the hill that rose to the north of the Palatine and west of Nero's lake rose 'the hated entrance hall of the cruel king', in Martial's words. It was decorated with gold and precious stones, and surrounded by a triple colonnade. In front, just north of the later arch of Titus, where the path to the Palatine turns off at right angles from the Sacra Via (the main avenue of the forum), stood the bronze Colossus, facing the forum and no doubt visible from many parts of the city. The Sacra Via was widened and straightened and given a steeper gradient as it rose towards the entrance to the palace. All along it were arcades and, behind them, great pillared halls 'giving the imperial palace what it had never had before, and was never to have again, a worthy entrance from the forum Romanum', as one archaeologist has put it[8]. And when one looked across Nero's lake one saw the monument to his deified predecessor converted into an ornamental nymphaeum – Nero's glory was not to be shared!

What was Nero's Golden House intended to be, and what place was it intended to have in Nero's reconstructed Rome? Suetonius concentrates on its luxury, emphasising the gold and jewels that adorned it, and the devices for showering flowers and perfumes from the walls of the dining rooms. Indeed, the luxurious taste of the time was in evidence in the name of the palace, derived from the generous use of gilt inside, and probably on the façade too. But Tacitus says explicitly that the wonders of the palace were not so much its jewels and gold, which were by then commonplaces of luxury, as its fields and lakes, and the

[5]   Cicero *Off.* 2. 60; Dio Chrys. 47. 15 addressing the citizens of Prusa in Bithynia.

[6]   See n51. It is not known what preceded Hadrian's temple of Venus and Rome on the site of the *vestibulum*. A Boethius, *The Golden House of Nero* (1960), 127 suggested the construction of a temple of the Sun.

[7]   This is the argument of M.P.O. Morford, *Eranos* 66 (1968), 158f.

[8]   B. Tamm, *Auditorium and Palatium* (1963), 101–6; van Deman, *MAAR* 3 (1925), 115f. The remark is by J. Ward Perkins, *Antiquity* (1956), 214.

impression of unspoiled nature created by its woods, open spaces and long vistas[9]. Suetonius elaborates on this aspect as well, noting the different kinds of animals and specifying that there were tilled fields, vineyards and meadows. Both authors remark too on the display of technical ingenuity. Suetonius speaks of the fountains and pools, and of the moving panels and spraying pipes of the dining rooms, adding that the most impressive of these rooms was round and rotated constantly like the world. The material remains support the Tacitean emphasis on layout, structural innovation and elegance, even delicacy of taste, as against sheer opulence.

Finally, both Suetonius and Tacitus lay particular stress on the size of the Domus Aurea, which is also the point of the contemporary epigram about moving to Veii, and of Martial's line 'one house took up the whole of Rome'. The current modern interpretation of the Domus Aurea as a rural villa in the centre of Rome accords with this dominant strain in the ancient criticism. It is a conception sufficiently grandiose and perverse in itself to explain the hostility engendered by Nero's building operations[10]. We do not need to follow scholarly flights of fancy and see, in the eventual design of the Colossus as the Sun and the rotating dining room that could have represented the heavens, hints that the Domus Aurea was planned to symbolise the rule of Nero the new Sun-god, making visible his association with Apollo and the Golden Age that had been celebrated at his accession[11].

It has been pointed out that the standard attacks on luxury that resounded through the Roman schools of declamation and filled the pages of Roman poets and philosophers had long included criticism of spacious country villas, of town houses that took up too much city land, and of technical ingenuity that subjected nature to luxury. Neronian literature itself abounds in such diatribes: in Lucan, in Petronius and particularly in Seneca. It may have been the building of the Domus Aurea itself which was the occasion for some of these generalisations, but they are so conventional that we should hesitate to infer from them that the palace was really excessive in opulence or colossal in size[12].

The starting point in estimating the extent of the buildings and park of the Domus Aurea is Martial's poem, written in the reign of Titus:

> Here where the heavenly colossus has a close view of the stars
> And high structures rise on the lofty road,
> There once shone the hated hall of the cruel king
> And one house took up the whole of Rome.

[9]   Suet. *Nero* 31; *Ann* 15. 42.

[10]   Nepos says of Atticus' house in the city that its charm lay in its park rather than its building (*Atticus* 13), but Atticus aimed, he says, to be 'elegans non magnificus' whereas Nero aspired to be both, the magnificence showing partly in the size of his palace and grounds.

[11]   The rural villa view is that of Boethius, *Golden House* and Ward Perkins *Antiquity* (1956), 209f who agree with Toynbee, *JRS* 38 (1958), 160–1 and Charlesworth, *JRS* 40 (1950), 71–2 in dismissing the ideas of H.P. L'Orange, *Symbolae Osloenses* (1942), 68f. See p.216.

[12]   The point is made forcibly by Morford in *Eranos* 66 (1968), 138f citing Elder Seneca *Controversiae* 2. 1 and 5. 5, 1–2 in particular. For Neronian authors: Lucan 10. 110–121; Petronius 120. 87–9: Seneca *Epp.* 88. 6–7; 88. 22; 90. 7; 90. 9; 90. 15; 90. 43; 115. 8–9 (size is stressed at 90. 43 and 115.8). Letter 90 is the one in which covert allusions to the Golden House are most commonly discerned, but in fact the parallels are not close enough: at 7, high buildings are the target (not a feature of the palace); at 9, panels heavy with gold are noted which may have been a feature of the palace though the main dining room had ivory panels, while 15, which is taken to refer to that room, has moving panels but they are not said to be of ivory and they display different scenes rather than sprinkle flowers (cf. Suet. *Nero* 31. 2). The pipes sprinkling saffron to great heights in section 15 do not suit what Suetonius says of pipes sprinkling unguents *desuper*. Cf. Plut. *Galba* 19.3 for such pipes elsewhere.

Here where rises the huge mass of the awesome amphitheatre
In sight of all was Nero's pool.
Here where we admire the baths built so quickly for our benefit
A proud park deprived the poor of their houses.
Where the Claudian temple spreads its wide shade
Stood the last part of the palace.
Rome is returned to herself and under your rule, Caesar,
The delights of their master have become those of the people.

(*Liber de spectaculis* 2)

We learn from this that the Domus Aurea extended from the summit of the Velian Hill (part of which was destroyed around 1930), across the area of the Colosseum, taking in the northern slope of the Caelian Hill and the slope of the Oppian. Evidence is also provided by the remains on the Oppian Hill west of the Sette Sale where the two large wings under Trajan's Baths have recently been more thoroughly excavated; those on the south-east of the Palatine under Domitian's palace where walls of the second Neronian palace cut into the remains of the Domus Transitoria; those just east of the Colosseum, in the valley between the Caelian and the Esquiline, where some rooms have been discovered[13].

The estimates of the extent vary considerably, but all agree that it covered a larger area than the Vatican city, which embraces about 110 acres. A conservative estimate is 125 acres; the one most widely accepted now gives the extent as 200 acres, about the same as that of Hadrian's villa at Tivoli[14]. Yet the important question is the nature of this imperial property: a private residential estate in the heart of the city, however large an extension Nero planned for Rome, would have still created problems for the movement of traffic. In making his calculations for the larger estimate given above, van Essen worked on two premisses: that Nero would follow the terrain as much as possible, and that he would want to be isolated. This led him to suggest that the Domus Aurea was a natural basin, with the lake at its centre and the summits of the surrounding hills for its limits, except on the east and south-east where it went up to the surviving section of the old Servian Wall of Rome.

The first premiss overlooks Nero's willingness to rearrange nature, as demonstrated at Subiaco and in the remains of the palace itself, which show that the Oppian Hill was trimmed to receive the northern and western rooms at least, while the Velia was cut and buttressed to accommodate the entrance hall. As to the second premiss, van Essen was prepared to use it, against the evidence of Martial, to extend the estate beyond the temple of Divus Claudius up to the summit of the Caelian Hill: Nero would not be overlooked from higher ground. But, even in its own terms, the argument is faulty, as the high podium of the temple seems designed to neutralise the slope of the hill. The question of being overlooked would not arise when Nero's nymphaeum was placed there: indeed it has been suggested that on the south side, facing the Colosseum, cascades

[13]   The remains are carefully catalogued by C. C. van Essen, 'La Topographie de la Domus Aurea Neronis', *Medelingen der Koninklijke Nederlandse Akademic van Wetenschappen*, Afd. Letterkunde 17. 12 (1954), 371f. Of the remains he attributed to Nero, the great cistern called the Sette Salle, east of the major remains on the Oppian Hill, is now thought to be wholly Trajanic, despite the fact that its orientation fits the Domus Aurea (L. Cozza, *Atti d. Pontif. Acad. di Archeologia*, ser. iii *Rendiconti* 47 (1974–5), 79). New excavations now show that the Oppian complex included an upper storey and extended further to the east (see p.141).

[14]   Van Essen (see note above), 4–13.

were arranged so that the maximum effect was derived from the elevation and the draining of the new branch of the Claudian aqueduct into Nero's lake[15].

It is time, however, to consider the theory of privacy. We have already remarked that, in accordance with Roman tradition, the Emperors conducted business in their own houses and villas. Now certain features of Nero's plans suggest that the Domus Aurea was not intended to be a private precinct. The Elder Pliny says that Nero rebuilt the temple of Fortune, originally consecrated by Servius Tullius, in a newly-discovered type of translucent marble and 'included it in the Golden House'. It must have been one of the buildings in the park, and, as a temple, it can hardly have been without public access[16]. When Gaius, as is alleged, took over the temple of Castor and Pollux in the forum as the entrance to his palace, his intention was that people would come there and worship him. And when Augustus bought up houses on the Palatine to enlarge his own, he promised to turn the property to public use, and built there the temple of Apollo[17]. Moreover, Nero is thought to have rebuilt the temple of Jupiter Stator which stood just south of his entrance hall and had been destroyed in the Fire of 64. What privacy would he have had with people attending the temple next door? And what of his expanded Sacra Via, which finished at his front door? One can hardly assume that the forum was to remain out of use, nor is it unlikely that the arcades and halls were to be used for commercial purposes, as had long been the case along the avenue. Then, on the east, we have already noted that the Domus Aurea may have been next to a rebuilt warehouse [...] – at least the land was not confiscated for another use – and beyond that, in the Piazza S. Clemente, a new building for the official mint may have been built in Nero's time. Not far away to the south stood Nero's grandiose market on the Caelian.

As part of his general reconstruction of Rome Nero could have had the idea of embellishing the central area with parks, groves and fountains. Here in his complex of imperial buildings he could hear audiences and do business, while his people would have access to him and to some of the buildings and grounds. Nero's *comitas* and *popularitas* must be remembered: he was not a man to deprive his public. Shortly before the Fire he held a public banquet in which he extended to the people pleasures normally confined to the few. Tacitus' sneer on this occasion, 'He used the whole city as his house', reminds one of the squib 'Rome will become a house'[18]. Nero may have felt he was opening his house to the citizens, while his critics felt that he was excluding the citizens from their city. After the Fire we find him offering public entertainment in his Vatican circus and adjacent gardens, dressed as a charioteer and mixing with the plebs[19].

When the conspirators of 65 were planning Nero's assassination they considered killing him, according to Tacitus, in the hated palace or in public, or when he was visiting the Campanian villa of Piso, where he frequently went without his guards. Yet Tacitus says that it was because the Emperor did not often leave his house and gardens that the conspirators eventually decided on the circus games, which the Emperor regularly attended, and where he could be easily approached in the holiday atmosphere. Tacitus appears to contradict himself here over the Emperor's general accessibility, but he probably had

---

[15]   A.M. Colini, *Atti d. Pont. Accad. Rom. di Arch.* Ser. III *Memorie* vol vii (1944), 137f.

[16]   Pliny *NH* 36. 162. I owe this reference and many of the ideas here about the purpose of the Domus Aurea to a paper and subsequent discussions with Nicholas Purcell.

[17]   Suet. *Gaius* 22. 1; Vell. Pat. 2. 81. On the public quality of temples see Pliny *Pan.* 47. 4–5.

[18]   Tacitus *Ann.* 15. 37.

[19]   *Ann.* 15. 44. The idea of privacy lies behind the interpretation of Lucillius' epigram on a theft of golden apples from the garden of Zeus as an allusion to some theft from the gardens of the Domus Aurea, but that interpretation is, in any case, implausible (see p.273, n31).

particularly in mind, in the second passage, the fact that Nero no longer attended the Senate regularly, for the Senate house would have been the expected venue for a tyrannicide modelled on the murder of Caesar.
The conspirators may also have considered, as the assassins of Gaius had, that the crowds at the circus made the Emperor's guards less effective than when he was in his palace or in the Senate[20].

In any case, nothing suggests that Nero meant to shut himself up in the Domus Aurea. One of the problems for the Pisonian conspirators may have been that after the Fire, with his palace damaged and under reconstruction, Nero was spending his time in imperial properties that were more private, such as the Servilian Gardens[21].

Thus the Domus Aurea park need not have prevented movement through the centre of the city, though doubtless the routes were changed. Even on the Palatine only a cryptoporticus connected the various imperial buildings: there was no need to weld them all into one enclosed complex, and they may have been intended to remain separate[22].

The Golden House was, nonetheless, an ambitious, probably an over-ambitious, project. Observers would have gained the impression that a vast complex was in hand, because the work did not proceed area by area. Though never finished, a vast number of buildings were started all around the central lake. Nero no doubt spoke with enthusiasm of the technical marvels that were in hand. The unsympathetic may well have reacted as one scholar who wrote, 'The Fire gave a mortally egocentric autocrat the chance to demand a unique monumental expression of what he considered his worth and position to be'[23].

The large remains on the Oppian Hill have by now lost most of their decoration. The grand apartments have been plunged in darkness since the foundations were laid for Trajan's Baths. Even before that, Vitellius and his wife were disappointed by the lack of decoration and the mean equipment of the palace. The Domus Aurea was left unfinished when Nero died, and the alterations made by Otho interfered with the grand architectural conception of its creator[24]. Even so, the construction and design still excite the admiration of architects and engineers by reason of the new exploitation of space and the creation of internal vistas. Two features, in particular, impress by their artistic and architectural originality: the five-sided trapezoidal court in the west wing, which was once matched by a similar one in the east wing, and the domed octagonal room in the centre with its five rooms radiating from it symmetrically. As the new excavations show, the palace originally had two floors, each of which displayed east-west symmetry and was interrupted by the two open trapezoidal courts. The two courts framed the central complex of rooms around the octagon which extended through the upper storey and could probably be viewed from the adjacent upper rooms as well as the lower ones[25].

[20]   *Ann.* 15. 52–3; Josephus *Ant. Jud.* 19. 76.

[21]   Tacitus *Ann.* 15. 55 attests his living in the Servilian Gardens in 65.

[22]   Tamm, *Auditorium and Palatium*, 72–5.

[23]   Suet. *Nero* 41; MacDonald, *Architecture of the Roman Empire*, 31.

[24]   Dio 65. 4; G. Zander, *Bollettino del centro di studi per la storia dell'architettura* 12 (1958), 47f.

[25]   This is the reconstruction of Fabbrini (n34) who notes the possibility that the octagon represented a modification of an earlier conventional plan. Her suggestion that Nero's mac aug dupondii (fig. 28) celebrate the design and mechanical ingenuity (*machina*) of his new palace is not only unlikely but untenable if MacDowall, *Western Coinages*, 59 is right to assign the earliest coins depicting this building to his Issue ii: it predates the Great Fire which stimulated the final redesigning of Nero's palace.

The octagon room thus formed the focus of the whole building. It is usually identified with the main circular dining room described by Suetonius, though there is no agreement on what elements rotated. It is notable, however, that the inside of the dome shows no traces of a decoration, and that the water that ran into the room to the north came in at a steeper gradient than would be necessary for a nymphaeum. Hence the suggestion that some of the water turned a device suspended through the opening in the dome, representing the changes of seasons on the vault. The two grooves on the outer surface of the dome will have served as tracks for the suspended device[26]. Whatever the explanation, the study of the Domus Transitoria and the Domus Aurea shows, to an even greater degree than our examination of the coinage, that Nero was an enthusiast who threw himself into grand projects and put at their service the latest Roman technology and the most advanced artistic ideas.

Secondary Source 2.4   J. Elsner, 'Constructing decadence: the representation of Nero as Imperial Builder'

(Source: Elsner, J. and Masters, J. (eds) (1994) *Reflections of Nero: Culture, History and Representation*, Chapel Hill, NC and London, University of North Carolina Press, pp. 112–27)

> There was nothing, however, in which he was more ruinously prodigal than in building.
>
> Suetonius, *Nero* 31.1[1]

On one thing the historical tradition hostile to Nero is agreed: his profligate excess surpassed even itself in his imperial buildings, and especially in the *Domus Aurea*, the imperial villa Nero built in the centre of Rome.[2] In this chapter, I compare posterity's representation of Nero's building activities with other imperial programmes of construction by other Julio-Claudian emperors. By placing the emperor's buildings within an ancient Roman debate on the nature of the principate, one can see architecture as three-dimensional and visual dynamic of self-presentation, in which rulers used buildings both as a method of self-presentation to the populace and as a means of distinguishing themselves from their imperial predecessors within what had rapidly become a tradition of successive emperors. Yet building was always an ambiguous theme in the invective of Roman moral rhetoric. As Julio-Claudian buildings became increasingly lavish, in the attempt to surpass previous emperors, they became increasingly open to the charge of luxury and decadence. Nero's very need to surpass his ancestors in imperial architecture primed the guns of those historians whose project was to condemn him.

Introduction

The fierce and productive academic debate in recent times on the nature of the Roman principate has tended to obscure the fact that there was an equally fierce – and perhaps still more interesting – debate on this same issue in ancient times.[3] In epic poetry, Lucan's *Bellum Civile* (however one chooses to read it, or chose to do so in the reign of Nero) is on some level an explicitly political riposte to the imperial politics of the *Aeneid*. In history, the works of Tacitus are

---

[26]   H. Storz–S. Prückner, *MDAI (R).*, 81 (1974), 323f.

[1]   An editor (especially) needs editing: I am grateful to Peter Garnsey, Valerie Huet and Jeremy Tanner for their suggestions.

[2]   See e.g. Griffin 1984 ch. 8 'The Tyranny of Art' pp. 119–42.

[3]   On the modern debate see e.g. Price 1980 pp. 28–43; Wallace-Hadrill 1982 pp. 32–48; Millar 1984 pp. 37–58; the essays in Raaflaub and Toher (eds.), 1990.

an extended meditation on the nature of imperial government from the standpoint of a neo-republican imagination. In drama, the *Octavia* – a rare non-Senecan tragedy to have survived from Roman literature – dramatises a debate on the principate between the characters of Nero and Seneca (vv. 440–592). Nero argues that the sword, the destruction of enemies and fear itself are the principal bulwarks of an emperor's power (vv. 443, 457–8); while Seneca argues the case for fostering one's subjects' loyalty and love (vv. 444, 457–8). As with Lucan's indebtedness to Virgil, and Tacitus' opening in the *Annals*, inevitably the debate turns on a comparison of Nero's reign with that of Augustus (vv. 472–532).

However, it turns out that Seneca and Nero subscribe to different versions and views of the Augustan principate. For Seneca,

> the first Augustus, his country's father, gained the stars and is worshipped in temples as a god. (vv. 477–8)

But Nero replies,

> He who earned heaven by piety, the deified Augustus, how many nobles did he put to death, young men and old, scattered throughout the world, when they fled their own homes through fear of death ... all by the proscription lists delivered to grim destruction. (vv. 504–9)

The meaning of the principate in ancient times was ambivalent, contested and open to debate. The existence of this Roman debate – attested as early as the reign of Nero by the *Bellum Civile* and the *Octavia* – is crucial. For it reminds us that we cannot regard imperial activity in isolation. Julio-Claudian emperors acted and were viewed in the knowledge that their office was in the direct line of their descent from Augustus.

In his moral epistle on mercy, addressed to Nero, Seneca explicitly compares the emperor with his predecessors:

> It is a mighty burden that you have taken upon yourself; no one today talks of the deified Augustus or the early years of Tiberius Caesar, or seeks any model he would have you copy but yourself ...
> (*De Clementia* 1.1.6)

Nero is burdened with the heritage of his office (despite, indeed because, 'no one today talks of his ancestors), yet he must act not as them but as himself. Ultimately, an emperor – always merely the next candidate to slot into the line of imperial purple – could not just emulate previous models, but had to create and foster his own image: 'the standard for your principate is the foretaste you have given' (ibid.) Seneca's keen awareness of the imperial problematic of tradition and innovation also motivates the implicit contrast between Claudius and Augustus in his *Apocolocyntosis*. There, writing about Claudius in a satiric vein, Seneca puts his condemnation at the court of heaven into the mouth of Augustus – implying that Claudius failed to live up to the imperial tradition he inherited (*Apocoloc.* 10–11). Just as Julio-Claudian portraits reflected the portraiture of Augustus (whether by imitation or innovation),[4] so their every gesture represented a new act in imperial self-definition, which could be directly compared with what had gone before. The fulfilment of the imperial office was beset by a permanent anxiety of influence.

---

[4]   On Julio-Claudian portraiture, see Ziss 1975 and Jucker 1981 pp. 236–316.

In this chapter, I concentrate on one specific but significant area in the public activity of the emperor – namely, the act of building in Rome. Nero himself was an outstanding builder, praised even by hostile sources such as Tacitus for the excellence of the rebuilding of those parts of Rome damaged by the great fire of AD 64 (*Annals* 15.43). In a remark recorded by a fourth-century historian, Nero

> was so effective for five years, especially in improving the city, that Trajan with justice declared that all other emperors fell far behind Nero's five years.[5]

Since such praise represents a rare match struck in the general darkness of history's subsequent abuse of Nero, his buildings certainly made a deep and at least in some respects positive impression – even on a hostile posterity. Before exploring them, and their textual representations, in more detail, let us briefly glance at the kind of activity which public building had become in the hands of the emperors, and how it was regarded.

Augustus' building programme had transformed the city of Rome.[6] In combination with Agrippa, he had reconstituted the visual environment of the city, not only in its ancient centre but also in the Campus Martius outside the pomerium, the traditional and augurally constituted boundary of Rome. By the time of Hadrian, this remarkable project of imperial construction had come to be a commonplace in descriptions of Augustus' reign. Hence Suetonius' well-known comment (*Aug.* 28):

> Since the city was not adorned as the dignity of the empire demanded ..., he so beautified it that he could justly boast that he had found it built of brick and left it in marble.

Not only did the first princeps build lavishly, but he also ensured that the edifices he constructed would forever be linked with their author's name. Apart from inscriptions on individual monuments, Augustus made his own record of the whole project of his buildings in Rome as chapters 19–21 of the *Res Gestae*, his autobiography. This was inscribed in two bronze columns engraved after his death in front of the mausoleum of the Julio-Claudian emperors, and copies were set up in temples elsewhere in the empire, notably in Asia Minor.[7] This two-fold Augustan programme in the realm of building – the actual construction of large numbers of prestige buildings and the careful public record of whom these buildings were inaugurated by – had a remarkable impact on the definition of

---

[5]   Sextus Aurelius Victor, *Liber de caesaribus* 5.1–2 (cf. also the *Epitome de caesaribus* 5.2–5) with Anderson 1911 pp. 173–8. My apologies for a longish note on the so-called 'quinquennium Neronis', or Nero's period of five (good) years. Following Victor, who is himself purporting to quote Trajan, it has become traditional to assume that Nero had five good years before he went bad, and that these years were associated with his building programme. The only conceivable good years in Nero's reign (according to the Tacitean-Suetonian account) were the early ones, good by comparison with what came later and good because Nero's regents, Burrus and Seneca, were in control. Unfortunately, these were not the years when Nero did much building. Accordingly, the debate has raged – was the quinquennium the first five years of Nero's reign, as argued by Lepper (1957) and Murray (1965), or the last, as argued by Thornton (1973), or indeed the middle ones, as argued by Hind (1971 and 1975)? All such argument assumes that the quinquennium must have existed and that we can believe a couple of fourth-century sources. One wonders. As Griffin points out (1984, p. 84), Nero had to be 'good' first in order to be bad later, and in order that the bad look worse. Here he conforms to the same pattern as Suetonius' Caligula and Domitian (*Gai.* 13–21, *Dom.* 4–10). Might one not suggest, as with so much else in the Neronian phantasmagoria, that the quinquennium Neronis is but another stitch in the tapestry of later myth-historical embroidery?

[6]   Gros 1976; Simon 1986; Zanker 1988; Favro 1992 pp. 61–84.

[7]   On the buildings section of the *Res Gestae*, see Sablayrolles 1981 pp. 59–77 and Elsner forthcoming.

the principate in Rome.[8] Buildings were the most direct, visual and experiential evidence of the emperor's activities. Thereafter no emperor could afford not to emulate the first princeps. The pattern of imperial building became – like that of imperial portraiture – one of emulation, imitation and improvement.

If Augustus' principate created the parameters of public and private activity by which the new role of emperor was to be defined, that of Tiberius established this group of imperial definitions through a basic continuity. The setting up of the *Res Gestae* in Rome, and its inscription in cities like Ancyra, Apollonia and Psidian Antioch in Asia Minor, were acts accomplished in Tiberius' reign. As Tiberian statements, they showed (no less than Tiberius' deification of Augustus)[9] the essential cohesion to be envisaged between the two reigns. As early as AD 30, the Roman officer Velleius Paterculus was concluding his *History of Rome* with a grandiose (if evidentially thin) peroration in the penultimate chapter on Tiberius as imperial builder.

> What public buildings did he construct in his own name or that of his family! With what pious munificence, exceeding human belief, does he now rear the temple to his father! With what a magnificent control of personal feeling did he restore the works of Gnaeus Pompey when destroyed by fire. For a feeling of kinship leads him to protect every famous monument. (II.130.1)

To be seen as a worthy emperor, Tiberius had to be perceived as a worthy builder.[10] Thereafter, in the writings of the Roman empire, it became a cliché of imperial history, biography and panegyric to enumerate at least some of their subjects' buildings. The apogee of this tradition is Procopius' *De aedificiis*, an entire panegyric devoted solely to Justinian's buildings.

A further element in the public dissemination of buildings under the principate was their representation on coins, as well as in inscriptions and literary texts.[11] This practice had begun in the Republic, but became assimilated to imperial propaganda under Augustus. It meant that prestigious edifices in Rome, whether built by the Emperor or not, could be associated with him in the perceptions of a large social stratum in the empire, through being represented on his coinage. By combining images of important buildings with brief texts announcing what they were, and on the coin's obverse, portraits of a particular ruler, such numismatic propaganda went a long way to establishing the image of emperors as builders. Augustus had a number of his most prestigious monuments marked in this way – his triumphal arches,[12] some of his temples,[13] his equestrian statues.[14] Later emperors chose to be represented not only on the obverse of coins with their own buildings (such as Claudius or Nero with their triumphal arches)[15] but also with earlier monuments, especially those set up by Augustus.

[8] cf. Millar 1984 pp. 57–8.

[9] On this see Vell. Pat. II 124.3, 126.1; Suet., *Aug.* 97 and 100.

[10] On the buildings of Tiberius, see Blake 1959 pp. 10–18.

[11] For an account of some aspects of 'the persuasive language of imperial coinage', see Wallace-Hadrill 1986 pp. 66–87.

[12] See Hill 1989 p. 53 (cf. Zanker 1988 pp. 55 and 188).

[13] Hill 1989 p. 27.

[14] ibid. pp. 66–7.

[15] ibid. pp. 50–1, 53–4. See also Kleiner 1985 pp. 99–138.

For instance a copper coin of Nero issued in Lyons, the main mint in the west of the Empire, shows Augustus' *Ara Pacis* on the reverse (see Plate 6).[16] Here not only was an important Augustus monument being associated with Nero, but its particular thematic resonances (to do with peace) were significant.

Yet the incorporation of public and private building into the very definition of the principate was tinged with ambiguity, even paradox. While mighty buildings were the rightful acts of great men, they were also – in Roman moral discourse – a sign of luxury, decadence and vice.[17] The grandeur of an emperor's buildings could signal his greatness, as in Strabo's contemporary account of Augustan Rome (*Geography* 5.3.8), Pliny the Younger's panegyric of Trajan (51–2) or Suetonius' *Life of Augustus* (28–9). But that very grandeur could be a sign of wanton, profligate and outrageous excess. Despite the approving remarks of Trajan and Tacitus on some aspects of Nero's building programme, it would be upon Nero as builder that the full weight of Roman rhetoric's moral censure of extravagant building would descend.[18]

This chapter, then, traces a double theme. On the one hand, I shall explore Nero as builder. That is, the emperor in his necessary (indeed, defining) role as one who initiated new and outstanding buildings in the city of Rome. This was not an easy role, since every move in it, every building, could be matched against the previous history of imperial building, the previous history of imperial self-definition in its most visual form. If an emperor's buildings fell short of the high standards set by his predecessors, then implicitly he was unworthy of his office. If he surpassed them, he risked the accusation of morally reprehensible luxuriousness. On the other hand, I shall examine the *representation* of Nero as builder in the historiographic tradition – that is, Nero's image as builder *after* his fall, when prosperity had already decided that he was wicked. I shall argue that the ambiguity implicit in the theme of building – coupled with Nero's deliberate construction policies – allowed his buildings to be rhetorically exploited against Nero as proof of his monstrosity, once the tradition had decided that his memory was to be damned.

Buildings and the rhetoric of imperial degeneracy

In Suetonius' *Life of Caligula*, the trope of imperial buildings plays an interesting role. Concluding his introductory account of Gaius' early life and reign (1–21), Suetonius lists his public works in Rome (chapter 21) – the temple of Augustus, the theatre of Pompey, the initiation of an aqueduct from Tibur and an amphitheatre. He mentions also Gaius' works at Syracuse (including the repair of the city walls and the temples of the gods), as well as his plans to rebuild the palace of Polycrates at Samos and the temple of Didymaean Apollo at Ephesus. The brief survey of buildings ends with Caligula's aim to construct a city in the Alps and to dig a canal through the Isthmus at Corinth. Essentially these projects fall into the classic categories for imperial building – centred primarily on sacred and secular constructions. The provision of buildings for

---

[16] Mattingly 1923 no. 361, p. 271, pl. 47.2. It seems more natural to assume that this coin, with its inscription ara pacis, should refer to the Augustan altar in Rome (with e.g. Platner and Ashby 1929 p. 31) than to invent an altar of Pax at Lyons solely on the evidence of the coin – as does Mattingly 1923 p. clxxx.

[17] A clutch of texts which denounce luxury through the image of luxurious building: Cato fr. 139 (in *Orationum Reliquiae* ed. M.T. Sblendorio Cugisi, Turin, 1982); Cic., *Pro Sest.* 43.49; Sall., *Cati* 12.3–4, 13.1, 20.11; Vell. Pat. II.33.4; Hor., *Od.* II.15, 18, III.1, 24, *Epist.* I.1.83–7; Petron., *Sat* 120.87–9; Sen., *Epist.* 90.8–10, 122.8. See especially the discussion of Catharine Edwards 1993, ch. 4: 'Structures of Immorality: Rhetoric, Building and Social Hierarchy'.

[18] For an account of this, focussing on the *Domus Aurea*, see Morford 1968 pp. 158–79.

leisure activities (such as the theatre and amphitheatre) is matched by public utilities (such as the aqueduct and walls of Syracuse). The construction of projects grandiose enough to be worthy of an emperor (the palace at Samos, the canal, the city in the Alps) is balanced by the temples in Rome, Syracuse and Ephesus. This is a carefully constructed and balanced list, on the lines of the rather longer one designed by Augustus for his *Res Gestae*.[19] None the less, it is a catalogue charged with potent and possible ambiguities pointing proleptically to the tyrant that Caligula would become. The palace at Samos explicitly recalls the tyrant Polycrates, the canal through the Isthmus evokes the canal at Athos dug by the Persian king Xerxes in his attempt to enslave Greece,[20] the city in the Alps suggests the Alpine feats of Hannibal who had attempted to conquer Rome.

Then, at the opening of chapter 22, Suetonius breaks off:

> So much for Caligula as emperor; the rest of this account must deal with the monster.

The acts of the monster include a number of building projects, listed separately from the previous list:

> He built out a part of the Palace as far as the Forum, and made the temple of Castor and Pollux its vestibule (22.2).

> He built a bridge over the temple of the deified Augustus, and thus joined his Palace to the Capitol. Presently, to be nearer yet, he laid the foundations of a new house in the court of the Capitol. (22.4)

This remarkable break from emperor to monster, and the ability of buildings to stand as evidence under either heading in Suetonius' rhetoric, is significant. The buildings of the monster are those which appear to transgress the precise and anciently established boundaries of function and situation, either by combining sacred and secular (including the temple of the Dioscuri into the vestibule of the palace, building a house in the temple of Capitoline Jove) or by uniting previously discrete and distinct parts of the city (the Palatine and Forum, the Palatine and Capitol).

Yet Suetonius' categories by which buildings are to be impugned for monstrosity are not stable. In his account of Augustus' public works (*Augustus* 29), Suetonius notes that the first emperor

> reared the temple of Apollo in that part of his house on the Palatine for which soothsayers declared that the god had shown his desire by striking it with lightning (29.3).

Gaius' linking of his own house with that of a god could not have had a better precedent, a precedent which the biographer appears to approve. Yet, if lightning had struck the house of Caligula, we can imagine what the portent would have been made to mean in Suetonius' rhetorical hands ... It was only the general success of Augustus, the fact the he was a 'good emperor', deified at his death, that allowed his house on the Palatine to stand posthumously for his good qualities. Likewise, had Caligula proved worthy to be a *divus* at his death, his building ambitions in the heart of Rome would not have been the acts of a monster.

[19]   See Elsner forthcoming for a detailed account.

[20]   Herodot. 7.22–4; cf. the reference to Caligula outdoing Xerxes' 'famous feat of bridging the Hellespont' at Suet., *Gai.* 19.

It is this quality of 'judgment through hindsight' that must make us wary of the textual tradition. The historians were above all rhetoricians, and buildings had the potential to occupy any position, positive or negative, in their highly rhetorical accounts. Above all, we need to worry when we find the 'evil emperors' lumped together as if their actions were simply and inevitably variations on the same theme – a series of reversals of the norms of *natura*. Within ten years of Nero's fall, the Elder Pliny wrote:

> Twice we have seen the whole city encircled by imperial palaces, those of Gaius and Nero, the latter's palace, to crown all, being indeed a House of Gold. (*Natural History* 36.111)

This passage is frequently quoted as if it reported the truth.[21] But whether it was really the case that both emperors attempted to ring the city with palaces, and whether such actions represented deliberate policy (with Nero emulating Gaius), what matters to Pliny is something quite different from factual veracity. In the context of a lament about modern extravagance, his account is a polemical attempt to associate what he implies are extreme acts of degenerate modernity with emperors whose names were already a byword for unrestrained excess. Pliny's whole argument is highly rhetorical. We learn that the 'lands of those who made this empire great occupied a smaller space than those emperor's sitting rooms' (36.111). Moreover, the *Domus Aurea* did not encircle Rome (except in Pliny's rhetorical flight of fancy); it linked the Palatine and Esquiline hills in the middle of the city.

In effect, almost as soon as Vespasian had taken over the empire, we can see in Pliny a highly mythologised and polemical version of Nero, in which his activities, his buildings and the nature of his principate become mapped – together with the principate of Caligula – onto a negative ideal of how not to be an emperor. Despite antedating Tacitus and Suetonius, Pliny (like the author of the *Octavia*) presents no more objective an account than they. Together, these writers provide a polemical rhetoric which hardly deserves to pass under the unproblematic guise of 'the evidence'. Nor can we rely on later sources (themselves reliant on Pliny and his Flavian contemporaries) such as Pausanias, writing in the second century AD of Gaius and Nero as a 'pair who sinned against the god' (*Description of Greece* 9.27.3–4).

Most commentators, especially those who look at the material remains of Neronian building (architectural, visual and archaeological), rather than at the writings of the ancient historians, are agreed that it represented an outstanding and innovative phase in the history of Roman art and architecture.[22] Those who have explored the economic and managerial implications of imperial building are likewise agreed on the general competence and good timing of Nero's construction measures in Rome.[23] These conclusions are a long way from the impression of outrageous excess on which our ancient literary sources unite. In this section I shall briefly outline a sketch of Neronian building policy in relation to the activities of earlier emperors.

It is clear that Nero's principate opted for a series of innovatory and even controversial gestures in the realm of public art. The Elder Pliny (no friendly

[21]   See e.g. Wiseman 1987 p. 409 or Purcell 1987 pp. 198–9. On the exaggeration of this text as an account of both Nero and Gaius, see Van Essen 1954 pp. 371–98, esp. p. 373.

[22]   Ward Perkins 1956 pp. 209–19, esp. p. 219; MacDonald 1965 pp. 3–46; Boethius and Ward Perkins 1970 pp. 211–16, 248–50; Kleiner 1985 pp. 73, 89 and 92.

[23]   See Balland 1965 pp. 349–93, esp. 391–3; Thornton 1971 pp. 621–9; Phillips 1978 pp. 300–7; Thornton 1986 pp. 28–44, esp. p. 39; Thornton and Thornton 1989 pp. 96–101, 119–20.

source, as we have seen, since he completed and revised his *Natural History* under the Flavians) remarks on Nero's colossi – not only the huge bronze statue which stood in the vestibule of the *Domus Aurea* facing the Sacra Via and the Forum (34.45–6), but also the enormous portrait painted on linen 120 feet high which he labels 'aN insanity of our age' (35.51). Nero's triumphal arch on the Capitoline Hill [...], voted in celebration of Corbulo's Armenian victories in AD 58, has been described as 'revolutionary' and 'remarkable'.[24] His baths were outstanding. As Martial wrote (also under the Flavians)

What is worse than Nero? What is better than his baths? (7.34.4).

From Claudius, Nero had inherited an extensive and effective series of pragmatic structural improvements in the city of Rome. Claudius had undertaken a number of major projects including the completion of the aqueducts started under Gaius (the Aqua Claudia and the Aqua Anio Novus),[25] the building of the harbour at Ostia,[26] and the draining of the Fucine Lake, 53 miles east of Rome.[27] These projects, along with the construction of granaries in both Ostia and Rome,[28] ensured stability in both water and grain supplies to the city.

No laudatory list survives of Nero's own buildings – such even as Suetonius includes in his account of Caligula the pre-monster. But from isolated references and archaeological excavation, some picture can be painted of his public building in Rome. This fits well with the range of projects planned by previous emperors. Nero completed the harbour at Ostia,[29] and went so far as to issue a coin in AD 64 depicting the harbour on the reverse (see Plate 8).[30] In addition to the arch, Nero dedicated a provision market, the Macellum Magnum, in AD 59, his new baths north of the Pantheon in the Campus Martius, and a gymnasium closely linked to the baths. Other significant public buildings included the amphitheatre in the Campus Martius erected in AD 57 and the completion of a circus begun by Caligula.[31]

These constructions are hardly out of keeping with previous imperial activity. They continue the policy of endowing the city with public buildings whose functions were highly suited to the needs and entertainment of the populace. Significantly, but not unexpectedly, we find the literary sources turning these monuments to rhetorical effect against Nero, despite the fact that they are little different from what we might have expected from any emperor – good or bad. For Suetonius, Nero's amphitheatre was the excuse to put 400 senators and 600 knights onto the stage (*Nero* 12.1). According to Tacitus, at the consecration of the gymnasium, 'oil was distributed to the equestrian and senatorial orders', which he acidly describes as a 'Greek form of liberality' (*Annals* 14.47). The gymnasium's main virtue, in Tacitus' account, was that it was struck by lightning and burned to the ground: 'A statue of Nero inside was melted into a shapeless mass of bronze' (*Annals* 15.22). All this is simply gratuitous – but it set the literary tone for what became (and still are) the standard rhetorical associations of Nero's buildings. By the third century,

---

[24]   Kleiner 1985 pp. 89 and 92.

[25]   Thornton and Thornton 1989 pp. 93–6; Blake 1959 pp. 26–8.

[26]   Thornton and Thornton 1989 pp. 77–91; Meiggs 1973 pp. 54–8.

[27]   Thornton and Thornton 1989 pp. 56–76.

[28]   Blake 1959 pp. 28–30.

[29]   Thornton and Thornton 1989 pp. 87–8, 96.

[30]   Mattingly 1923 nos 131–5, pp. 222–3, pl. 41.7.

[31]   On these projects see Blake 1959 pp. 33–6; on the gymnasium see Tamm 1970.

Philostratus could happily present 'the occasion of Nero's completion of the most magnificent gymnasium in Rome' as marked

> by the fact that Nero was in extra good voice when he sang on that day, and he sang in the tavern which adjoined the gymnasium, naked except for a girdle round his waist, like any low tapster. (*Life of Apollonius of Tyana* 4.42)

Thus a myth is born.

The principate's own presentation of these public buildings was sober by comparison. We have no Neronian texts to compare with the *Res Gestae*, but the coin record – an official and officially sanctioned document – is hardly outrageous. Just as Augustus had celebrated peace by closing the doors of the temple of Janus Geminus (*Res Gestae* 13), so Nero closed the gates of this temple in 66 and celebrated the event in a number of coin issues from both Rome and Lyons [...].[32] His own buildings were represented on coins mainly issued after the fire of 64.[33] They included the arch (coin struck in 64–5 [...]),[34] the Macellum Magnum (coin issued 64–6, see Plate 10),[35] and the temple of Vesta which Nero probably rebuilt after the fire (coin struck 64–5, see Plate 11).[36] Our literary sources do not record the reconstruction of this highly significant temple (despite attesting its destruction in the fire – Tacitus *Annals* 14.51), yet the coins suggest that Nero himself emphasised its importance.[37] These coins, in addition to those representing the Ara Pacis and the Ostia harbour, show a propaganda of typical Julio-Claudian balance, whereby honorific imperial monuments (such as the arch) are matched by public buildings of popular utility, such as the harbour and the market, and by the temples of Vesta, Janus and Pax Augusta. It is noteworthy that, while the texts never associate Nero with temple building or restoration, three out of the six coin types that have survived representing buildings associate the emperor with sacred edifices.

By contrast with (and indeed pointedly ignoring) all this, our literary sources focus on a radically different area of Neronian building. All Nero's gestures – whether innovatory or traditional – paled before what our ancient sources see as the outrage of the Golden House. In the words of Suetonius (*Nero* 31.1–2):

> He built a house stretching from the Palatine to the Esquiline, which he called the *Domus Transitoria*; and when it was burned soon afterwards, rebuilt it under the new name of the *Domus Aurea*. The following details will give some notion of its size and magnificence. A huge statue of himself, 120 feet high, stood in the entrance hall; and the pillared arcade ran for a whole mile. An enormous pool, more like a sea than a pool, was surrounded by buildings made to resemble

---

[32]   Mattingly 1923 no. 64, p. 209, pl. 39.17–18; nos 111–13, p. 215, pl. 41.1; nos 156–67, pp. 229–31, pl. 42.6–7; nos 198–204, pp. 238–9, pl. 43.8–9; nos 225–33, pp. 243–4, pl. 44.5–6; nos 319–22, p. 263, pl. 46.2; nos 374–5, p. 273, pl. 47.6; Hill 1989 pp. 10–11.

[33]   On the dates of the coin issues representing buildings, see Sydenham 1920 p. 63 (Ara Pacis: 60 or 64), pp. 91–2 (Janus Temple: 64–6), p. 97 (Arch: 64–5), p. 105 (Vesta Temple: 65), p. 106 (Macellum: 65–6), p. 108 (Ostia: 64–5); Mattingly 1923 p. clxviii (Macellum: 64–6), p. clxxiv (Janus Temple 64–7), p. clxxv (Vesta Temple: 64–5), p. clxxviii (Arch: 64–5); and Sutherland 1987 p. 82 (Ostia: after 64).

[34]   See Mattingly 1923 nos 183–90, pp. 234–5, pl. 43.3; Kleiner 1985 pp. 99–138.

[35]   Mattingly 1923 nos 191–7, pp. 236–7, pl. 43.5–7; nos 335–7, p. 266, pl. 46.6; Hill 1989 p. 40.

[36]   Mattingly 1923 nos 101–6, p. 213, pl. 40.10–13; Hill 1989 pp. 23–4.

[37]   It appears from Tac., *Hist.* I.43 that the temple had been rebuilt in time for Galba's ally Piso to be murdered there in early 69.

cities, and by a landscape garden consisting of ploughed fields, vineyards, pastures and woodlands – where every variety of domestic and wild animal roamed about. Parts of the house were overlaid with gold and studded with precious stones and mother-of-pearl. All the dining rooms had ceilings of fretted ivory, the panels of which could slide back and let a rain of flowers, or of perfume from hidden sprinklers, fall on his guests. The main dining room was circular, and its roof revolved slowly, day and night, in time with the sky. Sea water, or sulphur water, was always on tap in the baths. When the palace had been decorated throughout in this lavish style, Nero dedicated it, and condescended to remark: 'Good, now I can at last begin to live like a human being!'

Before looking more closely at the *Domus Aurea*, we should note that it belongs to a more strictly *private* sphere of imperial building than the temples, markets and theatres of the official documents and coins. Emperors did not represent their palaces, gardens or villas on their coinage, nor did they advertise details of their domestic buildings in official documents such as the *Res Gestae*. As the same time, imperial palaces were not 'private' in any modern sense of the word. Emperors concluded much of their official business in these 'private' residences – for instance meeting delegations of clients as is memorably recorded in Philo's account of the embassy of Alexandrian Jews to Gaius (*De Legatione* 181, 351f.). Under the Julio-Claudians, such 'private' spaces had become increasingly lavish and luxurious. The jewel-bedecked windows ordered by Gaius for his residence at the Horti Lamiani, while Philo and his colleagues trembled before the emperor's wrath (*De Legatione* 358, 364), have been matched by archaeological discoveries on the site of these gardens.[38] The remarkable grotto which served Tiberius as a dining room at Sperlonga,[39] and the extraordinary nymphaeum of Claudius recently discovered at Baiae,[40] only serve to confirm the extent and lavishness of such 'private' imperial luxury.

The *Domus Aurea* was in one sense a natural and direct continuation of this Julio-Claudian tradition. Its huge atrium and vestibule (in which the Colossus stood and towards which the Via Sacra was partly realigned and redirected) was a grand Neronian version of the patron's meeting place with his clients.[41] The luxurious excesses of the Golden House, against which the sources rail, are again in line with the general luxury of early imperial dining-rooms and villas. For instance, the nymphaeum of the *Domus Aurea* with its revolutionary ceiling mosaics depicting Ulysses and Polyphemus,[42] is iconographically and thematically related (as well as in terms of its innovatory lavishness) to the decor of the Sperlonga cave and the Baiae nymphaeum.

But while in itself the *Domus Aurea* may have been just one further step in the developing visual and architectural language of imperial luxury, in one crucial aspect it represented a radical act of innovation. Nero had placed a spectacular example of a lavish rural villa (the kind of villa suited to Sperlonga, Capri

---

[38]   See Cima 1986.

[39]   See Sauron 1991 pp. 19–42; Lavagne 1988 pp. 515–58; Andreae 1982 pp. 103–85; Stewart 1977 pp. 76–90; Conticello and Andreae 1974.

[40]   See Lavagne 1988 pp. 573–7; Andreae 1982 pp. 199–220; Zevi and Andreae 1982 pp. 114–56.

[41]   Tamm 1963 pp. 102–8.

[42]   See Lavagne 1970 pp. 673–721; Sear 1977 pp. 90–2; Lavagne 1988 pp. 579–88.

or Baiae) in the heart of Rome.[43] This, in retrospect, was to prove unforgivable. As Tacitus puts it (*Annals* 15.42):

> Nero turned to account the ruins of his fatherland by building a palace, the marvels of which were to consist not so much in gems and gold, materials long familiar and vulgarised by luxury, as in fields and lakes and the air of solitude given by wooded ground alternating with clear and open landscapes.

The outrage of *rus in urbe* (bringing the countryside into the city) was, like the building of villas into the sea,[44] a transgression of the discrete boundaries of *natura* approved by Roman custom and upheld by moral rhetoric. It represented an attempt, in Tacitus' words (*Annals* 15.42),

> to try the force of an art even against the veto of nature.

But the *Domus Aurea* added to this transgression a further confusion of boundaries hitherto experienced as distinct. Like the house of Caligula which impinged on the Forum and was ultimately linked by a bridge with the Capitol, one crime of Nero's palaces (committed by both the *Domus Transitoria* and the *Domus Aurea*) was to attempt to unite discrete and distinct spaces in the geography of Rome. Both Neronian palaces straddled the Palatine and Esquiline hills, with the *Domus Aurea* apparently incorporating most of the Caelian Hill too.[45] Not only was the Golden House represented as encroaching on the spatial integrity of the city, it was seen as having become the city. As Suetonius put it, purportedly reporting a contemporary epigram (*Nero* 39):

> Rome has become a house; citizens, emigrate to Veii;
> But watch out that the house does not extend that far too.

It was this usurpation of the city by the 'hated hall of a cruel king' which motivated Martial's jibe (*Liber de Spectaculis* 2.4):

> One house took up the whole of Rome.

And, to add insult to injury, the 'house' which had taken over the city was itself filled with 'buildings made to resemble citites' (Suetonius, *Nero* 31).

Conclusion

The relationship of the *Domus Aurea* to the 'monstrous' building of Caligula should make us wary. For Nero was, even in what posterity would later make out were the most scandalous excesses of his building, not as untraditional as the scholarly literature's emphasis on Neronian innovation may lead us to assume. On the contrary, everything about the *Domus Aurea* – lavish gardens, an attempt to link the Palatine with other hills in the city, luxurious decoration and fittings – all this was presaged by previous imperial building in Rome and in Italy. Nero simply went one step further than his predecessors, as he did in the design of his arch, and as he had to do in what I have suggested was an incremental visual discourse of building by successive emperors in the city. What is at stake is whether what Nero did was by definition outrageous by every standard of Roman taste and decorum (as the literary sources imply) or whether it *became* the supreme symbol for outrageousness only when (and because) Nero was overthrown.

---

[43]   See Purcell 1987 pp. 198–203; Griffin 1984 pp. 133–42.

[44]   For this particular assault on *natura* see Hor., *Od*. II.18.17–22; Papirius Fabianus in the Elder Seneca, *Contr*. II.1.11–12; Petron., *Sat*. 120.87–9.

[45]   On the topography of the *Domus Aurea*, see Van Essen 1954 and generally, Boethius 1960 pp. 94–128.

At the beginning of this chapter, I argued that imperial building was one of the emperor's most significant public activities, and that it encapsulated both the self-presentation of emperors by contrast with their predecessors and a public definition of their relationship with the populace. If we exclude the evidence of the literary polemics from Pliny and Martial to Tacitus, Suetonius and third-century writers like Dio Cassius and Philostratus (all biased against Nero and all probably embroidering on the same anti-Neronian sources), then there is little scandalous about his buildings. The range of kinds of monuments he constructed is traditional, the record of numismatic propaganda is sober and unexceptional, the innovations are all motivated by a tradition of imperial innovation in which Nero's moves were the next step. Moreover, no positive account of his works has been allowed to survive, although there must have been some.

My contention is that if Nero had not been overthrown in 68, if his reign had lasted as long as that of Augustus, or even that other philhellene builder Hadrian, there would have been nothing prodigal even about the Golden House. Certainly the history of imperial construction and the later topography of the city of Rome would have been very different. But the historian's rhetoric would have turned in the opposite direction – towards panegyric and not abuse. Instead, after the instabilities of 69, it fell to Vespasian to restore Rome.[46] His projects were traditional – for instance, the rebuilding of the temple of Capitoline Jove (sacked in the fighting of 69), a temple of Honos and Virtus, a temple of Peace. In part, his works specifically responded to Nero, contradicting with temples and public buildings the excesses of what Flavian writers were already portraying as a monstrously extravagant regime. The artificial lake of the *Domus Aurea* became the Colosseum, the temple of the Divine Claudius on the Caelian (which Nero had never got round to building) was completed, the colossus was rededicated to the sun. Vespasian's coins depicting buildings emphasised temples – both those he had built himself (like the Capitol) and previous sacred dedications, including the temple of Vesta restored by Nero.[47] Inevitably, given the image of Nero, Vespasian as builder and propagandist initiated a return to less daring and grandiloquent public gestures. Vespasian slotted into the tradition of the principate by not being another Nero, and by helping to construct a Nero like whom he could never be. As a result, Vespasian could be innovative by being conservative, and thus – as emperor – was perfectly placed to merit the approbation of the moral rhetoric of Roman historiography.

In effect, Nero only became an outrageous and prodigal builder when he fell from power. Then, the rhetoric of history turned against him and he was condemned in every respect – especially in the most visible and rhetorically potent elements in his reign, his private life and his public works. Essentially, the ancient historians made a brilliant and persuasive job of reversing causalities. Their combined argument was that the outrageous nature of Nero's actions, epitomised by murder and debauchery in private and by buildings and

[46]   On Vespasian's buildings see Homo 1949 pp. 365–81, Blake 1959 pp. 88–91 and Boethius and Ward Perkins 1970 pp. 217–24

[47]   Vespasian's coinage includes images of the restored temple of Jupiter Capitolinus (see e.g. Mattingly 1930 no. 614, p. 133, pl. 23.14; Hill 1989 p. 25), of the Augustan temple of Vesta on the Palatine (Mattingly 1930 no. 90, p. 17, pl. 2.17; Hill 1989 pp. 31–2) and the Ara Providentiae Augusti (Mattingly 1930 no. 611, p. 132, pl. 23.12; Hill 1989 p. 64), of the temple of Vesta in the Forum, restored by Nero (Mattingly 1930 no. 664, p. 151, pl. 26.9; Hill 1989 p. 23), and of the temple of Isis probably built by Gaius in the Campus Martius (Mattingly 1930 p. 123, pl. 22.7; Hill 1989 pp. 28–9). The famous coin showing the Colosseum was issued by Titus in 80–1 (Mattingly 1930 'Titus', no. 90, p. 262, pl. 50.2; Hill 1989 pp. 40–1).

theatrical antics in public, caused his fall. My suggestion is that, at least in the context of his buildings, their outrageousness, and the polemic poured upon them, were not a cause but, in fact, the result of his fall.

By being toppled, Nero did more than end the Julio-Claudian dynasty. He ended also the radical nature of early imperial experimentation with the city of Rome. The *Domus Aurea* became the ultimate, notorious, stage in the Julio-Claudian pattern of luxurious encroachment onto the rest of the city, begun as early as the extensions of Augustus' house on the Palatine into a palace under Tiberius. As such, and as the supreme monument of an emperor instantly vilified, it was – along with Nero's building projects in general – damned by the rhetoric of history.

Bibliography

Anderson, J.G.C. (1911) 'Trajan on the quinquennium Neronis' *JRS* 1 pp. 173–8.

Andreae, B. (1982) *Odysseus: Archaeologische des europäischen Menschenbildes*, Frankfurt.

Balland, A. (1965) 'Nova Urbs et "Neapolis", remarques sur les projets urbanistiques de Néron', *MEFR* 77 pp. 349–93.

Blake, M.E. (1959) *Roman construction in Italy from Tiberius through the Flavians*, Washington, D.C.

Boethius, A. (1960) *The Golden House of Nero*, Ann Arbor.

Boethius, A. and Ward Perkins, J.B. (1970) *Etruscan and Roman architecture*, Harmondsworth.

Cima, M. (1986) 'II "prezioso arredo" degli Horti Lamiani', in M. Cima and E. La Rocca (eds.), *Le tranquille dimore degli dei: la residenza imperiale degli Horti Lamiani*, catalogue for an exhibition of the same name in Rome (1986), Venice, pp. 105–44.

Conticello, B. and Andreae, B. (1974) *Die Skulpturen von Sperlonga*, Antike Plastik 14, Berlin.

Edwards, C. (1993) *The politics of immorality in ancient Rome,* Cambridge.

Elsner, J. (forthcoming) 'Inventing imperium: texts and the propaganda of monuments in Augustan Rome', in J. Elsner (ed.), *Art and text in Roman culture*, Cambridge.

Van Essen, C.C. (1954) 'La topographie de la Domus Aurea Neronis', *Mededelingen der Koninklijke Nederlandse Akademie van Wetenschappen* 17 pp. 371–98.

Favro, D. (1992) 'Pater urbis: Augustus as city father of Rome', *Journal of the Society of Architectural Historians* 51 pp. 61–84.

Griffin, M.T. (1984) *Nero: the end of a dynasty*, London.

Hemsoll, D. (1990) 'The architecture of Nero's Golden House' in M. Henig (ed.) *Architecture and architectural sculpture in the Roman Empire*, Oxford, pp. 10–38.

Hill, P.V. (1989) *The monuments of ancient Rome as coin types*, London.

Hind, J.G.F. (1971) 'The middle years of Nero's reign', *Historia* 20 pp. 488–505.

——(1975) 'Is Nero's quinquennium an enigma?', *Historia* 24 pp. 629–30.

Homo, L. (1949) *Vespasien: l'empereur du bon sens*, Paris.

Jucker, H. (1981) 'Iulisch-Claudisch Kaiser- und Prinzenporträts als "Palimpseste"', *JDAI* 96 pp. 236–316.

Kleiner, F.S. (1985) *The arch of Nero in Rome* (Archaeologica 52), Rome.

Lavagne, H. (1970) 'Le nymphée au Polyphème de la Domus Aurea', *MEFR* 82 pp. 673–721.

—— (1988) *Operosa antra*, Rome.

Lepper, F.A. (1957) 'Some reflections on the quinquennium Neronis', *JRS* 47 pp. 95–103.

MacDonald W.L. (1965) *The architecture of the Roman empire*, vol. 1, New Haven.

Mattingly, H. (1923) *Coins of the Roman empire in the British Museum*, vol. 1, London.

—— (1930) *Coins of the Roman empire in the British Museum*, vol. 2, London.

Meiggs, R. (1973) *Roman Ostia*, Oxford.

Miller, F. (1984) 'State and subject: the impact of monarchy', in F. Millar and E. Segal (eds.), *Caesar Augustus: seven aspects*, Oxford.

Morford, M.P.O. (1968) 'The distortion of the Domus Aurea tradition', *Eranos* 66 pp. 158–79.

Murray, O. (1965) 'The "quinquennium Neronis" and the Stoics', *Historia* 14 pp. 41–61.

Phillips, E.J. (1978) 'Nero's new city', *Rivista di Filologia* 106 pp. 300–7.

Platner, S.B. and Ashby, T. (1929) *A topographical dictionary of Rome*, Oxford.

Price, S.R.F. (1980) 'Between man and god: sacrifice in the Roman imperial cult', *JRS* 70 pp. 28–43.

Purcell, N. (1987) 'Town in country and country in town', in E.B. MacDougall (ed.), *Ancient Roman villa gardens* (Dumbarton Oaks colloquium on the history of landscape architecture 10), Washington, D.C.

Raaflaub, K. and Toher, M. (eds.) (1990) *Between republic and empire: interpretations of Augustus and his principate*, Berkeley.

Sablayrolles, R. (1981) 'Espace urbain et propagande politique: L'organisation du centre de Rome par Auguste (Res Gestae 19 à 21)', *Pallas* 28 pp. 59–77.

Sauron, G. (1991) 'De Buthrote à Sperlonga: à propos d'une étude récente sur le thème de la grotte dans les décors romains', *RA* pp. 3–42.

Sear, F.B. (1977) *Roman wall and vault mosaics*, Heidelberg.

Simon, E. (1986) *Augustus: Kunst und Leben in Rom um die Zeitenwende*, Munich.

Stewart, A.F. (1977) 'To entertain an emperor: Sperlonga, Laokoon and Tiberius at the dinner-table', *JRS* 67 pp. 76–90.

Sutherland, C.H.V. (1987) *Roman history and coinage 44 BC – AD 69*, Oxford.

Sydenham, E.A. (1920) *The coinage of Nero*, London.

Tamm, B. (1963) *Auditorium and palatium* (Stockholm studies in classical archaeology 2), Stockholm.

—— (1970) *Neros Gymnasium in Rom* (Stockholm studies in classical archaeology 7), Stockholm.

Thornton, M.K. (1971) 'Nero's new deal', *TAPA* 102 pp. 621–9.

—— (1973) 'The enigma of Nero's quinquennium', *Historia* 22 pp. 570–82.

—— (1986) 'Julio-Claudian building programs: eat, drink and be merry', *Historia* 35 pp. 28–44.

Thornton, M.K. and R.L. (1989) *Julio-Claudian building programs: a quantitative study in political management*, Wauconda, Il.

Wallace-Hadrill, A. (1982), 'Civilis princeps: between citizen and king', *JRS* 72 pp. 32–84.

—— (1986) 'Image and authority in the coinage of Augustus', *JRS* 76 pp. 66–87.

Ward Perkins, J.B. (1956) 'Nero's Golden House', *Antiquity* 30 pp. 209–19.

Wiseman, T.P. (1987) 'Conspicui postes tectaque digna deo: the public image of aristocratic and imperial housing in the late republic and early empire', in *L'urbs: espace urbain et histoire* (Collection de l'Ecole Française de Rome 98), Rome.

Zanker, P. (1988) *The power of images in the age of Augustus*, Ann Arbor.

Zevi, F. and Andreae, B. (1982) 'Gli scavi sottomarini di Baia', *La Parola del Passato* 203 pp. 114–56.

Ziss, K. (1975) *L'iconographie des princes Julio-Claudiens au temps d'Auguste et de Tibère*, Warsaw.

Secondary Source 2.5   Alan Cameron, 'Myth and society'

(Source: Cameron, A. (2004) *Greek Mythography in the Roman World*, Oxford, Oxford University Press, pp. 220–4, 228–38)

4: Popular Mythology

Some knowledge of myth was nonetheless widespread at a much lower social level. Greek mythology established itself early in Rome, as shown by the evidence of Republican drama. The themes of Ennius's tragedies are all from Greek mythology; in fact they are adaptations of Greek tragedies, and Plautus's comedies are full of mythological allusions. Eduard Fraenkel plausibly argued that many of these allusions were actually added by Plautus to his Greek originals.[1]

Before a characteristically acute and learned paper by Peter Wiseman, most of us probably thought that Julius Caesar's claim to descent from Venus through Aenas and Iulus was an eccentric fantasy, elaborated by Vergil in what was, after all, a poem. Wiseman showed that there were in fact a great many "Trojan" families among the Republican nobility.[2] The Geganii and Sergii claimed descent from Aeneas's followers Gyas and Sergestus, and the Nautii from Nautes, who received the Palladium from Diomedes. These traditions (mainly known to us from the Vergil scholia) were collected in two books entitled *De familiis Troianis*, by Varro and Augustus's freedman Hyginus.[3] Some of these traditions may have been no earlier than the first century, but since the patrician Nautii and Geganii disappear in the third and fourth centuries, respectively, others are surely much earlier.[4] Here is Wiseman's imaginative reconstruction of the audiences at which such legendary genealogies were aimed:[5]

> the dinner guests at a great house, listening to the anagnostes read from a not too rigorous work of history; the loungers in the exedra of the baths, as the poet recited his panegyrical epic; the Forum crowd, enjoying the splendor of a society funeral and listening to the orator declaim on the greatness of the deceased and of his family.

[1]   E. Fraenkel, *Elementi plautini in Plauto* (Rome 1960), 55–94; disputed by N. Horsfall, *Roman Myth and Mythography* (London 1987), 5 n. 25, who was rebutted by H.D. Jocelyn, *LCM* 17 (1992), 105.

[2]   Wiseman, "Legendary genealogies in late-republican Rome," *Greece and Rome* 21 (1974), 153–64 = *Roman Studies: Literary and Historical* (Liverpool 1987), 207–20 (with addenda on p. 381).

[3]   See Wiseman 1974, 153–4 = 1987, 207–8.

[4]   In favor of more recent origin, Horsfall in Bremmer and Horsfall 1987, 22–3; Erskine, 2001, 21–2.

[5]   Wiseman 1974, 159 = 1987, 213, with documentation.

There are two areas where we happen to be surprisingly well informed. First pantomimes, by far the most popular stage-stars of the early imperial Greco-Roman world. Pantomimes were dancers who performed to the accompaniment of flutes and a chorus. The pantomime himself did not sing but mimed a story from myth.[6] Fifty years ago E. Wüst compiled a list of some two hundred "titles," further expanded by M. Kokolakis. Margaret Molloy has recently produced a more balanced list of what she more plausibly styles "roles," which still runs to more than a hundred.[7] Every one is taken from Greek mythology.[8] We have already studied Lucillius's epigram on the bad pantomime who danced every part "according to the story" (καθ' ἱστορίην) except one. When doing Canace (who killed herself) he left the stage alive![9]

Interestingly enough, Lucian saw knowledge of all these roles in terms of literary culture rather than professional training. In his curious treatise On the Dance (§§ 35–7) he claims that the dancer must reach "the very summit of all culture (πάσης παιδεύσεως ἐς τὸ ἀκρότατον), and enjoy the favor above all of Mnemosyne and her daughter Polymnia." He devotes several pages to a comprehensive list of all the myths the dancer should know (§§ 37–63). Of course there is more than a touch of hyperbole here, but it is clear that pantomimes really did need to know at any rate the highlights of all the myths they might be called on to mime. Obviously they are more likely to have got this information from comprehensive mythographic handbooks than from allusions in the poets. After all, all they needed to know was the highlights of each story. Ps-Dositheus mentions three categories of people as "bearing witness" to the value of Hyginus's Fables: painters, teachers – and pantomime dancers.[10]

It is not surprising that educated aficionados of the dance took pleasure in watching the stories they knew so well re-enacted on the stage, but pantomimes were the rock stars rather than ballet stars of their age, popular idols with devoted fan clubs who often came to blows with the fans of rival pantomimes.[11] Evidently the fans too must have been familiar with at any rate the favorite roles of their heroes.

To move to another area of popular entertainment, gladiators were frequently named after warriors from myth. For example, Achilles, Ajax, Amphiaraüs, Eteocles, Hippomedon, Idomeneus, Meleager, Meriones, Orestes, Parthenopaeus, Patroclus, Perseus, Polydeuces, Pylades, Troilus, and Tydeus are all epigraphically attested.[12] It is natural to assume that some at least of

[6]   The best brief account is by C.P. Jones, *Culture and Society in Lucian* (Cambridge, Mass, 1986), ch. 7; see too Molloy 1996.

[7]   E. Wüst, *RE* 18.2. (1949), 847–9; M. Kokolakis, "Pantomimus and the Treatise Περὶ ὀρχήσεως," *Platon* 11 (1959), 3–56 at 51–5; Molloy 1996, 277–87.

[8]   Even if we count Nero's alleged wish to dance "Vergil's Turnus" (Suet. *Ner.* 54.1), that is hardly an exception.

[9]   *Anth. Pal.* xi. 254; O. Weinreich, *Epigramm und Pantomimus* (Sitz. Heidelberg 1948), 87–90; the last detail was παρ' ἱστορίην, "against the story."

[10]   Here are the two versions, correcting only the most obvious errors: ζωγραφία τοι γαροῦν τούτου τοῦ κόπου πολλοῖς τόποις δίδωσι μαρτυρίαν, ἀλλὰ καὶ οἱ γραμματικοὶ τέχνης ταύτης οὐ μόνον ἐπαινοῦσιν τὴν εὐφυίαν ἀλλὰ καὶ χρῶνται. μῦθοι μέν <τοι> τῶν ὠρχηστῶν ἔνθεν λαμβάνουσιν ἔπαινον καὶ μαρτυροποιοῦνται ἐν τῇ ὠρχήσει ἀληθινὰ τὰ γεγραμμένα/ *picturae igitur huius laboris multis locis dant testimonium, nam et grammatici artis eius non solum laudant ingenium sed et utuntur. fabulae quoque pantomimorum inde accipiunt laudem et testantur in saltatione vera esse quae scripta sunt.*

[11]   Briefly, my *Circus Factions* (1976), ch. VIII, esp. 223–5.

[12]   L. Robert, *Les gladiateurs dans l'orient grec* (Paris 1940), 299.

these names had a special reference; for example, that Achilles was a particularly fast runner (a fourth-century North African mosaic depicts a hunting dog appropriately named Atalanta);[13] that Meleager specialized in fighting wild boars; and that Ajax was a giant of a man.

On the other hand, gladiators called Narcissus, Hyacinthus, or Hylas, though no doubt proficient fighters, must have been young men conspicuous for their boyish good looks (everyone knows the dedications praising one evidently dashing young gladiator as *puellarum suspirium*, "the girls' heartthrob").[14] These names were no doubt chosen by those who ran the gladiatorial schools rather than the gladiators themselves, but their significance must have been obvious to spectators. Thus when Achilles was announced, people would expect some fancy running; when Ajax, that (like the modern wrestler André the Giant) he would take on several opponents at once. One monument records the manumission of two female gladiators, appropriately named Achillia and Amazonia.[15]

Such names also appear in the imagery of monuments to heroes of the hippodrome. One nice illustration is the opening of one of the many epigrams from a series of monuments to the greatest of all Byzantine charioteers, Porphyrius Calliopas, presumably from near the beginning of his long career.[16]

Ἀγχίσην Κυθέρεια καὶ Ἐνδυμίωνα Σελήνη
φίλατο· καὶ Νίκη νῦν τάχα Πορφύριον.

Cytherea fell in love with Anchises, and Selene with Endymion;
Now it seems that Victory has fallen in love with Porphyrius.

Another illustration is what Kathleen Coleman has characterized the "fatal charades" of the Roman amphitheatre, reenactments of mythical stories by condemned criminals.[17] Tertullian describes seeing Attis castrated, Hercules burnt alive, and Pluto hauling corpses out of the arena. According to Tertullian again, the gods of the pagans "dance the stories of myth" (*saltant ... historias*) in human blood at the gladiatorial shows.[18] Clement of Rome describes Christian women being martyred in the guise of the Danaïds and Dirce (who was tied to the horns of a bull).[19] Martial describes an Orpheus killed in the amphitheatre by the beasts he was supposed to be charming; a Prometheus hanging from a real cross (*non falsa pendens in cruce*) while a Caledonian boar tears at his naked flesh; a Daedalus without his wings being torn to pieces by a bear;[20] and Pasiphaë mating with a bull. "Whatever is told of in legend, the arena grants you, Caesar."[21]

---

[13]   Aïcha Ben Abed-Ben Khader et al. (eds.), *Image de Pierre: La Tunisie en mosaïque* (Ars Latina 2002), no. 159.

[14]   Robert 1940, 301; *ILS* 5142.

[15]   Robert 1940, 188–9, with pl. XII; for a full discussion of this monument, see now K. Coleman, *HSCP* 100 (2000), 487–500.

[16]   *Anth. Plan.* 337. 1–2, modeled on 357 by Leontius Scholasticus; for Porphyrius and his many inscribed monuments, see my *Porphyrius the Charioteer* (Oxford 1973).

[17]   K.M. Coleman, "Fatal Charades: Roman executions staged as mythological enactments," *JRS* 80 (1990), 44–73; see too Thomas Wiedemann, *Emperors and Gladiators* (London 1992), 84–89.

[18]   *Ad nat.* i. 10. 46–7; *Apol.* 15. 4.

[19]   Coleman 1990, 65–6.

[20]   Presumably (as Coleman 1990 argues, p. 63) the Daedalus figure was lowered into the arena by a crane as though flying and then left, without his wings, among the bears.

[21]   *Lib. Spect.* 29; 9; 10; 6.

It has sometimes been argued that these are just literary jokes, but Martial's *Liber Spectaculorum* was a collection of epigrams commemorating the games with which Titus dedicated the Flavian Amphitheatre in 80 AD.[22] The grim truth is that that these mythological tableaux really were acted out in the amphitheatre. Condemned men and women were dressed up to look like Orpheus (with a lyre), Daedalus (with wings), or Pasiphaë (with her bull). These elaborate charades would have misfired unless most of the audience was able to identify the pretend Orpheus and appreciate the horrific joke of his failure to charm real wild beasts.

If a pretend Pasiphaë mating with a real bull strains belief, we have Apuleius's account of the projected mating of Lucius the ass with a condemned murderess in the theatre of Corinth before she is thrown to the beasts. In the event Lucius seizes the opportunity of escaping first, but while he is waiting he watches an elaborately staged enactment of the judgment of Paris on the slopes of a Disneyesque wooden Mount Ida planted with real bushes, with a stream flowing down from its peak and real grazing goats for Paris to herd.[23] A beautiful boy dressed as an ephebe with two golden wings in his hair carrying a caduceus offers him a golden apple and nods his head as though passing on Jupiter's instructions. Then three female pantomimes appear outfitted as Juno, Minerva, and Venus, respectively, each miming the gift she will give Paris if he awards her the prize. Minerva is accompanied by two boys bearing arms, Terror and Fear. To the accompaniment of martial music she indicates to Paris with menacing glares and fierce gestures that if he gives her the golden apple he will become a great warrior. While Juno's gestures are lady-like (*nutibus honestis*), Venus, accompanied by a mob of little cupids and a chorus of young girls, gives a more languid performance, indicating that she will give Paris whichever girl he wishes, whereupon he presents her with the apple, and Juno and Minerva angrily leave the stage. What is so striking about Apuleius's vivid account of this tableau is the attention paid to its staging, to the use of props, gestures, dress, and music to tell the story. Anyone who knew the basic story could easily have followed the performance.

The importance of mythological knowledge at a lower social level is famously illustrated by Trimalchio's hilariously muddled identifications of the mythological scenes on his silver plate and in the Homeric passages declaimed by a troupe of actors. Notoriously, he describes Cassandra killing her children, Daedalus shutting Niobe in the wooden horse, Helen and her brothers Diomede and Ganymede, and Agamemnon marrying off Iphigeneia to Achilles.[24] It all seems hopelessly garbled, though (as Martin Smith pointed out) actually Trimalchio just gets a few key details wrong (it was Medea who killed her children, Pasiphaë whom Daedalus shut in a wooden cow, and Castor and Pollux who were Helen's two brothers; and Agamemnon only pretended to be planning to marry Iphigeneia to Achilles). Petronius's purpose was to depict a pretentious nouveau riche. But what is most interesting in the present context is the pretensions he illustrates: the cultural importance of Greek mythology.

22   J.P. Sullivan, *Martial: The Unexpected Classic* (Cambridge 1991), 6–12).

23   On this episode, see Ellen Finkelpearl, "The Judgement of Lucius: Apuleius, *Metamorphoses* 10. 29–34," *Classical Antiquity* 10 (1991), 221–36, accepting the basic verisimilitude of the Ida tableau but unfortunately confusing mime and pantomime throughout.

24   Petron. *Sat.* 52 and 59; see M.S. Smith's commentary (Oxford 1975), 165.

A less familiar illustration is Seneca's mockery of the vulgar millionaire Calvisius Sabinus, who "had a freedman's brain as well as a freedman's fortune".[25]

> His memory was so bad that at one moment or another the names of Ulysses, or Achilles, or Priam, characters he knew as well as we know our *paedagogi*, would slip his memory. No doddering butler [*nomenclator*] ever made so many errors not so much announcing as inventing people's names as he did with the Greek and Trojan heroes. But this didn't stop him wanting to appear a man of culture [*eruditus*].

Not only does Seneca apparently consider confusing mythological names as the worst sort of social gaucherie. He singles out mythological names precisely because they are the core components of a literary culture dinned into any well-brought-up boy from childhood.

We should also bear in mind that, while we smile at Trimalchio's wine-waiter dressed up as Dionysus (41.6–8), Varro reveals to us no less a person than the great Hortensius holding a picnic in his own game-preserve (*therotrophium*) at which an Orpheus, decked out in appropriate robes and harp, sang to the guests, whereupon "a multitude of stags, boars, and other animals poured around us." Elsewhere in his book Varro stresses the importance of feeding dogs properly, "so that they will not enact the story of Actaeon, and sink their teeth in their master."[26]

5: Mythology and Tourism

Wherever Greeks and Romans traveled in the Mediterranean world, they were likely to pass places famed in myth. Greece was a land rich in history, but it was the figures of myth who attracted most of the curious traveler's attention. Pausanias is naturally always ready with such information, often prompted by a statue, painting, or set of reliefs illustrating some mythological scene but no less often simply by arriving at a place with a mythological connection, however tenuous. For example: "the Kerameikos is named after the hero Keramos, the reputed son of Dionysus and Ariadne" (i. 3.1). Here is Pausanias on the Akropolis.[27]

> From this point the sea is visible, and it was here, they say, that Aegeus cast himself down and perished. For the ship that bore the children to Crete used to put to sea with black sails, but when Theseus courageously sailed off to fight the bull called the Minotaur, he told his father he would use white sails if he came back victorious.

As Lionel Casson has remarked, "this mythological digression, appended to the description of the imposing entry to Athens' finest sight yet running longer than the description itself, brings into sharp relief the fundamental difference between the modern and Pausanias' conception of a guidebook." Here is an excerpt from Casson's list of mythological sites and sights, mainly based on Pausanias:[28]

> At Salamis, the visitor was shown the stone where old Telamon sat and watched his sons, Ajax and Teucer, sail off to Troy; near Sparta, the point in the road where Penelope made up her mind to marry

---

[25] Sen. *Ep.* 27.5 (Campbell's Penguin translation, much adapted).

[26] Varro, *De agric.* iii. 13. 2–3; ii. 9. 8–9.

[27] Paus. i. 22. 5; L. Casson, *Travel in the Ancient World*[2] (Baltimore 1994), 295.

[28] Casson 1994, 233. All of the first and much of the second volume of F. Pfister, *Der Reliquienkult im Altertum* i–ii (Giessen 1909–12) is devoted to such sites and relics; see too L. Friedländer, *Darstellungen aus der Sittengeschichte Roms* i (Leipzig 1922), 450–3.

Odysseus; at Troezen, the spot where Phaedra used to spy on Hippolytus while he exercised in the nude ... the plane-tree in Phrygia in Asia Minor where Apollo strung up Marsyas for flaying; the olive-tree at Troezen where Hippolytus' chariot crashed, and the one at Mycenae under which Argos sat as he guarded Io; the cave in Crete where Zeus was born, and the one on Pelion where Chiron lived.

For less energetic tourists there were museums, such as the temple of Apollo in Sicyon described by Ampelius, which (he claimed) contained the following remarkable collection:[29]

The shield and sword of Agamemnon; the cloak and breastplate of Odysseus, the bow and arrows of Teucer; a chest of unknown contents placed there by Adrastus; the bronze cauldron in which Pelias was boiled; the letter of Palamedes; the skin of Marsyas; the oars and rudder of the Argonauts; the pebble that Minerva cast for the acquittal of Orestes ... the loom of Penelope.

Nor were educated Christians any less curious about such mementoes. Here is Sidonius, describing a voyage from Gaul to Rome in 467: "at Ticinum I went aboard a packet-boat (so they call the vessel) and travelled quickly down-stream to the Eridanus, where I had my laugh over Phaethon's sisters, of whom we have often sung amidst our revels, and over those mythical tears of amber ore."[30] And here is Procopius, visiting Beneventum in 536 in the retinue of Belisarius:[31]

This city was built of old by Diomedes, the son of Tydeus, when after the capture of Troy he was repulsed from Argos. And he left to the city as a token the tusks of the Calydonian boar, which his uncle Meleager had received as a prize for the hunt, and they are there even up to my time, a noteworthy sight and well worth seeing, measuring not less than three spans round and having the form of a crescent. There, too, they say that Diomedes met Aeneas, the son of Anchises, when he was coming from Ilium.

The Greek visitor was evidently impressed to find a western city with such strong Greek roots. In his *Periplus of the Black Sea* Arrian records having pointed out to him the peak in the Caucasus to which Prometheus was chained, as well as being shown two anchors from the Argo, one iron, the other stone. The iron one he judged too recent, but the stone one looked quite old enough.[32] Pausanias remarks that he had seen Niobe when climbing Mount Sipylos in Asia Minor: close up just a rock, but from further off "you seem to see a woman in tears with bowed head" (i. 21. 3). Pliny records that the skeleton of the monster to which Andromeda was exposed was brought to Rome from Jaffa by M. Scaurus, aedile in 58 BC.[33] It was widely accepted that this was the site of Andromeda's harrowing experience. Strabo, Pliny, Josephus, and Jerome all mention the impressions left by her chains in the cliffs where she awaited her doom, and Pausanias describes a blood-red spring where Perseus washed himself after killing the monster.[34] It is unimportant whether any of them actually believed the story. It is striking enough that five people from such very

[29]   Ampel. *Lib. Memor.* 8. 5 (the text is very uncertain toward the end).

[30]   *Ep* i. 5.3, trans. W.B. Anderson (Loeb).

[31]   *Bell. Got.* i. 15. 8–9.

[32]   *Periplus Eux. Ponti* 19. 5 (ii. 114. 10 Roos) and 11. 2 (ii. 110. 14 Roos).

[33]   Plin. *NH* ix. 11; Ascon. pp. 18–20 Clark.

[34]   Strabo xvi. 2. 28, p. 759; Plin. *NH* v. 69; Jos. *BJ* iii. 421; Jer. *In Jonam* 1. 3, p. 62 Antin; Paus. iv. 35. 9.

different backgrounds (Greek- and Latin-speakers, pagans, Jews, and Christians) all paid enough attention to remember and record the sight.

Geographical texts routinely allude to mythical traditions about the places they mention, even (perhaps especially) otherwise obscure places. Here is Strabo on a small city in Cappadocia called Comana: "it is thought that Orestes, with his sister Iphigeneia, brought these sacred rites here from the tauric Scythia, the rites in honour of Artemis Tauropolus, and that here also they deposited the hair [κόμην] of mourning, whence the city's name."[35] Even the much less learned *De chorographia* of Pomponius Mela offers the following on the stony Crau plain between the Rhône and Massilia in Gaul:[36]

> Here they say, Hercules was fighting Alebion and Dercynos, the sons of Neptune, and when his arrows had run out, he was helped by a rain of rocks at the hands of Jupiter, whom he had invoked. You would believe that it had rained rocks, so numerously and so widely do they lie scattered all over.

Ps-Apollodorus briefly alludes to the story, without mentioning the rocks, as much earlier did Aeschylus, without naming the sons of Neptune.[37] Improbably enough, Mela preserves the fullest known version of this obscure aetiological myth.

The most distinctive feature of Pausanias's countless mythological digressions is the frequency with which he cites sources—early and often recondite sources at that. Where did he get all this mythological lore? A recent study by Léon Lacroix plausibly traces much of it to local traditions, in particular to etymologies of place names and fanciful explanations of geological oddities and features of the landscape.[38] This may well be how many of the stories he reports originated, and he often refers to oral information, both from personal acquaintances and local guides.[39] A recent article by Christopher Jones has shown that these guides were not, as Preller put it, "very low people, induced by a small wage to undertake a rather demeaning trade, and only superficially acquainted with literature," but for the most part respectable local antiquarians.[40] Nonetheless much of the information Pausanias quotes not only derives from books but from books he took care to cite by name.

Lacroix saw a simple distinction between local and learned sources. What was not picked up from guides reflects Pausanias's wide general culture. Pausanias was certainly a cultivated man, undoubtedly familiar with a great deal of classical and archaic literature at first hand, but his direct sources must often have been more recent mythographers or mythographically orientated local historians and geographers. Let us look at the two examples Lacroix himself adduces: the citation of the *Foundation of Chios* by Ion of Chios for the mythological origin of the name of Chio (from χιών, a snowstorm); and the Atthidographer Cleidemus for damage done to the gilt image of Athena on a

---

[35]   12. 2. 3; see K. Clarke, *Between Geography and History: Hellenistic Constructions of the Roman World* (Oxford 1999), 299–300, 319–24.

[36]   *De chor.* ii. 78 = F.E. Romer, *Pomponius Mela's Description of the World* (Ann Arbor 1998), 91.

[37]   Ps-Apoll. ii. 5. 10 (with the useful notes in Carrière and Massonie 1991, 193); Aesch. F. 199 N²; quoted by Strabo ii. 4. 10; Gantz 1993, 408.

[38]   L. Lacroix, "Traditions locales et legends étiologiques dans la *Périegèse* de Pausanias," *Journal des savants* 1994, 75–99.

[39]   C. Habicht, *Pausanias' Guide to Ancient Greece* (Berkeley 1985), 144–5.

[40]   Jones, "Pausanias and his Guides," in S.E. Alcock, J.F. Cherry, and J. Elsner, *Pausanias: Travel and Memory in Roman Greece* (Oxford 2001), 33–9.

bronze palm-tree dedicated by Athens at Delphi (a flock of crows supposedly swooped down on the image and pecked away the gold when the Athenians were preparing their fateful Sicilian expedition).[41] Lacroix seems to have assumed that Pausanias drew his erudition directly from copies of Ion and Cleidemus. But no one who looks at the sources of the few surviving fragments of either (mainly lexicographers and Athenaeus) will find it easy to believe that original copies were still circulating for casual consultation in the mid-second century.[42] It is far more likely that Pausanias found both texts already cited in more recent mythographers.

A few more illustrations. First, on Messenia: "being anxious to discover what children were born to Polycaon by Messene, I read the *Eoeae* and the epic *Naupactia*, and the genealogies of Asius and Cinaethon as well." Since he goes on to regret that they did not satisfy his curiosity, Pausanias must actually have consulted these texts (which he also cites on other matters). Indeed Pausanias preserves most of what we know about Asius and Cinaethon. When discussing the sons of Medea, he cites Hellanicus, the *Naupactia*, Cinaethon and Eumelus.[43] But even granted that (unlike most of his peers) he had firsthand knowledge of all these texts, it is unlikely that he simply *remembered* their evidence on such precise points. There can (I think) be little doubt that his starting point was citations in more recent and accessible local mythographers—whom (here like his peers) he does *not* name. He may then have looked up such actual texts as he could lay his hands on,[44] but it is not a question of *either* mythographer *or* original texts. A few lesser *literatti* may have depended entirely on mythographers rather than texts, but the more scholarly (like modern scholars) will have used the one to lead them to the other.

Another example is the very beginning of his account of Athens (i. 2.1):

> As you enter the city, there is a monument to the Amazon Antiope. Pindar says she was carried off by Pirithoüs and Theseus, but according to Hegias of Troezen, when Heracles was besieging Themiskyra on the Thermodon and was unable to reduce it, Antiope fell in love with his companion Theseus and so betrayed it. ... But the Athenians claim that at the coming of the Amazons Antiope was shot by Molpadia and Molpadia was shot by Theseus.

The Pindar reference is to an unidentifiable lost poem (F 175), and this is the only reference to the otherwise unknown and undatable Hegias. "The Athenians" probably means one of the Atthidographers, perhaps Philochorus.[45] It is hard to believe that Pausanias had all this information at his fingertips. The likelihood is that he found it ready-assembled in a single well-documented mythographer whom (as usual) he does not name.

On the mythical history of Boeotia he cites verses from two purportedly archaic poets, Hegesinus and Chersias, both (he says) lost by his day and only known to

[41]   Paus. vii. 4.8; x. 15.5; *FGrH* 323 F 10 and 392 F1.

[42]   Plutarch too quotes both Ion and Cleidemus, but Ziegler puts both in his column of texts only doubtfully read at first hand: *Plutarchos von Chaironeia* (Stuttgart 1949), 275.

[43]   Paus. iv. 2. 1 and ii 3. 6–11; Bernabé, *PEG* i (1987), 115–6 (Cinaetho), 127–30 (Asius), 106–8 (Eumelus).

[44]   Two passages imply that he knew the *Arimaspea* of Aristeas of Proconnesus at first hand, but there can be little doubt that in reality, like us, he knew no more than what he had read in Herodotus (i. 24. 6; v. 7. 9; J.D.P. Bolton, *Aristeas of Proconnesus* [Oxford 1962], 32–3, 65).

[45]   On the surprisingly many and varied versions of the Antiope story, see Jacoby's notes on *FGrH* 606 F 1 (= Paus. i. 2. 1) and Philochorus 328 F 110 in *FGrH Suppl.* (1954), 439–40; also now Gantz 1993, 282–5.

him from the *History of Orchomenos* by Callippus. Huxley and West believe in these poets, but many others, notably Jacoby, think that Callippus invented both the verses and (in all probability) the two poets as well.[46] If so, yet another mythographer not above faking his references. Pausanias's scholarly instincts are underlined by his attempt to find copies, and the fact that he mentions his failure strongly suggest that he succeeded in finding copies of most of the other archaic works he cites.[47] But it was surely the mythographers (in this case Callippus) who pointed him in their direction in the first place.

6: Learning Mythology

So where did people acquire their knowledge of myth? We tend to assume that cultivated folk simply absorbed it from reading the classics, and up to a point many of them did, of course. No one can read Homer, Hesiod, Pindar, and the tragedians without picking up a lot of mythology. And naturally enough the later Roman poets often drew on their predecessors. At a lower social level, lesser folk must have picked up at least the outlines of the more popular stories from the theatre, or from statues, paintings, or mosaics.

But very few of the classics give a straightforward, much less complete narrative of even the most famous stories. To take the two richest classical sources of myth outside Homer and Hesiod, tragedy notoriously presupposes the antecedents of its plots (which is why the hypotheseis regularly supply background information), and Pindar is hardly less allusive than the Hellenistic poets, singling out the details in a story that best suited the patron and location of his poem—and often presupposing alternative versions. According to Geoffrey Kirk, this was because in the classical period "the myths were so well known that formal exposition was unnecessary."[48] Yet Aristotle claimed that even the best known myths were known to only a few.[49] Everyone knew their essence or outline, but there was no definitive narrative. In fact the essence of many a myth was simply one vivid, memorable, often shocking detail: Oedipus marrying his mother, Medea killing her own children; or a striking tableau: "Paris before the three goddesses, Theseus confronting the Minotaur in the heart of the labyrinth, Odysseus tied to the mast and listening to the deadly allurements of the Sirens' song."[50] The tragedians were often the first to single out specific episodes for detailed treatment (whence the mythographic importance of the tragic hypotheseis).

Parthenius's preface gives this very fact as justification for his own collection: the poets do not tell the stories completely or in their own right (αὐτοτελῶς).[51] Parthenius claims in his preface that his stories will enable his patron, Cornelius Gallus, "to put the most suitable of them into hexameters and elegiacs." Yet the truth is that Gallus was never likely to treat more than one or two as the subject for an entire poem. Every bit as important as mythical subject matter was myth as a source of imagery, comparisons, and similes in nonmythological

[46]   Paus. ix. 29. 1–2 and 38. 9; G.L. Huxley, *Greek Epic Poetry* (London 1969), 120–1; West 1985, 4; Jacoby on *FGrH* 385 (p. 180) and 331, *Suppl.* i (1954). 608–9; Bernabé's notes in *PEG* i. 142–4; West, *Greek Epic Fragments* (Cambridge, Mass., 2003), 32.

[47]   One archaic mythographic text we now know from the papyri to have been widely available in at any rate the early empire is the Hesiodic *Catalogue of Women*.

[48]   Kirk, *The Nature of Greek Myths* (Penguin Books 1974), 14.

[49]   τὰ γνώριμα ὀλίγοις γνώριμά ἐστιν, *Poet.* 1451*b*26.

[50]   Jasper Griffin, *The Mirror of Myth: Classical Themes and Variations* (London 1986), 14–5.

[51]   See the detailed commentary on this phrase in Lightfoot 1999, 368–9. [J.L. Lightfoot, *Parthenius of Nicaea: Extant works edited with introduction and commentary* (Oxford 1999)]

poetry—and oratory too (§ 7). Mythological allusions were supposed to be just that, allusive. They were not expected to *tell* the story but to evoke some aspect relevant to the writer's own context by a colorful or paradoxical detail. Everyone knew that Achilles was fierce, Odysseus cunning, Penelope faithful, but hardly anyone knew what stories lay behind Apriate, Harpalyce, Polycrite, and other obscure names found in the pages of Parthenius, and a full account served many useful purposes—including ethnics and patronymics for oblique references.

One of the reasons people turned to books like Parthenius and Antoninus Liberalis and the various Diegeseis was to acquire material for both solving and creating puzzling allusions. The citations provided will have varied in kind and purpose from work to work. When explaining a learned and allusive poet, it is actual sources that help the reader most. Thus for the first story in Callimachus's *Aetia*, the *Diegeseis* cite the *Argolika* of Agias and Derkylos and Aristotle's *Parion Politeia*, books that probably gave a more or less factual account of the custom Callimachus explains in his own way. But when writing for a poet (as Parthenius was) it would be helpful to add a few model illustrations of clever allusions to or uses of the myth in question.

Secondary Source 2.6   Paul Zanker, 'A miniature villa in the town'

(Source: Zanker, P. (1998) *Pompeii: Public and Private Life*, Cambridge MA and London, Harvard University Press, pp. 145–56)

As we have seen, the imitation of villa architecture in Pompeii in the first century B.C. was mainly limited to exploitation of sites with the best views on the surrounding slopes and isolated cases of luxurious interior renovation in the grandest houses in town. In the last decades of Pompeii's existence, however, the effect of villas and the décor and lifestyle associated with them spread to a very broad segment of the town's inhabitants. We find many different elements of villa architecture and decor in houses restored or remodeled[1] after the earthquake of A.D. 62,[2] although some of these features might not be recognizable at first glance as having been derived from this source.

As a rule the renovation or remodeling work was limited to the houses' gardens and peristyles. Let us begin by looking at a well-known house in the Via dell'Abbondanza (II 2.2; figs. 73 and 74) named after Loreius Tiburtinus, a

---

[1] I have based the dating principally on Maiuri, *L'ultima fase edilizia di Pompei* (Rome: 1942), passim, but his conclusions must now be considered outdated in part. Compare the critique by J. Andreau, "Le tremblement de terre de Pompéi," pp. 369ff; and F. Zevi, "Il terremotò del 62 e l'edilizia privata," in Zevi, ed., *Pompei*, vol. 2 (Naples: 1992).

[2] For recent studies on the dating of the earthquake, see Étienne, *La vie quotidienne*, pp. 15–16; J. P. Adam in F. Guidoboni, ed., *I terremoti prima del Mille in Italia e nell'area mediterranea* (Bologna: 1989), pp. 460–474; *Archäolgie und Seismologie: La regione vesuviana dal 62 al 79 d.C. Problemi archeologici e sismologici. Colloquium Boscoreale 1993* (Munich: 1995).

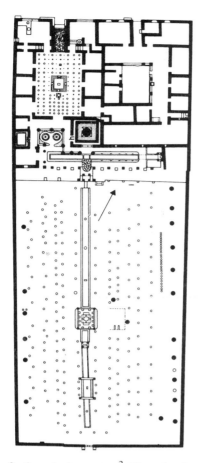

Figure 73 Plan of the "miniature villa" in the Via dell'Abbondanza (II 2.5). The garden of the relatively small atrium house was redesigned to imitate the grounds of a villa in miniature, with pergolas, fountains, porticos, and so on.

fictional character.[3] The sloping lot covers almost an entire *insula*, more than two-thirds of which is taken up by the garden. When viewed from the bottom of the garden, the living quarters appear mounted on a platform reminiscent of a *basis villae* (foundation wall; Cicero, *Letters to Quintus* 3.1.5). The structure is an instance of renovation in an older, medium-sized atrium house, which in the final period of the town's existence had a tavern occupying the front section. After the earthquake the house underwent

[3] For more on the subject see Spinazzola, *Pompei alla luce degli scavi nuovi*, vol. 1, pp. 369ff; A. Maiuri, *La casa di Loreio Tiburtino e la villa di Diomede in Pompei, I monumenti italiani*, ser. 2, fasc. 1 (Rome: 1947). The voluminous literature includes E. D. van Buren, *MemAmAc*, 12 (1935): 151–152; Jucker, *Vom Verhältnis der Römer zur bildenden Kunst*, pp. 28ff.; Schefold, *Die Wände Pompejis*, pp. 50ff.; H. Drerup, *RM*, 66 (1959): 164–165, and *MarbWPr* (1959), p. 14; H. Kähler, *Rom und seine Welt* (Munich: 1960), pp. 217ff.; F. Rakob in T. Kraus, ed., *Das römishce Weltreich* (Berlin: 1967), pp.184–185 and no. 85; Boethius and Ward-Perkins, *Etruscan and Roman Architecture*, pp. 315–316; McKay, *House, Villas and Palaces*, pp. 44–45; Castrén, *Ordo populusque*, p. 184; La Rocca et al., *Guida archeologica di Pompei*, pp. 240–241. Compare Jashemski's detailed discussion (with good documentation of the sculpture), *The Gardens of Pompeii*, vol. 1 (New Rochelle, N.Y.: 1979), p. 45; vol. 2 (New Rochelle, N.Y.; 1993), pp. 78–83. If the seal found in the first *cubiculum* to the left of the entrance (Spinazzola, *Pompei alla luce degli scavi nuovi*, vol. 1, p. 369 and fig. 414) is any indication, the house could have belonged to a D. Octavius Quartio, of whom nothing else is known (Della Corte, *Case e abitanti di Pompei*, 3rd ed. [Rome: 1965], pp. 370–371, no. 800, with fantastic combinations based on the inscriptions on the walls; Castrén *Ordo populusque*, p. 199, no. 285); F. B. Sear, *Roman Wall and Vault Mosaics, RM*, Ergänzungsheft 23 (Heidelberg: 1977), p. 93. F. Jung, "Gebaute Bilder," *Antike Kunst*, 27 (1984): 106ff.

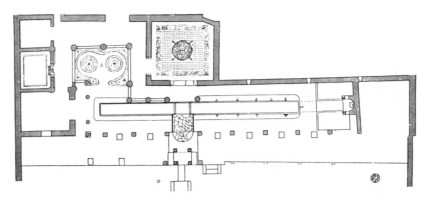

Figure 74   Plan of the terrace at the "miniature villa." Several elements of villa architecture are combined here in such a small space that they partly overlap.

extensive remodeling, most of it concentrated on the garden and the rooms adjacent to it. This work was not yet completed at the time of the eruption.[4]

The main room or *tablinum* behind the atrium was replaced by a kind of truncated peristyle, leading to a large, almost square dining room (*triclinium*, with three couches) on the left, and to two smaller rooms, one containing a shrine (*sacellum*), to the right. The plaster-covered columns of varying diameters stand at irregular intervals determined by the adjoining rooms. This truncated peristyle connects—but also collides and competes—with two further rows of roof supports, bringing utter confusion into the ground plan. A regular porch (*pronaos*) in front of the shrine has two columns between piers with engaged columns. The pier on the garden side is flush with a row of sturdy brick supports for the more than sixty-five-foot-long pergola extending across the rear of the house (fig. 75). The pergola shades a small ornamental canal, only about three feet wide, which runs along the axis of the shrine; it is spanned by two bridge-like structures and ends in a *biclinium* (dining area with two couches) with a fountain at the other end of the terrace.[5] We know from the collection of statues found here that the ensemble re-created in miniature the type of water-course (*euripus* or *nilus*) already popular in the villas of Cicero's era.[6] A surviving example on a monumental scale is the Canopus at Hadrian's Villa.[7]

A total of five elements derived from villa architecture and reduced to miniature size are thus combined and compressed, sometimes one inside the other, onto a terrace that is only twenty-two feet wide: (1) the truncated peristyle with the *triclinium* and day rooms (*diaetae*); (2) the shrine; (3) an aedicula to Artemis behind the fountain and above a *nymphaeum* (discussed below); (4) the watercourse associated with the pergola; and (5) the *biclinium* with the fountain-aedicula (fig. 76). All five are components of the expansive type

---

4   Maiuri, *L'ultima fase di Pompei*, pp. 152ff.

5   Paintings of villas suggest that such miniature bridges were extremely popular on the grounds. A watercourse (*euripus*) almost large enough for a villa is found at the Praedia of Julia Felix (II 4.3). Schefold, *Die Wände Pompejis*, pp. 53–54; La Rocca et al., *Guida archeologica di Pompei*, p. 244, with ground plan; H. Döhl, *Plastik aus Pompeji* (unpublished *Habilitation*, University of Göttingen, 1976), p. 101.

6   Cicero, *Ad Quintum fratem* 3.7.7 and *De Legibus* 2.2. Grimal, *Les jardins romains*, pp. 296ff. The Villa of the Pisones in Herculaneum offers two examples; see Crema, *L'architettura Romana*, p. 232, fig. 251; D. Mustilli, *RenAccNap*, new series, 31 (1956): 77ff.; Drerup, *MarbWPr* (1959), p. 3. Further examples can be found in Rakob, *RM*, 71 (1964): 182ff.; especially fig. 9.

7   S. Aurigemma, *Villa Adriana* (Rome: 1961), pp. 100ff.; Rakob in Kraus, ed., *Das römische Weltreich*, pp. 190ff. on fig. 30. Compare W. L. Macdonald, *Hadrian's Villa and Its Legacy* (New York and London: 1995), pp. 108ff.

Figure 75 An old photograph of the terrace at the "miniature villa," showing the collection of garden statuettes (now missing) lined up along the watercourse (*euripus*) spanned by a little bridge. The whole terrace is surmounted by a pergola stretching from a small shrine to Isis at one end to two masonry couches at the other. The paths are too narrow to permit two people to stroll side by side or in groups, an integral feature of the Roman villa.

of villa that opened up the house to the surrounding views and landscape and had become popular by the mid-first century B.C. at the latest.[8] The villas of Pliny the Younger are good examples of this type, as are some of the excavated houses in Campania and those depicted in wall paintings at Pompeii.[9] On the terrace of this particular house, however, the various components are squeezed into such a small space that two people cannot walk next to each other under the pergola without running up against a fountain, little bridge, pillar, or post at every turn, or tripping over the statuettes in the grass. A portion of the architecture has lost its original function.

The sense of constriction is increased by the excess of decorative painting and statuary. In the large *triclinium* there are two friezes above a wide panel painted to look like expensive multicolored marble incrustations.[10] A raised curtain painted in at the top of the picture is intended to heighten the illusion that the friezes are valuable Greek originals, and it gives the room the aura of a *pinacotheca* (fig. 77). The upper frieze (approximately two and a half feet tall) shows the labors of Hercules—probably following a Hellenistic model; the

[8] Noack and Lehmann-Hartleben, *Baugeschichtliche Untersuchungen*, pp. 205–206; D. Mustilli, *RenAccNap*, 31 (1956): 91ff.; Drerup, *MarbWPr* (1959), p. 9, where the typological "development," however, is in my view given too much emphasis. Clarke, *The Houses of Roman Italy*, p. 19; Mielsch, *Die römische Villa*, pp. 49ff.

[9] Pliny, *Epistulae* 2.17 and 5.6; Förtsch, *Archäologischer Kommentar zu den Villenbriefen*. Compare K. Lehmann-Hartleben's edition with commentary, *Lettere scelte con commento archeologico* (Florence: 1936), pp. 42ff.

[10] Spinazzola, *Pompeii alla luce degli scavi nuovi*, vol. 1, p. 390, fig. 443; vol. 2, pp. 973ff, plates 90–96. Compare Jucker, *Vom Verhältnis der Römer zur bildenden Kunst*, p. 28.

Figure 76   Masonry couches at the "miniature villa," with a "view" over the *euripus*. In the foreground one can see the slanted surfaces on which mattresses were placed. Behind them are an aedicula and two frescos with mythological motifs designed to look like framed paintings.

smaller frieze below contains scenes from the *Iliad*. This room, distinguished from others in the house by its very elaborate decoration, offered occupants a view through the Artemis aedicula and the lower part of the garden to the city and mountains beyond [...]. The *sacellum*, set off by two columns between piers with engaged columns, is also painted elaborately in the fourth style, this time depicting a wall. The figure of a priest of Isis on one of the inner walls and the diptych of Diana and Actaeon on the façade (along with the Egyptian terracottas found in the little garden in front of it) all suggest that the shrine was devoted to Isis/Diana. Her image probably stood in the niche on the back wall.[11] The architect had to dispense with a gable for the shrine, however, since it would have interfered with the pergola.

Small shrines, sometimes located in a garden, were quite common at larger villas; one need only think of the "Amaltheion" that Cicero so admired on the country estate of his friend Atticus in Epirus.[12] In the house we are concerned with here, the shrine was used as a kind of gazebo, from which one could look out the door toward the terrace and the watercourse, or through the window on the other side toward the lower part of the garden.

---

[11]   Spinazzola, *Pompei alla luce degli scavi nuovi*, vol. 1, p. 383, figs. 432ff.

[12]   Cicero, *Att.* 1.16.15 and 17; 1.13.1; *De Legibus* 2.3.7. Compare the shrine to Hercules in the villa of Pollus Felix near Sorrento: Statius, *Silvae*, 3.1. For excavated villas, such as the villa on Brioni, see A. Gnirs, *ÖJh*, 18 (1915): insert, 99ff. For the use of a shrine as a day room (*diaetae*) compare P. Williams-Lehmann, *Roman Wall Paintings from Boscoreale* (New York: 1953), p. 107, with further examples of "shrines" at villas on p. 123.

Figure 77 Wall painting in the reception room opening onto the terrace at the "miniature villa" (after Spinazzola; compare fig. 74). This *triclinium* was the most opulently decorated room in the house, and the owner could display his taste and learning in the frescos. The lower part of the wall imitates costly multicolored marble; it is surmounted by a frieze with scenes from Homer's *Iliad*. The main zone depicts the labors of Hercules. A painted raised "curtain" above these scenes is intended to suggest that they are valuable "paintings" that need to be protected from light, just as in some modern museum displays.

The statuary along the "banks" of the watercourse was adapted to the small format of the architecture.[13] The muses mounted on bases (fig. 78) are of normal statuette size—although there was apparently never a complete set—but the various figures in a seated or recumbent position and scattered about the grass are definitely miniatures (see fig. 75). They are also associated with a variety of different themes. The recumbent river god and the Sphinx are part of the usual watercourse decor; the herms were usually placed along garden paths. The little seated satyr belongs in a Dionysiac park, while the two sets of figures depicting hounds and quarry belong in a *paradeisos* (preserve for wild animals). The statuettes of the muses themselves belong in a *museion* (museum) of the type so frequently found at villas.[14] To this collection we should also add the little satyr in the pose of Atlas supporting the fountain, and there must have been a statue of Artemis/Diana intended as a cult image for the aedicula, since its gable bears a portrait of her (fig. 79).

[13]   Spinazzola, *Pompei alla luce degli scavi nuovi*, vol. 1, pp. 396ff., figs. 454–457, and 461; Döhl, *Plastik aus Pompeji*, pp. 149–150. The "boy with a goose" that has been turned into a *herakliskos*, or "little Hercules," is an interesting example of a change of taste on the part of the owner. The simple and familiar myth made the content of the Hellenistic masterpiece accessible. The bronze head between the claws of the Sphinx, which serves as a water spout, also creates a mythological link. Compare *Aquileia e Milano: Antichità Altoadriatiche*, vol. 4 (Udine: 1973), pp. 105ff., fig. 7; *Arte e civiltà nell'Italia settentrionale*, vol. 1 (Bologna: 1964), plate 28, no. 62; vol. 2 (Bologna: 1965), p. 146, no. 224 (I am indebted to H. Pflug for this reference).

[14]   Compare the "museum" in the park of Varro's villa near Casinum, which one should probably imagine as no more than a porticus decorated with the appropriate statues: Varro, *Res rusticate* 3.5.8. Compare also K. Schefold, *Pompejanische Malerei* (Basel: 1952), where the term is, however, understood in a very broad sense. I am indebted to R. Neudecker for pointing out to me a small poem found on the shaft of a herm that announces the equipping of such a garden "museum" at a villa on the Via Appia: see R. Paribeni, *NSc* (1926): 284.

Figure 78 Statuettes of two muses that stood along the *euripus* at the "miniature villa." They are copies of two statuettes from a famous Hellenistic group of all nine muses. As in the case of copies of paintings, such decorative statuary was intended to awaken associations of "Greek sculpture" and "art collections" in visitors.

In addition to these numerous sculptures there was no lack of wall paintings. The fountain aedicula, lined with pumice stone, is flanked by two large mythological scenes, one depicting Pyramus and Thisbe and the other a seated Narcissus [...].[15] An artist named Lucius proudly signed his name to them, although their quality is undistinguished. These frescos in the manner of panel paintings call to mind the passionate art enthusiast and collector Hortensius, who at his villa Tusculum made a shrine (*aedem fecit in Tusculano suo*) for Kydias' painting of the Argonauts (Pliny, *Natural History* 35.130). And there was still more: the entire length of the wall (over twenty-three feet long) to which the pergola was attached was covered with frescos depicting a variety of scenes—Orpheus charming the beasts, a hunting scene in a *paradeisos*, and Venus hovering above a shell on the sea.[16] These paintings and the statues of the muses on elaborate plinths were intended to give the airy pergola the flair of a lavish portico.

All this decoration and elaboration, however, represents only the upper level of the plan. From the terrace a flight of steps led down to the garden some three feet below, which measured approximately 180 by 95 feet. It was enclosed by a high wall and, like the terrace, bisected by a type of *euripus*. Pergolas and rows of shrubs and trees were arranged parallel to it. Similar paths ran along the brook on Varro's estate near Casinum (*Rustica* 3.9). The remains of a marble

---

15   Spinazzola, *Pompei alla luce degli scavi nuovi*, vol. 1, pp. 402ff., figs. 458ff.

16   Ibid., p. 391, figs. 444, 445; Schefold, *Die Wände Pompejis*, p. 53, no. 1. [...]

Figure 79 Aedicula with a *nymphaeum* in the garden of the "miniature villa." The aedicula, which was accessible from the garden terrace, originally contained a statue of Artemis, the goddess of hunting. The goddess was placed there in part as an allusion to the hunting preserves connected with great landed estates. The lower story of the structure, accessible only from the garden, is fitted out as a miniature *nymphaeum*. Such a composite, multipurpose structure is characteristic of the overall architectural and decorative style of the house.

table indicate that there was a round seating area, and a recumbent hermaphrodite must be the sole remnant of a group of sculptures placed in the borders.[17] As mentioned above, the *euripus* ran not down the middle of the garden but rather along the axis of the large dining room decorated to look like a *pinacotheca*. This canal was interrupted or spanned by several structures, and was also linked to the terrace pergola by a hybrid two-story construction, the upper portion of which we have already encountered as the Artemis aedicula. The lower story contained a miniature *nymphaeum*[18] with a fountain connected

[17]   Spinazzola, *Pompei allu luce degli scavi nuovi*, vol. 1, p. 411, figs. 470 and 478. (Figure 80 of this book shows the sculpture as placed by the excavators in a decorative but false position.) This is reminiscent of the ivy-covered statues that resemble gardeners at the villa of Cicero's brother (Cicero, *Ad Quintum fratrem* 3.1.5). Compare Jucker, *Vom Verhältnis der Römer zur bildenden Kunst*, p. 43, and M. Kunze, "Griechische Einflüsse auf Kunst und Gesellschaft im Rom der späten Republik und der frühen Kaiserzeit," in E.C. Weiskopf, ed., *Hellenistische Poleis*, vol. 3 (Berlin: 1974), p. 1611.

[18]   Spinazzola, *Pompei alla luce degli scavi nuovi*, vol. 1, p. 409, figs. 467–468.

to two water spouts: a mask of Oceanus and an Eros with masks sitting above the steps down which the water flowed.[19] There were also fish painted on the upper basin. To one side of the fountain Actaeon is shown watching Diana bathing, and as if all these were not enough mythological trimmings for one small fountain, on the narrow sides the artist added some small framed landscape scenes with shrines to Apollo and Diana. The room itself measures only about 9.7 by 3.2 feet, and with the fountain in it does not have space for even one couch.

At about the same time that this house was being remodeled, an owner of one of the terrace houses in the theater quarter (VIII 2.28) was building a *nymphaeum* on his property, in the form of a grotto just large enough to use and carefully placed to take advantage of the mountain view across the bay.[20] Thus the borrowing of elements from villa architecture proceeded in steps, and models for some features could already be found within the town.

To return to the miniature villa: the more than 160-foot-long water-course below the *nymphaeum* is divided into several sections. The water flowed first into a channel approximately 80 feet long with three jets of water spaced along it. Below this was a large pool lined with marble containing a square fountain in the middle, with steps on each side for the water to flow over and bases for twelve statuettes or vases around the edges (fig. 80).[21] Only 12 feet further on the channel is spanned by a decorative baldachin bridge, much too small for actual use. Below the bridge the watercourse then shifts direction slightly to point toward the gate in the wall at the bottom of the garden. Clearly there was already a path up to the house from this gate, and the watercourse was designed to run alongside it. By continuing his watercourse down this far, the owner also enabled passers-by to catch a glimpse of it through the gate. The lower channel below the canopied bridge is interrupted once, too, by a wider basin. Both it and the square pool higher up were probably shaded by arbors.

Thus the watercourse actually consisted of a series of separate pools of varying sizes connected by overflow troughs.[22] Once this has been recognized, the function of the pools becomes clear: they were fish ponds of the type popular at large seaside villas. Most likely they were painted in distinctive colors.[23] Varro and Cicero mention both the profits that could be made by raising fish and also the grotesque excesses to which some of these *piscinarii* were led by their passion for their favorite breeds.[24] Fish ponds represent another feature of villa life imported from the courts of Eastern potentates.[25]

In the case of the miniature villa in Pompeii, the clever arrangement of the fish ponds gave the owner a second watercourse! As we have seen, this excess was characteristic of the villa owner. We find the same principle of overkill with

---

[19] For the fountain figures compare B. Kapossy, *Brunnenfiguren der hellenistischen und römischen Zeit* (Zurich: 1969), pp. 40 and 60. For more on the popularity of *nymphaea* at villas, see Grimal, *Les jardins romains*, pp. 304ff.

[20] Noack and Lehmann-Hartleben, *Baugeschichtliche Untersuchungen*, pp. 70ff., 186, and 221ff.; N. Neuerburg, "L'architettura delle fontane e dei ninfei nell'Italia antica," *RenAccNap*, 5 (1965): 31, no. 35 and fig. 49.

[21] Spinazzola, *Pompei alla luce degli scavi nuovi*, vol. 1, pp. 410ff.

[22] Ibid., p. 412, fig. 472.

[23] Compare the basin painted with fish in the House of Epidius Sabinus discussed by Schefold, *Die Wände Pompejis*, p. 237.

[24] See the entry under "piscinia" in *RE*, vol. 20, part 2 (1950). Archeological examples are cited by G. Schmidt, *Il livello antico del Mar Tirreno* (Rome: 1972); Mielsch, *Die römische Villa*, pp. 23ff.

[25] D'Arms, *Romans on the Bay of Naples*, p. 41.

Figure 80 Marble fountain in the lower part of the watercourse at the "miniature villa" (compare fig. 74). This fountain interrupts the flow of the *euripus* and is too large in proportion to the other elements of the garden architecture. In the background a further aedicula is visible.

some miniaturized elements of villa architecture in the garden as on the terrace; in both places too many separate structures have been crammed into too small a space. Instead of distributing the decorative features around his garden—as the villa model would have suggested and his good-sized lot allowed—he first turned his fish ponds into a *euripus* and then added the *nymphaeum*, marble fountain, baldachin bridge, and pergola. His method did have one advantage, of course: it enabled him to survey the full complement of architectural splendors in his garden from the door of his dining room. Furthermore, the perspective made the entire layout seem larger than it was (although perhaps too much emphasis has been placed on such effects in recent studies).[26]

In this manner a country villa was re-created in miniature in Pompeii during the last decade of the town's existence. Perspectives actually intended for wider views are cunningly inverted—architectural elements borrowed from villas in the country or by the seaside are crammed together into a Walt Disney world. The elaborate garden is wholly out of proportion to the quite modest size of the actual living quarters; the remodeled section of the house is also characterized by a poor sense of proportion and a low level of artistic skill, in contrast to the "Neronian" wall paintings in the fourth style in the older section. The owner, eager to imitate the lavish world of villas he so clearly admired, preferred quantity over quality.

[26] In my view Drerup and Rakob overestimate the aesthetic component by interpreting the rigid perspectival arrangement as a stylistic phenomenon. If one imagines the aedicula filled by a statue or even a statuette similar in size to the two muses, then it would surely have blocked the view of the more distant elements in the series. And the fact that the lower part of the garden *euripus* is angled makes one even more skeptical: Drerup, *RM*, (1959) and *MarbWPr* (1959); Rakob, in T. Kraus, ed., *Das römische Weltreich* (Berlin: 1967).

Secondary Source 2.7   John R. Clarke, 'The villa as model for middle-class houses'

(Source: Clarke, J.R. (1991) *The Houses of Roman Italy 100 B.C.–A.D. 250: Ritual, Space, and Decoration*, Berkeley and Oxford, University of California Press, pp. 23–5)

Not every Roman lived in an ancestral domus or splashy villa. Particularly after the middle of the first century of our era at Pompeii and Herculaneum a great number of city houses were remodeled to imitate villas, but in miniature. This phenomenon, examined in depth by Paul Zanker,[1] often resulted in packing a great number of disparate and uncoordinated villa features into modest spaces. But instead of clearly framed views of distinct features like the fountains, statuary, and swimming pool at Oplontis, the visitor found a hodge-podge giving out mixed signals about the function and meaning of both individual space and the house as a whole.

Zanker cites the House of Octavius Quartio [...] as the prime exemplar of the "miniature villa."[2] The view from the fauces ends not in a tablinum, for there is none, but in a doorway leading to a three-sided portico surrounding a little garden. Having reached this area of the house, the visitor has entered a realm of mixed metaphors and hyperbole. To the left is the principal oecus, its larger entry focused, by means of a pavilion, upon a long canal that runs the length of the building lot. It is fed by a second, transverse canal running between two unusual spaces: at the west end is a small pavilion-like white room (perhaps a diaeta) outfitted as a little shrine, or *sacellum*, while at the east end there is an outdoor *biclinium* (a dining area with two couches). Zanker counts many built elements taken from villa architecture: the canal, or *euripus*, allusive to the Nile; the rear peristyle with oecus; the little temple or *aedicula* with images of Diana; and the biclinium with fountain. Add the many small-scale statues along the upper canal evoking gods as diverse as Isis, Dionysus, and the Muses, plus five different painted cycles on the exterior walls [...], two painted friezes from different epic sagas in the oecus, allusions to Isis in the sacellum, and one has an excellent example of the kind of bad taste that Cicero had decried a hundred years before.[3] While Cicero, aristocratic patrician, rejected statues of bacchants, Mercury, Mars, and Saturn as thematically unsuitable for an exedra dedicated to cultural pursuits, the owner of the House of Octavius Quartio built miniature grottoes, fountains, sanctuaries, and canals—and adorned them with statuary and frescoes allusive to a whole panoply of mythic cycles and religions.[4]

How did the ancient viewer experience such miniature villas? From the point of entrance into the peristyle garden, at the tablinum position, a person could walk either to the right or left. To the left he or she would encounter the smaller side entrance of the great oecus, probably used for both reception of business clients and convivial feasts. To the right the visitor would pass to the diaetae/sacellum, taking in the paintings both within the room and on its exterior. From here the view of the upper canal focuses on the biclinium. Statuary lined both sides of the canals, as it filled the little peristyle's garden. Making his or her way through this crowded Disneyland the viewer might also notice the big frescoes on the exterior walls. The next goal would probably be the oecus itself,

---

[1]   Paul Zanker, "Die Villa als Vorbild des späten pompeijanischen Wohngeschmacks," *Jahrbuch des deutschen archäologischen Instituts* 94 (1979): 460–523.

[2]   Zanker, "Villa als Vorbild," 470–480.

[3]   Cicero *Ad Fam.* 7.23.2.

[4]   For a critique of Zanker's position, see Jung, "Gebaute Bilder," 71–73.

commanding the carefully arranged view of the lower garden and its three-stage canal. A little bridge crosses the upper canal to reach the pavilion that marks the beginning of this long axis; beneath it, on the lower level, hides a little grotto sacred to Diana. Characteristically, the grotto is too small for a person to enter; it is an allusion to the great grottoes that graced large villas. Similarly, the canal may have doubled as a fish pond, the *piscinae* so important to Cicero and other villa owners.[5] One's walk though the lower garden included other surprises: the elaborate fountains that punctuate the canal and a statue of a hermaphrodite.

Other examples of villa imitations cited by Zanker, although less extensive than the complex of the House of Octavius Quartio, nevertheless document a new use of space stemming from new desires on the part of the patrons. If what had meaning in the large villas sinks to mere decoration in Pompeian gardens, it is because a new class, that of the entrepreneurial freedmen, was socially most active in this period. Like the rich former slave Trimalchio in Petronius's *Satyricon*,[6] these new bourgeoisie imitated the wealthy aristocratic upper class in their desire for the material trappings of wealth. The garden architecture, sanctuaries, fountains and resting spots, picture galleries, real and painted statues, landscape views, and even painted wild animal parks (*paradeisoi*) were all ways of possessing a bit of the luxury villa.[7]

Secondary Source 2.8   Verity Platt, 'Viewing, desiring, believing: confronting the divine in a Pompeian house'

(Source: Platt, V. (2002) *Viewing, Desiring, Believing: Confronting the Divine in a Pompeian House*, Association of Art Historians, Oxford and Malden MA, Blackwell Publishers, pp. 87–101, 107–11)

> Why did I see the thing? Why did I make my eyes guilty?
> Why, thoughtlessly, did I harbour knowledge of wrongdoing?
> Actaeon unwittingly beheld the naked Diana ...[1]

(Ovid, *Tristia* II.103–5)

The pleasures of voyeurism are vicariously experienced in a broad range of contexts in Roman art. One thinks of the observers painted within mythological tableaux in the frescoes of Campania, or the *frisson* created for the viewer of the Warren Cup by the boy's head peering round a door in the background.[2] The

---

[5]   John H. D'Arms, *Romans on the Bay of Naples* (Cambridge, Mass., 1970), 44.

[6]   John H. D'Arms, *Commerce and Social Standing in Ancient Rome* (Cambridge, Mass., 1981), 97–120; Wallace-Hadrill, "Social Structure," 43–44, 97.

[7]   Zanker, "Villa als Vorbild," 519–522.

[1]   'Cur aliquid vidi? Cur noxia lumina feci?
       Cur imprudenti cognita culpa mihi?
       Inscius Actaeon vidit sine veste Dianam ...'

[2]   For instance, the women observing the courtship of Mars and Venus in the House of M. Lucretius Fronto (Pompeii V.4.a), the townspeople crowding round Theseus and the dead Minotaur in the House of Gavius Rufus (VII.2.16), or the women watching the fall of Icarus in the House of the Priest Amandus (1.7.7). For a discussion of onlookers in Pompeian wall-painting, see D. Michel, 'Bermerkungen über Zuschauerfiguren in pompejanischen sogenannten Tafelbildern', *La regione sotterata dal Vesuvio: Studie e prospettive* (*Atti del Convegno Internazionale*, Nov. 11–15, 1979), Naples, 1982, pp. 537–98. For the Warren Cup, see J.R. Clarke, 'The Warren Cup and the Context for Representations of Male-to-Male Lovemaking in Augustan and Early Julio-Claudian Art', *Art Bulletin* 75 (1993), pp. 275–94; *Looking at Lovemaking*, Berkeley and London, 1998, pp. 61–78; J. Pollini, 'The Warren Cup: Homoerotic Love and Symposial Rhetoric in Silver', *Art Bulletin* 81 (1999), pp. 21–52.

voyeur within the image reflects the external viewer, so drawing one into the scene there depicted, yet simultaneously emphasizing our distance from and superiority to the thing beheld. We have the power to accept or reject the invitation; to view voyeuristically is to feel that one has a certain control over what is seen.[3]

However, as Ovid warns us in my epigraph, to view is not always to be a safely objective observer; sometimes, the object which one views can look back, and, caught in the act of observing, the viewer's vicarious position is undermined: we are actively implicated in the events which we behold. Actaeon's fate is not only a result of the fact that he saw what he should not have seen, but that Diana beheld him in the act of viewing. And, as Ovid insinuates with a hint of self-dramatization, myth and reality can mirror each other in disturbing ways.[4] As Bartsch's study of theatricality in the age of Nero has demonstrated, the relationship between performer and audience was often subverted in Imperial Roman society, to the extent that 'the categories of spectacle and spectator lose all stability.'[5] In such a culture, the gaze holds both power and danger for him who beholds, and who is beheld. The meeting of gazes can be an occasion fraught with anxiety about the confrontation of Self and Other and the potential for the onset of desire, shame, violence and the loss of autonomy.[6]

[3] 'The spectatorial role of a boy voyeur [on the Warren cup] intellectually connects the viewer of the *scyphus* with its engraved imagery, while giving him a sense of power over the spectacle that he beholds', Pollini, op. cit. (note 2), p. 39. For a study of voyeuristic power in the cinema, see J. Ellis, *Visible Fictions*, New York, 1992, pp. 45ff.

[4] Arguably, the boy-spectator on the Warren cup is also a potential participant in the action; both Clarke and Pollini suggest that he may be the next partner for the older lover portrayed on side B. Petronius also explores the way in which the voyeur is implicated in the actions he observes, in the Quartilla episode of the *Satyrica* (16–26), where the categories of spectator and performer in pornographic entertainment are broken down into general orgiastic chaos. Moreover, whereas Ovid links myth to reality through simile and exemplum, Petronius blurs the distinction between myth and reality to an even greater extent in the self-presentation of his protagonist Encolpius (see G.B. Conte, *The Hidden Author: An Interpretation of Petronius' Satyricon*, Berkely and Los Angeles, 1996).

[5] S. Bartsch, *Actors in the Audience: Theatricality and Doublespeak from Nero to Hadrian*, Harvard, 1994, p. 11. For further explorations of theatricality in Roman society, see B. Bergmann, 'The House of the Tragic Poet in Pompeii', *Art Bulletin*, June 1994, vol. 76, no. 2, pp. 199–218; B. Bermann (ed.), *The Art of Ancient Spectacle,* Yale, 1999; C. Edwards. 'Beware of Imitations: theatre and the subversion of Imperial identity', J. Elsner and J. Masters (eds), *Reflections of Nero: culture, history and representation*, London, 1994, pp. 81–97; C.P. Jones, 'Dinner Theatre', in W.J. Slater (ed.), *Dining in a Classical Context*, Michigan, 1991, pp. 185–98; A.O. Koloski-Ostrow, 'Violent stages in two Pompeian houses: Imperial taste, aristocratic response, and messages of male control', in *Naked Truths*, (eds A.O. Koloski-Ostrow and C.L. Lyons), London, 1997, pp. 243–66.

[6] In reading the images I discuss in this paper as a confrontation between Self and Other, I apply art-historical methods inspired by Lacanian theory of the Gaze and the psychological relationship between subject and object laid down in *The Four Fundamental Concepts of Psychoanalysis* (ed. J-A. Miller, trans. A. Sheridan, New York, 1977). The relationship of the self-emanating glance to the autonomous, externalized gaze of the world beyond creates a bipolar scopic field in which the subject's consciousness is created and defined by his status as the '*speculum mundi*' (p. 72); 'In the scopic field, the gaze is outside, I am looked at, that is to say, I am a picture.' (p. 106). The confrontation of the Self with an Other which embodies the externalized gaze by which he defines himself – the meeting of glance and gaze – is thus an occasion fraught with anxiety for the subject. It is such a confrontation which, I will argue, is explored by the paintings in the portico of Pompeii II.2.2–5.

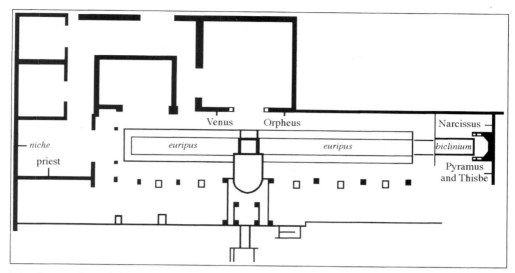

[Plate] 26   Plan of the portico area of II.2.2–5 (V. Platt).

In this paper I will explore the way in which the complexities of the gaze are explored by a series of 4th Style mythological paintings in Pompeii II.2.2–5 (called variously the House of Octavius Quartio, or Loreius Tiburtinus).[7] Here, issues of desire related to the power of naturalistic art are provocatively intertwined with religious iconography and the dimension of the symbolic in a manner which challenges and problematizes the viewer's response to the images with which he is presented. Architecture and decorative scheme work together so that the implicit dangers of voyeurism are presented as a series of tableaux sited within the world of mythology, which are ultimately made more relevant to the spectator through their juxtaposition with the imagery of cult. This creates a dynamic dialectic between viewer and image which raises interesting questions about the relationship between naturalistic art and religious modes of viewing. My reading of the images engages with the normative, male Roman viewer. Implicit counter-cultural viewings which take gender and class into account would doubtless function in different ways, but due to lack of space I concentrate on the way in which the images comment on visuality itself through the engagement of potential male heterosexual and homosexual desires.

At the back of Pompeii II.2.2–5, overlooking a long *euripus* (an ornamental water channel) adorned with sacro-idyllic features, a series of mythological paintings are arranged around a raised portico. This colonnaded area itself has a smaller *euripus* which stretches from a fountain in an *aedicula* flanked by dining couches (a *biclinium*) on the east side, to a small room on the west

---

[7]   The name Octavius Quartio comes from a bronze seal discovered in one of the cubicula of the house, and is associated with the owner of the house by Spinazzola (*Pompeii alla luce degli scavi nuovi* vol.I, Rome, 1953, pp. 369ff.); Loreius Tiburtinus, the name favoured by Della Corte, is based on fifteen electoral inscriptions on the house walls facing the Via Abbondanza, so, he argues, associating the house with the Tiburtini, one of the oldest and most wealthy families in Pompeii (M. Della Corte, *Una famiglia dei Sacerdoti d'Iside: M.M. Lorei Tiburtini*, Pompeii, 1930; *Pompeii: The New Excavations (Houses and Inhabitants)*, Pompei, 1943, pp. 92–9, no. 493; *Les nouvelles fouilles et l'amphithéâtre*, Pompeii, 1944, p. 91). There is no firm evidence to link either name with the owner of the house. For further information and bibliography, see K. Schefold, *Die Wände Pompeiis*, Berlin, 1957, p. 52, V. Tran Tam Tinh, *Essai sur Le Culte D'Isis a Pompéi*, Paris 1965, p. 43–5, G. Pugliese Carratelli & I. Baldassarre (eds), *Pompei: Pitture e Mosaici*, vol. 3, Rome, 1991: pp. 100ff., and P. Zanker, *Pompeii: Public and Private Life*, London, 1998, pp. 145–56.

[Plate] 27   The *aedicule* at the east end of the portico, framed by the Narcissus panel on the left, and the Pyramus and Thisbe panel on the right. Photograph: Soprintendenza Archaeologia de Pompei.

decorated with Isiac images (plate 26). The *aedicula* is framed by an image of Narcissus entranced by his reflection on the north side, and Thisbe committing suicide over the dying body of Pyramus on the south, while a lion runs into the distance (plate 27). The entrance to the Isiac chamber is framed by the figure of Actaeon attacked by his hounds on the north, and a crouching nude Diana on the south.

All three scenes depict a problematic confrontation, a meeting of gazes, between two individuals (in the case of Narcissus, between himself and his reflection), which results in death. The confrontations between self and other, lover and beloved which are presented in the panels of Narcissus and Pyramus and Thisbe, are reflected and magnified at the other end of the portico by the confrontation between Man and God in the larger forms of Diana and Actaeon, each isolated in a long panel flanking the doorway. Together the three scenes constitute a mythological and visual commentary on the power of the gaze. Moreover, each of these scenes is related to its context in such a way that is draws in the viewer, triangulating the relationship between subject and object so that we, as Ovid, will potentially fall prey to the dangers of viewing itself.[8]

---

[8]   For a discussion of the triangulation which occurs between lover, beloved and spectator in romantic art, see M. Bettini, *Portrait of the Lover*, Berkeley, 1999.

[Plate] 28   Panel depicting the artist's signature *Lucius pinxit* ('Lucius painted this'), Pompeii II.2.2–5. Photograph: Soprintendenza Archaeologia di Pompei.

All three myths can be found in close proximity in Books III–IV of the *Metamorphoses*.[9] As we do not find any visual images of Pyramus and Thisbe prior to the publication of the poem in the early first century AD, it is fair to say that Ovid was probably an inspiration at some stage in the selection and creation of the decorative scheme.[10] However, the images show significant departures from the literary text which demonstrates that the artist has not simply created a set of illustrations, but has independently selected and portrayed a set of mythological encounters as a unified group closely tied to their actual context.[11] That the painter of these images was conscious, and proud, of his role as their creator is demonstrated by the fact that he has signed his work (the only known example of a painter's signature in Pompeii) with the inscription '*LUCIUS PINXIT*', on the stone couch below the Pyramus and Thisbe panel (plate 28).[12] With the role of the artist thus emphasized, our role as viewer, and the viewing process itself, are thrown into relief. It is almost as if the artist, creating his paintings to be displayed and observed, is viewing us, as we view a set of images which are themselves about viewing; thus artist and spectator are implicated in the complex, anxiety-producing dialectic between observer and observed which the images explore.

The context of the paintings is one of *otium*; the extravagant use of water in the *euripus*, the *biclinium* and the long, carefully designed garden all evoke an atmosphere of cultured leisure. But the house is also self-consciously sited within the religious and the political spheres. The sacro-idyllic structures of the garden and portico (*tempietti, aediculae* and *nymphaea*) and the room decorated with Isiac paintings point to cult and ritual more than is usual in a

---

[9]   Actaeon: *Met*. III.138–252; Narcissus: *Met* III.339–510; Pyramus and Thisbe: *Met*. IV.55–166.

[10]   Pyramus and Thisbe first appear in Western literature as a tale told by one of the Minyeides in the *Metamorphoses*, perhaps inspired, as others in Book IV, by a story in Eastern literature. Although Pyramus is also part of a visual tradition in Asia Minor as a Cilician river god, he first appears with Thisbe, as in the Ovidian narrative, on wall-paintings of the 3rd and 4th Styles in Pompeii (the House of Venus in a Bikini – I.11.6; the House of M. Lucretius Fronto – V.4.a; IX.5.14). For a more detailed discussion, see LIMC: Pyramus.

[11]   Diana is not accompanied by the nymphs who protect her in Ovid's account, and Narcissus is alone, unlike many other depictions of the myth in wall-painting, the majority of which depict him accompanied by Echo or Cupid. The painter has chosen to concentrate on each confrontation in isolation. For Narcissus and Cupid see LIMC – Narkissos 27–44. for Narcissus and Echo see LIMC – Narkissos 45–55; of the Campanian wall-paintings listed in the LIMC, sixteen depict Narcissus accompanied by Cupid, Echo, or Nymphs and eight depict him alone.

[12]   CIL.IV.7535. For a discussion of Lucius and other paintings ascribed to him, see L. Richardson, jr., *A Catalog of Identifiable Figure Painters of Ancient Pompeii, Herculanium, and Stabiae*, Baltimore and London, 2000, pp. 147–53. The author identifies Lucius as primarily a painter of large hunting scenes (plus a few mythological panels), but does not rate him as an artist, going so far as to comment on the paintings in the portico, 'It is hard to imagine why anyone would want to claim responsibility for such incompetence' (p. 147).

domestic Roman house.[13] The relief carving of a *corona civica* (the oak-leaf garland which signified imperial religious authority) above the entrance to II.2.4 suggests that the insula was owned by an *Augustalis* (a priest of the Imperial Cult). This link to the imperial court is perhaps echoed by the Iliadic frieze in the oecus of II.2.2–5, which was a popular decorative feature among municipal elites in the first century AD after it was painted in Nero's *Domus Transitoria*.[14] The paintings are thus located within a nexus of relationships in Roman society, adorning the domestic space of a family conscious of its cultural, political and religious identities on both a local and national level. The wealthy municipal Roman both controlled and was subject to the gaze of society, was himself both viewer and viewed.[15] In a culture as visually aware, and as self-conscious, as that of first-century AD Italy, it is perhaps no surprise to find in the home of a high-profile townsman an emphasis on the potential dangers of such visuality.

Unusually for 4th Style Campanian wall-painting, each confrontation is depicted stripped of the voyeuristic subsidiary characters which often crowd mythological narratives as an audience within the frame with which the viewer can identify.[16] Moreover, Narcissus is not accompanied by Echo or Cupid, unlike many other Pompeian depictions; Diana has no nymphs to protect her, in contrast to Ovid's account. Each panel, typically of the 4th Style, brings its protagonists to the frontal plane as near-life-size figures rather than dwarfing them within a sacro-idyllic landscape. The panels fill the spaces they adorn and are not accompanied by subsidiary architectural ornament. They are all linked by the motif of water (Narcissus's spring, the meeting place of Pyramus and Thisbe, the pool where Diana bathes), but in each case, the water which defines the place of confrontation is provided by the *euripus* on the portico itself, and, with the exception of Narcissus's reflective pool, is not actually portrayed within the painting. In short, there is nothing to distract the viewer from the stark image each painting presents of a static meeting of gazes which coincides with, and even creates, the moment of tragedy. The large figures are not depicted with movement and vitality but instead are frozen in mid-action, projected into the viewer's space with a force which challenges and ultimately implicates us in their fate.

The motif of the desirous gaze which brings death is anticipated and framed by a panel on the north wall of the portico, of which only the bottom half remains, depicting Orpheus playing his lyre to a lion. He, too, is in the

[handwritten margin note: is an allusion to the "metamorphosis" enacted in Ovid.]

[13]   For a more detailed discussion of the garden, see W.F. Jashemski, *The Gardens of Pompeii, Herculaneum and the Villas Destroyed by Vesuvius II*, New Rochelle, NY, 1993, pp. 73–82. Isiac images are found in several domestic settings in Pompeii (see Tran Tam Tinh, 1964, op. cit. [note 7], *passim*). However, these are usually small votive statuettes, or painted details within more generally decorative schemes, perhaps a 3rd Style trend taking its lead from Imperial fashions. As Galinsky's analysis of Augustus' Isiac decorative schemes on the Palatine shows, the depiction of ritual objects within such schemes need not signify the actual cult practice of those that commissioned them. See Galinsky, *Augustan Culture*, Princeton, 1995, pp. 184–90, and M. De Vos, *L'egittomania in pitture e mosaici romano-campani della prima età imperiale*, Leiden, 1980.

[14]   See L. Richardson, *A New Topographical Dictionary of Ancient Rome*, Baltimore and London, 1992, pp. 138–9. Nero's dining pavilion incorporated small suites of rooms, one of which was decorated with 'small scenes from the Homeric cycle very delicately executed within a rich framework' of marble revetments (p. 138). In the House of Loreius Tiburtinus, a similar frieze depicting scenes from the Iliad is positioned beneath a large frieze depicting the Trojan exploits of Hercules, above a dado frieze of *trompe l'oeil* multi-coloured marbles.

[15]   See the bibliography referred to in n.4.

[16]   For the role of onlookers, see Michel (1982) op. cit. (note 2); for Cupid, Echo and Nymphs in Narcissus images, see n. 10.

Metamorphoses, where he is depicted in Books X and XI charming the trees and beasts with his songs of the fatal desires of other mythical characters, following his failed trip to the Underworld to rescue Eurydice.[17] And Orpheus too is often associated with watery contexts.[18] His own enterprise failed, significantly, due to his fatal glance at his beloved which caused her (second) death, and, ultimately, Orpheus's own violent murder at the hands of the women he subsequently spurned. Just like Narcissus, Pyramus, Thisbe, and Actaeon, Orpheus made a fatal mistake when he 'lovingly directed his gaze' (*'flexit amans oculos'* Met. X.57), which resulted in the destruction of both himself and his beloved. Orpheus being the artist *par excellence*, his song in the portico can be read as a symbol for the work of Lucius the painter, an artistic production warning of the dangers of the desirous gaze. Beside him was a (now-lost) panel of Venus standing on a conch shell, a personification of desire itself, forever reborn as our desires shift and change, and forever fired by the amorous gaze.[19] Together on the entrance wall of the portico, Venus and Orpheus act as a kind of prologue to the scenes of tragic viewing which take place within.

The image of Narcissus is a potent expression of the complex relationship between Self and Other, lover and beloved, viewer and image (plate 29). This is demonstrated not only by Ovid's account of the myth, but also by Philostratus and Callistratus, who both use ecphrasis as a means of exploring the visual paradox inherent in an image which portrays a viewer transfixed by an image.[20] The emphasis on reflection, reciprocity and ambiguity we find in the literary accounts is here communicated by the image's complex relationship to its context, through which Narcissus presents a twofold danger to the viewer. The painting's position next to the *euripus* is a reminder that the viewer might catch

---

[17] Met. X.I–XI.84. For a discussion of the portrayal of Orpheus in Ovid's *Metamorphoses* and Virgil's 4th *Georgic*, see W.S. Anderson, 'The Orpheus of Virgil and Ovid: *flebile nescio quid*', in *Orpheus, The Metamorphoses of a Myth*, (ed. J. Warden), Toronto 1982, pp. 25–50. For a review of Orpheus' representation in art, particularly as a paradigm of the artist and lover, and evocation against the evil eye, see I.J. Jesnick, *The Image of Orpheus in Roman Mosaic*, BAR International Series 671, 1997.

[18] Orpheus's severed head famously floated down the river Hebrus and over to the island of Lesbos (Virgil, *Georgics* IV.523–27, Ovid, *Metamorphoses* XI.1–66). Visual representations often site the musician near to water, most famously, perhaps, for Romans, the monument near the Suburra referred to by Martial, which seems to have taken the form of an elaborate nymphaeum surrounded by sculptures of Orpheus and the animals: 'Orpheus, sprinkled with water droplets commands a trickling theatre of entranced savage beasts' (Ep.X.20.6). For a more detailed discussion of Orpheus in watery contexts, see Jesnick, 1997, op. cit. (note 17), pp. 14ff.

[19] C.M. Havelock (*The Aphrodite of Knidos and Her Successors: A Historical Review of the Female Nude in Greek Art*, Michigan, 1995), discusses the importance of ritual bathing to the worship of Venus, emphasizing the fact that 'Water and bathing refreshed and regenerated the goddess of sex.' (p. 24) The ever-repeated motif of Venus's birth emphasizes her role as an ever-shifting arouser and potential facilitator of *eros*. As such, she personifies what Lacan terms the *'objet a'*, the object-causing-desire which mediates between the self and its actual object of desire. Just as Venus, the *objet a* is forever shifting and unfulfilled as with the satisfaction of each particular desire, we immediately desire something else; 'Desire is fundamentally caught up in the dialectical *movement* of one signifier to the next, and is diametrically opposed to fixation. It does not seek satisfaction, but rather its own continuation and furtherance: more desire, greater desire!' (B. Fink, *The Lacanian Subject: Between Language and Jouissance*, Princeton, 1995, p. 90).

[20] Philostratus, *Imagines* I.23; Callistratus, *Descriptiones* V. For an analysis of these texts, see J. Elsner, 'Naturalism and the Erotics of the Gaze: Intimations of Narcissus', in *Sexuality in Ancient Art*, ed. N. Kampen, pp. 247–61 and, for a broader analysis of Narcissus in Pompeii, see J. Elsner, 'Caught in the Ocular: Visualising Narcissus in the Roman World', in *Reflections of Narcissus*, (ed. L. Spaas), Oxford Berghahn 2000, pp. 89–110. For a discussion of the Narcissus myth in relation to Classical philosophy and optical theory, see S. Bartsch, 'The Philosopher as Narcissus: Vision, Sexuality, and Self-knowledge in Classical Antiquity', in *Visuality Before and Beyond the Renaissance*, ed. R.S. Nelson, Cambridge, 2000, pp. 70–99.

[Plate] 29   Narcissus, Pompeii II.2.2–5. Photograph courtesy of the Deutsches Archaeoligisches Institut.

sight of himself in the water and lose himself in solipsistic desire. Indeed, the background of the painting, with its combination of architectural detail, pool and leafy *locus amoenus*, is remarkably similar to the portico's setting between house and garden and there is every possibility that we, too, '*drawn by the beauty of the spring and the location*', will fall prey to the same fate (*Met.* III.414).[21]

Alternatively, the beauty of Narcissus's pale, undulating flesh might draw us into appreciative contemplation of his naked body, whether this be fuelled by voyeuristic desire to possess him or 'narcissistic' desire to be 'like' him.[22] Indeed, it is almost as if Narcissus is inviting us to lose ourselves in the contemplation of his image. Although the painting concentrates on the relationship between the boy and his reflection, excluding Echo and Cupid, Narcissus holds his head erect rather than looking down into the water.[23] His gaze is painted as if to look out into the viewer's space, triangulating the relationship, implicating us in his fate and raising the question of who, in fact, is seduced by whom. Drawn in by the beauty of the image, blinding ourselves to its artificiality and falling prey to the naturalistic deceit wrought by the painter, we too are '*seduced by the image of a shape we have seen*' (*Met.* III.416).[24]

However, when we glance away from the beautiful form of Narcissus to look more closely at the reflection which has so enthralled him, we find an ambiguous kind of image which complicates our reaction to the painting still further. The reflected face of Narcissus does not simply reduplicate his beauty upside-down, but is instead a more sinister angle, his eyes half-closed in an expression of languor, his reflection is a frontal, wide-eyed, almost distorted face with wild hair.[25] In his discussion of Lucius's oeuvre L. Richardson jr. assumes the

[21]   '*faciemque loci fontemque secutus*'.

[22]   The forces of the voyeuristic and scopophilic gaze are applied most effectively to erotic painting in Pompeii by D. Fredrick, 'Beyond the Atrium to Ariadne: Erotic Painting and Visual Pleasure in the Roman House', *Classical Antiquity*, vol. 14, 1995, pp. 266–88, following the Lacanian-inspired film theory of Laura Mulvey presented in 'Visual Pleasure and Narrative Cinema', *Screen*, 16.3 (1975), pp. 6–18, reprinted in C. Penley (ed.), *Feminism and Film Theory*, New York, 1988.

[23]   Most Campanian wall-paintings listed in LIMC – Narkissos, depict the youth looking down at his reflection or gazing into the distance, with the exception of our example from Pompeii II.2.2–5 (Narkissos 3), a panel in Pompeii V.2.1, and a panel in the Museo Nazionale in Naples (inv. 9388), which depict Narcissus looking up and out into the viewer's space (Elsner, 2000, op. cit. [note 20], p. 102; Balenseifen, K.32, 5; 32, 7: 32, 42).

[24]   Ovid's phrase '*visae correptus imagine formae*' brilliantly captures the conceit of an image which has a tangible power over the viewer. While '*correptus imagine*' means in the specific context 'seduced by a reflection', it also literally means 'seized by an image', so suggesting the potential violence of a situation in which the object beheld has direct, physical control over the beholder. The power of Narcissus himself to seduce or 'seize' the viewer is powerfully communicated by Ovid when he actually breaks off his impersonal narrative to address the boy in the second person ('credule ...:' *Met.* III.432–436), a motif which is picked up by Philostratus in his ecphrasis of an image of Narcissus in *Imagines* I.23.3 (*se mentoi* ...). As Elsner, 2000, op. cit. (note 20), p. 101, writes, 'Narcissus perishes in part because the sovereignty of subjecthood in looking out and controlling the world of the seen becomes inverted in a kind of paranoic catastrophe in which the seen looks back and controls as an object the viewer who looks out at it.'

[25]   As suggested by Elsner, ibid., p. 103.

[Plate] 30   Perseus and Andromeda, Museo Nazionale di Napoli. Photograph courtesy of the Deutsches Archaeologisches Institut.

deformities of the reflection are simply an example of bad painting.[26] Yet need we be so reductive in our reading of the image? The reflection is almost apotropaic in its grotesqueness, a warning perhaps of the potential danger of beholding oneself too closely; as in *The Picture of Dorian Grey*, the image presented to us might not be quite what we wish to see.[27] The distorted reflection also raises the question of what it is, in fact, that we desire; it is the reflection that has aroused Narcissus's love, but the reflection does not conform to the naturalistic ideal beauty of which Narcissus is meant to be a supreme example. Instead, it refers to quite a different visual tradition – that of the schematic,

[26]   Richardson, op. cit. (note 12), p. 147: Pyramus and Thisbe are, he writes, 'dreadfully badly drawn ... Narcissus is a little better, but not a great deal better, his gaze abstracted and directed upward, while his foreshortened reflection in the pool before him is more Medusa-like than seductive.'

[27]   Lacan himself, in his discussion of the relationship between the eye and the gaze, emphasizes the fact that 'what I look at is never what I wish to see' (Sheridan 1977, op. cit. [note 6], p. 103). The way in which we view the supposed object of our desire is distorted by the very fact that we desire it; the 'real' object is concealed by the desired, fantasized image we project onto it. The Gorgonian reflection of Narcissus raises several questions; does it represent Narcissus's fantasized projection of self, or does it reveal the 'real' Narcissus behind his skin-deep beauty? Or does it represent the difference between an image and its reflection in a way which undermines our confidence in the viewing process itself? For discussion of the difference between image and reflection in the context of ancient viewing, see J. Henderson, 'Footnote: Representation in the *Villa of Mysteries*,' in J. Elsner (ed.), *Art and Text in Roman Culture*, Cambridge, 1996, pp. 259–60, and Bartsch, 2000, op. cit. (note 20), pp. 73ff.

apotropaic Gorgon, an image which through its symbolic representation of 'the Other' has a fascinatory effect upon the viewer, which quite literally petrifies us, holds us captive.[28]

The Gorgon embodies the power of the gaze itself, and, as the myth of Perseus demonstrates, can only be safely viewed as a reflection. The intimate, and potentially dangerous, relationship between the gaze, reflection and desire is explored in Pompeii not only by images of Narcissus, but also by several images which depict Perseus and Andromeda beholding a reflection of Medusa's head in a pool of water, fascinated by the power of the monstrous Other which has brought them together (plate 30).[29] Although both images portray the ambiguous power of the Other both to fascinate and destroy, the Perseus and Andromeda scene is almost a reversal of the Narcissan tragedy. The force of the gaze has in fact made possible their union because its potential powers of destruction have been directed against a different representation of the Other in the guise of a sea-monster.[30] While the scene perhaps hints at a sinister force at work within the relationship between lover and beloved (the Gorgon is still worryingly present, and powerful), it yet emphasizes the safe 'otherness' of reflection, in contrast to the dangers of reality. However, in Narcissus's situation the categories of Self and Other, Reality and Reflection, have become confused; Narcissus has confronted the gaze of the Gorgonian Other within his very Self, and his misunderstanding of its nature will result in his own self-annihilation.[31]

With his static pose within the artfully created *locus amoenus* the youth does almost represent a stone image (as if he has been petrified by this Gorgonian reflection), a sculpture within a garden, as Ovid's Narcissus, who seems to be 'a statue shaped from Parian marble'.[32] The chilling nature of the confrontation of Self and Other may be made more palatable for the viewer by the naturalistic beauty of the image, and the distancing effect achieved by the representation of a possible sculptural image within a painted image. Yet it is this very naturalistic beauty which triangulates the relationship and draws the viewer's own gaze into its dialectic of desire, ultimately leading to our own confrontation of the fascinatory image in the pool. To confront our own 'Other', the image implies, all we need to do is glance into the *euripus* while we are dining, but to do so is to risk our own petrification.

---

[28]   Philostratus, too, implicitly refers to the Gorgon at I.23.4, where he describes his eye as 'charopon ... kai gorgon' ('shining and spirited'), implying a concentration of gaze which is almost terrifying in its feverish intensity. For this observation I am indebted to Jas' Elsner, in a discussion following the presentation of his paper on Narcissus at Corpus Christi College, Oxford, June 2000 (for details of publication, see note 13). He tells me that the 'gorgon' in Philostratus's text was pointed out to him by Sandrine Dubel.

[29]   L. Balenseifen, *Speigelbild in der antiken Kunst*, Tübingen, 1990, K.35–2, 4, 8 & 11.

[30]   The confrontation of Other with Other (Gorgon and sea monster) demonstrates the logic of apotropaism, by which an image metonymically representing evil is directed against evil itself in order to divert, or cancel out, its powers. See S.R.Wilk, *Medusa: Solving the Mystery of the Gorgon*, Oxford, 2000, pp. 145–181.

[31]   Psychoanalytical interpretations of the Gorgon relate its apotropaic power to the threat of castration and fear of female sexual potency (see Freud, 'Das Medusenhaupt: The Medusa's Head,' trans J. Strachey, in *The Standard Edition of the Complete Psychological Works of Sigmund Freud*, 18:105–6, London, 1961, discussed by Wilk, pp. 87–104). Arguably, Narcissus's self-infatuation can be interpreted as a retreat into sameness in order to avoid the sexual power of the Other (as Ovid suggests by entwining the myth with that of Echo); but as the distinction between Self and Other is elided, Narcissus ends up confronting in his reflection the very sexual powers from which he is seeking to escape.

[32]   Met. III.419: 'e Pario formatum marmore signum.' Callistratus literally concretizes this motif; his Narcissus is actually a sculpture painted within a picture, already petrified by the paralysing effect of his own desire.

As an image which explores the potential danger of viewing and desiring the Other, the painting of Narcissus sheds light upon the other images in the portico. Just as Narcissus is drawn into a tragic misunderstanding as a result of the desire which is aroused when he views the Other in the form of his reflection, so Pyramus's desire for Thisbe leads him to misinterpret her bloodied veil, and to commit suicide, thinking that she has been attacked by a lion (plate 31). In each situation, the gaze which has aroused desire has clouded judgement and brought about a tragic *méconnaissance*; both Narcissus and Pyramus have failed to read correctly the signs which characterize their confrontation with the object of their desire, and in each case, their failure to do so results in death.[33] Both images explore the complex way in which Self relates to Other, and the idea that the Other we behold and the Other we actually desire are rarely one and the same. While Narcissus illustrates an anxiety that desire for another is always in some form a sublimated kind of autoeroticism, the mutual suicide of Pyramus and Thisbe illustrates a situation in which desire for the other so annihilates our sense of self that we would rather die than live without our beloved.

Whereas Narcissus presents us with an image of sameness and hints at the desire aroused by the homosexual gaze, the tale of Pyramus and Thisbe is depicted as the union of physical, heterosexual opposites. Pyramus's dark, masculine, muscular body is contrasted with his beloved's pale, feminine, fleshy curves. Yet while the solipsistic gaze of Narcissus results in paralysis and dematerialization, the heterosexual gaze of Pyramus and Thisbe, which is focused upon a physical other, is portrayed in terms of active violence and bloody death. While Thisbe plunges a dagger into her chest over the bloodied body of her dying beloved, the lion which has interrupted and confused their rendezvous runs off into the distance. As with Actaeon and Diana, the potentially desirous gaze does not lead to sexual possession, but to death from phallic weapons and encounters with violent beasts; images of the wild and bestial are yoked to the human drama of violence and desire.[34]

[33]   My use of '*méconnaissance*' here is taken from Lacan's use of the term in his outline of the 'Mirror Stage theory' in which the 'misunderstanding' is that of the child who fails to realize that his reflection is not a unified 'Other', and thereafter defines himself through, and desires, a fantasy (the *objet a*), which he imagines will complete his own sense of lack (J. Lacan, 'The Mirror Stage as Formative of the Function of the I', in *Ecrits: A Selection*, trans. A. Sheridan, New York, 1977; also 'Of the Gaze as Objet Petit a,' in *The Four Fundamental Concepts of Psychoanalysis*, trans. A. Sheridan, New York 1977). The misreading of signs which characterizes the romantic confrontation in the cases of Narcissus, Pyramus and Thisbe demonstrates the confusion of the Mirror Stage as the lovers fail to distinguish between what they behold, and what they in fact desire. Narcissus's and Pyramus's desire for the *objet a*, the specular double which will fulfil their own fundamental lack, confuses their gaze to the extent that each actually perceives the opposite of what he is looking for. Thus Narcissus mistakes a reflection (the division of self), for a distinct subject (the doubling of self), and Pyramus misreads a sign for Thisbe's presence (her veil) as signifying her destruction.

[34]   The association here between romantic love and graphic violence reflects Ovidian language (where sexual penetration is compared to wounding in the story of Tereus and Philomela, Met. VI.527–30), and also anticipates the macabre fantasies of the Second Sophistic, particularly the images of sex and violence which imbue Achilles Tatius's *Leucippe and Clitophon* (see J.J. Winkler, 'The Education of Chloe, Hidden Injuries of Sex', in *The Constraints of Desire: The Anthropology of Sex and Gender in Ancient Greece*, New York, 1990, pp. 101–26; H. Elsom, 'Callirhoe: Displaying the Phallic Woman', in A. Richlin (ed.), *Pornography and Representation in Greece and Rome*, New York and Oxford 1992, pp. 212–30; and S. Goldhill, *Foucault's Virginity*, Cambridge, 1996).

[Plate] 31   Pyramus and Thisbe, Pompeii II.2.2–5. Photograph courtesy of the Deutsches Archaeologisches Institut.

The confrontation between Self and Other which is represented in each image necessarily involves a brush with the world outside our own subjective desires, which breaks through in the form of violence and, ultimately, death.[35]

Yes despite the imagery of unrestrained bestiality (enhanced by a large *paradeisos* scene of wild animals round the corner on the west side of the portico), destruction in each image emanates, disturbingly, from the Self. The lion is not directly responsible for the death of Pyramus and Thisbe – they themselves commit bloody suicide; Narcissus's fate is a direct result of his own self-fascination; Actaeon is killed at the hands of his own, tamed hounds. Hunting is a recurring theme in each painting (Narcissus, Pyramus and Actaeon are all depicted with long spears), an erotically charged activity which leads the hero into the ambiguous space of the *locus amoenus*, where anything can happen.[36] However, the weapons the youths carry help them little against the power of the gaze itself to entrap and ultimately destroy them. In each situation, death results from what each character has *seen*. Ovid's account of Pyramus and Thisbe repeatedly refers to their love as 'hidden'.[37] Yet when they finally arrange to meet, the lovers only behold each other in death. As in Ovid's text (but uniquely in Pompeian portrayals of the myth), Pyramus has not quite passed away; 'at the sound of Thisbe's name Pyramus raised his eyes which were heavy with death' (*Met.* IV.146–7).[38] Thus at the moment of self-destruction, the lovers' gazes finally meet in tragic recognition of their error. The consummation of their desire is denied and re-presented as suicide through

[35]   The failure of the world of language and signification (Lacan's 'Symbolic' realm) which characterizes the fate of Pyramus and Thisbe causes the emergence of the 'Real,' in the form of brute physicality and the biological events of violent wounding and death. Narcissus, however, ceases to exist because he is trapped in the world of the 'Imaginary', identifying with an image of sameness to the extent that he fails to submit himself to the Other (the process of 'Alienation', a necessary stage in psychological development, through which the individual becomes a subject within the 'Symbolic' realm). See Fink, 1995, op. cit. (note 19), pp. 50–55 and D. Evans, *An Introductory Dictionary of Lacanian Psychoanalysis*, London and New York, 1996, pp. 9, 82–4, 159–61, 201–3.

[36]   For an exploration of the erotically charged hunter motif, see A. Schnapp, *Le chasseur et la cité: Chasse et érotique dans la Grèce ancienne*, Paris 1997, pp. 247–57, 318–54.

[37]   'quoque magis tegitur, tectus magis aestuat ignis' (IV.64). 'nunc tegis unius, mox es tectura duorum' (IV.159).

[38]   *Ad nomen Thisbes oculos a morte gravatos Pyramus erexit.* Could Ovid's use of the verb *erigere* here have phallic connotations? Certainly the penetrative qualities of vision were linked to a certain extent in the ancient world with the phallic drive (see Bartsch, 2000, op. cit. [note 20], p. 75). The erotic power of the gaze in both Ovid's text and the Pompeian painting is thus linked to the phallic qualities of the weapons with which Pyramus and Thisbe paradoxically, and fatally, achieve the consummation of their desire.

(phallic?) stabbing; the object of the gaze and the object of desire coincide only at the moment of self-destruction.[39]

As with the image of Narcissus, the relationship between lover and beloved in the painting of Pyramus and Thisbe is triangulated with the viewer. The baroque combination of desire, nudity and violence creates an arresting, heady image, and we are drawn into the desirous gaze which is held within the painting. The two images function as a kind of diptych on either side of the *biclinium*; they offer an erotic choice to the diner within the ambiguous spaces of the constructed *locus amoenus*, which is constructed as a point within the triangulation of the homosexual or heterosexual gaze. The viewer can narcissistically identify with, or sexually desire, either the hard masculinity of Pyramus, the soft feminine curves of Thisbe, or the mediating figure of the effeminate Narcissus, who is both lover and beloved, active and passive, self and other.[40] Yet each erotic option lures the viewer into its dialectic of desire only to reveal the dangers of such confrontation. The distinction between active and passive, viewer and viewed, is broken down, as even the tough masculinity of Pyramus is shown to be mastered and penetrated by the desirous gaze in the form of the violent suicide which has lacerated his naked body. Thus whatever form of viewing we choose, we too will be potentially drawn into the dialectic of desire, will be, as is Narcissus, *seized by the image of a form beheld*.

While the two smaller images of Narcissus, Pyramus and Thisbe locate the dangers of confronting the Other in the power of the romantic gaze, the potential violence and tragedy they explore is reflected and magnified in the confrontation between man and god represented by Actaeon's fatal epiphany of the naked Diana (plates 32 and 33). To behold a divine being is to confront the Other in its most potent form. If to view something is to have a certain mastery over it, then Actaeon's visual possession of Diana is an example of the gaze at is most transgressive, particularly as his voyeurism is tinged with eroticism.

This particular visual representation of the Actaeon myth emphasizes the transgressive, violent power of the gaze more potently than any other example

---

[39]   For Lacan, the object-cause of desire is always missed, no matter what we do to attain it; it is the act of desiring in itself which is important. Desire is related to the drive, defined in terms of the demands of the Other according to which we identify ourselves and construct our fantasies. For Pyramus and Thisbe, once the Other by which they have identified themselves is perceived to be dead, the feeling of lack is such that their desire is transferred to a desire for death. For Lacan, 'every drive is virtually a Death Drive' because it is defined in terms of the symbolic world of language and signification which, because it exists independently of the individual self, cannot but emphasize our own mortality (*Ecrits*, op. cit [note 33], 1966, p. 848). Narcissus, Pyramus and Thisbe have failed to read correctly the signs of the symbolic world and it is meaningless to them; since the *objet a* can no longer be perceived as existing in this world, they can but turn to death. Interestingly, Lacan refers to death as representation itself; all drives lead to the death drive because they are 'organized by representation and representation implies the death of the thing' (M-H. Brousse, 'The Drive (II)', R. Feldstein, B. Fink and M. Jaanus (eds), *Reading Seminar XI: Lacan's Four Fundamental Concepts of Psychoanalysis*, New York, 1995, p. 114). Narcissus, then, dies when he confronts representation in the form of his reflected self. Wilks adds a yet more macabre note to the myth which his suggestion that the Gorgoneion (which Narcissus seems to confront in our painting) is actually a representation of death itself, based on the facial characteristics of a swollen corpse (pp. 109–17).

[40]   For a discussion of masculinity and effeminacy in Roman culture, see Clarke, 1998, op. cit. (note 2), Pollini, 1999, op. cit. (note 2), and C.A. Williams, *Roman Homosexuality*, New York and Oxford, 1999, pp. 125–59.

[Plate] 32 (left)   Diana, from the portico of
Pompeii II.2.2–5. Photograph: Soprintendenza
Archaeologia de Pompei.

in Pompeii. It is only in Roman art of the Imperial period that Diana is actually depicted nude; most earlier versions of the myth concentrate on the moment of punishment and depict Artemis/Diana as clothed.[41] However, although most painted examples in Pompeii portray a nude Diana open to visual possession by the viewer, they depict Actaeon's face appearing over a crag at the rear of the image.[42] Thus the viewer is given a privileged, and by implication, less transgressive view into the goddess' space, while the transgressive viewer within the myth is reduced to peering into the scene from an inferior position within the painting. Most 3rd Style representations locate the myth in a

[41]   For example, the Pan Painter's name vase, where the emphasis is on the clothed Artemis's violent revenge. The first literary account of the myth which identifies Actaeon's error to be his sight of the goddess bathing is Callimachus' 5th Hymn. Thereafter the motif of nudity and implied eroticism is used by Apollodorus (III.4.4), Ovid (*Met.* III.138–252; *Tristia* II.103–8), Seneca (*Oedipus* 751–63), Statius (*Thebais* III.201–5) and Apuleius (*The Golden Ass* II.4). The earliest surviving representation of the myth with a nude Diana is a chalcedony gem dated to the first century BC (Berlin Staatl. Museen FG 6435). Third Style landscape representations can be found in Pompeii IX.1.22 (the House of M. Epidius Sabinus) and IX.2.16 (the House of T.D. Panthera). See LIMC: Aktaion.

[42]   See Pompeii VI.13.19, VI.16.7 (the House of the Gilded Cupids) and IX.7.16 (the House of Fabius Rufus).

[Plate] 33 (right)   Actaeon, from the
portico of Pompeii II.2.2–5. Photograph:
Soprintendenza Archaeologia de Pompei.

sacro-idyllic landscape with very small figures, and often two tableaux – vision and punishment – within the same pastoral frame.[43]

As E.W. Leach has demonstrated, the variety of different forms of the Actaeon myth in art and literature 'shows it to have been an inherently flexible one with a high potential for incorporating moral ambiguity and an unusual susceptibility to individual interpretation'.[44] Lucius, our painter in Pompeii II.2.2–5, has selected and rejected various elements to create a unique tableau which absorbs and comments upon the dangers of the gaze in relation to the other panels in the portico, emphasizing the paintings' status as a unified group with a particular message for the viewer.

The house actually has two representations of the myth (dating to the same period and possibly both by Lucius). These form a unique pair in that each depicts the goddess and the mortal in separate panels flanking an architectural feature; the portico tableau is placed on either side of a doorway, and the second tableau is placed on either side of a fountain within a small *nymphaeum* in the garden below. Each is positioned close to water in an artificial *locus amoenus*, which brings the setting of the painting, with its motif of bathing, into the viewer's own space. Myth and reality are potentially confused, the artist's

[43]   See Pompeii I.9.5 (the House of the Orchard); VII.7.19; VII.15.2 (the House of the Sailor); IX.1.22 (the House of Epidius Sabinus).

[44]   E.W. Leach, 'Metamorphoses of the Actaeon Myth in Campanian Painting', *Mitteilungen des Deutschen Archaeologischen Instituts Roemische Abteilung*, Band 88, 1981, pp. 307–27.

[Plate] 34   Diana and Actaeon, from the House of the Orchard,
Pompeii I.9.5. Photograph courtesy of the Deutsches Archaeologisches
Institut.

ingenuity here reflecting and subverting the glorious paradox of Ovid's
description of Diana's grotto, where 'nature has emulated art with her own
genius.' (*Met.* III.158–9).[45]

Each tableau depicts Actaeon as a balanced opposite of the goddess, of equal
stature, with no other figures except his hounds, and on the same frontal plane
of the painting. We may contrast this with an example from the House of the
Orchard (Pompeii I.9.5), which depicts Diana within an extensive landscape
(plate 34). Although she bathes with her back to the viewer, she actually faces
Actaeon as he is attacked by his hounds in the background, while in the
foreground a voyeur figure within an architectural structure leans on a pillar
and surveys the tableau unharmed. The viewer of the painting, within the
architectural space of the house itself, is thus identified with the voyeur, rather
than with Actaeon, and the transgression is safely confined to the mythological
figures. The painting holds a certain *frisson* in that Diana has the potential

[45]   *Simulaverat artem ingenio natura suo.*

to turn and meet the gaze of the voyeur (and thus the viewer), so condemning us to the same fate as Actaeon. But crucially, the narrative of the painting is suspended so that she does not do so, holding the viewer in the suspended safety of vicarious transgression and confirming our (temporary) ocular possession of the scene. As John Ellis has written with regards to cinema, voyeurism 'demands that these things take place for the spectator, are offered or dedicated to the spectator, and in that sense implies a consent by the representation (and the figures in it) to the act of being watched'.[46] Thus the voyeur sanctions the viewing of the naked goddess.

However, in our portico, there is no voyeur within the image to justify our transgressive view, no receding plane within the picture from where Actaeon plays Peeping Tom, and no large landscape to diminish the force of the individual figures. Each is presented in almost lifesize proportion, facing the viewer on a frontal plane, demanding our attention. In contrast to the two smaller paintings, where the dialectics of the desirous gaze are held within the image, the static, frontal poses of Diana and Actaeon demand the viewer's direct engagement. Actaeon is not depicted mid-metamorphosis, with antlers, but as a fully human being, already attacked by his hounds at the very moment that he beholds the goddess. The encounter is made more immediate, emphasizing the power of the gaze itself, and the violence which immediately ensues.

The *méconnaissance* of the story is thus displaced from the hounds, which fail to recognize their master, to the actual transgressive moment of confrontation. Actaeon's stature emphasizes Diana's identity as a passive female figure open to the possessive gaze of the viewer. Yet the absence of a safe voyeur to justify the viewer's gaze means that we have only Actaeon with whom to identify, heightening our own unease and sense of danger in beholding the naked goddess. Moreover, in order to pass through the door which the figures on the portico frame, we must pass between Actaeon and Diana, so placing ourselves in the position of Actaeon and repeating this error.

The danger that we, too, will become transgressive voyeurs, is enhanced by the way in which Diana herself is represented. Facing the viewer, she bends down in a pose remarkably similar to the sculptural type of the 'Crouching Venus', her sinuous curves drawing the viewer's eye into the most intimate parts of her body (plate 35).[47] Rather than looking at Actaeon, she looks out of the painting into the viewer's space, while gesturing towards Actaeon as his hounds devour him. Thus we find that the goddess is communicating with us, demanding that we look at her, whilst simultaneously demonstrating what will happen to us if we *do* look at her. She is portrayed according to the visual language of the goddess of desire herself, a naturalistic form of representation which demands to be viewed and gains its power from its hold over the viewer.

---

[46]   J. Ellis, 1992, op. cit. (note 3), p. 45, quoted by Pollini, 1999, op. cit. (note 2), p. 39.

[47]   For examples of the 'Crouching Venus', see M.D. Brinkerhoff, *Hellenistic Statues of Aphrodite: Studies in the History of their Stylistic Development*, New York, 1978, pp. 35–55, and W. Neumer-Pfau, *Studien zur Ikonographie und gesellschaftlichen Funktion hellenistischer Aphrodite*, Bonn, 1982, pp. 213–14.

[Plate] 35   The 'Crouching Venus', Musée du Louvre. Photograph courtesy of the Bridgeman Art Library.

Thus, although as a naked, vulnerable form she is open to our visual possession, she also controls with disturbing power the way in which we view her, luring our gaze into a dangerous epiphanic confrontation.[48]

As the image of Narcissus has warned us, naturalistic representation, which seeks to replicate its prototype, can be deceptive and dangerous. If it is the aim of naturalistic art to replicate 'the Real', and if the representation of Diana is employing a recognized example of naturalistic art (the 'Crouching Venus'), then simply by looking at the painting, our gaze has tricked us into a transgressive viewing of the divine. It is a visual pun akin to the epigram about the Knidian Aphrodite where the goddess asks, 'Where did Praxiteles see me naked ...?'[49] Lucius thus emphasizes the power of the artist himself to capture and in some sense 'create' the divine, but in doing so, exposes us to the dangers inherent in such forms of representation. As if to emphasize the power of naturalistic deception, the pale, curvy nudity of Diana herself not only refers to the Crouching Venus but is also remarkably similar to that of Narcissus at the other end of the portico. For Narcissus, as for Actaeon, the lure of the naturalistic body resulted in death.

The viewer's potential transgression in viewing the goddess is made yet more immediate by the fact that Diana and Actaeon are depicted on separate panels. The first goddess passed by the viewer upon entering the portico would have been Venus on her conch shell. Being conscious of Venus and thus open to the dialectics of the desirous gaze, why should he not also assume the 'Crouching Venus' figure portrayed on her own in the panel to his right to be the goddess of love too? It is only by viewing and identifying Actaeon and his hounds that the viewer can then identify the crouching nude as Diana. Yet by then he has already committed himself to a transgressive viewing, because he has confused the goddess with the erotic dilemma of her divine opposite. Just as Hippolytus, that other young hunter in an erotic dilemma, the viewer is forced to make a decision between the two goddesses. But even in recognizing that dilemma, the viewer has already violated Diana's body with his gaze, and so repeated Actaeon's error. In attempting to identify the goddess and reading her through the Actaeon myth, the viewer finds himself playing the same guessing game as Pyramus and Narcissus, both of whom misread the signs of erotic confrontation and died as a result. By stylistically mirroring Venus and yet gesturing directly to Actaeon, Diana confuses the signs of our own confrontation with her so that the *méconnaissance* experienced by Narcissus and Pyramus is displaced onto the viewer and implicates us even more directly in Actaeon's fate.

[48] This paradox between the vulnerability of a nude image to the spectator's possessive glance, and yet the image's power to manipulate the way in which we view it, is famously captured by Praxiteles's Knidian Aphrodite. For a discussion of this image and the influence and power of the Knidia, see Havelock, 1995, op. cit. (note 19), *passim*; A. Stewart, *Art, Desire and the Body*, Berkeley 1997, pp. 96–105; R. Osborne, *Archaic and Classical Greek Art*, Oxford, 1998, pp. 230–5. For the female nude in general, see K. Clark, *The Nude. A Study in Ideal Form*, Princeton, 1956; J. Berger, *Ways of Seeing*, London, 1972; L. Nead, *The Female Nude: Art, Obscenity and Sexuality*, London, 1992; A.O. Koloski-Ostrow and C.L. Lyons (eds), *Naked Truths: Women, Sexuality and Gender in Classical Art and Archaeology*, London and New York, 1997.

[49] An epigram ascribed to Plato Junior and dated by D.L. Page to the first century AD, possibly contemporaneous with our paintings (*Further Greek Epigrams*, Cambridge, 1981, p. 82), discussed by Havelock, 1995, op. cit. (note 19), pp. 22–3, 62–3, 121.

Secondary Source 2.9   Lauren Hackworth Petersen, 'Disney World in Pompeii: the House of Octavius Quartio'

(Source: Petersen, L. Hackworth (2006) *The Freedman in Roman Art and Art History,* Cambridge and New York, Cambridge University Press, pp. 129–36, 261–2)

The well-known House of Octavius Quartio (II.2.2) remains the most extensively treated domus with which scholarship asserts the "villa as model" paradigm. Characterized by more than one scholar

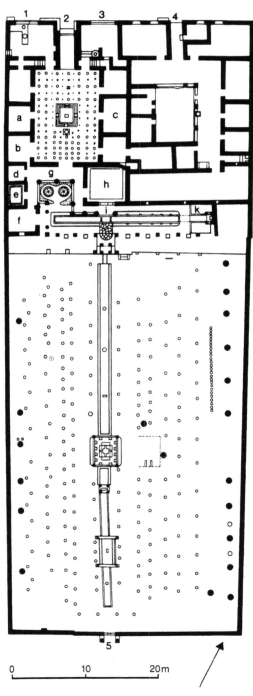

Figure 73   Plan of the House of Octavius Quartio, Pompeii. After John R. Clarke, *The Houses of Roman Italy, 100 B.C.–A.D. 250* (Berkeley, 1991), fig. 108.

as a "Walt Disney World,"[1] a notion that is rife with connotations of garish excess, the house stands out among other well-known residences in Pompeii (Figs. 73–75).[2] Its living quarters are remarkably small in comparison to its extensive garden space, which comprises roughly two-thirds of the total area of the house. In the postearthquake years, the remodeling effort of an ordinary, medium-sized atrium house centered on the garden area and on the decoration of its surrounding rooms, all indicating that the garden functioned as the focal point.[3] The expansive garden enlivened with statuary, water canals, pergolas, and fountains, seemingly extraordinary as far as Pompeian dwellings go, has inspired scholars to compare the effects of the house to the ill-conceived commissions of the fictional Trimalchio, who himself wantonly acquires all that he can of elite culture. In fact, modern views insist that the House of Octavius Quartio is emblematic of "freedman taste," owing to the emphasis the owners placed on the garden and to its perceived overdecoration and naive emulation of lavish villas. John Clarke sums up the sentiment succinctly: "If what had meaning in the large villas sinks to mere decoration in Pompeian gardens, it is because a new class, that of the entrepreneurial freedman, was socially the most active (in Pompeii) in this period. Like the rich former slave Trimalchio in Petronius's *Satyricon*, these new bourgeoisie imitated the wealthy aristocratic upper class in their desire for the material trappings of wealth."[4] The statement reveals much of what is embedded in modern constructions concerning good taste and outright imitation in domus decoration – freedmen, as epitomized by Trimalchio, lacked taste, and where we see a lack of taste, or shameless imitation, we can assume that the owner must have been a *libertinus*.[5]

It is undeniable that the House of Octavius Quartio shares many features found in villas of the elite – gardens, statuary, fountains, reception spaces – but here on a smaller scale than what villas could permit.[6] This last observation is to be expected given that villas were typically situated on property outside a city's walls (*villa suburbana*), as in the case of The Villa of Mysteries at Pompeii, or in the countryside (villa *rustica*), where space was plentiful for those who could afford it, as with the nearby Villa at Oplontis (Fig. 76); in contrast, domus, within city walls, were by their very nature limited, sharing multiple walls with neighbours. To be sure, villas maximized views outward toward landscapes and

[1]   Zanker 1998, 156 [Zanker, Paul. 1998. *Pompeii: Public and Private Life*. Trans. Deborah Lucas Schneider. Cambridge: Harvard University Press]; Clarke 1991, 207 [Clarke, John R. 1991 *The Houses of Roman Italy 100 B.C.–A.D. 250: Ritual, Space, and Decoration*, Berkeley: University of California Press].

[2]   For the fundamental study of the house, see Spinazzola, 367–434; and now Mariette de Vos, "II.2.2: Casa di D. Octavius Quartio," *PPM*, vol. 3, 42–108.

[3]   Zanker 1998, 145.

[4]   Clarke 1991, 25.

[5]   For example, Zanker 1988, 189, states that "to our modern eyes [the House of the Centenarian is] a grotesque potpourri," intimating that modern ideals supersede ancient perspectives.

[6]   The literature on Roman villas is vast. Some more notable studies, all with bibliography, include the following: Bettina Bergmann, "Art and Nature in the Villa at Oplontis," in *Pompeian Brothels, Pompeii's Ancient History, Mirrors and Mystery, Art and Nature at Oplontis, and the Herculaneum "Basilica"* (JRA Supplementary Series 47) (Portsmouth, RI, 2002), 87–120; D'Arms 1970 [D'Arms, John H. 1970. *Romans on the Bay of Naples: A Social and Cultural Study of Villas and Their Owners from 150 B.C. to A.D. 400*. Cambridge: Harvard University Press]; Harald Mielsch, *Die römische Villa: Architektur und Lebensform* (Munich: C.H. Beck, 1987); John T. Smith, *Roman Villas: A Study in Social Structure* (London: Routledge, 1997); Andrew Wallace-Hadrill, "The Villa as Cultural Symbol," in *The Roman Villa/Villa Urbana*, ed. A. Frazer (Philadelphia: University Museum, University of Pennsylvania, 1998), 43–53; and, more generally, Clarke 1991, 19–23; Hales, 61–93 [Hales, Shelley. 2003. *The Roman House and Social Identity*. Cambridge: Cambridge University Press].

the sea, whereas urban houses looked decidedly inward with views, when space permitted, to peristyle gardens.[7] The owner of the House of Octavius Quartio has brought a bit of nature into town, however, permitting him views of a veritable landscape and distinguishing him from many domus dwellers.[8] Three entertaining spaces capture aspects of villa living. Room *h*, the main reception room, is situated so that guests would have had visual access to a large aedicula, beyond which extended a water canal, running nearly the entire length of the garden itself (ca. 55 meters, a sizeable expanse within the crowded city). Diners could also experience nature closer at hand. The *biclinium*, situated at the eastern end of the terrace watercourse (perpendicular to the longer garden canal), had water as its main feature. In warmer weather, the mists from the fountain-aedicula at the head of the small waterway could cool diners (albeit limited in number to two or four based [on] the size of the *biclinium*), as could the mere proximity of water running gently between the two masonry couches.[9] Guests could also take in the collection of statuettes placed alongside the smaller canal (see Fig. 75). Meanwhile, a meal at the masonry *triclinium* within the garden itself[10] could permit a visitor a more intimate experience of nature – of the protective shade of the trees, the competing scents and colors of the flora, and the soothing sounds of water from the fountain near the middle of the large canal, all working together to create the impression that the property was isolated, if not removed completely, from the fray of city living (see Fig. 74). As ancient authors attest, such was the effect sought within their own villas. For example, Pliny the Younger extols villa living at his estate in Tuscany at the conclusion of his letter to Apollinaris.

> (F)or besides what I have already told you, the repose I enjoy here is more quiet and undisturbed than anywhere else. No summons to the bar; no clients at my gate; all is calm and still; which added to the

---

[7]   But see Zanker 1998, 142–5, for a discussion of terrace houses in Pompeii that had views of the landscape. Also see Clarke 1991, 235–50, for an analogous situation at Herculaneum (for example, the House of the Mosaic Atrium and the House of the Stags). On the importance of constructed views at Roman houses, see Lise Bek, *Towards Paradise on Earth: Modern Space Conception in Architecture: A Creation of Renaissance Humanism* (Rome: Analecta Romana Instituti Danici, 1980); Heinrich Drerup, "Bildraum und Realraum in der römischer Architektur," *RM 66* (1959): 145–74; Franz Jung, "Gebaute Bilder," *Antike Kunst* 27 (1984): 71–122. On gardens of Pompeii, see Jashemski [Jashemski, Wilhelmina F. 1979. *The Gardens of Pompeii, Herculaneum and the Villas Destroyed by Vesuvius*. 2 vols. New Rochelle, NY: Caratzas Brothers]; and, more generally, Linda Farrar, *Ancient Roman Gardens* (Stroud: Sutton, 1998); Nicholas Purcell, "Town in Country and Country in Town," in *Ancient Roman Villa Gardens*, ed. Elisabeth Blair McDougall (Washington, DC: Dumbarton Oaks, 1987), 187–203; Nicholas Purcell, "The Roman Garden as Domestic Building," in *Roman Domestic Buildings*, ed. Ian M. Barton (Exeter: University of Exeter Press, 1996), 121–51.

[8]   The House of Julia Felix, two blocks from the House of Octavius Quartio, remains the largest property found at Pompeii (it is sometimes referred to as a villa). It, too, includes an expansive garden space, occupying nearly an entire city block. See Valeria Sampaolo, "II.4.3: Villa di Giulia Felice," in *PPM*, vol. 3, 184–310; Jashemski, vol. 1, 43–8. In addition, lesser-known houses, such as those in Region I, namely, the domus at I.21.2 and I.22, among others, offered inhabitants extensive garden spaces despite the relatively small sizes of the houses themselves. Jashemski, vol. 2, esp. 61–73, describes a number of residence with large-scale gardens in Region I.

[9]   For an analogous situation, see the House of Neptune and Amphitrite at Herculaneum (Clarke, 1991, 250–63).

[10]   For the remains of the masonry *triclinium* in the garden, see Jashemski, vol. 1, 47; vol. 2, plan 25.

healthiness of the place, the clearness of the sky, and the softness of the air, make me enjoy the greatest vigor, both of mind and body.

(*Letters* 5.6.45)[11]

Here, Pliny's thoughts indicate that his villa was conducive to healthy living, both mentally and physically, and was thus necessary for politically active citizens as a way to get away from it all, if only temporarily.

Ordinary Romans could not afford such luxuries. Largely dependent on a city's commercial life for making a living, Romans were as bound to urban life as to their domus. Individuals of means could and did bring some of the comforts of villa living to their city residences, however, as the owner(s) of the House of Octavius Quartio did. Yet in analyses of this house, scholars tend to stress that this domus not only takes from elite culture – insisting on a trickle-down aesthetic – but that its owner(s) also "combined and compressed" so many features into a comparably small space that the house is rendered "tasteless."[12] To this end, Zanker, among others, rigorously compares ancient testimony, as well as material evidence from villas, with the House of Octavius Quartio, showing how it pales in comparison, feature by feature.[13] For instance, Zanker laments that the house's paths along the sculpture-filled upper terrace are too narrow for people to stroll side by side, as they could in villas where space was ample, while highlighting the fact that the large canal was cleverly disguised to conceal its true function – housing a series of fishponds (see Figs. 73–75).[14] Both fishponds (*piscinae*) and long watercourses (*euripi*) were frequently found among villa properties. One need only think of the fishponds at the dining grotto at the Villa at Sperlonga or of the canopus at Hadrian's Villa at Tivoli (Fig. 77).[15] To combine the two features into one smacks of overreaching and underachieving, however, and Zanker's message is unmistakable. The House of Octavius Quartio, although not connected to an ex-slave explicitly, is illustrative of "freedman taste" in domus decoration with Trimalchio's naïve affectations of elite culture constituting another basis for comparison.[16]

In addition, the House of Octavius Quartio contains references to Isis and things Egyptian.[17] Statuettes in the *viridarium* (g), which supplants the more traditional *tablinum*, included an image of Bes (an Egyptian rural deity), a Pharonic figure, and an ibis, sacred to Isis. Along the upper waterway, an image of a sphinx stood among traditional garden statuary, such as herms of

---

[11]   As translated in Pierre de la Ruffinière du Prey, *The Villas of Pliny from Antiquity to Posterity* (Chicago: University of Chicago Press, 1994), Appendix 2. *Nam super illa, quae rettuli, altius ibi otium et pinguius eoque securius: nulla necessitas togae, nemo accersitor ex proximo; placida omnia et quiescentia, quod ipsum salubritati regionis ut purius caelum, et aer liquidior accedit. Ibi animo, ibi corpore maxime valeo.*

[12]   Zanker 1998, esp. 156; Clarke 1991, 193.

[13]   Zanker 1998, 135–203. Also see Clarke 1991, fig. 114, where he lists the locations of the house's statuary and compares it with the "proper" settings.

[14]   Zanker 1998, 154–5.

[15]   On fishponds, see James Higginbotham, *Piscinae: Artificial Fishponds in Roman Italy* (Chapel Hill: University of North Carolina Press, 1997), esp. 55–64, for fishponds as emblems of social status; 210–13, for the *piscina* at the House of Octavius Quartio; and 201–10, for a discussion of other fishponds at Pompeii.

[16]   See Zanker 1998, esp. 201–3.

[17]   On the Egyptian themes in the house, see Clarke 1991, 194–201, esp. 196–7, for a discussion of the graffito found beneath the image of the Isiac priest, perhaps giving the name of a disciple of Isis. Also see Verity Platt, "Viewing, Desiring, Believing: Confronting the Divine in a Pompeian House," *Art History* 25.1 (2002): 87–112.

Dionysus, theater masks, and a river god, among others (see Fig. 75).[18] In nearby room *f*, the painted depiction of a priest of Isis – his head is shaven, and he holds a *sistrum* – and the retangular niche in the west wall have, as we saw, aroused speculation that this room was used as an Isiac *sacellum*. Last, but surely not least, the long canal in the garden has been likened to the Nile and has prompted some to fantasize that it was used to recreate the flooding of the Nile, playing an integral role in Isiac worship for the owners of the house.[19] Historians, citing the Isiac and Egyptian imagery scattered throughout the house, have thus been eager to identify its owners as Isiacs, typically construed, until recently, as those from the lower orders. As presented in the first chapter, both suppositions are not without their problems. Pictures and statues of Isis and things Egyptian infiltrated all strata of society and appeared in a variety of contexts making it difficult to separate Isiac worship from the more widespread cultural phenomenon of Egyptomania. Yet given the scholarly discourse, it would seem that the House of Octavius Quartio, perceived as a so-called Disney World of sorts and filled with Isiac imagery, could *only* have belonged to a lower-order individual – namely, a rich freedman.

The issue is further snarled because we know very little about the owner of the House of Octavius Quartio, even though, rather ironically, we refer to the house after its presumed owner. Once thought to belong to Loreius Tiburtinus based on some rather weak evidence, the house is now universally connected to Octavius Quartio on the basis of a bronze seal inscribed with the name D. Octavius Quartio (in the genitive), found in the potter's shop at the front of the house at the east side of the *fauces*, but not within the domus itself.[20] Attribution based on a single bronze seal is equally problematic; a portable object, the seal does not in and of itself identify the owner of the house so much as it may reveal the name of someone who frequented the shop, whether as a worker, an owner, or a customer. Even if the house did belong to Octavius Quartio – which remains a possibility – the perception of the house as being a "Disney World" potentially collides with what we know about the gens Octavia at Pompeii.[21]

Although the gens Octavia was not one of the city's more politically active families, it was one of Pompeii's veteran-colonist families, arriving in the late republican period. As such, one could safely argue that members of this clan were Romans to the core as evinced not only from their status as veteran-colonists but from the family's aedicular tomb at the Nuceria Gate, complete with a freestanding togate portrait of the father (at right) and his son in military attire (center) [...].[22] Visually the tomb displays male Roman citizens, as does the inscription, which indicates that Marcus Octavius was an *ingenuus*; he

---

[18]   See Clarke 1991, fig. 114.

[19]   On the flooding theory, Matteo della Corte, "I M.M. Lorei Tiburtini di Pompei," *Atti e memorie della società tiburtina di storia e d'arte* 11–12 (1931–2): 196–200; Tran Tam Tinh 1964, 45; Wild, 221. The water from the flooding would have been collected in the forty-four amphorae along the eastern side of the canal. For the more probable theory that the amphorae were used to store wine, see Spinazzola, 411–12.

[20]   Spinnazzola, fig. 414, for the seal. See Clarke 1991, 193–4, for synopsis and bibliography.

[21]   It should be noted that Spinazzola has discussed the house in overall favorable terms, although the recent trend has taken a different approach.

[22]   On the Octavii, see Castrén, 199. For the tomb, see D'Ambrosio and de Caro, "13OS," n.p. For a good summary of and ample bibliography on the effects of the veteran colonists within and about the city, see Zanker 1998, 61–81.

Figure 74   House of Octavius Quartio, view to the garden, Pompeii. Photo: Stephen Petersen (su concessione del Ministero per i Beni e le Attività Culturali – Soprintendenza Archeologica di Pompei).

Figure 75   House of Octavius Quartio, upper terrace with *euripus*, Pompeii. Photo: Soprintendenza Archeologica di Pompei, neg. C1276 (su concessione del Ministero per i Berni e le Attività Culturali – Soprintendenza Archeologica di Pompei).

Figure 76   Model of the Villa at Oplontis, by Victoria I. Photo: J. Stanton-Abbott.

Figure 77   Dining grotto and fish ponds at the Villa at Sperlonga. Photo: Stephen Petersen.

claims his filiation and voting tribe.[23] Complicating matters, however, is an individual, Vertia Philumina, who is identified in the same epitaph in no uncertain terms as a *libertina*. She is presumably the wife (and mother) and stands in the left niche dressed in proper matron attire (tunic and mantel). As the

[23]   The titular inscription reads: M(arcus) Octavius M(arci) f(ilius)/Men(enia) et Vertia <l(iberta)/ Philumina in loco/communi monument(um) communem sibei/posteriesque sueis fecerunt (Marcus Octavius, son of Marcus, of the tribe Menenia, and Vertia Philumina, freedwoman of a woman, built this communal tomb on communal property for themselves and for their descendants).

tomb testifies, a union between a colonist-*ingeunuus* and a freed slave seemed right at home within the daily fabric of Pompeii. It should therefore come as no surprise that visually nothing identifies this tomb as belonging in part to an ex-slave, save for the inscription. Indeed, Kockel characterizes the tomb as typical of those belonging to veteran-colonists at Pompeii; it is a multistory tomb with portrait statues placed in the aedicula, while *columellae* were placed below in the sockel.[24]

If the house at II.2.2 originally belonged to this family before being passed on to members of the gens or others altogether, this domus would likely reveal less about "freedman taste" than about the desire to create a home for a Roman family within a newly Romanized city. Even if this house belonged to another family or families entirely (free or freed alike), reading the dwelling in terms of what it lacks by way of rigorous comparison with villas and literary texts prohibits us from seeing the house, and others like it, for what it may have offered the inhabitants of the city. However, new investigations into domestic ensembles permit us to revisit houses in Pompeii, such as the House of Octavius Quartio, and to challenge the entrenched "villa as model" paradigm that has filled the city with ambitious (and naïve) freed slaves.[25]

Secondary Source 2.10   Alan E. Bernstein 'Useful death'

(Source: Bernstein A.E. (1993) *The Formation of Hell: Death and Retribution in the Ancient and Early Christian Worlds*, London, UCL Press, Chapter 4, pp. 107–29)

The previous chapters have presented three logically distinct but historically concurrent views of death. The tendency to regard death as neutral reflected an effort to confine the dead in storehouses or at the limits of the world, where they could not disturb humankind. Distancing them from the human community was more important than judging them. By contrast, the moral view, which seems to have followed but not replaced the neutral view of death, accentuated the effects that knowledge about the dead were considered to have on the morale and behavior of the living. This approach elicited attempts to categorize the dead and correlate certain fates after death with behavior in life. Many resisted these efforts at confinement and categorization by imagining ghosts in order to prolong their interaction with the dead. This refusal of categories pierced the boundary of death.

Although I know of no ancient discussion that delineates these three approaches as such, some sources debate the relative advantages of each view. In general, they interpret ideas, including religious beliefs, according to their effect on, or function in, society. Proponents of this method tend to accept or reject ideas more readily depending on whether they estimate that widespread adoption of those beliefs would cause people to live better—that is, obey the gods, honor their parents, serve the state, or rule their baser natures. This is the criterion of utility.

[24]   Valentin Kockel, "Im Tode gleich? Die sullanischen Kolonisten und ihr kulturelles Gewicht in Pompeji am Beispiel der Nekropolen," in *Römische Gräberstraßen Selbstdarstellung – Status – Standard*, eds. Henner von Hesberg and Paul Zanker (Munich: Verlag der Bayerischen Akademie der Wissenschaft, 1987), 194.

[25]   For example, one of the effects of Hales's recent study is her dissolution of the paradigm that Zanker so neatly established, namely, that domus dwellers fervently clung to elite models taken from villa design and decoration. [...]

This chapter, therefore, examines some explicit discussions in ancient literature of the relationship between beliefs about death and conduct in life. Hints of this important theme have already emerged. Plato said that death would be an escape for the wicked if there were no future life (*Phaedo* 107c). He also explained the deterrent effect of purified souls returning with knowledge of Tartarus (*Gorgias* 526). Virgil constructed his underworld to inform the future behavior of Aeneas. Now, before moving on to Jewish and Christian ideas of death and punishment after death, it is necessary to consider how the ancients of Greece and Rome analyzed the social and moral utility of their own religious traditions.

I do not mean to portray the ancients as reducing all ideas to their function. Yet the thinkers to be examined in this chapter noted the correlation between certain beliefs about the dead and the corresponding effects (whether beneficial or detrimental) on the society that accepted or rejected them. Another related premise claims that social order should by definition conform to the order of the cosmos: anything else would be chaos. Thus, correct belief about the nature of the world (including what happens after death) would advance the correct arrangement of society and the correct behavior of its members.

Some authors, such as Critias, Polybius, and Livy, state that the founders of their communities purposely devised myths to achieve a more tightly bound society whose members would cooperate more readily and exercise more self-control under the sway of these inventions than without them. Cicero held that correct understanding of the postmortem reward for patriots was part of what allowed the republic's great heroes to excel and, therefore, their descendants should also accept these beliefs. Lucian, too, operated under the assumption that recognizing the leveling effects of death would improve one's perspective in life. The authors discussed in this chapter agree that holding common beliefs about the afterlife binds a society together and enhances its propensity for virtue. Jewish and Christian authors do not make such statements in the period covered by this volume. Indeed, this feature of pagan philosophical self-consciousness usefully contrasts to an important aspect of divine providence in Judaism and Christianity. What the pagans attributed to human devising or themselves knowingly applied, Jews and Christians consider part of the providential working of divine justice.

Critias

Critias was an Athenian politician and playwright who lived from about 460 to 403 B.C.E. He was pro-Spartan and one of the Thirty Tyrants. Close to the Academy, he figured alongside Socrates in some of Plato's dialogues. He wrote a play called *Sisyphus* of which a surviving fragment contains a theory of the human origins of belief in the gods.

Critias posited two innovations in the transition from anarchy to the development of morals and respect for law. After an initial period of anarchy, men devised laws based on retribution to deter crime, but these checked only open offenses. The law could not control hidden deeds. Finally, "a wise and clever man invented fear (of the gods) for mortals." He devised a concerned and vigilant intelligence who could know whatever is thought or done. Critias's emphasis on fear implies that because no evil can escape these gods' notice, no evil will remain unpunished. Critias thus imagines the psychological effects of belief in such divinities. It was good for society, he suggests, to believe in these immortal, immaterial, knowing, and caring beings, for such "divinities" would deter crimes that no human agency could successfully prevent or prosecute. According to this view, their invention was a milestone in human history.[1]

Polybius

Polybius (c. 200–after 118 B.C.E.), the son of Achaean statesman, was raised in Greece but sent to Rome where he became attached to Scipio Aemilianus. He served as a Roman diplomat and emissary from Rome to Carthage, whose destruction he witnessed. In his *Histories* he considers Rome's attainment of world domination inevitable, but he also seeks human rather than purely fatal or providential causes for it. Considering the contribution of laws and institutions to the durability of regimes, Polybius notes a correspondence between the harmony of individual character and that of the social order, between the soul and the city. In constitutions "what is desirable ... makes men's private lives righteous and well ordered and the general character of the state gentle and just, while what is to be avoided has the opposite effect" (6.48.4).

Polybius believed that religions, or at least the beliefs acted out in rituals, could be contrived to serve the state and that the Romans were particularly adept at devising such rites. Thus, he considered the ability of Roman religion to incorporate the funeral rites of the individual *gens* or kin group, into the larger public reverence for the community's heroic dead as fundamental to the formation of Roman character and the success of Rome's expansion.

As an example of how to cultivate both personal and civic loyalty, Polybius singles out the burial practices of military heroes at Rome. In these ceremonies, the great man is laid out at the rostrum and publicly praised in such a way that the loss comes to be shared, he says, not only by the mourners but by the whole community. After interment, the death mask of the deceased is placed prominently in the house and, on public occasions, carried about the city. At a funeral of a descendant, all the death masks of a family's venerable ancestors are brought out, and the funeral speech praises not only the most recently deceased, but the whole lineage, beginning with the most ancient. Each ancestor is represented by an impersonator wearing a toga trimmed according to the level of magistracy attained, and these sit in special ivory chairs in front of the assembly, so that the whole community may commemorate the contributions of the venerable *gens* (6.54). The gallery of heroic "ghosts" arrayed before the community thus reinforces the prestige of the family in question and motivates others to emulate their example. "Who would not be inspired," he wonders, "by the sight of the images of men renowned for their excellence all together and as if alive and breathing?" (6.53.10; cf. 6.52.11, 55.4, 54.3). In this case, commemoration of notable ancestors, not classification of all the dead, is the operative model, whose utility Polybius praises.

Awe for distinguished forebears was not the only aspect of reverence that served the community. The Romans excelled over all other peoples, Polybius thought, in the depth of their religious convictions.[2] Their fear of the gods, which other peoples ridicule as superstition, "maintains the cohesion of the Roman State" (6.56.8). Were the state made up only of wise men, it would not have been necessary to cultivate this belief, but since the multitude does not know what it

---

[1]   Critias, fragment of the lost play *Sisyphus*, trans. Kathleen Freeman, in *Ancilla to the Pre-Socratic Philosophers* (Cambridge: Harvard University Press, 1948), 157–58. I thank Charles King for this and the following passage from Polybius.

[2]   Here is an opinion echoed in Cicero, *De natura deorum* 2.3.9, and made part of Jupiter's (self-serving) prophecy in Virgil, *Aeneid* 12.839–40.

wants, does not reason, and cannot contain its desires and passions, it must be checked by "invisible terrors and suchlike pageantry" (5.58.11).

The term "superstition" does not take full account of the benefits of these beliefs. It would be rash for his contemporaries to drop them, Polybius warns. Among the Greeks, where "notions concerning the gods and beliefs in the terrors of [Hades (*haidou dialēpseis*)]" are being abandoned, no official can be trusted with the smallest sum of money, though he be forced to find witnesses for every document and surround himself with auditors. Yet Roman magistrates, even those who deal with large sums of money, "maintain correct conduct just because they have pledged their faith by oath" (6.56.14). For Polybius, then, beliefs about gods and ghosts, should be judged not for their intellectual sophistication but for their utility. And as one who knew public life in both Greece and Rome, he thought Roman officials behaved more honestly than their Athenian counterparts because they feared the gods.

Lucretius

The Roman philosopher and poet Titus Lucretius Carus (99–55 B.C.E.) rejected the invisible terrors of future judgment which Critias and Polybius considered crucial to a society's discipline. These tales, he believed, chain the human mind in slavery to superstition; imagination is self-delusion. The correct understanding of how this world is related to the next, what happens after death, will liberate humankind from the crippling fears imposed by religion. There is no future judgment and, in the sense intended by the Orphics, Plato, and (later) Virgil, there is no transmigration of the soul.

In *On the Nature of Things*, he explains why these ideas are misconceptions. For Lucretius, as for his teachers Epicurus and Ennius, nature is a constant flux of material particles he called *semina*, "seeds" (1.59), which come together for a time to constitute a body if the particles are densely packed or a soul if they are rarefied.[3] At death, these combinations end, the particles scatter, and in the constant flux of matter, they form new bonds as each seed is recycled. The former union of body and soul which made up a human being ends. The recycled particles continue to exist, but no conscious person remains (3.847–61). These cycles go on independently of the gods (1.158). Punishment after death, therefore, is impossible. The tales about the underworld, postmortem judgment and punishment, gorgonian monsters, and chained Titans are mere figments of the imagination. Worse, these beliefs, Lucretius claimed, are based on guilt and the fear of death, which emotions are exploited by priests to ensure adherence to their cults, respect for their authority, and patronage of their shrines. This popular religion, what Lucretius calls "the old religions" (6.62), as fostered by priestly conspiracy, breeds fear and oppresses humankind (1.63–65).[4]

Whereas Critias maintained that the notion of postmortem scrutiny was consciously contrived to improve social behavior, Lucretius argued that belief in the gods arose from the consistency of our dreams, for people dream of strong and beautiful beings. Since the poets have described them the same way for so long and never shown them fearing death, we consider them immortal (5.1169–82). Ever since, humans have made themselves miserable by

---

[3]   For the place of Lucretius in the Epicurean tradition, see Diskin Clay, *Lucretius and Epicurus* (Ithaca: Cornell University Press, 1983), 197–98; also Dietrich Lemke, *Die Theologie Epikurs* (Munich: Beck, 1973).

[4]   In *Lucretius on Death and Anxiety: Poetry and Philosophy in "De Rerum Natura"* (Princeton: Princeton University Press, 1990), 14, Charles Segal argues that Lucretius is concerned to combat the terror of nonbeing rather than of the afterlife. Segal further discusses fear of the afterlife at 17–25 and 165.

imagining the gods as causes for what they do not understand (5.1185–87, 1194; cf. 1.151–54). The gods pursue only those who misunderstand them. They do not take vengeance on their victims. They haunt only the credulous souls who imagine them as spirits (6.71–79).

The correct understanding of divine sublimity exalts the gods beyond these petty concerns (such as punishing us for our misdeeds) and values their peace, their sublimity—in a word, their divinity (6.68–71). Lucretius himself evokes "nurturing Venus" as the provider of earth's bounty (1.1–5). In turning to Venus, however, he shuns Demeter, Persephone, and Hecate, the goddesses of fertility in the Eleusynian Mysteries, figures connected to the fear of death, whose exploitation he deplores. The love of Venus exhausts Mars and so brings peace (1.29–40). She offers herself to Mars, however, for her own purposes, unaffected by human prayers, beyond any wrath human beings imagine she might direct against them (44–49).

Who would fear death if people understood that neither their spirits nor their bodies, but only "pallid simulacra," survive to reach the Acheron (1.122)? In fact, what happens in death is analogous to sleep, when we feel no want of ourselves or of consciousness. Why should we feel it in death, when our mind and body will be even further scattered (3.919–30)? Like the body, the mind is mortal (3.831). "Therefore death is nothing to us" (3.830).[5] Even if our particles, after decomposition, were to be recomposed in exactly the same form, the very process of recomposition would preclude any continuity of feeling (3.847–61). Thus, "in death there is nothing for us to fear, nor can anyone be miserable who can not even exist, ... since immortal death has taken away our mortal life" (3.866–69).

Beyond the fear of simply being dead, Lucretius distinguishes the fear of punishment after death.[6] As the gods arose from our dreams, the fear of punishment after death emerged from our guilt. According to Lucretius, human society developed in orderly fashion until the discovery of gold, which engendered greed and conflict, particularly between the poor and the rich. But then, tired of strife, people framed laws to contain their ambitions. Later, they perceived that their earlier actions had exceeded the limits set down in the laws, and they began to fear punishment. For when one has practiced violence, the injury one has done usually reverts upon its author in the form of a fear of unintended self-betrayal "screaming in a nightmare or in feverish delirium" (5.1151–60; cf. 3.825–29). A combination of residual guilt and anticipated shame produces this emotion. The fear of death, like the dreams that induce us to believe in the gods, is wholly a product of the imagination.

Thus the famous punishments said to be administered in the underworld exist not there but in the living persons who fear them:

> There is no miserable Tantalus cringing beneath the great rock in the air above him and stilled by fruitless fear, as the story goes; rather [that rock] is the vain fear of the gods that afflicts mortals in this life and the fear of future blows with which destiny threatens us (3.978–83)[7]

---

[5]   For this slogan, see Barbara Price-Wallach, *Lucretius and the Diatribe against the Fear of Death: "De Rerum Natura" III 830–1094*, Supplement to *Mnemosyne*, 40 (Leiden: Brill, 1976); and Jean Salem, *La mort n'est rien pour nous: Lucrèce et l'éthique*, Bibliothèque d'histoire de la philosophie (Paris: Vrin, 1990).

[6]   Paul Eugène Lortie, "Crainte anxieuse des enfers chez Lucrèce: Prologomènes," *Phoenix* 8 (1954): 47–63.

[7]   Lucretius follows a different variant of the Tantalus legend from the one presented in Homer and Virgil.

Similarly Tityos is laid out *here* before us (3.992). The vulture gnawing his liver represents the anxieties that pierce his being. In passing, Lucretius sarcastically remarks that the bird would never find an eternity's worth of fodder in his victim's liver even if it covered the whole earth, nor would Tityos be able to bear the pain forever (3.984–95). Sisyphus "too is here in this life before our eyes" (3.995). The rock against which he labours is his unrealizable ambition for office and power. The Danaids, maidens cursed with the task of filling perforated urns, represent people unsatisfied by the fruits of life, brought in measure by the seasons. The holes in the urns in which they "carry" water are the gaps in their satisfaction with nature's bounty. "Cerberus, the Furies, the scarcity of light, and Tartarus belching frightening fire from his maw have never existed, nor can they" (3.1011–13).[8]

Where, then, do these fears come from? The answer is the same: from life itself (3.1014). The Roman state has punishments aplenty, rightly to be feared—prison, being cast from the high (Tarpeian) rock, lashings, executioners, pitch, metal plates, torches. But even without these, the mind dwells upon its deeds, applies goads to itself, and tortures itself with lashes, all the while fearing punishment in advance (3.1014–19). Thus, the human soul punishes itself through obsession not only with the imaginary torments described in myths but also with the real penalties of the judicial system. And in its guilt ("conscious of its own deeds" [3.1018]) it imagines itself, in advance, suffering penalties in death which it has so far escaped in life. There is no question, then, where the punishments come from. What seems remarkable to Lucretius is people's need to imagine themselves liable to such torments forever.

By contrast, Lucretius continues, the penalties of the judicial system will end. Yet adherents of the old religions consider finite punishments insufficient and insist on imagining that after death the punishments will be still worse. "At length the life of fools is made into a hell on earth" (3.1023). Lucretius interprets the popular fear of punishment after death as a correct perception of state-sanctioned penalties confused with torments from the mythical past, internalized by the guilt-ridden out of anxiety about having misdeeds discovered, and finally projected ahead into an afterlife when the gravity of the punishment will be intensified and, worse yet, unending. No effort to postpone it will work, nor will it diminish the time spent dead, for "that eternal death will nonetheless remain" (3.1091). The punishments after death are figments of the imagination; only death itself is eternal. And that is more peaceful than sleep![9]

Lucretius provides a rare opportunity to consider an ancient who denies the existence of any afterlife. For him the torments are allegorized representations of psychological problems. Sisyphus suffers indeed rolling his boulder, but not in the underworld and not in death. By comparing them to dreams, *On The Nature of Things* makes the beliefs promulgated by the regional Mediterranean cults entirely imaginary. The myths linking each shrine to its caretakers, the priests, gained credibility from their resemblance to the actual justice system of Rome and their traditional repetition by generations of poets and bards. Beyond the circulation of cultic myth and folklore were the written versions in Greek literature read by Romans. Yet these sources constitute the limit of their reality.

---

[8]   Gian Biagio Conte, "Il trionfo della morte e la galleria dei grandi trapassati in Lucrezio III, 1024–1053," *Studi italiani di filologia classica* 37 (1965: 114–32. See also André Desmouliez, "Cupidité, ambition, et crainte de la mort chez Lucrèce (De R.N. III 59–93)," *Latomus* 17 (1958): 317–23.

[9]   See Philip Mitsis, *Epicurus' Ethical Theory: The Pleasures of Invulnerability*, Cornell Studies in Classical Philology, 48 (Ithca: Cornell University Press, 1988).

Since in life these torments are confined to the judicial system, dreams, and classical (Greek) literature, they are invalid indicators about the nature of death, which we can under-stand only through philosophy (*ratio*). Lucretius thought only matter and death were eternal.

For Lucretius therefore, belief in gods, though supported by some psychological realities and aspects of institutional life, produces a debilitating subjection to imaginary terrors spawned by poets and fostered by greedy temple attendants. Clearly thinking in terms of cause and effect, Lucretius urged a life unencumbered by the emotional baggage of religion.[10]

Cicero

At first glance, Cicero would also seem to have no patience with the notion of punishment after death, for he is suspicious of all the gods, including those of the underworld.[11] If he disposes of the agents of postmortem retribution, he deprives the dead, or the wicked dead, of their tormentors. Clearly that is the impression he gives in *Pro Cluentio*. There, he calls "transparent fabrications and fables" the belief that "in the underworld there exists a site or a region devoted to the punishment of the wicked" and that a wicked man "would encounter there more persecuters than he left here." "Since all of this is false, as everyone knows," Cicero takes his discourse in another direction (171). He also implies in the fourth speech against Catalina (3.8) that these beliefs were a human invention that had long since lost their currency, typical, as they were, only of olden times.

The first debate in the *Tusculan Disputations* comes to the same conclusion.[12] The philosophical neophyte "A" contends that death is a great evil for humankind. The more experienced "M" undertakes to persuade him of the opposite view. First, however, M must remove any suspicion that A fears death because of the fables associated with a painful or punitive afterlife. You're not afraid of mythical beasts like the three-headed Cerberus, are you, he asks him, or of scrutiny by Greek judges such as Rhadamanthus and Minos, the rivers Styx or Acheron, or the torments of Sisyphus or Tantalus? Even the novice knows better: Do you think I'm crazy? (1.5.9). Again Cicero dismisses the underworld as unworthy of serious consideration by the sophisticates who frequent his villa. In fact, we are told, the underworld is empty (1.6.11).

Fears of the underworld may be put to rest when one understands how these erroneous beliefs arose. According to M, the mental capabilities of the human race have progressed. Only at the older, primitive stage was any belief in a punitive underworld necessary, and it sprang from reflections on nature, the source of all the knowledge of the ancients. They did not, however, understand the causes and principles behind the physical phenomena they observed. In this state of ignorance, they inferred from nighttime apparitions (ghosts coming back in dreams) that those who died and reappeared lived on after death

---

[10]   See the paraphrase in Segal, *Lucretius*, 35–36. Cf. Salem, *La mort*, 116. For Lucretius's direct attack on superstition, see 1.62–79; and M.J. Edwards, "Treading the Aether: Lucretius, *De Rerum Natura* 1.62–79," *Classical Quarterly* 40 (1990): 465–69.

[11]   See R.J. Goar, *Cicero and the State Religion* (Amsterdam: Hakkert, 1972); also Woldemar Görler, *Untersuchungen zu Ciceros Philosophie*, Bibliothek der klassischen Altertumswissenschaften, 2d ser., vol. 50 (Heidelberg: Winter, 1974).

[12]   For Cicero's philosophy, see A.J. Kleijwegt, "Philosophischer Gehalt und persönliche Stellungnahme in Tusc. I, 9–81," *Mnemosyne*, 4th ser., 19 (1966): 359–88; Olof Gigon, "Die Erneuerung der Philosophie in der Zeit Ciceros," *Entretiens Fondation Hardt* 3 (1955): 25–59. Paul MacKendrick, *The Philosophical Books of Cicero* (New York: St. Martin's, 1989), offers a summary (149–63) and a brief commentary (163–68).

(1.13.29). Moreover, this belief was not confined to the ancient Romans; it was accepted throughout the world. And what all peoples agree on should be considered a law of nature. Therefore, it is nature that inspires the belief that the dead live and continue to feel and experience a kind of life (1.13.30). Belief in reward after death for noble exertion in life, then, is the general consensus, and it would not have arisen without some natural basis. We should, therefore, accept it (1.16.35).

Since it is natural that we should believe that souls live on after death, we must learn what this afterlife is like, for ignorance has produced exaggerated fears, which appropriately occasion scorn (1.16.36). Because, in earlier times, people were unable to conceive of souls apart from bodies, they saw them as continuing to live underground, where they were interred, as if the corpses had not been burned before burial. Conceiving of the dead, including ghosts, as still joined to their bodies was a mental necessity for those who could not imagine an independent soul, and poets have built on this deficiency (1.16.37).

But with learning (*doctrina*) and the application of reason (*ratio*), says M, we can transcend this error. With the superior powers of conceptualization it brings, philosophy has led us away from these primal fears based on primitive myths. This realization has been accomplished in stages, with the help of Pherecydes of Syros, then his disciple Pythagoras, and finally by Plato (1.16.38).[13] Whatever its exact nature (1.11.24, cf. 1.17.41), once we can conceive of an immaterial, eternal soul, the whole question of death appears different (1.19.43–1.20.47).

Drawing directly on *Phaedrus* 245 and *Republic* 610–11, M claims that the soul is divine and demonstrably on a par with God, which fact renders the body unimportant (1.23.53–1.27.67). In this sense, as Plato said in the *Phaedo* (67c), the whole life of the philosopher is a preparation for death. Although they avoid committing suicide, the wise welcome death (*Tusculan Disputations* 1.30.74). Drawing on *Phaedrus* (246–47), M explains that after death, the soul goes either away from or toward the gods (1.30.72). In place of the scars Plato describes as visible on the naked soul in the form of a body (*Gorgias* 524), M imagines chains that permit the body to advance farther or not, depending on the degree to which the soul was liberated from ties to the body. Greater or lesser cultivation of the soul and control of the body, then, determines the length of one's restraints and the ability of one's soul to rise. Although there is no specific punishment for the wicked, this system of graduated reward distinguishes people's fates after death. No matter how high one rises, death frees the soul from the shackles of the body and only then does life truly begin, for "this life is death" (1.31.75.). Death, then, is a liberation—and therefore hardly an evil—since through its portals we either become gods or join the gods (1.31.76).

The debate "reported" by Cicero presents a theory of the growth of knowledge which accounts for the widespread belief, born of a more primitive age, promoted by the poets, and still accepted among the common people, which fosters fear of death and particularly the possibility of punishment in the earth, where Hades (or in his Roman form, Pluto or Dis) rules. In contrast, the philosophical view distinguishes body and soul in life and death. The fate of the soul has no relation to the fate of the body. The underworld, based on an assimilation with the grave, is not relevant. It is empty of souls (*Tusculan*

---

[13]   Cf. 1.21.49, where Cicero denies that Plato dispelled these errors.

Disputations 1.19.43–1.20.47). For those who care, the body experiences nothing, as Lucretius had already taught.[14]

Cicero devotes the remainder of the first dialogue to considering the alternative possibility, that the soul does not survive the body. Using Lucretius, he shows how, in that case, there would be no sensation (since the body can have no consciousness without the soul, and both are dead). The only afterlife this view affords the dead is in their reputation on earth (1.45.109). It is in fact intolerable to believe that the dead actually experience the pains of the underworld of which the crowd is convinced (1.46.111). This conclusion again reflects how Cicero's analysis builds on the distinction between the learned few and the gullible populace. The learned understand the principles of nature and have no need of myth; the ordinary people perceive nature directly, without the benefit of learning (*doctrina*), and hence remain prey to the poets' tales (or myths), which exploit their fears of the underworld.

Even though the underworld of torments is empty, heaven teems with heroes—but heroes of a special sort. It is the distinguished servants of their country who live on in glory. In his dialogue *On the Nature of the Gods*, Cicero again builds on his view that religious belief begins with the perceptions of the uneducated embellished by the bards.[15] As in the *Tusculan Disputations*, one important basis for the reverence we owe the gods comes from the respect universally accorded them, which derives in turn from their harmonious relationship with natural forces. The existence of the gods derives from the observations of nature by all and so must be accepted (*De natura deorum* 1.16.43; cf. 2.24.63). The question is not whether they exist but what they are like (2.5.13).

Whatever we eventually determine on this question, says Balbus, one of the disputants, it should be observed that religion, which he defines as "respect for the gods" (*cultus deorum* [2.3.9]), is good for social order and the expansion of the state for conquest is linked to *pietas* and respect for the auguries. He reports that generals who neglected the auguries failed, which shows that "those who submitted to the principles of religion extended the state by their command" (2.3.7–8). However the Romans measure up against other peoples in other areas of culture, Balbus says, they excel in one crucial regard: in their religion. Since most of the subject peoples in 44 B.C.E. might have thought it was in military organization, territorial expansion, and command that Rome excelled, Balbus here is firmly, though implicitly, connecting piety with military success (2.3.9).

The strict connection Balbus claimed between Rome's ancient religious devotion and its military success exemplifies the ancient technique of assessing ideas for their social utility, which is the subject of this chapter. Although the true cognoscenti do not take religious myths literally (indeed, he distinguishes between religion and superstition [2.28.72]), Balbus finds that reason can draw beneficial and useful principles from the observation of nature (2.28.70). Although the tales about the gods are false, conformity to the rituals that recognize the power of forces acknowledged the world over is not only

---

[14]   In this passage (1.21.48–49), Cicero pretends independence of Lucretius and Plato, though it is clear from preceding passages that they are the cornerstones of his argument: Plato, for the idea that the soul has a fate separate from the body (*Phaedrus* 245–47); Lucretius, for the idea that the body experiences nothing after death (*De rerum natura* 3.830–977).

[15]   On this work, see Martin van den Bruwaene, *La théologie de Cicéron* (Louvain: Bureaux de recueil, Bibliothèque de l'université, 1937).

beneficial but indispensible to the success of the noble order, the stability of the republic, and its military expansion.[16]

Selecting an example, Balbus—and Cotta does not challenge him on this point—blames the negligence of the nobility (2.3.9) for the public's loss of respect for the auguries, which it is their responsibility to maintain. According to Balbus, the ceremony's history in the republic's early days links traditional respect for the supernatural to the caste charged with administering its rites.

Whether it conforms to Cicero's private opinion or not, the theory outlined by Balbus evaluates religion in terms of its utility to the state. In his view, those political communities advance which conform in their ritual and social structure to the natural forces that govern the universe as these are understood by reason and enshrined in religion, though, where religion is concerned, the philosopher will distinguish true principles from the embroidery of popular proverbs, the myths of poets, and indiscriminate superstition. Nonetheless, because we can see certain physical truths through these principles, and because of the respect we owe tradition—remember the social utility of the auguries, mentioned at 2.3.9—it is our duty to uphold and venerate them (2.28.71). Balbus sharply distinguishes this grudging acceptance of religion from superstition. Whereas superstition accepts all these fables, religion is critical and selective (2.28.72).

We have seen in the previous chapter how Cotta attacked Balbus's conciliatory exposition by insinuating that the existence of Zeus, indeed of all the Olympians, depends on the likes of Cerberus. But Cotta disavows any intention of debunking the gods, for it would hardly be suitable for a philosopher to remove all belief in them (3.17.44). More important, as he did in the first of the *Tusculan Disputations*, Cicero makes his most critical disputant allow a crucial exception within the ranks of the divine—patriots: "We should declare against those who say that these gods whom we all honor piously and reverently were transferred from the human race into heaven not in fact but only in the opinions of men" (3.21.53). This is a theory dear to Cicero. He includes it in his summary discussion of death in *On Old Age* (21, 23) and with even greater clarity in that part of *On the Republic* (book 6), known as the *Dream of Scipio*, where it constitutes a veritable civic theology.[17] The deceased grandfather of Scipio Africanus appears to him in a dream and reveals the nature of the world in order that he might defend his country more steadfastly. Further, nothing pleases the gods more than those communities that rule themselves by the convocations and deliberations of men under the law, which are called states. It therefore follows (*certum est*) that the gods make special provisions for those who dedicate themselves to the well-being of these communities: "For all who defend, aid, and expand the fatherland, there is a specific place set aside in heaven, where the blessed will enjoy an unending age of happiness" (*De republica* 6.13).

Scipio's dream contains a revelation not touched on in the *Tusculan Disputations*. There, Cicero's disputant M observes that the country's ancient heroes lived in a purer age and perceived nature more directly than we do. Given that advantage, they behaved as if they (that is their souls) would enjoy future reward for service to the fatherland, and we should draw the appropriate conclusion by imitating their example: "And if we judge that the souls of those

---

[16]   Goar, *Cicero*, 117, observes that Cotta, the other disputant, also insists on upholding the traditional Roman rituals, even as he attacks much else that Balbus tried to salvage.

[17]   On this work, see Pierre Boyancé, *Etudes sur le "Songe de Scipion"* (1936; rpt. New York: Garland, 1987), 121–46; and Karl Büchner, *"Somnium Scipionis": Quellen-Gestalt-Sinn* (Wiesbaden: Steiner, 1976), 73–81.

who excel either by inventiveness or virtue, since they are the best by nature, and since they are also those who have served posterity best, and are most likely to be the best able to perceive the forces of nature, and since they have acted as if there is some consciousness after death, [we should too]" (1.16.35). But in *Scipio's Dream* Cicero makes his informant reveal the basis of their foresight: they have seen that future. That is how they were able to know that the soul lives on and that it is rewarded for devotion to the country's welfare. Heaven is not only the reward they attain; it is also the source from which they come—much like the orbiting souls of Plato's *Phaedrus*. As Cicero had the Elder Scipio say it: "Their governors and defenders come from that place [i.e., the heavens] and return there" (13). Although this shuttling back and forth between heaven and the country they serve no doubt diminishes their enjoyment of the "sempiternal" happiness, it explains their clearsightedness in advising posterity.[18]

The elder Scipio's revelation concerns more than the structure of the heavens. Clearly Cicero believes certain kinds of knowledge or belief will have behavioral consequences for those who share it. Thus the younger Scipio should know these things because, when they are known, even noble youths imbued with the traditions of their heroic forebears will dedicate themselves to these goals "with greater alacrity" (13). In the fictional dream, this link between belief and conduct motivated Scipio the Elder's communication of these truths to his grandson.

The contrast between his philosophical writings and his oratory, aimed at a wider audience, highlights the utility Cicero attributed to the link between belief and conduct. In his philosophical works, written in retirement, before his imprisonment and execution, Cicero denies the existence of punishment after death. There are no gods in the underworld. Nor do the dead experience the fate of their bodies. Thus, there is neither tormentor nor victim beneath the earth. However empty the earth's innards, heroes crowd the heavens. Those who devote themselves to the service of their country and imitate the ancestors of the Romans will attain unending glory after death. If they do not actually become gods, they will live with them (*Tusculan Disputations* 1.31.76). In expounding the apotheosis of patriots Cicero denies a systematic mapping of the underworld. He denies any space to the wicked, thus, as Plutarch would do later, consigning them to oblivion. In allowing Cotta to destroy the Olympian gods along with their chthonic counterparts, Cicero invents a heaven populated only by the gods of his choosing: outstanding servants of the (Roman) state. It would seem, therefore, that in Circero's view, only one destiny is possible after death: everlasting life for patriots. Such, at least, is the conclusion he reaches in his philosophical works.

Yet in the *Philippics*, whose purpose was to mold senatorial opinion against Mark Antony, he alludes clearly to the idea of divine retribution. Indeed, that fate already threatens Mark Antony as an enemy of the state. Men and gods work together for the preservation of the state, Cicero reminds the less philosophically sophisticated senators. Thus, public consensus must indicate the will of the gods. Although he feigns uncertainty about the reliability of the signs he sees, Cicero nonetheless affirms the state's safety and Antony's impending punishment (4.4.10).

Cicero is less roundabout describing the fate of Antony's troops. The orator assures the senators that, as warriors who died achieving victory for the

---

[18]   Goar observes, *Cicero*, 122, that the *Dream* provides an afterlife only for statesmen; nothing is said of the other souls.

fatherland, the dead men of his own side will dwell with the pious. Then, likening his opponents in a civil war to parricides for their offense against the fatherland, he guarantees the Senate that its enemies will pay for their crime with infernal punishment. Affecting to address the warriors slain in defense of the republic, he concludes: "Therefore, those impious ones whom you have killed will pay the punishments for their parricide in the underworld [*ad inferos*], but you, who have expended your last breath in victory, have attained the condition and the abode of the pious" (*Philippica* 14.12.32).[19] It is therefore clear that although in his philosophical works he found the idea of punishment after death distasteful and suited only to the incredulous, in his oratory he used it for political ends.

Now we understand why Cicero made Cotta hesitate. Divinities are not to be eliminated entirely, for their existence provides a reward for patriotic heroes. In philosophy leaders of the state may scorn the beliefs of the crowd and call then superstition, but as the situation with the augurs illustrates, they should set a limit to their disrespect. Statesmen do not want a multitude that believes in nothing. Then the people would lose respect for tradition and the authority claimed by the men who minister to it.

Livy

Livy, too, had a keen sense of the utility of religion for the state. A native of Padua born in 59 B.C.E., Livy came to Rome, where he devoted himself to his historical writing and died in 17 C.E. He gave public readings of his work, became friends with Augustus, and formed part of the literary circle that included Virgil, Horace, and until his exile, Ovid. His major work is a history of the Roman republic in 142 books collected into groups of ten, called "decades."[20] This work begins with the earliest legends "from the foundation of the city," a technique of organization that gives the work its title, *Ab urbe condita*. Immediately following his account of the establishment of a unified monarchy on the site by Romulus, Livy begins with this successor, Numa, and turns the subject from military consolidation to civilian foundation.

Inheriting a unified monarchy, Numa the legislator decided to instill a fear of the gods in the minds of the Romans in order to provide discipline that would hold the community together despite the lack of an external military threat. Since he knew he would gain no acceptance for his institutions without some little wonder (*miraculum*), he let it be known that he met nightly with the goddess Egeria, who advised him as to what ceremonies would most please the gods and how to dedicate a priest for each one (1.19.1). Livy built his theory of the function of religion into his historical account. Looking back from his vantage point, Livy imagined that Numa's stratagem served its purpose: the Roman state had been successful (from his perspective). Clearly, this fiction had called forth no retributive disaster from vengeful gods; rather, it had encouraged virtue among the citizens from the earliest days of Rome. Nor did Numa limit himself to the heavenly powers, Livy says; he also arranged to appease the chthonic forces, establishing ceremonies to placate the departed spirits of the dead (1.20.7).

More important than the historical nature of a decision Livy attributed to a legendary king is the readiness he must have assumed on the part of his audience to see the effectiveness of the innovation. Livy expected his readers

---

[19]   I wish to thank Lee Williams for calling my attention to this passage.

[20]   For an introduction to this work, see T.J. Luce, *Livy: The Composition of His History* (Princeton: Princeton University Press, 1977).

to see a likely correlation among conscious reflection, founding myths, belief in supernatural sanctions by the common people and a moral order consistent with military readiness in peacetime.

The scheme worked extremely well, Livy says. Concern for the gods (*cura deorum*) became so ingrained that the people perceived a heavenly spirit residing among them and they came to direct their affairs out of respect for promises and trust in one another rather than fear of the punishments stipulated by the laws (1.21.1).

Livy, then, assumes as plausible a notion that human reason can, by means of myth, instill a code of ethics that will regulate a voluntary association of citizens. He does not explain why the myth (or *miraculum*, as he calls it), "the little source of awe," should be necessary rather than the laws themselves or some philosophy of justice. He says only that the populace was uneducated (*rudis*) and inexperienced (*imperita*) in the arts of peace (1.19.4). Nonetheless, as Plato had before him, Livy attributed to the founders of the Roman monarchy, replaced by the republic, a fond concern for the stories that inspire right conduct. These, he suggested, lay at the basis of the Roman community. In his tale of Numa, Livy uses a theory of religion's social utility closely akin to that of Critias.

Utility in Lucian

Much of Lucian's art, as we have seen, consists in locating his audience in the underworld, so that it may appreciate the vanity of life from the perspective of the dead. Yet the viewpoint of the deceased must be imagined, and it is very clear that Lucian composes his shade's view of life from his own particular perspective. What is clearer from the underworld than from the surface is the value of the Cynic's outlook. However otherworldly Lucian's dialogues, whether in setting or perspective, both the writer and the audience are focused on earth. Lucian's model of the hereafter is not so much an otherworldly doctrine as a setting from which to "observe and prescribe for the sins of man" (*Downward Journey* 7). Because he advocates spreading a certain idea of the afterlife to change the beliefs and therefore the behavior of the living, Lucian forms part of the pragmatic tradition that considers religion useful.

In the *Dialogues of the Dead*, renowned underworld personalities attest that only Cynics face death calmly. Cerberus himself informs Menippus that Socrates' death scene was only for show: he was as frightened as the others on the bark across the Styx. The same authority assures Menippus that he alone confronted the passage into death with equanimity (4 [422]).[21] The crossing of the Styx in Charon's bark is a moment of truth. Lucian revels in the shrieks of hypocrites who reveal themselves as they part with their "possessions" to lighten the load for the crossing and enter the equality of death. The tyrant gives up his diadem and robes. The warrior lays down his arms. The philosopher relinquishes his quarrelsomeness and hair splitting; the rhetorician, his antitheses, balances, and periods (20 [366–74). There is no wealth, no ancestral title, no rank, no epitaph, and as Diogenes forces Mausolus himself to admit, no mausoleum among the dead (29 [431]). Lucian's lesson, therefore, is that these things are pointless in life too. He uses the poverty of death to teach simplicity in life.

Menippus sums it up: "In Hades all are equal, and all alike" (30 [433]). Socrates, famous for his snub nose and bald head, is unrecognizable, just a skull

---

[21]   Menippus hanged himself according to M.D. MacLeod in the Loeb edition of Lucian (7:117), citing Diogenes Laertius, *Lives of Eminent Philosophers* 6.100.

(6 [417]). Helen of Troy's beauty exists no more; she's all bone (5 [408–9]). Tireisias does not stand out as blind, because *none* of the skulls have eyes (9 [445]). Nireus and Thersites ask Menippus to determine which of them is better looking. He says he can't tell them apart. Then what of how we were? Menippus insists on seeing them as they are, as he would claim he did in life too (30 [433]).

To change the lives of his audience, Lucian draws freely on belief in judgment and punishment after death. In *Menippus*, the Cynic tours the underworld in the company of a Zoroastrian magus. They come to the court of Minos where the Poenae, Avengers, and Erinyes stand as assessors. The dead are brought in chains: procurers, publicans, sycophants, informers. The rich wear heavy, spiked collars. In a detail that comes from Zoroastrian literature, fitting for the guide in this dialogue, the dead are accused by their own shadows (11).[22] Yet, although Dion accuses him of many crimes and his shadow confirms the charges, Aristippus of Cyrene intervenes on behalf of Dionysius of Syracuse for his patronage of literature! (13). This, again, is the self-promotional aspect of Lucian's work. He favors the Cynics, and yet—for all he says about the rich—their generosity to authors weighs heavily in their favor.

Menippus and the magus come to the place of punishment: whips snap, fires burn, the rack creaks. Victims on the gibbet and the wheel moan and cry. Cerberus and the Chimera feast on the others. As he encounters dead men he knew, Menippus reminds them with gusto how wealthy they had been. The rich were often criticized for arrogant displays before the poor who stood outside the gates of private estates awaiting alms. Thus, Menippus chides the recently deceased rich for scornfully ordering their servants to close the gates to the many or, when they were in a good mood, appearing splendidly attired before the gathered hoi polloi and offering a hand or breast to be kissed (12).

What principles of punishment are at work here? Lucian presents his contrasts in graduated order. The guilty poor are chastised half as severely as the rich, being allowed periods of rest equal to their terms of punishment (14). Mausolus is given the same single square foot of space allowed any plebeian, but the man after whom imposing burial monuments derive their name must also bear the weight of his tomb (17). His earthly folly distinguishes him in death. In other cases, Lucian presents true reversal in the sense that the victims become the tormentors of those who persecuted them in life. Kings and their officers are reduced to poverty, and like the meanest of slaves, they are subject to blows from passersby. Xerxes, Darius, Polycratus, and other former rulers now are begging, reduced to dependency on their former subjects or people like them (17).

---

[22]   The Zoroastrian text is *The Book of Arda Viraf* or, in a recent publication, *Arda Wiraz Nanag: The Iranian "Divina Commedia"*, trans. Fereydun Vahman, Scandinavian Institute of Asian Studies Monograph Series, 53 (London: Curzon Press, 1986). Here a virtuous soul sees "his own religion and his own good deeds in the form of a [beautiful] girl" (194), and a wicked person sees "his own religion and deeds (in the form of) a naked whore" so tainted with spots she resembles "a reptile, most filthy and most stinking" (201). For an older translation see *The Ardai Viraf Nameh; or, The Revelations of Ardai Viraf,* trans. J.A. Pope (London: printed for Black, Parbury, and Allen, 1816), 52–101. In this version the demon that personifies the soul's evil deeds and thus afflicts it, is not a hag covered with blotches but "a form of the most demoniacal appearance; it had teeth like an elephant, and the nails of its hands and feet were like the talons of an eagle; his eyes were like blood, and out of his mouth issued volumes of pestilential vapour that mixed with the wind" (55). When questioned as to his identity, the demon answers: "I am your genius, and have become thus deformed by your crimes (whilst you were innocent I was handsome)" (56).

The simplicity and uniformity that death imposes on all has political consequences. The system according to which the poor as a class reverse dominance with the rich as a class, is endorsed by a plebiscite. Ruling now by force of numbers, the former poor imitate the *boulē* of the democratic city-states. The popular assembly approves a new law proposed by a certain Skull, son of Skeleton, of the deme Corpse and the tribe Anatomy. They provide that henceforth the rich should have their bodies sent below to be punished like those of other malefactors, but their souls should be forced to live in donkeys, transmigrating from ass to ass, bearing burdens under the "tender mercies" of the poor for a quarter million years, and only then being allowed to die (20). In this mode of justice one class exchanges its position with another so that victims come to dominate (20).

Whereas *Menippus* presents a reversal of classes, *The Downward Journey* offers a nearly direct confrontation of opposed individuals. The first of its two parts contrasts the deaths of its protagonists. The Cynic philosopher Cyniscus helps Hermes bring the tyrant Megapenthes down to the land of Hades. Poisoned by one of his cronies, Megapenthes is far too busy with all his schemes to be ready to die. He tries to escape from Hermes, who gathers up the dead, and must be brought down in fetters (3). Even at the shore of the Styx he tries to bargain with Clotho, one of the Fates, and then to bribe her for extra time. In the conversation, she reveals his great crimes (8–9). Cyniscus rebukes and threatens Megapenthes with his club as Hermes finally forces the tyrant on board Charon's boat (13). In life, annoyed because of the philosopher's frankness in denouncing his evil, Megapenthes had "come within an ace" of tying Cyniscus to a cross. Now Cyniscus takes satisfaction in seeing Megapenthes tied to the mast for the crossing of the Styx (13). Here is a near reversal of fates.

A cobbler named Mycillus, who had been working at his leather when summoned, accepts death much better. The cobbler had nothing on earth worth longing for, and now the prospect of death, where all are equal and justice is unbiased, looks good to him. "The tables are turned, for we paupers laugh while the rich are distressed and lament" (15). The cobbler had been the tyrant's neighbor, had seen all that went on in his house, and had counted him fortunate until the awful row he created at his death exposed the truth (16–17). The bark is full and Mycillus is not yet on board. Hermes offers him a ride on the shoulders of Megapenthes, which would create a dramatic inversion of their relationship in life, but Mycillus must pull an oar since he has not even a single obol with which to pay for the crossing. Urged by Hermes to lament his past life, he ironically bemoans the loss of hungry days and cold winters in tattered rags (20). The opening section, therefore, contrasts Megapenthes first to Cyniscus, notable for his right understanding, and then to Mycillus, remarkable for his simple life and his ability to learn from Megapenthes' negative example—exactly as Lucian's readers should!

In the second section, the setting is that of Plato's *Gorgias*. The three shades appear together before Rhadamanthus, who presides. Cyniscus insists on denouncing Megapenthes. The tyrant admits his public crimes but denies his more refined private vices. At the suggestion of Cyniscus, his bed and his lamp are summoned to testify, and these personal accouterments condemn him. Then, according to the reform of judgment procedures which Plato attributed to Zeus, the tyrant is stripped, and the testimony of bed and lamp is confirmed by blotches on his soul, which, as in Plato, signify his many vices. The punishment is that he should never get a drink of Lethe water, so that he must remember all he misses forever. As he must long for what he can never attain, he is sentenced to a place next to Tantalus (26–28). Under similar inspection, the soul of Cyniscus reveals some old, very faint scars that have been nearly eradicated by the practice of philosophy (24). The soul of Mycillus is entirely clear. Rhadamanthus sends Mycillus and Cyniscus to the Isles of the Blessed (24–25).

This Mycillus appears in another dialogue called *The Dream: or, The Cock*. Awakened from a dream of possessing the gold of his oppressive neighbor Eucrates by the crowing of his rooster, Mycillus rails at the bird, which, surprisingly, answers his scolding. The cock is Pythagoras in one of his many reincarnations, who instructs Mycillus about the folly of trusting in wealth. In the dialogue, however, Mycillus conveys his resentment of the ostentatious Eucrates and Simon, who hoard their own goods, steal from Mycillus, and extract extravagant displays of deference. Unlike *The Downward Journey*, *The Dream* provides no reversal of fortune. Mycillus simply sees how hollow are the "advantages" of the rich. When, in *The Downward Journey*, Rhadamanthus sends Mycillus to the Isles of the Blessed, he re-wards a victim who has learned to live simply in his modest condition. A similarity has been noted between this Mycillus and the Lazarus so conspic-uously neglected by the rich man in one of the parables of Jesus retold by the evangelist Luke.[23] In *The Downward Journey*, however, Mycillus "con-verts" after he dies and takes in the scene created by Megapenthes, and in *The Dream*, although his outlook is changed in life, Lucian does not portray his end. For this comparison to work well, one must combine the early conversion of Mycillus in *The Dream* with the sentence rendered in *The Downward Journey*.

Lucian, however, was no systematizer. His underworld is too porous. It is both a monarchy and a democracy. His shades can be tortured or punished or shamed or simply unhappy. No single, consistent vision rules. Lucian himself appears to warn interpreters against putting too rigid a construction on his dialogues. Proof comes in a dramatic judgment scene in the *Dialogues of the Dead* (24), which opens with Minos assigning punishments to the wicked and the Elysian Fields to the good. The pirate Sostratus objects to his sentence. Using reason, he forces Minos to admit that the Fates compelled him to live his life as he did. Since he was not responsible for his actions, he cannot be punished for them. Minos agrees, suspends his punishments, entreats him not to spread the word, and admits it is not the only contradiction he will find among the dead.

Whether because of punishment or simple confrontation with the reality of death, in Hades the dead now understand and lament their follies. They realize the worthlessness of possessions, the vanity of worldly ambitions. Lucian excoriates the schemers who hoped to inherit from aged, wealthy, childless benefactors who outlive the sychophants who courted them (14–19). Varying the theme of Tantalus, Lucian makes their deaths resemble their lives, as they come to Hades with their "open-mouthed greed," as if their thirst for wealth were about to be slaked (15 [345]). The only money allowed them in death is the penny they will surrender to the ferryman (21 [379]).

Not property but the consciousness of death should be the guiding principle of life, according to Lucian (3 [337]). He emphasizes this moral in the last line of *Charon* (24): "How silly are the ways of unhappy mankind, with their kings, golden ingots, funeral rites and battles—but never a thought of Charon!" (that is, of death). As Antilochus confides to Achilles, who is just as restless in Lucian's underworld as in Homer's, the key to life after death serves also for

---

23   For a careful study of these parallels, drawing particularly on *The Dream* and *The Downward Journey*, see Ronald F. Hock, "Lazarus and Micyllus: Greco-Roman Backgrounds to Luke 16:19–31," *Journal of Biblical Literature* 106 (1987): 455.

life: remain silent, "bear and endure it all," or else "become a laughing-stock" (*Dialogues of the Dead* 26 [401]). Or as Menippus tells Chiron the Centaur, who preferred life in the underworld to the boringly predictable sequence of seasons, night and day: One should do what "a sensible man is reputed to do—be content and satisfied with one's lot and think no part of it intolerable" (8 [436]). However bleak his prescription for happiness, Lucian still proclaims the superiority of life over death. Though Lucian has Diogenes chide him for it, an aged, crippled, deathly sick, and nearly blind man arrives at Charon's bark admitting that death frightens him and that he longs for the light (22).

As much as Lucian enjoys satirizing the beliefs of many, he subordinates his scorn for superstition to his didactic strategy. He portrays death to shape behavior and to teach moderation in conduct, frankness in speech, awareness of death, and the fundamental equality of all mortals.

The existence of this utilitarian approach to the afterlife in Greek and Roman antiquity is of the utmost importance, because it shows that this technique of analysis was available in the ancient world. Thus its absence from Jewish and Christian literature assumes all the more importance. Although they share with Greek and Roman philosophers the idea that humans should govern themselves according to the laws of the cosmos, Jewish and Christian writers regard their God as the creator of that universe and thus represent their ideas about the afterlife as a revelation of the truth by which their divinity rules the world. In the Jewish and Christian literature of antiquity, the principles of human government derive not from considerations of utility but from divine provision. In contrast, the Greek and Roman authors studied here present the elements of their world view as human discoveries, inventions, or in the worse cases, delusions. They accepted the notion that beliefs about the afterlife affect behavior. They actively participated in shaping those beliefs and sought thereby to improve the lives of the people around them.

Secondary Source 2.11   Michael Koortbojian, 'Adonis's tale'

(Source: Koortbojian M. (1995) *Myth, Meaning, and Memory on Roman Sarcophagi*, Berkeley, Los Angeles and London, University of California Press, Chapter 2, pp. 23–48)

Adonis's tale was an old one. The myth, evidently of oriental origin, had been told and retold by the Greeks in a variety of forms. The Romans adopted and adapted the tale, and by the mid second century—when the sarcophagi that are the focus of this study began to be produced—the story appears to have been among the most vital examples of mythology, one that found artistic expression in a wide range of Roman representations, both literary and visual.[1]

The abundant literary sources that survive testify to the tale's wide dissemination and its appearance in diverse genres. The myth comprised an elaborate narrative sequence, whose elements were extracted, and at times amplified, for presentation in new contexts. Some of the literary sources offer mere allusions to the myth in the proverbial form associated with commonplaces about the affairs of the gods.[2] Among the sources are also found ancient commentaries on these allusions, such as the explications provided in the scholia to Theocritus.[3] Still others present attempts at realistic, or

[1] See the materials collected in the articles by F. Dümmler, "Adonis," in *RE*, I; and B. Servais-Soyez, "Adonis," in *LIMC*, I.

[2] Cf. Hyginus, *Fabulae*, CCLI, CCLXXI; Ausonius, *Cupido Cruciatur*, 56ff.

[3] Theon, *Scholia in Theocritum Vetera*, I.109f., III.47f., XV.86 and 100ff.

"historical," accounts of the myth: some ancient authors recounted the genealogy of the ancient hero,[4] while others attempted to fix geographically the site of the river into which he was metamorphosed.[5] The myth also appears in ancient texts as a symbol or metaphor, thus suggesting a basic knowledge of the tale on the part of the authors' audience as well as a consensus about its broad significance and applicability in such a form.[6] And, finally, in some instances the tale of Aphrodite and Adonis forms a topos that served as the inspiration for literary composition.[7]

The most extensive account of the Adonis myth is that given by Ovid in his *Metamorphoses*. But even this must be combined with elements found in various other sources to provide a complete, if synthetic, narrative of the life and death of the hero.

The narrative begins with a tale of illicit passion, deception and their unfortunate consequences.[8] Myrrha, daughter of King Cinyras, was overwhelmed with desire for her father. With the aid of her nurse, she contrived to deceive him and, taking advantage of his drunkenness, fulfilled her extravagant passion under the cover of darkness. The passions of the father once incited, the act was repeated again and again. Finally, just as Psyche's discovery of Cupid had led to disaster, so the unwitting king, eager to know his consort, brought light to his bed and discovered his daughter. Chased from the palace by her outraged father, Myrrha pleaded with the gods to take her from both life and death, and they heard her petition. She underwent a metamorphosis, and Adonis, the offspring of this incestuous union of father and daughter, was born from the myrrh tree into which his mother had been transformed.

This first section of the full vita has the formal character of an independent tale, whose central figure is the hero's mother, and whose real focus is her passion, and her fate. Adonis's passion and fate—along with the divine ardor he inspired—emerge amid the story of this mortal youth beloved by a goddess:

> Excited by the beauty of a mortal, no more does she [Aphrodite] care for the shores of Cythera, nor does she seek again Paphos surrounded by the ocean deep, nor Cnidos with its abundance of fishes, nor Amathus laden with precious metals. She avoids even the sky: Adonis is preferred to heaven. She binds him to her, she is his companion.[9]

But the passion of more than one divinity was inflamed by the young Adonis. Not only Aphrodite was overcome by his beauty, but Persephone as well. Other

---

[4]   Hesiod, *Catalogues of Woman and EOIAE*, frag. 21 (surviving in Apollodorus, *Bibliotheca*, III.14.4); Antimachus, frag. 102.

[5]   Strabo, *Geographia*, XVI.2.18.

[6]   In the fourth century B.C. Plato used the "Gardens of Adonis" as a metaphor in the *Phaedrus*, 276b; in the late third century A.D. Porphyry employed Adonis to symbolize the harvest of fruits at maturity in his *Peri Agalmaton*, surviving in Eusebius, *Praeparatio Evangelica* III.11.12 (= frag. 7 in J. Bidez, *Vie de Porphyre: Le philosophe néoplatonicien*, 2 pts. [Leipzig, 1913]).

[7]   Cf. for example, Lucian, *Dialogi Deorum*, XIX (11).

[8]   Ovid, *Metamorphoses*, X.298ff.; Apollodorus, *Bibliotheca*, III.14.4; Hyginus *Fabulae*, LVIII; Antoninus Liberalis, *Metamorphoses*, XXXIV; Servius, *In Vergilii Bucolica*, X.18.

[9]   Ovid, *Metamorphoses*, X.529ff.; cf. Theocritus, *Idylls*, III.46ff.; Apollodorus, *Bibliotheca*, III.14.4.

ancient sources describe how the two goddesses disputed for his companionship and how Jupiter intervened to resolve their dispute by the decree of an annual cycle in which Adonis passed from the upper to the lower realm, his life parceled out between his two paramours.[10]

Aphrodite warned Adonis of the dangers of hunting wild beasts, but the youth failed to heed her counsel. Ignoring her warning, Adonis was drawn to the hunt, killed by a wild boar, and at his death transformed into a flower. According to other versions of the myth, Adonis's death resulted from his having incurred the wrath of other gods, and both Artemis and Ares were at times held responsible for his demise.[11]

The full mythological sequence is closed by the elaborate annual ritual of mourning instituted by Aphrodite in remembrance of Adonis's death, the *Adonaia*.[12] In this celebration of Aphrodite's love for the mortal youth, women reveled—even if, like the goddess, only briefly—in the re-creation of that love's erotic, sensual, indeed licentious aspects. There were rites of purification, and there was feasting, followed by lamentations, for which the women climbed to the rooftops, where they sang dirges over their small "gardens of Adonis," the young plantings whose brief life would be symbolically extinguished in the heat of the sun. Thus, as this botanical symbolism re-enacted Adonis's brief life, it echoed the metamorphic cycle from tree to flower within which the mythic action is set. According to legend, these rites culminated, albeit symbolically, in Adonis's resurrection.

The repertory of images

Just as in the majority of ancient texts, where elements from the overall vita were extracted and represented on their own, so too in the case of the monuments. Most instances of the myth in the visual arts represent single episodes.[13] Sometimes these are characterized by an epigrammatic concision similar to that which marks many literary allusions to the myth.[14] Other images, isolated from their narrative context, seem to have been intended to prompt one's recollection of the myth as a whole.[15]

---

[10]   The most important of the Greek sources for the Persephone episode are Apollodorus, *Bibliotheca*, III.14.4; Bion, I (*The Lament for Adonis*); and Theocritus, *Idylls* XV.86f. Cf. also the inscription from the grave altar of Pedana (*CIL* VI, 17050), with its allusion to Venus and Persephone's "battle" over a mortal's fate: Ingratae Venaeri spondebam munera supplex erepta coiux virginitate tibi Persephone votis invidit pallida nostris et praematuro funaere te rapuit. ... ("To ungrateful Venus I was making offerings as a suppliant, on the occasion when you lost your virginity, wife. Pale Persephone envied our prayers and snatched you away in an untimely death. ..."); translation from G.B. Waywell, "A Roman Grave Altar Rediscovered," *AJA* 86 (1982): 241.

[11]   For Artemis's role, see Apollodorus, *Bibliotheca*, III.14.4; for Ares's, see Servius, *In Vergilii Aeneidos*, V.72; Apthonius, *Progymnasmata*, II.10ff; Nonnos, *Dionysiaca*, XLI.204–211; *Anthologia Latina* (ed. Buecheler and Riese, I), 68 and 253.32ff. For further references in the writings of late antiquity (esp. Christian authors), see P.W. Lehmann, *Roman Wall Paintings from Boscoreale in the Metropolitan Museum of Art* (Cambridge, 1953), p. 46 n. 66.

[12]   For discussions of the *Adonaia*, see N. Weill, "Adôniazousai ou les femmes sur le toit," *BCH* 90 (1966); eadem, "La fête d'Adonis dans la *Samienne* de Ménandre," *BCH* 94 (1970); and cf. M. Detienne, *The Gardens of Adonis: Spices in Greek Mythology* (Atlantic Highlands, 1977). These rites would appear to be the point of Ovid's allusion at *Metamorphoses*, X.725f.

[13]   Cf. the materials presented in the survey by Servais-Soyez, "Adonis."

[14]   Cf., for example, ibid., nos. 12, 15, 19, 35.

[15]   Cf., ibid., nos. 33, 40.

Sculpted Roman sarcophagi focus, as is only appropriate, on Adonis's death, as the corpus of surviving examples that represent the myth reveals.[16] Yet other aspects of the tale, also pertinent in a funerary context, found no place in the story told by these monuments. The romance of the youth and the goddess, the goddess's urgent desire, and the implicit eroticism of the couple's love—each so eloquently expressed by Ovid—play a minor role on the sarcophagus reliefs. Nor does any reference to Adonis's incestuous origins have a part. And the theme of metamorphosis, so fundamental to the Ovidian account, makes no appearance either. On the single extant example that includes the Persephone episode, one of the major variants recounted by the Greek sources, this element of the fable is relegated to the ends of the casket where the scene augments but does not alter the significance of the myth as it was employed in the sepulchral context.[17] Finally, representations of the *Adonaia*, described in great detail by Bion and other Greek sources surely known in the Roman world—and with their imagery of rebirth, seemingly so well suited to a funerary setting—these too never appear on the sarcophagi.[18]

Thus the sarcophagus reliefs' representation of the myth had a unique character. For this selective rendition the artists excerpted the three scenes that pertained to the death of Adonis—his departure for the hunt despite Aphrodite's warning; the wounding by the boar; and his death in the goddess's arms—and presented this portion of the myth in the condensed form of an epitome. The tale's full complexity, transmitted by the numerous sources, remained part of the literary background and played scarcely any direct role in the form the tale assumed as it was adapted on the sarcophagi. For it was the death of the hero that provided the type: the close of Adonis's life—not the close of the complete mythological narrative in which that life was embedded—was linked to the death Adonis was enlisted to commemorate.

---

[16]   The Adonis sarcophagi were collected by C. Roberts in *ASR* III.1; a revised catalogue, by D. Grassinger, is due to appear as *ASR* XII.1. The following monuments may be added to those listed by Robert: fragments in Berkeley, Cologne, Manziana, and Rome and a casket in Rostock; see Koch and Sichtermann, *Römische Sarkophage*, pp. 131–133, with earlier bibliography. Note that cat. No. 18 in *ASR* III.1, listed as Adonis (following the 1904 British Museum catalogue of A.H. Smith), does not represent this myth: cf. now Walker, *Catalogue of the Roman Sarcophagi*, p. 23, no. 16, as "Hyas (?)" after Robert's suggestion (which still remains unconvincing).

[17]   This casket, now in Rostock (see W. Richter, "Der Adonissarkophag," *Festschrift Gottfried von Lücken* [Rostock, 1968]), is the only example among the Adonis sarcophagi on which the end panels play a clear role in the overall program and extend the temporality of the narrative displayed in the scenes of the front panel. That on the right end (Richter, plate 32) precedes the conventional sequence and depicts Aphrodite, holding the infant Adonis and seated between Zeus and Persephone; thus it represents the two goddessses' rivalry over the youth and the resolution of the case by the leader of the gods (cf. Apollodorus, *Bibliotheca*, III.14.4; Bion, I; Theocritus, *Idylls*, XV.86ff). The left end (Richter, plate 36) depicts an event subsequent to those on the front panel yet not found in any of the surviving sources: there Charon, identified by the rudder he holds, stands before the seated Adonis, and the boar's head hangs from a tree as a trophy to signal the scene's place in the narrative.
On one end panel of another sarcophagus a solitary figure is shown fighting a boar, a scene that may represent Adonis (see *ASR* III.1. no. 14, right end). Yet this is more likely a "generic" image of a hunter, such as those found on the end panels of another sarcophagus (cf. *ASR* III.1, no. 21); the significance of a fragmentary scene (*ASR* III.1, no. 17) is unclear; all were probably included as images appropriate to the mythological context.
The remaining end panels of Adonis sarcophagi display imagery derived from the decorative repertory of Roman art, such as the winged griffin (*ASR* III.1, no. 12; for the significance of which see C. Delplace, *Le Griffon de l'archaïsme à l'époque impériale: Étude iconographique et essai d'interpretation symbolique* [Brussels and Rome, 1980]), or Cupid and Psyche (*ASR* III.1, no. 14; for which see Chapter 4 below [not reproduced here]).

[18]   For representations of the *Adonaia* in ancient works of art, see Servais-Soyez, "Adonis," nos. 45–51.

Figure 4   Adonis and Aphrodite sarcophagus. Casino Rospigliosi, Rome.

One of the oldest of the Adonis sarcophagi, a relief that may be dated circa 150–160, is now found at the Casino Rospigliosi in Rome (Fig.4).[19] On its front panel the story is told in the three scenes that comprised the standard repertory, and which follow each other across the sarcophagus's front from right to left. In the first of these, at the far right, we see Adonis about to depart for the hunt despite Aphrodite's warning. At the center, conspicuously larger, is the depiction of the boar hunt and the wounding of Adonis. At the left, finally, Adonis languishes at the point of death in the arms of his goddess, in the company of her attendants, who stand by helplessly.

The representation of each of these three events is designed so as to appear separated from the next. The two scenes at either end are designated as interiors by a *parapetasma* stretched behind the figures that distinguishes them from the landscape setting of the hunt scene between then.[20] All three are framed as well by the poses of the figures, who focus their attention, and the beholder's too, on the individuated incidents of the tale depicted side by side. This effectively provides a transition between scenes, as the shift from one to another is marked by a sudden reversal of the figures' orientation.

Each of the scenes employed for the visualization of this tale was composed on the basis of established figural motifs.[21] This origin of the imagery accounts for both the visual and iconographic differences that separate the three scenes. Thus, in the continuity of the frieze as a whole, each depicted moment of the tale exudes the formal character of an independent tableau. Each of the scenes is treated as if it were a unit self-contained, without a necessary relationship to the others, and this serves to explain the subtle changes in scale between them. And in this fashion each of the three scenes is imbued with a formal clarity that is essential for the evocation of the narrative's symbolism and the establishment of its funerary significance.

The departure

In the first of the three scenes, the departure, the lovers confront one another face-to-face (Fig. 4). The distinction between the goddess and her mortal lover is inscribed, in both their poses and their statures. Aphrodite appears the taller of the two, and thus able to confront Adonis face-to-face, even though she sits while he stands. This subtle distinction in physical scale suggests the unequal relationship between goddess and man.

---

[19]   *ASR* III.1, no. 3.

[20]   On the highly conventionalized role of the *parapetasma* on late antique sarcophagi, see W. Lameere, "Un symbole Pythagoricien dans l'art funéraire de Rome," *BCH* 63 (1939); and cf. Engemann, *Untersuchungen zur Sepulkralsymbolik*, p. 39.

[21]   These shall be elucidated in the ensuing discussion.

Figure 5   Adonis and Aphrodite sarcophagus. Cathedral sacristy, Blera.

With similar gestures they debate the youth's intentions. Yet the differences to be read in these gestures are additional signs of their impending separation, of the divergent nature of their passions. As Adonis turns back toward Aphrodite, he signals his departure with his outstretched hand; with hers, the goddess reaches out and enjoins him to stay.[22]

On several of the reliefs (Figs. 5–7) Adonis appears nude before the draped goddess[23] – a characteristic reserved on the Casino Rospigliosi sarcophagus (Fig. 4) for the two other scenes. For although it is Aphrodite who is so often found nude in ancient works of art, where her physical beauty serves as a fitting attribute for the goddess of love, here nudity characterizes her mortal lover. Here he is the object of desire and the figure of sexual allure, with whom Aphrodite has so hopelessly fallen in love.

Adonis's nudity is another sign, perhaps the clearest, of the artificial, symbolic character of the scene. In the context of the myth, nudity is his proper *costume*, and in and around its conspicuous display are condensed the two conflicting aspects of the tale.[24] On the one hand, this nudity stands for the erotic nature of their divinely gifted union. It symbolizes—indeed literalizes—the appeal of *kalos Adonis*, to whom the goddess is so passionately drawn. On the other hand, Adonis's nudity is a sign of the innately heroic character of the mortal youth. As his nakedness distinguishes him from the other figures more properly attired for the hunt, it recalls Greek heroic forms and the ideals they represent and thus serves as a visual metaphor for his heroization.[25]

These relations of scale, of pose, and of nudity and dress are all forms of abstraction. They subtly divorce the actions and the motifs with which they are depicted from the specific narrative content of the myth. They are the stuff of art, not life; their usage undermines a response to the image that is confined to the categories of naturalistic representation, which such forms of abstraction so clearly contradict. These abstractions enlarge the image's frame of reference, for they render the essence of the characters' natures and interrelationships as general qualities. Such abstractions constitute a distinctive mode of visual representation, one that diminishes the roles of the protagonists as specific individuals and instead emphasizes their roles as types.[26] And as the types

---

[22]   This point is also made by Turcan, "Déformation des modèles."

[23]   *ASR* III.1, nos. 14, 15, 21; cf. also nos. 10 and 19.

[24]   On the various significances of nudity, see L. Bonfante, "Nudity as Costume in Classical Art," *AJA* 93 (1989).

[25]   See Zanker, *Power of Images*, pp. 5–8, on "heroic" nudity in early imperial art.

[26]   Cf. the comments of Hölscher, *Römische Bildsprache*, pp. 50ff: "Abstraktion der Inhalt und Typisierung der Form."

Figure 6   Adonis and Aphrodite sarcophagus. Casino Rospigliosi, Rome.

emerge with greater clarify, the themes they are meant to evoke—heroism, eroticism, and above all, *virtus*—are manifest with corresponding force.

Thus these abstractions introduce to the images another modality, which itself conveys additional significance. These abstractions are not derived from the myth, in the sense that they serve as aspects of its representation. Rather, they

Figure 7   Adonis and Aphrodite sarcophagus. Museo Gregorio Profano, Vatican.

are intended to suggest those fundamental traits and ideas that the tale and its protagonists are held to exemplify. These abstractions evoke—by association and by analogy—the grander scheme of significance in which the representation of the myth is meant to operate. By these means the designers of the reliefs have contrived to establish the visual composition according to the general structure of the plot, as opposed to the details of the story. "What happened" takes precedence over the specificity of "who did what, and to whom"; the general nature of events predominates over the specific actions of individual characters in particular tales.[27]

The emphasis on plot is confirmed by this formula of contrasting figures—female and male, seated and standing, dressed and nude—which duplicated the one established for the repertory of sarcophagus reliefs representing Hippolytus's refusal of Phaedra, a scene that focuses on a similar clash of divergent passions. The appearance of Aphrodite, regally enthroned, depended on the role the same motif played in the representation of Phaedra, who sits, with an eros in the pose of Skopas's famous *Pothos* at her knee, and declares her love for Hippolytus, who stands before her (Fig. 8).[28] Both myths tell of "love-struck" heroines—helpless in the throes of a passion whose

[27]   Cf. Aristotle's discussion of the plot of the *Odyssey* in *Poetics*, 1455b17–24; and see the comments of G. Else, *Aristotle's Poetics: The Argument* (Cambridge, MA, 1957), pp. 514–516.

[28]   The connection between the Adonis and Phaedra repertories is discussed by C. Robert, in *ASR* III.1, pp. 14f; further argument for the primacy of the Phaedra/Hippolytus imagery will be advanced below. On the recognizability of a "quotation" such as that of Skopas's *Pothos* employed here, see D. Boschung, "*Nobilia Opera*: Zur Wirkungsgeschichte griechischer Meisterwerke im kaiserzeitlichen Rom," *AntK* 32^1 (1989).

Figure 8   Phaedra and Hippolytus sarcophagus. Louvre, Paris.

fulfilment is denied them—whose pleas to their lovers are ignored. This same theme underlies the use of identical imagery in representations of the two tales.[29]

Roman aesthetics was marked by an appreciation of such borrowings, and Roman art often exploited such duplications of form for the purpose of display. Characteristic is a conspicuous taste for paired statuary, for example, the paired statues of Mercury and Mars from the *canopus* of Hadrian's Villa at Tivoli.[30] There the same constitutive elements of a common pose, derived from a fifth-century prototype—torso, legs, and extended right arm—were exploited equally for images of the two deities.[31] The *intentio*, given the context of their discovery, was clearly to establish a visible correspondence between the two, who are then distinguished by the prominent role given to their individual attributes. But in the case of the Aphrodite and Phaedra sarcophagus reliefs, the independence of the images from a joint context and the absence of individuating attributes suggest that the *intentio* of their visual similarity was to establish an intellectual correspondence—one of analogy. The basic elements of the two images—that complement of forms that constitute the motifs they share—thus were held to signal, not merely one story or the other, but the fundamental human relations exemplified in each scene and evoked by the figural types.[32] This interchangeability intimates the designers' cognizance of a parallel between both the protagonists and the plots of the two myths. Moreover, the implied analogy suggests that the crucial sense of the scenes transcended the details that distinguished the particular stories.

---

[29]   It is not only these two tales that are so conjoined amid the corpus of mythological sarcophagus reliefs. Long ago, J. Aymard ("La légende de Bellérophon sur un sarcophage du Musée d'Alger," *MélRom* 52 [1935]) pointed out the similar contamination of the Bellerophon imagery by that of Hippolytus.

[30]   E. Bartman, "Décor et Duplicatio: Pendants in Roman Sculptural Display," *AJA* 92 (1988).

[31]   Ibid., 224–225; J. Raeder, *Die statuarische Ausstattung der Villa Hadriana bei Tivoli* (Frankfurt am Main, 1983), pp. 87–88, plates 11–12; cf., further, M. Marvin, "Freestanding Sculptures from the Baths of Caracalla," *AJA* 87 (1983), for the paired statues of Herakles that stood in the Baths of Caracalla.

[32]   Thus the two variants of the enthroned Phaedra found on the sarcophagus reliefs and elsewhere should be distinguished: one represents her confrontation with, and confession to, Hippolytus; the other image, its sequel, depicts Phaedra with head turned away in resignation at the threshold of doom. On the ambivalence and multiple significance of the Phaedra motif, see now P. Ghiron-Bistagne, "Phèdre ou l'amour interdit: Essai sur la signification du 'motif du Phèdre' et son évolution dans l'antiquité classique," *Klio* 64 (1982); idem, "Le motif de Phèdre: Deux exemples d'un schema iconographique classique utilisé dans l'art hellénistique et romain," in *PRAKTIKA* (Athens, 1988).

The boar hunt

The gestures of Aphrodite and Adonis in the first scene on the Casino Rospigliosi sarcophagus (Fig. 4) also suggest the temporal dimensions of the frieze as they quite literally point the way toward the adjacent depiction of Adonis's subsequent fate. This is the boar hunt, which claims priority amid this representation of the cycle not only for its centrality but for the considerably larger portion of the relief it fills. The image conflates a sequence of moments and actions: the boar is shown attacking suddenly from its lair; Adonis has already fallen wounded, gored in the thigh; and his companions and their dogs attempt—too late—to fight off the beast. The damage has been done, but Adonis has not yet been vanquished. Although mortally wounded, the young hero is depicted rising up on his knees and raising an outstretched arm, as if to ward off the final assault of his foe, like many another ancient warrior summoning his remaining strength to make a "last-ditch stand"[33]. Despite his imminent death, to which his passion for the hunt has led him, his *virtus* shines forth in his refusal to succumb willingly to his fate.[34]

A group of six sarcophagi presents a variation of the hunt scene. On these reliefs Adonis lies slumped at the center, his apparently lifeless body supported by the arms of his companions, and Aphrodite makes a frantic appearance at the scene (Fig. 5; cf. Fig. 9).[35] Her entrance offers the counterpart to the charge of the boar, and together goddesses and beast frame the fallen figure of Adonis.

The arrival of Aphrodite at the side of her dying lover expands still further the temporal dimensions of this central scene. For Ovid tells how, having learned of Adonis's tragedy, she hurried to his side and sprang from her swan-drawn car, in visible agony at the sight of the youth, "his lifeless body lying amid his own blood."[36] Her intrusion on these reliefs reclaims for their visual narratives an aspect of the tale that had been ignored. As the textual sources clearly indicate, Aphrodite's arrival constitutes the first moment of a subsequent scene whose later moments may be represented on those sarcophagi where Aphrodite leans over the body of Adonis, taking him in her arms for the last time (Fig. 6).

Aphrodite makes no such appearance on sarcophagi of earlier date.[37] Rather than allow her inclusion to alter the established scene, the artists have performed an ingenious substitution, one that may have been inspired by the similar appearance of the personified figure of Virtus on the Hippolytus sarcophagi.[38] The onrushing figure of Aphrodite has seemingly inherited the

[33]   For the type of "man's last-ditch stand in the face of hopeless odds," see W.S. Heckscher, *Imago: Ancient Art and Its Echoes in Post-Classical Times. A Pictorial Calendar for 1963* (Utrecht, 1963), p. 14; cf. Homer at *Iliad*, V.309ff. (and see the commentary on these "falling-to-the-ground and moment-of-death formulas" in G.S. Kirk, *The Iliad: A Commentary. Vol. II Books* 5–8 [Cambridge, 1990], pp. 92f., AD loc.) and XI.355ff.; for the type's visualization, cf. the Fallen Warrior from Delos or the Wounded Gaul in the Louvre: see M. Bieber, *The Sculpture of the Hellenistic Age* (New York, 1955), figs. 422 and 431.

[34]   Adonis's battle with the boar, as a sign of his *virtus*, could even supplant the scene of his defeat, as in the fourth-century mosaic at Carranque, where only his wounded dogs, a broken lance, and the anemone growing at his feet suggest the battle's final outcome: see the catalogue entry in *Hispania Antiqua: Denkmäler der Römerzeit,* ed. A. Nünnerich-Asmus (Mainz, 1993), pp. 373–374 and plate 164b.

[35]   *ASR* III.1, nos. 14 and 20. This type includes nos. 13, 19, 21, and the fragment in Berkeley.

[36]   Ovid, *Metamorphoses*, X.721; cf. Bion, I.40ff.

[37]   *ASR* III.1, nos. 3, 4, 5, and 9.

[38]   As pointed out recently by P. Blome, "Funerärsymbolische Collagen auf mythologischen Sarkophagreliefs," *StItFilCl* 85 (1992): 1069.

Figure 9   Adonis and Aphrodite sarcophagus. Palazzo Ducale, Mantua.

position, the pose, and the gestures of one of the hunters who conventionally appear on the reliefs (cf. Fig. 4 with Figs. 5 and 9). The significance of his raised arm, poised to hurl his weapon, undergoes a form of inversion, and the gesture becomes a sign of her horror and an expression of her grief.[39] The gesture – the raised arm with open palm – provided a *pathosformula* that served as the physiognomic signal of her anguished mental state.[40]

The dramatic figure of Aphrodite increases the pathos of the scene and reinforces the contrast between this immortal and her now-fallen lover. Her presence imbues the scene with the vivid contrast, central to the entire cycle of imagery, between her fate and that of Adonis. The anguish of the goddess at the death of the hero discloses that, despite her passion, her divine powers have failed to save him from the perils of his mortality.

Exemplum virtutis

The focus of the hunt scene is the confrontation between man and beast. The idea of the hunt as a metaphor of battle had a long and venerable history.[41] It was thought to provide "an excellent training in the art of war," as Xenophon had claimed in the fourth century B.C.[42] In the same period that saw the rise of sculpted sarcophagi, the boar hunt became a staple of Imperial iconography, as it entered the Hadrianic triumphal repertory in the early second century.[43] Not only did the boar hunt appear in the monumental roundels that now embellish the Arch of Constantine, but Hadrian also issued bronze medallions with very

[39]   Cf. Bion, I.40ff.: "She saw, she marked his irresistible wound, she saw his thigh fading in a welter of blood, she lifted her hands and put up the voice of lamentation...."

[40]   For the term *Pathosformel*, coined by Aby Warburg ("Physiognomische Grenzwerte im Augenblick der höchsten Erregung [*pathos*] oder tiefster Versenkung [*ethos*]"), see, inter alia, his "Dürer und die italienische Antike," [1905], in A.M. Warburg, *Gesammelte Schriften*, 2 vols. (Berlin, 1932), II; the passage quoted is from a notebook from the years 1903–6, cited in E.H. Gombrich, *Aby Warburg: An Intellectual Biography* (Oxford, 1970), p. 179. On Warburg's concept of "energetische Inversion," see F. Saxl, "Die Ausdrucksgebärden der bildenden Kunst," [1932], in A.W. Warburg, *Ausgewählte Schriften und Würdigungen*, ed. D. Wuttke (Baden-Baden, 1992), esp. 420ff. Aphrodite's gesture displays precisely the range of significances that captured Warburg's attention; for other possible uses of this gesture, see below, Chapter 5, nn. 30–31 [not reproduced here].

[41]   See J.K. Anderson, *Hunting in the Ancient World* (Berkeley and Los Angeles, 1985) esp. chapter 1.

[42]   The quotation is taken from Xenophon, *Cynegeticus*, 12.1 (cited by Anderson, *Hunting in the Ancient World*, pp. 17f.). Cf. Polybius, *Historiae* XXXI.29.1ff (ibid., p. 85); Pliny's *Panegyricus* of the Emperor Trajan, 81.1–3 (ibid., pp. 101f.); and the reprise of Xenophon in Arrian, *Cynegeticus*, I.1ff. (ibid., p. 107).

[43]   See Anderson, *Hunting in the Ancient World*, chapter 6 ("Hunting in the Age of Hadrian"), esp. pp. 101–106.

similar iconography.[44] That the hunt continued to play this role in sepulchral symbolism is attested by the numerous sarcophagi which give prominence to similar images of the pursuit of other wild beasts, particularly the lion, as well as those representing the tales of boar hunters such as Adonis or Meleager.[45] The hunt was not only the focus of the mythological repertories, for its familiar motifs were detached from their narrative contexts and allowed to stand in isolation. In this sense the dead boar could even serve as a punning metaphor of *virtus* on a private gravestone, to allude to the deceased as *alter Meleager* (Fig. 10).[46]

In all these instances the hunt served as an exemplum—as both a sign of *virtus* and a model for conduct.[47] The consistent and conspicuous public display of these images suggests their function as *paradeigmagta*.[48] The power of such exempla lay in the ability of individual instances to demonstrate a general rule, and to accomplish this sufficiently well so that their intended public might be capable of recognizing the similarity.[49] The mythological exempla illustrate ancient events, which, as they were continually held up for emulation, were continually appropriated to serve new purposes in ever new contexts. And

[44]   For the Hadrianic roundels, see most recently, N. Hannestad, *Roman Art and Imperial Policy* (Arhus, 1986), pp. 204–206; see, further, R. Brilliant, *Gesture and Rank in Roman Art: The Use of Gestures to Denote Status in Roman Sculpture and Coinage* (New Haven, 1963), p. 130 (with earlier bibliography). For the bronze medallions with the boar hunt, see F. Gnecchi, *I medaglioni romani*, 3 vols. (Milan, 1912), III, plate 144, 12.

[45]   On the lion hunt as an *imago virtutis*, see A. Vaccaro Melucco, "Sarcofagi di caccia al leone," *StMisc* 11 (1966); B. Andreae, "Imitazione ed originalità nei sarcofagi romani," *RendPontAcc* 41 (1968–69): 166. For the relationship of Adonis to other "hunters" from myth, see J. Fontenrose, *Orion: The Myth of the Hunter and the Hunters* (Berkeley and Los Angeles, 1981), esp. pp. 167–174. On the familiarity of the hunt scene and its exemplary nature, cf. also the discussions of "la belle mort" in J.-P. Vernant, "La belle mort et le cadaver outragé," in *La mort, les morts dans les sociétés anciennes*, ed. G. Gnoli and J.-P. Vernant (Cambridge 1982); N. Loraux, "La belle mort spartiate," *Ktèma* 2 (1977). Cf. also Wrede, *Consecratio*, p. 150, on the nonmythological use of the lion hunt on sarcophagi; and B. Andreae, *Die Symbolik der Löwenjagd* (Opladen, 1985).

[46]   While Statilius Aper's grave monument depicts him standing triumphantly over the dead beast and thus likens him unmistakably to representations of Meleager, the inscription, with its pun on his name (*aper* = boar), invokes the parallel in a rather different fashion: Innocuus Aper ecce iaces non virginis ira nec Meleager atrox perfodit viscera ferro mors tacit obrepsit subito fecitq(ue) ruinam ... ("Lo, you lie here, innocent Aper! Your side pierced by neither the wrath of the virgin nor the spear of fierce Meleager. Silent death crept up suddenly, and brought destruction ..."); see *CIL* VI, 1975; Helbig[4] II (1966), 55–61, no. 1214 (with a different interpretation of the relationship between text and image). For the Meleager type alluded to on this monument, with the hero in triumph over the boar, see H. Sichtermann, "Das Motiv des Meleager," *RM* 69 (1962) and *RM* 70 (1963): 174–177; for the dead boar as the identifying attribute of Meleager, cf. *Anthologia Palatina*, VII, 421, and the motif's appearance on the monuments surveyed by S. Woodford in *LIMC* VI, "Meleagros," nos. 77–83, 91–97; and, further, the statue now in the Vatican: see Helbig[4] I (1963), 74–75, no. 97. Cf. also Quintilian's comments on such onomastic puns in the *Institutio Oratoria*, XI.2.30–31; and the discussions in T. Riti, "L'uso di *immagini onomastiche* nei monumenti sepolcrali di età greca," *ArchCl* 25–26 (1973–74); eadem, "Immagini onomastiche sui monumenti sepolcrali di età imperiale," *AttiLinc* (Memorie), ser. VIII, 21[4] (Rome, 1977).

[47]   *Rhetorica AD Herennium*, IV.49.62; Cicero, *De Inventione*, I.49. Cf. H.W. Litchfield, "National Exempla Virtutis in Roman Literature," *HSCP* 25 (1914). The traditional role of Meleager as an exemplum appears as early as Homer, where (*Iliad*, IX. 527ff.) he serves as the exemplum for Achilles; see R. Brilliant, *Visual Narratives: Storytelling in Etruscan and Roman Art* (Ithaca, 1984), p. 145.

[48]   Aristotle, *Rhetorica*, I.2.8 and especially II.20.1ff. For discussions of the literary employment of *paradeigmata*, see below, n.71.

[49]   See the discussion in J.D. Lyons, *The Rhetoric of Example in Early Modern France and Italy* (Princeton, 1989), pp. 12–15, 27.

Figure 10   Funeral monument of T. Statilius Aper. Museo Capitolino, Rome.

whatever the context into which they were inserted, they imposed a new,
specific, frame of reference—as it were, from within. Thus these mythological
exempla served as paradigms for the essentially mimetic character of human
action. Only when envisioned in the light of the legendary exploits of heroes

and gods can such human actions disclose their full significance and take their rightful place in the scale of human values vouchsafed by hallowed traditions.[50]

The use of exempla played a fundamental role in the rhetorical training of antiquity, especially in the "preliminary exercises," or *progymnasmata*, which were the standard course studied by Roman youths beginning as early as the second century B.C. and continuing without interruption into late Roman times.[51] Among these exercises the exemplary character of myth—and the persuasive power of exempla in general—held an important place, notably in the exercises known as *fabella, narratio, chria*, and *sententia*.[52] Training in such a curriculum no doubt produced, in addition to a ready familiarity with the standard rhetorical formulae, a predisposition to think in terms of these formulae. One was trained not only to use exempla effectively but to recognize and respond to them when they were employed.[53]

The transfer of exemplary rhetoric from the verbal to the visual realm played an actual part in the curriculum. *Ekphrasis*—the rhetorical technique of description that purported to present visual images through the medium of words—appears among the *progymnasmata* by the first century A.D.[54] But descriptions of images, paintings in particular, had played a crucial role in earlier literary forms. The most notable is perhaps the Hellenistic romance, where the encounter with a painted image establishes the theme, if not the plot, that is about to unfold.[55]

The visual exempla on the mythological sarcophagi could equally lay claim to the persuasive power that proficiency in these exercises might eventually provide the would-be orators. For beyond a specific skill in ekphrasis and the techniques related to it, the orator's transformation of the verbal to the visual lay at the heart of his enterprise. Among the greatest of the rhetorician's skills was his ability to bring the things of which he was speaking seemingly before the eyes of his listeners, so that these images might be imprinted firmly on their memories.[56] This was no less the concern of the designers of the sarcophagus images—and will be the subject of a later chapter.

---

[50]   J.P. Vernant, *Myth and Society in Ancient Greece* (London, 1980), p. 195.

[51]   See D. Clark, *Rhetoric in Graeco-Roman Education* (New York, 1957), esp. pp. 177–212. An English translation of the second-century B.C. *Progymnasmata* of Hermogenes appears in C.S. Baldwin, *Medieval Rhetoric and Poetic* (New York, 1928), pp. 23–38; for the sixth-century version of Apthonius, see R. Nadeau, "The Progymnasmata of Apthonius, in Translation," *SpMon* 19 (Ann Arbor, 1952). On the continuous use of these texts into late antiquity, see H. Marrou, *Histoire de l'éducation dans l'antiquité*, 6th ed. (Paris, 1965), p. 260.

[52]   Hermogenes, *Peri Muthon:* "Myth is the approved thing to set first before the young, because it can lead their minds into better measures" (trans. from Baldwin, *Medieval Rhetoric*, pp. 22–40); cf. Quintilian, *Institutio Oratoria*, V.11.19. For the use of exempla in the *chria*, see *Rhetorica AD Herennium*, IV.44.57. The names for the various exercises, while fixed in the Greek terminology, have various Latin translations; those employed here are taken from Quintilian, *Institutio Oratoria* I.9.1ff. and II.4.1ff.

[53]   See the discussion of the effects of Renaissance training with these texts in M. Baxandall, *Giotto and the Orators* (1971; Oxford, 1986), esp. pp. 32ff.

[54]   As E. Keuls, "Rhetoric and Visual Aids in Greece and Rome," in *Communication Arts in the Ancient World*, ed. E.A. Havelock and J.P. Hershbell (New York, 1978), 122 and n. 2, points out, however, paintings and sculptures do not seem to have appeared in these handbooks as explicit themes until the fifth century.

[55]   Ibid; see also M.C. Mittelstadt, "Longus: Daphnis and Chloe and Roman Narrative Painting," *Latomus* 26 (1967); G. Steiner, "The Graphic Analogue from Myth in Greek Romance," in *Classical Studies Presented to Ben Edwin Perry* (Urbana, 1969).

[56]   Quintilian, *Institutio Oratoria*, VI.2.23 and VIII.3.63.

Death in the arms of Aphrodite

The third scene on the Casino Rospigliosi sarcophagus represents Adonis's death in the arms of Aphrodite (Fig. 4). Here the two protagonists are depicted on the same scale, and signs of affection replace those of separation. The couple sit, embracing, their bodies mirroring one another as they are joined to share a single contour. Here the goddess lovingly lays her hand upon the dying youth's breast; on other reliefs she cradles his chin and caresses his cheek.[57]

There are a number of variants of this scene. Three of the reliefs lack the calculated symmetry of the end scenes displayed on the Casino Rospigliosi relief. On these sarcophagi the final moments of the drama appear to take place—as well they should, according to the sources—outdoors (cf. Figs. 6 and 11).[58] These scenes, as was pointed out above, conform more closely to the narrative, particularly as it is recounted in Ovid's *Metamorphoses*.[59] On several of the sarcophagi there are also indications of an attempt to tend Adonis's wounds, as on the example in Blera (Fig. 5), where a washbasin lies at the couple's feet. On some examples erotes take up the task (Fig. 9).[60]

All these images recall the plaintive spirit of Bion's *Lament for Adonis*, in which the goddess pleads for a final kiss from the expiring youth. In each of these variants of the scene he dies in the arms of his divine paramour, who is helpless to wrest him from his fate.[61] Thus the sarcophagus imagery for the myth dramatizes a series of apparent failures: Adonis's refusal to heed counsel, his failure to kill the boar and Aphrodite's inability to save him from death. Yet Adonis remains an *exemplum virtutis* because he represents a challenge to the awesome powers of ineluctable Fate.[62] Even the desires of the gods are subject to it, as the myth so plainly reveals. The valiant deed of the hero—his bold acceptance of the deadly challenge of the hunt—is sundered from its specific role in the mythological narrative, and stands as a sign of character.[63] The exemplary nature of the imagery in its sepulchral context transforms this series of apparent failures into a vehicle of heroic symbolism. In offering a heroic image of death, the sarcophagi thus recast the vision of an individual's life. For even Herakles died; *everyone* dies. These images acknowledge that in memory

---

[57]   *ASR* III.1, nos. 9, 12, 14, 15, and 17.

[58]   *ASR* III1.1, nos. 15 and 17. Cf. the scene of "final embrace" on the Casino Rospigliosi sarcophagus (Fig. 6) with a fragment from a wall painting, now in the Louvre: see Servais-Soyez, "Adonis," fig. 36 [...]. This painting employs the same motif for the couple and includes the boar running away. The scene of Aphrodite's last sight of the dying Adonis was paired in the ensemble to which this painting belonged with one depicting Orpheus's first glimpse of Eurydice as he found her in the Underworld: cf. P. Devambez, "Un fragment de fresque antique au Louvre," *MonPiot* 65 (1951).

[59]   *Metamorphoses*, X.717ff.

[60]   Cf. also *ASR* III.1, no. 5.

[61]   Bion, I.42ff; on the motif of the dying who give up their souls through the mouth, see R. Garland, *The Greek Way of Death* (Ithaca, 1985), p. 18; for discussion of the Roman continuation of this traditional idea, see Treggiari, *Roman Marriage*, p. 484 and n.6; cf. Statius's use of the motif at *Silvae*, V.I.195ff.

[62]   The *virtus* of Adonis was central to the discussion of the myth in J. Aymard, *Essai sur les chasses romaines, des origines à la fin du siècle des Antonins* (Paris, 1951), pp. 520–522.

[63]   Cf. Brilliant, *Visual Narratives*, p. 159, on the triump of Meleager and the similar "detachment of the heroic protagonist from the narrative context." See also J.-P. Vernant, "Death with Two Faces," in *Mortality and Immortality: The Anthropology and Archaeology of Death*, ed. S.C. Humphreys and H. King (London, 1981), on the Greek conception of commemoration, esp. p. 286: "The individuality of the dead man is not connected with his psychological characteristics or with the personal aspect of him as a unique and irreplaceable being. Through his exploits, his brief life and his heroic destiny, the dead man embodies certain 'values': beauty, youth, virility, and courage."

Figure 11   Adonis and Aphrodite sarcophagus (fragment). Museo Chiaramonti, Vatican.

it is the quality of life—and death—that survives and is worthy of commemoration and remembrance.[64]

The appearance of the embracing couple constitutes the only reference on the sarcophagi to that great eros that bound together goddess and mortal. The image of the intertwined pair—despite differences in its setting, in its pose, and above all in its obvious role in the narrative—endows this particular scene with an emotional tenor not unlike that of Ovid's description. The poet tells how Aphrodite entreated Adonis to lie with her, and how, "pillowing her head against his breast and mingling kisses with words," she tells him the tale of Hippomenes that concludes with her warning about the dangers of the hunt.[65] The motif regularly employed by the sarcophagus designers for the final scene of his death in the goddess's arms is strikingly reminiscent of scenes depicting the love of Aphrodite and Adonis in other works of ancient art. In the images displayed on vases, in frescoes, and in sculpture, the two lovers are often found wrapped in similar embraces, known as *symplegmata*.[66] It was the formulaic quality of the motif that allowed Theocritus to assume his readers would recognize the scene, in *Idyll* XV, where he speaks of a tapestry depicting Aphrodite and Adonis as they recline together in luxuriant repose.[67] A very similar scene could be employed for the depiction of Adonis's final moments, as in a fresco from Pompeii (Fig. 13). Not only is Aphrodite discovered coupled with Adonis in such as pose, but this same generic type of intertwined figures was also the standard formula for the representation of all of her love affairs, and those of other goddesses as well.[68] Thus as the final embrace of the two lovers depicts Adonis's death and Aphrodite's grief, it recalls—if only subtly—the imagery of the great love they once shared and have lost.

The sarcophagus designers clearly related this third and final scene of the cycle to the first of the sequence. On a number of the surviving Adonis sarcophagi, the first and third scenes are presented as pendants that frame the scene of the young hero's demise.[69] Both represent interior actions, indicated by the *parapetasma* stretched across the back of the relief ground (Fig. 4); each depicts one or both of the protagonists seated and on a larger scale than in the scene of the boar hunt. This "invention" of a new setting for the final scene may be regarded as one more example of the Roman taste for the display of pendants

---

[64]   Thus Patroklus dies, and even Achilles: *Iliad*, XXI.106ff.; cf. the comments of Nock, "Sarcophagi and Symbolism," p. 147. For the formulaic use of the Herakles proverb in Roman epitaphs, see R. Lattimore, *Themes in Greek and Latin Epitaphs* (Urbana, 1942), pp. 253–254. Cf. Ovid's epitaph for Phaeton (*Metamorphoses*, II.327–328), for even there the monument recasts the tale: "Hic situs est Phaeton currus auriga paterni/quem is non tenuit magnis tamen excidit ausis." For the significance of Phaeton's epitaph, cf. R. Turcan, "Les exégèses allégoriques des sarcophages 'au Phaéthon,' "in *Jenseitsvorstellungen in Antike und Christentum: Gedenkschrift für Alfred Stuiber* (1982), pp. 201f.—was this an early instance of the adage *De mortuis nihil nisi bonum*?

[65]   *Metamorphoses*, X.560ff.

[66]   See the materials collected in Servais-Soyez, "Adonis." My discussion of the *symplegma* is informed by a lecture given by Aileen Ajootian at the Archaeological Seminar of the Canadian Institute of Rome, May 4, 1988.

[67]   Theocritus, *Idylls*, XV. Cf the parody of such images in Plautus, *Menaechmi*, 144ff.

[68]   See the materials collected in A. Delivorrias et al., "Aphrodite," in *LIMC*, II; for Venus and Anchises, see E. Simon, "Umgedeutete Wandbilder des Casa del Citarista zu Pompeji," in *Mélanges Mansel* (Ankara, 1974), I, pp. 36–38, and III, plate 20. For the same motif employed in the representation of the Meleager myth, see the volute krater now in Naples, illustrated in K. Schefold and F. Jung, *Die Sagen von den Argonauten, von Theben und Troia in der klassischen und hellenistischen Kunst* (Munich, 1989), p. 54, fig. 35. For its use in the representation of Artemis and Hippolytus, see C. Robert, *Archaeologische Hermeneutik* (Berlin, 1919), pp. 222–227 and fig. 179.

[69]   *ASR* .III, nos. 3, 4, 5 and cf. 6, 10 and 17.

Figure 13   Adonis and Aphrodite. Wall painting. Casa d'Adonide ferito, Pompeii (VI, 7, 18).

since, as has already been observed, the literary sources for the final scene of Adonis's death call for it to occur in the grove where he was wounded by the boar. The formal role of the *parapetasma* is revealed most clearly on a fragment, now in the Vatican, where it appears stretched behind not only the figures but the tree that specifies their outdoor setting (Fig. 11).[70]

This visual complementarity of first and final scenes evoked a corresponding complementarity of sense and served to reiterate the significance of the departure scene. Each of these scenes suggest the inescapability of Adonis's fate. Just as Aphrodite was unable to prevent Adonis's departure for the hunt, so too she was helpless to prevent his "departure" from life. Only with the second

[70]   *ASR* III.1, no. 17.

of these scenes is the significance of the first fulfilled, as the expectations evoked by its imagery are realized. The artists' "invented" composition for the final scene imposed certain details on the story and sacrificed others to signal the analogy, which reveals the correspondence of both scenes as types of departure.[71] As in the case of the departure scene, here too the imagery evokes the tragic reality that even *heroes* die: to be loved by the gods is not enough to save them.

Beginning at the end

The recognized correspondence between the two scenes that open and close the tale—correspondence in sense as well as in form—explains the use of one or the other on the three surviving reliefs that depict only two of the three scenes of the cycle.[72] The visual repertory for the myth could be reduced yet remain effective because, despite depicting different narrative moments, these two scenes display the same typological character, share the same symbolic function, and represent the same idea—and therefore proved interchangeable.

Yet the elimination from the cycle of one scene or the other had a marked effect on the myth's representation and on that representation's significance. The final scene might be omitted, as on the sarcophagus at the Villa Giustiniani, for example (Fig. 14), with a resulting emphasis on the two remaining images of Adonis's failures: to heed the goddess's warning and to kill the wild boar.[73] The departure scene is given new prominence by the intrusion of foreign elements: Adonis is shown dressed and about to leave, leading a horse. The scene is nearly identical to those representing Hippolytus's departure from Phaedra (Fig. 9), which the Aphrodite and Adonis designers borrowed from the Phaedra repertory—just as they borrowed the enthronement motif with which this one was originally conjoined. Yet while Hippolytus hunted on horseback, Adonis—like Meleager—hunted the boar on foot and thus exemplified that brave hunter who stands alone in the face of danger.

Unlike the reuse of the enthronement motif, in which the specifics of the mythological narrative were abandoned in favor of the larger general significance of the image, in this instance the exchange of motifs gave prominence to details that undermined the grander sense of the scene. Once clothed (Fig. 14), the figure of Adonis forfeits the heroic connotations of nudity, as well as its erotic appeal. Deprived of this form of idealization and the schematic series of contrasts it established on other reliefs (cf. Figs. 5–7), this representation of the Adonis myth verges on the anecdotal. This "borrowing" should be regarded, not as another exercise in typology, marked by its characteristic quality of synthesis, but as an instance of contamination—one bred by a failure to comprehend the more profound connections between the two myths that had been established on other sarcophagi.[74]

---

[71] Cf. M.M. Willcock, "Mythological Paradeigma in the *Iliad*," *CQ 14* (1964): 142, on the invention of significant details by Homer to effect analogies and to provide parallels with the *paradeigma*. See also the related discussion in O. Andersen, "Myth, Paradigm, and Spatial Form in the *Iliad*," in *Homer: Beyond Oral Poetry*, ed. J.M. Bremmer, I.J.F. DeJong, and J. Kazloff (Amsterdam, 1987).

[72] *ASR* III.1, nos. 13, 19, and 20.

[73] *ASR* III.1, no. 13.

[74] See above, 34f., and below, 44, on the borrowings from the Phaedra sarcophagi. Cf. Brilliant, *Visual Narratives*, p. 159, for another appearance of this element of the Hippolytus repertory on the Meleager sarcophagus now in the cortile of the Palazzo Lepri-Gallo in Rome. On the overall problem of *contaminatio* in Roman sarcophagi, see Turcan, "Déformation des modèles," pp. 429ff.; cf. also the discussion of literary *contaminatio* with reference to Vergil, in A. Thill, *Alter ab illo: Recherches sur l'imitation dans la poésie personnelle à l'époque augustéenne* (Paris, 1979), pp. 71–87.

Figure 14   Adonis and Aphrodite sarcophagus. Villa Giustiniani [now Villa Massimo], Rome. [By kind permission of the owners, the Delegation of the Holy Land, Rome.]

The omission of the departure scene had a rather different effect, as can be seen on the sarcophagus in Mantua (Fig. 9). The two remaining scenes are divided by a pilaster, which marks the temporal shift and the change in setting from one to the next. The boar hunt here takes precedence, as it is expanded to fill almost two-thirds of the frieze.

The nearly centralized figure of Aphrodite, who rushes frantically to the side of her fallen lover, is the most prominent of many that crowd the relief. Amid the welter of forms she is distinguished by her naked torso and by her expansive gesture, which, as it crosses in front of the pilaster, seems to thrust itself beyond the boundaries of relief and enter real space. She is set apart by the reflective quality of her torso's smooth, polished surface, which contrasts decidedly with the busy interplay of light and shadow that characterizes the relief as a whole. The monumental quality of her upright form, which fills the relief from top to bottom, is further emphasized by its contrast with the pilaster, dwarfed alongside her. She visually dominates the frieze, and it is to her form that the viewer's eye is immediately drawn and his attention directed.

Thus the figure of Aphrodite, as it engages the beholder, effects an "entrance" to the story at its very center—with respect to the temporality of the narrative as well as the composition of the frieze. The goddess arrives dramatically, but too late to save Adonis—as the earlier moment of the disastrous hunt, with which her approach is coupled, makes clear. As the viewer scans across the frieze toward the right end, his eye led by the depicted movement of the central group of figures, he follows the story's unfolding, yet he seems to move backward in narrative time.

The retrospective character of the right-hand portion of the relief is recapitulated by the frieze as a whole. With this sarcophagus as with others the viewer's initial grasp of the relief as an integral form is supplanted by the perception of the multi-scened frieze's distinct elements. Perception oscillates between the poles of whole and part: the synoptic view of the whole, dominated by its compositional pattern of forms, dissipates with the recognition of the subjects represented and the individuation of distinct scenes. As the narrative movement of each scene's figures merges into the overall compositional pattern, focus on the segments gives way to the perception of a single totality.[75]

Cognizance of this phenomenon of perception in antiquity is implicit in a celebrated passage of Flavius Josephus. In his account of the triumphal procession upon the return to Rome, Josephus describes the huge painted

[75]   On the interrelation of synoptic and sequential perception of the sarcophagus reliefs, see Brilliant, *Visual Narratives*, pp. 161–162. A concise discussion of these issues, with respect to the complex organization of the imagery of Trajan's Column, is found in S. Settis, *La Colonna Traiana* (Turin, 1988).

banners, called *pegmata*, that depicted scenes of the war and "portrayed the incidents to those who had not witnessed them as though they were happening before their eyes."[76] Yet the description of the depicted subjects that follows offers merely a sequence of topoi, recounted without any sense of chronology. The integrity of the individual *pegmata* vanishes as Josephus recites their contents, displayed in a series of thematically related fragments, which the reader—like the beholder of the triumph—must reassemble into a coherent vision of the war.[77]

The artists responsible for the Mantua sarcophagus clearly exploited this interplay between synoptic vision and discriminating focus. The initial view of the whole is disrupted by the prominence of Aphrodite, whose figure commands attention. Nevertheless, the general movement of the figures in the frieze draws one's vision away toward the right end. This movement underscores the natural impulse to read the linear progression of the entire narrative, following the model of writing from left to right. As the beholder begins to scrutinize the imagery and ponder its significance, his scansion of the entire panel begins invariably at the left end, and therefore the first scene confronted as he surveys the frieze represents the end of the story. The contemplation of the imagery thus expands, with respect to form and to content, simultaneously forward and backward, as well as spatially and temporally. For on the Mantua sarcophagus—just as on the majority of the early Adonis reliefs—while the experience of the imagery moves from left to right, the temporal sequence of the mythological narration is displayed in the opposite direction, from right to left.[78]

In their narrative solutions, the sarcophagus designers demonstrated great ability and willingness to take advantage of this phenomenon of scansion, so fundamental to visual narration, which was inherent in the pictorial organization of the sculptures' form. One of the most complex of these solutions may be discerned on a relief now in the Vatican (Fig. 15).[79] This sarcophagus displays in a different form the contamination of the Aphrodite and Adonis repertory by that of the Phaedra and Hippolytus sarcophagi.[80] On the right is the familiar boar hunt; on the left, however, the imagery seems to have become confused. Once again the borrowed horseman motif appears; but instead of extending the departure scene as it had on the Giustiniani sarcophagus (Fig. 14), here it is appended to the motif of embracing lovers—customarily the final scene of the cycle.

While the integrity of the hunt scene is rendered with great clarity, there are no formal divisions between the two elements that make up the left-hand side of the frieze. The figure who stands at their juncture actually seems designed to link them. He turns with his head toward one, and with his outstretched arm he gestures toward the other, instigating a sequence of implied movements that intimate a continuity of these elements with the scene of the hunt at the right side of the frieze. In this conflation of scenes, Adonis, identifiable by his nudity, appears twice. This double presence, as it indicates the continuity of the narrative, represents the first two of three distinct moments depicted on the

[76]   Flavius Josephus, *Bellum Iudaicum*, VII.139ff., esp. 147–148 (trans. H. St. J. Thackeray, in *LCL* ed. [Cambridge and London, 1927; 1967]).

[77]   Settis, *La Colonna Traiana*, pp. 232–234. Cf. the similar painted panels mentioned by Herodian, *Historiae*, III.9.12, VII.2.8.

[78]   *ASR* III.1, nos. 3, 4, 5, 6, 9, 10, 20, and the sarcophagus in Rostock.

[79]   *ASR* III.1, no. 12.

[80]   Turcan, "Déformation des modèles," pp. 430–431.

Figure 15   Adonis and Aphrodite sarcophagus. Galleria Lapidaria, Vatican.

relief: Adonis, first in the arms of Aphrodite, then leading his horse toward the hunt, and finally (at the other side of the frieze) wounded by the boar. Thus the Vatican sarcophagus, despite its formal similarity to the Guistiniani example, is actually another variant of the more customary three-scene reliefs.

The very placement on the Vatican sarcophagus of the couple's final embrace imbued it with a certain ambiguity. The motif that had conventionally served to depict the wound tending is thus stripped of both its poignancy and intimacy as its sense is undermined.[81] Its visual conjunction with the departure motif, and the repeated appearance of Adonis that results, produce a false sense of the temporal relation between the two conflated scenes. The scene that is chronologically first seems to follow visually from that which is chronologically third. Installed as on the Mantua sarcophagus (Fig. 9) at the left end of the frieze, where scansion of the visual narrative begins, the Vatican sarcophagus's scene of final embrace thus constituted *both* the beginning and the end of the tale: the beginning, as one confronts the narration on this monument; the end, as one recognizes the subject that is narrated (Fig. 15).

This conception of the myth's narration on these sarcophagus reliefs—since it appears on more than one example—is unlikely to have been the result of a mistake on the part of the workshops that produced them. In the conflation of different scenes, just as in the transfer of motifs from other mythological subjects, one should recognize the artists' awareness that both the departure and the final embrace had ultimately the same significance for the sepulchral interpretation of the myth. In both scenes, Adonis is about to depart from the goddess who loves him, despite her desire to prevent their separation, a desire made palpable on the

<hr>

[81]   Thus Blome, "Funerärsymbolische Collagen," pp. 1067f.

reliefs by the erotic overtones of the *symplegma* motif. Such are the limits of even divine love; such is the extent and the power of Fate.[82]

That the visualization of the story on the sarcophagi might begin at the end is not in itself surprising. The rhetorical device may be as old as storytelling itself.[83] More specifically, the artists were free to reorder the progression of scenes on the reliefs because the Adonis myth, like most moralizing tales, was understood retrospectively, with its conclusion already established. Indeed, the images' moral significance and exemplary value depend on this, and it is the reason that such familiar myths—and moral tales in general—are invoked again and again.[84] This conception of the myth's character helps to explain the right-to-left order of the scenes on those sarcophagi where the narrative cycle begins at the point of the frieze that for the viewer is ordinarily the end. The awkwardness of this entirely conceptual order, at odds with the demands of the conventional sequence of the visual narrative, was understandably jettisoned and the scenes on the sarcophagus reliefs displayed in chronological order from left to right. Yet its reappearance on the Vatican sarcophagus suggests the value of such a disruption of custom as a device to prompt renewed attention to the myth's significance. As the rearranged scenes are read from left to right, their distinctive temporal disjunction compels a new consideration of the narrative—and of the way that narrative has been represented. The final scene becomes not merely the starting point for the tale that is recalled by these images, but the vantage point from which the myth they relate is to be understood.[85]

The visual composition for the three scenes of the cycle established an analogy between its beginning and end. This thematic reiteration, in even this abbreviated redaction of the myth, recalls the use of repetition to bracket episodes in epic compositions.[86] The epitomization of the tale is fulfilled by this implication of closure, which endows these extracts from the myth with a sense of unity and completeness.

Yet the same visual means that allowed the artists to effect this sense of closure also served to expand the connotations of the myth's imagery. With the transposition of compositional motifs from the depiction of one myth to that of another, the artists gave greater emphasis to those elemental plots that were

[82] Blome's suggestion ("Funerärsymbolische Collagen," pp. 1067f.) that this conflation of scenes represents a stage in the progressive transformation of the myth's narration on the sarcophagi, when the right-to-left reading of the early reliefs is reversed, depends entirely on his belief that the Vatican relief must be dated earlier than the Giustiniani example; both works are, however, generally dated to the same period (ca. 170–180?) and the argument fails to explain why such a stage—if it is without other significance—would be required in such a development.

[83] See E.W. Said, *Beginnings: Intentions and Methods* (Baltimore, 1975), and, most recently the volume entitle *Beginnings in Classical Literature*, ed. F.M. Dunn and T. Cole (Cambridge, 1992).

[84] Cf. the related discussion of the historiated bowls in Settis, *La Colonna Traiana*, pp. 226–229, 235.

[85] A more comprehensive system of classification than that proposed by Robert in *ASR* III.1 is implicit in my argument. This system would distinguish the permutations in the order of the scenes on the sarcophagus fronts, omissions from or additions to the basic repertory of three scenes, as well as the deliberate disruption of a continuous presentation of the narrative sequence. Robert's first "class," with its 3–2–1 temporal sequence of the scenes, would provide the largest grouping (*ASR* III.1, nos. 3, 4, 5, 6, 9, 10[?], 20[3–2], and Rostock); its reversal, a 1–2–3 sequence, or its reduction to 1–2, forms another group (nos. 13, 14, 19, and perhaps the fragmentary no. 17); variant orderings, such as 3–1–2 (no. 12) or 1–3–2 (no. 21), are thus distinguished, as are those examples which introduce additional scenes (no. 15 and perhaps Rostock).

[86] See B.A. van Groningen, *La composition littéraire grecque* (Amsterdam, 1958), pp. 51–56, on the technique of ring composition.

shared by more than one tale. In this fashion the artists established visual analogies among different myths based on their narratives' related plot structures, rather than on their individual stories' details. Generalized motifs such as the *symplegma*, familiar from a host of representations of related themes, provided the sarcophagus designers with visual forms that had both their own established significance and connotations extending beyond the story lines of the tale they were enlisted to depict.

These are the basic strategies by which the sarcophagus designers effected the grand analogies that formed the raison d'être of so much funerary symbolism. And it was by these means that the artists freed themselves from the bondage of the codified visual programs for their myths and allowed their powers of invention free rein. These strategies permitted the artists not only to alter the way a myth was depicted, but to recompose the tale to reflect its insertion in a sepulchral context. As the images themselves suggested associations between tales, they provided the structural guidelines for their interpretation. In these pictorial renditions of myth one must recognize works of art unburdened of a subservience to texts so that they might produce original and profound effects of their own. Those who viewed these images were intended not merely to recognize the myth but to grasp that the sculpted figures and their actions exemplified certain ideas and values that are the true subjects of the sepulchral symbolism: these are tales told with concepts as well as with characters. The three scenes of the Aphrodite and Adonis repertory collectively render a story of heroic *virtus*, the *amor* of the gods, and the conquest of both by the power of Fate. The reliefs must be conceived as the manifestation of these themes. The real significance of their epitomizing form of narration is revealed only if their stories are considered as the vehicles, rather than as the content, of the sepulchral message.

Secondary Source 2.12   Susan Wood, 'Mortals, empresses and earth goddesses'

(Source: Kleiner, D.E.E. and Matheson, S.B. (eds) (2000) *I Claudia II: Women in Roman Art and Society*, Austin, University of Texas Press, pp. 77–99)

Demeter and Persephone in Public and Private Apotheosis

Many recent studies of antiquity, including some in the present volume and its predecessor, have addressed the "construction of gender" in various historical periods; that is, society's creation of a set of expectations about the appropriate traits of character and forms of behavior for men and women.[1] Such stereotypes and socially established norms of conduct were often taken at the time to be natural and inevitable but were in fact dependent on and varied according to cultural and historical circumstances. Examination of these gender constructs is important and necessary, exposing as it does the fallacious and often contradictory logic behind the assumptions of many antifeminists that nature, or God, has placed some inevitable restrictions on the freedoms and opportunities available to women. On the other hand, our understanding of ancient societies (or of modern ones, for that matter) is not complete if we do not also examine the other side of that coin: the ways in which certain intractable biological facts about human existence affect all human cultures, producing some patterns of behavior, particularly of religions belief and ritual, that are remarkably universal and consistent. Some of these facts include sex, as opposed to gender (the biological facts of copulation and reproduction, rather than the elaborate

---

[1]   E.g., N.B. Kampen, "Gender Theory in Roman Art," in Kleiner and Matheson, *I, Claudia* 14–24.

structures of behavior and social roles that surround these activities), physical danger, illness, and mortality. Walter Burkert published a masterly examination of the biological origins of much religious behavior; I propose in this essay to examine in particular the fears, and religious responses to those fears, that have their origins in the sexual vulnerability of females.[2] Rape and sexual murder are, of course, dangers to all human beings, male or female, young or old, but the nature of female physiology causes women to be more aware of the danger than men, and causes the parents of young girls, in particular, to fear for the safety of their children.

Contemporary American culture has produced some mythologies of its own that express such anxieties, one of which has received extensive examination in the recent book *Abductions*, by John Mack, a psychologist who treats patients who claim to have been abducted by extraterrestrials. To the great dismay of many of his professional colleagues, Mark appears to believe that on some level of psychological reality, at least, the events that his patients describe have really occurred. I will leave it to others to debate phenomena such as self-hypnosis and false memory, but whatever the merits of Mack's conclusions, the narratives that he recounts do display a remarkably consistent pattern: the patients usually claim to have been visited by the extraterrestrials while in bed asleep (i.e., in a passive and vulnerable state), carried helplessly aboard alien spacecraft and subjected to barbaric experiments, often involving sexual violation. By way, perhaps, of compensation, the aliens then grant them enlightenment on some issue such as ecology or world peace and finally return the victims to their beds, apparently unharmed, until they "recover" the memory of the event at some later date. Some are also convinced that their children are being abducted on a regular basis, and one man claims to have seen his infant son aboard an alien spacecraft.[3] Many of these "experiencers," despite their conviction that they have been brutally victimized, also seem to regard these abductions as something like a religious experience: another popular book on the subject bears the title *Communion*.[4] It is easy for nonbelievers in U.F.O. mythology to laugh at these claims, yet they give voice to real and profound fears of death, of rape, and of losing a child. Reaction to such terrifying realities can take the form of destructively superstitious behavior, of which Americans have recently witnessed another horrifying example in the nationwide witch-hunts for child-abusers that began with the case of the McMartin School.[5] These fears, however, can also manifest themselves in a more benign spirituality and in a range of behaviors between those benign and destructive extremes.

Stories of alien abduction display remarkable consistency with mythological patterns throughout history. Carl Sagan has already documented their resemblance to medieval stories of incubi and succubi.[6] They also resemble the

[2]   W. Burkert, *Creation of the Sacred: Tracks of Biology in Early Religions* (Cambridge, Mass. and London 1996).

[3]   J. Mack, *Abduction: Human Encounters with Aliens* (New York 1994) 178–79.

[4]   W. Streiber, *Communion: A True Story* (New York 1987). On the conviction of experiencers that they have a spiritual mission, see Mack (supra. n.3) 181–87, 230, 247–56, and passim. A fairly representative statement is on p. 253: "It seems to me that Eva is a pioneer with a global mission of healing and peace."

[5]   D. Nathan and M. Snedeker, *Satan's Silence: Ritual Abuse and the Making of a Modern American Witch Hunt* (New York 1995) passim. See esp. pp. 29–50 on the origins of panic, and 147–54 for an instructive comparison to the interrogation of children and use of their testimony in the Salem witch trials.

[6]   C. Sagan, *The Demon-Haunted World: Science as a Candle in the Dark* (New York 1995) 115–33.

very familiar topos in Greek and Roman mythology of rape by a god, in which some powerful being attacks and abducts a human or a less-powerful deity, carrying the victim forever away from the life that he or she once knew but giving the abductee some form of immortality, in another shape or another sphere of existence. Images of such episodes, like the rape of the daughters of Leucippus by Castor and Pollux, or Selene descending from her chariot to embrace Endymion who would then sleep forever, proved understandably quite popular in funerary art.[7]

Among these numerous myths, however, the rape of Persephone held special pride of place in Greek and Roman religion. As recorded in the *Homeric Hymn to Demeter* and in Ovid's *Metamorphoses* and *Fasti*, Hades, the god of death, seized and carried away Persephone as she was picking flowers with her companions. Her mother Demeter, goddess of the earth and of fertility, then searched for her missing daughter, and during her quest received hospitality from Celeus, whom she rewarded by curing his sick child Triptolemos. She then attempted to go farther and give the boy immortality, a scheme that his mother inadvertently frustrated, but although Demeter failed to make the child immortal, she promised that she would one day grant to him the secrets of cultivation of grain. When Demeter finally learned from the nymphs that her daughter was in the underworld, she won Persephone's release and return to the world of the living, on condition that, because she had eaten pomegranate seeds in the underworld, she must return for part of every year to the realm of the dead.[8] This fable of death and seasonal regeneration appears to have been the central event that the mysteries of Eleusis re-enacted for the enlightenment of the initiates. Unlike most mythological rapes, it involves a definite resurrection: not immortality in some other plane of being but a return to life in this world. Moreover, the myth is striking for its female character: a dominant theme of the *Homeric Hymn to Demeter*, and of the cult at Eleusis, is the loving bond between mother and daughter and the association of both with the seasons, fertility, and cultivation of grain, traditionally women's work.[9]

A feminist theologian has tried to compose a kinder, gentler, "prepatriarchal" version of Persephone's descent to the underworld, in which there is no rape and the goddess goes voluntarily to care for the souls of the dead.[10] But as John Mack's patients intuitively recognize when they recount their experiences of alien abduction, the story will not work without the rape. The fear of death,

---

[7]   J. Bayet ("Hercule Funéraire," *MEFR* 39 [1921–1922] 228–29) gives a useful categorization of the types of myths that appear most commonly on Roman sarcophagi. The largest category is "enlèvements" (abductions). Another large category is "amours divines et immortalité," some of which are essentially rapes, although the god does not carry away his or her victim. Koortbojian 63–113.

[8]   *Homeric Hymn to Demter*; Ovid *Met.* 5.341–678, *Fast.* 4.417–620. The detail that Demeter cured Triptolemos of a near-fatal illness before attempting to give him immortality may be a late addition; the hymn does not mention it, but Ovid *Fast.* 4.529–44 narrates it in some detail.

[9]   See E.H. Spitz, "Mothers and Daughters: Ancient and Modern Myths," *Journal of Aesthetics and Art Criticism* 48 (1990) 411–20.

[10]   Charlene Spretnak, quoted by M.L. Keller, "The Eleusinian Mysteries of Demeter and Persephone: Fertility, Sexuality and Rebirth," *Journal of Feminist Studies in Religion* 4 (1988) 39–40. It is possible that some of the terracotta plaques from Locri record a version of the myth in which Persephone voluntarily weds Hades, but this interpretation is far from certain: a figure who rides in a dove-drawn chariot is probably Aphrodite rather than Persephone, and the great majority of the Locrian *pinakes* that represent the chariot group of Hades and Persephone follow the standard iconography. Some that represent a beardless young man and a woman who is not struggling may portray a mortal couple at their marriage rather than the mythological scene. In any case, the sexual union with the male ruler of the underworld remains a central element of the Persephone story. See Zuntz 164–68, and Cohen 125–126, figs. 51 a and b and 52.

expressed as the horror of violation, is central to the meaning of the myth and to the cathartic experience of the initiate. Rape is a shattering reality for countless victims, a danger of which all women become aware at an early age and for that very reason the most powerful possible metaphor for helplessness in the face of some event or force of nature beyond human control. In Cohen's study of rape scenes in ancient art, she rightly advised modern analysts to recognize the literal as well as metaphorical meanings of these representations: what the viewer sees first is a scene of violent abduction, and one responds to this image before intellectualizing the scene as a reference to life, death, and the seasons.[11]

The mysteries of Eleusis, with all of their emotional and psychological resonance continued to be celebrated throughout the Roman imperial period. Many emperors, along with countless Roman citizens, became initiates, and at least three emperors lavished architectural patronage on the site.[12] Ovid devotes long passages in two of his poems to the myth of Persephone and Demeter and seems familiar with the rites of Eleusis.[13] Cicero describes Eleusinian initiation as raising mankind from a brutish to a civilized existence, providing a source of joy in life and a reason to die with hope.[14] Somewhat closer to home for Italians, the island of Sicily claimed possession of the very spot where Persephone vanished into the underworld, at the spring of Kyane, where one of the earliest cult images of the goddess was found, a sculptured head in the Daedalic style of the late seventh or early sixth century.[15] This image and numerous terracotta votive statuettes and plaques attest the enormous popularity of the cult of Demeter and Persephone in Sicily and in southern Italy.[16] Non-Greek peoples of Italy also enthusiastically embraced this myth, especially in funerary art.[17] The story of Persephone was, in short, not only thoroughly familiar to most Romans of the imperial period but deeply entrenched in the religious traditions of their homeland. For many men and women of all classes, the myth was also associated with the profound religious experience of initiation at Eleusis.

---

[11]   Cohen 118. See also W. Burkert, *Ancient Mystery Cults* (Cambridge, Mass and London 1987) 12–29, on the function of mystery cults in answering personal needs, in particular alleviating the fears of death or future disaster; see esp. 21–22 on the cult at Eleusis.

[12]   Suet. *Aug.* 93: Dio Cass. 51.4.1; Augustus was an initiate. For a history of the site in Roman times, see K. Clinton, "The Eleusinian Mysteries: Roman Initiates and Benefactors, Second Century BC to AD 267," *ANRW* II.18.2 (1989) 1499–1539, and G. Mylonas, *Eleusis and the Eleusinian Mysteries* (Princeton 1961) 155–86. See in particular p. 156 on the sack of the sanctuary in AD 170 by the Kostovoks and the subsequent restoration by Marcus Aurelius; 162–66 on the Greater Propylaea, probably completed during the principate of Marcus Aurelius, and 183–186 on projects sponsored by Hadrian.

[13]   Ovid *Met.* 5.332–678, *Fast* 4.417–620. In *Fast.* 4.535–36 , Ovid mentions that the initiates at Eleusis break their fast at nightfall, as did Demeter on her arrival at the house of Celeus. If Ovid knew what the initiates do, he had presumably been initiated.

[14]   Cic. *Leg.* 2.14.36; see Keller (supra n. 10) 27.

[15]   Ovid *Met.* 346–61, 409–24, *Fast.* 4.419–21. On the Laganello head from the sanctuary near the spring of Kyane: G.P. Carratelli ed., *The Western Greeks*, exhibition catalogue, Palazzo Grassi, Venice, March–December 1996 (Venice 1996) 675 no.72; *LIMC* IV[1] 862 no. 189 (as Demeter); Zuntz 71; E. Langlotz and M. Hirmer, *Ancient Greek Sculpture of South Italy and Sicily* (New York 1965, originally published as *Die Kunst der Westgriechen in Sizilien und Unteritalien* [Munich 1963]) 48, 251, with earlier literature pl. 3.

[16]   Zuntz 70–89 on the importance of cult in Magna Graecia, 89–178 on Sicilian terracotta votives. Terracotta statuette from Medma: Zuntz frontispiece, xi. Terracotta reliefs from Locri: Zuntz 164–168; Langlotz and Hirmer (supra n. 15) 271, pls. 71–75; Carratelli (supra n.15) 701–702 nos. 166.I–166.VI.

[17]   Lindner 49–54 nos. 34–41; L. Sperti, *Rilievi greci e romani del Museo Archeologico di Venezia* (Rome 1988) 130 under no. 40.

It is only to be expected, then, that Persephone (also known as Kore, "The Maiden") has a special association with the funerary monuments of men and women, both in Greek and in Roman art, and that in those of women there would be an implied identification of the goddess with the deceased, whose mourning relatives might hope that she, like the goddess, would enjoy victory over death in the form of a happy afterlife. Two Archaic Greek statues of the early sixth century BC, the well-known Berlin Kore and the more recently discovered statue of Phrasikleia, were undoubtedly tomb makers and probably represent the deceased rather than the goddess Persephone, yet the young women appropriate some of her attributes, like the polos headdress decorated with flowers.[18] The Berlin Kore carries another of the goddess's attributes, the pomegranate. Phrasikleia carries a flower, like the ones on her headdress; flowers, with their self-evident meaning of youth, vitality, and potential sexuality, are an important element of the story of Persephone. The spilled and abandoned flowers that she left behind form a powerful image of untimely death in literature and in the visual arts.[19] The inscription found with this statue indentifies it as "the marker of Phrasikleia. I shall always be called "Maiden" (Kore), since the gods gave me this name instead of marriage."[20] The wording of the inscription, like the attributes and iconography of the figure, seem to blur the distinction between her identity and that of the queen of the underworld. Since the unmarried Phrasikleia must have died very young, her situation bore special comparison with that of Persephone, and the grief of her bereaved parents to that of Demeter. Six centuries later, when sculptured sarcophagi became popular in the Roman empire, the identification of the deceased with Persephone enjoyed popularity once again (fig. 5.1). Long before the manufacture of these tomb monuments, however, Demeter and Persephone had long been associated in Roman art with mortal women, not only to express hopes for their existence after death but often to honor and heroize them while they were still alive.

During the Roman imperial period, visual association of living or recently deceased women with goddesses became an acceptable, and eventually a common practice, both for private individuals and for women of the imperial family. Identification with Ceres was one of the earliest such forms of apotheosis, and one of the most enduringly popular, perhaps because the goddesses of the earth, with their intimate connection to the daily lives and survival of humans, seemed especially appropriate for assimilation with mortals.[21] In most cases, the meaning of the association is simple and direct: Ceres is a goddess of fertility and the mythological archetype of the loving mother and protector of the young. The primary social role of aristocratic and imperial Roman women was to perpetuate their families by bearing children. One of the earliest such identifications with Ceres to be clearly attested in coins

---

[18] See B.S. Ridgway, *The Archaic Style in Greek Sculpture* (Princeton 1977) 109, n. 32, on the implied identification of the deceased with the goddess and the significance of the *polos* as a mark of divinity. Persephone wears a *stephane* decorated with flowers in several of the terracotta plaques from Locri, including the one that represents her enthroned as queen of the underworld beside Hades and another in which she looks on as a girl picks pomegranates. See supra n. 16, for references.

[19] See Ovid *Met.* 5.398–401.

[20] J. Boardman, *Greek Sculpture, The Archaic Period* (New York and Toronto 1978) 73; Ridgway (supra n. 18) 109, n. 32. See also Cohen 134–35 for the special significance of a reference to Kore in the monument of a young girl who died unmarried.

[21] See Mikocki, passim, esp. 90–94.

FIGURE 5.1   *Sarcophagus with the Rape of Persephone*. Rome, Museo Capitolino inv. 249. [photograph: Deutsches Archäologisches Institut, Rome, Inst. Neg. 62.806]

and inscriptions is that of Livia, the wife of Augustus and mother of Tiberius.[22] Two centuries later, a handsome statue of the empress Julia Domna, the mother of the emperors Caracalla and Geta, presented her with the attributes of the goddess, and this statue had obviously been an object of love and veneration for the people of Ostia, since the circumstances of its find suggest that it was carefully buried to protect it from destruction.[23] The volume of extant material attesting identification of actual women with the chthonian goddesses is far too great for a comprehensive survey here. Let us examine, however, some early examples that demonstrate how such associations became acceptable.

[22]   Identifications as Ceres Augusta: *CIL* X, 7501; *CIL* XI, 3196 (the latter is definitely datable to AD 18, during Livia's lifetime); W.H. Gross, *Julia Augusta: Untersuchungen zur Grundlegung einer Livia-Ikonographie* (Göttingen 1962) 43–47, 106–31; B.S. Spaeth, "The Goddess Ceres in the Ara Pacis Augustae and the Carthage Relief," *AJA* 98 (1994) 88, n. 206; Mikocki 18–21, 151–54 nos. 1–26 for epigraphic and numismatic evidence.

[23]   Statue of Julia Domna as Ceres, Ostia: Kleiner, *Roman Sculpture* 326, 327, fig. 291, 354, with literature; Bieber, *Copies* 166 figs. 740–41; R. Calza, *Scavi di Ostia* 9: *I ritratti romani dal 160 circa alla metà del III secolo D.C.* (Rome 1977) 50–51 no. 63, pls. 49–50. Epigraphic evidence for identification of the deified Julia Domna as NEA ΔHMHTHP: *CIG* II, 2815 and 3642. On the "priestess of Ceres" type that this statue follows, and its many replicas in both imperial and private portraits, see Bieber, *Copies* 163–67, figs. 728–33, 738–40. This statue follows Julia Domna's latest portrait type and may postdate her death and deification. Mikocki (141) notes that during the Julio-Claudian dynasty, identification of living women with Ceres was popular but that during the second and third centuries, it became more common for women, both imperial and private, who had died.

Augustus had become an initiate at Eleusis at a pivotal time in his career, shortly after his victory at Actium in 31 BC but before he secured his final victory over Egypt.[24] His devotion to the cult and its personal meaning to him were probably sincere, but for Augustus, sincerity was never inconsistent with political opportunism, and he undoubtedly recognized the prestige of the cult and the propagandistic value of the beloved goddesses. The earliest known portrait statue of his wife Livia in the Greek-speaking eastern part of the empire stood along with a statue of himself at Eleusis that must have been set up soon after his initiations in 31, even though Livia would certainly not have been with her husband at that time. It is clear, however, that both members of the imperial couple had a special relationship to the sacred site from the very beginning of Augustus's regime. Livia definitely did accompany Augustus on a later trip to the Greek world in 19 BC, when he attended the mysteries again, requesting a special repetition of the ceremonies for his benefit, even though it was not the usual time of year for their celebration. No literary accounts record whether or not Livia became an initiate on this occasion, but it would have been rather surprising if she had not. A more unexpected and shocking event, however—the suicide of one of the initiates—may have over-shadowed other more routine occurrences at that celebration in 19 BC and caused our sources to omit mention of them.[25] Whether or not Livia was an initiate, the identification of her with Ceres that pervades her portrait imagery may have its origins in her husband's special devotion to the cult of Eleusis.

The beautiful maternal goddess of the Ara Pacis Augustae is a very eclectic being who will probably never receive an identification that satisfies everyone.[26] She displays, however, many aspects and attributes of Ceres.[27] These allusions were undoubtedly intentional, whether or not "Ceres" is the name by which we should call this goddess. This eclectic being, in turn, bears a subtle but undoubtedly intentional resemblance to a living woman on the same monument: the emperor's wife Livia, in the south processional frieze, wears a veil, a vegetal crown under the veil, a coiffure with a simple middle part (not the prevailing fashion at the time) and long, cascading locks that hang down behind her ears to her shoulders, an element that did not become common in actual fashions until years later.[28] During the principate of her son Tiberius, while Livia was still alive, coins and inscriptions refer to her as "Ceres Augusta," and

---

[24]   Dio Cass. 51.4.1.

[25]   Rose, *Dynastic Commemoration* 140–41 no. 71; Clinton (supra n. 12) 1507–1509; Dio Cass. 54.9.10 on the celebration of the rites in 19 BC and the public suicide of an Indian man named Zarmaros, who had just been initiated.

[26]   See K. Galinsky, "Venus, Polysemy, and the Ara Pacis Augustae," *AJA* 96 (1992) 457–75. See in particular pp. 471–72 on the syncretic associations of Venus with Ceres and of Ceres with Tellus.

[27]   Spaeth (supra n. 22) 65–100.

[28]   Spaeth (supra n. 22) 88–89, fig. 14. I arrived independently at the same conclusion. See also R. Winkes, *Livia, Octavia, Iulia (Archaeologica Transatlantica* 13, Louvain 1995) 49 and 156 no. 79.

at least some cameo gems that represent her with the corn-ear crown may also date to her lifetime.[29] The emperor's daughter-in-law Livilla, the mother of his twin grandsons, probably also appears on a group of cameos with the poppy and corn-ear crown and in two cases with her all-important babies as well.[30] The identification of Livilla's likenesses is problematic, but if these gems do represent her, they must certainly date to her lifetime, since she died in disgrace in AD 32, executed for alleged involvement in the murder of her husband, and would certainly never have been honored after her death.[31]

Cameos are a relatively private and intimate medium in which more explicit deification may be possible than in public coinage or sculpture. More public apotheoses of living women appear in the following principate, that of Caligula, who made his dynastic and monarchical intentions clear from his earliest days in power. The living women of his family, who represented the hope of perpetuation for the Julian family, thus received extravagant public honors. His favourite sister Drusilla, whom he named as the heir to the empire in his will, appears on a coin of Smyrna with the corn ears and poppies either of Demeter or of Kore, and her only fully preserved statue follows a Classical Greek type known as the Kore Albani.[32] It is in this guise, with slight variations necessitated by representation in relief, that Persephone appears on the fifth-century Greek sculpture known as the "Eleusinian relief," as she and Demeter bestow the gift of agriculture on Triptolemos and send him on his mission.[33] Drusilla was the first Roman woman to be deified after her death, but both of these representations almost certainly date to her lifetime: the coin from Smyrna bears the names of magistrates of the year 37, and the statue, like at least two other portraits of Drusilla, was recut at some point after its manufacture to add an attribute, the beaded *infula* that crosses her forehead and hangs to her shoulders. The only possible motivation for the recutting was Drusilla's death and deification, at which time her images required some additional mark of sanctity. The statue in its original form must then have presented Drusilla not as a *diva* but as the emperor's living heir and associated her with Persephone as a fertility goddess and restorer of life to the earth in spring. When Caligula named Drusilla as his heir, he had recently suffered a life-threatening illness. The

---

[29] Identifications as Ceres Augusta: see supra n. 22.
Cameos possibly datable to Livia's lifetime:
A. Florence, Museo Archeologico no. 26, inv. 14549, *LIMC* IV 905 no. 172, with earlier literature, s.v. Demeter/Ceres (S. De Angeli); W.-R. Megow, *Kameen von Augustus bis Alexander Severus* (Berlin 1987) 255 no. B17, pl. 13.9; Mikocki 157 no. 41, pl. 2.
B. Florence, Museo Archeologico no. 177, inv. 1453, onyx cameo, H. 0.048. Jugate portrait of Tiberius, laureate, and Livia, wearing a crown of poppies and corn ears behind a crescent diadem. The presence of Tiberius and Livia together on the gem suggests that both were still alive when it was made. Mikocki 157 no. 40, pl. 2, with earlier literature; Megow (supra) 179–80 no. A49, pl. 10.10. The dating and interpretation of the Gemma Tiberiana remain highly controversial. It is certain that Livia appears here with the attributes of Ceres, but it is less certain whether the gem belongs to her lifetime or later. See Mikocki 157–58 no. 45, pl. 7, with earlier literature.

[30] Mikocki 34–35, 174–75 nos. 161–64, pl. 4, figs. 161–63; Megow (supra n. 29) 29–31, 295–97 nos. D22–D26.

[31] Tac. *Ann* 4.3–8, 11; Suet. *Tib.* 62.1; Dio Cass. 58.11.6–7.

[32] Coin from Smyrna: D. Klose, *Die Münzprägung von Smyrna in der römischen Kaiserzeit* (*AMUGS* 10, Berlin 1987) 15, 217–19 nos. 1–36; W. Trillmich, *Familienpropaganda der Kaiser Caligula und Claudius* (*AMUGS* 8, Berlin 1978) 123. Statue in Museo Gregoriano Profano: for a full discussion of the identification of this statue, with earlier literature, see S. Wood, "Diva Drusilla Panthea and the Sisters of Caligula," *AJA* 99 (1995) 471–82, figs. 15–17. On the coins and the statue, Mikocki 42–43, 184 nos. 223, 224, pl. 27. Mikocki discusses the various identifications of the statue but favors the identification as Drusilla.

[33] Eleusinian relief: Athens National Museum. *LIMC* IV 875 no. 375, with earlier literature, s.v. Demeter (L. Beschi).

political urgency of naming a young, apparently healthy and fertile successor to renew the Julian family in the event of his death must have been compelling to him and to the viewers of the statue.

Although Claudius presented a more restrained public image of himself and his family, public identification of living women with goddesses had clearly become acceptable by this time, since his last wife Agrippina the Younger appears as Demeter on coins of the Roman mint, the medium through which imperial likenesses received perhaps their widest public distribution. When the profiles of Agrippina appear on the reverses of the aurei and denarii of Claudius from the Roman mint, and on the obverses of coins that represent her son Nero on the reverse, she invariably wears the corn-ear crown.[34] In the Greek-speaking East, where notions of divine kingship had deeper traditional roots, such an identification also appears in monumental public sculpture, on a relief panel of the Sebasteion of Aphrodisias, where Agrippina as Ceres-Demeter clasps the hand of a figure of Claudius in the guise of Zeus.[35]

Cameos, as usual, can express the identification even more extravagantly: one such work in the Cabinet des Médailles represents the imperial couple as Triptolemos and Ceres, bestowing the gifts of prosperity on their grateful subjects.[36] Agrippina here has an oddly small and misshapen head, suggesting that she has been recut from an image of the previous wife Messalina. If so, then the idea of associating the emperor's wife with Ceres predated his marriage to Agrippina the Younger. During the short period at the beginning of Nero's principate when Agrippina still enjoyed considerable power, she continued to appear in the guise of Demeter in both public and private works of art. On a cameo vase, the young emperor and his mother appear in the dragon-drawn chariot of Triptolemos and Demeter, just as Claudius and Agrippina had done on the earlier gem, and the message is the same: that the blessings of prosperity flow to the people from the generous and fertile imperial family.[37] In the Neronian gem, there may be an added implication: the emperor's mother stands in the same relationship to him as the mighty goddess to her younger, mortal protégé.

During the principate of Claudius, deceased women of the imperial family also began to appear in public art with explicitly goddesslike attributes, and for them, too, Ceres and Proserpina were some of the most popular objects of identification. Drusilla had been the first Roman woman deified, but her cult was short-lived, ceasing to serve any useful political purpose after the coup that ended Caligula's principate. Livia would have been the most obvious first choice for deification, and indeed she was worshiped as the goddess Ceres

---

[34]   *RIC* I²; 125 no. 75, 126 nos. 80–81, pl. 16; A. Banti and L. Simonetti, *Corpus Nummorum Romanorun* XVI (Florence 1978) 65–75 nos. 1–17 (aurei) and 86–94, nos. 33–46 (denarii). Agrippina also appears with the corn-ear crown in a jugate portrait with Claudius on tetradrachms from Ephesus, pp. 77–81 nos. 18–23. See also Trillmich (supra n. 32) 55–59, pl. 11, figs. 11 and 15, and Mikocki 39, 179–80 nos. 192–201, pl. 5, nos. 192, 195.

[35]   Mikocki 39, 180 no 202; R.R.R. Smith, "The Imperial Reliefs from the Sebasteion at Aphrodisias," *JRS* 77 (1987) 106–10 no. 3, pls. 8–9.

[36]   Paris, Bibliothèque Nationale, Cabinet des Médailles 276: Megow (supra n. 29) 207 no. A86, pl. 27.3; Mikocki 39, 180 no. 203, pl. 9.

[37]   Lindner III, pl. 24.2; *LIMC* IV¹ 902 no. 138, s.v. Demeter/Ceres (S. De Angeli); Mikocki 180–81 no. 205.

Augusta in some provincial cities after her death, even before her official consecration, but Drusilla's untimely death caused her unexpectedly to "jump the queue."[38] It remained therefore to Claudius to deify his grandmother Livia, a wise political move for him, since his kinship to her was far closer than to Augustus. Sculptures that associate Livia not only with Ceres but with syncretic beings like Ceres-Fortuna undoubtedly helped to promote this politically useful new cult.[39] Claudius also did not neglect his own mother, Antonia the Younger, who never received official consecration but who nonetheless appears on coins wearing the corn-ear crown[40] and in at least one statue of the Kore Albani type.[41] This, too, is a syncretic image with attributes of Aphrodite, a goddess with whom Persephone had deep and ancient associations, especially in Italian cult.[42] Since the statue of Antonia as Persephone-Aphrodite appeared in a group with statues of her two grandchildren Octavia and Britannicus, her association with goddesses of fertility was especially appropriate.[43]

Such allusions to the chthonian goddesses often appear as well in portrait statues of non-imperial women, both living and dead. At least one surviving statue attests the use of the Kore Albani type for portraits besides those of Drusilla and Antonia Minor.[44] The Large and Small Herculaneum Women, which probably represented Demeter and Kore respectively, became very popular prototypes for portrait statues.[45] One of the earliest such adaptations appears in the statue of Nonia Balba, the daughter of a local philanthropist who

[38] An example of "unofficial" worship of Livia includes a small but prominently located shrine dedicated to Ceres Augusta in the theater of Leptis Magna. The colossal cult image, although highly idealized, appears to be a portrait of Livia wearing the turret-crown and corn-ear and poppy garland: a syncretic combination of the attributes of Ceres, Cybele, and Tyche. See G. Caputo and G. Traversari, *Le sculture del teatro di Leptis Magna* (Rome 1976) 76–79 no. 58, with full earlier references, pls. 54–55; D. Kreikenbom, *Griechische und Römische Kolossalporträts bis zum späten ersten Jahrhundert n. Chr., JdI–EH* 27 (1992) 180–81 no. III 39, pl. 11.c; J.A. Hanson, *Roman Theater Temples* (Princeton 1959) 59–60, figs. 21–22, on the shrine.

[39] Statue of Livia as Ceres-Fortuna:
A. Ny Carlsberg Glyptotek inv. 1643. Winkes (supra n. 28) 119–20 no. 43; Poulsen I 73–74 no. 38, pls. 60–63; Gross (supra n. 22) 118–19; Mikocki 22, 159 no. 53, pl. 11.
B. Louvre, MA 1242. Winkes (supra n. 28) 148–50 no. 74; Mikocki 22, 159 no. 51, pl. 11, with earlier literature.
Capitoline bust of Livia-Ceres: Fittschen-Zanker III 3–5 no. 3, pl. 2.3; W. Eck, K. Fittschen, and F. Naumann, *Kaisersaal: Portraits aus den Kapitolinischen Museen in Rom* (Köhn, Römische-Germanisches Museum, 23 April–22 June, 1986) 56–57, photo p. 29. For a discussion of Livia's "Ceres Type" and catalogue of extant replicas: Fittschen-Zanker III 4, 5, n. 10, under no. 3.

[40] *RIC* I²; 124–25 nos. 65–68, pl. 15; *BMCRE* I 180 nos. 109–14; Trillmich (supra n. 32) 69–77 nos. 1–32, pl. 6.

[41] B. Andreae, "Le Sculture," in G. Tocco Sciarelli ed., *Baia: Il ninfeo imperiale sommerso di Punta Epitaffio* (Naples 1983) 54–56 no. 6, pls. 122–23, 126–30; B. Andreae, *Odysseus* (Frankfurt 1982) 202–207.

[42] Zuntz 164–68.

[43] Andreae (supra n. 41, 1983) 56–60 nos. 8–9, figs. 156–57, 163; Andreae (supra n. 41, 1982) 207–208.

[44] Munich Glyptothek 208. B. Vierneisel-Schlörb, *Klassische Skulpturen des 5. und 4. Jahrhunderts v. Chr.* (Munich 1979) 163–73 no. 15, figs. 74–79.

[45] M. Bieber, "The Copies of the Herculanium Women," *ProcPhilSoc* 106 (1962) 111–34; *LIMC* IV 853 no. 62, s.v. Demeter (L. Beschi). Doubts have been raised about whether the Hellenistic originals did in fact represent Demeter and Persephone; they were recently discussed by Catherine de Grazia Vanderpool in "Clothes and the Woman," presented at the annual meeting of the Archaeological Institute of America/American Philological Association (AIA/APA), 28 December 1997, abstract *AJA* 102 (1998) 362.

rebuilt the basilica of Herculaneum and was consequently entitled to decorate it with statues of himself and his family.[46] The group probably belongs to the principate of Tiberius, thus predating even the earliest extant imperial statues in the guise of Persephone or Demeter. It is possible that Nonia Balba had already died by the time the group was dedicated and so was singled out for special honor, but her statue appeared in a definitely non-funerary context.

When portrait statues follow these Hellenistic prototypes but do not actually hold the attributes of Demeter and Kore, it is not certain whether the original meanings of the statues were uppermost in the minds of their patrons and sculptors.[47] The dignity and quiet stance of the figures may simply have lent themselves well to images of elite women. The Large Herculanium Woman was, however, undoubtedly understood by Roman patrons to represent Demeter, since statues of this type, including portrait statues, frequently hold her attributes of the corn ears and poppies.[48] This type was, moreover, extremely popular not only in public statues of aristocratic women but in funerary statues and reliefs, sometimes appearing on grave stelai and sarcophagi along with other portraits that followed the type of the "Small Herculaneum Woman." In these settings, the two types clearly seem to identify actual mothers and daughters with the Eleusinian goddesses.[49]

In funerary art, the story of the rape of Persephone retained all its emotional power and indeed was one of the most popular subjects for mythological sarcophagi. A large number of sarcophagi represent the rape in a pattern so consistent that although the artists and patrons introduce some variations into the formula according to individual needs and wishes, all must be at least loosely based on a common model (figs. 5.1, 5.2).[50] In every case, the central scene is that of Hades in his chariot, carrying his struggling victim away, while Persphone's companions react with gestures of alarm. Hot on his heels, the goddess Athena grips the arm of Hades and attempts to hold him back, sometimes assisted by Artemis. These warlike virgin goddesses had become part of the myth at least by the fifth century BC, when Euripides, in a choral strophion of the *Helen*, mentioned their efforts to aid Demeter's search for her daughter, and the decision of Zeus to thwart them.[51] On a number of sarcophagi, another deity intervenes: Venus, who has set the chain of events in motion by inspiring the lust of Hades, grips Athena's shield and pulls her back,

---

[46]   On the Balbus group: J.J. Deiss, *Herculaneum: Italy's Buried Treasure*,[2]; (New York 1985) 158–66; E.R. Barker, *Buried Herculaneum* (London 1908) 155–57, figs. 12, 14. On the female statues and the dating of their hairstyles: K. Polaschek, "Studien zu einem Frauenkopf im Landesmuseum Trier und zur weibliche Haartracht der iulisch-claudishcen Zeit," *TrZ* 35 (1972) 162–64; Bieber, *Copies* 150, pl. 116, figs. 683–87.

[47]   J. Trimble, "Greek Style, Roman Statues: The Small Herculaneum Women," presented at the annual meeting of the AIA/APA, 30 December 1995, abstract *AJA* 100 (1996) 389–90; Mikocki 92.

[48]   Bieber, *Copies* 153; Bieber (supra n. 45) 124; *LIMC* IV^1 853 no. 62, s.v. Demeter (L. Beschi).

[49]   Bieber, *Copies* 153 (on a funerary statue from the Isola Sacra of Ostia) and 154–56 on stelai and sarcophagi; Bieber (supra n. 45) 128–33. An example of a stele that shows portraits of an older and younger woman in the Large and Small Herculaneum Woman types is an Antonine stele in Athens, now built into the wall of the Small Metropolis: Bieber, *Copies*, fig. 718. A similar pairing appears in a sarcophagus now in the Palazzo Colonna: Bieber, *Copies* 155 figs. 721–23.

[50]   *LIMC* IV 901 nos. 126–34, s.v. Demeter/Ceres (S. De Angeli); Koch-Sichtermann, *Sarkophage* 175–79 no. 38; B. Andreae, *Studien zur römischen Grabkunst* (Heidelberg 1963) 47–48, for a catalogue of representations of the rape of Persephone in Roman funerary art.

[51]   Euripides *Helen* 1313–18.

FIGURE 5.2   *Sarcophagus with the Rape of Persephone.* Florence, Galleria Uffizi inv. 86. [photograph: Deutsches Archäologisches Institut, Rome, Inst. Neg. 72.120]

so that the rape scene becomes a three-way tug-of-war-between virginity, sex, and death.[52] Behind the central group, Demeter mounts her dragon-drawn chariot and begins her long pursuit, brandishing the torches that will light her way, but ahead of the central group, Hermes Psychopompus is already directing the chariot of Hades into the underworld.

Sculptors and workshops could of course introduce variations into the formula: for example, some show Hades holding Persephone at a diagonal, with her head forward toward the horses, so that her legs kick out behind the group (fig. 5.2), while others show her standing more upright but leaning backward with her torso and brandishing her arms.[53] Place personifications like Tellus, Oceanus, Caelus, mountain gods, and nymphs may appear to help set the scene, and some sarcophagi also include the scene of Hades pouncing on Persephone as she picks flowers (fig. 5.1), but all follow this basic format with a fair degree of consistency. Given its ideal adaptation to a long, continuous rectangular field, the sequence of figures as we see them on sarcophagi was probably created specifically for this type of monument, but some of the figure groups, in particular the chariots of Hades with Persephone pursued by Athena, and of Demeter with her torches, have older origins.[54] The work that inspired the adaptations in stonecutters' pattern books was most probably a celebrated painting by Nicomachus that had been brought to Rome and displayed in the Capitolium until it was accidentally destroyed by fire, probably in 64 or 69.[55] Until then, the work would have been available to Roman patrons and artists for observation and emulation. After its loss, however, as artists worked from copies of copies and adapted them to a variety of media, spaces, and surfaces,

[52]   Lindner 113–14. The presence of Venus is constant in the sarcophagi that she classifies as Group C, pp. 76–80 nos. 93–104 and pp. 113–14. Venus also appears on some sarcophagi of Lindner's Group D, pp. 81–82 nos. 106, 109, 110. On the role of Venus as instigator of the rape of Persephone: Ovid *Met.* 5.363–84.

[53]   For a complete discussion of the typology and categories of these sarcophagi, see Lindner 64–86, 108–14. Figure 2: Galleria Uffizi, Florence, inv. 86. *LIMC* IV[1] 901 no. 128, s.v. Demeter/ Ceres (S. De Angeli); Sichtermann-Koch, *Mythen* 57 no. 60 with earlier references, pl. 147, figs. 2, 3, pl. 148, fig. 2, pls. 149, 150, 151, fig. 1; Lindner 77, no. 94. An example of the sarcophagi in which Persephone reaches backward with her arms in Walters Art Gallery, Baltimore, inv. 23.219. *LIMC* IV[1] 901 no. 132; Koch-Sichtermann, *Sarkophage* 177, 263, fig. 204; G. Koch, "The Walters Persephone Sarcophagus," *JWalt* 37 (1978) 74–83; Lindner 64–65 no. 68.

[54]   Koch (supra n. 53) 79.

[55]   Pliny *HN* 35.108; Lindner 11. On the relationships of this famous lost painting to extant works, including the Hellenistic frescoes in Tomb B at Vergina and later Roman versions in sculpture, mosaic, and painting, see Lindner 30–34 no. 21, and 108; J. Oakley, "Reflections of Nicomachos," *BABesch* 61 (1986) 71–75; Sperti (supra n. 17) 130 under no. 40.

the composition almost inevitably evolved into diverse versions. Venus, for example, as she intervenes to stop Athena's rescue effort, is probably a Roman invention, reflecting a version of the story best known from the *Metamorphoses* of Ovid.

One of the earliest replicas of this composition is not a sarcophagus but a small ivory plaque from Pompeii, apparently a decorative attachment of a small cupboard, possibly an inlay into a door or more probably a vertical handle.[56] Whatever its precise function, it must have been visible from both sides since both are decorated (fig. 5.3). Because of the small scale of the plaque, the scene must be divided into two: the chariot of Hades as he carries away his victim on the convex side, and the pursuing figures of Demeter, Artemis, and Athena on the reverse. This plaque has a companion piece of identical shape that represents more problematic mythological scenes, but scenes that may, if my interpretation is correct, present striking parallels and contrasts to the story of Persephone that would explain why they have been paired (figs. 5.4–5.5). The outer, convex side portrays a woman wearing a diadem and long chiton and holding a scepter, sitting on a birthing chair while a midwife kneels in front of her to deliver her child (fig. 5.4).[57] Given the small scale and somewhat mediocre carving of the ivories, the scene is difficult to interpret, and some have seen it as a doctor tending the wound of a male warior, but all the figures in the scene do appear to have breasts and to wear long female garments.[58]

Other sculptural works that unambiguously represent birthing scenes display very similar compositions: a simple terracotta plaque from the tomb of a midwife at the Isola Sacra of Ostia, for example, shows the mother sitting more or less upright on a birthing chair, an assistant standing behind her to support her upper body, and a midwife reaching between her legs.[59] Several biographical sarcophagi represent the moment immediately after the birth in a very similar format: the mother in a birthing chair, the attendant behind her, and the midwife in front of her, this time holding the infant in her hands and

[56]   Naples, Museo Nazionale Archeologico inv. 109905B. *LIMC* IV 901 no. 135, s.v. Demeter-Ceres (S. De Angeli); Lindner 88–89 no. 155, 105, pl. 18.1; V. Spinazzola, *Le Arti decorative in Pompeii e nel Museo Nazionale di Napoli* (Milan, Rome, Venice, Florence 1928) 224, pl. 33; P. Williams Lehmann, *Roman Wall Paintings from Boscoreale in the Metropolitan Museum of Art* (Cambridge, Mass. 1953) 58, fig. 39; A. Sogliano, "Rilievi di Avorio," *Giornale degli Scavi di Pompeii* n.s. 3 (1874) 12–16; Hans Graeven, *Antike Schnitzereien aus Elfenbein und Knochen in photographischer Nachbildung* (Hannover 1903) 39–46 nos. 25–28.
This plaque and its companions were discovered in Insula 2, Regio I of Pompeii on 27 June 1873, with other ornaments that evidently belonged to an object described in the excavation report as "un piccolo armadio." Sogliano suggests that the plaques decorated the fronts of drawers and that the inner sides are more badly damaged due to the contact with the objects inside the drawers. Graeven suggested the interpretation as vertical handles, attached by the holes in their lower borders, although they could have been reused at some later date.

[57]   Naples, Museo Nazionale Archeologico inv. 109905A. Koortbojian 53–56, fig. 17. Luisa Musso, "Il Trasporto funebre di Achille sul rilievo Colonna-Grottaferratta," *BullComm* 93 (1989–1990) 14–16, fig. 11, with full earlier literature; Koch, *Meleager* 118, n. 5; *LIMC*[1] 227 no. 43 and I[2];, pl. 168, s.v. Adonis (B. Servais-Soyez); Spinazzola (supra n. 56) 224 and pl. 33; Lehmann (supra n. 56) 57–58, fig. 38. On the significance of the midwife scene: N.B. Kampen, "Social Status and Gender in Roman Art: The Case of the Saleswoman," in D'Ambra, *Roman Art in Context* 124, originally published in M.D. Garrard and N. Broude eds., *Feminism and Art History* (New York 1982) 60–77. Reference to Pompeiian plaque is on p. 70.

[58]   Spinozzola ([supra n. 56] 224) describes this as the wounding and death of Adonis, an interpretation following by Lehmann (supra n. 56) 57–58, Servais-Soyez in *LIMC*[1] 227 no. 43, and partially by Koortbojian 53–56. Graeven (supra n. 56) proposes that it represents the scene of Homer's *Iliad* E 336, in which Aphrodite, while attempting to intervene in battle, is wounded by the spear of Diomedes.

[59]   Kampen, *Image and Status* 69–72, fig. 58, and Kampen (supra n. 57, 1993) 124, 126, fig. 49.

FIGURE 5.3 *Ivory Plaque with the Rape of Persephone.* From Pompeii, Naples, Museo Nazionale Archeologico 109905B. [photograph: Deutsches Archäologisches Institut, Rome, Inst. Neg. 66.1837]

preparing to bathe him.[60] This version of the birthing scene has the advantage of depicting the individual of greatest interest to the artist and patron (the child, the rest of whose life is depicted in the other scenes on these monuments) and also allows a more dignified presentation of the mother than in the plaques that recorded the profession of midwives. In these sarcophagi, the mother is modestly covered, her skirt drawn down over her legs. The ivory plaque likewise depicts the mythological mother modestly, with all but her lower legs concealed, and probably shows the moment before the birth, as the midwife reaches toward the patient's groin or possibly washes her in preparation for the delivery, since she is holding some round object in her hand that might be a sponge. (This object appears too small to be an infant's head, but that possibility cannot be altogether ruled out.) The ivory plaque shares as well another feature with birthing scenes on some sarcophagi: the presence of a figure at the far left who has no evident task to perform in the delivery. On sarcophagi, there are often three such figures, one of whom writes on a globe, as though to record the astrological destiny of the newborn. In different contexts, they can bear the attributes either of the Muses or of the Fates.[61] The figure on the Pompeiian plaque may, then play a similar role, foretelling the fate of the child.

On the other side, two helmeted men lift the nude body of a dead or dying comrade, as an old man laments in the background, lifting the limp arm of the fallen man (fig. 5.5). This is a very stereotypical scene that could represent the death of any number of heroes and has numerous precedents in Greek vase painting.[62] One of the closest extant parallels in Roman sculpture is the tiny relief of the ransom of Hector's body on the *Tabula Iliaca* in the Museo

---

[60] Kampen, *Image and Status* 33–44. Some especially good and clear examples include the sarcophagus of a child in Paris, Musée du Louvre MA 319: Kampen, *Image and Status* 34, 37, 76, 147 no. 23 (with earlier literature), fig. 8.

[61] Kampen, *Image and Status* 37, 38–39, text fig. 1.

[62] Koch, *Meleager* 34. See also *LIMC* VII¹ 697–698 nos. 3–15 and *LIMC* VII²; nos. 3–15, pls. 520–523, s.v. Sarpedon (D. von Bothmer).

FIGURE 5.4   *Ivory Plaque with the Birth of Meleager (?)* From Pompeii, Naples, Museo Nazionale Archeologico inv. 109905A. [photograph: Deutschen Archäologisches Institut, Rome, Inst. Neg. 66.1838]

FIGURE 5.5   Reverse of plaque shown in figure 5.4: the dying Meleager carried by his companions. [photograph: Deutschen Archäologisches Institut, Rome, Inst. Neg. 74.1337]

Capitolino, a small marble plaque that illustrates every book of Homer's *Iliad* in abbreviated form with extensive inscriptions.[63] Virtually the identical group—the limp body with its head toward the viewer's right, the two men facing inward toward him and bending to lift him, and the mourning figure behind him—occurs in the uppermost register at the far right, where an inscription identifies the dead man as Hector. In the fifth register from the bottom, however, a very similar composition appears, this time identified as the death of Patroclus, whom his companions are hoisting into a chariot. Because of the battlefield setting, the mourning old man is absent, but he can appear in the death scenes of Achilles, Hector, Meleager, Paris, or virtually any young hero to represent the hero's father or his pedagogue as the narrative demands. The dead

---

[63]   *Tabula Iliaca*: miniature relief in very fine grained white marble, 0.25m. H., 0.28 W., left part of composition lost. Museo Capitolino inv. 316. Musso (supra n. 57) 14, fig. 7, with full earlier references; *LIMC* I[1] 105 no. 433; 129–30 nos. 543, 547; 135 no. 572; 179–80 no. 845a, s.v. Achilleus (A. Kossatz-Deissmann) and *LIMC* IV[i] 493 no. 93; 494 no. 105, s.v. Hektor (O. Touchefeu); Helbig[4] II 1266; Stuart-Jones 165–72 no. 83.

hero in this case must, however, be someone whose fate is intimately connected with the birth scene on the other side, since on the analogy of the Persephone plaque, these must be two episodes of the same story. The artist, moreover, has gone to great pains to give them parallel compositions: both sides have a total of four figures, of whom three direct their attention to a seated or semireclining figure in the middle, and the midwife bends toward her patient in much the same manner as the warrior on the other side bends to lift the feet of his fallen comrade. The oak tree behind the woman on the birthing chair adds a vertical element to the composition at the same position as the old man on the other side.

Of the possible candidates, therefore, Achilles and Meleager seem the likeliest, since both of these men had portentous births. In both cases, the Fates appeared to their mothers and warned them of their son's deaths: Thetis learned before his conception that Achilles would die young in battle, while Althaia heard on the day she gave birth that Meleager would live only as long as a brand that was at that moment burning in the fire. Both mothers attempted to defeat fate: Thetis by dripping the infant Achilles in the Styx, Althaia by seizing the brand from the fire, quenching the flames, and putting it safely away. But in both cases, the effort ultimately failed. Thetis neglected to dip Achilles' heel in the Styx, while Althaia, when she learned years later that Meleager had killed her brothers in battle, threw the brand back into the fire and caused his death.[64] Both of these stories would make appropriate pendants for the Persephone plaque, since all three myths deal with mothers whose children are fated to an early death but who can exercise some control over that fate. Demeter, in this pairing, is the archetypal good mother, whose loyalty to her daughter never flags and who wins in the end at least a partial victory over death. If Thetis is the mother on the second plaque, then she too is an exemplum of maternal love, although her effort to save Achilles is less successful. If she is Althaia, on the other hand, she embodies the opposite qualities from Demeter: she is the treacherous mother who brings about both her son's destruction and her own.

Which mother and son, then, do the plaques depict? In favor of Achilles are the extant examples of the scene of his birth, although none exactly match the birth scene on this plaque, whereas representations of Meleager's birth are otherwise unknown.[65] A fragmentary relief from the first century AD, half of which survives in Grottaferratta, the other half in the Palazzo Colonna at Rome, shows the death of a hero in a manner almost identical to the Pompeii plaque, although with additional figures that the small scale of the ivory plaque did not allow; Luisa Musso has advanced arguments for the identification of this marble relief as the death of Achilles.[66]

On the other hand, by far the most common use of this visual topos in Roman imperial sculpture is for the death of Meleager, whose life and death were an

[64] On the accounts of the birth of Achilles and prophesies of his fate, see *RE* I 225, s.v. Achilleus (J. Escher-Bürkli). Catallus 64.323–81: the Fates predict the entire life of Anchilles at the wedding of Peleus and Thetis, implying his early death in battle in lines 362–64. The earliest version of the story that Thetis bathed him in the Styx to make him invulnerable in Statius *Ach.* 1.133–39, 269–70. At least one representation of the birth of Achilles in the visual arts shows the Fates present: a mosaic of the fourth–fifth century AD at Nea Paphos, Cyprus. *LIMC* I^1 42–43 no. 3; I^2; pl. 56, no. 3. s.v. Achilleus (A. Kossatz-Deissman).
On the birth and death of Meleager: Ovid *Met* 8.451–547. The birth of Meleager: 451–59. Althaia's vengeance: 460–514. Death of Meleager: 515–25. Lament, funeral, suicide of Althaia: 526–47.

[65] *LIMC* I 42 nos. 1–4 for birth of Achilles; 43–45 nos. 5–18 for his bath in the Styx, s.v. Achilleus (A. Kossatz-Deissmann).

[66] Musso (supra n. 57) 9–19, figs. 1–5; Koch, *Meleager* 118.

FIGURE 5.6 *Sarcophagus Fragment, Showing the Dying Meleager Carried by His Companions*. Rome, Museo Capitolino inv. 619, mid to later second century. [photograph: Deutsches Archäologisches Institut, Rome, Inst. Neg. 68.3477]

enormously popular theme for sarcophagi (fig. 5.6).[67] All of them represent the group moving from left to right rather than from right to left, and the men carrying the hero's feet face away from rather than toward the body, since they are already walking toward their destination rather than lifting him. The earliest of these monuments must be at least sixty or seventy years later than this plaque and probably follow a version of the scene created specifically for narrative friezes with their traditions of continuous physical movement from one scene to the next. The left–right reversal of the scene, likewise, is a common adjustment in adaptations for sarcophagi, dictated by the convention that the action of the story should flow from left to right, the direction in which the Latin language was written and the direction of great narrative friezes like the Columns of Trajan and Marcus Aurelius. In a similar manner, most painted and mosaic versions of the rape of Persephone show the chariot of Hades in motion from right to left, but all but five extant sarcophagi reverse the direction of movement.[68]

The bulk of the evidence, in my opinion, favors an identification of the Pompeiian plaque as the birth and death of Meleager. The pendant plaques, then, would present didactic examples of the good mother, Demeter, and the

[67] Koch, *Meleager* 106–18 nos. 73–111 catalogues 37 examples of the scene of Meleager carried home by his companions; the Museo Capitolino sarcophagus inv. 619 is 113 no. 88, pl. 81.c.

[68] Lindner 74–76 nos. 88–92, pl. 23, catalogues the five examples of Persephone sarcophagi in which the action moves from right to left.

evil mother, Althaia. The literal power of life and death that any mother exercises over a helpless infant is both awe-inspiring and terrifying, and these two plaques would represent those two extremes of motherhood. The context of the find suggests that the luxurious object to which these plaques belonged was some item of female use, such as a jewelry box.

Unlike the plaques, most later objects that represent the myth (mosaics, paintings, cinerary urns, altars, and sarcophagi) do have recognizably funerary functions. In many cases, there is no way to know whether the bodies that once lay in these tombs were male or female, but funerary altars of the late first and early second centuries sometimes include the chariot group of Hades carrying off Persephone as a little vignette above or below an inscribed tablet, and in these cases at least, it is clear that the myth was considered equally appropriate for men, women, or married couples.[69] Centuries earlier, Etruscan patrons had represented the myth on the cinerary urns of both men and women, since six of the eight examples that Lindner catalogues have lids that represent reclining male figures.[70] When the deceased was a woman, however, the identification of her with the young goddess could become explicit, through the use of her portrait face on the figure of Persephone, as in a sarcophagus of the mid third century AD in the Museo Capitolino (fig. 5.1). Here, the myth has been changed almost beyond recognition, from a scene of violence and violation to a joyous wedding procession in which Persephone appears to be a fully voluntary participant. Instead of kicking and brandishing her arms, the dignified figure stands up in the chariot, holding her veil like a traditional bride.[71] The designer of this monument suppresses the cruelty of the abduction in favor of a more optimistic vision of death as a beginning of a happy afterlife. Heracles, the veteran of many journeys to the underworld, is prominent among the wedding guests leading the chariot, and the dog Cerberus at his feet reminds us of one of his better-known triumphs over death. It is he, rather than Hermes Psychopompus, who closes off the scene, as the final figure at the far right of the frieze: a physical embodiment of the "happy end." Even in this sanitized version of the myth, however, it is impossible to ignore the grief and rage of the survivors: Demeter still pursues, and Artemis and Athena still attempt to intervene.[72]

Portraits appear as well in a mosaic from a family mausoleum of some years earlier, probably the later second century.[73] Here, Persephone's face is missing, but her shocked companion who kneels on the ground beside the chariot group

---

[69] Lindner 60–63 nos. 56–66. Of the altars with inscriptions, two (nos. 57 and 58) are of women, four (nos. 59, 60, 62, and 63) of men, and two (nos. 61 and 65) of couples. The altar of Marcus Antonius Asclepiades and Julia Philumen, Lindner's no. 61, has been published with a good illustration of G. Daltrop, "Bildnisbüsten von Ehepaaren an römischen Grabaltaren," *Eikones: Festschrift Hans Jucker* (Bern 1980) 87, pl. 27.2. I am indebted to Eve D'Ambra for calling this altar and the publication to my attention.

[70] Lindner 49–52 nos. 34–41 for a catalogue of Etruscan sarcophagi with the rape of Persephone. Nos. 34 and 38 have lids with reclining female figures; the remainder are male.

[71] P. Blome, "Zue Umgestaltung Griechischer Mythen in der Römischen Sepulkralkunst. Alkestis-, Protesilaos- und Proserpinasarkophage," *RM* 85 (1978) 449–57, esp. 451 on the significance of Heracles.

[72] See Cohen 123–24 for an analysis of a similarly romanticized version of the rape of the Leucippidae on a red-figured hydria by the Meidias Painter. Here too, one of the "victims" behaves like a fully willing participant in an elopement, but there are still tensions and contradictions in the iconography that indicate that the Meidias Painter was conscious of the more familiar and brutal version of the story that he was trying to soften.

[73] Helbig[4] II no. 1674; H.P. L'Orange and P.J. Nordhagen, *Mosaik von der Antike bis zum Mittelalter* (Munich 1960) 47, pl. 24.B; Lindner 58 no. 50, pl. 14.1.

wears the contemporary hairstyle fashionable at the time of Faustina the Elder. Possibly, both of these figures represent girls of the family who died young. As they appear here, however, the scene seems to express one sister's loss of the other. Alternatively, the figure of Persephone could have been purely ideal, in which case the only "real" figure in the picture, the portrait-companion, would be a mortal witness to the scene, emblematic of the universality and inevitability of death. In either case, since Demeter's chariot does not appear in his composition, the portrain-companion allows for the presence of a surviving mourner who can emphasize the impact of the scene. The four seasons in the medallions at the corners of the decorative border of the floor could remind the viewer of Persephone's eventual return in spring, but this mosaic differs from the Capitoline sarcophagus in refusing to gloss over the violence of the scene. Indeed, this mosaic bears a striking resemblance to the Hellenistic fresco at Vergina that represents the rape of Persephone with particular poignancy. There is good reason to believe that this mosaic, like that fresco, is one of the most faithful extant copies of the famous lost painting by Nicomachus.[74]

The rape of Persephone is not the only context in which the goddess appears on sarcophagi and funerary monuments. She can be presented iconically, as the queen of the underworld, as for example on a relief from Ostia, now in the Vatican. The small scale and concave shape of this work strongly suggest that it originally stood in a niche of a small family tomb or similar sort of shrine.[75] The divine couple sit facing the viewer on an ornate double throne, Persephone holding the torch of the Eleusinian rites and Hades holding a scepter, but the two are characterized as rather different beings. Hades is almost rigidly frontal, although he inclines his face slightly toward his bride, and he holds his scepter vertically. Persephone, although equally majestic, seems a little more gracefully relaxed and reacts more affectionately to her husband, placing her left arm around his shoulders and holding the torch diagonally in the crook of the right. Both her gestures parallel those of the little nude winged boy beside her, who stands in an even more relaxed, off-balance pose, with a torch in the crook of his right arm, his legs crossed, and one hand resting on the back of the throne behind Persephone's shoulder. A corresponding figure of a girl on the opposite side, falsely restored as Isis, stands by a water jar. Since an Eros with a torch is a standard image for Hymenaeus and the water jar is part of the apparatus of a wedding ceremony, this relief could represent the sacred marriage of Hades and Persephone, although the solemn frontality of the figures argues against a narrative content.

The characterization of Persephone as the more gentle and emotional of the two gods, however, is something that occurs again when the enthroned underworld gods appear in narratives. They can appear in this way amid mythological scenes, as on the Velletri sarcophagus, in which the iconic group takes its place in the middle of the upper register, directly above the scene of the rape of Persephone, and demonstrates the triumphant transformation of Persephone into the mighty goddess of the underworld (fig. 5.7).[76] The enthroned couple can

---

[74]   Lindner 32–33, 58 no. 50, 108; Oakley (supra n. 55) 73, fig. 4. On the Vergina fresco, see also Cohen passim, esp. 122–23.

[75]   Vatican, Vestibolo Rotondo inv. 1137, marble, heavily restored, 0.95 m. H., 1.06 W. Helbig[4] I, 195–96 no. 253.

[76]   Velletri sarcophagus: Kleiner, *Roman Sculpture* 259, 265, with earlier literature, figs. 229–30. On the group of the enthroned underworld gods: Andreae, *Studien* 26–32; on the scene of the rape of Persephone, pp. 45–47.

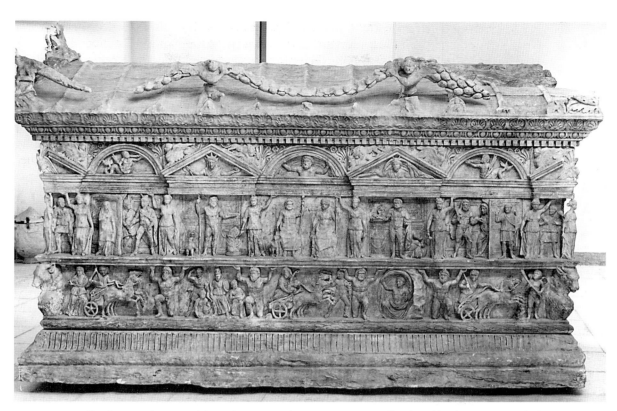

FIGURE 5.7   *Velletri Sarcophagus.* Mid to alter second century. From Velletri. Velletri, Museo Capitolare. [photograph: Deutsches Archäologisches Institut, Rome, Inst. Neg. 59.53]

also appear among biographical or quasibiographical scenes concerning the deceased.[77] On a Trajanic sarcophagus lid in the Museo Capitolino, which appears today set on a box to which it does not belong, Hades and Persephone sit facing frontally in the central panel, as on the Velletri sarcophagus, but to the viewer's right we meet two figures in contemporary dress and hairstyle, seated side by side on their marriage bed, apparently saying their farewells (fig. 5.8). On the other side panel we meet the same couple on their knees, entreating the three Fates, presumably without success. The wife appears once more in single, upright figure to the viewer's left of the central group, while Hermes Psychopompus appears on the corresponding panel on the other side, apparently to lead her from the bedroom scene to the underworld. The woman does not directly interact with the underworld gods themselves or entreat them for mercy, but they appear to interact both with her and with the viewer, extending their right hands with the palms exposed. This is a universally understood human gesture of friendly welcome and, from a more powerful being, of clemency. Hades and Persephone thus become characters in someone else's story: the rulers of the underworld who will judge the souls of the dead and display mercy to those who deserve it.[78]

They also play this role in several mythological sarcophagi. The sarcophagus of Gaius Junius Euhodos and Metilia Acte (fig. 5.9) states unambiguously that the underworld gods will show clemency toward deserving mortals like the mythological heroine Alcestis, a mortal who shares with Persephone the important trait of a return from death.[79] Unlike Persephone, she voluntarily

[77]   Sarcophagus lid: Museo Capitolino inv. 723. Helbig[4] II 213–14 no. 1406 (B. Andreae); Andreae, *Studien* 27 no. 16, 31–32.

[78]   Andreae, *Studien* 30–32.

[79]   Andreae, *Studien* 44. Vatican, Museo Chiaramonti inv. 1195.

chose to offer her life in place of her husband's and was rewarded for her valor by rescue from the underworld. In Euripides' tragedy, Heracles liberates her by wrestling Death into submission, but the designers of some Roman sarcophagi clearly have another idea. In these versions, the underworld gods voluntarily agree to release Alcestis, as they will presumably also grant an afterlife to Euhodos and Metila, whose portrait faces appear on the figures of the mythological couple.[80] Here, the underworld gods actively participate in the scene of the heroine's return. At the viewer's right, Persephone stands, leaning over the throne of Hades, placing an arm around his shoulder and obviously entreating, while Hades gestures acquiescently. The goddess who returns from the dead every spring, it appears, has both the will to take mercy on mortals and the power to intercede for them with her more severe husband; the torch that she holds in her right hand in this sarcophagus recalls both wedding torches and the ceremonial torches of the Eleusiniuan mysteries and remind us of her role as a goddess of rebirth. Behind the group of Alcestis and Heracles returning from the underworld, the three Fates, recognizable by the open scroll that one of them holds in her hand, look on with apparent approval, turning their heads toward Admetus-Euhodos as he clasps hands with Heracles. The Fates often appear in Roman funerary art as the "accusatores," or prosecuting attorneys, in the judgment of the souls of the dead, on the lid of the sarcophagus in the Museo Capitolino, for example (fig. 5.8), and in frescoes of the hypogeum of Vibia and Vicentius, to be discussed below.[81] In the case of Alcestis-Metilia, it is evident that the "accusatores" have been thoroughly won over by the forces of clemency.

Persephone plays the part of intercessor for the dead in at least one more mythological sarcophagus, another story of a mortal who won a temporary release from the underworld.[82] The mortal this time is male, the hero Protesilaos who died on the beaches of Troy, the very first victim to fall. His wife Laodamia so impressed the gods with her grief and devotion that they permitted Protesilaos to return from the dead for a one-day reunion with his bride. A handsome sarcophagus in the church of S. Chiara in Naples (fig. 5.10) devotes the main facade to the scene of the return of the hero, but the short sides represent his first arrival in the underworld, and his return to the realm of death after the reunion with Laodamia. In the arrival scene, Protesilaos approaches a group of Hades and Persephone much like the group on the Euhodos sarcophagus. Hades sits majestically on his throne, while a rather provocatively dressed Persephone stands beside him, an arm around his shoulder, and gestures toward him. This time, she turns her face toward her protégé (or client, to use the term that would have occurred most readily to a Roman viewer) rather than toward Hades, but in this relief, as in the Euhodos and Metilia sarcophagus, one requires no imagination to understand her actions. She is exercising the sacred and traditional right of a wife to influence her husband. To hammer the point home, a little figure of Amor stretches out his arms to draw Protesilaos toward his divine patron.[83]

---

[80] *LIMC* I¹ 535 no. 8, 536 no. 16, with full earlier literature, and *LIMC* I²; pls. 401.8, 401.16, s.v. Alkestis (M. Schmidt); Bloe (supra n. 71) 441–45; S. Wood, "Alcestis on Roman Sarcophagi," AJA 82 (1978) 499–510, and "Alcestis on Roman Sarcophagi: Postscript," in D'Ambra, *Roman Art in Context* 96–99; Sichtermann-Koch, *Mythen* 20 no. 8, pls. 16, 17.2, 18, 19; Calza, *Ostia* 9 (supra no. 23) 27–29 no. 31.

[81] Andreae, *Studien* 31–32.

[82] Sichtermann-Koch, *Mythen* 65–66 no. 70, pls. 168.1, 171; Blome (supra n. 71) 445–49.

[83] Andreae, *Studien* 37.

FIGURE 5.8 *Sarcophagus*. The lid depicts the underworld gods, center, the deceased couple, to the right, and the couple entreating the Fates, to the left. Early second century, probably Trajanic. Rome, Museo Capitolino inv. 723. [photograph: Deutsches Archäologisches Institut, Rome, Inst. Neg. 62.796]

FIGURE 5.9 *Sarcophagus of Caius Junius Euhodos and Metilia Acte*. Ca. 160–170, from Ostia. Vatican, Museo Chiaramonti inv. 1195. [photograph: Deutsches Archäologisches Institut, Rome, Inst. Neg. 72.590]

Persephone can thus inspire hope in two ways: first as an example of a being who overcomes death and second as a goddess who perhaps because of her own dual nature, not only as the awesome and terrifying queen of the underworld but as the bringer of renewed life, can grant such a victory to others. The sarcophagus in the Galleria Uffizi in Florence that depicts the rape of Persephone on its main frieze (fig. 5.2) implies such a message by associating the goddess with at least one and more probably two mortal women who either returned from the underworld or secured a return for a loved one. Graceful figures of the seasons decorate the corners of this box, reminding the viewer of the cycle of life and death that Persephone represents and drawing the viewer's attention around to the short ends, which as usual are a little more summarily carved than the main frieze but still display considerable attention to

FIGURE 5.10   *Sarcophagus Depicting the Myth of Protesilaos and Laodamia*. Short end: Protesilaos before the underworld gods. Naples, Church of S. Chiara. [photograph: Deutsches Archäologisches Institut, Rome, Inst. Neg. 62.876]

iconographic detail. On one side is Hermes leading a veiled woman, and on the other, Heracles, leading a similar figure in the opposite direction. The latter can only represent Alcestis returning from the dead. The group on the other end of this sarcophagus is more problematic: most scholars have interpreted it to represent Alcestis on her way to the underworld, before her release, but Andreae believes that this figure could be Laodamia, who committed suicide after her brief reunion with Protesilaos in order to be with him forever. Despite its somber ending, her story thus has certain parallels with that of both Alcestis and Persephone: the notion that death can be overcome and that the love of a married couple can extend beyond death. The iconographic message of the Florence sarcophagus is more oblique than that of the monument of Euhodos and Metilia, but nonetheless it suggests to the viewer through the juxtaposition of scenes that Persephone's death and resurrection is the archetypal victory that allows mortal heroines like Alcestis and Laodamia to hope for clemency from the rulers of the underworld.

Persephone's role as a potentially merciful intercessor for the dead lasted well into the fourth century and after the establishment of Christianity. In the small underground tomb of a woman named Vibia, we see Vibia escorted into a clearly Christian paradise by a Good Angle.[84] On the center of the barrel vault above this lunette, however, Vibia approaches the enthroned figures labeled by inscriptions as Dis Pater (that is, Hades) and Aeracura (another name for Persephone). This time it is Alcestis who seems to act as an advocate for the deceased, whom she escorts. The clear implication is that the gods can take mercy on other virtuous mortals, just as they did for Alcestis. And here too, the deceased can be identified not only with heroines but with the goddess herself.

---

84   Andreae, *Studien* 49–50; M. Borda, *La Pittura Romana* (Milan 1958) 347, photo p. 348; J. Wilpert, *Die Malereien der Katakomben Roms* (Freilburg im Breisgau 1903) 144, 392, pl. 132. See in particular p. 392 for discussion of the inscriptions.

On another panel of the vault, Hades carries away his victim, in the traditional iconography for the rape of Persephone, but the inscription tells us that this is the ABREPTIO VIBIES, the abduction of Vibia. The inscription above her entry into paradise, INDUCTIO VIBIES, obviously a parallel construction, emphasizes the "happy end" of Vibia's passage to the next world. Here, then, the painter invokes the myths both of Alcestis and of Persephone herself to express the hope that the deities of the underworld will display clemency to Vibia and grant her a happy afterlife.

Let us now briefly review some of the salient characteristics of Demeter and Persephone and compare them to the female saint who eventually replaced them in the hearts of Christians. Demeter is a mother whose child dies an untimely death but then miraculously rises from the dead in spring. Through her exemplary virtue as a loving and loyal mother, Demeter gains the power to defeat death. She is often represented as a beautiful but melancholy figure, veiled and seated in a quietly meditative pose.[85] The similarity of her images to those of the Virgin Mary are obvious. Bieber has documented how Christian artists adapted the type of the "Large Herculaneum Woman" for images of the Madonna.[86] Another statuary type of Demeter, the veiled figure that was popular for portraits of aristocratic and imperial women including Sabina and Julia Domna in the statues found at Ostia, was also transformed into a Madonna in at least one medieval work of sculpture.[87] Persephone is a virgin who dies but then ascends from the world of the dead, in her physical body. Like the Virgin Mary, whose sacred month is May and whose altars and images are traditionally decorated at that time with fresh flowers, Persephone has a special association with spring and renewal and is often represented with garlands of flowers. She, also like the Virgin Mary, has the power to intercede for mercy toward the dead and can be depicted majestically, as an enthroned queen. The Virgin Mary thus appears in significant ways to incorporate the characteristics of both goddesses, through her unique status as virgin and mother.

The human psychological need for something like the myth of Persephone, and for divine figures with the characteristics of the two Eleusinian goddesses, appears not to have ended with the suppression of the cult at Eleusis in Christian times, nor was it by any means unique to Greek and Roman culture. The Mesopotamian goddess Inanna-Ishtar, who likewise is a goddess of fertility, journeys to the underworld, but her vengeful sister Ereshkigal, the goddess of the Land of No Return, entraps her, strips her of her jewelry, clothes, and divine powers, and torments her with all forms of misery.[88] To secure her rescue, Ea, the goddess of wisdom, creates a clever and handsome eunuch (or, in the Sumerian version of the story, a pair of sexless beings) who ingratiates himself with the queen of the underworld and tricks her into agreeing to Inanna's release. This myth does not use the image of sexual aggression for the death of the goddess, but it does share with the story of Persephone the theme of sterility and drought that devastate the earth while the goddess Inanna is dead and the return of the earth to fertility with her return to life. Here too, as in the story of

---

[85]   Representations of Demeter seated, veiled, with a melancholy expression: *LIMC* IV¹ 858 no. 122 (the fresco in the tomb at Vergina); 859 nos. 138, 140, 143 and p. 862 nos. 190–91 for examples in sculpture. S.v. Demeter (L. Beschi).

[86]   Bieber, *Copies* 155, figs. 648–49.

[87]   Bieber, *Copies* 167.

[88]   "Descent of Ishtar to the Nether World," *The Ancient Near East*, James B. Pritchard, ed. (Princeton 1958) 80–85; D. Wolkstein and S.N. Kramer, *Inanna: Queen of Heaven and Earth: Her Stories and Hymns from Sumer* (New York 1983), translation of text 52–89, commentary 155–69. For an analysis of the narrative patterns of the myth, see Burkert (supra n. 2) 61–62.

Persephone, the goddess's freedom from the underworld is not complete, and she, like Persephone, also becomes in part a goddess of death. The powers of the underworld demand a sacrifice in exchange for her; she gives them her husband Dumuzi but then barters for an agreement that will let him spend half of every year in the underworld, while his sister spends the other half there in his place. The structural similarities to the myth of Persephone are obvious, and they are not, I think, the result of direct borrowing of the mythology from one culture by another. Rather, they probably owe their similarities to the fears that all human beings share and to the hope that drought, famine, and death can be overcome.

Those fundamental human concerns, and their mythological expressions, remain as strong in our secular modern society as in ancient ones. The realities of life that the myth attempts to express (the inevitability and terror of death, and the inexplicable cruelty of a violent or untimely end) have not changed. The story of Demeter and Persephone deals specifically with one of the harshest types of bereavement: the loss of a beloved child who has not yet fulfilled her potential in life. Phrasikleia's grieving relatives understood the special relevance of the myth to their emotional state when they commissioned the statue and inscription that implied the assimilation of that young, unmarried girl to the goddess, and so did Noelle Oxenhandler, in her 1993 essay "Polly's Face" in *The New Yorker*.

I began this essay with references to imaginary abductions, but I end with a very real one: 12-year-old Polly Klaas, who was playing with friends in her home when an intruder kidnapped her at knifepoint and later raped and murdered her. In the months following her disappearance and before the discovery of her body, the citizens of Petaluma, California, made very effort to find her, but virtually the only effort possible was to post pictures of the missing girl in the hope that someone would see and recognize her. Oxenhandler describes how after a certain point, these photographs took on almost the property of cult images. I can offer no more eloquent testimony to the eternal power of the myth of Persephone than to quote her words about Polly Klaas:

And here we touch upon the cosmic horror of this crime: kidnapping has to do with the invasion of the "bright" world in which children chatter and play . . . by another world, the dark world of unspeakable sorrows, the underworld. Part of the horror of Polly's story is how swiftly these two worlds connected, how easily the dark world made its claim—as when, in the ancient myth, a crack opened up in the earth, and golden-haired Persephone, who had been happily playing with her companions, vanished with the dark figure of Hades into the ground. "This child is the light of our lives," Polly's mother was quoted in the newspaper as saying—speaking the language of Demeter, goddess of earth and growing things, who when her daughter vanished cast the shadow of drought upon the whole world. The photographs of Polly show a child as beautiful as Persephone: flowing hair, soft, dark eyes; a radiant, dimpled smile. ... And, as those of us who remain here grow accustomed to her face, which everywhere denotes her absence, we cannot help participating in her transfiguration. Even as we refuse to give up hope for her return, we find ourselves going in and out of the bank, the post office, the bookstore, turning a girl into a goddess.[89]

Note

Thanks to the American Academy in Rome, where I completed most of the work on this article, for permitting me to stay as a visiting scholar and to a

[89]   N. Oxenhandler, "Polly's Face," *The New Yorker* (29 November 1993) 95–96.

number of friends and colleagues both at Oakland University and at the American Academy whose suggestions and information facilitated my research: in particular, Bettina Bergmann, Ada Cohen, Robert Cro, Eve D'Ambra, Katrina Dickson, Christine Kondoleon, and Louisa Ngote. Christina Huemer, Antonella Bucci, and the library staff of the American Academy in Rome also offered me invaluable assistance. Magda Cima of the Direzione dei Musei Capitolini generously facilitated my study of a mosaic in the closed section of the Palazzo dei Conservatori; I am especially grateful to her for her kind cooperation on short notice. I owe thanks also to the Deutsches Archäologisches Institut in Rome for the use of their photographic archives.

Abbreviations of frequently cited works:

ANDREAE, *Studien*
B. Andreae, *Studien zur römischen Grabkunst* (Heidelberg 1963)

COHEN
A. Choen, "Portrayals of Abduction in Greek Art: Rape or Metaphor?," in Kampen, *Sexuality in Ancient Art* 117–35

KOCH, *Meleager*
G. Koch, *Die Mythologische Sarkenphage 6: Meleager* (Berlin 1975)

KOCH-SICHTERMANN, *Sarkophage*
G. Koch and H. Sichtermann, *Römische Sarkophage* (Munich 1982)

KOORTBOJIAN
M. Koortbojian, *Myth, Meaning and Memory on Roman Sarcophagi* (Los Angeles and London 1995)

LINDNER
R. Lindner, *Der Raub der Persephone in der antike Kunst* (*Beiträge zur Archäologie* 16, Würzburg 1984)

MIKOCKI
T. Mikocki, *Sub Specie Deae: Les impératrices et princesses romaines assimilées à des déesses: Étude iconologique* (Rome 1995)

SICHTERMANN-KOCH, *Mythen*
H. Sichtermann and G. Koch, *Griechische Mythen auf Römische Sarkophagen* (Tübingen 1975)

ZUNTZ
G. Zuntz, *Persephone: Three Essays on Religion and Thought in Magna Graecia* (Oxford 1971)

Acknowledgements

Grateful acknowledgement is made to the following sources.

Primary Sources

Introduction

Primary Sources I and II: Melville, A.D. (trans.) (1990) *Ovid: The Love Poems*, Oxford, Oxford University Press. By permission of Oxford University Press.

Block 1

Primary Source 1.1: Isbell, H. (trans.) (1990) *Ovid: Heroides*, Harmondsworth, Penguin. Copyright © 1990, H. Isbell. Reproduced by permission of Penguin Books Ltd.

Block 2

Primary Source 2.1: de Sélincourt, A. (trans.) (1960) *Livy: The Early History of Rome*, with an intro by R.M. Ogilvie, Harmondsworth, Penguin. Copyright © The Estate of Aubrey de Sélincourt, 1960. Introduction copyright © R.M. Ogilvie, 1971.

Primary Sources 2.2 and 2.3: West, D. (1991) *Virgil: The Aeneid, A New Prose Translation*, Harmondsworth, Penguin. Introduction and translation copyright © David West.

Primary Source 2.4: 'The Art of Love: Book 1' from Green, P. (trans.) (1982) *Ovid: The Erotic Poems*, London, Penguin. Copyright © Peter Green, 1982.

Primary Sources 2.5 and 2.11: Graves, R. (1957) *Gaius Suetonius Tranquillus: The Twelve Caesars*, revised with an intro by M. Grant, Harmondsworth, Penguin. Copyright © 1957, R. Graves. Reproduced by permission of Carcanet Press Ltd.

Primary Source 2.6: Grant, M. (trans.) (1956) *Tacitus: The Annals of Imperial Rome*, London, Penguin. Copyright © 1956, 1959, 1971, 1973, 1975, 1977, 1989, Michael Grant Publications Ltd. Reproduced by permission of Penguin Books Ltd.

Primary Sources 2.7 and 2.10: Reprinted by permission of the publishers and the Trustees of The Loeb Classical Library from Cary, E. (trans.) (1925) *Dio Cassius: Roman History/Vol. VIII*, The Loeb Classical Library, vol. 141, Cambridge, MA, Harvard University Press. Copyright © 1925 by the President and Fellows of Harvard College. The Loeb Classical Library® is a registered trademark of the President and Fellows of Harvard College.

Primary Source 2.15: Reprinted by permission of the publishers and the Trustees of The Loeb Classical Library from Gummere, R.M. (trans.) *Seneca: Vol. VI*, The Loeb Classical Library, vol. 77, Cambridge, MA, Harvard University Press. Copyright © 1925 by the President and Fellows of Harvard College. The Loeb Classical Library® is a registered trademark of the President and the Fellows of Harvard College.

Primary Source 2.18: Kenney, E.J. (ed.) (1998, 2004) *Apuleius: The Golden Ass: A New Translation*, London, Penguin. Translation, introduction and notes copyright © E.J. Kenney, 1998.

Primary Source 2.19: Sullivan, J. (trans.) (1965, 1969) *Petronius: The Satyricon and The Fragments*, Harmondsworth, Penguin. Copyright © 1965, 1969, J.P. Sullivan. Reproduced by permission of Penguin Books Ltd.

Primary Source 2.21: Geer, R.M. (trans.) (1965) *Lucretius: On Nature*, Bobbs-Merrill Company Inc.

Primary Source 2.22: Reprinted by permission of the publishers and the Trustees of The Loeb Classical Library from King, J.E. (1960) *Cicero: Tusculan Disputations/Vol. XVIII*, The Loeb Classical Library, vol. 141, Cambridge, MA, Harvard University Press.

Secondary Sources

Introduction

Secondary Sources I and II: Auden, W.H. (1966) *Collected Shorter Poems 1927–1957*, London, Faber and Faber. Copyright © 1939 by W.H. Auden (Secondary Source I) and 1936 by W.H. Auden (Secondary Source II). Used by permission of Curtis Brown Ltd. All rights reserved. 'Musée des Beaux Arts' copyright 1940 and renewed 1968 by W.H. Auden. 'Twelve Songs: IX', from *Collected Poems* by W.H. Auden, copyright © 1976 by Edward Mendelson, William Meredith and Monroe K. Spears, Executors of the Estate of W.H. Auden. Used by permission of Random House Inc.

Block 1

Secondary Source 1.1: Buxton, R. (2007) 'Tragedy and Greek myth' in Woodard, R.D. (ed.) *The Cambridge Companion to Greek Mythology*, Cambridge and New York, Cambridge University Press. Copyright © Cambridge University Press 2007. Reproduced with permission.

Secondary Source 1.2: Taplin, O. (2007) *Pots and Plays: Interactions between Tragedy and Greek Vase-painting of the Fourth Century BC*, Los Angeles, CA, J. Paul Getty Museum. By kind permission of Oliver Taplin.

Secondary Source 1.3: Cameron, A. (2004) *Greek Mythography and the Roman World*, New York, Oxford University Press.

Secondary Source 1.4: Frazer, Sir J.G. (1949) *The Golden Bough: A Study in Magic and Religion*, London, Palgrave Macmillan.

Secondary Source 1.5: Csapo, E. (2005) *Theories of Mythology*, Malden, MA and Oxford, Blackwell Publishing. Copyright © 2005 Eric Csapo. Reproduced with permission of Blackwell Publishing Ltd.

Block 2

Secondary Source 2.1: Slayman, A. (2007) 'Fact or legend? Debate over the origins of Rome', *Archaeology*, vol. 60, no. 4, July/August 2007. Reprinted with permission of *Archaeology* magazine, www.archaeology.org. Copyright © The Archaeological Institute of America, 2010.

Secondary Source 2.2: Reprinted by permission of the publisher from *Nero* by Edward Champlin, Cambridge, MA, The Belknap Press of Harvard University Press. Copyright © 2003 by the President and Fellows of Harvard College.

Secondary Source 2.3: Griffin, M.T. (1984) *Nero: The End of a Dynasty*, London and New York, Routledge. Copyright © Miriam T. Griffin.

Secondary Source 2.4: Elsner, J. (1994) 'Constructing decadence: the representation of Nero as Imperial Builder' in Elsner, J. and Masters, J. (eds) *Reflections of Nero: Culture, History and Representation*, Chapel Hill, NC and London, University of North Carolina Press.

Secondary Source 2.5: Cameron, A. (2004) *Greek Mythography in the Roman World*, Oxford, Oxford University Press.